America's Youngest Warriors
Volume II

More stories about the
young men and women who served in the
armed forces of the United States of America
before attaining legal age

Compiled and edited by

Ray D. Jackson and Susan M. Jackson

Published by the

Veterans of Underage Military Service

ii

First paperback edition, 2003

Library of Congress Control Number: 2002100396

ISBN 0-9656093-2-4

For more information or to order additonal books, please write:

Veterans of Underage Military Service
VUMS Book Project
710 East La Jolla Drive
Tempe, AZ 85282-5355

This book is dedicated to the memory of those youngsters, most of them unknown to all but their families, who died while serving in the armed forces of the United States of America before attaining legal age.

These are the few we know about:

Felbert E. Williams, Jr.	*1926-1942*
Norman E. Gibbs	*1927-1942*
Morris H. Wilson	*1927-1943*
Robert W. Fox	*1927-1943*
Jack Cook	*1929-1945*
"Chick" Harris	*1930-1945*
Huey P. French	*1935-1950*
Dan Bullock	*1953-1969*

Their stories are told on pages 1-5.

"You don't have to be very old to grow up fast."

Admiral Jeremy Michael Boorda,
underage veteran.

Contents

Contributors to Volume II

A Note to the Reader

Shortly before the fifth annual reunion of the Veterans of Underage Military Service (VUMS) in San Antonio in March 1997, we received the first 1,500 copies of *America's Youngest Warriors* from the printer. Pre-publication orders for the book had been filled, and copies were on sale at the reunion. The reception to the book was beyond our most optimistic expectations. It was so heartwarming to see 60- and 70-year-old men and women scurrying around getting their copies autographed by those whose stories were in the book. They could have been compared to a bunch of excited high school freshmen with their first yearbook.

Even before the reunion was over we were asked, "When are you going to do another volume?" Our response was, "Not in the foreseeable future!" At that time the questions came mostly from VUMS members who had not submitted a story. Since 1997, the membership of the VUMS has increased considerably. As new members became acquainted with the book, many asked when another volume would be published, wanting to tell their own stories. Meanwhile, sales of the book continued at a steady pace, and a second printing was necessary, so another 1,000 copies were printed in March 1999.

Such an enthusiastic response to the book from both the contributors and their families convinced us of the value of recording the stories. We realized that for many, their story in the book was the only recognition and record of their underage service. It reaffirmed our belief that the men and women who "rushed the cadence" to serve their country so young deserve special recognition, and that their stories should continue to be recorded.

In editing this second book, we used the same procedures as we did with the first. After receiving the original story, we edited for content and format and returned it to the contributor for review, revision, and approval. Some stories required several drafts, several mailings back and forth, and often phone contacts, to verify that the final version was satisfactory to both the contributor and to us. We relied totally on the contributor for content and accuracy. After a permission-to-publish form was signed by the contributor, only minor changes for style and format were made in the final version.

Over the years we have learned of eight young men who were killed in action prior to their 17th birthday. We decided early on to dedicate this book to the memory of those youngsters, but soon realized that a single dedication page as is normally used in books was not sufficient. Instead, we added a chapter of short biographies of these young men.

The majority of men and women who served underage now consider it a badge of honor to have done so. However, there are still some who are fearful that the government might be "out to get them" for their fraudulent enlistment. In an attempt to assure them that it is now perfectly safe to admit to underage service, we included the chapter titled "Nothing to Fear."

Jack Cannon, now of Raton, New Mexico, who provided the watercolor of the flag used on the cover of the first book, kindly gave his permission to also use it again for Volume II.

There is always the question, "What exactly is an underage veteran?" The VUMS definition of an underage veteran is one who was sworn into a branch of the armed forces *before* reaching the age of 17 for men, and before reaching the age of 20 for women who served prior to 1948.

The U. S. Army Air Corps became the U. S. Army Air Forces (with an *s*) on 20 June 1941. On 18 September 1947, the U. S. Air Force was formed as a separate service. Although officially the Army Air Forces, the term "Air Corps" was commonly used until 1947. Thus, VUMS members who submitted stories for this book frequently stated that they served in the Army Air Corps. In the first book, and in this one, we have used the official term "U. S. Army Air Forces" to the consternation of many who considered themselves to be in the Army Air Corps.

In the first book, we filled in partial pages with what we called "VUMS Notes." They were a variety of interesting incidents about various aspects of the military which were not included in the stories. In this book, anecdotes or unusual incidents, both humorous and serious, observed or experienced by VUMS members are used as fill-ins. They begin with the title, "INCIDENTally."

Ray D. Jackson and Susan M. Jackson

The Few we Know About

The number of underage military personnel who perished in war is unknown and impossible to determine. Locating information about those who were killed in action before reaching the legal age of enlistment is very difficult. Military records are of little use because a fictitious birth date would have been used when the individual joined underage. It is by chance that one hears about the sacrifice of these youngsters, with the major sources for such information being family and friends. Therefore, we will never know how many young men and women lost their lives in the service of their country before reaching the legal age for enlistment.

During the past ten years, the identities of only eight young men who were killed in action before their 17th birthday have become known to the Veterans of Underage Military Service. Their stories follow. They are probably typical of the stories of all the unknown youngsters to whom this book is dedicated.

Felbert E. Williams, Jr., was born in Sunflower, Mississippi, on 29 November 1926. He enlisted in the U. S. Army on 25 September 1941 and was soon sent to the Philippines. According to Army records, he gave his birth date as August 1923. In the Philippines, he was assigned to Company G, 31st Infantry Regiment. He was captured on Bataan and survived the infamous Bataan Death March, but fell to the ravages of dysentery and died on 2 June 1942 in a Japanese prisoner of war camp. He was 15½ years old.

Information about Felbert Williams was provided by his cousin Philip Logan of Manassas, Virginia, in a 1995 letter to the Veterans of Underage Military Service.

Norman E. Gibbs of Peoria, Illinois, joined the U. S. Marines shortly after the attack on Pearl Harbor. Born on 27 June 1927, Gibbs was 5-foot 10-inches tall, and weighed 150 pounds when he faked his way into the Marines at age 14, with his mother's approval. He was killed when a transport exploded near Guadalcanal on 28 December 1942. He was 15 at the time of his death. In an article about Gibbs in the 2 February 1943 edition of the *Peoria Journal-Transcript*, his mother was reported to have said that the boy was so enthused about his enlistment that she didn't have the heart to spoil it by revealing his correct age. Gibbs is buried in the Camp Butler National Cemetery, Springfield, Illinois.

Information about Norman Gibbs was taken from the VUMS newsletter, The Underage Veteran, *Volume 3, No. 4.* The Underage Veteran *was later renamed* America's Young Warriors.

Morris H. Wilson was born into a poor family in northern Michigan on 13 April 1927. Home life was not pleasant for Morris. His dad would berate him and embarrass him in front of others. At age 15, he changed his birth certificate to reflect his age as 17 and obtained his parents' signatures on papers to enlist in the Navy. He was sent to Great Lakes, Illinois, for boot camp, then to Connecticut where he was assigned to the submarine, USS *Dorado* (SS-248). In several letters to his mother he indicated that he was beginning to regret his decision to enlist. His parents made no attempt to get him out.

The USS *Dorado* sailed from New London, Connecticut, for Panama on 6 October 1943. She did not arrive at Panama, nor was she heard from at any time after sailing. The standard practice of imposing bombing restrictions within a specified area surrounding unescorted submarines was in effect, but a patrol plane out of the U. S. Naval Operating Base, Guantanamo, Cuba, received faulty instructions about the location of the restricted area surrounding the *Dorado*. At 8:49 p.m., 12 October 1943, the aircraft dropped three depth charges on an unidentified submarine. About two hours later, the plane sighted another submarine and was fired upon. A German submarine was known to be operating near the scene of these two contacts. Because the lack of evidence, the Court of Inquiry was unable to reach definite conclusions about the loss of the *Dorado*. It is likely that Morris Wilson died as a result of friendly fire.

Information about Morris Wilson was obtained from his niece, Carolyn Wilson of Bokeelia, Florida. Information on the events leading up to the loss of the USS Dorado *was obtained from the website* www.subnet.com/fleet/ss248.htm.

Robert W. Fox, of Kansas City, Missouri, was determined to enlist in the Marines at age 15. He was born on 11 July 1927. In a letter to his friend, Hank "Jupe" Paustian, he outlined his plan:

Kansas City, Mo.
August 25, '42

Dear Jupe:

I thought I would write you & tell you that I'm not going to the Marines with you. Both Dad & Mom backed out so I am going to run off & join under an assumed name. I have talked with her about running off & she said she would rather have it that way. She said she would not trace me & have me come back. She wants me to write her & she won't tell Dad where the letter came from.

I'm going to get some money first so I can bribe some old man & woman to sign my papers.

I've already told them if they didn't sign my papers by Friday that I was going to run off. Dad just laughed and said that I was just talking thru my hat. But that is where he is wrong. I've made up my mind as what I am going to do & I'm going to do it.

I think I'll go to Topeka and sign up there.

I hope you pass your physical in San Diego. I'll try to look you up there.

Bob

4

Bob Fox was successful in getting his parents' permission and joined the Marines with his friend in August 1942. He was killed in action on Tarawa on 20 November 1943, four months past his 16th birthday.

Hank Paustian of Lawrence, Kansas, with the permission of Bob's sister, June Fox August of Tucson, Arizona, furnished the information above, including a copy of Bob's letter.

Jack Cook was orphaned at a young age and was later adopted. At age 14, he enlisted in the Army and made his adoptive mother promise that she wouldn't notify the Army that he was underage. He was assigned to Company F, 513th Parachute Infantry Regiment, when it was formed at Fort Benning, Georgia. He was wounded in action on 30 March 1945 near Potthof, Germany, and died of wounds on 6 April 1945 at the age of 16. A few days after he was wounded, his company commander received an order to get him off the line because of his age. His adoptive mother's conscience had bothered her so much that she went against Jack's wishes and reported his age to the authorities. Jack was posthumously awarded the Silver Star for gallantry in action that led to his death.

Information about Jack Cook was obtained from the 17th Airborne Infantry Division Association as reprinted in Military, *April 1998, p 16.*

"Chick" Harris, who lied about his age to get in the Marines, died on Iwo Jima on 19 February 1945 at the age of 15. He was killed soon after leaving his landing craft. Some information, but not his first name nor his home town, can be found on page 158 of James Bradley's book, *Flags of Our Fathers.*

Huey P. French of Childress, Texas, wanted to be a soldier from the time he was very young. Childhood games with his siblings had a military theme, and Huey was the leader. As he grew older, he lost interest in school and just wanted to be a soldier. He joined the U. S. Army in March 1950, just a few weeks after his 15th birthday.

Huey completed basic training at Fort Ord, California, and later in the year he was assigned to Company C, 32nd Regiment, 7th Infantry Division. In November 1950, his division landed at Iwon, Korea, and moved up to the eastern side of the Chosin Reservoir. As the Chinese entered the war in force, the troops were surrounded, and in the ensuing battle, Corporal Huey P. French was killed in action. He was manning a machine-gun position at the time. He died on 2 December 1950 at the age of 15.

Huey's twin sister, Joan French Blackburn of San Antonio, Texas, furnished the information above.

Dan Bullock was born in Goldsboro, North Carolina on 21 December 1953. He adjusted his birth certificate to read "1949" and enlisted in the U. S. Marine Corps on 18 September 1968. Although he did not have the consent of his parents, his enthusiasm about the service kept them from notifying officials about his age. In early 1969, Dan joined Fox Company, 2nd Battalion, 5th Marines in Vietnam. Three weeks after arriving in that country, Bullock was with his company in bunkers when they were attacked by the enemy. Bullock and three others died; 20 were wounded.

A story in the 13 June 1969 issue of *The New York Times* broke the news that Pfc. Dan Bullock was only 15. It was claimed that he was the youngest American serviceman to be killed in action in the Vietnam War.

In 1999, Bullock's friend, Franklin D. McArthur, Jr., founded the Pfc. Dan Bullock Foundation. The foundation objectives are to honor Dan Bullock by erecting a statue of him, providing an adequate headstone, and providing scholarships in his name to children of honorably discharged or active-duty members of the United States Armed Forces.

Information about Dan Bullock was obtained from the Dan Bullock Foundation's website, www.pfcdanbullockfoundation.org, and from Mr. Franklin D. McArthur, Jr.

Nothing to Fear

An important function of the Veterans of Underage Military Service is to assure veterans who served underage that there is nothing to fear, that the government is not "out to get them." In fact, most underage veterans now recognize it as a badge of honor to have circumvented the system in order to serve their country before they could legally do so. When Allan Stover founded the VUMS in 1991, he received many letters from underage veterans who were afraid they would get in trouble if anyone found out that their enlistment was fraudulent. One letter warned him that ... "the government can come down hard on you, and it is possible to be sued for all the money you have collected." The unsigned letter ended with, "You all better think about it before you go public."

To allay these fears, Stover wrote to the various branches of the military services asking about their policies relative to underage service. He received responses from the Army, Air Force, Navy, and Marines, clearly stating their policy, which was that underage veterans had nothing fear. Stover was somewhat taken aback by the response from the Coast Guard, the branch in which he had enlisted in at age 14. The letter from the Coast Guard Director of Personnel stated that he retained the right to prosecute Stover at any time. After an exchange of letters, the director said that he wouldn't prosecute, but that he retained the right to do so.

Stover then wrote to the Commandant of the Coast Guard and included copies of the correspondence with the Director of Personnel. In his letter, he said that he was ready to turn himself in to the Commandant for arrest and trial, but that he would bring a host of TV reporters with him. The response from the Commandant was immediate. He said that there had been a misunderstanding and that the Coast Guard's policy was the same as the Navy's.

Title 10, United States Code Armed Forces, and Title 32, United States Code National Guard, (As amended through April 6, 1991) address the issue of crediting minority service. Section 1039 of the Code states:

> For the purpose of determining eligibility for retirement or transfer to the Fleet Reserve or Fleet Marine Corps Reserve, entitlement to retired or retainer pay, and years of service in computing retired or retainer pay of a member of the armed forces, and service which would be creditable but for the fact that it was performed by him under an enlistment or induction entered into before he attained the age prescribed by law for that enlistment or induction, shall be credited.

If the United States Code states that time of service performed under an enlistment or induction entered into before attaining legal age can be counted towards retirement, it is obvious that the government is not "out to get" underage veterans.

Further evidence that underage veterans have been forgiven is a commendation to the Veterans of Underage Military Service that was placed in the Congressional Record on 27 February 1996 by the Honorable Owen B. Pickett, Member of the U. S. House of Representatives. The first paragraph of the commendation states:

> Mr. Speaker, I rise today to pay tribute to an often unacknowledged group of veterans that deserve recognition. Each of the members of this group joined the military and fought to defend this country before they were of legal age to do so. These brave and courageous young men have been represented in every war in which the United States has been involved. Most of the current members fought in World War II.

Several prominent members of the U. S. Congress have joined the VUMS. Sadly, two are now on the deceased roster. Congressman Bob Stump of Arizona, Chairman of the House Armed Services Committee, and former Chairman of the House Veterans Affairs Committee, served in the Navy at age 16. The story of his underage service appears on page 264 of the first volume of *America's Youngest Warriors*. The late Congressman Joe Moakley of Massachusetts, former Chairman of the House Rules Committee, and later Ranking Member of the Rules Committee, enlisted in the Navy at age 15 and served in the South Pacific during World War II. He died on Memorial Day 2001 after serving nearly 30 years as a Member of Congress. Several eulogies for Congressman Moakley that were broadcast nationally noted that he served in the Navy at age 15. Senator Mike Mansfield of Montana served as Majority Leader of the U. S. Senate longer than anyone before him, and later served as Ambassador to Japan for 12 years. Mansfield joined the Navy at age 14, the Army at age 15, and the Marines at age 17. Senator Mansfield died on 5 October 2001 at the age of 98.

With the publicity that underage veterans have received during the past decade, and the number of prominent Americans who served underage, these veterans should have no reason to fear "getting caught."

The
Stories

The following pages contain 200 stories contributed by members of the Veterans of Underage Military Service. The age and branch of military service at time of the enlistment is indicated under each name, for underage service only. Many contributors joined one branch of the military while underage, but re-enlisted and served in other branches later on.

Because of the large number of contributors, and because of the long time span and the number of events covered, it would have been impractical to check all factual details. Therefore, we have relied completely on the contributors for the content and accuracy of their stories.

The sequence in which the stories appear is based on the date of first enlistment while underage. The first story is from a veteran who joined the Army in 1917 during World War I, and the last story is from a veteran who joined the Marine Corps in 1969. Most of the stories are from the era spanning World War II, the Korean War, and the Vietnam War. All but a few contributors furnished a picture with their story.

Willis E. Earl, Sr.

Age 16 – United States Army

I was born in Gardiner, Oregon, on 4 June 1900. My father was a master mechanic with the Southern Pacific Railroad following his previous careers as a stagecoach driver and a steamboat

> About two weeks later, my parents caught wind of what I had done...

captain. My brother was a civil engineer with the railroad. At the age of 12 they got me a job building track between Coos Bay and Eugene, Oregon. Mr. Taylor was the engineer on the work train. I told him that I wanted to do what he did. He put a word in for me and I got a job at the roundhouse in Portland. At age 16, I took a room at a boarding house there.

After a few months, I told the foreman that I thought I should go to war. I asked him that if I did, would he give me my job back when I returned. He agreed. I walked over to the Portland Armory, and on 1 May 1917, I enlisted. I told them I was 19, even though I was only 16, and they did not question me. That very

day I was sent to the Army barracks in Vancouver, Washington. About two weeks later, my parents caught wind of what I had done and sent my aunt and uncle over to fetch me.   My uncle was a prominent attorney in the area and as it turned out, he and the commanding officer knew each other! The officer told my uncle to leave me in the Army, since it would mean a dishonorable discharge to get me out, and the war would be over in six months anyway. He felt that I would never leave

the Vancouver barracks, much less see action in France. That was that.

I was immediately sent to Kelly Field, Texas. It was nothing but a desert then. I was assigned as an office orderly for the commanding officer. I did not wait long before asking him to send me to France.

He said, "No!" About three weeks later, I worked up enough nerve to ask him again. This time he was very angry and responded, "If you want to go over there so badly and build latrines, then go!" I was transferred to the 55th Aero Squadron (later designated the 467th) and sent by train to Long Island, New York.

On 13 October 1917, we embarked on the S. S. *Pannonia*. After a voyage of 17 days, which was marked by exceptionally heavy weather and a submarine attack on the convoy, we landed at Liverpool. After crossing the channel to France we marched 16 kilometers with full pack to Issoudun, France. Camp was made by strewing straw on the ground in some empty hangars. We made the best of it for about six weeks until we constructed barracks.

Our squadron was made up of men who in civilian life were mechanics, carpenters, clerks, professional and commercial workers. We turned a mud hole into a well-ordered camp with power houses, roads, a sewage system, running water, and a network of buildings that could shelter 15,000 troops. We were proud of our efforts, and I made it from private to corporal fairly quickly. Being a bit of a rebel though, I lost that rank a time or two. I was once even demoted to buck private for almost breaking a guy's arm.

On 13 May 1918, the squadron was ordered to St. Jean-de-Monts, on the Bay of Biscay. We were to turn this wilderness into an aerial gunnery school. Because of our record and experience gained at Issoudun, Army headquarters had the confidence in us to pioneer this work. By summer's end there was a complete and modern camp in every sense of the word. I became a sergeant for about four weeks, but was again demoted for allowing my workers too many breaks.

By now our squadron realized and regretted that we were never going to see the front lines. But it was here at the Bay of Biscay that I and another fellow were able to make a bit of a difference in someone's life. After work one day, a friend and I went to the beach. We were lying there relaxing when over the ocean comes this sputtering plane, obviously in trouble. It crashed out a ways in the surf. We realized that there was not a soul around, except us, and we must move quickly if we were to help the pilot. We swam out to the plane and found the pilot unconscious, bleeding, and face down in the water. Together, we dragged him out of the plane and swam to shore with him. During the rescue, I took some sort of hit to my left eye and had to be sent to Nantes to have it looked at. That is the most action I saw while in France.

Our work was completed and again our squadron was on the move, this time toward the front at Chaumont. However, events brought the hostilities to an end with the signing of the armistice. While awaiting orders to return to America, the flu epidemic hit our squadron hard. Three of our men died. I got it pretty badly and nearly died there myself. While recuperating in the hospital, my squadron was sent to Brest, France, and was preparing to embark for home. I begged to be released so I could go with them. The doctor said, "If you can go down and put in a day's work as kitchen police, I'll let you go!" I did, and he held to his word.

The USS *Rochester* brought us home and I was discharged as a corporal on 25 March 1919.

I am currently the oldest known blood donor in the U. S. I have been a member of American Legion Post #1, Portland, Oregon, since 1919, and am a life member of the 40et8 Club. On 4 June 2000, I celebrated my 100th birthday. At that time I found out that the Veterans Administration still had my birthday as being born in 1897. They thought I was 103! Isn't that something?

Willis Earl returned home to Oregon and went back to the Southern Pacific Railroad where his job was waiting. He attended Oregon Agricultural College for a year (OAC is now OSU). He worked his way up to an engineer and became the road foreman of engines. In 1945, he retired from the railroad and began a career in electronics, eventually started his own business. He retired for the last time in 1968. Willis lives in Vancouver, Washington, near his family.

Frank Woodruff Buckles

Age 16 – United States Army

I was born on my father's farm north of Bethany in Harrison County, Missouri, on 1 February 1901. My father retired in 1905 and bought property in the small town of Coffey, where I started school. In 1910, he

> ..., the old sergeant advised me that the Ambulance Service was the quickest way to get to France, ...

bought a farm in Vernon County, near Walker, Missouri, where we enjoyed country living. In December 1916, we moved to Dewey County, Oklahoma, near Oakwood. I was 15 at the time, and I accompanied a boxcar load of draft horses and equipment to the farm. I knew that my father was planning to arrange for a man to take the horses to Oklahoma. He would be paid $20 and transportation back to Missouri. I asked my father if I could do the job, and he agreed. My parents came later by automobile.

In the charming little frontier town of Oakwood, population 300, I worked at the bank, lived at the hotel, and went to high school. On 6 April 1917, the United States entered the Great War and patriotic posters appeared in the post offices.

When summer vacation came, I was invited to the Kansas State Fair in Wichita. While there, I went to the Marine Corps recruiting office to enlist. I said that I was 18, but the understanding sergeant said that I was too young; I had to be 21. I went to Larned, Kansas, to visit my father's mother who was living with my aunt and uncle who owned a bank in Larned. A week later, I returned to Wichita and went to the Marine recruiting station. This time I stated that I was 21. The same sergeant gave me a physical examination, but kindly told me that I was just not heavy enough. I tried the Navy and passed the tests, but they were perhaps suspicious of my age and told me that I was flat-footed.

I decided to try elsewhere, so I went to Oklahoma City. There I had no luck with either the Marines or the Navy. I then tried the Army, but was asked for a birth certificate. I told them that the public records were not made of births in Missouri at the time I was born, and my record would be in the family Bible. They accepted this and I enlisted in the Army on 14 August 1917. Thirteen of us were accepted at the recruiting station and given rail tickets to Fort Logan, Colorado, where those who were accepted were sworn into the regular U. S. Army. My serial number was 15577.

In choosing the branch of the Army in which to serve, the old sergeant advised that the Ambulance Service was the quickest way to get to France because the French were begging for ambulance services. I followed his advice and was sent to Fort Riley, Kansas, for training and trench casualty retrieval and ambulance operations.

The unit that I went overseas with was called the First Fort Riley Casual Detachment, which consisted of 102 men. The ranking officer was a sergeant. I have a photo of this unit taken at Fort Riley.

We sailed from Hoboken, New Jersey, via Halifax, Nova Scotia, in December 1917, aboard the HMS *Carpathia*, the vessel famous for the rescue of the White Star Liner, *Titanic*, on 15 April 1912. Some of the officers and crew who made the rescue were aboard the *Carpathia* and were not averse to describing the rescue.

We docked in Glasgow, Scotland, and our unit continued on to Winchester, England, to await cross-channel shipment to France. A unit of the 6th Marines was operating Camp Hospital No. 35 near Winchester. Our unit was forced to replace the Marines who were sent on to France.

While in England, I drove a Ford ambulance, a motorcycle with sidecar, and a Ford car for visiting dignitaries. Others walked. After some weeks in England, I requested a meeting with the commanding officer of the area, Colonel Jones of the 6th Cavalry. I asked to be sent to France, and he explained to me that he, too, wanted to go to France but had to stay where he was ordered.

I finally got an assignment to escort an officer to France who had been left behind by his original unit. In France, I had various assignments and was at several locations. After Armistice Day I was assigned to a prisoner-of-war escort company to return prisoners back to Germany.

After two years with the AEF (American Expeditionary Force), I returned home on the USS *Pocahontas* in January 1920. I was paid $143.90, including a $60 bonus.

I went home to visit my parents, then decided to get a quick education in shorthand and typewriting at a business school in Oklahoma City. After four months of school, I got a job at the post office, working 4:00 p.m. to midnight. I was paid 60¢ an hour. In one month, I had enough money to take the train to Toronto, Ontario, Canada, where I got a job in the freight soliciting office of the White Star Line Steamship Company. I also had a night job with the Great Northwest Telegraph Company.

During the winter of 1921, I went to New York and got a job in the bond department of the prestigious Bankers Trust Company at 5th Avenue and 42nd Street. I used as my reference the Oakwood, Oklahoma, bank where I had worked at age 15.

The steamship business had more appeal for me, but first I had to have some experience at sea. I got my first sea job with the old Munson Line as assistant purser of the ship, *Western World*, bound for Buenos Aires. I spent several years with the Grace Line, in both cargo and passenger ships on the west coast of South America, where an intimate knowledge of the countries and language was required.

In 1940, I accepted an assignment to expedite the movement of cargoes for the American President Lines in Manila. Unfortunately for me, my stay was extended by the Japanese invasion of the Philippines in 1941. I spent three and a half years in Japanese prison camps at Santo Tomas and Los Baños. We were rescued by the 11th Airborne Division on 23 February 1945.

Life in San Francisco was pleasant after World War II. On 14 September 1946, I married Audrey Mayo of Pleasanton, California. She was born on a ranch, and my people were landowners and farmers for generations, so we decided it was time to give up foreign assignments and come back to the land. We came to Gap View Farm near Charles Town, West Virginia, in January 1954, to reside in the area where my forefather, Robert Buckles, his wife, and 15 other families settled in 1732.

Frank Buckles continues to work on his farm and still drives to town at the age of 101. His wife Audrey passed away. They have one daughter, Susannah. Frank lives near Charles Town, West Virginia.

Daniel L. Sjodin

Age 14 – Minnesota National Guard

I was a bugler in the Boy Scouts in my hometown of Aitkin, Minnesota, where I was born on 28 April 1919. The bugler in the local National Guard unit transferred to another city and

> I led a 36-bomber mission on Memorial Day 1944, and it was especially memorable.

they needed a bugler real bad. They came to me and asked me to join. I told them that I couldn't because I was only 14 years old. They asked me to get my parents' permission and they would sign me up as age 18. My parents approved, and I joined Company B, 135th Infantry Regiment, Minnesota National Guard, on 10 February 1934.

I worked a paper route, and in 1935 I earned enough money to buy a 1928 Model T Ford for $16. I fixed it up, painted it, and in 1936 I sold it for $32, which I thought was pretty shrewd. While in high school, I worked at the Gambles store in Aitkin, and continued with the store after graduating.

The 135th Infantry Regiment was mobilized in 1941 before the attack on Pearl Harbor and sent to Camp Claibourne, Louisiana. It was 30° below zero the night we left Minnesota. Three days later, we were in 90° Louisiana heat, and we changed into summer uniforms fast!

After a few days at Camp Claibourne, three of us from Aitkin transferred to the Army Air Corps to become pilots. I trained in California, New Mexico, and Idaho. I was made an instructor pilot and later became a squadron commander in a B-24 group that was forming. I was promoted to captain in 1943 and was given command of 20 bombers and their crews. After training in Nebraska, we flew to South America and on to Africa. Two thirds of the squadron was sent by two ships to Italy, but one of the ships was attacked and we lost 154 officers and men.

I flew my first mission out of Africa in early 1944, with the 485th Bomb Group. I flew a total of 50 missions over Germany in a B-24. I led a 36-bomber mission on Memorial Day 1944, and it was especially memorable. We bombed a refinery, wiping it out, and destroyed 17 German aircraft, with the loss of only one bomber. We received a Presidential Unit Citation for that raid.

I remained in the Air Force and obtained a regular commission in 1947. At that time, I had to correct my age on the records. I flew a C-54 aircraft during the Berlin Air Lift in 1948. We carried coal, flour, electrical supplies, and other cargo from Rhein Main Air Base, Frankfurt, Germany, to Templehof Air Base in Berlin, Germany. Every three minutes a plane would land loaded with needed supplies for Berlin. The Russians finally lifted the blockade due to the successful airlift.

I retired from the Air Force on 31 November 1961 as a lieutenant colonel after serving a total of 28 years.

Dan Sjodin was awarded the Distinguished Flying Cross for leading the Memorial Day 1944 raid, the Air Medal with three oak leaf clusters, and a number of other service medals. He earned a degree in history and political science from the University of Minnesota in 1957. He was a charter pilot for the University of Minnesota and sold life insurance for Midland Mutual Life Insurance Company. Dan and his late wife Virginia had three children. He lives at Mille Lacs Lake Isle, Minnesota, in the summer and in Harlingen, Texas, in the winter – the best of two worlds.

Dave E. Severance

Age 15 – Colorado National Guard

I was born on 4 February 1919, and grew up in Colorado, far removed from either ocean. I had been inspired to make a career of the military when I watched our Fourth of July parades. A local company of the

> ..., the colonel yelled at him, "See if you can get a larger flag."

Colorado National Guard would pass by in a truck decorated as if it were a gun position, firing blanks from their Browning water-cooled .30-caliber machine guns.

In December 1934, Jim, a high school buddy, told me that one could enlist in the National Guard by telling them he was 18 years old. On 11 December 1934, Jim and I were at the Guard meeting in the Armory. Both of us were tall for our age, and there were no questions asked. We became members of Company M, 157th Infantry Regiment, 45th Division, Colorado National Guard. I was 15 years old. What I didn't know for several years was that Captain George Irvin, the company commander, went by to see my father the next day and asked him if my enlistment met with his approval. He answered in the affirmative. Our pay was $1 per drill, a far better job than working in the hay fields for $1 per 12-hour day. A two-week summer drill was like going to summer camp. What a thrill it was for a 15-year-old kid to fire live ammunition from a .30-caliber machine gun!

I was selected by Captain Irvin to attend a West Point prep school at Fort Warren, Cheyenne, Wyoming, in the summer of 1937. The wrong answer to a yes-or-no question during my physical exam changed my whole life. I told the doctor I had suffered from hay fever earlier in my life, and I was disqualified. I stayed in touch with Captain Irvin until the day he died. He was promoted to colonel and assigned as General Hershey's assistant in the Office of Selective Service. I had so much respect for him that even after I was promoted to colonel, I still called him Colonel Irvin.

After a year at the University of Washington in Seattle, I returned to Denver, Colorado, and on 1 October 1938, I enlisted in the Marine Corps. When the recruiting officer asked me why I wanted to be a

Marine, I told him I wanted to fly. He said it was no problem, that all I had to do was to tell the drill instructor when I finished boot camp, and he would send me across the bay to the Naval Air station, North Island, and they would make an aviator out of me.

Sergeant William A. Searight, our senior drill instructor, was a handsome, calm, stately, and efficient Marine. He had three hashmarks (12 years' service), not unusual in the pre-World War II Marine Corps. During the last week of training, I asked to see him. When I repeated what the recruiting officer had told me, it was as if he were a thermometer filled with red mercury. The red started with his neck and flushed to his face. I did a non-regulation about-face and reached the door just ahead of his toe. Later, he did approve my request to attend Sea School.

After two years at sea, I returned to the Marine Corps Recruit Depot, San Diego, as a corporal in the 8th Marine Regiment. Six months later, July 1941, I was on my way to the Naval Air Station, Lakehurst, New Jersey, for paratroop training. About a week before completing my training, I was running up the two-flight stairway from the basement of the Marine barracks building. As I grabbed the railing post to swing around to the second flight, I crashed into somebody and knocked him flat on his back. The first thing I saw when I looked down was the two silver "railroad tracks" on his collar. I had knocked down a Marine captain! On second look, it was not just any captain, it was my Denver recruiting officer. He refused help in getting to his feet, so I apologized and took off. I saw this officer on many occasions in later years, but I do not believe he recognized me as the Marine who knocked him down on the Lakehurst stairs. As for me, I felt I had evened the score somewhat.

In early 1943, I was a sergeant in the 3rd Marine Parachute Battalion at Camp Elliott, San Diego, California. In order to be placed on the Headquarters Marine Corps Platoon Sergeant List one had to ask the commanding officer for a recommendation. Once I discovered that sergeants junior to me were making the list, I asked my battalion commander for a recommendation. He told me to go to town and have a passport photo taken (for 35¢) and return. When I next entered his office with my passport photo, he asked if I would rather be a second lieutenant than a platoon sergeant. Naturally, I chose the senior rank. With the Marine Corps in the process of building up from a strength of about 18,000 to over 400,000 men, they needed a number of second lieutenants. They had started a school for second lieutenants in the back country of Camp Elliott, called Green's Farm.

On weekends we returned to our barracks wearing small "OC" (officer candidate) pins on our collars. At first, we were being saluted by lieutenants and captains who were not familiar with the OC pins which, at a distance, looked like a major's emblem. Obviously, they chewed us out when they discovered their error. We soon made it a practice to salute all officers at a distance of about 30 yards!

Our unit sailed for the South Pacific in March 1943. On 4 December, we landed on Bougainville to support the 3rd Marine Division. I was a platoon leader. The day after landing, our units moved out to occupy Hill 1000 outside the 3rd Marine Division's perimeter. Four days later I had my platoon on a patrol behind a ridge adjacent to Hill 1000. My mission was to determine if any Japanese forces had reached the ridge. We discovered that they had when we were ambushed. Fortunately our units had trained against such attacks, and before long our fire power drove the Japanese from their ambush site. Our conservative estimate was that we had killed 16 of the enemy. Our loss was one killed.

In February 1944, all Marine parachute units were disbanded and I took command of Company E, 2nd Battalion, 28th Marine Regiment, 5th Marine Division, at Camp Pendleton, California. On 19 February 1945, our regiment landed on Iwo Jima over Green Beach, the beach closest to a 455-foot volcano called Mount Suribachi. By the evening of 21 February, we had destroyed the enemy defending the base of the volcano. On the morning of the 23 February, my battalion commander sent a four-man patrol up Suribachi. They reached the top with no resistance. He then called me and told me to send him a platoon-size patrol with my executive officer, First Lieutenant H. George Schrier, in charge. This 40-man patrol was to see how far up Suribachi they could go before being fired on by the Japanese. If they should reach the top, the battalion commander told Lieutenant Schrier as he handed him a small flag, they were to raise the flag.

The patrol climbed without opposition, and upon reaching the top, found a piece of pipe and raised the small flag. A Marine photographer, Sergeant Louis Lowery, accompanied the patrol, and once the flag was up, he took a photo with the men who raised it placed around the site. At about that time, several Japanese soldiers emerged from their caves, and before they were cut down, tossed several grenades at the Marines. One grenade landed near Sergeant Lowery. He leaped over the edge of the volcano and slid down about 30 feet. Other than scratches, he was not hurt. Although his camera was damaged, his film survived.

Almost simultaneously on the beach below, Lieutenant General Holland Smith and Secretary of the Navy James Forrestal were looking at the flag. Secretary Forrestal stated that he would like to have the flag as a memento of his visit. When this word reached my battalion commander, he said, "Hell, no! He can't have our flag. We put it up there and we are going to keep it." He had a scheme. He sent Second Lieutenant Alfred (Ted) Tuttle to the beach to obtain a second flag. Tuttle said that, almost as an afterthought, the colonel yelled at him, "See if you can get a larger flag."

When Tuttle returned with a large ceremonial flag, the colonel gave it to a detail from Company E that was preparing to string telephone wire to the top of the volcano. The detail included Sergeant Mike Strank, Corporal Harlon Block, Pfc. Ira Hayes, and Pfc. Franklin Sousley. With them was Pfc. Rene Gagnon, who was a Company E runner taking fresh batteries to Lieutenant Schrier's patrol.

Arriving on the beach shortly before Sergeant Strank's detail started up the volcano, was Associated Press photographer, Joe Rosenthal. He and two Marine photographers headed for the volcano, unaware that Sergeant Strank was carrying a second flag to the top. Sergeant Bill Genaust was carrying a movie camera with color film, and Joe Rosenthal and Pfc. Bob Campbell had still cameras. Part way up the mountain, the trio met Sergeant Lowery coming down to look for another camera. He told them that he had already photographed the flag-raising, but that the view was terrific. The trio decided to continue to the top. Arriving, they saw Sergeant Strank's group tying a flag to another pipe. Assisting the five Marines who carried the second flag up the volcano was Pharmacist's Mate Second Class John Bradley, a Navy corpsman, who had been with the first patrol.

Rosenthal was told that the small flag would be coming down as the larger one was raised. Genaust took a position about three feet to the right of Rosenthal, so they could both film the larger flag being raised. Bob Campbell moved to where he could photograph both flags as they were moved. Genaust asked Rosenthal if he was in his way. As Rosenthal turned his head to the right to answer, he caught movement out of the corner of his eye, and turned to frame the flag in his view-finder. He had just enough time to shoot one picture. He said he waited until the flag reached its "peak," apparently referring to the wind unfurling the flag. The resulting picture would become a Pulitzer Prize winner and be acclaimed as one of the most reproduced photos in history. Eventually, it was the inspiration for the Marine Corps War Memorial, which was dedicated on 10 November 1954, in Arlington, Virginia.

Company E would remain on the front lines on Iwo for 33 of the 36 days of combat. Company casualties, which were comparable to other front-line companies, reached 80 percent.

After World War II, I requested flight training and spent two years learning to fly. Subsequently, I served in a number of positions: as an instructor in the Aviation Section, Marine Corps Schools, Quantico, Virginia; as a night-fighter pilot of both propeller and jet aircraft in Korea, flying 69 night missions; with the Inspector General's staff, Headquarters Marine Corps; as commander of a jet squadron with atomic-weapons delivery capability; Operations and Training Officer, Naval Forces, Continental Air Defense Command, Colorado Springs, Colorado; as G-1, 1st Marine Air Wing in Japan; and as commanding officer of the Corps' largest Marine Air Reserve Training Command at Floyd Bennett Naval Air Station, Brooklyn, New York. I was serving as Assistant Director of Personnel, Headquarters Marine Corps, at the time I retired in 1968.

Dave Severance was awarded the Silver Star for his actions on Iwo Jima, as well as the Distinguished Flying Cross and four Air Medals for his Korean Service. He has been a volunteer at the Veterans Administration and a volunteer aircraft restorer at the San Diego Air and Space Museum. Since 1974, he has served as Secretary-Treasurer of a once 1,000+ man association of World War II Marine and Navy paratroopers. In June 1996, he and his wife Barbara were invited to Washington, D.C., by the Commandant of the Marine Corps where Colonel Severance carried the Olympic Torch from near Arlington Cemetery to the Marine Corps War Memorial before a crowd of 4,000 people. Dave and Barbara have four children and seven grand-children. They live in La Jolla, California.

Fred F. Eubanks, Jr.

Age 15 – Texas National Guard

My good buddy "Goose" Walker and I decided to join the National Guard when I was 15. We lived in Kingsville, Texas, at that time. I was born in Mart, Texas, on 20 October 1919. "Goose" and I joined Company G, 141st Infantry,

> I was told not to do it that way, but it worked!

36th Division, Texas National Guard on 9 June 1935, in Robstown, Texas. We hitchhiked from Kingsville to Robstown and back to attend meetings. We went to summer camp at Camp Hulen, in Palacios, and Camp Bullis, in San Antonio. I remained in the Guard until 30 August 1938.

After high school graduation in 1937, I went to Texas A&I College, then to the Schreiner Institute, after which I worked as a roughneck for Magnolia Petroleum. I married in 1941, and in 1942, we moved to Houston, and I joined the U. S. Marine Corps. At first, I was denied enlistment because my right eye did not pass the medical examination. I copied the eye chart, memorized all seven lines, and passed the eye exam in Houston, in San Antonio, and in San Diego.

At boot camp, although I was left-handed, I became a right-handed shooter and fired a record rifle score which got me a $5-a-month pay raise and early promotion to private first class. After boot camp, I was assigned to the Camp Mathews Rifle Range as chief instructor at the pistol range. I was promoted to corporal in 1943 and was selected to go to NCO Officer Candidate School in San Diego, then to Quantico, Virginia, for a commissioned officers' school.

After I was commissioned as a second lieutenant, I was sent to Camp Pendleton, California, to set up an infantry weapons training school. In 1944, I was ordered to the 2nd Marine Division on Saipan, Marianas Islands, where I was assigned to the 6th Marine Regiment. Shortly after I arrived, the regimental commander, Colonel Gregon A. Williams, asked me if I would like to form a regimental scout-sniper platoon. I thought that was a supreme honor. I was permitted to select "shooters" from anywhere in the regiment or the replacement draft that had just arrived. I assembled 40 top-guns. We were assigned to clean out enemy soldiers from caves and shoreline areas that had been by-passed during the fighting.

Colonel Williams called me in one day and told me we were going in to Nagasaki, Japan, as the first amphibious wave. He said I was to train my platoon half days as scout-snipers and half days as MPs. If we didn't encounter resistance on landing, I would become the Regimental Provost Marshal and my men would be MPs. That was the case, and we became MPs.

In 1950, I was en route to Camp Pendleton with my wife and daughter from the shooting matches at Quantico, Virginia. We stopped at a team-shooter's parents' dude ranch in Colorado for about five days. As we were leaving the ranch, I asked my wife to turn on the radio, and we heard the news that North Korean troops had crossed the border into South Korea. We went straight back to Camp Pendleton.

I arrived in Pusan, Korea, on 2 August 1950 as the executive officer of Company A, 1st Battalion, 5th Marines, 1st Provisional Marine Brigade. We fought in the Pusan Perimeter until early September, then we went aboard ship to join the rest of the 1st Marine Division to make the landing at Inchon on 15 September 1950.

We landed on Red Beach. I was on the left flank, right in front of a North Korean pillbox. People in front of me were being killed. I saw the two apertures they were firing from, so I went in between them. A young Marine in front of me was shot in the neck. I called for help, but the young man died in my arms. After he died, I got mad. I started throwing grenades into the apertures, but the Koreans would throw them back. So, I would pull the pins and hold the grenade for several seconds before throwing it. A Marine with a flamethrower that I had called for came up, but he was hit. I took the flamethrower, put the muzzle into the hole, and turned on the fuel. When the tank was almost empty, I sparked it and the pillbox blew up. I was told not to do it that way, but it worked!

As we moved inland, we ran into another pillbox. While I was attacking it, I was shot through the knee. I was evacuated to Japan and spent about three months in the hospital.

I returned to the States and spent the next few years as a training officer at Quantico, then joined the 6th Fleet for a tour of duty in the Mediterranean. My most memorable rifle and pistol team was a "pick up" from the 6th Fleet that won the Mediterranean Challenge Trophy from the British at Malta in 1958! Admiral Cassidy, commander of the 6th Fleet, asked me to form a team of Navy and Marine shooters from the fleet and challenge the British. His orders were to, "Beat the Brits!" I assembled a team and began training them. I told them that there would be no smoking, no drinking, and no liberty until after the match. We began training at 0500 every morning and trained all day. The training paid off; we won the trophy. Needless to say, the admiral was pleased – the British were not.

I returned to Camp Lejeune, North Carolina, and joined the 6th Marines just in time to be deployed to Lebanon for three months in 1958. During the Cuban missile crisis, I led Battalion Landing Team 2/2 as an expeditionary force. I later became an instructor in amphibious warfare at the Marine Corps Staff and Command College at Quantico. I was also range director at Camp Perry, Ohio, for the National Rifle and Pistol Matches for three years. In 1965, I went to Vietnam, served a year there on the MACV staff, then returned to the States and retired in 1966 as a lieutenant colonel. I served three years in the Texas National Guard and 24 years in the Marine Corps.

Fred Eubanks was awarded the Silver Star for his actions at Inchon and the Purple Heart for wounds received there. As a three-war veteran, he earned 28 other medals and ribbons, and was exposed to nuclear radiation and to Agent Orange. Throughout his Marine Corps career, he participated in and directed rifle and pistol matches and was frequently a medalist, earning the Distinguished Marksman Medal and many other marksman awards. After retiring from the Marine Corps, he was a foreign service officer in Vietnam for the Department of State for five years. Currently, he uses his background in marksmanship as a Texas certified, concealed-carry handgun instructor. Fred and Mildred, his wife of 60 years, have a daughter and two grandsons. Fred and Mildred live in Kerrville, Texas.

Leigh R. Wilson

Age 14 – Missouri National Guard

I was born in Corning, Missouri, on 2 November 1920. I enlisted in the Missouri National Guard, Battery C of the 128th Field Artillery Regiment, on 7 September 1935. It was a month and 23 days before my 15th birthday. I was a bugler and a captain's orderly in my first duty.

> They dropped 20,000 civilians on us and told us to make a division out of them.

We were mobilized in November 1940 and sent to Camp Jackson, now Fort Jackson, South Carolina. In the spring of '42, I went to Field Artillery OCS and was commissioned a second lieutenant. My next assignment was to the cadre of the 102nd Infantry Division at Camp Maxey, Texas. They dropped 20,000 civilians on us and told us to make a division out of them. It took us about five months, but we made a division out of them. At that point, I had volunteered for overseas duty. They had asked for volunteers among single lieutenants to report to Pittsburgh Replacement Depot, San Francisco, California.

We were told that this was an emergency replacement, and they were in a hurry. We arrived at the depot and stayed for six weeks, the usual "hurry up and wait." I was put in charge of a platoon of 80 to 85 lieutenants. I called roll every morning, and if there was no duty I just turned them loose.

I joined the 27th Infantry Division, which was originally a New York National Guard unit, in Hawaii. We set up defensive positions and conducted amphibious training in preparation for the Central Pacific offensive. We fought in the Gilberts and the Marianas. Saipan was quite an operation. Two Marine divisions and the 27th Infantry Division took 21 days to take the island. There is a lot of history in that operation.

On the final day, the Japanese commander summoned all Japanese who were left on the north end of the island. There were quite a few civilians, women and children, apparently. That morning he had 5,000 people equipped with everything from nice weapons to bayonets tied

to a stick.   He ordered them to attack us, which they did.   The
commander proceeded to commit suicide, and many civilians jumped
off the cliff.

Anyway, about 5,000 Japanese started their attack at 4:00 o'clock
in the morning of the final day of the operation. Lo and behold, they
hit my regimental combat team.   They just about wiped out two
battalions of the 105th Regiment, and in an area about 1,500 yards
deep, there were probably at least 3,000 Japanese bodies and 2,000
American. It was not pleasant when we got back in there.

We left Saipan for Espiritu Santo in the New Hebrides to lick our
wounds and reorganize. From there it was to Okinawa. We landed
without much problem because the Japanese commander had elected
to pull off the beaches. We turned south and ran into what was called
the Naha-Shuri line where the Japanese had positions dug in clear
across the island. This turned out to be a rough operation, but we did
secure the island. Our regimental combat team suffered about 2,500
casualties.

After the island was secure, we were mopping up the north end
when I got orders to go home. After a 30-day leave, I was to report
back to Okinawa to get ready for the Honshu operation. We were to
enter Osaka, with the 11th Airborne on our right. So I went home. I
left everything there, didn't bring any bags or anything. About two
weeks after I was home, Harry Truman saw fit to drop the bomb. A
few years later, I had the opportunity to thank him personally for that.
And I still thank him.

I joined the 129th Field Artillery after the war. I helped form what
was to become Battery D of the 129th in Independence, Missouri.
Harry Truman dedicated our armory. Not only that, but he came to
Maryville, Missouri, at the time I commanded the 129th Field Artillery
Battalion and dedicated our new armory there. Bess and Margaret
came with him. We had a nice conversation with him.

I commanded that battalion for about nine years. I helped form the
135th Artillery Group, which I commanded for 9 or 10 years. I was
Division Trains Commander in the 35th Division for one year and then
had a 5-year tour as Assistant Adjutant General of the Missouri
National Guard.

I retired as a brigadier general in 1980. My retirement orders
stated that I had 45 years, 1 month and 23 days of service. I have

been very fortunate. I was able to stay in contact with the Guard as chairman of the Insurance Trust for a number of years. Counting the Insurance Trust time, I served a combined 61 years with the Missouri National Guard and the U. S. Army. I am very thankful for that service.

Leigh Wilson was awarded the Army Distinguished Service Medal and the Legion of Merit, along with numerous other service medals. He attended Northwest Missouri State University from 1937 to 1940, and graduated from the University of Missouri in 1952 with a B.S. in business administration. Northwest Missouri State University conferred him an Honorary Doctor of Pedagogy degree on 26 July 2001. During his civilian career, Leigh was president of Wilson Court Inc., president of the Wilson Restaurant Corporation, vice president of the A-C Lighting Security Inc., and president of the Maryville Industrial Development Corporation from 1961 until 1988. His wife Barbara died in 1982. They had six children, one of whom is deceased. Leigh lives in Springfield, Missouri.

Alton Q. Kilmon

Age 16 – United States Army

I was born in Poulson, Virginia, on 14 September 1919. There were few jobs because of the Depression, so I decided to join the Army. A friend who had enlisted at Fort Monroe brought me an application. I filled out all but the blank for the birth date. After a lot of begging and pleading, my mother and dad signed it for me. After they signed, I filled in my birth date as 14 September 1917, and took it to a notary public, who was a friend. He signed it, wished me luck, and didn't even charge me a notary fee.

> *"Sergeant, I'm General Marshall; I would like to see your facility."*

I was sworn into the Army at Ft. Monroe, Virginia, on 25 February 1936, and assigned to A Battery, 2nd Coast Artillery Corps. I received basic training at Ft. Monroe, and my first assignment after basic was at the Boat House, where the Submarine Mine Depot was.

In 1940, I attended the Coast Artillery School at Ft. Monroe, and after completion of the school I was assigned to A Battery, 71st Antiaircraft Artillery Battalion. I served in the antiaircraft defense of Washington, D.C., from 5 January 1942 until the spring of 1944. Our unit was stationed at a small compound on the Washington side of the Lincoln Memorial Bridge, not far from the U. S. Army Headquarters on 14th street. Across the Potomac River, construction of the Pentagon had gotten underway the year before.

There were several antiaircraft batteries at the compound which were manned 24 hours a day. One Sunday morning in 1942, I was checking positions at the detachment's sentry box, when an officer rode up on a horse. "Sergeant, I'm General Marshall; I would like to see your facility." the officer said. I replied, "Yes, sir! I recognize you, but I need some identification." General Marshall dismounted and produced the required identification. We then toured the facility. General Marshall stayed about an hour, drank coffee, and visited with the soldiers. Before he left, he told me that he would like to come by the compound to visit and relax whenever he had a chance. Of course, I told him that he would be welcome, but I never thought that it would happen. After all, George C. Marshall was Chief of Staff of the Army and had many pressing duties to occupy his time.

The following Saturday, I got an inkling that the general was serious because he had his driver leave off a basketful of fruit for the soldiers. The general did become a frequent visitor, usually on Saturdays or Sundays. His driver would bring him to the compound and wait while the general would drink coffee and visit with us, walk the grounds, or just rest on a bunk in the barracks.

Early in 1943, I was told to report to U. S. Army Headquarters with a detail of soldiers. The headquarters was being moved to the Pentagon and my detail's job was to move the personal desk of General Marshall. Following his move to the Pentagon, the general continued his weekend visits to our compound.

Later in 1943, I was transferred to Camp Shelby, Mississippi, and assigned to the 588th Engineer Bridge Company. We went to Germany in the fall of 1944. I served in Germany until October 1945 and came back to the States for a 90-day furlough.

I reported back to Ft. Monroe, and in the summer of 1946 I was assigned to a service unit at Ft. Moultrie, South Carolina, at Charleston. At this time a National Guard unit which was on active Army duty was manning Ft. Moultrie.

In the fall of 1946, I was ordered to the Pacific for the atomic bomb tests. Upon receiving the orders, I went to the personnel office and questioned why I was ordered overseas when there were at least ten persons in the outfit with the same MOS (Military Occupational Specialty) who had never been overseas. With no answers given, I proceeded to the Post Commander's Office. I knocked on the door and went in. He asked me if he could help me. I explained what I felt was wrong in being sent back overseas. This man had been a prisoner of the Japanese. His eyes were damaged during his time as a prisoner, so he had to read with a magnifying glass, which he was doing at the time I went into the room. After hearing my explanation, he called in someone from personnel, and then he told me I was excused and to forget about the Pacific.

In December 1946, I was placed on orders to go to Leghorn, Italy. There I was assigned to the 88th Infantry Division, 913 Field Artillery Battalion, in Gorizia, Italy. Gorizia was under martial law at this time due to a dispute over the border between Italy and Yugoslavia.

About midsummer of 1947, the dispute was settled and I was detailed to take a convoy of trucks to an infantry battalion and move the battalion to the city of Trieste, which had been made a free territory. I reported to Major McPhearson, the battalion commander, completed the move in two days, then returned to Gorizia.

In December 1947, I returned to the States and was assigned to the 82nd Airborne Division at Ft. Bragg, North Carolina. When I refused to go to jump school, they allowed me to be discharged early, and I decided to quit the Army.

I returned to Hampton, Virginia, in September 1948, and went to the Submarine Mine Depot at Ft. Monroe to look for work as a civilian. There I found many soldiers that I had served with from 1936 to 1940. The commanding officer was a lieutenant when I was there in the early years. He told me that there were no jobs for civilians, but if I would re-enlist, there was a job in the Army for me. I re-enlisted immediately and never lost a day of service.

I served at the Submarine Mine Depot until January 1950, when it was deactivated. General Tuftoy, the chief of ordnance, came to brief us on our new assignment. The general had served there previously as a lieutenant.

All graduates of the Coast Artillery School were assigned to the Redstone Arsenal in Huntsville, Alabama. There we did research and development on guided missiles. Most of our work was on the Redstone missile, which carried our first man into space.

In the spring of 1952, I went to the Pentagon in Washington, D.C., to the office of the Chief of Ordnance, and was assigned to the Joint Task Force at the Navy Research Laboratory, Washington, D.C. In the late summer of 1953, we went to Eniwetok for the first hydrogen bomb test. When I returned from the tests, I was assigned to Sandia Base in Albuquerque, New Mexico, where I entered a school for the study of nuclear weapons. When I met my commanding officer for the first time, I remembered that he was the major whose battalion we moved to Trieste in 1947. Of all the men under whom I served in my Army career, Colonel Mac was the best.

In December 1954, the 15th Ordnance Battalion was transferred to Wierhof, Casern, Germany. I stayed there until 31 March 1957, when I retired. The years 1950 to 1957 were the best years of my service, which I thoroughly enjoyed. During my time in the service I had my ups and downs, but I would do it all over again for my country.

Alton Kilmon received a number of commendations from the Army, the Navy, and the U. S. Civil Service. After retiring from the Army, he worked for 16 years at the Fort Monroe Post Engineers Department. Alton has two children, six grandchildren, and six great-grandchildren. He lives in Hampton, Virginia.

✓ *INCIDENTally* — *Ouch!* – While serving on the USS *Dortch* during World War II, our chow was very limited: dehydrated vegetables, dried milk, powdered eggs, mutton and goat cheese from Australia. The bread always had weevils in it. When we got our first liberty back in the States, four of us went to a nice restaurant and ordered all the good things we had missed. Our waitress was attractive and very congenial. I made the comment, "For two cents I'd bite her on the butt." One of my buddies produced two cents and said, "Doc, I dare you." When she returned, I bit her, expecting to get slapped and asked to leave. Instead, she turned around and said, "Nice, isn't it?" I was so embarrassed I could have crawled under the table. – *Charles R. Johnson.*

34

Albert E. Crane

Age 14 – Oregon National Guard

My military career began in 1936 and ended
in 1972. I enlisted in Company F, 2nd Battalion,
162nd Infantry Regiment, 41st Infantry (Sunset)
Division, Oregon National Guard, on 16

> *That 1-year tour became five years.*

November 1936, at Portland, Oregon. I told them that I was 18, but
I was only 14. I was born on 6 January 1922. That was it! No birth
certificate or parental permission was required. I found out later that
several men in the company were underage.

My motivation for enlisting was twofold: curiosity, and getting paid
$12 every three months. That was a lot of money for a teenager to
have in those days. Having money to buy new clothes reduced the
problem of wearing hand-me-down, ill-fitting, clothing. However, there
must have been some patriotism involved. How much, I don't know.
Later, I was selected as an honor guard for the colors during parades.
Each parade was an emotionally moving experience for me.

Summer active-duty training in 1937 was at Camp Clatsop on the
coast of Oregon. In 1938, it was at Fort Lewis, Washington. I also
attended the Citizens' Military Training Camp at Vancouver Barracks,
Washington, in 1938. That was the year a spooked mule destroyed a
machine gun and a two-wheeled gun cart while running down a hill.

Early in 1939, I dropped out of high school and left home. The
Spokane, Portland, and Seattle Railroad hired me as a "gandy dancer"
on a section gang a few miles south of Pasco, Washington. The formal
title for the job was "Maintenance of Way Employee." A lot of hard
work was the simplest description of the job.

I was discharged from Company F in October 1939 and re-enlisted
in January 1940, the day after my 18th birthday. I did not attempt to
change my age in my service records at that time. In the fall, I
received that famous letter from President Roosevelt (as did many
others) telling me that my unit was going on active duty for one year.
That 1-year tour of duty became five years.

The division was sent to Camp Murray, near Fort Lewis,
Washington. One day, another private and I discussed our future

during the year of training ahead. We agreed that promotion to corporal was all that we could expect. Both of us were commissioned officers by the time the war was over.

Rumors about an extension of active duty beyond our 1-year obligation were disturbing to many. Vehicles and buildings were marked with "OHIO." This implied that the men were going "over the hill in October" as deserters. The 2nd Battalion had been on a field exercise and we were to return to camp in trucks. As we approached the trucks we could see "OHIO" marked on them. The battalion commander was not amused at what he saw. He sent the trucks back to the motor pool and made us walk the 10 miles back to camp. Our active-duty period was extended indefinitely, but I do not recall any "OHIO" desertions.

Within hours after the Pearl Harbor bombing, we were on guard duty in the Seattle, Washington, area. Within a week, elements of the division were spread throughout the coastal areas of Washington and Oregon, on guard duty.

In February 1942, the 162nd Infantry Regiment, and other elements of the division, moved to Fort Dix, New Jersey, by train. In March 1942, we shipped out of the Brooklyn Navy Yard aboard the SS *Santa Paula* and the SS *Uruguay* as part of a convoy heading south, through the Panama Canal. We arrived in Melbourne, Australia, after a "forty days and forty nights" trip. I could never figure out why we were sent from the West Coast on such a roundabout way to get to the South Pacific.

By the end of May 1942, the division was assembled near Seymour, north of Melbourne, at a World War I Australian Army camp. It seemed that we ate mutton stew three times a day for weeks. In February 1943, the 162nd Infantry Regiment landed at Oro Bay, Papua, New Guinea. We route-marched up the coast to a place called Gona, a short distance northwest of Buna. A few weeks there patrolling and building defense positions was a prelude to intensive combat starting in June 1943 in the Salamaua – Lae area on the shores of Huan Gulf. After 76 days of continuous combat, the 162nd Regiment and other elements of the division returned to Rockhampton, Queensland, Australia.

In October 1943, I was selected for officer candidate school, even though I did not have a high-school diploma. I had worried about my first-enlistment lie for seven years. It was time to clear the record. The company commander listened to my story and sent me to the battalion adjutant. I filled out a form, and my records were corrected. The only penalty I suffered was a partial pay reduction because Congress had enacted a law against underagers. Full pay was reinstated many months later, with no retroactive pay authorized.

I completed OCS at Camp Columbia, near Brisbane, Australia, in May 1944 and was assigned to the 32nd Infantry (Red Arrow) Division as a second lieutenant. The division was at Aitape, New Guinea. On arrival, I was assigned to Company L, 127th Infantry Regiment. There was plenty of combat in the following days.

In October 1944, I was evacuated to a hospital in Lae, New Guinea, with infectious hepatitis. I rejoined the division on the Villa Verde Trail on Luzon, the largest northern island of the Philippines. I was assigned to Company G, 127th Infantry Regiment. We had 119 days of intensive combat before Lieutenant General Tomoyuki Yamashita surrendered to the 128th Infantry, 32nd Division, on 2 September 1945. General Yamashita, supreme commander of the Japanese troops in the Philippines, was known as the "Tiger of Malaya," and the "Butcher of Bataan." We renamed him the "Gopher of Luzon," because his troops dug covered spider-holes and elaborate tunnel systems for hiding and protection.

I was discharged from active duty at Fort Bliss, Texas in October 1945. I had served 38 months and 10 days overseas. I joined the 49th Infantry (Argonaut) Division of the California National Guard in 1948, and retired as a lieutenant colonel in 1972.

Al Crane was awarded the Bronze Star and the Combat Infantryman's Badge. He also earned a number of service medals. From 1945 until 1951 he worked as a foreman on a 500-acre farm near Modesto, California. In 1951 he enrolled in San Jose State College under the GI Bill and received a B.A. and a secondary teaching credential in 1954, followed by an M.A. in 1960. He taught biological science at San Jose City College for nearly 30 years. In December 1972, Al married into a ready-made family of five girls and one boy. The boy is now a retired Marine Corps major. He and is wife Virginia have twenty-five grandchildren and two great-grandchildren. Al and Virginia live in Fallbrook, California.

Jehu P. Malone

Age 14 – United States Army
Age 16 – United States Army

When I was born in Chicago, Illinois, on 19 February 1923, my father named me Jehu Peter Paul Patrick Malone. I'm sure he named me after three saints figuring that was as close to Heaven as I would ever get. He may have been right!

> We asked if I could add my two years of honorable service to my age and be classified as 18.

During my first semester of high school, I hit a teacher. This was in September 1937, and hitting a teacher was a real no-no in those days. I was sent to juvenile court, and the judge gave me a choice. I could go to reform school, or quit school and try to find work to help my family, which consisted of my father, mother, and older brother.

In those days, you could quit school at age 15, and I was close to that. I had been taking Junior ROTC in school and liked it so much I thought that I would eventually like to attend the U. S. Military Academy at West Point and make a career of the Army. Knowing that I could never get into the Academy with reform school on my records, I chose to drop out of school and to go into the Army when I was old enough. There was always a chance that I could take the entrance exams for the Academy, but it would be hard without a high school diploma.

My ROTC instructor, a regular Army sergeant named A. D. Lee, talked with my parents. He told them that he might be able to help me, as I had shown promise in ROTC. He took me to the recruiting station in Chicago to talk to a recruiter. Sergeant Lee explained the problem and told him of my wish to join the Army. The following dialog ensued:

The recruiter asked me, "When will you be 18?"

I replied, "February 19, 1941."

He said, "I don't want to hear that! When will you be 18?"

Again, I said, "February 19, 1941."

"One more time. When will you be 18?" he asked.

This time I said, "In February."

He said, "That's it! Let's make out the enlistment papers."

The recruiter filled out the form and had Sergeant Lee sign it as though he knew my true age to be 17. I'm sure Lee knew that I was just 14.

I was assigned to a horse-drawn 75mm cannon in an artillery unit. The only horses I had ever seen were pulling milk and ice wagons. I didn't know anything about horses, but I learned very fast that there were two kinds of equine animals: horses and mounts. A horse was used to move the guns, a mount was what you rode.

After almost two years of service, I was called in to the battery commander's office. "Are you 19 or 16? We have checked and found that you enlisted fraudulently," the commander said. They gave me a minority discharge.

I went back home and went back to school. A few weeks later, I hit the same teacher that I had hit two years before. Knowing that I couldn't stay in school, I went to Sergeant Lee and asked him if there was any way that I could re-enlist. He talked to someone at the recruiting office about my problem. If you are over the maximum age for enlistment, but have already served honorably, you can deduct those years from your age. We tried it the other way. We asked if I could add my two years of honorable service to my age and be classified as 18. The recruiting office sent a request for a waiver to the adjutant general. The adjutant general's office sent a telegram to the effect that no one had ever posed that question before, but if we could deduct, we could add.

I enlisted on 13 December 1939. I was 16 years old. I was assigned to the Medical Company of the 1st Infantry Regiment at Camp Jackson, South Carolina. We maneuvered from South Carolina to Texas, and then to our home station at Fort Francis E. Warren, Wyoming. I was transferred to the station hospital and became a surgical technician.

In February or March 1941, I was sent to Camp Clatsop, Oregon, as part of the cadre. I had made private first class, with specialist first class. I wore one stripe up and six rockers underneath. My monthly pay was $30 for private first class and $36 for specialist.

About that time they did away with the specialist ratings and came up with the technical ranks.

In May or June 1941, the 1st Battalion, 37th Infantry Regiment was assigned to Dutch Harbor, Alaska. On 7 December 1941, war was declared and the telegram we got contained a sentence saying, "Outposts will be sacrificed for the good of the nation." This made you feel real good, knowing that you were one of the outposts they were referring to.

We withstood the bombings by the Japanese on 3 and 4 June 1942. This was when the first Japanese Zero fighter was shot down and recovered in one piece, more or less. I understand that it was brought back to the States, repaired, and flown all around the States. It had the original meatball insignia, and no one ever noticed, nor reported it!

When the war ended, I was on assignment to the Treasury Department on a special war-bond tour. There were teams of us that went to every state, with the sole purpose of selling war bonds. One man, Chuck Kelly from Pittsburgh, was a Medal of Honor recipient. He would auction off the blue-ribbon bar to the person who pledged to buy the most bonds. He would give that person the blue-ribbon bar, then later would tell that person that it was the only one he had, and he would really be out of uniform without it. Nine times out of ten, the person would give it back. Actually, he had a cigar box half-full of the blue-ribbon bars. He sold a lot of bonds that way.

I was discharged on 8 August 1945 and returned to high school. I was older than some of my teachers. While in high school, I had to get permission from the Veterans Administration and the Board of Education to miss three days of school so I could get married and have at least two days for a honeymoon.

I was not doing well in high school. I had the same teacher that I had hit twice before. Rather than get into more trouble, with the principal's permission, I went to the Chicago Board of Education and took the GED test. I passed with flying colors and again re-enlisted in the Army.

I went to officers candidate school at Fort Riley, Kansas, in 1948. I had to straighten out my age before they would accept my application. I graduated as a second lieutenant, Ordnance Corps. I went from a branch with no weapons (medical) to a branch where I was an automotive-platoon and small-arms maintenance officer. I resigned in 1954, in lieu of a court-martial. When I re-enlisted again, I served as a recruiter, an infantry medic, a National Guard advisor, and finally, an ROTC instructor at Marquette University. I retired on 31 May 1962.

I was recalled to active duty in July 1966 and was sent to Korea. I returned to civilian life in 1968. I was informed in the year 2000 that I had been advanced on the retired list to the rank of second lieutenant, with 28 years and 3 months' difference in back pay. That came out to be a substantial amount of pay. It also increased my monthly pay quite a bit.

"Doc" Malone received the Combat Medical Badge along with the usual medals one gets in 30 years. He maintains that the name of the badge is a misnomer because medics are non-combatants, according to the Geneva Convention. After he retired from the Army, he was employed by the Wisconsin Employment Service (he called it the Enjoyment Service), working mainly with veterans. He retired from service with the state of Wisconsin in 1983. Doc and Betty, his wife of 56 years, have one daughter, two sons, one granddaughter, and two great-grandsons. They live in Merrillan, Wisconsin.

Lyle J. Bouck, Jr.

Age 14 – Missouri National Guard
Age 16 – United States Army

I was born in St. Louis, Missouri, on 17 December 1923, and like most families during the Great Depression, our family was very poor. My father was a World War I veteran and had served in the National

> I asked what we should do. The reply was, "Hold at all costs!"

Guard. He knew that the Guard paid a dollar a day and served three meals a day at the two-week summer camp. At his suggestion, my brother Robert and I joined the 138th Regiment, 35th Infantry Division, on 3 August 1938. Robert was 19, but I was only 14. I never had to lie about my age because nobody ever asked me. I was handed an application and I signed it. The Guard needed bodies for the summer maneuvers and many members dropped out after summer camp. However, I enjoyed summer camp and decided to stay in. I made the drill nights and the summer camps of 1938, 1939, and 1940.

We were activated into the U. S. Army on 16 December 1940, one day before my 17th birthday. We were sent to Camp Joseph T. Robinson, Little Rock, Arkansas, where I was the supply sergeant. I became the transportation sergeant during the Louisiana maneuvers. Our one year of active duty was almost completed when the Japanese attacked Pearl Harbor. We were ordered to remain on active duty for the duration plus six months.

The 35th division was ordered to the West Coast where the 138th Regiment was separated from the division and sent to the Aleutian Islands. I thought that Dutch Harbor, Alaska, was the most dismal place on the face of the earth. I was also at Umnak, Cold Bay, and Kodiak. It was so cold that I searched for any means of escape. Although I had only completed my freshman year in high school, I applied for OCS (officers candidate school). I completed my application for OCS by simply filling in the proper space indicating that I had completed high school. When I was accepted for OCS, I had my records brought up to date and my age corrected. Until that time, my underage status was never mentioned.

I completed OCS at Fort Benning, Georgia, on 26 August 1942 and was commissioned a 2nd lieutenant. I was 18 years old. I remained at Fort Benning as a small-unit instructor for two years. I was transferred to Camp Maxey, Texas, where I became the platoon leader of the I&R (Intelligence and Reconnaissance) Platoon, 394th Regiment, 99th Infantry Division. There was only one man in the platoon who was younger than I was. We were sent overseas in the fall of 1944.

We were on the line near Lanzerath, Belgium, on the night of 15 December 1944. This was the location where the 1st SS Panzer Division was to spearhead the German counteroffensive that would soon become known as the Battle of the Bulge. They were to break through and reach the Meuse River within the first 24 hours. Hitler had personally selected SS Lieutenant Colonel Jochen Peiper, Heinrich Himmler's adjutant, to direct the spearhead. Peiper was commanding officer of the 1st SS Panzer Regiment. The crack 9th Parachute Regiment of the 3rd Parachute Division was to punch a hole in the American lines to allow Peiper and his tanks to speed to the Meuse and capture the bridges before the Americans had time to destroy them.

My 18-man platoon was on a hillside overlooking the town. A tank-destroyer outfit was in the town. The next morning the Germans opened up with an artillery barrage. We were the target for a time, then they began firing at targets behind us. I watched the tank-destroyer outfit hurriedly leave the town, so I took a few men and went into Lanzerath, which had no more than 10 houses, and found a vantage point on the top of a building. Looking down the road beyond the town, I saw a column of German troops heading toward us. I radioed this information to headquarters, but they didn't believe me. I asked for artillery, but none came.

We watched the German troops enter the town and waited for them to come into our range of fire. I again asked battalion headquarters for artillery fire, but they said there were no guns available. I asked what we should do. The reply was, "Hold at all costs!"

The 18 of us were in log-covered foxholes and in perfect position to ambush the column. We waited until the lead elements had passed, and I was about to give the order to fire when a little blond girl with red ribbons in her hair dashed out of a house and pointed out our position to the Germans. Our ambush was ruined and the firefight began. The paratroops kept coming straight down the road in perfect order. They were easy targets. The range was so close that we could see their faces. We kept firing and repelled three attacks by the Germans. By mid-afternoon, there were many bodies in front of us. One of our men was killed and over half were wounded. We ran out of ammunition and were captured as we attempted to withdraw.

We were taken to a café that had been set up as a first-aid post. We were held in a room that was the German forward-command post and were spectators as the Germans tried to determine where the American force was that had stopped their advance. I couldn't understand what the Germans were saying, but I learned later that Colonel Peiper had ordered the paratroop commander to give him a battalion of infantry to ride with his tanks so he could make the breakthrough. They didn't realize that the 18 of us had stopped an entire parachute battalion.

I had been wounded and was on a stretcher when a cuckoo clock in the café struck midnight. I had just turned 21. I mumbled to myself, "What a hell of a way to become a man!"

The day after we were captured, Colonel Peiper ordered 210 American prisoners of war to be killed. This became known as the Malmedy Massacre. Peiper was later tried and found guilty of the massacre.

We were packed aboard a POW train that reached the marshaling yards at Limburg, Germany, on 23 December 1944. British bombers blasted the rail yard that night and blew up the boxcar just ahead of the one I was in. I didn't know it at the time, but Kurt Vonnegut, Jr., now a famous author, was on the same train. We met for the first time 50 years later.

We were taken to a prison compound on a hilltop overlooking Hammelburg, Germany, and were jammed into a 20-foot by 20-foot concrete vault with shower heads on the walls. We had heard that the Germans were gassing captives, so we were greatly relieved when only water came from the nozzles.

On good days we subsisted on meager portions of watery turnip soup, hard black bread made from potatoes, barley, and sawdust, and cooked beet jam. On bad days we got nothing, or perhaps a vile broth of dehydrated vegetable tops with a slimy film of white maggots floating on the top. We dubbed the broth "the Green Hornet."

A harrowing experience occurred on 27 March 1945. General George S. Patton's son-in-law, Lieutenant Colonel John K. Waters, was a prisoner at our camp. A 350-man armored column of the 4th Armored Division drove 60 miles through the German lines in an attempt to liberate us. When the American troops arrived, the German guards fled. We were liberated, but Colonel Waters was not among us because he had been hospitalized. On our way back to the American lines, we were surrounded by a massive German force and recaptured. I was shipped to Moosburg, a camp near Munich. We were liberated on 29 April 1945 by the 14th Armored and the 99th Infantry Divisions. I weighed 112 pounds and had hepatitis.

I was brought back to the States and shipped to O'Reilley General Hospital in Springfield, Missouri, where I regained my health. I was released from active Army duty on 31 December 1946, but remained in the Missouri National Guard until 15 January 1951.

Lyle Bouck was awarded the Distinguished Service Cross in 1981, 37 years after the battle in which he distinguished himself. He also earned the Silver Star, the Bronze Star, the Purple Heart with two oak leaf clusters, and the Combat Infantryman's Badge. He and the 17 men in his platoon received a Presidential Unit Citation for stopping the German advance on 16 December 1944. They have been credited with significantly delaying the timetable of the German offensive that began on that day. (Details of this action and Lyle Bouck's heroic exploits appear in a number of books including: The Bitter Woods, *by John Eisenhower;* A Time for Trumpets, *by Charles McDonald;* Citizen Soldiers, *by Steven Ambrose;* Best Stories from World War II, *by C. Brian Kelly;* Blood Dimmed Tide, *by Gerald Astor;* Key to the Bulge, *by Stephen M. Rusiecki;* Massacre at Malmedy, *by Charles Whiting; and* Twenty Five Yards of War, *by Ronald J. Drez. Drez devotes 30 pages to the action at Lanzerath.)*

After the war, Lyle earned a doctor of chiropractic degree from Missouri Chiropractic College. He practiced his profession in St. Louis for 51 years before retiring in 1999. In 1946 he married Lucille Zinzer, a grade school classmate. Lyle and Lucy have five children and twelve grandchildren. They live in St. Louis, Missouri.

Jerome A. "Jerry" Gettler

Age 15 – New York National Guard
Age 16 – United States Army

I was born in Brooklyn, New York, on 15 February 1924. At the time I was born, my dad apparently had a fairly responsible job with a manufacturing company. We moved to Toledo, Ohio, in

> *It was easy to join. We simply signed a statement that we were 18 years old.*

1930 and lived there for about a year, then returned to New York. That was the year my dad lost his job, and the Depression was in full gear. Times were tough! Sometimes my dad worked at three jobs at the same time, bringing in meager amounts from each.

I inherited a paper delivery route from an older brother who had inherited it from our oldest brother. Life consisted of getting up at about 5 a.m., in the winter stoking the coal fire in the basement, delivering the papers, fixing breakfast, and going to school. After school, papers were delivered on the second route. This was seven days a week, year-round, for $5 a week, of which $4 went to the family to help with the food bill.

My elementary education was at a Catholic school where students were highly disciplined. I walked to school, more than a mile each way. My mother was an excellent cook. She prepared potatoes in many ways. Potato pancakes were a favorite. Things got so desperate at one point that my mom had me take her wedding ring to pawn. I took it to a pawn shop and got $10 for the ring. One Christmas when we couldn't afford a Christmas tree, I put in extra time peddling  magazines at the Long Island Railroad Station and earned the 50¢ to buy a tree.

In 1939, when I was 15 years old, I was pals with a couple of boys who were a year or two older than I was. They knew of boys who were joining the National Guard and going to drills and summer camp.

This sounded interesting and a way to earn a few extra dollars and get away for two weeks. So on 13 June 1939, I enlisted in Company G, 165th Infantry Regiment, 27th Division, New York National Guard. This was the regiment that was known as "The Fighting 69th" during World War I, and of which a movie of the same title was made. It was easy to join. We simply signed a statement that we were 18 years old. No verification was required.

In 1940, the U. S. Congress passed a draft law that included the induction to active duty of reserves and National Guard units for one year of service. Since I was 16 and still underage, I could have opted out of active duty. However, since I had less than a year left to complete high school, I discussed the options with my parents. I could get out of the Guard and finish high school, then face the draft as soon as I turned 18. Or I could go in with people I knew and get my year of service out of the way. My parents agreed that I might as well go, and they consented to my staying in.

Our division was inducted into active federal service on 15 October 1940. We were sent to Fort McClellan, Alabama. By the time I was 17, I was a rifle platoon sergeant, and I was assigned to a training cadre established for training of the draftees who we were getting in to bring the division up to full strength.

Before our year of active duty was up, the Congress passed another law extending our tour from one to three years. During our long, hot, and tough maneuvers through the hills and fields of Arkansas and the bayous and snakes of Louisiana, there was almost a mutiny in the ranks. An informal club was formed in protest of the tour extension. This was the OHIO club, "Over the Hill in October." Shortly after returning from maneuvers, we were granted furloughs to go home for Thanksgiving. This helped to diffuse the mutiny, and before it could start up again, the attack on Pearl harbor changed everything.

Within five days we were on a troop train heading west. Five days later we were in Southern California pulling guard duty around the West Coast aircraft plants. This is when I realized it would be a long war. Watching those planes take off and land gave me the bug to join the Air Corps. I was now 18 years old and could legally apply for aviation cadet training. I took the exams and passed. My orders for transfer to cadet training came through only one day before my outfit shipped out from Fort Ord for overseas. I was unassigned, and fortunately, I got four months of furlough time before there was an opening in the cadet training program.

After three grueling days of qualification testing to determine if we were best qualified for pilot, navigator, or bombardier, I learned that I was accepted for pilot training. From there it was pre-flight training at Santa Ana, California, then primary at Santa Maria, California, where 50 percent of the class washed out. I almost washed out just before soloing, but that, and other events, are subjects for a much longer story. After that, I was very fortunate and seemed to sail right through flying school, getting exactly what I wanted: twin-engine fighter training in P-38s. On 28 July 1943, I graduated from flight school at Williams Field, Arizona, as a second lieutenant, and had earned my silver wings.

After graduation we went through transition training at Muroc, California, later named Edwards Air Force Base, then on to the North Island Naval Air Station at San Diego where we got some very intensive combat transition training. It was here, where for a few terrorizing seconds, I thought I would be killed when another P-38 ran into me on the runway and sheared off both tail booms of the P-38 that I had just landed.

In early November 1943, I was flown to Australia, then on to New Guinea where I was assigned to the 433rd Fighter Squadron of the 475th Fighter Group, "Satan's Angels." This was the only P-38 fighter group formed outside of the United States, and it was the highest scoring of all the P-38 fighter groups. We have our own museum at the March Air Force Reserve Base in California, and a web site at www.475thfg.org. Major Dick Bong, the country's leading ace with 40 victories, got five of them flying with the 475th. The country's second leading ace, Major Tommy McGuire, with 38 victories, was also the product of the 475th and was installed in the Aviation Hall of Fame in the year 2000.

All of our missions were either over water or jungle, and they ranged from escorting bombers, to fighter sweeps, to strafing barges and ammunition dumps, and to covering rescue operations. I completed 37 missions before I dehydrated and lost 30 pounds in a matter of a couple of days. After my second bout of this, I was hospitalized again and was returned to the States. Subsequently, I put in some time flying the P-63 King Cobra, and the B-26 Marauder.

After tours of duty at Walla Walla, Washington, Ontario, California, and Mountain Home, Idaho, I went on terminal leave. My effective date of discharge was 29 August 1945, about 45 days short of five years from first entering active duty that was supposed to last for one year.

Jerry Gettler was recommended for the Air Medal, but still has not received it. After his discharge, he first worked in construction, then as a veteran's group organizer-recruiter. From there he took a job with General Foods Corporation where he was encouraged to go to college. He took night classes in accounting and law at Southwestern University in Los Angeles. He entered the accounting field and worked at high-level positions in a number of large companies. He was a partner in a business venture that had its offices in the Watergate Building in Washington, D.C., at the time of the burglary of the Democratic National Committee offices. He was vice president of finance (CFO) then executive vice president (COO) of the Aerol Company, Los Angeles, and later, vice president of the Advanced Ground Systems Engineering Company of Long Beach. He was with North American Aviation Division of the Rockwell Corporation where he served as senior-contracts and proposal administrator. His final business venture was in computerized employment services. He retired in 1997 and moved to Maryland where he has two grown children. Jerry and his companion Catherine live in Hagerstown, Maryland.

Vernon E. Greene

Age 16 – United States Army

I was born in Bluefield, West Virginia, on 11 May 1923, the middle child of nine surviving children. When my father died in 1938, I did as my older brother had done: I dropped out of school at the age of 15 to work in the coal mines and add income to the family. As I recall, the daily wage was just short of $5. We were required to report to work every Monday through Friday, but we were sent home if we weren't needed. The fortunate ones were needed about three days per week. My oldest brother was my shift boss, and this made my work more difficult. He put extra pressure on me so that other workers would not think he was showing favoritism. I was caught between a rock and a hard place.

> These were the days when a jam sandwich could be two slices of bread jammed together.

Generally, my mother prepared breakfast and supper meals with the anticipation that leftovers would take care of lunch. These were the days when a jam sandwich could be two slices of bread jammed together. The younger folks in the family were disappointed when the preacher came for Sunday dinner because he would often be seated in their place, and there would be less food available.

By mid 1939, at the age of 16, I was going to work not knowing whether I was going to earn a wage each day or not. I decided to become a soldier. I wanted to move away from the coal dust and the daily risk of losing life or limb in the mines. I knew that I was too young to enlist without an adult's signature, and I knew that my mother would not sign for me. My oldest sister signed for me, and on 18 October 1939, I was en route from Bluefield, West Virginia, to Fort Thomas, Kentucky. I became a member of Company M, 10th Infantry Regiment, 5th Infantry Division. I was not to become familiar with the terms "basic training," "boot camp," and "advanced training," until I returned from Iceland in 1943. Upon enlistment, I was sent directly to Company M of the 10th Infantry.

Our division moved to Fort Benning, Georgia, for maneuvers in the spring of 1940. This was followed by maneuvers in Louisiana and Texas, the largest peacetime field maneuvers in U. S. history. That fall, we moved to Fort Custer, Michigan, and occupied new wooden barracks. This was our first permanent shelter in over a year. By this time I had been promoted to corporal and was a machine-gun squad leader.

In the fall of 1941, we arrived in Iceland to augment the British forces that had been rushed there after the Germans took Norway. During our stay in Iceland, we called our regiment the 10th Labor Regiment instead of the 10th Infantry Regiment because we worked 12 hours per day, seven days a week. We unloaded ships, built fortifications, manned defensive positions, and patrolled the beaches.

At a 4:00 a.m. reveille formation one morning in early December 1941, just as the first sergeant was about to dismiss us, he hesitated, then said, "Oh, yes! The Japanese bombed Pearl Harbor. Dismissed." That is how we learned that we were at war.

I was promoted to sergeant and appointed section leader of two machine-gun squads. Shortly thereafter, I was selected for the Infantry Officers School at Fort Benning, Georgia. I did attend OCS, but I did not graduate. I did not tell anyone this, I just kept it locked up inside me for 57 years. This is a wonderful opportunity to let it fly away.

I was assigned to the 78th "Lightning" Division at Camp Butner, North Carolina. Company M, 311th Infantry Regiment became my home until I returned from Europe for the second time during World War II. I was promoted to first sergeant at the age of 20.

In September 1944 we were at sea, headed for England. Four weeks later we were in Belgium, and by December we moved into Germany. The 311th Regiment had its initial introduction to combat on 9 December 1944, in the Hurtgen Forest, one of the bloodiest battlegrounds of the war. By 23 December, our defensive position covered about 12,000 yards of the north shoulder of the Bulge. We had Germans on three sides of us, but we stayed there until 30 January 1945.

On 11 December 1944, the 78th Division was ordered to seize the town of Schmidt and the Schwammenauel Dam. The execution of this order was delayed by the German counteroffensive, now known as the Battle of the Bulge. In late January 1945, we began our drive to capture Schmidt. I was still a first sergeant, but was assigned to be the platoon leader with four machine-gun squads. At the time of the capture of Schmidt, I would never have believed that I would be revisiting it many years later, as a friend rather than a foe.

While the 311th was in division reserve in Schmidt, I received orders to go to regimental headquarters, take a bath, get a clean uniform, and report to the adjutant. I did as I was told. At regimental headquarters, I was formally discharged from the enlisted ranks of the Army of the United States and told to report to the 78th Infantry Division Headquarters. There I was given a hot meal and a bed, and was instructed to get breakfast early and be ready to meet Major General Edwin P. Parker, Jr., our commanding general, at 0800 the next day.

The next morning, General Parker swore me into the Army of the United States as a second lieutenant and placed a gold bar on the appropriate place on my collar. The adjutant read that I was commissioned "for the duration of the war plus six months." The general then took the crossed rifles (the infantry branch insignia) from the collar of a lieutenant colonel and placed them on my collar opposite the second lieutenant bar. Looking back, I wonder if I had made it at Fort Benning in 1942, how long my tour would have been. I passed "the duration of the war plus six months" by some length. I retired in 1974 as a colonel, not from the Army of the United States, but the United States Army.

Then it was back to Company M, 311th Infantry, and the war. We were on our way to the Rhine River, and within a month we would be on the east bank of that mighty river. The day after the 9th Armored Division had captured the bridge at Remagen, our regiment was ordered to cross the bridge to help expand the bridgehead on the east side. We were across the bridge less than 24 hours after it had been captured. Ours was the first infantry regiment to cross the Rhine.

Our division was part of the First Army that conducted a pincers movement to encircle the Ruhr Valley, Germany's richest industrial district. The climax of our regiment's drive was the capture of

Wuppertal on 16 April 1945. We did not know it, but this was our last day of combat. Our unit had been in combat for 130 continuous days.

After V-E day, the 78th Division was sent to Berlin as part of the occupation force. I had let it be known that I wanted to remain in the Army after the war, so I was transferred to the 70th Infantry Division, which was scheduled to be deployed to the Far East for the invasion of Japan. I was enjoying myself in France when the Japanese surrendered.

In September 1945, we boarded a ship in northern France and sailed for New York. When we arrived, Red Cross ladies greeted us with smiles, coffee, and doughnuts. Everyone appeared happy and we were greeted with an unhesitating handshake or a pat on the back. What a contrast this welcome was compared with the silent treatment we received upon returning from Korea. A greater contrast was provided by some of our citizens who met us as we returned from Vietnam with posters and shouts, calling us killers and murderers.

In May 2000, 55 years after leaving the battlefields of Europe, I had the privilege of visiting those same battlefields. I made a special trip to the Raffelsbrand area to view the site of the recently discovered remains of a 311th soldier who had been reported missing in action. He was last seen alive on 13 December 1945. I visited two cemeteries where thousands of American soldiers were buried. In the town of Schmidt, the townspeople surprised me with a party on my 77th birthday. There was music, dancing, and plenty of German food and drink for everyone. It is a pleasure to reflect on these significant and formative years gone by. The recollection of ice-covered foxholes has dimmed, but the friendships formed during common danger remain forever bright.

Vernon Greene was awarded the Silver Star, the Legion of Merit, two Bronze Stars, the Meritorious Service Medal, four Air Medals, the Joint Service Commendation Medal, the Army Commendation Medal, the Combat Infantryman's Badge, the Republic of Vietnam Cross of Gallantry, a Master Parachute Badge, Belgium and Republic of Vietnam Parachute Badges, and a number of service medals. He taught in several colleges and high schools after retiring from the Army. He and Elizabeth Stafford, whom he married in 1948, had five children. They later divorced. Vernon and his present wife Jerrie, whom he married in 2001, live in Fayetteville, North Carolina.

David L. Johnson
Age 15 – United States Marine Corps

I was raised in Jackson, Mississippi, although I was born in Pine Bluff, Arkansas, on 12 August 1924. As a kid, I was mean as the devil. There was a Ford dealership in Jackson that kept its display cars unlocked,

> *I weighed less than 100 pounds at the time I was rescued.*

and even left the keys in the cars in the back row. Some of us boys would push a car in the front row aside, then get in the car with keys and go for a ride. The cars that had keys didn't have much gas, so we would ride around for a while until the gas got real low, then we would return the car. But one night we wrecked a car, and we were caught and charged with stealing cars.

To get out of the mess I was in, I went to the Marine recruiting office, told them that I was 18, and was sworn into the Marine Corps on 12 January 1940. At that time the services were desperate for men, so they didn't ask many questions.

At New Orleans, Louisiana, we were put on a train for San Diego, California, and boot camp. I was given $6 for food during the 2-day train trip. I wrote to my mother and told her, "You will never guess how much money they gave me to eat on!"

After boot camp, we spent several weeks at the rifle range in La Jolla, then went aboard a ship and sailed to Mare Island in San Francisco Bay. We waited several weeks at Mare Island for USS *Henderson* to arrive and take us to Shanghai, China. We arrived at Shanghai on 1 May 1940. I was assigned to E Company, 2nd Battalion, 4th Marine Regiment. Captain Lewis B. "Chesty" Puller was the acting adjutant. He had been serving on the cruiser *Houston* before joining the 4th Marines. Puller was with us about a year, then was promoted to major and was sent Stateside.

Our pay was $21 per month. We were known as "the millionaires of Shanghai" because of the extreme poverty in the area. We could buy almost anything and have money left over at the end of the month. Tailor-made suits cost $5.

I stayed in Shanghai until September 1941 when 200 or 300 men of the 4th Marines were sent to the Philippines to join up with the 1st Separate Marine Battalion. At that time the Marine Corps consisted of two brigades, one on the East Coast and one on the West Coast.

In the Philippines, we were stationed at Sangley Point, near the naval base at Cavite, where we guarded oil tanks and the radio-transmitter towers. The remainder of the 4th Marines came to the Philippines around the 1st of December and went to Olongapo.

It was 8 December 1941 in the Philippines when Pearl Harbor was bombed. We were bombed two days later, and most of our aircraft were destroyed on the ground. The day the war started, a Colonel Adams came to our company and picked a sergeant and 20 men to be assigned to two squadrons of old Navy PBY aircraft. Within a few days, all our aircraft were shot down and we returned to Manila. No one knew what was going on, and no one knew where the 4th Marines were. There was total confusion. We didn't know where we should go. At this time Manila was declared an open city. We went to the docks and got a ride on a tugboat to Corregidor. When we arrived, our sergeant located the headquarters and an Army major told him to take us to the topside barracks and guard MacArthur's headquarters at the end of the long barracks. The major also fed us some malarkey that Corregidor couldn't be bombed because of all the 3-inch antiaircraft guns they had. On 29 December, we were bombed and MacArthur moved his headquarters into the main tunnel from topside.

Meanwhile, the 4th Marines were moved to Corregidor and I was assigned to A Company, 1st Battalion. By this time, our battalion included men from the Army, Army Air Forces, Navy, and some Filipinos. Our company CO, Major Lang, had previously been a Marine aviator and had lost a leg, so he couldn't fly. He was killed during the shelling of Corregidor before the invasion.

On Corregidor, the defensive artillery had been set up during the Spanish-American War to protect the entrance to Manila Bay, so all the guns faced seaward. The Japanese came in from the rear and we had no long-range guns to face them.

During the Spanish-American War, Admiral Dewey had brought over 12-inch mortars which were installed in the fortifications near the sea. They were used to block the mouth of Manila Bay. Bataan fell on 9 April 1942 and the Japanese brought a hundred or so batteries of 105mm artillery pieces and 50 or 60 240mm howitzers to fire on Corregidor, which was about three or four miles across the bay. We had only one or two 155mm guns that were operational. The guns would fire four or five rounds, then quickly move to another location. The Japanese had observation balloons that spotted the fire and would notify their artillery on Bataan. The massive Japanese artillery barrage that followed would flatten the area.

We were situated on high ground about 50 feet above the beach. We were fed each night after dark and were also given a can of fish, sausage, or C-rations, and two slices of bread, which we could save for the next day or play it safe and eat right away, because some of the guys were always hungry.

The Japanese infantry landed at night, and the current caused them to drift from their intended landing area to one where we were right above them on the high ground overlooking the beach. We inflicted many casualties on the invading troops, but they prevailed. Corregidor was officially surrendered at 12:00 p.m. on 6 May 1942, but the word didn't get out to the troops for some time.

About an hour and a half after the surrender, I was wounded. I was shot in both arms and in my hip. I crawled to a tunnel that housed a Navy radio station. When I reached the big metal doors, I called out and three guys came out and got me. There were about 150 men in the tunnel. Over a hundred of them were wounded, and there was only one corpsman, a Navy chief pharmacist's mate, to care for them. He did a great job. I have forgotten his name and have never heard what happened to him.

I was kept in a hospital on Corregidor for about a month after our capture, then transferred to Bilibid prison in Manila. About 1 July, I was moved to the Cabanatuan prison camp where I stayed until 1944. In the last part of 1944, I was moved to Fort William McKinley for about a month, then back to Bilibid where I was liberated by American troops. I weighed less than 100 pounds at the time I was rescued.

The Army immediately started flying their former prisoners of war back to the States, but the Navy didn't. They said that they would take care of their own men. We were taken to the port area and loaded aboard two British transports, the *Ajax* and the *Achilles*. When we 'reached the Philippine island of Mindinao, we were unloaded. Finally, we boarded an Army transport, but they would not allow our dog Sochow on board. So, one of the Marines went ashore and found a Marine air base and got Sochow a ride back to San Diego where, after a long career with the Marines, he was buried on the Marine Base. We went to New Guinea, picking up Army troops along the way. When we finally made it to San Francisco, all the parades were over.

We were in San Francisco for about a month, mostly waiting for transportation, which was hard to come by at that time. They treated us royally. They put a number of us former POWs in a drawing-room car. When we stopped in Los Angeles, I got off the train and didn't make it back in time. When I missed the train, I went to buy tickets and found that they were unavailable at any price. At this time, the return of the prisoners of war was on the front page of all the papers, and that was the only reason that I got a ticket to New Orleans. I caught another train and was on my way to the East when it was announced that President Roosevelt had died.

At first, I decided to stay in the Marines and was stationed at the Navy Yard in Philadelphia. Then I decided to get out, so on 16 January 1946, I was discharged with 100 percent disability.

David Johnson was awarded the Purple Heart, but not until 1956. He also received the Bronze Star, as all survivors of Corregidor and Bataan did. His civilian career included working for an engineering firm out of Scranton, Pennsylvania, which sent him to Eugene, Oregon. He was in the auto-parts business in Los Angeles, then went to Phoenix, and on to Grand Junction, Colorado, where he was involved in uranium exploration. After working in the grocery business, he started his own firm in Pearl, Mississippi, constructing storm windows. He is semi-retired. David and Ruth, his wife of 43 years, have two living children, three grandchildren, and six great-grandchildren. They live in Pearl, Mississippi.

Robert L. Riley
Age 16 – Indiana National Guard

I joined the National Guard when I was 16 years old. I had to fib a little, but I got in! That was 17 January 1940. I was in the Guard until September 1940 when I was found out and I was given an honorable discharge.

> Now, to a "landlubber," a swell is a huge wave!

I was working at the Alcoa plant in Lafayette, Indiana, when World War II broke out. My friends were joining the service, so on 5 May 1942, I joined the Navy. I was sent to Great Lakes, Illinois, for six weeks of boot camp. From there, I went to the University of Minnesota and was assigned to the ship's company as a chauffeur.

I was assigned to the Naval Armory in Chicago, Illinois, for seven months' duty on the USS *Wolverine*, one of two aircraft carriers the Navy had on Lake Michigan. The other carrier was the USS *Sable*. Both had been converted into carriers and had 600-foot flight decks. About 18,000 pilots qualified for carrier landings on these two ships. After service on the *Wolverine*, I was transferred to Lido Beach, Long Island, New York, for amphibious training, then went to Little Creek, Virginia, for the completion of my amphibious training.

I was assigned to the USS *Lejeune*, a Navy transport ship, and we sailed for Europe in a convoy of 37 ships. I was beginning to wonder if we would make it to Europe because we ran into a storm in the North Atlantic in which the swells were 50 feet high. Now, to a "landlubber," a swell is a *huge* wave! We landed in Helensburg, Scotland and stayed there a short time. We were then was transported by rail to Southampton, England, and went aboard the *LST-498*.

LSTs are 325 feet long and 50 feet wide. They go right up to the shore, open the bow doors, and drop the ramp so that tanks, jeeps, and trucks can drive right on shore. At the time, they were the largest landing craft in use. I spent my time on the *LST-498* going back and forth between Normandy and England.

When the war ended in 1945, I was sent back to Exeter, England, then to Southampton where I boarded the *Queen Mary* for the trip back home. That was the largest ship I ever did see! When they marched us down to the dock to get on board, I asked where the ship was. One of my friends said, "Right beside you!" I thought it was a building, it was so big. The *Queen Mary* brought 15,000 troops back on that trip.

I was discharged at Great Lakes, Illinois, on 7 October 1945. This was the end of my Navy career — 3 years and 5 months, and many memories, some good, some very bad.

Robert Riley received two certificates from the French government for his service in Normandy. He moved to California after his discharge and went to work for Lockheed Aircraft Company as a structure mechanic on the F-104 fighter. He also worked on the C-130, the S3A, the C-5A, and the F117A Stealth fighter. He retired in 1985. His wife passed away in 1997 after along illness. Robert has four children, six grandchildren, and two great-grandchildren. He lives in Sylmar, California.

Harvey H. Reese

Age 15 – Georgia National Guard
Age 16 – United States Army

I was born in New Rochelle, New York, on 5 September 1924. I enlisted in the 179th Field Artillery, Georgia National Guard on 19 February 1940. I was 15½ years old and tall for my

> *I spent Christmas night outside on duty with my best friend, my 30-caliber carbine.*

age. My age was not questioned. I wanted to wear the uniform and I wanted the $1 we received for each drill at the Atlanta City Auditorium.

On 5 August 1940, our unit went on maneuvers in Louisiana for three weeks. I was assigned to KP the entire time. I washed and cleaned pots and pans from 3:00 a.m. until midnight. The only good thing that resulted from this KP duty was that I was promoted to private first class after the maneuvers were over.

On 24 February 1941, our unit was mobilized, supposedly for one year. I was attending high school at the time, and I persuaded my father and mother to allow me to go in the Army for one year. I could have gotten out of it if I had told my commanding officer my true age.

I was sent to Camp Blanding, Florida, for basic training. On the morning of 7 December 1941, I was lying on my bunk when several men came running down the battery street shouting that the Japanese had bombed Pearl Harbor. Later that night, I was given a Browning automatic rifle and assigned guard duty. I was to guard the vehicles at the motor pool.

I was assigned to radio school after basic training was completed. I learned the Morse code and was promoted to corporal while there. The following year I was selected as cadre to train men of the 16th Field Artillery Brigade at Camp Gruber, Oklahoma, as radio operators.

I was promoted to sergeant while at Camp Gruber. After the training was completed, I was assigned to Headquarters, 15th Corps Artillery, at the Desert Training Center, Camp Young, California. The training took place during the hottest part of the year. The thermometer registered up to 120 degrees even when in the shade. The strenuous physical training all of the Corps Artillery members underwent made the sun seem unusually hot and the sand unusually deep.

In late November 1943, our unit left Camp Iron Mountain for three weeks of desert winter-training maneuvers. Men of the 18th Field Artillery will long remember those winter maneuvers, which many still say were much more strenuous than any experiences they had in combat. The sandstorms, the freezing weather at night, the many moves on dark nights, the foxhole and trench digging, remain in our memories. After winter training, we settled down to await orders for overseas.

On 18 March 1944 we entrained at Freda, California, for Camp Shanks, New York. Ten days later, we boarded the British ship *Mauritania* in New York City. We made the crossing to England in nine days despite the fact that enemy submarines made it necessary for our unescorted ship to change course frequently and travel many extra miles.

The ship docked at Liverpool, England, on 8 April 1944. After a night's ride on a crowded British troop train, we found ourselves in Chepstow, Monmouthshire, South Wales, where we spent three weeks. Members of our group were impressed by the beauty of the Welsh and English countryside, but we were depressed by the damp, cold weather which seemed to persist in spite of the calendar's contention that spring had arrived.

We moved northward on 29 April and camped on the outskirts of Ludlow, Shropshire, England. We lived in tents on the banks of a small stream. The dampness and chill of the English air seemed to increase rather than decrease as summer approached. On 2 June 1944, we started towards the marshaling area on the English Channel near Southampton.

On 8 June we embarked for the trip across the English Channel to Normandy. We arrived at Omaha Beach on the morning of the 9th and found it impossible to land because of a severe storm reported to be the most severe storm that had hit the Channel in 80 years. We finally left the LST (landing ship, tank) on 10 June by climbing onto the floating docks.

Our first assignment was at La Duvalerie where we directed fire for the VIII Corps Artillery. This was where we were first introduced to the German 88s. We were in close association with the men of the 82nd Airborne Division who, in our eyes, were already seasoned veterans.

Our unit played a significant part in the breakthrough at St. Lo. We were attached to the 9th Division at the time. We were later attached to the 1st Division when the push across France and Belgium began. On 27 August 1944, we crossed the Seine River at Ris-Orangis, marched down the Champs Élysées in Paris, and continued on to a place southeast of Chevregny. We continued on through France, ending up in Krauthausen, Germany, by 2 October. By the end of November we were at Mausbach, Germany.

The 18th Field Artillery Group was at Weisweiler, Germany, when we received the news of the German breakthrough into Belgium that became known as the Battle of the Bulge. Our group made a 12-hour, 80-mile march on narrow, shell-torn roads filled with heavy traffic to get to Somme Leuze, Belgium, to help drive the enemy back into Germany.

On Christmas Day 1944, we had moved south to Bohon, Belgium, and spent Christmas there. It was extremely cold, and snow was on the ground. I spent Christmas night outside on duty with my best friend, my 30-caliber carbine. I also had a 50-caliber machine gun, but it was frozen, and I doubt that it would have fired if I had had to use it. Throughout January we were in general support of the 18th Airborne Corps, reinforcing the fires of the 82nd Airborne Division. On 26 January 1945, we moved 25 miles north and took up a position at Born, Belgium. On the road to Born we stopped at the village of Saint Vith, Malmedy, Belgium. The rumor we had heard earlier, that a group of American soldiers had been slaughtered, appeared to be true. In a field were approximately 200 dead American soldiers all covered with snow. A graves-registration unit had put a white tape around the area to keep others from walking among the dead. We learned later that the dead soldiers were from the 285th Field Artillery Observation Battalion that had been attached to our unit.

In early February we began our march back into Germany. We were assigned to general support of the VII Corps, reinforcing the fires of the 8th and 1st Infantry Divisions. During March, the 18th Field Artillery Group kept moving toward the Rhine River. By 8 March we were in Cologne, Germany. Our group had the distinction of being the first field-artillery group to cross the Rhine, crossing at Lannesdorf under cover of artificial fog.

In April we were attached to the 18th Airborne Corps and reinforced the fires of the 78th Infantry Division. After serving as part of the 1st Army for over a year, the 18th Field Artillery Group became a part of the 9th Army on 6 May 1945. On 7 May 1945, we received word of the unconditional surrender of Germany.

I was discharged from the Army on 31 October 1945 and returned to the Technical High School in Atlanta, Georgia. After graduating, I enrolled at Georgia Technical College, and in 1948, transferred to the University of Georgia. I joined the Georgia Air National Guard on 11 April 1948. On 27 December1950, I was given a direct appointment as a second lieutenant and was called to active duty on 8 January 1951. My first active duty station was at Sewart Air Force Base, Tennessee, where I was a personnel officer. Later assignments included Lowry Air Force Base, Colorado, and Pope Air Force Base, North Carolina.

I attended the Air Command and Staff College at Maxwell AFB, Alabama, and later was assigned overseas duty at Wheelus Field, Tripoli, Libya. From Libya, I served a tour at Wiesbaden AFB, Germany, and returned to the States in August 1959. After a tour at Truax Field, Wisconsin, I was assigned to the Los Angeles Air Defense Sector as director of personnel. I retired from the Air Force at the rank of major on 1 March 1966. Later, I joined the California State Military Reserve as a major and was soon promoted to the rank of lieutenant colonel.

Harvey Reese earned five battle stars on his European-African-Middle Eastern Campaign Medal during World War II. While in the Air Force, he was awarded the Air Force Commendation Medal and an Air Force Outstanding Unit Award. After retiring from the Air Force, he worked as a retail store manager in Agoura, California, retiring from that position on 10 May 1980. Harvey and his wife Kathryn have three children and two grandchildren. They live in Simi Valley, California.

Wayne A. Kuschel

Age 16 – United States Army

I was born in Ellsworth, Wisconsin, on 6 December 1923, during the early years of the Depression era. I was fortunate to attend good schools from the first through the eighth grades. Bernice Pace, my teacher in several grades, was the sole reason that I did so well in

> *I had to do lots of convincing to get my parents to sign my enlistment papers.*

my endeavors. She poured academic knowledge into my brain. I received my diploma from the eighth grade in 1938.

Mrs. Pace wanted me to attend high school, but I thought that I was too smart for that, and that I didn't need any more education. I worked on several farms for $6 per month, with room and board. In the early part of 1940, I was driving a cattle truck when I noticed a billboard advertising the U. S. Army with "see the world, adventure," etc.

I went to the Army recruiting office and spoke to a recruiter. He sold me on the idea of enlisting, then asked me how old I was. I said that I was 17 and going to be 18 in December 1940. He looked at me and said, "You have to be over 18. Come back next week, and if you are 18 and going to be 19 in December 1940, you have a place in the Army." He gave me two papers to have my parents sign: one for age and dependency, the other for guardian approval.

I had to do lots of convincing to get my parents to sign my enlistment papers. I worked on the subject for over a week. They finally agreed, and in turn, I promised to send money home to help support them. My friend, Judge John C. Christenson, notarized my papers. He would later be a chief judge at the Nurenburg trials.

I was sworn into the Army on 12 June 1940 at Fort Snelling, Minnesota. I was 16 years old. We were issued clothing, received about 15 days of recruit training, and put on a troop train for Fort Lewis, Washington, where I was assigned to Company M, 15th Infantry Regiment. We finished recruit training and I was assigned as a truck driver, with additional duties on a machine-gun crew.

In November 1940, my mother's health was deteriorating, so the doctor requested that I be transferred to Fort Snelling to be closer to her. I arrived at Fort Snelling on 6 December 1940 and was assigned to the Antitank Company, 3rd Infantry Regiment. Winter was well on its way and we participated in winter-training operations.

In May 1942 we were placed on alert for movement to an undisclosed destination. We boarded troop trains and headed east, arriving at the Boston Port of Embarkation. Our movements were under tight secrecy and security. We boarded the SS *Dorchester* and left Boston harbor in foggy weather.

We had numerous abandon-ship drills, as many as two a day. It seemed like drills were always called at chow time. We passed through "torpedo alley," an area where the German submarine wolf packs were active, without being attacked. When we arrived at our undisclosed destination, it was Fort Pepperall, Newfoundland.

I was promoted to corporal and assigned as a driver for the company commander's staff car. In February 1943, I was promoted to sergeant and assigned as the regimental commander's driver. In August 1943, I heard that the 8th Airways Communications had two openings in its ranks. I requested a transfer to the Air Forces, but I had to take a reduction in rank to private.

I was transferred and soon regained corporal's stripes. I became assistant crew chief on Major General Carl Brandt's UC-45 aircraft. I couldn't get enough flying experience. I bummed rides on the B-18, the A-20 (or DB-7), the OA-9, and the C-47 aircraft, and no one asked me about my background.

On a trip with General Brandt, I was asked to be his co-pilot. He became interested in me and asked me if I cared enough about flying to enter the cadet program. I told him it was my dream to become a pilot, but that I only had an eighth-grade education. His comment was, "Nonsense, you have very good common sense."

I requested a pre-cadet test. One prerequisite was that I had to have a birth certificate. By this time I was over 21 and no one pressed the issue of my fraudulent enlistment. It took numerous copies of my birth certificate sent to various agencies to correct my birth date on all the records.

I passed all the tests and returned to the United States in February 1944 for aviation cadet pilot training. I reported to the 59th Training Group at Keesler Field, Biloxi, Mississippi, for cadet classification, then was sent to a college-training detachment in Alliance, Ohio, for 12 weeks of refresher courses in subjects associated with flying. No one could advise us of our flying status, and we thought it was a stall job. Perhaps they had all the flying personnel required at the time.

The next stop was Independence Army Air Field, Kansas, a desolate spot. We remained there just swapping BT-13s from one side of the field to the other. We just knew that our flying career was over. One day we were sent to the San Antonio Aviation Cadet Center, San Antonio, Texas. Here we studied all subjects essential to flying. But it seemed that I was always on the wrong list and didn't get into actual flying.

A surprise was in store for 47 of us cadets. We were called by name, then marched to an isolated wooden building with guards all around it. Secrecy was the word of the day. A major walked in the room, introduced himself, and told us about the secret project he was involved with. It was the B-29 Superfortress. We were chosen to be flight engineers on the B-29s. It sounded intriguing and a challenge to me, so I signed on the dotted line. At least, I would be flying!

We were sent to Amarillo AAF, Texas, for pre-flight engineer training. When I first saw a B-29, I thought it was the biggest airplane in the world. I was proud and honored to be assigned to the largest heavy bomber in the world. I knew that my father was inspecting and testing the engines for the B-29, which was a big boost to my morale. The course was highly technical, but I passed with a superior rating and graduated on 11 June 1945.

We went to Hondo AAF, Texas, to receive training in B-29s, but due to the shortage of aircraft, we trained in converted B-24s. We graduated on 22 July 1945. What a hassle! What was to have been six or seven months had lengthened to 18 months. We were now preparing to fly to the Far East and enter the war with Japan. On completion of the training, I was commissioned a second lieutenant.

We went to Roswell, New Mexico, for training in B-29s, and were assigned to a permanent crew. Finally, we went to Lincoln AFB,

Nebraska, to pick up new aircraft. By this time, the atomic bombs had been dropped on Japan and the war was over.

In early 1946, I was sent to Wright Field, Dayton, Ohio, where I was assigned to cargo test and maintenance. On occasions, I flew with Major James H. Doolittle, Jr., son of General Doolittle.

After many months of flight testing, I applied for flight training, was accepted, and reported to Randolph Field, Texas, in September 1947. We were the first U. S. Air Force class to fly the new AT-6 trainer. I soloed after about 21 hours of instruction and graduated as a full-fledged multi-engine B-25 pilot on 8 October 1948, 56th in a class of 227. I thought I did quite well with my eighth-grade education!

After graduating from pilot training, I went back to Wright-Patterson AFB, Ohio, and was assigned as a flight-test maintenance officer. In late 1949, the military budget was cut, and since I was a reserve officer, I was caught in the reduction-in-force. In January 1950, I re-enlisted as a technical sergeant and was shipped to McClellan AFB, California, as a flight engineer, but was soon reassigned to Davis-Monthan AFB, Tucson, Arizona. I was with the 64th Bomb Squadron, which flew B-50s.

I was promoted to master sergeant in 1951 and soon recalled to active duty as a pilot and flight engineer with the rank of first lieutenant. I was assigned to the 325th Bomb Squadron, flying B-36 aircraft. After numerous missions and long flights, I began to develop problems with my eyes. I was transferred to Biggs AFB, Texas, where I worked with a C-124 flight simulator. My eyes continued to change, so I took a maintenance officer's position with the 97th Bomb Wing.

In early 1954, I filled a maintenance officer's position in the 6486th Wing Inspectors Office at Hickam AFB, Hawaii. I returned Stateside in 1957 and reported to March AFB, Riverside, California. In July 1960, I retired at the rank of major.

Wayne Kuschel accepted a position with the U. S. Army Aviation Systems Command, Saint Louis, Missouri, a short time after his retirement from the Air Force. He held several executive management positions with the agency and retired from there in 1979. His wife Dorothy died in January 2002. Wayne lives in Henrietta, Texas.

Wallace R. Marston

Age 16 – United States Army

Because of the Depression, there just weren't any jobs available around Dunedin, Florida, where I was born on 23 December 1923. I joined the Army because I was looking for a home. I lied

> As our homemade flag was raised, it unfurled – and boy, it was a beautiful sight!

about my age and was sworn in on 6 September 1940 at the age of 16. I was not asked for any document to prove my age.

My first unit was Company E, 67th Armored Regiment, 2nd Armored Division, at Fort Benning, Georgia. The 2nd Armored was commanded by General George S. Patton. I was sent to Fort Knox, Kentucky, to attend radio operators school. I was there from 1 November 1940 until 31 January 1941. After graduating from radio school, I returned to Fort Benning.

I left Fort Benning on 1 June 1941 and reported to Camp Polk, Louisiana. My new unit was Company B, of the 753rd GHQ Tank Battalion. They had maneuvers in Louisiana in 1941 in which I did not participate. The 192nd Tank Battalion, a National Guard unit, took part in the maneuvers. They were scheduled to be sent to the Philippines. They needed some replacements to bring it up to full strength, and I was one of the replacements. I joined the 192nd in September 1941, and we headed straight to California.

In California, we were issued winter clothing, which indicated to us that we were headed for Alaska. We left San Francisco in the latter part of October 1941 on the transport *Hugh L. Scott*. We stopped at Pearl Harbor and spent about a week there waiting for a cruiser to escort us to our destination. Three days before we were to debark, we were told that we were going to the Philippines.

We landed at Manila in the Philippine Islands, on 20 November 1941, "Roosevelt Thanksgiving Day." We called it a "Roosevelt

Thanksgiving" because that was the first year that Thanksgiving was celebrated on the third Thursday of November instead of the fourth Thursday. President Roosevelt changed the date to give more time between the Thanksgiving and Christmas holidays. We were told that we would be served a Thanksgiving dinner, but they just gave us some hardtack and sent us off to Clarke Field. This was 17 days before the attack on Pearl Harbor.

We cleaned and mounted the guns on our tanks. We heard about the attack on Pearl Harbor and immediately deployed our tanks around Clark Field. About eight hours after hitting Pearl, the Japanese bombed and strafed Clark. For some reason, they caught our planes on the ground and destroyed them. Only the one or two that were on patrol at the time were not hit.

Our tanks were sent to Lingayen Gulf to help repulse the invasion. By the time we got there, the enemy was well established. We lost our lead tank, but I think the crew got out and were captured. We covered the infantry as they retreated down the Bataan Peninsula. We fought the Japanese all the way. We ran out of food and were eating anything we could get our hands on – lizards, snakes, monkeys, anything. We fought until we were finally overwhelmed. I thought that we were going to fight to the finish, but someone decided that we couldn't put up an effective resistance, and there was no use sacrificing any more lives. We had a mass surrender at Mariveles Air Field on 9 April 1942.

The Japanese marched us from Mariveles to San Fernando, a distance of about 70 miles. There were artesian springs along the way, but if anyone stopped to get a drink, he would be shot. We were not given any food until the fifth day, then it was a bowl of rice. This was the infamous Bataan Death March. At San Fernando, we were stuffed into railroad cars and taken to Camp O'Donnell. Many men died of suffocation in the cars. On 1 June 1942, I was transferred to Cabanatuan prison camp and held there until September 1943 when I was shipped to Japan. During the time I was at Cabanatuan we buried 2,700 men.

I was taken to a prison camp at Hirohata, about 30 miles south of Osaka, Japan, where I worked as a slave laborer in a steel mill. We did not know of the atomic bombs, but on 15 August 1945, the Japanese commander, who had lived in the United States and spoke good English, called us in formation and announced that the steel mill was shutting down for a two-week vacation and the workers would get a rest. We knew something was up because a steel mill just doesn't shut down during a war.

On 23 August, we painted the letters "PW" on the roof of a building so they could be seen by aircraft. Soon after, a flight of Navy Hellcats really put on an air show for us. The planes flew so low that the pilots would wave to us. They dropped some cigarettes and candy to us. One of the packages had a message that the war was over and told us not to get violent. We would be rescued soon.

A representative of the International Red Cross, a Swede, came to the camp on 30 August and told us that the Japanese had surrendered. We asked if we could have a little more rice. He turned to the Japanese commander and said, "Give them the keys to the storeroom. Who in the hell do you think won this war!" Our cook was from Texas. When he got the rice, he started cooking immediately. He said, "You bastards, you wanted more rice. I'm going to give it to you by the bucketful." Before the rice was cooked, B-29s with the words "PW Supplies" painted on the wings came over and started dropping 50-gallon drums full of everything from tooth picks to toilet paper. We had chocolate and all types of canned goods. We started to eat and many of us got sick because our stomachs were not used to such rich food. We finally had to make a sign to the B-29s not to drop any more because we had more than we could handle.

The Swede from the Red Cross told us that on 2 September the Japanese were going to sign the surrender documents, and on that date we could fly the American flag if we had one. Fortunately, the parachutes that were used to drop the supplies to us came in several colors. About a half dozen of our group took the parachutes and made a very beautiful American flag. All the guards left on the night of 1 September because they had been very cruel to us. They brought in new guards the next morning. The guards stacked their rifles and everything was ready for lowering the Japanese flag and raising the American flag. It was a beautiful day with a soft breeze. As our homemade flag was raised, it unfurled – and boy, it was a beautiful sight!

For the next few days, we would go to town, ride trains to other towns, then come back. We would gather swords from Japanese officers that we saw on the streets. We stayed in camp until 9 September. When the liberation party came in, we didn't know what to think. The men were yellow-skinned and wore strange helmets. The only helmets that we knew about were of World War I vintage. We had heard that the Russians had entered the war and thought that they were coming. When the lead man got close to us, he said in a deep Georgia drawl, "How long ya-all been here?" We knew then that they were Americans. Their skin was yellow from all the atropine they had been taking to prevent malaria.

We were put on a train for a 24-hour ride to Yokohama where we were treated to hot showers, hot meals, and new clothes. We were loaded on LCVPs to be taken to a ship in the harbor. Many of the men were too weak to climb the rope ladders to the deck of the ship. Some Marines just put them on their shoulders like gunny sacks and climbed up the ladder with them.

The ship took us to the Philippines where we stayed about a week. During this time we had to give affidavits because all of our records had been lost. We then began a three-week journey home. The last few days the ship would only make three or four knots because they had to wait for a berthing space in San Francisco Bay. About 3:00 a.m. one morning we heard a commotion and went topside. We could see the lights of San Francisco! No one went below decks again because we were afraid that if we did, the lights wouldn't be there when we came back up.

I was sent to Letterman General Hospital for a week or so, then put on a hospital train for Augusta, Georgia. During the five days on the train crossing the United States, I felt that I had died and gone to heaven – it was so great to be home. In Augusta, a big hotel had been converted into a hospital. I stayed there for a few days, then went back to Dunedin, Florida. No one knew I was coming; there was no one to welcome me. But I was home! I was discharged from the Army on 9 June 1946.

Wallace Marston worked in the grocery business for a time, then went into the construction trade and became a building contractor. He went back into the grocery business later, running three convenience stores. His health deteriorated, so he retired at age 45. He has two children, a son and a daughter. Wallace lives in Altoona, Florida.

Walter F. Ram

Age 16 – United States Army

The year was 1940; I was 16 years old and anxious to get into the U. S. Army. I was looking forward to the excitement and the adventure. I was born in Nogales, Arizona, on 20 December 1923. I changed

> The buildings at Stalag 17 were old, with large windows, but no glass.

the date on my baptismal certificate to read 20 December 1921 and somehow convinced my parents to sign the enlistment papers. I was sworn into the Army on 24 September 1940 for a period of one year. I was sent to Fort Sill, Oklahoma, for basic training, then on to Camp Barkley, Abilene, Texas. We participated in the Louisiana maneuvers of 1941.

I didn't really like the infantry, so when my year was up, I took my discharge. Within a few days, I signed up for the Army Air Corps, still using 1921 as my birth year. I went to radio school in Illinois, and later to gunnery school and became a radioman-gunner on a B-24. The Air Corps was expanding rapidly in 1942, and I was assigned to a B-17 crew in a newly formed group. I turned 18 about this time and had my records changed to my correct birth year.

In January 1943 we were scheduled to fly to North Africa. Our squadron left Salina, Kansas, with a destination of Keesler Field, Mississippi. We developed engine trouble and were forced to land at Jackson, Mississippi. We learned later that our aircraft had been sabotaged. Iron filings had been put in the engine oil. Most of the aircraft in our squadron suffered the same fate.

It took three months to get new engines in our aircraft. Meanwhile, we were quartered at the Hidleberg Hotel in Jackson, and we had a wonderful time. By the time the engines were replaced, our orders were changed, and we were to go to England. In early April 1943, we went to Bangor, Maine, then to Goose Bay,

Labrador, and on to Iceland and Scotland. We ended up at Bassingborn, England, as the 10th Crew of the 331st Bomb Squadron of the 94th Bomb Group.

I flew my first combat mission in late April. We received quite a bit of flak, and while our aircraft was being repaired, I volunteered to take the place of the radioman on another aircraft for my second mission. On my third mission with my regular crew, while over the target, we were hit in the right outboard engine. We started back to England but couldn't keep up with the other planes in the flight. We were slowly losing altitude all the way back and just made the coast of England. We came in over a line of trees and crash-landed in a field. The entire crew made it out safely. The aircraft that I had flown on my second mission lost a wing over the English Channel and crashed. We saw four or five parachutes, but I don't think any of the crew survived.

On my sixth mission our target was Keil, Germany. On the way to and from the target our 50 aircraft had to contend with an estimated 200 Nazi fighter planes. We were the last plane in the flight – "tail-end Charlie." Other aircraft that were to be near us had aborted, but our pilot was determined to make the raid. We were the first to be attacked by the enemy fighters. We were hit and the pilot was killed. This was about 9:15 in the morning of 13 June 1943. I was near the middle of the aircraft, manning a top gun. There was an explosion in the bomb bay and I was thrown against the side of the plane. I was wounded, my face was burned, and my oxygen mask was blown off. I realized that we had to bail out, so I started to put my parachute on. Because of my head wound and the lack of oxygen, I was having trouble getting ready to bail out, so when my parachute was on, the ball-turret gunner just threw me out of the plane. I must have been partially conscious because I had to pull the ripcord. The next thing I knew I was looking up at a nurse through a hole in a bandage that they had put over my face. I was in a German civilian hospital and was treated very well. They left another hole near my mouth so I could drink through a straw.

Later I was sent under guard, by train, to Frankfurt. We spent the night on the train in the station at Hamburg. The next day I was taken to the interrogation center in Frankfurt. That night the British bombed the train station in Hamburg.

I was put in a very small room with a small wooden bed. I could barely walk because my legs had been injured when I hit the ground after bailing out of the aircraft. A man in a black uniform came in the room. I think that he was a Gestapo agent, but I'm not sure. He took out some papers from his briefcase, then asked me my name. I gave him my name, rank, and serial number. He asked questions about what outfit I was from, what my commander's name was, where I was trained, etc. I answered, "I don't know," to all his questions except when he asked for my name, rank, and serial number. Finally, he got so angry that he stood up, pulled out his gun, and pointed it at my head. I thought for sure that he was going to shoot me. He held it there for a while, then put it back in its holster. He gathered up his papers, put them in his briefcase and said to me, "You fool, you should have been killed instead of just wounded."

From there they took me to a hospital in Berlin where I stayed until September. When my sores healed they sent me to a POW camp for British prisoners in Poland. I stayed there about two days and they took me back to Berlin. I was put with several other American POWs and put on a train. At every city the train stopped they would take us off and march us through the middle of town. The people would shout at us, calling us names. One I remember is, "Chicago gangsters!"

When we reached Ausburg, they took us from the train and marched us by a German hospital that treated wounded German fliers. We marched through throngs of Germans who were very angry that we had wounded their German soldiers. We were surrounded, and it was obvious that the populace was out to hang us. We didn't have enough guards to protect us. We were very lucky when a truckload of German soldiers came and rescued us from the crowd. They took us out of town in trucks and put us on a train.

Our destination was Munich, but we had to walk much of the way. Along the way we passed a camp and saw starving people clutching the barbed wire and watching us. I didn't know it at the time, but it was Dachau. We arrived in Munich and stayed there about a month. Then they loaded us in the 40-and-8 cars (40 men or 8 horses), but they put at least 80 of us in each car. We couldn't move around. We had no food or water, just a bucket for a toilet. It took about 12 hours to reach Vienna, Austria, where they kept us in the cars for three days without food or water. Finally, we reached our destination, but we had to walk the last three miles uphill to our new home – Stalag 17. This was a large prison camp that housed American, British, and Russian POWs.

Getting food was our biggest problem at Stalag 17. When I was shot down, I weighed 160 pounds. When I came out after two years of imprisonment, I weighed 97 pounds. They fed us rutabagas, old, moldy, and full of maggots. At first, we would scrape the maggots to the side, but later on, we began to eat them; after all, they were boiled. They would give us a slice of bread a day. What saved us was that our government sent us parcels through the Red Cross. The parcels weighed 11 pounds and contained a can of Spam, a can of corned-beef hash, a box of crackers, a can of cheese, a can of powdered milk, a can of margarine, a chocolate bar, and two cigarettes. I didn't smoke, so I traded cigarettes for food. The parcels were delivered infrequently and each had to be shared by three or four people. The Germans kept many of the parcels.

The buildings at Stalag 17 were old, with large windows, but no glass. There was no insulation and no hot water. In the winter we would have to take freezing cold showers with snow coming in the windows. That was really cold! I was thrown into solitary confinement for two weeks one time. I was given one container of water and one slice of the black bread each day. When I came out of there, I was still in a prison camp, but I felt like I was free.

We stayed in Stalag 17 until about 20 March 1945 when they made us go on a forced march. We didn't know where we were going. We had heard that Dresden, Germany, had essentially been obliterated by British and American bombers, and that this had so incensed Hitler that he had ordered all POWs to be killed. We marched for days and had to scrounge for food. One day our guards made us go to the side of the road and wait for another group coming from the opposite direction to pass through. They were Jewish prisoners, and they were in very bad shape. We felt sorry for them. There was no flesh on their faces and their clothes were in tatters. One fell to his knee right in front of me. He looked at me as if to ask for food. All I had was water, so I started to move toward him to give him a drink. A big guard kicked me off the road, then turned and shot the prisoner in the head. We learned that whenever one of the Jewish prisoners couldn't walk anymore, he was shot. A wagon came behind the group picking up bodies. There were about 4,000 prisoners that left Stalag 17, and at least 300 are unaccounted for today. They must have been shot while scrounging for food. The sad thing was that the war was almost over.

We finally came to Branau, Austria, and that is where we were liberated. I think it was 5 May 1945. We could see a German town across the river. The houses had white flags on them. Then we saw a bunch of jeeps coming. The GIs quickly disarmed our guards. We were told to do whatever we wanted. We took the guards' guns and went into Branau looking for food. We forced a baker to open his shop and also raided a wine cellar. However, we couldn't eat or drink very much because our stomachs were so small.

The Army soon took control of us and took us to an airfield where a bunch of C47s were lined up. They flew us to Rheims, France, put us in a barracks, made us strip and throw away our clothes, and had us take a good hot shower. We were issued new clothes, then we went to a mess hall. We could only eat a little at a time, but we ate every two hours.

We were taken by train to Le Havre, then by ship to New York. I was given 63 days' leave and 17 days of travel time to report to San Pedro, California, where I was discharged in September 1945.

Walter Ram was awarded the Air Medal, the Purple Heart, the Prisoner of War Medal, and a number of other service medals. After his discharge, he completed high school and earned a college degree in business administration. He owned and operated an agricultural produce business in Nogales, Arizona for many years. He learned to fly and piloted his own aircraft. Walter and Katherine, his wife of 50 years, have three sons and six grandchildren. They live in Tubac, Arizona.

Robert A. Brown

Age 16 – United States Army Air Corps

I was born in Fairfield, California, on 24 August 1924, and enlisted in the U. S. Army Air Corps on 2 October 1940 at San Francisco, California. I was 16 years old, but I coerced my parents into signing that I was 18. I was stationed at Hamilton Field,

> My worst experience was seeing three Americans decapitated by a Japanese soldier.

California, where I was assigned to the 34th Pursuit Squadron, and trained as a medical technician.

The 34th Pursuit Squadron departed for the Philippines aboard the USS *President Coolidge* on 1 November 1941, arriving in Manila on 20 November 1941. Our squadron was dispatched from Nichols Field, outside of Manila, at night on 30 November 1941, to a newly constructed dirt runway at Del Carmen, west of Clark Air Base. We were the only runway or airfield that was not attacked on 8 December 1941 because the Japanese didn't know we were there. However, I was at Clark Air Base having a tooth filled on 8 December, and luckily, I survived the bombing and strafing of the airbase.

On 10 December 1941, our squadron commander, 1st Lt. Samuel H. Marrett, along with several other P-35s, took off for a strafing mission on Japanese ships at Vigan, on the west coast of Luzon. Lt. Marrett peeled off at 12,000 feet, picked out a tanker, and strafed as he approached sea level. When he pulled up, the tanker blew up and the force of the explosion took his wings off. He was the first of our squadron to be killed in action.

Japanese fighters followed our planes back to our base and worked us over real good. Most of our aircraft were destroyed, but there were no casualties. A miracle!

We retreated towards Bataan to Orani with five flyable aircraft on 25 December 1941. On or about 2 January, our planes headed south for Australia and we never saw them again. We retreated to Bataan, and on 6 January 1942, we were issued World War I-vintage rifles. We were assigned a new commander, and were told that we were now in the 71st Provisional Infantry and would take up beach defense at Km (kilometer) Post 192 on the west coast of Bataan. We learned real quick that the Japanese were already there and dug in along the beach. At this point, the 17th Pursuit Squadron was being dispatched to Km Post 200, and since they had no medical personnel, I was directed to join them. When we arrived, we encountered the same situation. The Japanese were already there.

Thus began the "Battle of the Points" on Bataan with Air Corps units fighting as infantry. The only machine guns available to us were those that we salvaged from the wings of our aircraft. We resisted two amphibious landings and eventually, after four weeks of fighting, killed over 2,000 of the enemy. We were called "The Flying Infantry."

Our sister squadron, the 21st, commanded by Captain William Edwin Dyess (for whom Dyess AFB, Texas, is named), plus the 20th Pursuit Squadron and remnants of the 3rd Pursuit Squadron, also fought with us on the Points. Captain Raymond A. Sloan, Commander of the 17th Pursuit Squadron, was killed in action on 11 February 1942. His last words were, "This is one hell of a way for a $10,000 pilot to die."

The 17th was pulled out in late February for a much-needed rest and assigned to beach defense on the southern tip of Bataan. At that point we were very tired, hungry, sick, and had no medicine for malaria, dysentery or beri-beri. Our rations had been cut to one-third. We stayed there until the surrender on 9 April 1942.

The surrender of Bataan was the beginning of hell! The prisoners were marched to a prison camp 70 miles away, without food or water. This would go down in history as the infamous Bataan Death March. The brutality of the Japanese was unbelievable. Seeing your own men being shot or bayoneted – and one could do nothing about it! My worst experience was seeing three Americans decapitated by a Japanese soldier. I made the 70-mile march in four days, arriving at Camp O'Donnell on 14 April only to see 1,500 men die in a 30-day period. The lowest death rate per day that I am aware of, until my departure from Cabanatuan on 6 October, was 13.

We departed Manila on 8 October 1942 on board the "Dysentery Ship," *Totoru Maru*, and arrived at Pusan, Korea, on 8 November 1942. We went by rail to Mukden, Manchuria, arriving on 11 November 1942. I weighed in at 80 pounds.

I learned to speak Japanese, which helped in the treatment of the prisoners by Japanese doctors. I received three written commendations from the Japanese camp commander for my efforts in behalf of the ill and wounded.

Mukden POW camp had 19 killed and 54 seriously injured during a B-29 bombing raid on 7 December 1944.

In May 1945, all American colonels and generals who were captured in the Philippines, along with all British and Dutch colonels and generals, were brought to our POW camp. Colonel James O. Gillespie, M.D., who was the highest ranking doctor in the Philippines at the time of the Japanese invasion, was one of the officers brought to our camp. Colonel Gillespie became aware of my work, and after liberation, reported it to the U. S. War Department. I received a letter of appreciation from the War Department, signed by Major General Edward F. Witsell, the Adjutant General, commending me for my efforts in helping my fellow POWs.

We were liberated by a six-man OSS team and the Russians on 20 August 1945. It was a happy 21st birthday for me on 24 August 1945. I retired from the Air Force as a chief master sergeant on 6 October 1969, with 29 years of active service.

Bob Brown was awarded the Bronze Star, three Presidential Unit Citations, two Air Force Commendation Medals, the Meritorious Service Medal and a number of service medals. He was featured in the Air Force Times "Outstanding Airmen" program in1956. Bob is the youngest living survivor of the Bataan Death March. The lack of food during his three and a half years as a POW adversely affected his health. His feet and legs are a constant source of pain. Bob lives in Challenge, California.

Marvin F. "Rusty" Foster

Age 13 – Texas National Guard
Age 13 – United States Army
Age 16 – United States Navy

I was born in Los Angeles, California, on 10 July 1927. My mom and dad were both medical doctors, so my upbringing through the Great Depression was relatively comfortable. At the ripe old age of 11 or so, I developed a wanderlust to see what was on the other side of

> ..., he figured that the discipline and structure might be just what I needed...

the mountain, a wanderlust which remained with me most of my life.

My first few forays from home were on Greyhound buses, freight trains, and/or by hitchhiking, which took me to many parts of our great country. Shortly after my 13th birthday, I was in the hobo jungle associated with the El Paso, Texas, railroad yards. A group of Texas National Guard soldiers approached a group of us young "knights of the road," and a corporal asked if any of us were interested in joining the National Guard. They were from Company H, 2nd Battalion, 141st Infantry Regiment, 36th Division, Texas National Guard.

At the time I thought why not, another adventure. I was big for my age and I could easily pass for 16 or 17. I lied and told the recruiter that I was 18, that my name was Joseph Carlton, and that I was an orphan. He was eager for recruits, so he didn't question me too closely. He took us to a tent camp nearby and "swore us in," not even asking for a birth certificate. This was about 15 October 1940. We were issued uniforms and equipment used by the Army in the 1930s, i.e., boondocker shoes, wrap-

around leggings, riding britches, a shirt, and a campaign hat that resembled what some state troopers wear today.

After three or four weeks of basic training in marching, Army regulations, etc., we were informed that the 36th Division had been called up and made a part of the regular Army. Here I was now, at age 13 years and 4 months, a soldier in the Army of the United States of America. Wow!

A short time later, we were sent to Camp Bowie, Brownwood, Texas, where all the units of the 36th Division were assembled for training. Because I was in a light weapons machine-gun company, I was taught how to field-strip and shoot the .45-caliber pistol and the .30-caliber machine gun. The machine guns were water-cooled and were transported on carts pulled by two soldiers. We also had BARs (Browning Automatic Rifles) and were issued updated uniforms and equipment.

After about seven months, I figured it was time to move on before they found out my true age and who I really was, so I went AWOL. When they eventually figured things out, the Army wrote my dad a letter inquiring about me and explaining what I had done. The letter said that due to my age, and the fact that a corporal had given me the oath instead of a commissioned officer (as required), no further action would be taken.

During the rest of 1941 and 1942, and into the summer of 1943, when World War II was going full bore, I still had that restless itch for travel and adventure. I wanted to be part of the war effort. I was still too young to join, so I kept busy at school and traveling. I was a constant frustration to my parents, who wished that I would live a more conventional lifestyle. I worked here and there: as busboy, dishwasher, theater usher, bellhop, railroad track layer, log skidder for a saw mill, milking cows, on a cattle ranch, at a bottling company, at a laundry and rug cleaners, etc. I even got involved with some delinquent stuff.

In the spring of 1943 the war was turning in our favor. While I was still attending high school, and after my 16th birthday, I approached my dad about joining the Navy. He was against it at first, but after some thought, he figured that the discipline and structure might be just what I needed to get my life back on track. So we got a copy of my birth certificate and changed a "7" to a "6". My birth certificate now read 10 July 1926.

I enlisted in the Navy at age 16 in 29 November 1943 for a 4-year minority cruise. I went to San Diego for boot camp, then to Texas A&M for radio school. While waiting at the U. S. Navy Amphibious Base, Oceanside, California, for assignment, they made me the camp bugler because I played the trumpet.

I was sent to Milne Bay, New Guinea, in June 1944, on the USS *Day Star*, a converted Navy troopship, to join a PT (Patrol Boat) squadron. After a few weeks there, I was sent to a harbor near Finschhafen, New Guinea, where I joined PT-238 of Motor Torpedo Boat Squadron 20. I did the radio, flags, and blinker-light communications, and manned a gun while on patrol.

Soon after the invasion of the Philippines, we moved to San Jose, Mindoro, Philippine Islands. Our job was to patrol around the islands of Mindoro, Leyte, Marinduque, Samar, Luzon, Panay, etc. Most of our action was sneaking into areas at night, shooting up a 60mm magnesium flare, then strafing enemy shore encampments. Occasionally, we'd launch a Mark 13 torpedo at a Japanese ship.

One of the highlights of our stay in the Philippines was the 4 July 1945 Regatta, which was a 10-mile race between the fastest boat from eight PT boat squadrons. We won the race hands down, averaging close to 60mph. We were heroes for a few days.

When the war ended in August 1945, our base exploded in celebration. There were five-inch star shells bursting in the air, and 60mm flares, flare guns, and small arms being fired. There was brandy from the first-aid kits and 190-proof alcohol from our torpedoes.

I returned to the States on a CVE (baby aircraft carrier) in January 1946. We docked in Seattle, Washington, and I went by train from there to Terminal Island Receiving Center near Los Angeles, California. While on a 30-day leave, I met and married my wife. I was honorably discharged in June 1947.

After a period of unrest and various jobs, I re-enlisted for a 2-year hitch on 1 December 1948. I was sent to Tsingtao, China, and was a signalman and quartermaster on the flagship of a destroyer squadron. We left China in April 1949 because of the advancing Communists. I was assigned to a small fuel ship which sailed to Okinawa, Guam, Kwajalein Atoll, then by plane to Oahu, Hawaii.

I was honorably discharged for the second time on 28 February 1950 and joined the reserves. The Navy didn't need my rating for the

Korean War, so I wasn't called up. I have always loved my country and I am proud and honored that I was able to serve her. If called upon again to defend her, I wouldn't hesitate.

Rusty Foster entered college on the GI Bill in September 1950 and earned a B.A. in languages (Spanish and Russian) from California State University, Fullerton. He also attended Talbot Theological Seminary, La Mirada, California. His education also included other schools and technical institutes. He learned to fly on the GI Bill and went to Mexico as a pilot-missionary. He also flew as an airline pilot, air-taxi pilot, crop-duster, and fire-fighter. He spent two years in the drug-eradication program in Mexico with the Narcotics Assistance Unit, U. S. Department of State. He has been a pastor and Bible teacher for 50 years. Rusty and Johanna, his wife of 55 years, have three children, six grandchildren, and three great-grandchildren. They reside in Palm Desert, California.

✓ *INCIDENTally* — *No sympathy!* – After receiving several shots on the second day of boot training in 1943, both arms were heavy. I was 15 years old, feeling sorry for myself, and seeking sympathy, when the chief said, "Those feeling bad, step forward." I joined several others in stepping forward. Our reward was a Johnson bar and the task of waxing our barracks floor. It was a learning experience that lasted through my 21 years in the Navy. – *Arnold L. McLain.*

Travis L. Surratt

Age 15 – United States Army

I was raised on a West Texas cotton farm. No job opportunities existed in this rural area at that time, so I decided to enlist in the Army, although I was only 15 years old. I listed my age as 18 and my mother signed the necessary

> On New Year's Day 1944, a championship game took place which we called the Irish Potato Bowl.

papers. I was sworn into the Army on 22 November 1940 in Lubbock, Texas. I was born on 9 January 1925.

I was sent to Fort Sam Houston, Texas, and finished basic training at Dodd Field, which had been an airbase during World War I. We lived in tents for eight weeks. Our mess hall was located in an old airplane hangar.

After recruit training, I was assigned to Company F, 38th Infantry Regiment of the 2nd "Indianhead" Division at Fort Sam Houston. In November 1942, the division was transferred to Camp McCoy, Wisconsin. We spent the entire winter of 1942-43 on skis, literally traversing the Iron River and Iron Mountain area of what is known as Michigan's Upper Peninsula.

In October 1943, we went overseas, landing at Belfast, Northern Ireland. At that time, General George Patton's Third Army was stationed there. My company was billeted in Newry, about two miles from the Free State of Ireland. My platoon was billeted in the Orange Hall there. Our mess hall was in an old abandoned church which had been built in 1502.

We stayed in Ireland until April 1944. We used our time having track meets, daily calisthenics, and 25-mile weekly hikes. We formed a football league. Space was limited to practice or train because there was no private land available. We managed to play about 10 football games. On New Year's Day 1944, a championship game took place which we called the Irish Potato Bowl. The game was considered quite an event at the time. I participated in that momentous game, and we won, 6-0. I still have clippings and pictures about the game that were published in the *Stars and Stripes*.

In April 1944, we were transferred to Cardiff, South Wales, to become part of General Bradley's 1st Army, which was destined to be in the invasion Army at Omaha Beach.

We landed at Omaha Beach about 6:30 a.m. on D-Day plus one, 7 June 1944. Our landing craft was sunk by German shellfire. The 2nd Infantry Division traveled 1,750 miles, from Omaha Beach to Pilsen, Czechoslovakia, and fought in five major battles.

I served 4 years, 9 months, and 19 days in the Army, most of that time with Company F, 38th Infantry. I was a platoon sergeant in charge of a heavy-weapons platoon. We had two machine-gun squads and three 60mm mortar squads, for a total of 35 men.

I received an honorable discharge at Fort Sam Houston, San Antonio, Texas, on 10 August 1945, at the age of 20.

Travis Surratt was awarded the Bronze Star with oak leaf cluster, the Combat Infantryman's Badge, and a number of service medals. He began his work career on 2 January 1946 as a roustabout with the Phillips Petroleum Company. He worked his way up the ladder over the years, becoming a pipeline inspector and later supervising the building of gasoline plants, chemical plants, refineries, and helium plants in many locations around the country. He lived and worked in England when Phillips Petroleum was laying pipelines under the North Sea. He was district superintendent for the Permian Basin at the time he retired after nearly 40 years with the company. Travis lives in Odessa, Texas.

A. J. McKinney

Age 15 – United States Navy

I was born at Fort Blackmore, Virginia, on 12 March 1925. In 1940, when it became apparent that war was imminent for our country, several young

> ... *the captain decided that we should all abandon ship.*

men where I lived in Clincho, Virginia, a coal mining area, decided to enlist in the military. We felt that it was our patriotic duty to help defend our country.

When I enlisted, my parents, along with the general manager of the coal mine where my father worked, agreed to say that I was born on 12 March 1923, which made me appear to be 17 instead of 15. Since I was always quite large for my age and I always associated with an older group of young men, it was not hard for me to be accepted.

We left Virginia by train for Nashville, Tennessee, where we were taken to the naval recruiting station. I was sworn into the U. S. Navy as an apprentice seaman on 7 January 1941, on a minority cruise. A minority cruise was one in which you agreed to serve until your 21st birthday. I was 15 years, 9 months, and 25 days old.

Several of us left Nashville for the Naval Training Center, Norfolk, Virginia, on the same day we were sworn in. After boot camp, I requested to attend the naval electrical school and was accepted.

Upon completing electrical school, I was assigned to the USS *McCawley* (AP-10). Later, the ship was designated an attack transport and listed as APA-4. We were anchored in Chesapeake Bay when Pearl Harbor was attacked on 7 December 1941. We transported Marines and made several training landings at Little River, North Carolina.

In late December 1941, we went to the Brooklyn Navy Yard where British-style communications were installed on our main mast and the ship received a camouflage paint job. We loaded Army troops in New York and joined up with a convoy of some 47 ships which were staging in Halifax, Nova Scotia. We joined a convoy of many ships that were headed for Reykjavik, Iceland, where we discharged troops and cargo, then boarded Marines who were returning to the United States. We arrived back in New York in late February 1942, debarked troops, and left for Norfolk, Virginia. We departed Norfolk in early April 1942 with Marines aboard and destination unknown.

We went through the Panama Canal in early May 1942 and arrived in Samoa, debarking Marines at Pago Pago and Apia. On 18 May 1942, we departed Samoa, bound for New Zealand on a mission of war. We arrived in Wellington, New Zealand, on 22 May 1942. Admiral Turner came aboard, and the *McCawley* became his flagship.

We departed Wellington with Marine Raiders aboard on 27 July 1942. We held maneuvers in the Fiji Islands, then attacked Guadalcanal on 7, 8, and 9, August 1942. After the initial invasion, we made numerous troop and supply trips to Guadalcanal from New Caledonia.

We made the invasion of Rendova, one of the Solomon Islands, on 30 June 1943. We successfully unloaded our troops, equipment, and supplies, and were departing Rendova via the Blanche Channel about 4:30 p.m. when we were attacked by Japanese torpedo planes. We took a hit on the port side of the engine room. Admiral Turner, his staff and all of our crew, with the exception of 65 of us in a repair party, abandoned ship. By 7 p.m., we had only about one foot of freeboard at the stern and the captain decided that we should all abandon ship. The USS *McCalla*, a Fletcher-class destroyer, came alongside and we climbed a rope ladder to the destroyer's deck. Within a few minutes, our ship took another torpedo and sank. We lost 15 shipmates who were in the engine room at the time. We learned later that the last torpedo was from one of our own PT boats. After we were aboard the *McCalla*, a torpedo from a PT boat went beneath her. We departed Blanche Channel at full speed.

I had just made electrician's mate first class and was one of 42 first class and chief petty officers to return to the States for further assignment. We arrived in San Francisco on 16 August 1943. I was given a 30-day leave, with orders to report to the Submarine Chaser Training Center (SCTC) in Miami, Florida, as an instructor. I was there for about three weeks when I was notified that I was being transferred to Orange, Texas, to help put the USS *Thomas J. Gary* (DE-326) in commission. I requested and was granted a meeting with the executive officer of SCTC. My question was, "Why was I being reassigned to sea duty when there were many first class electrician's mates who had never been to sea?" As I recall, he was a very kind officer. He said to me, "Son, we need sailors with your experience to put ships in commission and help win this war."

I spent my time on the DE-326 making convoy runs to the European and the African war theaters. I studied and worked very hard and was promoted to chief electrician's mate on 1 November 1944, after serving 3 years and 10 months in the Navy. At that time my true age was 19 years, 8 months, and 19 days. I believe that I may be one of the youngest in the U. S. Navy to hold that rank.

I left the DE-326 on 18 February 1945 and was assigned to the Naval Research Laboratory in Washington, D.C. When the war was over, I requested a discharge on points. I received an honorable discharge at Bainbridge, Maryland, on 8 October 1945.

A. J. McKinney earned five battle stars on his Asiatic Pacific Medal and one battle star on his European Theater Medal. After his discharge he was employed as an electrician on high-voltage lines with a coal strip-mining company and was soon promoted to a management position. He worked as superintendent of roads and grounds for Pan American Airways at Cape Canaveral, and later as superintendent of equipment maintenance for B. B. McCormick & Sons, in Jacksonville, Florida. He went next with the Liberia Mining Company, a subsidiary of Republic Steel Corporation, and worked in Liberia, West Africa for five years. When he returned to the States, he worked as superintendent of maintenance for the Raymond International Corporation in Puerto Rico, then was transferred to Houston, Texas. As equipment supervisor, or troubleshooter, he traveled extensively to the company operations in the Middle East, Africa, New Zealand, South America, the Caribbean Islands, and throughout the United States. He retired on 1 January 1988. A. J. and Alma L. Eames were married on 15 June 1946 by Dr. Frederick B. Harris, who was Chaplain of the U. S. Senate during the war. They have two sons, four grandchildren, and one great-grandchild. A. J. and Alma live in Port St. Lucie, Florida.

Harry H. Ferrier
Age 16 – United States Navy

I was born in Springfield, Massachusetts, on 23 January 1925. My father died, and he was buried on my thirteenth birthday. The next three years were difficult. My mother remarried in 1940 and I decided to enter the naval service. With the help of my mother and a friend, I altered my birth certificate and enlisted in the Navy on 28 January 1941.

> Of the 21 aircraft in that attack, ours was the only one to return, ...

After recruit training and completion of aviation radio school, I was assigned to Torpedo Squadron Eight (VT-8), USS *Hornet* (CV-8). In early 1942, VT-8 was divided into two units. The larger unit embarked on the *Hornet* with fifteen Douglas TBD-1 Devastators. A smaller group, known as the receiving detail, remained at the Naval Air Station, Norfolk, Virginia, to receive the new Grumman TBF-1 aircraft. I was assigned to the TBF group as a radioman third class, qualified in aircraft.

Our group of six TBF-1 aircraft arrived at Pearl Harbor too late to join the *Hornet* before she sailed on 28 May. Instead, we were assigned to Midway Island, while the larger unit with fifteen TBD-1s was on the *Hornet*. On 4 June 1942, VT-8 was one of the first American aircraft squadrons to attack a large force of Japanese aircraft carriers that was about 150 miles west of Midway. This was the beginning of the now famous Battle of Midway.

The entire squadron of 21 aircraft was involved. The TBFs and the TBDs made their attacks separately, with the TBFs attacking at 7:00 a.m. I was a radioman-gunner in a TBF piloted by Ensign Bert Earnest, with my friend, Aviation Machinist Mate Third Class J. D. Manning, as turret gunner. When we approached the enemy carriers, a swarm of Japanese Zeros attacked us. Manning was killed and I was wounded and knocked unconscious. Ensign Earnest, also wounded, somehow brought the plane back to Midway.

Of the 21 aircraft in that attack, ours was the only one to return, and we were so shot up that when we landed at Midway, we went into a ground loop. All 15 TBDs were lost. Ensign George Gay was the only TBD pilot who survived. Of the 48 pilots and crewmen of VT-8 who flew into battle, only three of us survived: Ensigns Earnest and Gay, and myself. VT-8 was the first aircraft squadron to receive a Presidential Unit Citation during World War II. The TBF was named "The Avenger" following the Battle of Midway.

After the Battle of Midway, I was assigned to Torpedo Squadron Three (VT-3). VT-3 had also been decimated at Midway, although its losses were not as severe as VT-8. In July 1942, we embarked on the carrier USS *Enterprise* (CV-6).

The *Enterprise* and its embarked air group participated in the invasion of Guadalcanal on 7 August 1942. It remained in the area supporting the Marines and patrolling the area in search of Japanese forces. On 24 August 1942, during combat air operations, the *Enterprise* sustained three bomb hits which partially disabled its flight deck. The aircraft that I was in, piloted by Ensign Fred Mears, landed back aboard following the attack.

A couple of days later, my aircraft and several other flyable TBFs were sent to Henderson Field on Guadalcanal to support the Marines. Within days, VT-8, which had been on board the carrier USS *Saratoga*, also came ashore as a result of the *Saratoga* having been torpedoed. I was once again in VT-8 and flying with Ensign Earnest, my pilot during the Battle of Midway.

In December 1942, VT-8 returned to the United States and was decommissioned. Following a 30-day leave, I reported back to San Diego, California, and was assigned to Bombing Squadron Six (VB-6), which was then re-forming. Eventually, VB-6 and VB-3 were combined into VB-5 and assigned to the new carrier, USS *Yorktown* (CV-10). From May 1943 until May 1944, VB-5 participated in numerous battles in the Pacific theater. I was promoted to chief petty officer on 1 April 1944.

I was commissioned an ensign in January 1945, shortly before my 20th birthday. I voluntarily reverted to CPO in June 1946 and was assigned to Weather Reconnaissance Squadron 3 at NAS, Miami, Florida. I spent four hurricane seasons flying as a radioman and radar operator in Consolidated PB4Y2 Privateers.

I was again commissioned an ensign in 1951, during the Korean War and attended aviation-electronics officers school. I then taught about the electronic triggers for nuclear weapons at the Armed Forces Special Weapons Project in Albuquerque, New Mexico. I participated in two atmospheric nuclear-weapons tests in the Nevada desert.

I accepted a permanent commission as an ensign LDO (limited duty officer) in 1955. During the Vietnam War, I made three combat cruises aboard the amphibious-assault helicopter carrier, USS *Princeton*, in support of U. S. Marine troop operations.

I retired from the Navy as a commander on 1 September 1970, after nearly 30 years of service.

Harry Ferrier was awarded the Distinguished Flying Cross, the Purple Heart, three Air Medals, and four Presidential Unit Citations. The four PUCs were for service with Torpedo Squadron Eight, the USS Enterprise (CV-6), the First Marine Division (Reinforced), and the USS Yorktown (CV-10). On Veterans Day, 11 November 1997, he was inducted into the Combat Aircrew Roll of Honor aboard the USS Yorktown Naval Museum at Charleston, South Carolina, and was conferred another signal honor on 1 October 1998 when the Confederate Air Force, Midland, Texas, inducted the aircrew of the Grumman Avenger, TBF-1, BuNo 00380, into the American Combat Air Crew Hall of Fame. Following his retirement from the Navy, Harry became involved in local politics. He served on the Oak Harbor School Board, the Island County, Washington, Planning Commission, and as Island County Auditor. He married Christie A. Ferrier in 1945. They had two children, four granddaughters, and now have three great-grandchildren. Christie died in April 1989. In March 1990, he married the former Evelyn Koetje. Harry and Evelyn live in Oak Harbor, Washington.

Charles E. White

Age 15 – United States Navy

My parents were living in St. Petersburg, Florida, when I was born on 4 January 1926. Within a year after my birth, we moved back to Lauderdale County, Alabama, where all of our family lived. My father died in 1930 when I

> I made up my mind that I would get in the Navy someday.

was 4 years old. That left my mother to raise three kids. With the help of a good garden, a milk cow, some chickens, and a small widow's pension, we managed to survive the Depression.

When I was about 10, I saw a magazine that had colored pictures of some gold, silver, and blue Navy aircraft flying off a carrier. I said to myself, "Boy, that's really something. That's for me!" I made up my mind that I would get in the Navy someday.

In the late fall of 1940, I was running with a crowd of boys who weren't really the best. I was beginning to be a problem for my mother. I told her that I thought that I could get into the Navy, but she resisted it for a long time. Things were just getting worse, so I went to see the Navy recruiter at the post office in downtown Florence, Alabama. He said, "You don't have a birth certificate, so you'll have to get me a letter from the superintendent of schools to prove your age." I went to the high school and obtained a letter from the superintendent. I took the letter down to the hardware store where my next-door neighbor worked, put it in his typewriter, fixed it up like I wanted it, and went across

the street and joined the Navy! Of course my mother had to sign the papers. She did a lot of thinking, praying, and consulting with her sisters, but she signed. I was sworn into the Navy on 27 May 1941. As it turned out, it was probably the best thing I could have ever done.

I went to boot camp in Norfolk, Virginia. They found out that I played the bugle, so while all the other boots were out hitting the grinder every day, I went to the band barracks and practiced with the training station's drum-and-bugle corps. After boot camp I was anxious to get out of Norfolk. I went to see an old chief at the assignment desk and told him, "Man, I'm ready to get out of here. Put me on a ship, anything!" He said, "You get back over to the barracks and shut up. I'm going to do you a favor that you're going to thank me for the rest of your life."

Sure enough, I got a set of orders to VP-84 (Patrol Squadron 84) at Breezy Point, near Norfolk. They didn't even have airplanes yet, so they asked for volunteers to go to Key West, Florida, with VP-81. I was there when the war started. We heard the news about the attack on Pearl Harbor about 1:00 in the afternoon. By that evening, we had a 50-caliber machine gun mounted at each corner of the hangar and everywhere else we could find to put one.

While at Key West, I noticed young, white-hat sailors running around with wings on their chests, so I found out about naval aviation pilots. I said, "My God, That's for me! I gotta do that!"

In May 1942, German submarines sank 37 ships right in our patrol area in the Gulf of Mexico and the Caribbean. Our aircraft brought back some of the survivors of ships that were sunk. In July 1942, I was transferred to Norfolk and assigned to VP-82. They flew the Lockheed Hudson, which the Navy called a PBO. Soon after I arrived, the squadron got new aircraft, the PV-3. These aircraft had new radar systems, and they needed radar operators, so I went to the three-week school at the Cavalier Hotel in Virginia Beach, Virginia. While at Quonset Point, Rhode Island, I took the physical and requested to be sent to flight school, but they wouldn't submit the request until I had been with the squadron for a few months.

I finished the radar course and rejoined the squadron which was at Agentia, Newfoundland, at the time. My plane commander wrote a recommendation for me to attend flight school and sent it off in January 1943. It came back within a month, and on 1 April 1943, I left for flight school. I had just turned 17 and was a petty officer second class.

I was among a group of enlisted sailors and Marines that completed flight preparatory school at Natchitoches, Louisiana, then went to Kilgore, Texas, for training to see if we could fly or not. From there it was to Athens, Georgia, for pre-flight, then to Dallas, Texas. Here we flew the N2S "Yellow Peril." We would look up and the sky was just black with airplanes coming in and trying to land. That set some of us to wondering if we were doing the right thing or not. From Dallas, we went to Pensacola, Florida, for some flight time in the SNV "Vultee Vibrator." We were waiting for transportation to Whiting Field, Florida, for the instrument program on 6 June 1944, D-Day in Europe.

I finished my training and received my wings on 24 October 1944. I was promoted to aviation pilot first class. Enlisted pilots were called APs (Aviation Pilots) and officers were called NAs (Naval Aviators). Enlisted pilot wings were the same Navy wings of gold as the officer pilots, but we had to buy ours; officers were presented theirs. Flight training for student enlisted pilots was the same as student naval avaitors.

I was sent to Hawaii where I flew SBD5s off Ford Island, then moved to Barbers Point where we got the new SB2C aircraft. There were three other enlisted pilots in the squadron. With the war over, in early September we were transferred to VJ-14 at Ford Island where we flew the Martin Marauder, towing antiaircraft targets.

I flew from various locations in Washington and California, then went to Guam in October 1946. We made 3-week trip to China, stopping in Shanghai and Tsingtao. We were on a photo mission. The Communists were sabotaging the Peking-Mukden Railroad, and the brass wanted to get some idea of where the Communists were hanging out.

In 1947, I returned to the States to re-enlist and ended up at Key West, Florida, in VX-1 an antisubmarine development squadron. I flew the PB4Y2 for a couple of hundred hours. I spent about a year in Port Lyautey, Morocco, then went to Memphis, Tennessee.

They abolished the AP rating in 1948 and everyone had to go back to a basic rating. I obtained the rate of AC (Air Controlman), but I was still a pilot. I was a petty officer first class for 7½ years before I made chief in May 1952. Many times I was the plane commander with an officer as a co-pilot. Whenever we would go cross-country and stop somewhere, they had a car waiting for the officer. They would tell me, "You can catch a bus over there to the barracks or to the chow hall."

While I was at Memphis in 1953, I obtained a green instrument card, which I used for the remainder of my time in the Navy. There were three instrument ratings at that time. A red card didn't do you any good at all. You had to stay on the ground with that. The white card was the standard instrument rating. You could fly on instruments with the white card, but you had to have a clearing authority, someone other than yourself, to sign your flight plan. A green card signified that you had the instrument skill and expertise to sign your own clearance. About that time almost all enlisted aviation pilots had green cards.

I spent three years in Naples, Italy, flying all sorts of aircraft. In November 1959, President Eisenhower was about to leave for India, Pakistan, and Afghanistan. We were to transport an advance party to wherever he was going to stop. We left in a R4D8 transport plane on Wednesday and spent that night in Cairo, Egypt, Thursday night in Dhahran, and arrived in New Delhi, India, on Friday afternoon. They shipped five Marine helicopters to Karachi. We had to haul the ground crews from there to Kabul, Afghanistan. The helicopters could only fly about 250 miles and we had 1,000 miles to go. We made four stops before arriving in Peshawar, Pakistan.

We had Captain E. P. Aurand, the naval aide to the President, with us. He was a test pilot before he got the job with President Eisenhower. The only approved entry into Kabul was to go from Kandahar, which is in southwest Afghanistan, and fly up a valley to Kabul. There was no instrument or night flying in Afghanistan at that time. As we headed for Kabul, the clouds kept getting lower. We were about 15 or 20 minutes from Kabul, but had to go through a mountain pass. The ceiling was down to about 200 feet. I was flying the airplane. The naval aide to the President said, "Go on and dart through that pass. It's only a couple of minutes on to Kabul." Of course, I wouldn't do that. I circled two or three times, and you just couldn't see anything on the other side of that pass but snow. A lieutenant commander, part of our crew, kept telling us, "Don't go in there! Don't go in there!" I wasn't about to go in there.

We backtracked down the valley and crossed the mountains to Peshawar, Pakistan, and spent the night. The next morning we went through the Khyber Pass to Kabul. When we got there we found that they had had a real good snowstorm. We had violated their flight rules by entering Afghanistan through the Khyber Pass. We had to go to the ambassador, who went to the king of Afghanistan, to get permission to leave.

We left Naples on 4 July 1960 and headed home. I checked in at Memphis in mid-July and stayed there until I retired from the Navy on 16 October 1962.

Charlie White worked as a flight controller at the FAA Jacksonville Air Route Traffic Control Center, Hillard, Florida, from shortly after his retirement from the Navy until 1974. Then he sold real estate in Key West, Florida, and later in North Carolina. He retired from that endeavor in 1983 and moved back to Florida. In 1998, he was elected president of the Silver Eagles Association, a fraternal organization of former Navy, Marine Corps, and Coast Guard enlisted pilots, and served three years. Charlie and Gloria, his wife of 53 years, have three children, six grandchildren, and one great-grandchild. They live in Pensacola, Florida.

✔ *INCIDENTally* — **Last rites!** – When I was in Army basic training at age 14, I got very sick with spinal meningitis. An Army chaplain thought that I was an officer's kid. He told me later that he had given me last rites. I guess the last rites didn't work because at age 74, I'm still here! – *Jerome A. "Jerry" Moore.*

Joseph L. Alexander

Age 14 – United States Army

I grew up in San Antonio, Texas, where I was born on 25 August 1926, and given the name Joseph Trejo. I lived with my grandmother and an aunt in a cold and loveless

> I was a 15-year-old prisoner of war!

household. I was told that I was illegitimate, and that my mother had died when I was very young. This was hard to cope with, and I became scrappy and mean. Other kids were not allowed to play with me because I was so mean. Their parents said that I'd wind up in prison someday – I did – but not the kind they were thinking of. When I was 14 years old, I went with my grandmother to Fort Sam Houston in San Antonio, to enlist in the Army. They didn't ask for a birth certificate or any kind of personal records. All they did was ask me was whether I wanted to sign up, and I said yes. That was it!

I was sworn into the Army on 7 July 1941. I wanted to be an infantryman, but I was assigned to the Army Air Corps which had been renamed the Army Air Forces about three weeks before. It would be years before I knew that there had been a name change. I was sent to a civilian airfield in Albuquerque, New Mexico, now Kirtland Air Force Base, for basic training. I was trained as an ordnance maintenance technician. My first duty station was at Clark Field, in the Philippines. I was assigned to the 440th Ordnance Aviation Bombardment Squadron. My job was to load bombs on B-17s.

About the time that Pearl Harbor was bombed and the war started, my true age was discovered. The first sergeant said that a war zone was no place for a 15-year-old, and that I would be sent back to the States as soon as transportation could be arranged. I was scheduled to leave on a troopship that was evacuating civilians from the

Philippines, but the ship never left the dock. It was bombed by the Japanese.

There was a war to be fought, and the fact that I was underage was forgotten. Everyday the Japanese made low-level runs on Clark Field, strafing and bombing the base. Half of our bomber force was lost and there was a heavy loss of lives. Our squadron moved to Mindanao, another island in the Philippines, which was about 500 miles south of Luzon. The enemy didn't let up, and we were under attack almost from the time we arrived there.

In May 1942, General Jonathan M. Wainwright, Commander of U. S. Army Forces Far East, surrendered the Philippine Islands. I was a 15-year-old prisoner of war! For me, death may have been a kinder blow, but I didn't know it at first. The Japanese soldiers split us into groups and herded us into various camps. There were no barbed-wire fences. They fed us reasonably well. They were rough on us, but they weren't mean.

Three months later we were told that we would be going to Japan. I was scared and I broke down. Others also panicked and cried. We just didn't know what the hell was going to happen to us. It wasn't long before we found out. They herded us aboard ship like cattle and treated us like animals. We were packed into the ship's hold so tightly that there was barely room to stand. We were denied the use of toilet facilities and the stench became unbearable. The only food was hardtack. We were three months at sea and were twice torpedoed by American submarines. More than 1,000 men had boarded ship in Mindanao; less than half ever saw American soil again.

When we arrived in Japan, about 500 of us were taken to the seaport city of Kawasaki to work in steel mills that were turning out structural components for ships. We were forced to work from dawn until dark, seven days a week. The only meal each day was a cup of maize – dried corn usually used for chicken feed. To be sick was not allowed; manpower was needed in the mills. We were always subjected to constant beatings at the whim of the guards. They used walking canes and cudgels to make their points.

Many times after a long day had ended, the guards would make us stand at attention all night, put us outside in the cold, or threaten to kill us because one of them wasn't happy about something we said or did. The next morning we would go to work without any sleep or anything to eat. This would go on for two or three days before they would give us something to eat, but we never got to rest.

We marched to work before daylight and would pick up orange peelings or whatever we could find on the street to eat. If we saw trash cans along the way, we would search them for food and eat whatever we found. If the guards caught us doing this, they would beat us for stealing. A delicacy for us was to crisp orange peels on ingots of hot steel in the mills.

I was at Kawasaki for about a year, then some of us were moved to the neighboring city of Shinagawa. The treatment there was not better. We were marched to the city's steel mills or to the harbor to load 100-pound bags of rice on barges. The more work we did, the more was expected of us. In spite of our weakened physical condition and mental anguish, we kept going or suffered the consequences.

One time, the guards put a Marine in a pit and beat him over the head without letup. I don't know what the man had done to so infuriate the Japanese, but they beat all of the hair off his head. However, the Marine did not die and they did not break him! After that, for some reason, the Japanese feared him and left him alone. They called him "Superman."

We had been captured on Mindanao by the fighting troops, regular soldiers, and they treated us fairly. The men guarding us in Japan were the home guard or reserves who had not the slightest feeling for us. At times the Japanese guards would strike up a conversation with us and talk to us about the United States. They would tell us about the schools they had attended in the States, then turn around and beat us for no apparent reason.

After a year and a half at Shinagawa, I was moved to Omori. It wasn't long before we discovered where the food was stored. We stole food from a big warehouse, most of it sugar. The guys would find the oddest places to hide the food – under their armpits, taped to their stomachs, carried inside papers, etc. The guards would shake us down, and if they found anything, they would beat the hell out of us for stealing. Sometimes they would come in at three in the morning, wake up the whole camp, barracks by barracks, and have us all stand at attention because someone was caught stealing.

At Omori, a Japanese warrant officer found out that I was the youngest prisoner. I guess he felt sorry for me because I was so young.

I was detailed to take care of the chickens for the guards. I picked up the nickname "Chicken Boy," but I put my position to good use. I stole eggs and took them back to the guys. We ate them raw. I didn't steal chickens because I knew that the guards kept a close count of them.

Occasionally we came across an English-language newspaper that gave us an idea of how the war was progressing. In spite of being cut off from the rest of the world, we had an idea that the war was drawing to a close. The real indication of this was that the guards started treating us more humanely.

We learned through the grapevine that the atomic bombs had been dropped, and that the war was over. We woke up one morning and all the guards were gone. We didn't know how to act. We started running around cheering, hugging each other, and crying. We broke into the storehouse where they kept the food. Some of the men were thirsting for revenge and wanted to go into the city and kill everyone in sight. When the American B-29s dropped 50-gallon drums of food to us, we knew it was definite. The war was over. We were free!

Amid the joy of our release, there was still tragedy. Some of the starving men could not restrain themselves, and in their eagerness to satisfy their hunger, gorged themselves with the food and died from the shock to their systems. A few days later, American ships sailed into the harbor to pick us up. We were crying, laughing, and hollering. They told us the war was really over and gave us cigarettes and anything else we wanted. Aboard ship, we were given physicals and clean clothes. I was covered with lice. We were covered with lice almost the entire time we were in captivity. It was a real pleasure to have a hot shower after 3½ years of occasionally being doused with a bucket of cold water.

We were flown to a hospital in Manila and everyone was real nice to us. The mess halls were open 24 hours a day. I had turned 19 in Japan, just at the time we knew that the war was over. I weighed 85 pounds.

At Letterman General Hospital in San Francisco, I called my grandmother in San Antonio. I learned that she had been informed that I was dead. I had been gone more than a year before she learned that I was alive. She was glad to hear from me. My next stop was the Brooke Army Medical Center at Fort Sam Houston, San Antonio. I spent almost two years in Army hospitals before I returned to active duty.

While a patient at the medical center, I learned that the cold, impersonal woman I had known as my aunt was really my mother. It was a deep shock. She had been married, then abandoned, and wasn't able to cope with approaching motherhood. I came to grips with the truth, and to erase the stigma of illegitimacy that I had lived with all my life, I legally claimed the name of the father I had never known. I had my records changed accordingly. Joe Trejo was no more. Now I was Joe Alexander. I am grateful that I had the opportunity to come to an understanding with my mother before her death.

I returned to active duty and was assigned to the motor pool at Kelly Air Force Base. I had three short tours at other places, but when I retired as a technical sergeant at age 37, I had spent 17 years at Kelly.

I still smile when I see a plaque honoring World War II dead that is on a wall in my old high school. My name is on it! It was not easy to readjust after so many years as a prisoner, but I did. When I see the American flag, I still get tears in my eyes.

Joe Alexander was awarded the Purple Heart for wounds received on Mindanao. After he retired from the Air Force, he remained at Kelly AFB as a civilian employee. He worked in the supply and logistics area, and in the distribution directorate. He retired again in 1980. He was national commander of the American Defenders of Bataan and Corregidor for the years 2000 and 2001. Joe and his wife Norma have two sons and two grandchildren. They live in San Antonio, Texas.

Walter Howard Lewis

Age 16 – United States Navy

Hitler marched into Poland in 1939 and I lost my mother that same year from a heart attack. I had two brothers and two sisters living when she died; the oldest was seventeen and the youngest nine. Our father was a train engineer on the C&O

> *I sold what books I had to the high school bookstore ... and left home with two of my friends.*

Railroad. He was determined to keep us together, but he was gone a great deal of the time.

My older sister Mickey was 15 years old. She and I kept house for Dad. She cooked his meals and I helped her with the housework. It was amazing that she could do all this because she was crippled by infantile paralysis. She had a game leg and walked with a crutch. We lived in Lexington, Kentucky, where I was born on 20 June 1925.

My dad and I did not get along very well because he began to drink heavily after Mother died. It was difficult staying at home and trying to go to high school because I never knew what he would do when he got drunk. Before my mother died, I was an honor student in high school, but I lost all interest without her to motivate me. I tried, but I didn't have books half the time, so I finally quit school. I sold what books I had to the high school bookstore on 4 December 1941 and left home with two of my friends. We hopped a freight going south but made it no further than 80 miles from home. We had gone through a tunnel that was a mile and a quarter long on top of a boxcar. All three of us nearly suffocated. Needless to say, we found our way back home on 6 December 1941. Dad was glad that I was back. I started to feel better about home after I was cleaned up and had a good night's sleep.

My whole life changed the next day. We were in the neighborhood ice-cream store when we heard that the Japanese had bombed Pearl

Harbor. The three of us, and two other friends, decided to join the Navy. We went to the recruiting station on 8 December 1941. The recruiter signed up two of my friends who were of age. He asked me how old I was and I told him that I was 18. He said that he didn't believe me, but if I was, I should get my birth certificate, come back in the morning, and I could go with the two he had already accepted.

I went from the Navy recruiting office to the Board of Health that afternoon and obtained a copy of my birth certificate. I took it home and eradicated the top of the five in 1925, matched the ink, and changed the year to 1923. I was sworn into the Navy on 12 December 1941.

That night I told my dad that I had joined the Navy. He said that he wouldn't let me go, and that he would tell them that I was underage. I told him that I would leave home and never come back if he wouldn't let me go. He told me that I was a man, and that he would not help me get out if I changed my mind. The day that my older friends and I got on the train at Union Station, my father saw me off. He had tears in his eyes as he hugged me. He said he wished he had stopped me. I told him that I loved him and that I would be O.K. My other two underage friends who didn't get in then, later went to sea, one in the Navy when he became 17 and the other in the Merchant Marine when he was 15. The 15-year-old was the only one of the five of us who didn't make it back. He died on the docks in Pearl Harbor helping to unload war supplies from his ship.

I became a Navy signalman and served on four ships, two Liberty ships and two tankers. The first ship I served on was torpedoed by a German U-boat on our way to Russia via Capetown and the Persian Gulf. We took a torpedo in the stern ammunition magazine. We had to abandon ship because we were dead in the water and couldn't defend ourselves. We were 375 miles southeast of St. Thomas, Virgin Islands. After five and a half days in very rough water, we were picked up only 25 miles from there. We lost three Navy gun crewmen and one Merchant Mariner. The gunners' quarters were above the ammo magazine and the Merchant Mariner had borrowed a hammock from one of the gunners and swung it under the gun tub outside of the gunners' quarters.

I went on to serve on an oil tanker, another Liberty ship, which by coincidence, was the SS *Pearl Harbor*, and a gasoline tanker, before I was hospitalized and then honorably discharged on 3 March 1944 at the Great Lakes Naval Hospital.

Howard Lewis earned the Combat Action Ribbon and other service medals for his service during World War II. After his discharge, he went back to high school and finished his education. He went to work for a trucking company while he was in college, and stayed with that company until he retired. He was a terminal manager in Lexington, Kentucky, for the last 20 years of his 33-year career. He married Doris Ann Glass when she was 17 and he was 22. They have five daughters, a son, and eight grandsons. Howard and Doris live in Lexington, Kentucky.

✓ **INCIDENTally** *— Cheers!* – I was a Merchant Marine sailor aboard the SS *Netherlands Victory* in 1944. When we arrived at Pearl Harbor, we were told that there was a 10:00 p.m. curfew for all military personnel in Honolulu. That night a group of us were in a bar when a Navy chief and two shore patrolmen came in checking passes and running the soldiers and sailors out of the bar. When they came to us we said, "Merchant seamen." He asked for the ship's pass, then said, "*Netherlands Victory* – are you guys Dutch seamen?" One fast thinker in the group replied, "Yo, yo, Nederlander!" The chief said, "OK, glad to have you guys with us, we're only checking Americans." The word was quickly passed to the rest of the crew. *– Patrick H. Taylor.*

Clinton D. Keel

Age 16 – United States Navy

I was raised at the foot of the Cumberland Mountains in Warren County, Tennessee. My actual birth date is 14 December 1925, but the birth date that I used to get into the Navy was 7 December 1924. When I enlisted, I

> ..., to my dismay, the mother blurted out, "Little boy, where did you steal that uniform?"

weighed 115 pounds, was 5 foot 7 inches tall, and wore a size-7 shoe. I did not own or have any need for a razor. My mother died in 1933 at the age of 24. Since I never got along very well with my stepmother, my father was pleased to help me inflate my age and assist me in getting out of their hair. I was sworn into the Navy on 15 December 1941.

I spent two months in boot camp at San Diego, California, and then I was assigned to the USS *Aldebaran* (AF-10). After one year aboard the *Aldebaran*, I was sent to Boston, Massachusetts, where I was assigned to the USS *Lexington* (CV-16). Then it was back to the Pacific. The Lexington was torpedoed and badly damaged at Kwajalein. We returned to Bremerton for repairs and then went back into action. We were hit by a kamikaze on 4 November 1944 and I received multiple burn and shrapnel wounds. I spent time on various hospital ships and in hospitals, but I was returned to duty.

I was assigned to the USS *Colbert* (APA-145). The *Colbert* struck a floating mine while riding out a typhoon in the China Sea. We lost all power and had to be towed to Buckner Bay at Okinawa. I was on Okinawa when the war ended. I was sent back to the States and discharged on 8 December 1945.

During my first year or so in the Navy, I was in constant fear of my age being discovered and I would have to return home in disgrace. This didn't happen, but my age and youthful appearance did present many problems. I studied hard and became a boatswain's mate at age 18. Older men did not relish taking orders from a kid. It was a difficult task – but somehow, it worked out.

While I was still an apprentice seaman, I was in the lobby of a theater in San Francisco. I noticed a mother and her daughter staring at me. In a short while, they moved in my direction and I felt certain that they were coming over to make my acquaintance, and that their visit would be a friendly one. The daughter was about my age; my pulse rate increased and my imagination ran wild. When they approached, to my dismay, the mother blurted out, "Little boy, where did you steal that uniform?" My ego was splattered, my dream world went up in smoke. I'm certain that my face changed color. I think I muttered a few words and made for the exit.

Well, I did survive the age problems, the typhoons, the mines, the torpedoes, and the kamikaze. Here I am at age 76, in as good a shape as I could expect to be, when all is considered. Whatever success I may have achieved in life, I attribute to my military service, especially to the order and discipline I learned, and to the GI Bill.

Clinton Keel returned to high school, finishing at night while working in a dental laboratory during the day. After graduation, he enrolled at the University of Tennessee. He became a housewares and hardware manufacturers' agent and pursued this line of work for 43 years, retiring at age 71. Clinton and Jean , his wife of 55 years, have four children and nine grandchildren. They live in Madison, Tennessee.

Richard T. Towner, Jr.

Age 16 – United States Army

I was an apprentice union steamfitter at age 15, in Rochester, New York, where I was born on 28 July 1925. Shortly after my birthday in 1941, several friends and I took

> I was to be a member of the Army's Navy!

the ferry that used to run between Rochester and Coburg, Ontario, Canada. I wanted to join the Royal Canadian Army, so I went to the armory, but it was closed. I told the guard that I wanted to join the Canadian Army and gave him my name and address. This was on Saturday, and the following Tuesday a letter came from a Canadian recruiting officer, and my dad blew his top at me!

All was forgotten until 7 December 1941. After I heard about the attack, I said, "Dad, I am going to join the Canadian Army". He said, "Like hell!" Well, that worried him and he said, "If you're going to join an army, it will be the American Army." So he told me to get my birth certificate and he would fix it so it would pass the recruiters, and it did! All this was about 9 December and I left for training on the 15 December 1941.

When my mother heard about what he had done, her Irish temper flared. She swore that she was going to kill him for altering my birth certificate. To this day, my oldest sister does not believe that her father would do such a thing.

When I went to the recruiting offices on 9 December, I was going to join the Marines, but the line was so long it wound around the block. I tried the Navy, but the lines there were also very long. I went to the Army recruiting office and found only about ten men waiting in line, so I went in to join the Army. The recruiter looked at me and said, "You look like you are too young, but there is nothing wrong with this birth certificate."

I was sent to Camp Upton, New Jersey, for boot camp, then reported to Fort Eustis, Virginia, to attend a school on aircraft search and sounding systems. After graduating, I reported to the 7th Coast Artillery at Fort Hancock, New Jersey, for training in planting ocean mines.

While I was in training, one of the 1,500-pound anchored mines broke loose and washed ashore at Asbury Park Beach, New Jersey. My unit was sent to retrieve the mine. We loaded it into a 6x6 truck and headed back to camp. While driving in town, the truck driver braked to avoid hitting a car. I was standing in the back of the cab and in front of the mine. It broke loose over the blocking and pinned my left calf to the steel bulkhead.

They rushed me to the base hospital and put the muscle and veins in my leg back together. After the surgery, Captain Kloin woke me up and told me I was not an 18-year-old. I said, "Sure I am." He knew better and reported it to the colonel, who was the base commander. After I was released from the hospital, I was ordered to report to the colonel's office. He told me he could send me home or keep me because my dad had signed for me. I told him that I wanted to stay and go to France because I had always heard my dad talk about the time when he was in France during World War I.

After being released from the hospital, and after my encounter with the colonel, I was sent to Point Pleasant, West Virginia, for assignment to the United States Army Mine Planter-*16*. I was to be a member of the Army's Navy!

I served aboard the USAMP-*16* as a deck hand and then as quartermaster. I was later assigned to the engineering "black" gang where I served as a boilerman and oiler. We were sent to the Caribbean Sea to mine all shipping lanes east and west and up and down each coast near the Panama Canal.

While aboard ship, I was promoted to technician fifth grade. Most of the crew were former merchant seamen who had been drafted into the Army. After three years aboard ship, I was sent Stateside to a ranger base for 18 weeks of combat training. I became a machine-gun squad leader. We were shipped to Attu Island, Kisha Island, and Shemya Island in the Aleutians to prepare a B-29 base as part of the invasion of northern Japan. I was there two months, the atomic bombs were dropped on Japan, and the war was over.

I returned to the States and was discharged on 8 November 1945. I returned home to resume my apprenticeship as a union steamfitter. I re-enlisted in the Army in November 1948, but I obtained a hardship discharge in 1949 because I could not support my family on Army pay.

Dick Towner returned to his trade and worked 40 years as a steamfitter with the Steamfitter and Plumbers Local 13 in Rochester, New York. He moved to Florida after his retirement in 1981. In 1996 he was inducted as an honorary chief petty officer in the Exalted Order of Chief Petty Officers, USN, the largest maritime fraternity in the world. Dick and Joan, his wife of 55 years, have five children, seven grandchildren, and one great-grandchild. Their youngest son is a Navy chief petty officer. Dick and Joan live in Flagler Beach, Florida.

✔ *INCIDENTally* — ***Please stay away!*** – My cousin, Ellis Anderson, was stationed aboard the battleship USS *New Mexico*. Our paths crossed twice – once at Leyte, and again at Okinawa. Each time I saw the *New Mexico*, it had been hit by a kamikaze. I took my landing craft over to his ship to see if he was okay, and both times he survived without injury. Approximately 60 men were killed by the kamikaze at Okinawa. When I came aboard after the second hit, Ellis said, "Len, I don't think I want to see you anymore. Each time you come around, we get hit!" — *Leonard E. Anderson.*

Leo Peltier

Age 14 – United States Army

I was born in Spokane, Washington, on 12 May 1927, and raised in Eureka, Montana, as an adopted son. As a kid, I was out of control, as out of control as you could get in the late '30s and early '40s. I would probably

> *When General Patton ran out of gas, we fueled his tanks.*

have been sent to reform school had I not gone into the Army.

My older brother Alford took me and his son to Kalispell, Montana. We were planning to join the Navy, but the recruiter wasn't in that day, so we joined the Army. I told the recruiter that I was 18, but I was only 14. I was given papers to take home for my father to sign. He did, and I was sworn into the Army on 19 December 1941.

I was sent to San Diego, California, for basic training, then to Oakland, California, and on to Boston, Massachusetts. From there we went to Iceland. That was the time that the Germans were raising havoc with shipping in the North Atlantic. I witnessed the torpedoing of American ships by German submarines.

I spent about a year and a half in Iceland. That is where they caught up with me about my age. I had turned 16. I could have been sent home for falsifying records, but the Army declared me "essential." We shipped out from Iceland to Scotland and went by train to England. I was put in a replacement depot for a mobile antiaircraft unit.

Our unit landed in Normandy 15 days after D-Day. Truck drivers were desperately needed after the breakthrough at St. Lo, so many of us became truck drivers. At one time, we had five first sergeants driving trucks. The Red Ball Highway was started to ship supplies to the front. With two men per truck, we drove 24 hours per day, stopping only to eat and refuel. At night, we drove under near black-out conditions. When General Patton ran out of gas, we fueled his tanks. Later we switched from using 2½-ton trucks to 24-foot semis. Our unit shipped members of the 101st Airborne Division from France to the front lines during the Battle of the Bulge.

While at St. Trond, Belguim, we were nearly surrounded by the Germans during their last big offensive. This is the area where the Germans were firing V-1 rockets at England. The foggier it got, the more they fired.

One time I saw General George Patton. He was in his jeep, with escort jeeps in front and behind him. Both escort jeeps had 50-caliber machine guns.

After the Battle of the Bulge, we shipped bridges and other equipment as the Allies moved into Germany. We placed pontoons on the Rhine River and put together a bridge. After crossing the Rhine, we hauled engineering supplies to the front and hauled German POWs back. We could haul about a hundred prisoners in the 8-foot by 24-foot semis. I had not been around Germans before, but I found that they were just like anybody else. They were doing what they thought was right, just like we were doing what we thought was right.

Our unit found a factory in western Germany where Poles were forced to work. Most of the Poles were young women, and most were sick. They had not been fed very well. The factory had a retractable smoke stack that was lowered during the day so Allied bombers would not know it was a factory.

We were in Luxembourg, on the way to Rheims, France, when we heard the news that the Germans had surrendered. Everyone was whooping and hollering. We asked what was going on and they said, "The war is over!"

From May to September 1945, we hauled lumber from Belguim to Rheims for tent cities. From there we went to Marseilles where we boarded a ship for New York City. I was sent to Camp McCoy, Wisconsin, where I was discharged on 1 November 1945. I was given a train ticket back to Montana.

Leo Peltier went back to school after his discharge from the Army. He graduated from Lincoln County High School in Eureka, Montana, in 1948. He moved to Redmond, Oregon, in 1957 and was a distributor for Signal Oil. Later, he operated an appliance store and was in the appliance repair business. Leo lives in Redmond, Oregon, in the summer and spends the winters in Mesa, Arizona.

John M. Bohannan

Age 16 – United States Navy

I was born in Cleveland, Texas, on 7 May 1925. We lived in a number of places in south and southeast Texas while I was growing up. After the attack on Pearl Harbor, I wanted to join the Navy, but I was only 16. I talked my dad into going to the recruiting office with me.

> I can say that I never saw anything in my life as pretty as the Statue of Liberty.

He told the recruiter that I was 16. The recruiter took him into another room to talk to him. Dad told the recruiter, "I won't lie to get that boy into the service, but I will say that he is closer to 17 than he is to 16." So the recruiter put down 1924 as my birth year and my dad signed the papers without looking at them.

I was sworn into the Navy on 4 January 1942, 28 days after Pearl Harbor. I was closer to 17 than 16, but just barely. I spent four weeks at boot camp at Norfolk, Virginia, then I was sent to gunnery school in Little Creek, Virginia. After gunnery school, I was assigned to the U. S. Navy Armed Guard as a gunner on transports and cargo ships that were outfitted with surface and antiaircraft guns.

A group of us was sent to the Brooklyn Navy Yard for assignment to a gun crew and a ship. My first ship was an oil tanker with one 4"-50 caliber surface gun of World War I vintage. We had an eight-man crew and a coxswain who was a 3rd class boatswain's mate for a commanding officer. We made one trip from New York to Houston, Texas, and brought back a load of crude oil.

I got off of the ship in New York and was placed in another gun crew. We were assigned to the *Summelsdyke*, a Dutch combination passenger and cargo ship. We carried ammunition, food supplies, and the 14th Naval Construction Battalion to the South Pacific. Our first stop was at Tongataboo, a British-owned island in the Friendly Island Group. We unloaded some cargo there and some of the

Seabees, then went on to Espiritu Santo where we unloaded ammo, a deck cargo of tanks and small boats, and the remaining Seabees. We then went to Tocopillo, Chile, and filled our empty cargo holds with caustic soda to take back to San Francisco.

After we returned to the States, I went on leave, then reported to the Armed Guard Center at Treasure Island, San Francisco, California. I was assigned to the *William T. Coleman*, a new Liberty ship. We had a 20-man gun crew and two signalmen. Our gunnery officer was Daniel E. Sullivan, a former San Francisco police officer.

We left San Francisco on 18 December 1942, sailed across the Pacific Ocean, through the Indian Ocean, the Red Sea, through the Suez Canal, and into the Mediterranean Sea, all without an escort. We stopped at Alexandria, Egypt, where we unloaded part of our cargo, then sailed for Tripoli, Libya, with gasoline and ammo for the British 8th Army.

We were tied up between two British ships in Tripoli harbor on 19 March 1943. The *Ocean Voyager*, an English Liberty ship, was on our port side and a British corvette was on the starboard. A German Junker-88 aircraft attacked and hit the *Ocean Voyager* and the corvette. We pulled away from them because they were both burning, and both sank later. At about 3:00 a.m. the next morning, the boilers on the *Ocean Voyager* blew up and a 7½-ton chunk of cherry-red hot steel hit our aft-starboard life raft. I had just walked out from under the raft. I was picked up and slammed down, striking the left side of my head on the steel deck. I couldn't hear anything for 20 or 30 seconds, then hearing returned to my right ear. I have not heard anything in my left ear since that time. There were no medical personnel on board, so my injury wasn't treated.

While the ship was being loaded in Alexandria for our next trip to Tripoli, one of the members of our gun crew saw several cases of Scotch whiskey stacked on the dock. It was to be loaded on our ship to be taken to the English officers in Libya. Somehow or other, two cases of that *good* Scotch found its way into our ammo locker. Most of us ended up with a bottle or two in our gun tub. We thanked the generosity of the Queen's armed forces.

We shuttled back and forth from Alexandria to Tripoli three or four times until July 1943, at which time we joined the armada for the invasion of Sicily. On 10 July we were the 19th ship into the harbor at

Avola, Sicily. We stayed there 11 days and fought off 86 air raids. We did get minor damage to our propeller from a bomb. It cut our speed down from about 15 knots to about 7 knots. We crossed the Atlantic and landed in New York. I can say that I never saw anything in my life as pretty as the Statue of Liberty.

At New York, I received orders to report to Treasure Island, San Francisco, again. I was given a 28-day delay en route. My ear was bothering me all this time. After I reported in to Treasure Island, I went to the sick bay. The first doctor treated me for an earache and sent me back to duty. After three trips to sick bay, they finally realized that something was wrong with my ear and put me in a hospital. I was put on limited duty and stayed in the Navy until the war was over. I was discharged on 4 September 1945 at New Orleans Louisiana. I have had five operations on my ear since, but never recovered my hearing.

John Bohannan worked in law enforcement after his discharge from the Navy. He was a patrolman in Port Arthur, Texas, and Texas City, Texas. He worked for the federal government as a security officer for about four years and later became chief of police in Hillsboro, Texas. After 17 years as a police officer, he went into sales. He sold municipal supplies until he retired in 1977. John and Mary Jo, his wife of 44 years, had one child (now deceased), two grandchildren, and two great-grandchildren. They live in Forest Hill, Texas.

Fred J. Webb

Age 16 – United States Army

I was born in Toledo, Ohio, on 10 September 1925. While I was in high school, the progress of the war seemed to go against the Allies. So on 3 February 1942, I walked out of school before noon and hopped a bus for

> *I completed nine missions, then a tiny mosquito did me in.*

downtown Toledo, Ohio. We had traveled about five blocks when the bus pulled over to the curb and the driver got out. We noticed that he walked over to a bench and talked to the bundled-up person sitting there. There had been about 16 inches of snowfall the night before. The driver returned to the bus and informed us that it was a lady sitting on the bench, and she was frozen stiff. The driver said that he would stop at the next public phone and call the police. This was my first encounter with a dead person. I felt very bad inside.

When I arrived downtown, I visited the Navy recruiting station. The sailor there looked me over, paused several times, and finally asked, "How old are you?" I told him that I was 18 years of age. He smiled. We proceeded into an adjoining room where they gave me an eye exam. "That's it, kid," the sailor said, "Your eyes are a little under what's required to enlist in the U. S. Navy. Come back when they get better. Just eat a lot of carrots and your vision will improve. Come back then." I walked out of the Navy recruiting station and proceeded to the U. S. Army recruiting station which was a couple of blocks away.

The Army recruiter looked at me with a smile and asked how old I was. Although he doubted that I was 18 years of age, he handed me some papers for me to fill out and have them signed by my dad before a notary public. Then I was to bring the papers back to him. I went home and told my dad that if he signed the papers before a notary, I was in the Army. My dad doubted that I could get in, but he was tired of me insisting that I could. Finally, Dad gave in and took me to a notary. I raised my hand and swore to all the facts on the recruitment form. My dad was still smiling, thinking that I would be home that afternoon because the truth would prevail sooner or later.

I took the signed forms back to the Army recruiting station, but before I got there, I took my pen and traced over the typed date of birth to make it 1923 instead of 1925. The recruiter noticed the trace-over of the original date of birth and asked me about it. I told him that my folks made a mistake and my dad traced over the date. The sergeant smiled and said, "Son, there is a train leaving here tonight and here are your meal tickets. There is a restaurant across the street, so go and eat a good dinner. It takes several hours for the train to get to Fort Benjamin Harrison in Indiana, where you are going."

I went across the street to the restaurant and met up with three or four other recruits who were already eating. We boarded the train later and joined a large number of soldiers who had boarded at other locations. Early the next morning we arrived at Fort Benjamin Harrison. A regular infantry outfit was stationed there at that time.

After several days of waiting to be called for an examination, I began to worry about them finding out about my forged paper. On the fourth day, they finally called my name and I joined the groups, dropping my shorts and presenting my arms for shots, etc. On the fifth day, 12 February 1942, I was sworn into the U. S. Army.

Next, I boarded a train for Wichita Falls, Texas, where I was taught to drill and spent many days taking tests. When this was all over, they put me on another train and shipped me to Chanute Field, Illinois, for training. I learned several trades such as welding and sheet-metal work that would come in handy later. I was with the ground crew fixing up B-25s most of the time.

From Texas, I was sent to the Columbia Army Air Forces Base in Columbia, South Carolina. I pulled guard duty and loafed a lot, but as luck would have it, I talked a squadron commander into taking me up for a plane ride. A gunner showed me the ropes with a machine gun. I liked what I saw and wanted to become a gunner, but the Army had other thoughts as to where I belonged. I would be trained as a gunner later. So, it was back to the ground crew for a while.

We were loaded on another train in Columbus and arrived at Camp Kilmer, New Jersey, in the middle of the night. A few days later, we were put in trucks, taken to a dock and unloaded beside a troopship, which we boarded. The next morning, I went topside and looked out at the Statue of Liberty in the distance. Emotions flooded my eyes and brain as I realized that this was the beginning of the great adventure I had been told about.

We landed at Oran, North Africa, and that night we marched from the port and arrived at Goat Hill in the morning. It was raining like cats and dogs all the way. Many enlisted men and officers fell out and went to streams to soak their blistered feet. Several gray-haired members of the column helped those marching who had trouble with their back packs. The metal buckles on the field packs pushed into their shoulders, and after a while, really hurt.

I volunteered for guard duty the next day. The Arabs had taken U. S. Army uniforms and shoes from shallow graves and were boldly wearing them. This stopped when we started guarding the graves of U. S. Army casualties. That was the last of my guard-duty days.

By this time, 12 March 1943, I was often flying. I volunteered many times to fill in as a waist gunner when one was needed. We flew from various fields in Morocco, Algeria, and Tunisia. We moved to Italy in October 1943. I was stationed at Grottaglie, Amendola, and Vincenzo. In April 1944, we moved to Corsica.

I was in the engineering department of the 448th Bomb Squadron. My primary task was to make sure the squadron aircraft were always ready to take off for missions. I worked around the clock many times, patching holes in B-25s. The squadron suffered many casualties and replacements were slow to come in. Many times I was called to fill the waist gunner position. When they had a full crew, it was back to patching holes in the aircraft for me.

While in Italy, I completed nine missions, then a tiny mosquito did me in. I got malaria and became a chronic malaria patient, so finally they sent me back to the States, where I was hospitalized at the Kennedy Veterans Hospital in Memphis, Tennessee. The hospital was receiving so many men who had been wounded in the hedgerows of France that they needed beds. They called my father and asked him if he would take care of me if they sent medication home with me. My father said, "Send him home!" I went back to Toledo, Ohio, and recovered my health.

I was given a certified disability discharge on 22 September 1945 and received disability checks for five years.

Fred Webb was awarded the Bronze Star for his actions in the Italian campaign, and he earned a number of other decorations, including two Distinguished Unit Citations. After he recovered his health, he enrolled at the University of Southern California where he received an A.B. in theater arts. He worked in the broadcasting field for 55 years as an announcer, program director, and general manager. Fred and his wife Margaret have three children, three grandchildren, and two great-grandchildren. They live in Chattanooga, Tennessee.

✔ *INCIDENTally — The square needle!* – I will never forget the first day I arrived for boot camp in 1955. At the airport in San Antonio, we were put on a civilian bus for the trip to Lackland AFB. The bus driver was a character and talked the entire trip. He told us that he had served in the Air Force and we would really like it once boot camp was over. He went on to say that the worse thing was the shot in the testicles to prevent venereal disease. He also said that they had to use a square needle to be effective. Being only 16 and not used to an adult leading me on like that, I believed him. It was after the oldest guy in our squadron, a former British seaman, told me that, "The bloke was only pulling your leg," that I was able to sleep soundly. I still kept a sharp eye out for square needles when we went through the shot lines. – *George E. Ferguson.*

Jack T. Venables

Age 15 – United States Marine Corps

The story of my underage military service is closely entwined with that of my brother, James W. Venables. My brother and I both joined the Marine Corps when we were 15 years old. We said that we were born in Farwell, Texas, because we had been told that

> It was amazing how quickly I was able to get my rifle back together again.

the Hall of Records there had been destroyed by fire. Actually, we were both born in California – my brother in Bakersfield on 1 August 1925, and I in Visalia on 1 September 1926. In the picture below, I am standing behind my brother.

Jim joined the Corps in June 1941. He shipped out from San Diego for Samoa in January 1942 as a member of Item Company, 8th Marines, 2nd Marine Division. During the war, he went on to serve in the 6th Marines, Scouts and Snipers, and as an MP in Wellington, New Zealand. He landed on Guadalcanal in December 1942 and later fought on Tarawa and in the Saipan campaign.

Following the war, Jim stayed in the Marine Reserves and was called back for Korea. He served in a tank outfit – I don't know which one. By the time the Korean War was over, he had racked up enough years in the Corps that he decided to stay in until he was eligible for retirement. Vietnam erupted before he retired, so he ended up in that war also. Fortunately, he was a supply sergeant by then. He eventually retired as a master sergeant. Although he received no medals for heroism, he served his country extremely well and will always be an unsung hero to me. Regrettably, I lost my best friend to heart disease on 29 March 1991.

With full assurances from my trustworthy recruiting sergeant that I would be assigned to my brother's unit, I joined the Corps on

2 March 1942, at the age of 15. Following boot camp at San Diego, I was assigned to Fox Company, 10th Marines, 2nd Marine Division. Although it was not the same unit as my brother's, at least we were in the same division. The 10th Marines was an artillery regiment. I was a battery recorder, which involved receiving orders for the gun coordinates, recording them, and passing them along to the gunners at the appropriate time. After Guadalcanal, I trained as a gunner and that became my job until I left the 10th Marines.

I landed on Guadalcanal on 4 January 1943. While Jim and I were on Guadalcanal we got together for the first time since the war had begun. He came back to my gun site and we had a wonderful reunion! The two months of jungle fighting were etched on his face and he had lost a lot of weight, but it was still great to see him still in one piece.

When the island was secured in mid-February, we were shipped to New Zealand for R&R and further training in preparation for Tarawa. Both of our units were stationed at McKay's Crossing, near Paekakariki, about 30 miles from Wellington. We arranged for liberty at the same time and boarded the small-gauge railroad train for the trip to Wellington. Because we both had contracted malaria on the Canal, my brother always carried a thermometer with him. While on the train, we started to feel lousy, and in checking our temperatures, we learned that we each had a fever. By the time we reached the city, our temperatures were very high and there was no doubt we were having a malaria attack, so we checked into a military hospital. We were started on a 10cc dose of quinine every four hours, around the clock. Talk about bitter! There was a little guy who came around each day asking, "Any flute today, mista?" We used all of our liberty money buying fruit to chase the bitter taste of the quinine.

We both attempted to call our units to tell them we were in the hospital, without success. The telephone lines were always tied up. A hospital staff member said that he would report where we were, but he didn't! When we returned to camp, our respective captains called us in for an explanation for our absence. Each of us explained what had happened, told them that the phone lines were always busy, and that the hospital representative was to have reported for us. We were told in no uncertain terms that it was *our* responsibility to report our whereabouts. Although both of us were up for promotion to corporal, our failure to report our whereabouts resulted in our being passed over for promotion.

After Tarawa (Betio) was secured, a buddy and I went looking for my brother. I had been told that the 6th Marines were mopping up the other islands. With the tide out, we had no problem walking from island to island. We spent several hours trying to catch up with Jim's unit. The sun was unbearable and my buddy began to complain, so we finally gave up and started back to our unit. By that time the tide had started to come in, and we found ourselves wading between islands. The tide kept rising. As the water reached neck-level, forcing us to carry our rifles high above our heads, a group of laughing Marines in an amphibious tractor came by and plucked us out of the water. Later I learned that my brother had already returned shipboard. Although the casualties were high, thankfully, neither of us had been wounded.

Saipan was also an extremely rough beachhead due to the enemy guns hidden on Mount Tapotchau. The Japanese were looking down our throats. They had gun coordinates for what appeared to be every inch of the beaches and the entire island. Several of us ended up on the beach the first night in a large shell crater with tracer bullets flying over our heads and shells landing nearby.

The next day, we moved inland and dug our gun emplacements and some very large foxholes. We covered the foxholes with logs and what dirt we could find. We were being shelled one day, and as the bursts hit the trees above us, we dove for our foxhole. It happened that I was the last one in, and a shell exploded fairly close to us. I thought the flash from the shell had blinded me so I yelled, "I can't see, I can't see!" A buddy yelled, "Open your eyes!" I did and was happy to learn that I was not blind. That story may be corny, but it's true.

My final combat was the landing on Tinian in support of the 6th Marines. We met no resistance on the beach, and aside from one incident, the campaign, for me, was uneventful. One day I was sitting on one of the sand bags surrounding our gun emplacement, with my rifle apart, cleaning it. A group of Marines came by and started flushing out Japanese soldiers that were hiding in corn stalks right in front of our gun! It was amazing how quickly I was able to get my rifle back together again.

I saw Jim on Saipan, and again in Hawaii. He had a malaria attack on Saipan and did not make the Tinian operation, so we couldn't get together there. My brother served 36 months overseas and I served 25 months.

We were both in and out of the hospital with malaria. When I returned to the States, I was sent to a camp in Klamath Falls, Oregon, for rehabilitation. To be released, you had to pass a tolerance test, which consisted of spending a week carrying a full pack and a rifle, climbing and marching around the hills all day. I passed the tolerance test and was given a choice of duty, so I chose the Marine Corps Supply Depot in San Francisco where my brother had been assigned. This was my final duty station, and it was fantastic! We were there when the war ended. I was discharged after completing a 4-year minority cruise on 12 March 1946 at the age of 19 – an old man!

Jack Venables went back to high school after his discharge from the Marines. He earned a diploma, married Esta Finkbeiner, and started college under the GI Bill. Their two daughters, Gaye and Janet, were born before he graduated. He worked part-time, first as a busboy, then as a waiter, and finally as a bellhop at the Shattuck Hotel in Berkeley, California. Jack received a degree in business administration from Armstrong College in 1950. He then began working as a claims adjustor for Farmers Insurance Group. He transferred to the sales department in 1955 and served as a division manager, regional sales manager, and director of life-insurance sales before he retired in 1992 after 42 years with the company. Jack and Esta live in Merced, California.

William P. Mazzoni
Age 16 – United States Navy

My father operated a meat market in Chicago, Illinois, where I was born on 14 April 1926. On hot summer nights

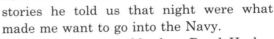

For four weeks they thought that I might be dead.

during the 1930s, everyone sat on their front porches because there was no air conditioning or television. One evening, a sailor who was home on leave was sitting with his parents on their porch across the street. We weren't used to seeing sailors in our neighborhood in those days, so my friends and I went over to talk with him. He told us many sea stories and talked about the places he had been. We noticed that he had on a white campaign ribbon. He explained to us that he was with Admiral Byrd when he went to the North Pole. Of all the stories that he told, I can remember that one the most. My friends all went in the Coast Guard, but I am sure the

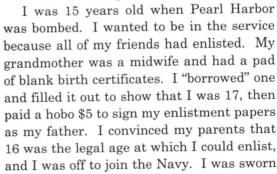

stories he told us that night were what made me want to go into the Navy.

I was 15 years old when Pearl Harbor was bombed. I wanted to be in the service because all of my friends had enlisted. My grandmother was a midwife and had a pad of blank birth certificates. I "borrowed" one and filled it out to show that I was 17, then paid a hobo $5 to sign my enlistment papers as my father. I convinced my parents that 16 was the legal age at which I could enlist, and I was off to join the Navy. I was sworn into the Navy on 1 May 1942 and sent to the Great Lakes Naval Training Center for boot camp.

After boot camp we were shipped to Pearl Harbor. We were to be assigned as replacements on ships that were shorthanded. We refueled there and proceeded to Guadalcanal. There were 40 sailors on board, and we each had orders for what ship we would be assigned to. The rest of the men were Marines who were going to be part of the ground forces. Four of us were assigned to the USS *Vincennes*.

Everyone else had been deployed and we were waiting for our ship. While we were waiting, we received word that the *Vincennes* had been sunk.

At that time, my parents received a telegram telling them that I was missing in action. For four weeks they thought that I might be dead. Finally, the Navy straightened out who was on the ship and who wasn't, and they let my parents know where I was. I didn't have any idea what was going on, even when an MP came looking for me. They put me on a cargo ship that dropped me off at New Caledonia. It was there that I learned that the Navy knew I was underage. They were very unhappy with me, and I was sure they were going to send me to prison. If my mother hadn't contacted the Red Cross, no one would have found out that I was underage. I was sent home and discharged in December 1942.

In April 1943, shortly after my 17th birthday, I re-enlisted in the Navy. I was assigned to the USS *Wharton* (APA-7). We carried mostly Marines and participated in the landings in the Marshall Islands, Saipan, Guam, and Okinawa. I was part of the deck force. We manned the guns and operated the landing crafts. My battle station was on a 5-inch gun. These were guns that they had taken off other ships. I was the hot-shell man. I had to wear asbestos gloves because I was supposed to catch the hot shell casing and throw it overboard.

I was also part of the crew on the landing craft. We carried the Marines in to the beach and carried the wounded out. The hardest part of all was seeing the condition of the wounded. There were men who were burned so badly that they begged me to shoot them. The suffering I saw changed my life, and I never took things for granted again.

I was aboard the *Wharton* for two and a half years. When the atomic bomb was dropped, we were at Pearl Harbor preparing to load troops for what we were sure would be an all-out attack on Japan. Now that the war was over, instead of loading troops, we took casualties back to the States. I made one more trip on the *Wharton*. Then I had enough points to be discharged. The *Wharton* went to one of the shipyards to be outfitted for the atomic test at Bikini Island. The scientists had brought a lot of test equipment to be installed.

I was discharged from the Navy on 12 February 1946.

Bill Mazzoni owned and operated a trailer park for several years, then went into the salvage business, buying overruns and surplus stock. He started the business in his home, but soon expanded into a rented building and called his store "Bargain City." He sold the business and is semi-retired. Currently, he works part-time delivering pizzas for Pizza Hut. When all employees were asked to fill out an evaluation form that asked what his future plans were, he wrote, "I want to work two more years at Pizza Hut, save my money, and go to medical school to be a brain surgeon." One of the powers-that-be from Pizza Hut came to Beloit to shake the hand of the ambitious young man. When he saw that Bill was older than he was, they all had a good laugh. Bill and Marilyn, his wife of 50 years, have three children, seven grandchildren, and two great-grandchildren. They live in South Beloit, Illinois.

Charles R. Johnson
Age 16 – United States Navy

I was born in Hollis, Oklahoma, on 5 April 1926. When I was six months old, my parents moved back to Carrollton, Texas, where they were raised. I attended school in Carrollton through my sophomore

> I heard a yeoman say, "Chief, this birth certificate has been changed."

year of high school. I was unhappy at home and wasn't doing well in school, so I left home and hitchhiked to southern California when I was 15 years old. I washed dishes and waited tables in and around Los Angeles, Pasadena, and San Bernardino. From California, I went to Portland, Oregon, where I worked as a busboy, as a waiter, and in other jobs until March 1942.

War had broken out, so I returned to Carrollton to enlist in the Navy. I sent to Oklahoma for my birth certificate and asked a friend who was taking typing to help me alter it. We used ink eradicator and changed the date, but it didn't work very well, and the change was obvious. After talking with my parents, and having them agree to sign for me, I went to the Navy recruiting office in Dallas, Texas. While waiting in the passageway, I heard a yeoman say, "Chief, this birth certificate has been changed." The chief replied, "If he wants in that bad, let him go."

Later that day, 26 June 1942, we were sworn in and left that night by train for San Diego, California, and boot camp. After boot camp, I completed hospital corps school and was transferred to the U. S. Naval hospital in Bremerton, Washington. The food was much better there than we had in boot camp or in hospital corps school. The first morning, I filled my tray to overflowing. When I ate all I could hold, I lined up to dump the leftovers on my tray in the trash can. The chief in charge was nearby. He told me to go back to the mess table and finish my breakfast. He said, "The rule here is take all you want, but eat all you take." I finished breakfast at 9:00 a.m.

On 11 November 1942, I received orders to Farragut, Idaho. Another corpsman had orders to Pearl Harbor. He lived near Farragut, so we arranged to trade orders. I went to Treasure Island, California, and boarded the USS *Mt. Vernon* for transportation to Hawaii.

Pearl Harbor was still cluttered with debris and sunken ships. The sunken hulks of the *Arizona* and the *Utah*, one on each side of Ford Island, were stark reminders of the Japanese attack almost a year before. Waikiki Beach was strung with barbed wire. I was stationed at the Kaneohe Naval Air Station and the Eva Marine Corps Air Station, across the island from Honolulu. The closest thing to taking a ride in a dive bomber was to take the Oahu Transit bus over the Pali to Kanehoe Bay.

In 1943, I was transferred to Midway Island (10,000 men and no females) where I did a 10-month tour. While there, I was promoted to pharmacist's mate 3rd class and reached my 17th birthday. Midway was used as a staging point for bombing raids on Japanese-held Wake Island. Several different kinds of planes were used for these raids. On one occasion, an Army Air Forces B-24 was used. They were experimenting with low altitude skip-bombing. During the raid, the pilot was killed, the co-pilot blinded, the navigator wounded, and the plane was flown back by a gunner. Wake Island was a real hot spot!

I was transferred to the USS *Dortch* (DD-670) while it was in Pearl Harbor for repairs. We left Pearl to join Admiral Halsey's Third Fleet. I had just had my 18th birthday. We operated primarily with Task Force 38.3 through most of 1944 and 1945.

While the Third Fleet was engaged in covering the invasion of the Philippines, the carriers launched a long-range bombing strike on part of the Japanese fleet. On their return, they reported that an enemy battleship, a carrier, two cruisers, and a destroyer, were left damaged and limping away. About this time, Admiral Halsey received word that the Seventh Fleet was in trouble and needed help. Halsey departed the task force with the battleships, leaving word for the cruiser division to hunt down and sink the damaged Japanese ships.

That afternoon the carrier was sunk, and that night the cruiser was located and sunk. When the battleship was sighted, the *Dortch* was ordered to make a torpedo run. We went in close and fired a spread of five torpedoes. The battleship went from "dead in the water" to a speed of 12 knots, and disappeared!

While on radar-picket duty off Tokyo, the *Dortch* ran into two Japanese destroyer-escorts. Our radar control was not working and we were under orders to maintain radio silence and not use star shells. We did the best we could and made hits on one enemy ship while we sustained several hits. We lost three men that night, and several of the personnel sustained injuries. The next day we conducted burial at sea ceremonies.

Our squadron of destroyers was relieved by a squadron of new destroyers and we were assigned to the Seventh Fleet to support the invasion of Iwo Jima. After Iwo Jima, we returned to the States and the *Dortch* went into dry dock for overhaul.

Upon arriving in San Francisco, I went to the hospital corps office at ComWestern Sea Frontier. A warrant officer asked if he could help me. I replied, "I would like some of that stuff I've heard about." He asked, "What is that?" I replied, "Leave, and shore duty!" He asked when was the last time I had had a leave and I told him, "I haven't ever had leave." He turned and asked one of the corpsmen to pull my record. After reading it, he told one of the personnel to type up a set of orders. I was to have a 30-day leave and was to report to the recruiting office nearest my home to await further assignment. I had been at sea for 32 months.

After I returned to the ship, the executive officer felt that I had gone over his head in going directly to ComWest Sea Frontier, so he delayed my leave and transfer for 15 days. During this time, the CO and half the ship's crew were on leave. "Open gangway" had been declared – if you didn't have duty, you had liberty. I checked every day for 15 days to see if my orders and leave were ready and was told each time that the executive officer had not signed them.

I finally went on leave, and after 30 days I reported to the recruiting office in Dallas, Texas. The yeoman asked me if I wanted to apply for transportation expenses to my next duty station. I said yes, and he handed me a quarter and told me to take the bus to the Naval Air Station in Dallas.

Thirty days after reporting to NAS Dallas, I was involved in an auto accident and was transferred to the naval hospital in Norman,

Oklahoma. While hospitalized, I requested and received every kind of leave they had to offer.

In February 1945, I returned to active duty in Dallas. On 1 April 1946, I went to the personnel office and asked when I would be discharged. The yeoman said, "Doc, you had enough points to be discharged six months ago." I told him that if he would double check, he would see that I was regular Navy and due for re-enlistment. I re-enlisted on 5 April 1946.

A month later I was transferred to a naval air and pre-flight school in Ottumwa, Iowa. In October 1946, the Navy requested volunteers for flight medical school in Pensacola, Florida, and I volunteered. After I completed the school I was assigned to the naval hospital at Pensacola, where I stayed until June 1948.

I reported to the Naval Air Facility, Honolulu Airport, Oahu, in June 1948, where I served in the aviation medicine office. In mid-1949, the facility was decommissioned and I was transferred to VR-8, a transport squadron. Our squadron was one of the first from the Naval Air Transport Service to be assigned to MATS (Military Air Transport Service). After moving to Hickam Air Force Base, I was assigned to an Air Force evacuation squadron on temporary duty for 15 months. We used C-54s (R5Ds) for medical air evacuations in the Pacific area. Our patient holding areas were: Guam; Clark Air Force Base, Philippines; Haneda Air Force Base, Tokyo; and Kadena Air Force Base, Okinawa. While serving with the 1453rd Military Air Evacuation Squadron, I was assigned to Haneda Air Force Base, Tokyo, for four months. Our job was to load and offload patients from planes and to assist with the screening of outpatients being evacuated.

Upon returning to Hickam Air Force Base, I received orders to the Naval Air Technical Training Center, Memphis, Tennessee. En route to the States we learned that hostilities had broken out in Korea. I just knew that my orders would be cancelled, but they weren't. I was assigned to the Naval Air Technical Training Center, Memphis, Tennessee, from June 1950 until May 1952, then was transferred to NAS Dallas. My father was terminally ill at the time.

I received orders to board the USS *Sicily* (CVE-118) in May 1953, and we departed for the Far East. We returned to San Diego in February 1954 and decommissioned the *Sicily* at San Francisco in September 1954. I went back to Hawaii where I was stationed at

Barbers Point and later Ford Island.   I returned to Dallas for recruiting duty in 1956.   In 1960, I received orders to attend the Field Medical School, Camp Pendleton, California, and served with the Marines on Okinawa until I retired from the Navy on 3 August 1961.

Charles Johnson sold cars and became part-owner of a Ford-Mercury dealership after retiring from the Navy. Later he sold automobile warrantee policies, and retired for the second time at age 63. On 7 December 2001, he received his high school diploma during a special veterans graduation ceremony at Carrollton High School where he had attended before entering the Navy. Charles and Louise, his wife of 49 years, have one daughter, two grandchildren, and one great-grandson. They have lived in Spring, Texas, for the past 29 years.

✔ *INCIDENTally* — *Playing it safe!* – While at Fort Benning, Georgia, in 1944, the request went out for men to apply for officer candidate school. My first inclination was to volunteer, so I checked it out and began filling out the forms. My mind went into gear, thankfully, when I came to the part about providing five character references. Now tell me, where would this lying, fraudulent enlistee get five people to lie for him? I gave it up and went back under cover. – *Walter Holy.*

Herman I. "Ike" Hargraves

Age 16 – United States Navy

I was born in Beaumont, Texas, on 11 February 1926, the second of four children. My father was a carpenter and worked for the Yount Lee Oil Company. He owned a four-acre truck farm which allowed him to provide

> Being the hard-headed kid that I was, I took leave anyway.

for his family. Growing up during the Depression was a challenge. School did not mean very much to those who were trying to feed their families. I played football at school, but nothing else really interested me.

Although times were hard, I grew up with a close-knit group of friends. One of my friends, Lee Duke, had joined the Navy and was stationed at Pearl Harbor on 7 December 1941. I remember when the president told the nation about the Japanese attack. Several days later, we learned that Lee had been killed in that attack.

A few months went by and Boozy Cope and I decided that we would join up. He was 17 and old enough to join, but I was 16, which was too young. In order to enlist I had to have a birth certificate or a letter from a parent saying that I was 17. I don't remember how I got the letter, but I did. I was sworn into the Navy on 9 July 1942 and was off to boot camp in San Diego, California.

After boot camp, I had a short leave to go home, then returned to San Diego and boarded the transport ship *Mount Vernon*, which took us to Pearl Harbor. Upon arriving in Pearl, I was assigned to the USS *Ramsey*, an old World War I destroyer that had been converted into a minelayer. We were sent from Pearl Harbor to the Aleutian Islands, off the coast of Alaska. During the voyage, Tokyo Rose said on her radio broadcast that we had been sunk and all hands were lost. Of course, we had not been sunk, but we went to general quarters and stayed at general quarters all the way to Adak, Alaska.

After laying mines and picket patrolling off Adak harbor for some time, the *Ramsey* and several other destroyers was given the task of towing torpedo boats from Adak for their use in attacking the Japanese fleet at Kiska, in the southern end of the Aleutian chain. On our return to Adak we were standing special sea detail and general quarters. As we approached the harbor, two bogeys (unidentified aircraft) were reported off the port bow at three o'clock. We watched the fast-approaching aircraft that turned out to be two Lockheed P-38s of the Army Air Forces. As we watched, a sailor near me said, "Boy, the war won't last long with planes that fast!" Actually, for us, the war had not really started.

Just before Christmas, we convoyed the Navy supply ship *Jupiter* back to San Francisco where the *Ramsey* went into dry dock. I was taken by some kind of ailment and was transferred to the hospital at Treasure Island. After being released from the hospital, I was stationed in downtown San Francisco. During this assignment I got married. After a bout with appendicitis, I was transferred across the bay to the General Engineering and Dry Dock Company, to commission the minesweeper, USS *Champion.*

I became ill again and was taken back to the hospital on Treasure Island. I think my sickness was related to malaria that I had as a kid. When I was released from the hospital, I was sent to Seattle, Washington, to attended gunnery school and fire-fighting school. After completing that training, I was assigned to the USS *Fanshaw Bay* (CVE-70) which was a small escort aircraft carrier stationed at Astoria, Oregon.

While at Astoria, Oregon, I requested leave to visit my wife in San Francisco. The gunnery officer said that I could have leave, then later changed his mind. Being the hard-headed kid that I was, I took leave anyway. Needless to say, that was a big mistake!

After some time in the brig, I was returned to active duty. I was sent to Port Moresby, New Guinea, and arrived there in mid-1943. From there I went to work at the newly established destroyer repair base at Hollandia, New Guinea. I remained at Hollandia until the time the atomic bombs were dropped on Japan. We left Hollandia and went to Manakana in the Philippine Islands, across the bay from

Tacloban. I returned to the States toward the end of 1945 and was discharged from the Navy at Camp Wallis, Texas, near Galveston.

Before 60 days had passed, I re-enlisted in the Navy and was stationed at Green Cove, Florida. During this time, we mothballed half of the Sixteenth Fleet on the St. Jones River. My first marriage had ended in divorce, and while at Green Cove, I remarried. We had a son who was born at the Jacksonville Naval Air Station, Florida.

I was discharged and returned to Beaumont, Texas, where I worked at the Pine Grove Golf Course. After divorcing my second wife, I decided I wanted to see what Korea looked like, so I went back in the Navy. I participated in putting the hospital ship, USS *Haven*, back in commission, then it was off to Korea.

After my third discharge from the Navy in 1951, I enlisted in the reserves. I was married again in 1953 while working at the Brown and Root Tank Plant in Houston, Texas. During the Cuban missile crisis, the Navy sent me a notice that my enlistment would expire in seven days, and I would have to re-up. I told my wife that I would wait and not re-up. Within two weeks I received my final discharge. With my active duty and reserve time, I served 17 years, 4 months and 23 days in the Navy.

Ike Hargraves worked as a pipe supervisor in the petrochemical construction industry. He retired from Brown and Root Inc. in June 1991 with over 30 years of service. Ike and his wife Betty live in Conroe, Texas. They have one son and two granddaughters.

Royal Q. Zilliox
Age 16 – United States Marine Corps

I was born in San Antonio, Texas, on 21 January 1926. On 28 July 1942, at the age of 16, patriotism called, and posters of dress blues convinced me that I should join the Marines.   Since I

> The nightly raids by "Washing Machine Charlie" made our life interesting, ...

wanted to join and not be checked on, I assumed the name of Charles F. Black. I just pulled this name out of a hat. Next, I changed my birth date so I would be 18. I told the recruiters that I was an orphan, which was true. They had the court appoint a guardian for me and he signed the papers. It took me a few days to get used to answering to my new name.

In September 1942, after completing boot camp, I was assigned to the 1st Platoon, Battery A, 3rd Special Weapons Battalion, at Camp Pendleton, California. My platoon was originally attached to the 9th Marine Regiment of the 3rd Marine Division.

One of my most memorable times was a liberty in Los Angeles. I had gone to the USO and was asked if I wanted to go to a party. Naturally, the answer was yes. It was at this party that I first encountered Communism. There were many people there attempting to convince us that we were fighting that war to save Russia and to preserve Communism. I was young, but I knew that I did not like the ideology that those people were expounding. The only thing I liked about that night was that I

was served liquor without being asked for an ID. Oh, yes, I had to pay for the drinks.

Our battery was shipped to New Zealand with the 3rd Marine Division in January 1943. Auckland, New Zealand, was by far the greatest liberty port I was ever in. In July 1943, we arrived at Guadalcanal and were deployed for antiaircraft defense. The nightly raids by "Washing Machine Charlie" made our life interesting, although laughable. Ours was a 40mm antiaircraft battery and we never had the opportunity to fire in anger while on Guadalcanal.

On 1 November 1943, I went ashore on Bougainville with the first wave to scout gun positions for the platoon's antiaircraft battery. Although the Japanese force that defended Torokino Point was small, they fought to the last man. The truth is that the initial landing suffered more from the high waves on the beach than from the enemy. We lost about a third of our landing craft that day. When we dug in for the night, I was tired. My foxhole mate said he would take the first watch. He must have been jumpy since he did not awaken me until morning. What woke me was someone near us who started shooting. After a few seconds, he began to yell, "Snake!" It was not a Japanese soldier.

Two days later, on 3 November 1943, we were preparing for a counterattack by the Japanese. That night we watched a naval battle about 50 miles offshore. The next morning we were informed that our Navy had been victorious. However, early in November, the Japanese sent a large force of fighters and bombers against us. Our fighters stopped some of them, but many came at us. I don't know how long the firefight lasted. It seemed to be over as soon as it started, yet it also seemed to last forever. When the air-ground battle was over, a Marine Corps photographer came running to us through the smoke created by the gun fire. He told us that we had shot down one of the bombers. None of us had seen all the action because too much was going on, and the smoke from our gun was too dense. We turned in the kill, but our fighter pilots claimed that they shot down all the enemy planes that day. We never did get to paint that "Rising Sun" on our 40mm gun.

We returned to Guadalcanal in January 1944. The next month I entered the hospital. I remained a patient in various hospitals until I was discharged for medical reasons in November 1944.

After I was discharged, I sent papers to the Marine Corps and had my name and birth date corrected on all my records. No problems.

Royal Zilliox used the GI Bill to attend Utah State University, the University of Utah, and Southern Methodist University where he received a B.S. in mathematics in 1959. He worked as a geophysicist for 10 years, then in the computer industry for 35 years. He helped organize the Lone Star Chapter of the 3ʳᵈ Marine Division Association and served as vice president, then president, of the national 3ʳᵈ Marine Division Association. He is currently chairman of the division's Memorial Scholarship Fund. He married his "child bride" in 1955. His favorite story is that she was in the third grade when he entered the Marine Corps. Sadly, she passed away in 1995, after 40 years of marriage. Royal lives in Dallas, Texas.

✓ *INCIDENTally* — **Toothache!** – In 1951, while I was serving with a Marine Air Wing in Korea, a wisdom tooth needed some attention. I went to the dentist's tent and was told to sit in a portable dental chair that was essentially just a few pipes held together. The dentist, a Navy lieutenant, had a friend visiting him. The two were in a deep discussion and the dentist was drinking a beer. He prepared a syringe to deaden my mouth. He held a beer can in one hand and the syringe with its huge needle in the other. He took a sip of beer and waved the syringe up and down to emphasize the point he was making to his friend. I sat there petrified, or maybe it was terrified. The needle looked so big, and I didn't know how much beer the dentist had drunk. After making his point he turned to me, said, "Open up," and inserted the needle to deaden my mouth. The discussion between the two continued, and more beer was consumed. After about ten minutes, the dentist picked up his instrument, turned to me and expertly removed the wisdom tooth. I don't know whether it was because I was so terrified, or he was such a good dentist, but that tooth extraction was by far less painful than any that I have had since. – *Ray D. Jackson*

R. Joseph Madonna

Age 16 – United States Navy

I was raised in Chicago, Illinois, where I
was born on 26 December 1925. When
World War II broke out, I was anxious to
enlist and see the world. I went to the
Chicago City Hall and told them that I had

> ..., I received a message
> from the Marine Corps
> that I was AWOL.

lost my birth certificate and wanted a duplicate. I told them that I
had been born in 1924. Naturally, the search didn't turn up anything,
so they issued me a new one. I convinced my mother to sign it, and
away I went.

I went to the Navy recruiting station in Chicago and enlisted. The
recruiter didn't suspect anything, but in those days, if you could still
breathe, you were O.K. I was told to go home and wait until I was
called. I also went to the Marine Corps recruiting office and enlisted.
Again, I was told to go home and wait until I was called. The Navy
called first. I was sworn in on 3 August 1942 and sent to the Great
Lakes Naval Training Station for boot camp.
Our training was very short, and I was
shipped to Norfolk, Virginia, where I was
assigned to the oiler, USS *Winooski* (AO-38).
We sailed from Norfolk in time to make the
North African invasion on 8 November 1942.
I had been in the Navy for three months at
the time of the invasion.

My ship, the *Winooski,* was torpedoed on
11 November 1942, three days after the
landings. The ship was badly damaged, but
we were able to sail to Gibralter where it
was put in dry dock to be repaired. I stayed at Gibralter for three
months, spent my 17th birthday there. I returned to the States and
was assigned to another oiler, the USS *Cossatot* (AO-77), which was
commissioned on 20 April 1943 in Baltimore, Maryland. Being part of
the original crew, I was now a plank owner. This meant that after one
year aboard, all of the original crew was entitled to a celebration. By

this time, *Cossatot* was known as "the galloping ghost" of the North Atlantic, because we had been listed as sunk, and because number 77 was the same as that of the great football player, Red Grange.

When my ship was being repaired in dry dock at Gibralter, I received a message from the Marine Corps that I was AWOL. Evidently, the Navy and Marines didn't know about my dual enlistment. We all got a big laugh out of that. I guess our ship's captain straightened it out, because I never heard any more about it. I don't know how the Marines traced me to Gibralter.

In April 1944, on the anniversary date of our commissioning, we were anchored outside the harbor at Oran, Africa. The captain allowed all plank owners to load one of the large whaleboats with food and beer and sail to the beach for our anniversary celebration. While loading the beer, some of the crew got into the cases and soon were pretty stoned. My good friend, Edward J. Coons, wanted to beat the whaleboat to the shore so he jumped overboard and started swimming toward the beach, not realizing how far out we were. The undercurrent was very strong, and we could see that he was in trouble. I jumped in after him. When I reached him, he was going down. I dived down, grabbed him by the hair, and tried to pull him to the surface. He panicked and started fighting, punching me heavily around the waist and groin.

About this time the sea became very heavy, and the waves were getting higher and higher. A summer squall had come up. I was now very exhausted and was sinking with Ed. I could no longer hold him up and had to let him go. By this time the storm had intensified and the whaleboat had lost sight of us, and they were having their own problems trying to stay afloat. They had turned the flag upside down as a distress signal. Luckily, someone had the presence of mind to throw a life ring out. With my last bit of strength, I finally reached the surface and spread my arms out and miraculously fell on the life ring. If that ring hadn't been there, I would have sunk back under the waves also. The crew pulled me aboard and we were later rescued. My friend's body was washed ashore the next day. We all attended his funeral and gave him his final salute. He was buried in the Oran cemetery.

I served on oilers for my remaining time in the Navy. I was discharged on 6 February 1945.

Later I learned that the submarine that torpedoed the *Winooski*, the U-173, was sunk off Algiers five days after damaging our ship. Last year (2001), I was put in touch with a lady in California whose uncle was a crewman on the U-173. She has sent me photos of her uncle, the captain of the U-173, and the sub itself. She also sent a German submarine flag and a roster of the crew. In turn, I have sent her mementos from the *Winooski*. Small world!

Joe Madonna earned the Combat Action Ribbon and two battle stars for his European, African, Middle East theater ribbon. He worked as lead supervisor for a terminal transport company and later owned several restaurants and bars. Joe and his wife Joanne have three sons and seven grandchildren. They live in Kankakee, Illinois.

✓ *INCIDENTally* — *A small world!* — As my cousin and I were standing on the deck of the USS *New Mexico* at Leyte Gulf, a P-38 fighter plane made what appeared to be a simulated strafing pass at one of the Essex-class carriers anchored nearby. As the plane pulled out of the dive, it rolled over on its back and came down the flight deck, setting the carrier on fire and destroying several planes. Many years later, I told this story to my business partner who had been a P-38 pilot in the Pacific. He told me that the P-38 pilot who crashed into the carrier was from his squadron. — *Leonard E. Anderson.*

Jacklyn H. Lucas

Age 14 - United States Marine Corps

My father, a Plymouth, North Carolina, tobacco farmer, died when I was 10 years old. I resented his death, and I guess I resented a lot of things because I became a real mean kid. By the time I was 11 years old I was so rambunctious that my mother sent me to the Edwards Military Academy in Salemburg, North Carolina. The discipline at Edwards helped to straighten me out and I became a cadet captain by the time I was 13.

> "Maybe he was too damned young, and too damned tough to die."

When the Japanese bombed Pearl Harbor, that did it for me. I was determined to join the Marine Corps and fight the enemy. I tried to enlist, but I couldn't fool the recruiters. I turned 14 on 14 February 1942 and was still determined to get into the fight. During the summer I told my mother that I was going to enlist and that I was going to sign her name to the enlistment papers. I told her that she could try to stop me, but if she did, I'd find another way. She agreed not to try to stop me on the condition that I finish my schooling when I was discharged.

I went to the Marine recruiting office in Norfolk, Virginia, and told the recruiter that I was 17. I passed all the exams and when they gave me the papers for my mother to sign, I signed them. I was 5-foot 8-inches and weighed 185 pounds, but less than six months past my fourteenth birthday. I was sworn into the Corps on 6 August 1942.

Boot camp at Parris Island was a snap. Three years in a military school had prepared me very well for the Marines. The weather was hot and humid at Parris Island in August and September, so the DI would have me drill the platoon while he stood in the shade of a tree. You can imagine what the troops would have thought had they known that it was a 14-year-old kid drilling them.

After boot camp I went to Camp Lejeune, North Carolina. I did well in the heavy machine-gun school and was detailed to the training command. This was not what I had in mind when I joined the Corps; I wanted to fight. When the rest of my unit was ordered to San Diego I was supposed to stay at Camp Lejeune, but I packed my seabag and got on the back of the train and stowed away to California. A sergeant discovered that I didn't have any records, but it was more trouble to send me back to North Carolina than to keep me, so they kept me. Shortly after arriving in San Diego, we sailed for a staging area in Hawaii.

At Camp Catlin on Oahu, I made a mistake. In a letter to my 15-year-old girlfriend in Swanquarter, North Carolina, I mentioned that I was also 15. Apparently a mail censor noticed this and I was ordered to report to the colonel to explain things. Confronted with my letter, I had no alternative but to admit my age. I told the colonel that if I was discharged from the Marine Corps, I would join the Army. I guess the colonel believed me because he didn't have me discharged, but he wouldn't let me go into combat. My unit left for Tarawa, but I was stuck at Camp Catlin.

This was a frustrating time for me. I had enlisted to fight, and here I was, stuck in Hawaii. I noticed that men who got into trouble and spent some time in the brig were frequently transferred to a combat outfit. This looked like a way out for me. My dad had taught me to box when I was a kid and I have always been a scrapper. It was time to put my 18-inch biceps to use. In 17 trips to town, I got into 17 fights. I provoked a fight anytime I could and was locked up a number of times. I mashed up a sergeant and was sentenced to 30 days on bread and water.

After I got out of the brig one time, a buddy and I decided to celebrate. We shanghaied a truckload of beer from the ship's stores and treated our company. The troops had worked their way through ten or twelve GI cans full of iced brew and it looked like we needed some more, so a pal and I went back for more. We were too inebriated to operate efficiently and the police caught us.

While I was in the brig after the beer-hijacking incident, I decided that this course of action wasn't getting me anywhere, except the brig. While listening to the radio I heard Tokyo Rose say that troopships at Pearl Harbor would soon be heading for Iwo Jima. So on 9 January

1945, I packed my seabag, went to Pearl Harbor, and caught a Higgins boat that was headed for the USS *Deuel* (APA-160). I was lucky; my cousin Samuel Oliver Lucas was aboard. With Sam's help, I hid in a landing craft and slept on the weather deck for 29 days. I knew that I would be listed as AWOL for 29 days, but after 30 days, I would be considered a deserter. That day I turned myself in to Captain Robert H. Dunlap, Sam's company commander. Captain Dunlap took me to Colonel Pollock and told him the situation. The colonel said to me, "I'd like to have a whole shipload of Marines that want to fight as bad as you." I was assigned to C Company, 1st Battalion, 26th Marines, 5th Marine Division, Captain Dunlap's company. I did not inform the colonel that I was 16 years old

The ship stopped at Saipan and a Marine was taken ashore with appendicitis. I was issued his rifle and gear. On 14 February 1945, I turned 17, but there was no party for me on the *Deuel*. On 19 February we hit the beach at Iwo Jima. Shells were flying, people were being blown apart, and bullets were everywhere. This was just where I wanted to be. I was as anxious as ever to fight and kill as many of the enemy as I could. During the first two days, we suffered 5,370 casualties, killed and wounded.

The next day we were making our way toward the Japanese airstrip on the plain northeast of Mount Suribachi. We stopped to pound an enemy pillbox and jumped for cover into one of two parallel trenches that led to it. To our surprise, there were 11 Japanese in the other trench. They were too close to put our rifles to our shoulders, so we opened fire offhand. Just after I shot the second enemy soldier, my rifle jammed. I looked down to try to get the damned thing to work when I saw the grenades. I hollered, "Grenades!" and dove for them. I smashed my rifle butt against one, drove it into the volcanic ash, fell on it, then pulled the other one under me. I was there to fight, and we were there to win. You do what you have to do to win. It was not in me to turn and run.

The volcanic ash and the good Lord saved me. If I'd been on hard ground, that thing would have split me in two. There was just one explosion, but one was all I could handle, and I had trouble handling that one. It blew me over on my back, and it punctured my right lung, but it never knocked me out. It also got me in the thigh, neck, chin, head, chest, right arm, and hand.

The rest of the team sprinted down the trench, turned and fired down the other trench, killing the Japanese soldiers. I was lying on my back with my right arm twisted so far underneath me that I thought it had been blown off. My mouth and throat filled with blood and I probably would have drowned if I had lost consciousness. My left hand was the only thing I could move and I kept moving it to show that I was alive. A Marine from another unit came up and I was afraid I would be shot because I was barely recognizable as an American. The Marine called for a corpsman, and while he was working on me, a Japanese soldier popped up from a hole in the trench. The corpsman shot him and continued to work on me.

A mortar barrage on the edge of the trench delayed the stretcher bearers. When they finally carried me off, one stumbled and dropped his end of the stretcher. I split my head open on a rock. I looked up at him and smiled to let him know that I knew what he was trying to do, and that I appreciated it. I could see that he was exhausted.

On the evacuation beach a corpsman covered me with a poncho for shelter from the elements. I thought, "Oh, Lord, I'm dead!" Then the morphine took hold and I passed out. As they were hoisting me aboard an LST, they nearly dropped me into the sea. Someone caught my foot and pulled me aboard. I was put in the hold of the LST with hundreds of other wounded until there was room for me on the hospital ship, the USS *Samaritan*. Before the ship sailed for Guam, the American flag went up on Suribachi. The word was passed throughout the ship and I felt as jubilant as I could be. I had fought for my country and I felt a great deal of pride in that. My only regret was that I didn't get to stay there longer to kill more Japs.

Aboard the hospital ship a surgeon said, "Maybe he was too damned young, and too damned tough to die." I went under the knife 22 times, and there are still about 200 pieces of shrapnel in my body, some the size of 0.22 bullets. The only time I was ever knocked out in my life was when they gave me an anesthetic. After seven months in hospitals, I was in good enough shape to be discharged.

Jack Lucas received the Medal of Honor from President Harry S. Truman on 5 October 1945. When the President said to him, "I'd rather be a Medal of Honor winner than President of the United States," Jack replied, "Sir, I'll swap with you." Jack earned the Medal of Honor at the age of 17 years and 5 days. He was the youngest U. S.

Marine ever to be awarded the nation's highest honor, and the youngest recipient since the Civil War. Captain Dunlap, who took Jack into his company, also earned the Medal of Honor on the same day that Jack did. Jack also received the Purple Heart for his wounds. He still sets off metal detectors in airports from the shrapnel he carries in him. True to his word to his mother, Jack finished high school and graduated from college. During the Vietnam War, Jack accepted a commission in the Army and served for six years, leaving the Army as a captain in 1965. In 1985 Jack returned to Iwo Jima. In his words: "I wanted to walk on the beach without having to duck." In 1995, during the State of the Union address, President Clinton recounted Jack's heroic action on Iwo Jima and introduced him, along with a son and grandson, to the joint session of Congress which gave him a standing ovation. He has four sons, a daughter and seven grandchildren. One son, a West Point graduate, served two tours as a captain in Vietnam. Jack lives in Hattisburg, Mississippi.

President Harry S. Truman awarding the Medal of Honor to 17-year-old Pfc. Jack Lucas, USMC, 5 October 1945.

Donald A. Sehmel

Age 16 – United States Marine Corps

I was born in my grandparents' home on a farm in Puyallup, Washington, on 14 August 1925. I grew up on a small farm in Rosedale, a part of Gig Harbor, Washington, during the Great Depression.

> *I wondered why all the Marines were yelling, "You'll be sorry!"*

Starting at age 13, I worked at odd jobs on weekends and during summer school vacations for 10¢ an hour. The money I earned was used to buy school clothes. I had two older sisters who also worked during the summers.

I had a great childhood, except that my mother died when I was 12. I fished and learned to shoot and hunt. I was returning from a local duck-hunting outing on 7 December 1941 when I heard about the bombing of Pearl Harbor. I wanted to join the Marines but my dad would not let me fib about my age.

I finished my junior year of high school and was president of my class that year. That summer, I found a job as an auto-mechanic helper and floor sweeper for 25¢ an hour. That was big pay because of the war. I kept nagging about joining the Marines, and finally my dad said he would sign for me. I signed up on 7 August 1942 at age 16.

I took my first train trip to San Diego, California, and boot camp. I wondered why all the Marines were yelling, "You'll be sorry!" when we got to the recruit depot. I soon found out! I handled boot camp well; I kept my mouth shut and did what I was told. Boot camp was finally over, and on graduation day we were given our eagle, globe, and anchor emblems and were called Marines for the first time.

We trained until February 1943 when we shipped out to join the 1st Marine Division which had left Guadalcanal for Australia just a few months before for rest and rehabilitation. We trained a lot, but we had great liberty for the next few months while being made a part of the "Old Breed." There was much pride in being a Marine and part of the 1st Marine Division. I was assigned to M Battery, 4th Battalion, 11th Marines and was trained to be a forward artillery observer.

We left Australia on Liberty ships for parts unknown. The ships did not have heads below decks nor chow facilities. The heads were made of wood hanging over the rail of the ship. Food was C-rations and sandwiches for the two weeks it took to get us to New Guinea. We trained in New Guinea and experienced our first bombing by enemy aircraft. We watched many air battles.

My first combat was at Cape Gloucester, New Britain, on Christmas Day 1943. The naval gunfire, the bombing and strafing of the beach, and the air battle that was going on were extremely interesting. When we landed, I was struck by the smell of the beach, the acrid smoke from the shells and bombs, and the stench of the swamp.

I was attached to the 3rd Battalion, 1st Marines. We went to our right in a column along a narrow trail in the general direction of the air strips. I looked out to sea and saw dive bombers working over the ships. All at once a destroyer was hit, broke in half, and sank within a minute or two. Years later I learned that the destroyer was the USS *Brownson*. Over 100 sailors went down with the ship.

We were involved with small firefights over the next day or two as we advanced. The rain and mud were terrible. Our biggest battle was at a place called Hell's Point. I became aware of how valuable tanks were when attacking dug-in troops and pill boxes.

My next duty was with the 3rd Battalion, 5th Marines, commanded by Colonel Lew Walt. It was an attack on Aogiri Ridge and what was known as the East-West Trail.

After Cape Gloucester, we went to an island called Pavuvu, 60 miles north of Guadalcanal, for four months of training in preparation for our next operation, Peleliu, which we hit on 15 September 1944. We were told that this operation would be short and sweet, but it was long and bloody. We left Peleliu in November and went back to Pavuvu for rest and more training among the rats and land crabs that were prevalent there. Many of us were troubled with malaria.

We went to Guadalcanal for maneuvers and more training, getting ready for our next campaign. We boarded ship and rendezvoused with others at Ulithi, in the Caroline Islands. While we were there, an aircraft carrier, the USS *Franklin*, passed us on the way to the harbor. She was shot to hell and still smoking from the fires. She had been hit by kamikaze off Japan.

On Easter Sunday, 1 April 1945, April Fools' day, we landed on Okinawa. It was supposed to be a bloody landing – April Fool! Hardly a shot was heard. There were a lot of air battles with kamikaze planes, but it was easy going for us for three or four weeks, then things got bad! My worst time came at Kunishi Ridge with the 7th Marines. Finally, the campaign ended and we went to the north end of the island to rest and train for the invasion of Japan.

We were told that a new kind of bomb had been dropped on Japan. Then a week later, another one was dropped. The war ended on 14 August 1945, my 20th birthday, and I was alive. A great day!

The 1st Marine Division was going to China, and I was going back to the States, but there was no transportation. We finally left for the States in October, after experiencing two typhoons. I went back to Camp Pendleton and was discharged on 23 December 1945.

Don Sehmel received a letter of commendation from Major General William R. Rupertus, Commanding General, 1st Marine Division, for meritorious service in maintaining communications between an infantry unit and its artillery support under heavy enemy fire on Cape Gloucester. After his discharge, he worked in an automobile garage for a year or so, then enrolled at the University of Washington under the GI Bill. He graduated with a degree in pharmacy, worked for a drug store in Tacoma, Washington, for five years, then opened his own store. After 20 years he closed the store and became a real-estate broker and worked in that field for 20 years, retiring at age 70. Don and Mary Ellen, his wife of 55 years, have three sons, five grandchildren, and one great-grandchild. They live in Gig Harbor, Washington.

Ray F. Tegeler

Age 14 – United States Navy

I was born in Houston, Texas, on 25 August 1927. In July 1942, my older brother and I went to the Houston shipyard to try to get a job. They would not hire us because my brother was about to be drafted and I was too young to work there.

> When I returned ... the draft board came after me claiming that I had not registered ...

We left the shipyard and went to the Navy recruiting office in Houston and enlisted in the Navy. We were sworn in on 10 August 1942. I was 14 years old and my brother was 18 years old. I told them that I was 17, and my dad signed the papers. There were no questions asked about my age.

We went to boot camp in San Diego, California, for approximately five weeks. We were sent to Pearl Harbor for a short time, then on to Midway Island where we spent nine months. From there, it was Ford Island, then Pearl City, Hawaii.

My brother and I were very lucky. We were able to stay together until we came back to the States in April 1945. We were on our way back when we got the word that President Roosevelt had died.

When we arrived at Treasure Island we were scheduled for a 30-day leave. In formation one morning, the chief said that the Navy was looking for volunteers for the frogmen, who are now called Navy Seals. The school was to be in Florida and would last for 12 weeks. We would get an extra 30-day leave, 15 days' delay en route on the way to Florida, and 15 days after finishing school.

Six of us stepped forward. Then the old chief started telling us how tough the school was. He told us not to let the extra 30-day leave get us into something we might not want. By the time he finished his speech, all six of us had stepped back. I probably couldn't swim that good anyway.

Upon reporting back to duty after our leave, they split us up. I was stationed in San Francisco on shore duty. I was an "old salt" by then. I was honorably discharged from the Navy on 15 October 1945, at the age of 18. When I returned to Houston, the draft board came after me, claiming that I had not registered for the draft. I had to show them my discharge papers as proof that I had been in the Navy for more than three years.

Writing about my Navy days and comparing my experiences with some of the "sea stories" that are told makes me feel like I was in summer camp.

Ray Tegeler retired from the International Longshoreman's Association, Local 1273, at the Port of Houston in 1982 after 31 years of service. He and Lelia, his wife of 48 years, have three daughters, one son, five grandchildren, and four great-grandchildren. Ray and Lelia live in Brazoria, Texas.

Charles N. Sharpe

Age 16 – United States Marine Corps

I was born in Mount Pleasant, Tennessee, on 16 June 1926, the youngest of eight children. Four children were born to my father's first wife, and four to my mother. Six weeks after I was born, my parents separated.

> I was in the first wave of Marines to hit the beach at Tarawa.

My mother took the four of us to live with my grandmother in Johnsville, Tennessee. My mother died in 1935, and my grandmother and an uncle continued to raise us. When my grandmother died in 1940, the state made me go live with a sister. We were both too young to get along, so I went to live with an older sister. I still felt lost, so with the help of a brother, I got my sister to say I was 17 and she signed the papers for me to enlist in the Marine Corps.

I was sworn into the Marines on 4 September 1942 and was on my way to the Marine Corps Recruit Depot, San Diego, California, for boot camp. After boot camp and 30 days of mess duty, I was sent to Camp Linda Vista, California, where I joined the 2nd Anti-tank Battalion. Following a short period of training, we went to San Diego where on 23 February 1943, we embarked for the South Pacific.

We went to Wellington, New Zealand, and after a short time there, our battalion was disbanded and we were used as replacements for the 2nd Marine Division. I was assigned to George Company, 2nd Battalion, 2nd Marine Regiment. I was in the first wave of Marines to hit the beach at Tarawa and participated in the invasions of Saipan, Tinian, and Okinawa. We were the first occupation troops at Nagasaki, Japan. I stayed at Nagasaki until 23 October 1945 when we embarked for San Diego. We were

sent to Camp Pendleton for a short stay, then transferred to Camp Lejeune, North Carolina, where I was discharged on 12 December 1945. I served 3 years, 3 months, and 8 days in the Marine Corps. Of that time, 2 years, 8 months and 21 days were spent in the Pacific theater.

While I was on Saipan, my sister noticed that my brother, W. E. Sharpe, and I had the same APO address. He was with the Navy Boat Repair Unit 3245 on Saipan. She wrote to my brother who had his commanding officer look up where I was. We got to spend some time together before I went to Okinawa.

Charles Sharpe became a truck driver and joined the International Brotherhood of Teamsters. He was a business agent and had other duties with the Teamsters during his 43-year career. Charles, a widower, helped raise ten children and has over forty grandchildren. He lives in Nashville, Tennessee.

✓ *INCIDENTally* — **Halt!** – In 1942, while I was in boot camp at the Naval Training Center in San Diego, I overheard a chief telling of an incident that happened the night before while he was making his rounds checking on guard posts. As he approached a seaman who was standing "clothesline watch," the seaman said, "Halt – who goes there!" Both stood there for a while and finally the chief said, "Son, haven't you forgotten something?" The seaman replied, "Yes sir, but you're going to stand there until I think of it or I'll beat the hell out of you!" – *Charles R. Johnson.*

Cecil E. Hutchinson
Age 16 – United States Navy

I tried to join the CCC (Civilian Conservation Corps) when I was 14 because I wanted to work, and the $21 a month looked good to me. They asked me my age and I told them 14. They told me to come back in three

> *"Just how old are you if you served on a wooden ship?"*

years. It never occurred to me that I was too young to work. I had worked in the woods helping to fell trees from the time I was 10 years old.

Meanwhile, my home life deteriorated. I was born in Thorp, Washington, on 21 July 1926, in the same house that my father was born in. My parents divorced when I was about 5 years old, and my mother moved all over Washington and Idaho. I started the first grade in Harrah, Washington, but was pulled out and restarted that grade the next year in Shoshone, Idaho, then moved back to Enumclaw, Washington.

By the time I was 15, I knew it was time to leave. My stepfather was very abusive. I paid a lawyer in Auburn, Washington, $5 to make out a sworn affidavit that my name was Eugene McPherson and that I was 17 years old. My mother gave me her permission and she signed my enlistment papers. I was sworn into the Navy on 25 September 1942.

I went through three weeks of boot camp at San Diego, California, in Company 42-596. After boot camp, I was transferred to San Francisco with a 9-day delay en route, which gave me time enough to go home to Auburn. While I was there I visited my old grade school. They called an assembly of the entire school and had me tell them "all about Navy life!" I, with just four weeks in the Navy and no shipboard experience, was to tell them all about Navy life! All that I could do was to tell them about boot camp.

When I tell people that the first U. S. Navy ship I served on was an old wooden ship, the USS *Crocket*, they think I am stretching the truth a bit and ask, "Just how old are you if you served on a wooden ship?" It was an old Sacramento River boat made entirely out of wood, and it had a large paddle wheel on the stern. Actually, it was tied to a wharf, and the Navy used it to supply heat for buildings on the base. It also served as our mess hall. While there, we put the USS *ARD-8* into commission. It took 21 days for the *ARD-8* to be towed to the submarine base at Pearl Harbor, where we repaired submarines and destroyers. I was a quartermaster striker and helmsman. In port, my work was on the signal bridge.

I was sent from Pearl Harbor to Bremerton, Washington, to pick up a newly constructed escort carrier. I was sent to gunnery school at a Coast Guard station on the Washington Coast while waiting for the new ship. The school lasted two weeks. It also involved ship and aircraft recognition, not only of our allies, but of German, Japanese, and Italian ships and planes. A picture would flash for three seconds, and we had to identify it in daylight and darkness. I thought I would never get through that school.

The USS *Attu* (CVE-102) was commissioned in Astoria, Oregon, in late 1943. As we were backing out into the harbor, the engines quit. The *Attu* never got out of Astoria as long as I was aboard her. I don't remember all the reasons why, but I was sent to the USS *Matankau* (CVE-101) and put her into commission. I was a plank owner on the *Attu*, the *Matankau*, and the *ARD-8*. We were allowed one ship's boat and one jeep on the ship. When we left the States, we had three boats (all marked #1) and three jeeps (all marked #1) aboard.

The shakedown cruise for the *Matankau* was to the Southwest Pacific. We passed close to Guadalcanal, went up to Manus Island north of New Britain, and then east of New Guinea, then back to a Long Beach, California, shipyard for repairs. At Long Beach, I was transferred to the Corpus Christy Naval Air Station, Texas, where I joined a seaplane squadron that flew the PBMs (Patrol Bomber, Martin) seaplanes. We trained in antisubmarine warfare in the Gulf of Mexico and the Atlantic Ocean.

Because I had been a quartermaster striker, I was put in charge of the daily meteorology charts and wrote up the weather maps for the squadron. I received flight pay until I transferred to the beach party.

I was a good swimmer and they needed men to swim out to the seaplanes and remove their wheels when they were put into the water, and then swim out and reattach the wheels when the planes returned from their mission. On many days we put the aircraft in the water in the very early morning and retrieved them near midnight that night. I got a good suntan during the daytime. One night, during the beginning of a hurricane, we swam out in the dark to help bring about 15 planes onto the beach and secure then.

I was discharged from the Navy on 30 January 1946. I sailed with the Merchant Marine for a time, then re-enlisted in the Navy in November 1947. I was assigned to the USS *Myles C. Fox* (DD-829). We spent the winter of 1948-49 in Tsingtao, China, and were one of the last American warships to leave there when the Communists took over. In 1950, I was transferred to the USS *Piedmont* (AD-17) and spent several months in Hong Kong providing radio communications for the American Legation, enabling them to maintain contact with the State Department in Washington, D. C.

We had just returned to Subic Bay in the Philippines from Hong Kong in June 1950 when the Korean War started. We were at the landing at Inchon, and we were the first American warship to return to San Diego after supporting the landing. When the Chinese came into the war, we went back to Korean waters. I was there and in Japan until I was discharged from the Navy in 1951.

When I went back in the Navy in 1947, I had my records changed to my real name and age. The Navy grunted and threatened a lot, but they did change everything. I may be the only man with Navy discharges under two different names with the same serial number!

After my second discharge from the Navy, I was passing through Oregon and stopped to see my great-uncle Tom. He talked me into staying for the winter and go horse logging with him in the spring. I didn't get out of Oregon for several years, and when I did, I had a wife and three children, none of which I had planned on. During my unplanned stay in Oregon, I joined the 41st Infantry of the Oregon National Guard. I attended the Army radio-repair school at Fort Benning, Georgia, and was assigned as the communications sergeant with Company F, 162nd Infantry, 41st Infantry Division. I was also a team sergeant in the 301st Army Special Forces Airborne, a reserve outfit. There were A-teams, B-teams, and C-teams, with the A-teams being the smallest, having about 12 men each. There was one team in Seattle, one in Los Angeles, and one in Boise, Idaho. We came together every year at Fort Bragg, North Carolina, for training and jump school. I served until July or August 1960. I had hurt my back in a logging accident and could no longer keep up with the training.

In conclusion, it has always seemed strange to me how a lifetime could be condensed to just a few lines. As a pastor, I have noted this in obituary columns. How do we put down the feelings, the smells, the excitement, and the fears of those times so new generations may comprehend the times we lived in?

Cecil Hutchinson worked in law enforcement as a deputy town marshal and as an undercover agent going after cattle rustlers in eastern Washington and Idaho. He has been a pastor since 1973 and has served as pastor of several churches. He was director of the Yakima Calvary Rescue Mission in the 1970s. At present, he is the director of the Lewis County Gospel Mission in Chehalis, Washington. Cecil and Winnie, his wife of 49 years, have three children and six grandchildren. They live in Chehalis, Washington.

Adam C. Istre
Age 15 – United States Navy

I was born in Lake Arthur, Louisiana, on 8 January 1927. When I was about a year old, my people moved to a little town called Gueydan, Louisiana, to the east of Lake Arthur. We lived on a small farm

> ... they told me I hadn't been born because they had no record of my birth.

right outside of town. I was raised speaking French. When I started school I couldn't even laugh in English, and my teacher could not even laugh in French. That was really something. However, with my teacher's help, I did learn how to speak English to a degree, and I did manage to get through the first grade and continue my education. During my school years, I worked on a farm and a ranch. I worked during holidays, before school in the morning, after school in the evening, and during vacation time.

I was in the eighth grade at the age of 15 and wasn't doing too good as a student. I decided that my country could make better use of my talents. When I tried to enlist, I couldn't furnish a birth certificate because I was delivered by a midwife and a record wasn't kept. I was asked for a baptismal certificate, but the church in which I was baptized had burned down. I went to the Social Security office and listed my birth year as 1925 on the application for a card. This presented a problem for me later in life, but with the card, and with the fact that my mother didn't know how to read or write, it was rather easy to get by the recruiter. I signed my mother's name on the forms.

I was sworn into the U. S. Navy on 2 October 1942. I took boot training at Great Lakes Naval Training Station, Illinois. They had just finished building a new camp called Camp Green Bay. There was no heat, no hot water, and no bunks. Everyone had to sleep in hammocks. A lot of guys got up in the mornings with broken fingers and broken toes because they had fallen out of their hammocks during the night. The older guys who had to shave really had a bad time. However, we all got through that O.K.

Then came the time that they gave everybody a choice of what they wanted to do in the Navy. I was given a choice of either the submarine service or commando training. Coming off of a farm and a ranch, I thought I was pretty tough, so I decided to take commando training. We were sent to the big blimp hangar at Moffett Field, Mountain View, California. After I had been there for a few weeks, I found out that I wasn't near as tough as I thought I was. We completed this training in March 1943, and we went aboard ship getting ready to head for the South Pacific. There was a dentist on board who had lived in my hometown for a long time. He recognized me and told me that I should go home. He also told the commanding officer. So on 25 March 1943, I was discharged and sent home.

After I became 17, on 2 February 1944, I re-enlisted. This time I went through boot camp at the Naval Training Center at San Diego, California. This was a real Sunday picnic after the cold barracks at Great Lakes and after taking commando training. I had a nice warm bed to sleep in. It was just as good as being in my room back home.

After boot camp, I was put aboard the USS *Wasp* and we headed for the Pacific. Our first stop was Honolulu, Hawaii. At the receiving station in Honolulu, I was assigned to the USS *PC487,* which was a pursuit craft. We operated around the Hawaiian frontier, along the shoreline off of Honolulu. Pearl Harbor was our main base of operation. Besides patrolling the shorelines of Oahu, we escorted submarines away from the Hawaiian Islands for six to eight hours to give them a running start. We also escorted supply ships around the Pacific to the various islands below the equator and did weather patrol in the Aleutians. We maintained those duties until the end of the war. After the war, the *PC487* was given to Russia

Those of us with enough points to get out of the service were rotated back to the U.S. aboard the *PCE(R)851.* We went through the Panama Canal and up the East Coast to New London, Connecticut. I shipped over for another two years on 8 February 1946 and went home on leave.

Upon returning to duty after leave, I was stationed at the Fargo Building in Boston, Massachusetts. My job was running prisoners from the Fargo Building to the Naval Disciplinary Barracks in Norfolk, Virginia. I did this for a short period of time, then I was assigned to the USS *Yosemite* (AD-19). We made a shakedown cruise to Guantanamo Bay, Cuba. On returning from Cuba we pulled in to Casco Bay in Portland, Maine, and dropped anchor there.

We received Rear Admiral Beatty on board. He was the COMDESLANT (Commander Destroyers Atlantic). I worked for him as a personal boat skipper. I took care of his gig and also his barge. I did this for a good period of time, then I was asked if I wanted to take a European tour aboard the USS *Yellowstone (AD-27)*. I agreed to go because I wanted to see Europe.

While aboard the *Yosemite*, I had qualified as a diver, so one of my jobs aboard the *Yellowstone* was to inspect the hulls of destroyers that were tied alongside. Another diver and I would check the hulls for nicks and scrapes, and check the rudders, propellers, shafts, etc.

We made a good-will tour to several ports in Italy, Gibralter, Spain, and Turkey. While docked at Naples, Italy, the Italian Navy requested help in breaking up an Italian warship that had been sunk during the war and was blocking part of the harbor. Another diver and I placed demolition charges at specific locations in the sunken ship. When the charges were detonated, they were able to remove the pieces and clear the area. For our help in doing this, we were invited to one of their four-masted ships to have dinner with the Italian crew. I think we got a little lit, because they were passing out champagne right and left.

When we returned to Boston, Massachusetts, my enlistment was up. I decided I needed to go home for a while, so I took my discharge on 16 December 1947 and returned to Gueydan, Louisiana.

I went back to the ranch and worked there until an Army recruiter came by. He questioned me about my service in the Navy and told me that they were in dire need of a boat skipper in Galveston, Texas. The Army had an R&R center at Fort Crockett which provided deep-sea fishing boats for people who were on R&R. He talked me into enlisting, which I did on 22 June 1949. I was sent to Fort Crockett. I stayed there for a number of months. That is where I met my wife-to-be, Beverly Jane Alexander. We were married and settled down in Galveston until they closed the fort.

I was transferred to Fort Worden, Washington, on 3 March 1950 and was put in charge of running a ferry between Fort Worden and

Canada. When my wife was expecting a baby, we thought it would be a good idea if I were to get a discharge and go back to Galveston. We were having a hard time financially. They gave me an honorable discharge on 19 May 1950.

Years later, my work required that I obtain a passport. I went to the passport office and was told that I needed a birth certificate. I went to the Department of Vital Statistics in New Orleans, and they told me I hadn't been born because they had no record of my birth. I was told to get statements attesting to my birth from three people who had known me all my life. I did this and was issued a birth certificate with my true birth date on it.

Solving the passport problem was simple compared to the problem with Social Security after I retired. I had never taken the time to give the Social Security people my true birth date. When I signed up for Social Security retirement, I used my true birth date. The clerk put everything in the computer, then turned to me and said, "Do you know anybody else with your name?" I told him no. He said, "The computer says that you were born in 1925. How do you explain this?" I told him the story about enlisting at age 15. I was told to go home, get the birth certificate and my passport, and report back to him. After more checking, he said, "I can't give you full credit and you won't get the amount you would have received with a 1925 birth date." I said, "I don't want money that I don't have coming to me."

Changing records to get in the service early caused some complications in my later life, but I'm forever thankful that I was given the chance to serve my country in both the Navy and the Army. Anyone who hasn't spent time in the military has really lost out on a great life experience.

Adam Istre returned to Galveston and was hired by GMX Exploration to run an old ex-Navy minesweeper for gravity meter surveys in the Gulf of Mexico. About two years later, he went to work running a supply boat in the Gulf for the Forrestal Oil Company and the Superior Oil Company. In 1959, he was hired by Otis Engineering to help them get started in the boat business and to help train personnel. By then he held a master's license for ships up to 500 tons. He worked for Otis for 32 years, retiring as a field superintendent in 1991. Adam and Beverly Jane, his wife of 53 years, have three sons and six grandchildren. They live in Houma, Louisiana.

Charles H. Owens

Age 14 – United States Marine Corps

I was born in La Fayette, Georgia, on 29 March 1928. I joined the CCC (Civilian Conservation Corps) in 1942, just before it was disbanded. I used the discharge I

> *It was a long jump, like falling into hell.*

received from the CCC to prove my age when I joined the Marine Corps on 7 October 1942, in Chattanooga, Tennessee. I was 14 years old. I enlisted because it was the thing to do at the time. Patriotism was more prevalent than it is today.

I was sent to sea school after boot camp and then joined the Marine Detachment on the USS *New York*. I was not happy aboard ship, so I asked for a transfer to the 43rd Replacement Battalion. I joined A Company, 1st Battalion, 7th Marines, 1st Marine Division in May 1944.

We landed on Peleliu on 15 September 1944. I was 16 years old. I was in one of the first waves of troops to land. When we hit the beach, I went over the side of the amphibious tractor. It was a long jump, like falling into hell. The noise of the incoming fire was such that voice contact was almost impossible. The artillery, antitank, mortar, machine-gun, and small-arms fire was dealing out death to the assaulting Marines, and particularly to those who chose to remain on the beach.

Suddenly, I heard a very loud, booming, voice, a voice so loud that one could hear it over all the noises of battle, a voice that I would never forget. I looked up and saw a Marine major carrying a Thompson submachine gun, strolling up the beach. The major had his insignia in plain sight on his collar, rather than hidden on the underside in order not to attract enemy snipers. As he came upon a group of us huddled together in fear, he shouted, "Get off this beach or I'll shoot your butt!" His voice still rings in my ears today.

We were caught between fear of the intense Japanese fire and the wrath of the major. The choice was easy – we jumped up and moved inland on the double. I learned later that the next Japanese mortar barrage exploded precisely where we had been lying. Later I was wounded, spent a few days on a hospital ship, then returned to my outfit.

We landed on Okinawa on 1 April 1945 and fought in that campaign. After the war, we were sent to north China. When I returned to the States, I re-enlisted and served as a rifle platoon sergeant with both G and H Companies, 3rd Battalion, 7th Marines, in Korea, where I was wounded again. In 1954, I was assigned as a DI (drill instructor) at the Marine Corps Recruit Depot, San Diego. I completed a second tour as a DI there in 1958. I retired after 20 years of active duty in 1962. In 1966, I was asked to return to active duty and was sent to Vietnam where I joined the 3rd Marine Division. We were in the Dong Ha area near the DMZ. I retired from the Corps for the last time in 1968.

In my years as a Marine I saw many deeds of heroism in combat, but none that even came close to the performance of that major on the beach at Peleliu. Forty-eight years later, I learned who that major was. My account of that day on Peleliu is in Bill Ross's book, *Peleliu: Tragic Triumph*. A Marine, W. H. Brockington, read Ross's book and realized that the major could only have been his friend, Lieutenant Colonel Arthur M. Parker, Jr, USMCR (retired). Brockington and Col. Parker visited me in Georgia in October 1992. It was a very moving reunion. The major's physical appearance had changed considerably, but that same booming voice was still a part of him. It is hard for me to describe how emotional that meeting was.

Chuck Owens was wounded in action three times. He received the Purple Heart with two gold stars (three awards) and earned a Commendation Medal with Combat "V" for his actions in Korea. After retiring from the Marine Corps as a master sergeant (E-8), he worked for the Roper Corporation, a subsidiary of General Electric, in La Fayette, Georgia. He earned an associate degree from Northeast Alabama State Junior College in 1977. Chuck and his wife Eva, have a son and a daughter. They live in La Fayette, Georgia.

Kenneth E. Appel

Age 15 – United States Coast Guard

I was born in a log cabin in Pearre, a small town in Washington County, Maryland, on 21 March 1927, the oldest of six children. My mother's relatives made up a large number of the population in that area. When I was 4, we moved to Little Orleans, a town a few miles away in Allegheny County. We visited back and forth by way of the Western Maryland Railroad passenger train. That was always a thrill because many of the local residents would meet the train every day to see who got off or on, to collect the mail, and to exchange gossip.

> I would hear about the war from young sailors who would come in and talk about their adventures.

Work was almost non-existent until President Roosevelt created the WPA, CCC, etc. My father was partly disabled due to an eye injury, and he didn't have work as a carpenter, his usual trade. There was little building going on due to the Great Depression, so he took a job

as a timekeeper for the WPA. We took advantage of the abundance of fish in the Potomac River and wild game in the woods around us. My mother baked loaves of bread and rolls, and canned vegetables from a small garden. When I was 12 years old, I picked apples in the nearby orchards for 5¢ per bushel. My cousin and I collected bottles and sold them to a couple of moonshiners that we knew. Not many people around us were any better off than we were.

Everything changed when the Japanese bombed Pearl Harbor. Everyone wanted to do something for the cause. I was in a high school where the main course of study was agriculture. I couldn't see much future for me in that since we had only about an acre of land and a chicken coop with just enough chickens to provide eggs for us.

I talked my dad into letting me travel to Washington, D.C., with an older boy who had quit school earlier and was working in a fast-food restaurant there. I was soon working in the same place as a dishwasher. I was promoted to counterman, and then to night manager. I was not yet 15.

I would hear about the war from young sailors who would come in and talk about all their adventures. They sounded so patriotic. I wished that I could get in the Navy, too, but even though I was 6- feet tall and weighed 165 pounds and was bigger and stronger than many of them, I was still only 15 years old.

I decided to ask my parents to sign a paper stating my age as 17. They refused, telling me how dangerous that could be. I tried again and again to get them to sign, but to no avail. Then I thought of the Coast Guard. They didn't know much about it, so I told them that I understood it was mostly guarding the coast and there was little chance of going to sea. I don't know if they believed what I told them, but they finally relented. We found a notary public to notarize their signatures, and I was on my way to enlist in the U. S. Coast Guard on 10 November 1942.

After some hard boot-camp training at Curtis Bay in Maryland, I was put aboard an old bay steamer headed for Norfolk, Virginia. At Norfolk, headquarters sent me back to Maryland and I was assigned to beach patrol at Ocean City, Maryland. This was not quite what I was hoping for. We patrolled the beach and the boardwalk night and day, watching for any German saboteurs who might use the rubber boats from their submarines to come ashore. Residents had to keep windows covered after dark, and we patrolled with no lights.

In order to let as many men as he could have Christmas off, the chief walked the beach with me on Christmas Eve. We talked about my duty and I told him I had hoped to be assigned to a Coast Guard cutter and sent to sea. I wanted to see more action and maybe mix it up with a few submarines. The chief told me how lucky I was to have a safe billet like I had, but he knew that I'd rather have sea duty. Well, I didn't have to wait long. On 31 December 1942, at 1 a.m., a Coast Guard truck pulled up to the station loaded with men. I was awakened and told to pack my sea bags right away and join the others in the open truck.

It was cold and raining as we rode to the Cape Charles ferry where we warmed up a little, but we were still wet when we left the ferry and were taken to the waterfront. We were loaded aboard two LCVPs (Landing Craft Vehicle and Personnel) with some very rough-looking Coast Guardsmen. It was my first clue that I wasn't going to be on a cutter. Instead, we were taken to a large ship, the USS *Leonard Wood*, which was camouflaged with paint and rust spots. "APA-12" was painted on the bow.

I knew that I would like this ship. She was the flagship of our amphibious group. The crew was made up of Coast Guardsmen with a Navy commodore and his staff. I was assigned to the 1st Division, the closest division to the bow. My billet was trainer on a twin 40mm antiaircraft gun during sea watch, and bowhook in a LCVP during invasions and maneuvers.

Early in 1943, we did night-landing training with the Army and Marines off Cove Point, Maryland, on the Chesapeake Bay. In late May or early June, we left Norfolk, and were not told where we were headed. We reached a French naval base near Oran, Algeria, where we stayed until we headed out to invade Sicily on 10 July 1943. It was at night and the seas were extremely heavy. My LCVP lost steering as we hit the beach. After the troops were out, the boat broached and we had to be towed back to the ship for repairs. The repairs didn't take long and we went back to the beach with more troops. This time the rudder broke again and the boat filled with water. Being stranded, so to speak, I took a 30-caliber light machine gun off the stern and set it up around a hole I had dug in a sand dune. Most of the boats that weren't sunk had returned to the ship, and the Army troops, except for a few working on the beach, had gone inland.

I heard a plane, which turned out to be a Messerschmitt 109, strafing up the beach. It was unbelievably low, and when it got nearer I could see the full belly of the plane. I pulled the trigger and let him have a stream of bullets. The plane made a long arc, crashed into the sand, and caught fire. The pilot never left the plane. It took a long time for me to talk about that event, but as time goes by, it does become easier.

It wasn't unusual for boat crews to be left behind when a ship left an invasion site. We would then catch a ride on another ship or find another way back to our own ship. I got a ride on the USS *Alcyon* back to Oran where I rejoined the *Leonard Wood*.

We returned to Norfolk on 3 August 1943 and left the next day for Honolulu via the Panama Canal and San Francisco, arriving in Honolulu on 26 September 1943. We left Pearl Harbor on 10 November and arrived at Makin Island about 10 days later and took part in the initial assault on Makin. I remained at Makin in the boat pool for about 60 days, then went via a Liberty ship on an overnight passage to Tarawa, where I went aboard the aircraft carrier, USS *White Plains*, for a trip back to Pearl Harbor. I was assigned to the USS *Arthur Middleton* (APA-25) in May 1944.

A few days after boarding the *Middleton*, we left for Eniwetok in the Marshall Islands, arriving there in June of 1944. We left there for Saipan where we took part in the initial assault on 15 June 1944. We left Saipan on 18 June, bound for San Diego where we picked up Marine replacements for the battle on Saipan. After receiving word that the island was secure, we dropped the troops off in Hilo, Hawaii, and returned to Pearl Harbor. We left for Eniwetok in September 1944, and went on to Manus in the Admiralty Islands. From there we went to Leyte in the Philippine Islands and participated in the initial assault there on 24 October 1944.

From Leyte we proceeded to Hollandia, Dutch New Guinea, and on to Halmahara in the Dutch East Indies. We returned to Leyte, then went back to the Admiralty Islands. From there we went to New Britain in the Solomon Islands, and finally, back to Manus Island.

At Manus, I received mail informing me that my father was dying of cancer. I really wanted to see him, and at that time I didn't know how bad it was. The executive officer gave me a transfer in lieu of an emergency leave because the Red Cross could not obtain verification of my father's illness. I flew in a Navy C-54 from Negros Island to San Francisco via Kwajalein Island, Johnson Island, and Pearl Harbor. I boarded a train in San Francisco and arrived in Maryland in January 1945 only to find that my father had been buried three weeks before.

I celebrated my 18th birthday on 21 March, having seen action against Italians, Germans, and Japanese. I received an honorable discharge on 12 October 1945 at Norfolk, Virginia. I was in the Coast Guard for nearly three years and never served on a Coast Guard vessel, only on U. S. Navy ships. I am proud to have served in the

Coast Guard during World War II and would happily do it over again to help this great country.

Ken Appel earned the Combat Action ribbon, a Navy Unit Commendation ribbon, the European theater ribbon with one battle star, the Asiatic-Pacific theater with three battle stars, and the Philippine Liberation Medal with one battle star, all before his 18th birthday. After his discharge from the Coast Guard, he passed the Maryland state examination and received his high school diploma and studied business at Catherman's Business School. He went to work for the Kelly-Springfield Tire Company as an accountant, but he did not like office work. He worked for the Western Maryland Railroad for several years, then became an inspector for Tidewater Fisheries. He patrolled the Chesapeake Bay, Patuxent and Potomac Rivers, enforcing fishing, oyster, and crabbing laws. In 1955 he was employed by the Naval Ordnance Laboratory and put in charge of a 64-foot harbor-defense boat that was used to recover air-dropped ordnance such as mines and torpedoes. He was general foreman of the boat group, but he had to relinquish that job when he developed malignant melanoma and had to stay out of the sun. He then became a real-estate broker and still works at that profession. Ken and Marie, his wife of 55 years, have two daughters, one son, two granddaughters and one adopted grandson. They live in Dowell, Maryland.

Marvin E. "Bud" Law

Age 15 – United States Navy

My dad was in the Army and I was living with my mother in Alva, Oklahoma, where I was born on 11 August 1927. My mother did the best she could with me, but I was not the easiest person to take care of. I was getting in trouble at school and was not doing very well with my grades.

> He was wrong there! I was never sorry that I joined the Navy.

One day in November 1942, I went to town to get a hamburger at the local pool hall. On the way back to school I met a friend from school who was going the other way. When I asked him where he was going, he informed me that he was on his way to the Navy recruiting office to enlist. He asked me to go with him to the recruiting office. I said, "I have to get back to school, I'm already late." Then I said, "Oh what the hell, I'll go with you anyway." He was a senior and old enough to enlist, while I was a 15-year-old freshman.

While he was filling out the paperwork, I was sitting back reading all the recruiting material. When he was finished and went into the next room to take a physical, the recruiter said to me, "You are next!" I tried to explain that I was just there as support for my friend. He said, "Come on, you would make a good sailor." So, I took him at his word and enlisted.

My mother wouldn't sign for me, so I hitchhiked to Fort Sill, Oklahoma to see my dad and ask him to sign. He did not hesitate one minute. I told him that he would never be sorry that he signed for me. He informed me that *he* wouldn't be sorry, but *I* probably would. He was wrong there! I was *never* sorry that I joined the Navy.

I went to Oklahoma City for my final physical and was sworn in on 23 November 1942. I was sent to San Diego, California, for boot camp. I had my first meal in the Navy on Thanksgiving Day, and what a good meal it was! I finished boot camp and was sent to the receiving station to await assignment. I was doing all kinds of duties while there, including sweeping and keeping the barber shop clean. I told them that I could cut hair, and the first thing I knew, I was a barber. I didn't like being a barber because I wanted to go to sea.

Later, I got into a little trouble and the captain asked me why I did what I did. I told him that I wanted off the base and on a ship. He told me that my wishes would be taken care of. Within two days, I was aboard the light cruiser, the USS *Concord* (CL-10). I was a very happy sailor.

We left that night for the South Pacific. On board was Rear Admiral Richard E. Byrd and his staff. We were to go to several South Sea Islands to survey for American air bases. When we were at sea for about 10 days, an explosion occurred in the aviation gasoline-storage area, killing 24 of my shipmates. The explosion knocked out the ship's steering for a short time and ruined all of our refrigeration, causing much of our food to spoil. The cooks did what they could to improvise meals, which wasn't much.

We continued the cruise, going to the islands of Tahiti, Bora Bora, Pitcairn, and the Easter Islands. On our way to Panama for major repairs, we buried our 24 shipmates at sea.

After the burial, we stopped in Lima, Peru, for supplies. The crew got one night's liberty. What an experience for a 15-year-old boy from Oklahoma! We went on to Panama where the ship underwent overhaul for three months. From Panama, we headed straight for the Aleutian Islands in the North Pacific. We stopped at Adak, then went on to Attu, our patrol base. Our purpose for being there was to help protect the Aleutian Islands and Alaska.

By this time I was 17, and I thought I would make myself legal with the Navy. I went to see the chaplain and told him my story. He checked and found that they would send me back to the United States and discharge me, then in 90 days, I could re-enlist. I didn't like that idea, so we agreed to just forget the whole thing.

We made several runs to the Kurilie Islands of northern Japan, and bombarded several of the islands. We went to the Sea of Okhotsk as part of Task Force 92 to bombard Paramushiri on 12 August 1945. On that day, the USS *Concord* fired the last salvo of World War II.

The USS *Concord* was the first ship to have the honor of laying a wreath on the Tomb of the Unknown Soldier at Arlington National Cemetery, which was performed by Navy personnel for the first time. We were also honored to be the first Navy ship to have a plaque in the Arlington Memorial.

The *Concord* was decommissioned in January 1946, and I was discharged from the Navy as a radioman third class on 20 January 1946 at Norman, Oklahoma. I went back in the Navy for a short time during the Korean War and served on an LST. I am very honored to say that I am a veteran of the United States Navy.

Bud Law received the Combat Action Ribbon and a number of other service medals. He returned to Oklahoma and started driving trucks, mostly from Oklahoma to California. General Motors built an assembly plant in Oklahoma in 1981 and Bud worked there for 10 years. He retired at age 65. He has attended every reunion of the crew of the USS Concord *since 1986 and has been reunion president four times. Bud and Jennie, his wartime pen pal and wife of 56 years, have four children, nine grandchildren, and nine great-grandchildren. They live in Moore, Oklahoma.*

Walter E. Brown

Age 15 – United States Navy

I was raised in the Flatbush section of Brooklyn, New York, where my twin brother and I were born on 15 December 1926. We were the youngest of ten boys and one girl. I was going to grammar school when

> ... I took my original certificate, folded it right on the date of birth and kept folding it until it looked pretty good.

the war started, but 10 months later, when I was in my first year of high school, my two buddies and I decided to try to enlist. I changed my birth date on my baptismal certificate, but I did a bad job. I went to my church and I got another certificate for $1. I did a bad job of changing the dates on that one also, so I went back to the church and got another. I messed that one up, too, so I took my original certificate, folded it right on the date of birth and kept folding it until it looked pretty good.

When I went to enlist, the recruiter looked at the certificate and asked if it said 1924. I said yes, so I passed. I was only 5-feet 6-inches tall and weighed 122 pounds. I guess they needed bodies. I had to get permission from my parents. I talked my mother into signing, but my father didn't want to let me go. He relented and signed when I told him that I would be stationed at Floyd Bennett Field in Brooklyn after boot camp. Now all I needed to do was to get out of high school so they wouldn't be checking up on me. I waited until the last day before I was to leave for boot camp, then told my teacher a lie. I said that my folks were breaking up and I was going to live in New Jersey with my cousin, so they sent my school records to her house. I left the next day, 27 November 1942, for boot camp at Bainbridge, Maryland.

After boot camp, I went to the Radio Corporation of America radio school in New York City. After graduation, I went aboard a troop transport, the *Frederick Funston* (APA-89), and we sailed for North Africa. We landed at Oran and experienced some air raids while there.

In July 1943, we landed at Sicily; then in September 1943, we landed at Salerno, Italy. After landing troops, we took wounded soldiers back to the hospital in Oran. We had some burials at sea. After leaving the wounded at Oran, we went to New York for about a month, then we went on to the Pacific. At Pearl Harbor, I was transferred to an *LCI*-462 (landing craft, infantry), and we prepared for the invasion of the Marshall Islands. After the Marshalls, we made the landings at Saipan, Tinian, and Guam. After a stop at Pearl Harbor, where our ship was converted to a rocket ship, we made landings at New Guinea, Leyte, Luzon, and the last big one, Okinawa. We battled the kamikaze for weeks on end!

I was sent back to the States and got home just in time for VJ Day. Later, I was sent to France and England where we picked up an LST (landing ship, tank) that had been on lend-lease. We stayed around Europe for a while, then we went back to New York where I was discharged in May 1946.

I was recalled to the Navy in January 1951 and assigned to the aircraft carrier, USS *Tarawa* (CV-40). I was discharged for the second time in 1952.

Walter Brown returned to New York and went to work for the Stagehand Union. He worked as a stagehand on Broadway shows, and for the last 30 years of his career, for the NBC Television studios. He quit smoking and started jogging in his late 40s, entered races in Central Park, and became a three-time national champion for his age group. He has run in about 80 marathons and completed several 50-mile and 100- kilometer runs. He retired to Florida in 1989 and still runs five to six miles on most mornings. Walter and Florence, his wife of 55 years, had three children (one son is deceased) and six grandchildren. They live in Vero Beach, Florida.

Howard C. Blair

Age 15 – United States Navy

I was born in Geneva County, Alabama, on 5 October 1927. I joined the U. S. Navy on 8 January 1943 at age 15. I didn't have a birth certificate, but my mother signed for me. I was 62 inches tall and weighed

> *... the inspecting officer would invariably stop and ask me how old I was.*

110 pounds, the lower limit for both. My size caused me a lot of unwanted attention while in boot camp at San Diego, California. The chief said, "You men will shave every day." Then he looked at me and said, "Although some of you wont need a blade in the razor." I was stopped almost every time I left the building by some officer who would ask my age. I dreaded inspections because, as the smallest man, I was last on the back row and the inspecting officer would invariably stop and ask me how old I was. I would respond, "Seventeen, sir," until the last inspection during boot camp. By this time I was so tired of saying "seventeen" that I responded, "Sixteen, sir." The commander patted me on the back and said, "You will make a fine sailor."

After boot camp, I was sent to hospital corpsman's school. In August 1943, I went to Espirito Santo in the Pacific where I was waiting for assignment to a Marine unit as a hospital corpsman. My mother became worried about my serving with the Marines, so she obtained a birth certificate from the Alabama State Health Department and sent it to the Navy. This got me out of the Marines. After about 30 days, they called me in and said that there was a Navy regulation that allowed boys as young as 14 to sign on as cabin boys with parental consent. I was told that the regulation was still in effect and that they were going to let me decide whether to get out or stay in the Navy. I asked that if I were to stay in, where would I go. They told me that they would put me on an aircraft carrier that was in the bay. I agreed to stay in and spent my 16th and 17th birthdays aboard the USS *Prince William* (CVE-31).

While aboard the *Prince William*, a wise chief told me to send my birth certificate through channels and ask them to correct my date of birth. He said that the war was still on and that they would okay it then, but if I decided to stay in the Navy after the war, I might not have the opportunity and might be charged with fraudulent enlistment. He was right. My birth date was corrected on my records.

After the war, I went back to the States to school, then back to the Pacific as a corpsman on medical evacuation flights over the Pacific. I went to Japan, China, the Philippines, and all the islands. I left the Navy after five years' service and returned home. Alabama hadn't changed much. My father was still sharecropping, so I joined the Air Force. I went to Germany for the Berlin Airlift. When I came back to the States I went to Medical Laboratory School at Fort Sam Houston, Texas, and now it seemed that I had to work 24 hours a day.

After 10 years in the Air Force and 22 months without a day off, I got out. I joined the Army Reserves. I retired in 1987 at age 60 with the rank of sergeant major.

Howard Blair went to work for Pfizer Inc. as a technical representative and then as a regional supervisor. His job required him to travel extensively. He has been in all 50 states. Being retired military has been very beneficial to him. He has had four major surgeries, including a bypass, all at the Wilford Hall Air Force Medical Center in San Antonio, Texas. He has four sons and five grandchildren. Howard lives in San Antonio, Texas.

Jack E. Reid

Age 16 – United States Army Air Forces

I was one of three children being raised by a single mother who worked 10 to 12 hours a day to feed us. I was born in Eldorado, Illinois, on 15 March 1926, but we moved so frequently between Illinois and Indiana that

> The food was so bad we would have fought our way off the ship.

I never attended less that three different schools during each of my elementary years. One exception was the fifth grade. That year I wrote an essay on cancer that won second place in the state of Indiana.

I quit school after the eighth grade to work and help my mother with the bills. I was large for my age and I lied about my age to get work. I helped paint and wallpaper, and finally got a job in a machine shop. The friends that I acquired were all three or four years older. I really thought I was a big shot. We drank and roamed the streets. I quickly found out they were no good, just trouble waiting to happen. We were thrown in jail for public intoxication, loitering, and vandalizing.

We passed the draft board office one day and one of the guys said, "You know, we have only a few days left to register for the draft, we may as well do it now." All agreed and started to enter the office, all but me. I was trying to figure out what to do. They all said, "Come on, Reid, don't be a chicken." So I went in thinking I could get by without actually registering. That did not happen. A lady sat me down and filled out the form for me. "How old are you?" she asked. With five of my friends there, I said, "Eighteen." No one asked for any proof of birth.

Later that year, when I received my "greetings," I discussed it with my mother. She said, "Let me think about it for a couple of days." She also told me to decide what I wanted to do. A couple of days later, she asked, "What do you really want to do?" I told her I found out that

I could get an allotment for her that would help a lot, and I thought I ought to go. She answered, "You know I don't like the guys you run with, so I think you ought to go also."

I reported to Fort Benjamin Harrison and was sworn into the Army on 15 January 1943. I was put on a train and sent to Jefferson Barracks in St. Louis, Missouri, for six weeks of basic training. I was rebellious, having had no father figure since I was seven. I really needed the discipline, and I got my share of it because I deserved it. I received an early education on KP, latrine duty, campground cleanup, breaking up stones from a quarry, and keeping my nose on a brick wall while the others marched. We lived eight to a tent. It was winter, and it snowed that year. If anyone's area was not perfect at tent inspection, the offender got a weekend pass and the other seven did not. After my weekend pass, I rapidly learned how to keep my area perfect.

After basic training, we were put on a troop train. I don't think anyone knew where we were going. We went west over the Rocky Mountains, then south, then east to Mississippi, then west through Texas, then back up to the Rockies, then back to Texas where we finally stopped at the Pyote Air Force Base, a B-17 training base. Pyote, Texas, was a tiny town that had only a couple of houses and two or three bars, all owned by the same man who had decided to get rich off the servicemen. He did this by serving name-brand beer and wine the first hour (he opened at 6:00 p.m.), and after that he served brands we never heard of.

I was assigned to the motor pool office. My job was to keep track of all vehicles. We lived in barracks, and I got to know the other soldiers pretty well. They were a nice bunch of guys, honest, friendly, and they worked hard. It was Pyote where I changed from a potential hoodlum to a straight-arrow guy. There was only one rebellious incident after that.

On my day off, I was sleeping-in when I was awakened by the duty sergeant. He told me to get up, and I told him it was my day off and I was sleeping-in. This went back and forth several times until my rebellious nature kicked in and I informed him that if I got up, I'd kick his ass. When I got up later, there was a note for me to report to the first sergeant. He chewed me out pretty good. He agreed I was right, but a soldier cannot refuse a direct order. The duty sergeant then told me that I had to clean out the weeds around the barracks. I was in a "get even" mood, so I asked him how he wanted me to get rid of the weeds. He said, "I don't care how you do it, just do it!" I obtained some kerosene and poured it around the barracks, lit it, and stood back to wait on the fire department. The next day, I was up for a court-martial. I was found guilty and restricted to the barracks for 30 days. I went to the chaplain, explained everything, then told him that I was underage and asked if I should tell the captain and go home. The chaplain said, "Jack, you can probably go home, but you can bet you will be drafted on your 18th birthday, and they'll put you in the infantry." I figured he was right, so I just tried to do a good job and forget it.

We were sent to Salina, Kansas, to train on B-29s for about six weeks. Then we were sent to Sioux City, Iowa, to form groups to go overseas. From there we went to Wilmington, California, and went aboard ship. It was a fast ship, so we had no escort. We changed course every six minutes to reduce the chances of a submarine torpedoing us. We were only allowed on deck about eight hours a day and that time was spent standing in line for our two meals a day. The food was so bad we would have fought our way off the ship.

We stopped in Sydney, Australia, for about eight hours. We were let off the ship, but just on the dock. We left Sydney, bound for Bombay, India. At Bombay, we were put on a train and traveled across India to Calcutta. About 100 of us boarded trucks, bound for Asansol, India, which was 200 miles back toward Bombay. We arrived in Asansol late at night and no one knew that we were coming. We ate C-rations for dinner. The next morning we found out that we were in the First Air Commando Group. The largest plane they had was a B-25. We had been trained on heavy bombers for the past year and a half.

The 1,200-man First Air Commando Group was designed to be completely self-sufficient. We had gliders, B-25 light fighter bombers, C-64 evacuation planes, Piper Cubs for reconnaissance, P-47 fighters, P-51 fighters, P-38 fighters, and C-46 cargo planes. The Commando Group had first priority. If it was available, the Commandos had first choice. We even had a commercial ice-cream machine. Everyone loved that!

Colonel Phillip Cochran, our CO, and cartoonist Milton Caniff were personal friends. Caniff had been there before we arrived and had painted comic-strip murals all over the Officers' Club. He drew a comic strip, "Terry and the Pirates," that loosely followed the career of our Colonel Cochran. The hero in the comic strip was Colonel Flip Corkin. Jackie Coogan, a famous child movie star and ex-husband of Alice Faye, was one of our glider pilots. After the war, he played in a popular TV show, "The Munsters."

The Air Commandos had complete control of the air over Burma. The gliders had made drops of troops and supplies in Burma. Later, most gliders were destroyed by a big hurricane. They were so light that tiedowns did not help. The gliders were just torn apart by the wind. The Air Commandos, using our C-46s, hauled mules, pipe, jeeps, and whatever supplies were needed to Burma and over the hump to China. The pilots were amazing. The pipe was loaded to about two feet from the top of the aircraft. The pilots would crawl over the pipe to the cockpit, then pipe was loaded to the very top. When they landed, the pipe had to be unloaded before the crew could get out. If they had an emergency, there was no way out. They were brave young men.

Colonel Cochran was sent to Africa and I heard that he was promoted to general. Colonel Gates replaced him. Things went on routinely, as far as I could tell. Two Red Cross ladies came to the base. They picked up donuts and coffee at our mess hall, then were driven by a soldier around the base selling the donuts and coffee. I did not like paying, but I was told that the ladies were friends of Colonel Gates, so shut up.

I was in ordnance, and my responsibility was to maintain the required inventory of vehicles and to keep track of them. We had vehicles in India, Burma, and China, so this was not an easy task. My lieutenant told me that if the pilots said a vehicle was lost in action, my job was to get a replacement. I made a trip to Calcutta each week for vehicles. My lieutenant liked to smoke and drink. He gave me, a private first class, control over our office and I enjoyed it. I met many officers. They all wanted a jeep to drive around, so they came to me. I noticed that we were losing many jeeps in action, but I did not really question it.

We were at an outdoor movie, sitting on 5-gallon gas cans, when VE day was announced. Gas cans flew everywhere. It was a happy night. The war with Japan seemed to go on and on. Some of us were put on orders to go to China. We were to have out duffel bags at the airport at 6 a.m. the next morning. As I arrived at the airstrip, they announced that the war was over and we could all go back to our regular jobs. What a relief! I figured we'd be home in a few weeks, but the First Air Commando Group was in for a big shock: the entire group was restricted to base.

I learned later that we had a technical sergeant in the personnel office who was really a captain, and a captain in administration who was really a major. They were undercover intelligence officers and had been stationed with us for a year looking into our "lost in action" supplies and vehicles. Our Colonel Gates had recruited pilots and others, and formed a huge black-market operation. They had sold stuff, including my jeeps, in three countries. The intelligence people were bringing guys back from the United States who had been involved in the operation.

They checked me out because of my job, but I didn't know anything about it. I was cleared by the intelligence officers and sent home. I was discharged in January 1946. Six months later I met Lieutenant Colonel Fox, the Commando's adjutant, at a Greyhound bus station in Indianapolis, Indiana. He told me he had been cleared and was on his way home. He said they court-martialed the black-marketeers right on the base. That was the last I ever heard of it. I never saw it in the papers or on the news.

I had a wonderful life, due entirely to my underage military service.

Jack Reid entered a bricklayer apprentice program after his discharge. He moved to Texas to work as a bricklayer for the Dow Chemical Company in Freeport, then he started a masonry contracting business in Lake Jackson, Texas. He was part-owner of a lumber company for a time, then became involved in a TV and appliance business, which he operated for 41 years and sold in 1991. He was a councilman and the mayor of Lake Jackson, chairman of the Lake Jackson State Bank, a church deacon, a director of the Chamber of Commerce, a member of the Houston-Galveston Area Council, and served on a number of other boards and committees. Jack and Henrietta, his wife of 52 years, have three children and eight grandchildren. They live in Lake Jackson, Texas.

Thomas J. Craig

Age 16 – United States Navy

When America declared war following Japan's surprise attack on Pearl Harbor, I was 15 years old, having been born on 2 May 1926. One year later, most of my buddies, who were a year or more older than me, were either enlisting in the military, being drafted, or awaiting call-up.

> *He nearly fell off the platform when I told him that I had joined the Navy.*

I was still 16 and determined not to be left behind. I quit high school, and with my parents' consent, altered my birth certificate to make me 17 years of age. Actually, Mom made the change, and it didn't turn out too good. In retrospect, maybe her heart wasn't really in it. Anyway, I found my baptismal certificate and made the change on that.

On 2 February 1943, I was sworn into the U. S. Navy at the recruiting station on Wall Street, in New York City. During the physical exam, it was discovered that I had a number of small cavities in my teeth. I was told to get them filled before I could leave for boot camp. Over the next week or so, I sat in the dentist's chair for the drilling and filling of all the cavities, with no pain killer. It was a rough experience, but I was determined to get to boot camp. I didn't want to jinx what I was doing, so before I left, I told hardly anybody in the old neighborhood (the upper West Side of Manhattan) that I was joining the Navy.

I left for boot camp in Newport, Rhode Island, on 17 February 1943. We were taken by subway from Wall Street to Grand Central Station. At the Times Square Station we marched in a column to the shuttle train over to Grand Central. By chance, I passed a buddy from the neighborhood who asked, "Where the heck are you going?" He nearly fell off the train platform when I told him that I had joined the Navy and was heading to boot camp. We joked about that later when we were home on leave at the same time. He had joined the Army.

With the war on, troop movements were a military secret. So when we left Grand Central Station that morning, we were not told which boot camp we were going to. That was not revealed until we were most of the way up the east coast of Connecticut. Prior to that, there was much speculation among those of us on the train. We didn't know whether we would go to Great Lakes, near Chicago, or Sampson, in upstate New York, or Newport, Rhode Island. Judging by the route we were taking, we had just about guessed that our destination was Newport by the time they finally revealed the secret.

I went through the nine weeks of boot camp with lingering concern in the back of my mind that I might be discovered before I reached my 17th birthday. I made it through and was granted my first choice of training, aviation radioman school in Jacksonville, Florida. Following radio school, I completed air gunnery school in nearby Yellow Water, Florida, and operational training in the TBF Avenger in Fort Lauderdale, Florida. In February 1944, I joined Torpedo Squadron 44 at Quonset Point, Rhode Island. Several months later, Fighter Squadron 44 joined us in Sanford, Maine. Shortly after that, we were sent to the Pacific as Air Group 44.

We relieved Air Group 32 aboard the aircraft carrier, USS *Langley*, just in time to take part in the Battle for Leyte Gulf. I participated in two of the four torpedo attacks our group made during this battle. In this and subsequent campaigns in the Philippines, Formosa, the China Sea, and Okinawa, I flew off the carrier a total of 35 times, 18 of which were bombing missions.

I flew in the rear of the Avenger where I operated the radar and armed the bombs or torpedoes prior to the attack. During the attack, I manned the 30-caliber machine gun in the tail. The pilot, in addition to aiming and releasing the bomb load, could fire two 50-caliber machine guns mounted in the wings. Just above me and to the rear of the pilot was the turret gunner with a 50-caliber machine gun.

Our squadron flying complement was 13 pilots and 26 aircrewmen. By the time we were relieved in February 1945 we had lost nine pilots and 17 aircrewmen. A tenth pilot went home on crutches with injuries suffered when the Langley was hit with a bomb in January 1945. One of the 17 aircrewmen turned up as a POW in Japan at the war's end. Fighter Squadron 44 also lost nine pilots.

I feel fortunate to have been among those lucky enough to come home. Of course, it wasn't all luck. I did a lot of praying each time we dived at our target at nearly 300 miles per hour.

The USS *Altamaha*, a smaller carrier, was our transportation back to the States. Following a memorable passage under the Golden Gate Bridge, we disembarked at the Alameda Naval Air Station. Oakland proved to be a great liberty town during the 10 days or so that we were there. A welcomed 30-day leave at home followed.

After the leave, I wound up back at the Naval Air Station in Fort Lauderdale, Florida, where I was an instructor for several months. My request to return to squadron duty was granted and I was sent to the Naval Air Station, Grosse Isle, Michigan, to join Torpedo Squadron 97. While I was there, Japan surrendered. That night I remember riding down Woodward Avenue in downtown Detroit on the top of a car. It looked like New Year's Eve in Times Square as thousands of people came out to celebrate.

The Navy offered early release to those holding certain awards. I took advantage of that and was honorably discharged on 15 September 1945.

Tom Craig was awarded the Distinguished Flying Cross and the Air Medal with gold star for a second award. Following his discharge, he completed his high school education and later attended the University of Connecticut at Stamford. In 1951 he became a radio announcer and newscaster. In 1972, he settled in Cincinnati, Ohio, where he worked as a television general-assignment reporter for WLWT-TV, the NBC affiliate there. He retired from the station on 1 January 2001 after 28 years. He was involved with broadcasting for about 50 years. In 1994, Jeanne, his wife of 32 years, passed away. Tom lives in Cincinnati, Ohio, in the home he and his wife shared over the years and the same home Jeanne, a Cincinnati native, grew up in. He keeps in close touch with his stepson who lives in nearby Indian Hill.

John P. "Pat" McManus
Age 15 – United States Navy

I was born in Culver City, California, on 5 December 1927. I had two brothers and four sisters. This was a difficult time to grow up because of the Depression. I can't remember a time that I didn't work. I sold

> *I was so mad that I felt I had to get into the war in some way.*

flowers house-to-house when I was 4, sold magazines house-to-house until I was 9, shined shoes until I was 12, and set pins in a bowling alley and caddied on a golf course until I was 14 years old.

I was caddying on 7 December 1941, two days after my 14th birthday. When I heard that the Japanese had bombed the fleet at Pearl Harbor, I had no idea where Pearl Harbor was. I had a strong feeling for the Navy because I lived in Long Beach, California, and used to shine a lot of the sailors' shoes. They had money during hard times, so they were good customers.

I was so mad that I felt I had to get into the war in some way. A friend of my brother Dan had got into the California State Guard at age 16, so I talked Dan into going in. In March 1942, when he was 16 and I was 14, we told the recruiter that we were both 18, and we went right in. We didn't even go home to get any papers signed. They cut our hair, gave us uniforms and a 1903 Springfield rifle, sent us to a training camp, then posted us as guards at the Golden Gate Bridge in San Francisco.

By December 1942, it was obvious that the Japanese weren't going to invade California, so I talked Dan into going over the hill and joining the Navy. By the time we got back down to southern California, the State Guard was trying to catch us, so it wasn't very hard to talk our mother into signing the papers for us to join the Navy. I was 15 by then and Dan was 17. He was old enough to go in, but we had to say that he was just about to turn 18 and I had just turned 17. If he had said he was 18, he would have had to have a draft card.

My mother signed papers that we were both 17 and also one that said she hadn't seen my father for seven years. When we took our physical, Dan didn't pass because his two front teeth had been knocked out. So I had to go on without him. I was sworn in on 14 February 1943. Dan got his front teeth replaced and came in three weeks later. About five weeks into boot camp, I got an emergency leave because my dad was dying. Dan got leave also, but when we returned, I was sent overseas and he went back to finish boot camp.

I went to Australia. aboard the *LST474*, then was assigned to a minesweeper, the *YMS50*. We were involved in some invasions in New Guinea and New Britain. I was a pointer on a 20mm gun. Very exciting! I was aboard the *YMS50* for a year and a half. Eight weeks after I left her, she struck a mine and sank.

I went back to the States where I was assigned to the crew that put the USS *Niagara* (APA-87) into commission. We went back to the Philippines and Okinawa. I was at Okinawa when the war ended. We went to Yokohama, Japan, for the surrender, then back to the Philippines to get more soldiers and took them to Hokkaido, Japan. We then went to Saipan and picked up some Marines and took them to China.

We returned to the States, went to the Philippines, then went back to Hawaii where the *Niagara* was designated as one of the target vessels for Operation Crossroads to test the effects of the atomic bomb on Navy vessels. You had to volunteer for this operation, and I did. I was in the Able and the Baker shots. The Able shot was dropped from an aircraft and the Baker shot was underwater. Both were awesome and worth seeing.

I went back to the States and was assigned to the destroyer USS *R. B. Anderson* (DD-786). I was discharged from the Navy in March 1947.

Pat McManus went to Guam as a civilian to work for the Morrison-Knutsen Construction Company after his discharge. He later joined the Merchant Marine. He is still working as a sales manager for the R. A. Biel Water Improvement Company. Pat and Terry, his wife of 51 years, have five children, six grandchildren, and one great-grandchild. They live in Farmington, New Mexico.

Jesse W. Crow

Age 16 – United States Army

As the son of a World War I veteran and a grandson of a Civil War veteran, I always wanted to be a soldier. I quit high school in my freshman year. About two years later, I went to the draft board and signed up, telling

I never knew for sure how the Army learned of my age, ...

them that I was 18 years old. This was on 11 February 1943, which was the day and month I put down for my birthday, along with the year 1925. I was born on 11 June 1926 in New York City.

I was sworn into the Army on 26 February 1943, took basic training at Camp Roberts, California, then volunteered for the paratroops. I went to Fort Benning, Georgia, for jump school, and from there to Fort Bragg, North Carolina. I was assigned to the 506th Parachute Infantry Regiment of the 101st Airborne Division. We went to Camp Shanks, New York, and from there to Aldbourne, England, during 1943.

While I was with the 506th in England, I was a member of the regimental rifle team. We competed with British Airborne units. Colonel Robert Sink, our regimental commander, had his troops compete in an assortment of different sports, which was good for morale. At one event against the British paratroopers, they gave each of the rifle-team members a pair of British jump wings, like the ones they wore on their caps. I still have mine, but one of my buddies broke the crown off.

In February 1944, my age was discovered and I was returned home and given a minority discharge. I never knew for sure how the Army learned of my age, but I believe that it was my mother who informed them. In an old trunk of my mother's, I found a letter she had written to me but was returned to her marked "unable to deliver." This was while I was in England. Folded with the letter was my birth record.

I'm sure she must have reported my correct age soon after this, but she never told me that she did.

I went back into the Army in October 1944. After retaking basic training, I was refused an assignment to a paratrooper unit; instead I was sent to the 9th Infantry Division. I served with that division until after the war. When it came time to come home, I enlisted for more than a year of occupation duty.

I was discharged from the Army in January 1947. I am proud that I have been able to serve my country in both war and peace.

Before I left England in 1944, about 21 members of my platoon, the 1st Platoon, Company A of the 506th Parachute Infantry Regiment, signed a British one-pound note for me. I brought it home, but it was lost. Fifty years later, I found it! I immediately initiated a search to locate my buddies who had signed the note. I was able to trace the whereabouts of all but two. Six were killed in action, ten have died since the war, and three of us are still living. The three of us now keep in touch.

Jesse Crow was awarded the Bronze Star, the Combat Infantryman's Badge, Parachute Wings, and a number of other service medals. He worked for the Illinois Department of Transportation for 32 years. In 1974, he was named as one of 50 outstanding Illinois state employees, selected statewide and from all departments. Jesse has three children and three grandchildren. He lives in De Soto, Illinois.

Bert L. Frey

Age 15 – United States Merchant Marine

I was born a Native American in Jefferson County, Colorado, on 5 February 1928. I was given to the Frey family to raise when I was young. From what I have learned, this was a common practice during the Depression years.

> We decided that we would sign each other's papers.

My early years were spent in Red Feather, Colorado. Later, the Frey family moved to Dallas, Texas.

In the spring of 1943, I skipped school and went to downtown Dallas. I was wearing my ROTC uniform, and until that time, I had thought of myself as a kid. While walking down a street, a prostitute stopped me and asked me if I wanted some sex. She apparently mistook me for a GI. I thought, if I could fool a prostitute, I could fool a recruiter.

I decided that I would go into the service, so I went to the Marine Corps recruiting office. I filled out the papers and returned them to

the recruiter. He gave me some additional papers to be filled out by my parents and informed me that I had to bring the papers back, along with a copy of my birth certificate, proving that I was 17. Well, that was a problem because I was only 15.

I met another young man who was 16 and had run away from home. He was also trying to get into the service. We both knew that we could not get our parents to sign for us. We decided that we would sign each other's papers. We then shopped for a cheap lawyer who would make us a fake birth certificate. While we were doing this, we heard that the Merchant Marine was recruiting 16-year-olds. I still wanted to be in the Marine Corps, but my buddy wanted to go into the Merchant Marine. He finally convinced me that it was the thing to do.

On the day that we enlisted, 16 March 1943, I left home in the morning and met my buddy. We now had the necessary papers and birth certificates, so we were able to take our physical. We both passed and were told to be at the recruiting office at five o'clock Friday morning. That morning, I walked out of the house and never looked back. We were put on a train and shipped to St. Petersburg, Florida, for basic training.

On the first day in basic we took another physical, a basic-knowledge test, and started our marching and discipline drills. Because I had these skills from ROTC, I was made guidon. Every day we had classes and drills, as well as physical fitness. We had classes on seaman terms and learned the requirements for surviving in a lifeboat. After three weeks we took lifeboat training, both rowing and sailing. After completing lifeboat training, we shipped out on a sailing ship and learned to rig the sails. I thoroughly enjoyed the great feeling of sailing. We spent two weeks at sea, then returned to base for additional written tests to determine the sea classification we were qualified for.

I qualified for radio school and was sent to the Merchant Marine Academy at Kingspoint, New York, for training. After one week in school, I found that I had failed the Morse code. I couldn't tell a dit from a dah. I was sent before the Academic Board. They determined that I would do better in the engineering department. Every morning after that, I was delivered to Pier 37 in New York Bay, where I worked as a fireman on a Scotch marine boiler on a ferry boat. In the afternoon, I took classes on the mechanics of the boiler system.

After three weeks, I received my engineering department certification and was assigned to a coal-burning ship. We went to England with supplies. After my first assignment I worked for various shipping lines and later contracted with the Army Transport Command. Our ship assisted in landing supplies on Juno Beach. While we were unloading the ship, I went out on the deck and saw the horrors of war and the smell of death. I will never forget it.

Around the 13th of August 1944, we left for the invasion of southern France. Our ship was hit in the Bay of Marseille. I never knew what happened. I was oiling a bearing one minute and the next thing I knew I was in a lifeboat. We lost 35 men.

After I was released from the hospital, I returned to duty as a ship's master electrician for a West Coast shipping firm. We delivered supplies to the Aleutian Islands.

During these times I realized that I needed to go back to high school. After 27 months in the Merchant Marine, I went back and completed my education.

In 1947, I joined the Marine Corps and served one enlistment. I was a Marine security guard at Quantico, Virginia, and helped train some troops from Turkey and New Zealand. The Turks were fearsome warriors.

At first, I was not going to include my picture for this story, but I decided to when I remembered an incident in boot camp. I kept looking at this guy in another platoon, and he kept looking at me. During a break, I started walking towards him when I realized why I thought I knew him. I was looking at a mirror image of myself. We became good friends, and even traded IDs for going on liberty. We went separate ways after basic training, and I never saw him again. If anyone recognizes this picture, please contact me. I have always wondered what happened to him. It is quite possible we were brothers – but that is another story.

Bert Frey is a consulting electrical-safety engineer, a career that he started as an electrician aboard ship. He was the electrical inspector for the city of Dallas for 25 years, 17 of the years as an assistant chief inspector. He taught classes and wrote two electrical-training textbooks for the Dallas Independent School District. He was the chief electrical inspector for the city of Tyler, Texas, for 10 years. In 2001, he retired as CEO of the Independent Electrical Contractors. He also served on the State Electrical Exam Board for eight years. Bert and his wife Barbara have raised seven children and two step-children. They live in Tyler, Texas.

James F. Kearns

Age 16 – United States Navy

I was born in Somerville, Massachusetts, on 26 August 1926. My dad was in the Navy and at sea much of the time. My mother died in 1940 and I went from pillar to post

> I received my recommendation for warrant officer from Captain John S. McCain, ...

until World War II started. In March 1943, my aunt went with me to the parish priest (who had bad eyesight) to get a copy of my baptism record. When the priest asked what year was on the record, my aunt said 1925. He said, "Oh, yes, now I remember," and wrote 1925.

I returned to Newport, Rhode Island, and went to a recruiter who happened to be a former student of my dad's in torpedo school. He said, "What the hell are you doing here?" I told him and he said, "Let's see the proof that you are 17." I showed him the baptismal record. Then he said, "Does your dad know about this?" Naturally, I answered yes. I was sworn into the Navy on 16 March 1943.

My next stop was the Naval Recruit Training Station at Sampson, New York. Six weeks later, and after a week's leave, I reported to the Naval Armed Guard Training Center, Little Creek, Virginia, for four weeks of gunnery training.

I served on four Merchant Marine ships, a T-2 tanker, and three Liberty ships. We supported the invasion of Italy at Salerno and the Normandy invasion. I made six Atlantic convoy crossings and received my baptism to enemy action just before my 17th

birthday. On our last trip across the Atlantic we had 400 German prisoners of war aboard. We offloaded them at Boston in January 1945.

The next month was spent making a fast trip to California where I was assigned to a pool of personnel and sailed immediately for the Western Pacific where I was assigned to the *LST-49*. It was a fast trip in a slow boat. Okinawa was a nice place to visit, but not a place where you would like to spend much time.

Being a regular Navy sailor, I was relief for the reserves who were shipped wholesale Stateside right after the war ended in 1945. We took the *LST-49* from Shanghai to Subic Bay in the Philippine Islands for decommissioning. I caught another ship back to China, where I was assigned to the *LST-1033* and spent the rest of my enlistment. We pulled all kinds of duty, including United Nations' relief runs from Shanghai up the Yangtze River to Zhenjiang, China. We became the mail ship on the Taku Bar near Tientsin in North China. We made guard-mail runs to Peking (Beijing). I spent Christmas of 1945 at the American Embassy in Peking. What a party we had! I left the ship in Tientsin and traveled Stateside for discharge.

I had planned to re-enlist within the 90-day period required to retain my rating of gunner's mate second class. However, it was 93 days before I went to the recruiting office. I was told that I could re-enlist, but as a seaman. I decided not to, so I got a job and joined the reserves. I could take only so much as a civilian, so in 1948, I re-enlisted in the regular Navy and started over as a seaman. I was assigned to the USS *Livermore* (DD-492). From there it was onward and upward.

In 1950, I participated in the recommissioning of the USS *New Jersey* (BB-62) and served on her for two years. In November 1951, we relieved the USS *Missouri* in Korea. Later, I was assigned to the USS *Salem* (CA-139), which was serving as the flagship of the commander of the Sixth Fleet. After a time on the *Salem*, I was transferred to the Naval Training Center at Bainbridge, Maryland, as a company commander for recruit training and graduated six companies. My next assignment was to the USS *Albany* (CA-123) in 1956.

While serving aboard the *Albany*, I received my recommendation for warrant officer from Captain John S. McCain, later Admiral McCain and father of U. S. Senator John McCain. In 1958, the *Albany* was to be converted to a Talos-missile ship. As a result, I had a choice of duty and transferred to the USS *Cassin Young* (DD-793). I received my appointment as CWO-1 (gunner) while on the *Cassin Young*. Upon receiving my appointment, I was ordered to report to the USS *Suribachi* (AE-21) as ship's gunner and cargo officer. Later, while aboard the *Suribachi*, I received a commission as an ensign, with my date of rank adjusted to the date that I became a warrant officer.

In 1964, I became a plank owner of the USS *America* (CVA-66) where I was a fire-control officer for the Terror surface-to-air missile system. In the ensuing years, I served on a number of other ships and had shore duty a few times. Some great things happened to me during my naval career. I retired as a lieutenant commander in March 1974 with 31 years of service. Not bad for a high school dropout!

Jim Kearns was awarded the Bronze Star and the Navy Commendation Medal. He earned two battle stars in the European theater, one in the Pacific theater, one for Korea, and he received a number of other service medals. After his retirement, he and a friend established the Atlantic Marine Surveyors Company Inc. He still surveys yachts, but only on a word-of-mouth basis. He has two sons and six grandchildren. For the past 12 years, Jim has lived on his yacht moored at the marina in Norfolk, Virginia, next to the Naval Amphibious Base. He says he just cannot get away from the Navy's haze-grey.

Gerald "Jerry" Siegel

Age 16 – United States Army

When I was 2 years old, my family moved to New York City from Baltimore, Maryland, where I was born on 20 July 1926. When was 16 years old, the war had started and my father took a job in a shipyard in Baltimore, so we moved back there.

> Thirty-three years later, I made a pilgrimage back to the places where I had fought during the war.

All my friends were in New York, my older brother was already in the Army, and I was very unhappy with the school situation in Baltimore. Everywhere I looked I saw men in uniform. I decided that I wanted to be one of them. In those days, it was required that you register for the draft when you were 18 years old. On 13 February 1943, I registered for the draft and told them that I wanted to go into the service immediately. No one questioned my age, and on 16 March 1943, I was drafted. I told my parents that if they disclosed my age, I would run away to Canada and join the Canadian Army (at that

time, I am not sure I knew where Canada was). In any case, they must have believed me because they remained silent.

I was sent to Camp Buttner, North Carolina, where I became part of the 78th Infantry Division. After basic training, most of the men in my unit were shipped out, but I remained part of the cadre and actually took basic training three times. The first two groups we trained were shipped out after basic training, but the third group remained with the division.

By this time, I had become a radio operator and was assigned to Headquarters Battery, 78th Division Artillery. The division went on maneuvers in Tennessee, then was sent to Camp Pickett, Virginia, and from there to Camp Kilmer, New Jersey. We shipped overseas, landing in Southampton, England. From there we went by train to

Bournemouth, England, where we boarded LSTs for the trip to France. We landed at Normandy long after it had been secured; in fact, all of France and most of Belgium had been liberated.

On 13 December 1944, the 78th Division, known as the Lightning Division, smashed into the Seigfried Line, capturing Kesternich, Simmerath, and Rollesbroich. On 17 December, the Battle of the Bulge began, and the 78th, on the northern flank, held its lines. On 30 January 1945, the Lightning Division attacked the mighty Schwammenauel Dam which controlled the flooding of the entire Roer Valley. Within the next 11 days, 78th Division troops drove elements of six German divisions before them, crashed through the Seigfried line, captured Schmidt, pushed all the way to the Roer, and captured the dam.

On 23 February 1945, the 78th, as part of the Ninth and First Armies, swept across the Rhineland and crossed the Rhine within eight days. We crossed on the Ludendorf Bridge at Remagen, the first infantry division to cross the Rhine. After crossing the Rhine, the First and Ninth Armies joined up to form a giant pincer movement that encircled two German army groups. This became known as the Ruhr Pocket. By 17 April, the pocket had been virtually eliminated. The division captured 47,581 prisoners, including seven general officers. After 132 days of combat, the 78th was pulled out of the line and put in a rest area. While we were in the rest area, the war in Europe ended. During the course of the war, the 78th Division had destroyed 237 pillboxes, captured 57,214 prisoners, seized 213 German towns, and captured 471 square miles of ground. After the surrender, we occupied Berlin.

In early December, we stayed in Hoeselt, Belgium, where we were warmly greeted by the now liberated Belgians. A little 14-year-old tugged on my sleeve and begged me to stay in her home, which I did for two months. I was discharged from the Army on 24 January 1946.

Thirty-three years later, I made a pilgrimage back to the places where I had fought during the war. When I arrived in Hoeselt, I found that little girl. She was now a 48-year-old grandmother. Needless to say, it was a very wonderful and heartwarming reunion. Since then, I have made fifteen additional trips to Belguim, and she and her family have all visited me in America.

In 1995, I was invited by the Belgian government to attend ceremonies celebrating the 50th anniversary of the liberation of Belgium. At the ceremony, I was awarded two medals, one from the Village of Werm, and one from the City of Hoeselt.

Jerry Siegel took full advantage of the GI Bill of Rights, completed high school, went to college, and graduated from law school. He practiced law for many years, served two terms as a police magistrate in Baltimore, and served four years as a member of the Maryland Legislature. He retired in 1988 and now lives in Eustis, Florida, with his wife Lona. They have four children and five grandchildren.

✔ *INCIDENTally* – **Fire when ready!** – During armored basic training at Fort Knox, Kentucky, in 1946, we were sent to the tank range for our first live ammo target practice. This 118-pound, skinny, 15-year-old tanker was about to perform. I was a bit nervous (scared) to say the least. The sergeant yelled, "Fire when ready!" I put my eye to the scope and moved the barrel toward the target, closed my eyes, and fired. The tank shook and rocked. I thought it blew up – wow, it was loud! Outside the tank, someone yelled, "Scott, get down here." I jumped off the tank, knowing I was in trouble. The crew patted me on the back and yelled, "You hit the target and destroyed it!" I was now a scared hero with a tear in my eye. I never told them that I had my eyes closed when I fired. – *Scott L. Webb.*

John Laws

Age 15 – United States Navy

I was born in Wichita, Kansas, on 1 June 1927. When I was 5 years old, my family moved to Olympia, Washington, where my father started a business. This was

> *I was so impressed with his uniform and his sea stories, I decided that I wanted to join the Navy.*

during the middle of the Depression, and life was very hard. We sold the business and moved to Tacoma, Washington.

As a youth, my dad served three apprenticeships and became a master brickmason, master concrete-finisher, and a master carpenter, but he could not read or write. When the WPA started, he was hired as a foreman at $85 per month. Normal WPA wages were $55, so we were able to live pretty well for the time. I sometimes worked as a helper in my dad's construction business. I also worked in a furniture factory when I was 12 years old. My friends and I picked berries, apples, and cherries. It didn't take long doing that for me to realize that there had to be something better.

Our house bordered McChord Air Base. Three days after the Japanese attack on Pearl Harbor, the MPs came and moved us away from the base.

My mother's favorite cousin, who had been in the Navy for thirty years, came to visit. I was so impressed with his uniform and his sea stories, I decided that I wanted to join the Navy. My uncle helped me talk Mother into signing the consent forms.

I went to the recruiting office with two of my buddies. We walked in and a chief said, "Two 15-year-olds and one 16." "No, sir," I lied, "I'm 17." One of my friends said that he was 17, but the other one said, "I just came in with them." I recently discovered that he did enlist, still underage, at the same time as my brother.

I was sworn in on 18 March 1943 and was sent to Farragut, Idaho, for boot camp. From there I went to machinist school at the University of Kansas. After completing the school, I went to Pearl Harbor where I was assigned to a commandeered Hudson River boat. This boat had a three-foot-wide bumper at the waterline which made a terrific ride in rough seas. I arrived on Palmyra Island late in 1943 for a 1-year tour of duty.

I had been on the island for about six months when I was assigned to mess duty for a month. One day I was working on the line serving mashed potatoes. I served a sailor a scoop of potatoes, but he didn't move. Not knowing exactly what to do, I gave him a second helping of potatoes. The sailor still didn't move, so I gave him a third helping. When he still didn't move, I looked up to tell him to move on and was shocked to find that the sailor was my brother whom I hadn't seen for over a year. He was serving on a ship that was loading fuel, became ill, and was sent to our hospital. We served together for about five months but were separated after the ruling that brothers couldn't serve together. This ruling came as a result of the death of the five Sullivan brothers who were all serving on the same ship when it was sunk.

I was sent to San Diego where I went aboard a transport to go to the Philippines. I was assigned to the USS *Baltimore* (CA-68). The bow of the *Baltimore* was heavily damaged in a typhoon off Okinawa, so we were sent to Pearl Harbor for repairs. From Pearl I went back to San Diego and was reassigned to the USS *Gosselin* (APD-126), where I remained until I was discharged in August of 1946.

I was a civilian until March 1948, but I began to remember the good times, so on 22 March I re-enlisted. Then I remembered the bad times. I was sent to Guam where I served a year with the 103rd Naval Construction Battalion. Then it was back to San Diego where I was assigned to the USS *Collett* (DD-730). I served on the *Collett* until my discharge in March 1950.

John Laws was in the trucking business with his brother for about 10 years, then he went into construction. Currently, he is a painting contractor. John and his wife Pat have six children, six grandchildren, seven great-grandchildren, and two great-great-grandchildren. They live in Montgomery, Texas.

Emilio L. LaBate

Age 15 – United States Marine Corps
Age 16 – United States Navy

I was born in Brooklyn, New York, on 13 September 1927. My father died when I was 5 years old, and my brothers and I worked to help our mother. In early 1943, at age 15, I was driving a truck for a major

> *I had no intention of joining the military – I just needed a driver's license.*

oil company and I needed a driver's license. I went to the license bureau in Brooklyn and they told me that I had to have a draft card before they would issue me a license. I went to the draft board and told them that my name was Léo E. LaBate and that I was 18. I got my draft card, then went to the license bureau and got my driver's license. I had no intention of joining the military – I just needed a driver's license.

Three months later, at the age of 15, I was drafted! I was inducted into the Marine Corps on 6 April 1943 and was sent to boot camp at

Parris Island, South Carolina. After boot camp, I went home on leave for a couple of days. While I was home, a truant officer came to the door and asked for me. He told me to go back to school. I told him a few things, using a few choice words. When my leave was up, I reported in to a Navy depot near Dover, New Jersey, where I had been assigned. I was there for five or six months, then someone found out how old I was, and I was given an honorable discharge.

I went into the Navy a few weeks before my 17th birthday. I told them that I was 18 because I knew that my mother would not sign for me. This time I enlisted as Emilio L. LaBate. After boot camp, I was assigned to the USS *Bremerton* (CA-130), which was to be commissioned in Camden, New Jersey. I was a plank owner on the *Bremerton*, but I didn't show up for the commissioning ceremonies. My mother came from Brooklyn for the ceremony, but she couldn't find me, and I was looking for her while the ceremony was taking place.

We did a shakedown cruise to the Caribbean. On the way back we were heading for Portland, Maine, when we hit a whale. The bow of the ship was damaged, so we put into Boston for repairs. We then went to the South Atlantic and stopped at Rio de Janeiro. While we were being escorted out of the harbor by some Brazilian ships, we were told that one of their ships was torpedoed. We just kept going.

When the war in Europe was over, we went through the Panama Canal and to Pearl Harbor. We anchored next to the sunken USS *Arizona*. One morning just as I was heading to the shower, a tanker rammed our ship right in the area where the shower was. I got out of there fast! Many men were killed or injured in that collision. After our ship was repaired, we joined Halsey's Seventh Fleet in the Western Pacific. About that time, the war with Japan was over.

We survived the typhoon of October 1945 and went to Shanghai, China. We patrolled the river and detonated mines by shooting at them. We helped clean up the port and helped get Japanese troops aboard ships and sent back to Japan. We made a trip to Korea, and I got to see the Great Wall of China.

I was discharged from the Navy on 1 April 1946 and returned to Brooklyn. My mother had five sons in the service during World War II: Earnest was in the Army Air Forces, I was in the Marines and the Navy, Vincent was in the Seabees, Michel was in the Army, and Anthony was in the Merchant Marines. Of the five of us, Vincent was the only one who was wounded and awarded the Purple Heart. I understand that there were more men of Italian decent in the armed forces during World War II than any other ethnic group.

Emilio LaBate began working as a hod carrier after his discharge from the Navy. He soon became a plasterer and started his own contracting business in 1960. At one time he owned and operated eight 10-wheeler trucks and two caterpillar tractors. He was a subcontractor on portions of the train tunnels under the World Trade Center Towers. In the late 1970s he developed cancer and sold his business. He was cured of the cancer and since then has enjoyed a retired lifestyle. Emilio and Frances, his wife of 54 years, have three children and five grandchildren. They live in Brooklyn, New York, in the summer and Sunny Isles, Florida, in the winter.

Kenneth D. Mann

Age 16 – United States Navy

I was born in Scranton, Pennsylvania, on 23 August 1926. My father was a building contractor along with my grandfather. Both went broke during the Depression. We moved to Philadelphia in 1931 as my father

> We were given the oath by an old-time movie star, Harry Carey.

was able to get work at a Texaco gas station in Hatboro, Pennsylvania. However, he became quite ill and we moved to California. I remember the five- or six-day trip driving across the country. We stayed in the car except for one or two nights, and we ate Velveeta cheese and crackers during most of the trip.

When we got to Los Angeles, we lived in "Mrs. Marian's" boarding house, all of us in one room. This was at the height of the Depression. My father got a job selling wholesale liquor in South Los Angeles, and we then could afford to move into an apartment. About this time, my father's illness progressed and he died in 1936. My mother remarried about a year later. My stepfather was really a good guy and I had no problems along that line. I was going to Los Angeles High School and was there when 7 December happened.

I really disliked high school, and I was a lousy student to boot. A buddy and I would skip school every chance we got and would go downtown to the movies. He used to con his mother into writing excuses for both of us. About this time, my mother became very ill and was hospitalized off and on. Several of my neighborhood friends who were 17 were joining the Navy and the Marine Corps, not waiting for the draft. Since I disliked school, was anxious for adventure, and filled with pure patriotism, I decided at age 16 to try to join the Navy.

A friend of mine told me that if I did not present a birth certificate, the recruiters would give me a document that would take its place if

I could give a good reason for not having one. When they asked me for a birth certificate at the recruiting office, I said, "I tried to get one but couldn't because the courthouse in Pennsylvania where I was born had burned down and all records of my birth were lost." The recruiter then gave me an official document that said "Age Certificate." He said, "Just take it home, have your mother or father fill it out, get it notarized, and bring it back."

I talked my mother into letting me join. I think she agreed because she was so ill. Both she and I filled out the form and took it to the Bank of America office where we banked, had it signed and notarized, and I took it back to the Navy. I had no problem; they accepted it without question.

I was sworn into the U. S. Navy on 28 May 1943 on the steps of the Federal Building in Los Angeles. We were given the oath by an old-time western movie star, Harry Carey. Since Los Angeles was so close to Hollywood, it was common practice to have a movie star participate in the swearing-in programs.

I was put on a bus for boot camp in San Diego. After eight weeks at the U. S. Naval Training Center, San Diego, I was selected to go to radio school, which was my first choice of schools. I had been a ham-radio operator as a kid, and I was quite good at receiving and sending Morse code. I was sent to the University of Colorado in Boulder for the radio course. I graduated in the top five of the class, and as a result I was promoted to radioman third class. Because I had done so well in radio school, I was selected to attend radio intelligence school at Bainbridge Island, Washington, to learn how to intercept Japanese "katakana" radio code, which was more complicated than the standard Morse code. Bainbridge was the intercept station that had copied the infamous Japanese "winds" message. This was a top-secret activity. We did not even talk about it amongst ourselves when we were not on duty. We took a special oath not to divulge our participation in this activity for 50 years. Now, of course, there are numerous books and movies telling about the whole operation.

When I graduated from this school, I was sent to FRUPAC (Fleet Radio Unit, Pacific), which was operating from Wahiawa on the island of Oahu. From there, I was assigned to task-force duty as part of the admiral's flag staff.

FRUPAC was part of Naval Intelligence, OP-2-G, which was the organization that intercepted Japanese "katakana" radio messages and was responsible for the intelligence information that made it a victory at Midway. FRUPAC also intercepted the Japanese-radio message that told where Admiral Yamamoto was going to be, and the Army sent up P-38s and shot him down. I did not participate in the Midway or the Yamamoto intercepts, but FRUPAC, under Commander Rochefort, made these victories possible.

I was in five major campaigns in the Pacific: Kwajalien, Guam, Saipan, Tinian, and Okinawa. While performing radio-intercept duties, I was attached to Admiral Marc Mitscher's flag staff while on the USS *Bunker Hill* and the USS *Enterprise*, both of which were hit by kamikazes. I ended up in the water after the hit on the *Bunker Hill*, but I was picked up quickly by one of our destroyers, along with hundreds of other guys. There were 396 killed and 264 wounded out of a crew of 3,000. This was 11 May 1945.

I ended up in Tientsin, China, then returned to the States where I was discharged a radioman first class on 28 May 1946.

I entered the University of California, Los Angeles, in September 1946 and enrolled in the brand new U. S. Air Force ROTC Program. I graduated in 1950 and was commissioned a second lieutenant in the U. S. Air Force Reserve. I requested active duty to go to pilot training. I served a tour in Korea with a B-26 light-bomber group. Upon my return to the States, I was sent to the USAF Arctic Navigation School to be cross-trained as a radar-navigator. After this training, I was sent to St. John's, Newfoundland, the headquarters of the Northeast Air Command. I spent three years flying around the Arctic and flew one of the first aircraft to land at Thule, Greenland, to help establish the base there. We flew the first construction workers from Westover Air Force Base, Massachusetts, to Thule, Greenland, for the building of that base. After three years in the Arctic, I returned to inactive duty with the reserve and retired as a colonel in 1980.

Ken Mann became an agent for the Internal Revenue Service, Department of the Treasury. His main job was investigating tax-evaders, non-filers, and other tax violators. His last 10 years of government activity were concentrated on drug and money-laundering cases. He retired from government service in 1994. Ken has a son and a daughter. He lives in San Juan Capistrano, California.

King D. Ross

Age 16 – United States Marine Corps

I had two older brothers in the Marines and I wanted to serve my country, too. I was born in Washington, D.C., on 22 December 1926. We later moved to Manhattan in New York. When I was 15, I used an older, deceased

> I met my older brother Charlie during the Okinawa battle.

brother's birth certificate and filled out the papers and passed the Marine Corps physical, but my parents wouldn't sign for me.

When I was 16, I had a friend white-out the "6" on my birth certificate and make a photostat of it. I typed a "5" in place of the "6", and enlisted in the Marine Corps on 16 June 1943. This time my dad signed for me, but I signed my mother's name. They were taking in so many men at that time that I had to wait until August to get into boot camp.

After boot camp at Parris Island, South Carolina, I was picked to be a range coach and a drill instructor. On the advice of my older brothers (already Marines), I declined both, hoping to see combat. I did!

I was a radio operator with Headquarters and Service Battalion, 2nd Marine Division, during the Saipan and Tinian operations, and was a member of K Company, 3rd Battalion, 1st Marines, 1st Marine Division, during the battles for Peleliu and Okinawa. I met my older brother Charlie during the Okinawa battle. He was with the 6th Marine Division.

I was discharged from the Marine Corps on 6 May 1946 and said to myself, "No more uniforms!" Two years later, I was a New York City police officer.

King Ross was awarded the Navy and Marine Corps Commendation Medal, three Presidential Unit Citations, the Combat Action Ribbon, and rated four battle stars on his Asiatic-Pacific service ribbon. After his discharge, he attended Brooklyn College, and in 1948, became a

New York City police officer. He served for 10 years as a uniformed patrolman and 10 years as a detective. As a member of the NYPD, he earned three Excellent Police Duty awards, a Meritorious Police Duty award, and a Department Commendation. He is a member of the NYPD Honor Legion. After leaving the police department, he moved his family to Australia where he became a state housing officer. After two years, they returned to the States, where he worked as a chauffeur and bodyguard for a large bank for 10 years. His last 12 years of employment was as a Special Deputy U. S. Marshall (court-security officer). He has been married for 52 years to, in his words, "the most beautiful woman I ever saw." King and Joanne have three children. They live in Oakdale, New York.

✔ *INCIDENTally — **The glue did not hold!** –* In 1944, my 14-year-old friend and I were determined to enter the service. We registered for the draft and gave a fictitious age. We pledged to each other that we would stick together. Upon receiving orders to report for induction, we went to Portland, Oregon and reported in at 0800. At 1100, my brother, who unbeknownst to me, had enlisted in the Marines, reported in. My 14-year-old friend went to the Marines with my brother. So much for the pledge to serve together. – *Walter Holy.*

Dorwin G. Dean

Age 15 – United States Navy

I was born in Spokane, Washington, on 6 December 1927. We moved to Everett, Washington, in 1939. My stepfather took a job on the railroad in El Paso, Texas. I didn't want to move, but my mother convinced me

> *Needless to say, it was a long and fearful night for many of us.*

that I should. I had completed eight grades of school and didn't want any more. By the time I spent six months in Texas, I was ready to go anywhere. Although I was living alone and had a fair job, I just didn't make the change very well. I knew that the chances were good that I could get in trouble.

It took all that a full-grown know-it-all could say or do to convince my mother that her helping me get into the service would be the lesser of two evils. Years later, I would be in her shoes under similar conditions. With her help, I was sworn into the Navy on 21 June 1943.

I had it all figured out. I wanted to take boot training at Farragut, Idaho. Surely, they wouldn't send me to a facility as close as San Diego, California, but they did. I was in Company 43-224. After boot camp I wanted to serve in a ship's company, but the wheel of fortune put me in the amphibious forces.

I was sent to the destroyer base in Coronado, California, and introduced to the Higgins boat. When our training was over, we were sent to Fort Ord, California. I think they were juggling us around for valid reasons, but we couldn't believe that we would be sent to an Army camp. We were there only for a couple of weeks and didn't do any work except participate in a parade for a general. However, liberty in Monterey and Salinas was great. I guess the locals liked the color change of the uniforms.

The playing around was over and we boarded a train for San Francisco. We marched from the train station down to the

Embarcadero, to Pier 43. A Liberty ship, the *George W. Julian*, awaited us. I had had two 12-hour liberties in San Diego, one while in boot camp and the other at the amphibious base, and two or three liberties at Fort Ord, but no boot leave. My grandmother lived in Oakland and expected me to come see her. When we reached the ship, we were told to board, to billet down, and that there would be liberty tomorrow. We were now officially the Standard Landing Craft Unit 24. The next morning, 10 October 1943, at 1:15 a.m., we felt the ship shudder. That woke us up, and we made a mad rush topside. The Golden Gate Bridge was drifting right over the top of us as we sailed out.

Fifteen days later, we disembarked on Fualefeke Island, one of the Ellice Islands, which also included Funafuti Island, where there was an airstrip. We inhabited Fualefeke for about five months. We built a pier, shot a few wild boars on another island, and did in many, many little green lizards with our machetes. The Japanese dropped a few bombs on us a couple of times. Right after the first bombing run, five boys stood in front of the captain's tent. They were all underage. I had a few mixed emotions myself! I knew one of the kids who was underage. They all left the island, but I don't know what happened to them.

We left the Ellice Islands in early April and arrived at Pearl Harbor on Easter Sunday morning. We received lots of rest and recreation for the next five months. While we were there, six LSTs in the West Loch blew up. They were gearing up for the invasion of Saipan and were loading ammunition. There were many killed and wounded.

Our outfit was getting smaller because boat crews were being assigned to task forces. We joined up with Standard Landing Craft Unit 36 and were assigned to Task Force 58. MacArthur was going back to the Philippines, so we landed troops at Dulag, Leyte, Philippine Islands on 20 October 1944. The troops cleared the beach fairly fast so we didn't have much to do but stay out of trouble. That afternoon I relaxed on deck and happened to get my legs severely sunburned. Later, it looked like the enemy was going to try and come in behind us, so we went back on the beach and dug in. There was enough happening to keep us occupied all afternoon.

About dark, one plane dropped one bomb on a fuel and ammunition dump a short way down the beach from us. A little while later, we heard that there was a small group of our troops trying to get to where we were, but the burning dump held them up. They didn't want to go through the jungle because of snipers. There was an LCVP broached on the beach, and it seemed to us like a good idea for us to get it in the water and go pick up those men. There were a lot of our ships at anchor that were on alert for Japanese landing craft. We could see their guns tracking us as we went along the beach. The burning dump lit up the area some, so we slid in where we could. We could see the troops, but they never made a break for it. Maybe they thought we were Japanese. We never did find out.

During that escapade I got punctured in the leg with shrapnel, but I had no idea that I was hit because my legs were so severely sunburned and swollen that I couldn't feel it. It got kind of serious later. The next morning, we started out just as some enemy dive bombers came over. We headed for a barge that was loaded with crates, barrels, and machinery. We slid alongside of the barge just as one of the planes made a run at us. After he passed overhead, we raised our heads and saw the word "gasoline" stenciled on the barrels. Oops!

The night of 29 October 1944 was beautiful. I had bedded down in the well deck of an LCM. I woke up after midnight in pitch-blackness, heavy rain, and gale-force winds. In time we could see one light, and that was all. We had no control of the craft, so it had to be fate that saved us from that storm. The light was on a Liberty ship, the *David Gaylord*, and lying alongside of her was a pontoon barge loaded with long pilings. Needless to say, it was a long and fearful night for many of us. It was shaping up for us to be at the grand finale in Japan, but I'm glad the big boys got there first and dropped the bomb before then. I was discharged at Bremerton, Washington, on 3 March 1946.

Dorwin Dean was a long-haul trucker for most of his working life. He and Rose, his wife of 41 years, have a combined family of six children, ten grandchildren, and three great-grandchildren. They live in Battle Ground, Washington.

206

Arnold L. McLain
Age 15 – United States Navy

This story should be titled "Underage Military Service, an Old Family Tradition." My uncle, my father, and I, all served in the Navy while underage.

> *My parents did not appreciate my action, but took no steps to have me released.*

The town of Kannapolis in Cabarrus County, North Carolina, was founded shortly after 1900 when the Cannon family established a textile factory there. In 1912, my grandmother and her four children moved from their mountain home in Alexander County and settled in a company-owned house in Kannapolis.

My uncle Raymond McLain, my mother's brother, at the age of 15, decided that he would rather see the world than be tied down working in a textile mill, so he enlisted in the Navy in 1916. His Navy career was short-lived as his mother had him discharged after only a few months. Raymond returned to Kannapolis and worked in the Cannon Mills for some 40 years.

My father, Maurice Story McLain, was born on 16 November 1904 in Alexander County, North Carolina. In the fall of 1920, at age 15, he enlisted in the Navy. He received basic training at Hampton Roads, Virginia, and was in President-elect Warren G. Harding's inaugural parade in 1921. He was hospitalized with a severe case of measles, probably in the spring of 1921. He also came down with the flu. In those days, measles and the flu were quite serious illnesses. Apparently, at that point, the

Navy became alarmed and notified his father. He arrived on the scene about the time the disease was brought under control and had him released from the service. They returned to their mountain home in Alexander County, North Carolina. In early 1923, he came to Cararrus County and went to work in the Cannon Mills.

I was born on 18 July 1927 and grew up in Kannapolis. At age 16, I was expected to begin working in the Cannon Mills. Somehow, in June 1943, my 16-year-old cousin Bruce and I talked his dad and my Uncle Raymond into signing enlistment papers for us to join the Naval Reserves. This was on 23 June 1943, 25 days prior to my 16th birthday. My parents did not appreciate my action, but took no steps to have me released. My father apparently remembered his own underage service years earlier.

I completed boot camp with Company 4328 at Bainbridge, Maryland, and on 4 September 1943, I was assigned to training at the Naval Operating Base, Norfolk. I became a crew member of the USS *Samuel S. Miles* (DE-183) on 9 October 1943. The *Miles* was commissioned at the Brooklyn Navy Yard on 4 November 1943. I served on the *Miles* in the central and south Pacific areas for 16 months. We participated with the Third and Fifth Fleets in 13 landing operations, earning eight battle stars and two stars for the Philippines Liberation.

We returned to San Pedro, California, on 22 July 1945. I was assigned shore duty at the Naval Air Station, Willow Grove, Pennsylvania, from November 1945 until June 1946. I enlisted in the regular Navy in January 1946. I served brief tours at the Naval Air Station in Ottumwa, Iowa, in Jacksonville, Florida, and in Memphis, Tennessee. In August 1948, I was assigned to the USS *New Kent* (APA-217). I also served on the USS *Randall* (APA-224), USS *Menard* (APA-201), and the USS *Comstock* (LSD-19), with a tour at the Naval Air Station, Jacksonville, Florida, after serving on the *Randall*.

I earned two battle stars in the Korean War and served in the Vietnam area during the summer of 1954. I participated in the underwater Pacific nuclear tests (Operation Wigwam) in 1955 while serving aboard the *Comstock*. I was stationed at the Naval Amphibious Base, Coronado, California from June 1956 until August 1958. I went aboard the USS *San Joaquin County* (LST-1122) at San Diego, California, in September 1958. The *San Joaquin County* was transferred to SERVFORPAC at Sasebo, Japan, in March 1959 and converted to a support and station ship at a Guam shipyard. On 1 September 1959 she sailed for Japan and was stationed at Iwakuni. I served there until May 1962. Later, I served on the USS *Apache* (ATF-67) and the USS *Molala* (ATF-106). I was promoted to chief boatswain's mate in September 1960. I retired from the Navy on 1 July 1964 at San Diego, California, after 21 years of service.

Arnold McLain was employed by the North Carolina Driver's License Section in Johnston County from the time he retired from the Navy until July 1990. He was assistant district supervisor in Wayne County when he retired in 1992. He has been active in the Fleet Reserve Association, the American Legion, and the Boy Scouts of America. During his 35 years with the Scouts, he received the Silver Beaver, Vigil, and Founder's Honor awards. Arnold and his wife Lila have two daughters and five grandchildren. They live in Smithfield, North Carolina.

✓ *INCIDENTally* — **Promotion!** – When I joined the National Guard in 1940, I would go to the Armory to play basketball with the other fellows for a couple of hours. The government paid us one dollar per drill for being there. Later, while on maneuvers in Louisiana, I spent the entire three weeks on KP, cleaning pots and pans, peeling potatoes, and starting fires under the containers to boil water for the sterilization of mess kits and gear. Advancing in rank was a matter of luck. One day the first sergeant came over to three of us who were on KP and said that he had a promotion for one of us. We flipped a coin and I won. That is how I became a private first class. – *Harvey H. Reese.*

Jack C. Harper

Age 16 – United States Navy

I was born in Long Beach, California, on 17 June 1927. When I was 4 years old, my parents moved from California to Arkansas. Today this seems to me to be a "Grapes of Wrath" in reverse. However, my dad had lost

> ..., I was awarded five battle stars, all before my 18th birthday.

his job in California and thought that he could find work in Arkansas. Unfortunately, this did not happen and our lives only became more difficult.

I had been going to school and working at various jobs, but the hours were too demanding, so I dropped out of school in early 1942 to work full-time in a furniture shop. The age limit was 16. I told them that I was 16 and they accepted me. I worked there for a year.

On my 16th birthday, I asked my dad to sign the papers for me to join the Navy. He was happy to oblige. On 28 June 1943, I was sworn into the Navy and sent to San Diego, California, for boot camp. After completing boot camp, I went to the naval base at Coronado for amphibious training. Upon completion of the training, I was assigned to Standard Landing Craft Unit 4 as a machine gunner on LCMs. We went to Pearl Harbor in October 1943 where I had more training in landings and in gunnery practice.

I participated in the amphibious landings in the Gilberts, Marshalls, Marianas, Pelileu, and Okinawa. Fortunately, I was never wounded, although we lost several of our boat crew members from the original group. Because of my age, I felt that God watched over me.

I very well remember the terrifying experiences I had during that period. The first was landing with the first wave in the Gilberts; the second was being stranded on Roi-Namur on 12 February 1944 when the Japanese bombed us; and finally, the nightly kamikaze raids at Okinawa. During the period from November 1943 until April 1945, I was awarded five battle stars, all before my 18th birthday. This can't be a record, but it's a pretty good average considering that I got the third one on my 17th birthday at Saipan. It was the biggest birthday party I ever had!

During this period, I served on the *LST-482*, the USS *Belle Grove* (LSD-2), SS *Cape Georgia* (a merchant ship as a temporary boat crew), USS *Kenmore* (AKA-221), and the USS *San Diego* (CL-52). I received my first leave in July 1945 after returning from Okinawa. That is a long time to be away from home when you are so young.

I was discharged on 6 December 1945, enlisted in the Naval Reserve, finished high school, and requested active duty. By March 1948, I hadn't heard from the Navy, so I re-enlisted in the regular Navy. Unfortunately, I was the sole support of my mother and sister, so in May 1949, I requested an early discharge.

I got out, but I wasn't happy. I really hadn't adapted to being a civilian yet, so I joined the Air Force Reserve and again requested active duty. Finally, in early 1951, I was called up and sent to Alexandria, Louisiana. That is where I met my future wife.

I was released from active duty in 1952 and returned to Phoenix, Arizona, where I went to work for the Mountain States Telephone and Telegraph Company. I joined the Arizona Air National Guard and became a load master on four-engine transport aircraft. I also trained to be an aerial-refueling boom operator. During my time in the Guard, I flew 3,000 hours to destinations such as Europe, South America, and Alaska.

In 1966, we started flying regularly scheduled supply trips to Vietnam. Talk about a tough schedule! We would depart Phoenix on Thursday, and 12 days and 100+ flying hours later, we would return to our regular civilian job. One trip would consume all allowable flight hours for a month. It still seems strange to think about leaving Phoenix, going to places like Hawaii, Wake Island, Japan, Okinawa, the Philippines, and Vietnam, then report back to your civilian job — all in less than two weeks!

I retired from the National Guard on 15 July 1973 at the rank of master sergeant. Many new and exciting things have happened to me, but none equal my military experiences. I feel very fortunate to have been a part of helping America retain her freedoms that so many take for granted. Few know of the sacrifices that were made by men, women, and boys such as we.

Jack Harper started working for Mountain States Telephone and Telegraph Company as a lineman in 1952. He held numerous assignments within the company and was security manager at the time of his retirement in 1982. Jack is one of the five original members of the American Legion Post #6 Color and Honor Guard in Prescott, Arizona, who perform military honors for families of deceased armed-forces veterans, and do flag-raisings and colors-postings at numerous schools. He is also involved with DARE (drug-alcohol abuse education) programs. Jack and Bobbie, his wife of 51 years, have two sons and three grandchildren. They live in Prescott, Arizona.

✔ *INCIDENTally* — *A reverent team.* — Stuck on a scrub pine tree after being wounded, I was waiting for something to happen when a strange voice called out, "Luster!" Soon, two Navy corpsmen were standing over me making plans to get me off that noisy O-bong-ni (5 hills) ridge line (South Korea, August 1950). Soon, one was in my face calling my name to be sure I was still alive. Struggling down and across a red clay ditch, they worked me toward the road. Babbick wanted to rest a little, but Green refused saying, "We have to get him back." We came to one more red clay ditch that was steeper than the last one. One pushed from under and the other pulled from above. Babbick shaded my face while Green went for a litter. An M-26 tanker offered to take me back on his machine. Green said, "No, thanks." After they put me in a jeep ambulance, I realized that I had heard not one word of profanity during all of the arguments and the struggle to get me off that ridge. What a pair! They must have come from a seminary. Babbick was later killed in action and Green was wounded. I can never forget that reverent team. — *Herbert R. "Lefty" Luster.*

Joseph Homko

Age 16 – United States Army

I was born in East Allen Township, Pennsylvania, on 28 March 1927. I was bored with school. I thought the war would be over soon and I would miss out on the big adventure, so I quit high school

> *I was the youngest in my company and the second youngest in the division.*

during my junior year and registered for the draft, telling them that I was 18. When I registered, I volunteered for early induction. I was called up on 30 June 1943. I was sent to the induction center at Fort Dix, New Jersey. I volunteered for airborne duty and was transferred to Fort Benning, Georgia, where I was assigned to the 513 Parachute Infantry Regiment of the 13th Airborne Division.

I became a member of Company A of the 513th. I was the youngest in my company and the second youngest in the division. My MOS was

1st machine gunner. This meant that I had to carry a machine-gun receiver which weighed about 35 pounds. After about eight months my age was discovered, and I was discharged on 27 February 1944, one month before my 17th birthday. The 513th was transferred to the 17th Airborne Division about the time I was discharged, so I consider myself a member of the 17th Airborne.

At age 17, I passed the physicals for both the Marines and the Navy, but the quotas were filled for both services, so I had to wait. After about three months, the Navy called and I headed for boot camp. After boot camp, I went aboard the heavy cruiser USS *St. Paul* and was assigned to the gunnery division. I spent about 18 months on the *St. Paul*, 4 months in the Atlantic and 14 months in the Pacific.

I was discharged from the Navy in May 1946.

Joe Homko sailed in the Merchant Marines for six months after his discharge from the Navy. He then became an auto mechanic with a

Chrysler auto dealership. He became a toolmaker and an engineering technician. He has been a machine-shop proprietor for nearly 20 years. He was recognized for his tool-making expertise in the 20 October 1969 issue of American Machinist. *Joe and Winona, his wife of 50 years, have three children, two girls and one boy, and three grandchildren, two girls and one boy. Joe and Winona live in Oxford, New Jersey.*

✓ *INCIDENTally* — **Retarded, sir!** – When I was recalled to active duty in 1966, I ended up in Korea. I was told that I had to take the medical proficiency test if I wanted some extra money in my pay. I went to Seoul and reported to a very young warrant officer. He asked for my ID card, and I gave it to him. When I was recalled, they gave me the prefix "RP" before my serial number, instead of the usual "RA." The warrant officer looked at my ID and said that there was no such designation as "RP." I answered very respectively that that was what they had assigned me in Washington. He insisted that there was no such thing. He said, "What does RP stand for?" By this time my temper was building up and I snapped back with, "Retarded Personnel, sir!" There were six other retreads with me and they all gave the same answer, "Retarded Personnel, sir!" I thought the warrant officer was going to wet his pants, he was so mad. To this day, I don't know what it RP stood for, whether it was recalled, retired, or as I said, retarded. – *Jehu P. Malone.*

James J. Leftwich

Age 13 – Texas State Guard
Age 14 – United States Coast Guard
Age 16 – United States Coast Guard

I was born in Waco, Texas, on 3 February 1929 as the Great Depression was shifting into high gear. When I was a few months old, my family moved to Chicago where

> In spite of being an eighth-grade dropout, I was selected as the outstanding officer candidate...

my dad had found a job. That job played out before the year was over. We moved to Oklahoma, then to Tyler, Texas, and finally to Dallas where I finished the eighth grade. Education had become a burden, and I decided that I knew all that I needed to know. I was constantly getting into trouble for playing hooky to go to the Dallas Public Library.

I joined the Texas State Guard when I was 13 years old. I had a great time driving the jeeps and heavy trucks to the frequent drills and bivouacs. Several of the guys from the Guard company decided to join the service, so we went downtown to join the Marine Corps. It turned out that I was color-blind and was immediately rejected. Next, I tried the Navy; same thing – color-blind. The Coast Guard recruiter was right next door, so that looked like the next try, but I had to get around the color-blind problem some way. While the Navy recruiter was out to lunch, I "borrowed" the test book with all the colored dots. I took it home, and with the help of some of my buddies, memorized all the pages. Each page had a particular clue, which made it easy. I passed the color-blind tests and all the other tests for the Coast Guard.

Dad signed my enlistment papers after I had convinced Mom that the Coast Guard didn't do anything more dangerous than guard the coast. I was sworn into the Coast Guard on 20 July 1943, and along with eight others, boarded a train the next day for St. Augustine, Florida and boot camp. When I went to pick up the train ticket at the recruiting station, I left the color-blind test book in the men's room, after wiping off the fingerprints.

It was an exciting day when we arrived at St. Augustine and boarded a bus for the training station, which was the old Ponce de Leon Hotel that had been taken over for the duration of the war. It was a pretty fancy place.

After graduating from boot camp, my first assignment was to the Cape Canaveral Beach Patrol Station, which was located at the lighthouse at Merritt Island. When not on patrol with my dog, I would climb to the top of the light tower and watch the passing ships through binoculars. I could see across the island to the west and watch torpedo bombers take off from the Banana River Naval Air Station. The owner of Merritt Island came by the station one day and wanted to sell some of the land to the crew of the station. I was making $54 a month at the time, but I didn't want to be a landowner, nor did any of the crew. We were too smart to buy all that sand and palmetto bushes that are now NASA's Kennedy Space Center.

After a few months, I tired of cleaning up after Doberman Pinschers and German Shepherds, so I put in for sea duty. A few weeks later, I reported to an 83-foot sub-chaser boat in Port Everglades, Florida. This was the first boat I had ever been aboard, and to me it seemed like a large ship. The first day at sea, we were assigned to escort the SS *Sea Train Texas* to Havana with a load of railroad cars. I was seasick from the time we left Port Everglades sea buoy until we passed Morro Castle. I did not like to be seasick, decided that I never would be again, and I wasn't during my entire career in the Coast Guard. There was a lot of very ugly weather waiting for me down the road. All of the antisubmarine patrols after that convoy trip were fun. I would take my turn in the bilge of the boat on sonar watch. I never got sick, even when the chief boatswain's mate blew cigar smoke down the voice tube from the bridge, which he loved to do.

My boat was transferred to Miami after a few months and I was sent for special training at the Sub-Chaser Training School. Two weeks before finishing my training, I was ordered to report to the USS *Escatawapa* (AOG-27), a Navy gasoline tanker that was outfitting in

Brooklyn, New York. On 18 August 1944, the USS *Escatawapa* was commissioned. We had 10 officers and 51 enlisted men aboard. I was a seaman second class. Years later, I would serve with two of these officers, one of which became a rear admiral, the other a commander. At that time I was Lieutenant Leftwich, not a seaman second class. They were more surprised than I was. A 14-year-old kid one day, and the next time you see him, he is commissioned. Amazing!

We set sail on 9 September 1944 toward Norfolk, Virginia, for further sea trials and training in formation with the USS *Ranger* and several cruisers and destroyers. We were hit by a severe hurricane on 16 September while off Cape Henry and went inside Chesapeake Bay to anchor until the storm passed. That day, the Coast Guard cutters *Jackson* and *Bedloe* capsized off Cape Hatteras with few survivors. One year later, that storm would be looked back upon as a "piece of cake" in comparison with the typhoon which blew the *Escatawpa* ashore on the Japanese island of Kyushu with engines going full speed ahead. That event occurred nine days after the atomic bomb had been dropped on the Kyushu city of Nagasaki.

We operated in the Norfolk area, training and preparing for our journey to the Pacific. We fully expected to be in combat by the end of the year at the latest. We sailed from Norfolk on 6 October 1944 and joined a convoy bound for the Panama Canal. On 12 October, Columbus Day, we passed San Salvador Island at dawn. We were close enough that I could see the Christopher Columbus Monument by using the large telescope which we kept on the signal bridge. I was excited about the coincidence. Columbus also first went to sea at age 14. As we approached Panama, the ship received orders to proceed to Aruba to load a full cargo of 100-octane aviation gasoline for the Panama Canal Station. This was our first of many cargoes.

In later years, when I read the novel, *Mister Roberts*, I thought back to see if I could remember Heggen or Logan as being crew members on the *Escatawpa*. I could identify Mister Roberts, the captain, and the crew members easily. To borrow a phrase from *Mister Roberts*, we spent months "going from Tedium to Apathy" and back to Pearl Harbor. Mr. Roberts was my division officer and I worked for Sam the Signalman, but his name had been changed from Tony. We were beginning to think that Johnson Island would be our closest approach to combat, but orders eventually came for us to proceed to Eniwetok with a convoy of small auxiliary ships. We continued the "Tedium to Apathy" routine for a while longer, but one lengthy trip to Tarawa broke the monotony somewhat.

On 25 March 1945, at anchor in Eniwetok lagoon, I was injured by the explosion of a flare mortar on the flying bridge, and my journey to glory ended. I was transferred to the Navy infirmary on the island. I cried when I saw the *Escatawpa* sail the next day for the invasion campaigns that I wanted to participate in.

After being patched up, I was transferred to the Aiea Heights Naval Hospital at Pearl Harbor, and later to Oaknoll Naval Hospital at Oakland, California, then to the Navy hospital at Norman, Oklahoma. I had already been certified as physically qualified for re-enlistment, in spite of losing two fingers at Eniwetok, but I had too many points, and I was in the Coast Guard Reserve, so I was told that I would have to be discharged. I was sent to St. Louis, Missouri, where I was discharged on 8 August 1945 at the age of 16. I requested to re-enlist in the regular Coast Guard, but the request was denied. I hitchhiked home to Dallas and wrote some letters to the Commandant of the Coast Guard, with the help of a Dallas recruiter. I re-enlisted in the regular Coast Guard on 4 December 1945, still at the age of 16.

My first postwar assignment was to the USCGC *Primrose*, a small buoy-tender that worked out of Galveston. I requested a transfer and received orders to report to the USCGC *Mojave* in Boston. It was an interesting assignment with lots of hard work and long watches at sea. When the *Mojave* was decommissioned, I transferred to the USCGC *Tampa*. My assignments after that were aboard cutters assigned to weather patrol out of Boston, New York, Los Angeles, and Honolulu.

In 1957, I was accepted in officers candidate school and transferred to the Coast Guard Academy at New London. In spite of being an eighth-grade dropout, I was selected as the outstanding officer candidate and received the Superintendent's Award, an engraved officer's dress sword. I guess all that hooky time spent at the Dallas County Library paid off.

Upon graduation on 1 October 1957, I was assigned to the USCGC Minnetonka (WPG-47) which was based in Long Beach, California. I was back in my old business of Pacific weather patrols. In 1960, while serving in Hawaii, I came across reports that people were being denied retirement benefits based upon underage enlistments being classified as fraudulent. I began a campaign to reverse this ruling by addressing a letter to the Commandant of the Coast Guard, requesting clarification of my status. The reply was that since I had twice enlisted fraudulently, the time of those enlistments could not count toward retirement. This involved the time of my first enlistment in 1943 and all subsequent enlistments up to the time I became of legal age for enlistment. However, I received information and opinions through the grapevine that I had enough support at high levels in the Coast Guard and in the General Accounting Office to enable me to receive a favorable ruling. My purpose was not to just receive a favorable ruling for me, but for all others in the same situation. I requested assistance from Senator Ralph Yarborough and Congressman W. R. Poage of Texas. With the assistance of these fine representatives, the U. S. Coast Guard Commandant, and the people in the General Accounting Office, legislation was eventually passed to classify all underage enlistments as creditable service. This battle enabled me to retire on 31 January 1964 at the grade of lieutenant, with 21 years of service. I hope that other underage veterans became aware of this opportunity.

Jim Leftwich worked for the Texas Highway Department for a year, then accepted a position as a corporate pilot for a manufacturing company near Waco. He had learned to fly while stationed in Hawaii. When the company went bankrupt, he returned to the sea, obtaining a chief-mate's license. He started as a third mate, soon became second mate, then chief mate, and finally, a master. His first job as ship's master was aboard a large tanker. It was ironic that on this tanker, one of the 27 tanks carried more cargo than the 27,000-barrel capacity of the USS Escatawpa, *the ship that got him started in the tanker business. After serving as master of tankers for 22 years, he retired and dropped both anchors in Waco, where it all began. Jim and his wife Mamie have four children and six grandchildren. They live in Hewitt, Texas.*

David N. Showalter

Age 15 – United States Marine Corps
Age 16 – United States Army Air Forces

On Sunday morning, 7 December 1941, I was sauntering down the main street of Milwaukee, Wisconsin, listening to the Christmas music being broadcast over the loudspeaker

> *I decided to join any service that would have me, no matter how devious the process.*

system. A solemn voice interrupted, stating that Pearl Harbor had been attacked by Japan.

At age 14, I was too young to be admitted to any of the services, so in January 1942, I joined the Civil Air Patrol. This did not satisfy my patriotic urge to fight for my country. When my sister married an Air Forces pilot in July, that did it! I decided to join any service that would have me, no matter how devious the process. My height was 5 foot 8 inches, my weight was 140 pounds, and my age was 15.

Being a crafty lad, I altered my birth certificate to make me old enough to enlist. It originally showed that I was born on 8 January 1927 in Green Bay, Wisconsin. I confided my plans to a buddy who was 17, and he decided to go with me. We both skipped school, feeding one another courage on our way to the Marine recruiting station. We were both accepted and were sworn in on 23 July 1943. I could hardly contain my joy as I prepared for my adventure. My parents were divorced and I was certain that my mother and grandmother, with whom I lived, had no idea that I had joined the Marines and planned to sneak off. Little did I know.

Proud and excited, I boarded the train on my way to boot camp. Barely one hundred miles later, the train pulled to a stop. I looked through the window, and to my astonishment, recognized my very large mother, accompanied by an equally large Marine sergeant. As I cringed in humiliation, they boarded the train and approached me amidst a car full of recruits. Norine, my very large mother, caught me by the ear and in a commanding voice said, "Come with me, young man!" Having no choice, I went. That was the end of my Marine career. I learned later that my 17-year-old buddy lost his life on Iwo Jima.

Back to high school I went, biding my time. In November 1943, with the same birth certificate, I joined the Army Air Forces and qualified for pilot training as an aviation cadet. I made it safely to Fort Sheridan, Illinois. The Army cut my hair, took away my clothes, and sprayed me for lice. Doctors and dentists prodded and poked, punctured me with needles, and painted numbers on my body with iodine. The proud moment finally came when I received my uniforms and equipment.

Several days later, we boarded a troop train with triple-decker bunks. It took four days and nights to reach our destination. The train would often be put on sidings to let priority trains carrying troops, ammunition, and war materials speed by. At some daytime stops in small towns, the ladies served us homemade donuts and cookies.

We finally arrived at Sheppard Field, Texas, where I spent 12 weeks learning to be a soldier. Being 16 years old, and having often bicycled 40 miles on weekends to hike and squirrel hunt, I had determination to endure the 20-mile hikes while other "legitimate" recruits had to be taken back to the base in the meat wagon. General Hap Arnold attended my graduation at which there were 4,999 other soldiers.

The next stop was Aloe Army Air Field in Victoria, Texas, an advanced-flying school. Finally, my dream came true, I thought. But it was not to happen. Just prior to completing my cadet training, Norine, my enormous mother, discovered my whereabouts and contacted my commanding officer, relating the information that I was underage. One more humiliation! Four months from my 18th birthday, against my wishes and protesting all the way, I was given an underage honorable discharge at Fort Sheridan, Illinois.

While at Fort Sheridan, I was put in charge of a large barracks of underage boys, also waiting to be sent home. At this time, the Stearhead Infantry Division was being rotated from Europe to the Pacific. Those in charge would not give the veterans passes to go into town. I felt that this was highly discriminative and decided to remedy the situation. After rifling through as many desks as I could get into, I finally found 50 blank passes and a validating stamp. I filled them out and we escaped. I will not reveal the name of the town where we celebrated – they may still be looking for us 57 years later! We sneaked back, drunk as hoot owls. These seasoned veterans made me an honorary member of their unit. I was questioned by our group captain the following day. Of course, I knew nothing. However, the twinkle in his eyes led me to believe that he knew the truth.

Home *again*! By now I was 5 foot 11 inches and weighed 150 pounds. Knowing that in a few months I would turn 18 and be drafted, I enlisted in the Navy Air Cadet program, expecting to be trained as a pilot. Upon my arrival at the Navy Air Technical Training Center in Memphis, Tennessee, I discovered that I was a seaman second class, a combat aircrewman trainee on torpedo bombers, not in pilot training. Never trust a recruiter! The war ended soon, I was finally 18 years old, and I received a regular honorable discharge, not an underage one.

Space does not allow me to review my experiences in the Wisconsin Air National Guard as a tow-target operator over Lake Michigan in 1947-48. I joined the Air Force again as an aviation cadet in 1950 and was discharged because of allergies.

I used my altered birth certificate one more time, in 1946. I needed it to prove that I was 21 years old in order to marry. My enormous mother attended the wedding but did not rat on me this time. If I ever alter my birth certificate again, it will be to make me younger, not older.

David Showalter died on 30 March 2002, shortly after completing his story for this book. He had been a retired building contractor, a member of AMVETS, the American Legion, and in both the Sons of the Union Veterans and Sons of the Confederate Veterans organizations. Both David and Elizabeth, his wife of 56 years, were deeply involved in volunteer activities. They had four children and one grandchild who is in the Army Signal Corps.

Howard E. Ketcham

Age 15 – United States Navy

I was born in Boonville, Indiana, on 28 July 1928. When I was 14 years old, I was hopping freight trains and traveling all over the country. When I told my mother that I wanted to enlist in the Seabees, she said, "Well, son, at

> *I was in the South Pacific by the time I was 15½years old.*

least I will know where you are." So during the second week of July 1943, I went to Evansville, Indiana, to join the Seabees. The recruiter ask me how old I was and I told him that I was 16, but that I would be 17 on 28 July. He told me to come back with written permission when I was 17.

On 28 July 1943, my 15th birthday, I returned to the recruiting office with a phony permission form and was sworn into the Seabees. I went to boot camp at Camp Perry, Virginia, then to advanced training at Gulfport, Mississippi. After the advanced training, we boarded a troopship, the *Azalea City*, at Gulfport in December 1943.

We went through the Panama Canal and on into the Pacific with just our troopship and three destroyer-escorts. About halfway to New Hebrides, the seas became very heavy, all troops were ordered below, and all hatches were secured. We soon found out why. We were in a very bad typhoon. Fuel fumes were very strong in the hold. As we lay on our bunks, we thought that we were going to capsize. The next morning we were dead in the water. There was some damage above deck.

I was in the South Pacific by the time I was 15½ years old. We landed in the Russell Islands, then Guadalcanal, then the Admiralty Islands, and finally, back to Guadalcanal. On Guadalcanal, a small group of us were attached to the 6th Marine Division. Shortly after that, we joined with a huge convoy at Ulithi Island and sailed for Okinawa.

We landed on Okinawa at dawn on Easter Sunday, 1 April 1945, with the 6th Marine Division. I was 16 years and 8 months old. Okinawa was the last island I was on. I spent a total of 23 months overseas. I was discharged on 16 March 1946.

I often thought that I was only one of a very few who were underage in World War II, but I now know that there were many of us in that category. During my time in the service, I never told anyone my real age. I kept the secret until later in life when I retired after 44½ years on the railroad. I just received my high school diploma from the state of Florida, which is honoring all World War II vets who dropped out of high school and went to war.

Howard Ketcham went to work for the railroad as a locomotive fireman after his discharge from the Navy. This time he was paid to ride the trains. When he retired from the railroad, he had to change to his true age on the insurance policies and the Railroad Retirement Board. Howard and his wife June live in Fenwick, Ontario, Canada.

John W. King

Age 14 – Alabama State Guard
Age 15 – United States Coast Guard

I was born in Birmingham, Alabama, on 17 May 1928. In January 1943, at the age of 14, I joined the Alabama State Guard. I don't remember what lies I told to satisfy the age limit. It was more important for the State Guard to recruit than to worry about age.

> *It was not unusual to find either a full orchestra, or at least a string quartet, playing during our meal.*

We met at the Birmingham Armory during the evenings and all day on Saturdays. This worked out fine for me because I was enrolled in my first year of high school and was taking ROTC. In the summer of 1943, I attended summer camp with the State Guard at a training camp on Dauphin Island, Alabama. During training, I qualified on the rifle range with the old Springfield 1903 and the 45-caliber sub-machine gun.

My family life was quite hectic. My mother was in the final stages of cancer and my father was an alcoholic. I was determined to get into the service to get away from home. My best friend had just joined the Coast Guard at the age of 15. I convinced my mother that the Coast Guard was the same as the Sea Scouts, and she agreed that I should join. I went to the recruiter and got an application and filled it out, stating that my age was 17. I signed my mother's name and notarized the application with a notary seal that I had found in a junkyard.

On 6 August 1943, I took the train to St. Augustine, Florida, to attend boot camp. When the train arrived, I learned that there were six of us recruits aboard. We were met by a petty officer and loaded on a horse-drawn tourist wagon for the ride to the Coast Guard training facility. The wagon stopped in front of the most beautiful hotel I had ever seen, the Ponce de Leon Hotel, which had been built by the millionaire industrialist Henry Flagler as a winter home for rich people from the north. Much to my surprise, we were off-loaded and led into the hotel.

It was at the Ponce de Leon that we were billeted and we received our basic training. Each morning we would march from the hotel to the Castillo de San Marcos, a fort that was built in 1695. Then we would be divided into groups and assigned to separate rooms in the fort for individual subject training. In the evening, we returned to the hotel where we would be led into the main dining room for dinner. It was not unusual to find either a full orchestra, or at least a string quartet, playing during our meal.

During my three months of boot camp, I was on the boxing team. At the completion of boot camp, I was promoted to seaman second class and transferred to Sheepshead Bay, New York, where I continued to box. Only now my training was under the supervision of Jack Dempsey, the former world champion.

I attended signalman school at Sheepshead Bay, and upon graduation, I was promoted to signalman 3rd class. I believe I was the youngest petty officer in the Coast Guard at that time.

My first duty station after signal school was the Coast Guard Station, Key West, Florida. I was assigned to the signal tower where we controlled the arrival and docking of all vessels. I also served on missions with the antisubmarine fleet as a signalman aboard the cutter CGC83492.

In the summer of 1944, I was transferred to New Orleans, Louisiana, for duty aboard the Coast Guard cutter Blanco-W125. The Blanco was the largest sailboat on active duty in the U. S. Navy during World War II. Our mission was to sail from New Orleans, through the Gulf of Mexico into the Atlantic, on submarine patrol. We were able to sail without engine noise and stay on station for long periods of time.

In civilian life, the Blanco belonged to the president of Pabst Blue Ribbon Beer. She was a typical luxury yacht. I was assigned my own stateroom. As the only signalman aboard, one of my duties was to change the signal identification lights on the main mast, which was about 100 feet in the air. To me, this was one of my favorite duties, to climb the mast to the crow's nest and set the lights. I was also assigned as a gunner on the 3.5-inch gun. We did make contact with enemy subs, and when we did, we called the Air Force to bomb them.

When the war was over, the *Blanco* was decommissioned in Charleston, South Carolina. My total Coast Guard service from 1943 to 1946 was 2 years, 7 months and 18 days.

After being discharged, I returned to Birmingham and lived with my sister for a short time. While there, I studied for and completed my GED. The next two years I spent attending colleges in Alabama and Mississippi. My college results were less than desirable, so I enlisted in the Army.

Upon completion of Army basic training, I was promoted to corporal and assigned as a physical-training instructor and as NCOIC of a gym for Combat Command A, Fort Knox, Kentucky. One of my duties was to supervise the training of the boxing program for basic trainees. Another duty was to operate the gym, which included boxing instruction and various games such as shuffleboard, table tennis, and billiards. I made my spending money playing pool. My immediate boss was Master Sergeant McAfee. One of the assignments he gave me was to paint the pool tables pink. After several weekly inspections, he confronted me about the paint job. I told him I had no intentions of painting the tables pink, and I asked for a 10-day leave. I got the leave, and while I was gone, he had me transferred to Japan.

In Japan, I was stationed at Camp Zama, which was known as the West Point of Japan. There I attended Japanese language school. During this period I was promoted to sergeant first class (E-6). My unit, the 14th Regiment of the 24th Infantry Division, was transferred to Korea as the 14th Regiment of the 25th Infantry Division. At this time, I was the platoon sergeant of the Counterfire Platoon. My unit participated in the withdrawal from North Korea and the stabilization along the DMZ. I led the platoon through the battles for Kumwah Valley, Hill 1052, and Heartbreak Ridge. I was given a battlefield commission as a second lieutenant in 1951.

As an infantry officer, I had many interesting assignments. I taught at the Infantry School at Fort Benning, Georgia, served as a platoon leader and company commander with the 20th Infantry in Panama, and was selected to attend the Armor Advanced Course at Fort Knox, Kentucky. While at Fort Knox, I ran across Sergeant Major

McAfee and thanked him for having had me transferred to Japan back in 1949. Of course, he greeted me as, "Captain, sir!"

In 1961, after graduating from the Advanced Armor Course, I was reassigned to Fort Benning as a tactics instructor and live-fire demonstration presenter. In 1963, I was selected to attend the Air University at Maxwell AFB, Alabama. This was a very interesting year. It gave me an opportunity to understand and appreciate the role the Air Force plays in warfare.

From Maxwell AFB, I was transferred to Fort Bragg, North Carolina, for military advisory training and attendance at the Vietnamese Language School, and then was assigned to Vietnam where I became Chief of the Popular Forces Motivation Indoctrination Program. My group of three split "A" Special Forces teams were assigned throughout Vietnam, training the Popular Forces in tactics and weapons, equipping them and advising during many battles. Upon completion of my tour I was assigned to the Pentagon.

My first two years at the Pentagon were spent as a program and budget officer and as a congressional-affairs officer for the Chief of Army Research and Development. I participated in the preparation of the Army R&D budget and assisted in presenting the budget to the U. S. House of Representatives and the U. S. Senate. After two years, I was reassigned to the staff of the Chairman of the Joint Chiefs of Staff. I was the senior emergency-action officer at the National Military Command Center. Specifically, my job was to facilitate the passing of information in matters of extreme emergency between the Chairman of the Joint Chiefs, the President of the United States, and the Commanders in Chief throughout the world. One of my specific duties was to alert the Chairman and the President of any nuclear missile launches, including the potential targets, from information received from the North American Air Defense (NORAD) at Cheyenne Mountain, Colorado. I was in daily contact with the office of the President, Secretary Henry Kissinger, and General Al Haig. It was important that I be able to contact the President immediately.

I retired as a lieutenant colonel on 31 January 1971, 27 years after my underage enlistment in the Coast Guard. During my service, I was able to acquire a B.S. in industrial management with an area of concentration in engineering from Samford University, Birmingham, Alabama, a master's degree in business administration, and a doctorate in business administration from George Washington University, Washington, D.C. My only comment here is that we who joined underage were aiming for greater things.

John King was awarded the Bronze Star, the Air Medal, the Joint Services Commendation Medal, the Army Commendation Medal with two oak leaf clusters, the Vietnamese Cross of Gallantry with silver star, the Combat Infantryman's Badge with star (Korea and Vietnam), and a number of other service medals. After retiring from the Army, he worked as a realtor and progressed to opening his own building and real-estate company, KY Homes, building single-family homes. Later, he joined National Homes Manufacturing Company, retiring from that company in 1982. During the time he was in the home-building industry, he was instrumental in the construction of some 3,000 homes. He then served as a senior vice president for builders' services at 1st Western Mortgage, a national mortgage banking company. During his tenure, he established offices in Washington, D.C., Maryland, Virginia, and Florida. He purchased the East Coast offices from 1st Western and renamed the company Network 1 Inc. Ultimately, he sold the company and retired in 1990. John and his wife Marti have a combined family of six sons, one daughter, and two grandchildren. They live in Ormond Beach, Florida.

Gerald F. Barlow
Age 15 – United States Navy

It was many years ago, yet it seems like only yesterday that a boy of 15 was turned into a man almost overnight. I ran away from Saint John's Orphanage in Brooklyn, New York, and used my older brother Harold's birth certificate

> I was being treated like a man, not a 15-year-old boy!

to join the Navy. Looking back, I now know that this was the best thing I could have done. I was just a smart-ass kid from Brooklyn, with no formal education, no trade, and no place to live. My life didn't begin the day I was born, which was 30 March 1928; it began on 25 August 1943, the day I joined the Navy.

I was sent to boot camp at the Great Lakes Naval Training Center, Illinois. When some of the men were complaining about how hard it was, I was thanking God each and every day, thanking Him for a wonderful future that I didn't think I would have had. No longer did I have to worry about how I was going to eat and where I was going

to sleep. No longer would I be by myself, and no more lonely days and nights. I knew from the start that I was going to get through boot camp, no matter how hard it was. No one could possibly know how proud and happy I was. I was being treated like a man, not a 15-year-old boy!

After boot camp, I was sent to Boston, Massachusetts, to await the commissioning of the carrier, USS *Wasp* (CV-18). The commissioning took place in the South Boston Dry Dock on 24 November 1943. While aboard ship, I worked in many different departments, from the flight deck working with planes, to the gunnery department, to the mess hall and galley. I wanted to learn as much as I could about the Navy and the ship I was on. The most wonderful thing about this was that I had *friends*! I had not had friends in a very long time.

There were about 3,000 men and 100 aircraft aboard the *Wasp*. Just knowing that I was part of this team gave me a wonderful feeling of pride and satisfaction that is almost impossible to describe. During the time I was aboard this ship, we were involved in many of the major battles that took place in the South Pacific. Our ship and crew received the Navy Unit Commendation for action against the enemy Japanese forces from May 1944 until August 1945.

On 19 March 1945, off the coast of Kyushu, Japan, a Japanese plane dropped a bomb on our ship. We lost over 100 men during this engagement. I couldn't believe what happened next. The captain sent for me, and for the life of me, I couldn't figure out why. He couldn't possibly know how old I was. How could he? No one else knew. How wrong I was! The captain informed me that he had received notice from the Navy Department that I was underage and he was to put me off the ship at the first port of entry in the United States to await an underage discharge. My whole world began falling apart.

I had been through too much to let anyone send me back to St. John's Orphanage. Since I had nothing to lose, I asked the captain for permission to speak. When he gave me permission, I said, "Captain, when general quarters was sounded, I went to my 20mm gun station and fought alongside of everyone else, and you didn't hear me say that I was only 15 years old. I stayed on that gun for many hours and ate Spam sandwiches like everyone else. I could have been one of the men who were killed. I did everything that was asked of me and did it well. There were some men who were in fights, but I wasn't one of them. Please, look at my record, tell me what I did wrong aboard your ship. I beg you, please don't take my life away. I fought for you, and if I am worth saving, fight for me."

After my discourse, the captain agreed to send a dispatch to the Navy Department requesting that I be allowed to remain in the Navy. The Navy agreed, and I was sworn in under my correct name. When I went back to my department, I told everyone, "Don't call me Harold or Hank anymore. From now on, just call me Jerry."

Boy, did I have a lot of explaining to do! They couldn't believe the story I was telling them. Then the questions started: What did you do during the six months prior to joining the Navy? Why did you leave the orphanage? Lots of questions and not enough answers.

I was on the *Wasp* from 24 November 1943 until 5 January 1946, then I was transferred to another carrier, the USS *Philippine Sea.* In January 1947, we took Admiral Richard E. Byrd to the South Pole. At that time we were part of Task Force 68, "Operation High Jump." I couldn't believe that this was happening to me. I read about Admiral Byrd in my history book. Never did I dream that by the time I was 18 years old I would have been in a world war and was now with Admiral Byrd on the way to the South Pole.

I was aboard the *Philippine Sea* from 11 May 1946 until 5 January 1948. Later, I served on other ships, including the carrier, USS *Leyte.* While aboard the *Leyte*, I took a test for a commissioned officer. I passed, was promoted to chief warrant officer, and sent to supply-corps school in Athens, Georgia. I also attended an instructor training school and then became an instructor at the Great Lakes Naval Training Center, back where I started.

In 1964, at the age of 35, I retired from the U. S. Navy as one of the youngest commissioned officers to do so. After a rough beginning, I am proud of the way my life turned out.

While in the Navy, I took the GED and completed two years of college. However, no school could have given me a better education than the one I received from the many different men I came in contact with. I owe the men on my first ship, the USS *Wasp*, more than they will ever know, and I thank them for giving me the life that I now have. They were my family, and they taught me well. The only regret I have is not being able to say thanks to my friends who were killed in the bombings of the *Wasp*. Somehow, I think they know.

Jerry Barlow earned eight battle stars on his Asia-Pacific theater ribbon, the Combat Action Ribbon, and a number of other service medals. After he retired from the Navy, he went to work for the Harry M. Stevens Corporation, a sports caterer, and retired from that position in 1991. Jerry and Beverly, his wife of 54 years, have six children, eleven grandchildren, and five great-grandchildren. They live in Toms River, New Jersey.

Charles W. Squires

Age 16 – United States Navy

I was born in Aberdeen, Washington, on 26 February 1927. We moved to Monroe, Oregon, sometime in 1929 and I started school there. My father was a truck driver but had to quit the

> *I spent the next seven months in terror that someone would find out that I was only 16.*

trucking business and go to work for the railroad. We moved to Crescent Lake, Oregon, then back to Springfield, Oregon, where we lived until 1940. My father died that year.

During my sophomore year in high school, I went on my own and supported myself until I joined the Navy. A good friend of mine got his draft notice, so I drove him to Portland, Oregon, where we visited the Navy recruiting office. The chief handed us an enlistment blank and I filled it out, putting my age as 17. The chief said that I was not old enough to join without my mother's signature. I went home and my mother said, "By golly, I think I'll sign it. At least I will know where you are."

That night I drove back to Portland, was sworn into the Navy on 21 September 1943, and was off to boot camp at Farragut, Idaho. I spent the next seven months in terror that someone would find out that I was only 16. After boot leave, I was picked for gunnery school at Lake Union, Seattle, Washington.

After completing gunnery school, I was sent to Astoria, Oregon, where I served on a precommissioning detail. Our job was to clean all the guns and spare parts and bore-sight the 5-inch guns on the stern of several CVEs (baby aircraft carriers) that were being readied for commissioning. I decided that was not exciting enough for me, so I put in for destroyer school. In a few weeks, I was sent to Bremerton, Washington, and put on a troopship going to San Francisco. I spent about four months in destroyer school on Treasure Island, then was assigned to the USS

Shields, a brand-new destroyer being commissioned in a shipyard in Bremerton, Washington.

On 6 May 1945, the *Shields* left for the Western Pacific. We stopped at Pearl Harbor, then escorted some ships to Ulithi. We went to Leyte in the Philippines on 10 June 1945. A week later we were underway for Brunei Bay, Borneo, where we reported for duty on 17 June.

On 26 and 27 June, the *Shields* was on station in Brunei Bay and shelled entrenched Japanese forces, in support of Australian assault troops. On 2 July, we escorted ships back to Leyte Gulf. We went into dry dock at Leyte, then departed for Subic Bay to rejoin the 7th Fleet. On 24 July we returned to Brunei Bay in the company of the USS *Metcalf* and the HMS *Bonaventure*.

On our return to the Philippines, the *Shields* and the *Metcalf* were diverted to pick up survivors of the oiler *Chestatee*, which had hit a mine in the Balabac Straits. After debarking these men at Puerto Princesa, Palawan Island, we proceeded to join the fleet in Manila Bay on 29 July.

In company with nine other destroyers and six cruisers, the *Shields* conducted maneuvers from 31 July to 2 August, then returned to Subic Bay. Four days later we were assigned to the Philippine sea frontier and were anchored on station when we received the news of the Japanese surrender.

After the war was over, we sailed for Okinawa and encountered a typhoon en route. We arrived at Okinawa on 2 September, and five days later we joined up with various units of Task Force 78 in the Yellow Sea and went to Jinsen, Korea. We then patrolled the north China coast, stopping at the ports of Tsingtao, Chefoo, Weihawi, Port Arthur, and eventually, Shanghai. The Communists and Nationalists were watching each other, but they were really not fighting at that time.

I had enough points for discharge, so I was transferred to another destroyer, the USS *Herndon* (DD-683). There was only one other signalman aboard the ship, so he and I stood four-on and four-off watches during the trip back to San Diego. I was very glad to get there. I was offered a promotion to signalman second class if I would stay aboard the *Herndon* while it sailed to the East Coast. I asked the captain if I had a choice, and he said I did. I told him that I would like to go home. I went aboard an APA and sailed to Bremerton, Washington, where I was released from active duty on 8 January 1946. I stayed in the reserves.

I re-enlisted in the regular Navy in October 1950. I was assigned to the USS *Preston,* which was being recommissioned at Long Beach, California. After a shakedown cruise, we sailed for the East Coast through the Panama Canal. We docked at Newport, Rhode Island, then they sent us for more underway training. We finished that, and I was transferred back to the West Coast and went aboard the USS *Brinkley Bass* (DD-887). We made two trips to Korea. We spent some time with the fleet and patrolled Tin Can Alley in Wonsan Harbor. We managed to get shot at a couple of times, but they evidently had the wrong gun crew, because we weren't hit.

We went back to the States and I was transferred to electronics school. I put in a year at that, but decided to go back to the fleet. I liked signalman-quartermaster much better than electronics.

I was assigned to the USS *Mahoning County* (LST-914). We made a resupply run to the Arctic for the DEW (Distant Early Warning) line. That was an interesting trip. After that I went aboard the USS *Orange County* (LST-1068). That is where I banged my leg up and ended up in a hospital.

I served aboard the USS *Noble* (APA-218), the USS *Summit County* (LST-1146), and the USS *Plumas County* (LST-1083). While I was aboard the *Plumas County*, we went to the Marshall Islands with a lead-lined room on our tank deck. We had a team of scientists aboard from a New York university. They monitored all the natives and all the flora and fauna for radioactivity.

I got my first and only tour of shore duty at the Naval Reserve Training Center at Fort Douglas, Utah. I met and married my wife there. We went to Guam where I spent two years at the Air Navigation Office.

Then it was back to sea duty aboard the USS *Alvin Cockrell* (DE-366). It was a reserve training ship stationed at Alameda, California. That was interesting duty. From the *Cockrell*, I went to the seagoing tug, USS *Hitchiti* (ATF-103). I tell you she was the busiest tug in the Pacific. During the first 18 months I was aboard, we were underway 15 months. It was good duty. She was an excellent ship with a good skipper and a good crew. We went to Vietnam and salvaged a merchant ship that had run aground. It took an entire squadron of us about 10 days to salvage the ship, but we did it. We made a couple of trips to DaNang and one to the Mekong River.

Finally, after 23 years in the Navy, I retired as a chief quartermaster in April 1970.

Chuck Squires returned to the Pacific Northwest and worked for several lumber companies as a logging-truck driver. Chuck and Loretta have a combined family of four children, seven grandchildren and six great-grandchildren. They live in Nampa, Idaho.

✓ *INCIDENTally* — *Snakes alive!* – In Vietnam in 1963, the U. S. Army had no realistic idea of how to protect an outpost. We were in the north, just south of Hue, when the war began to get serious. Our military geniuses decided that digging trenches around our tented compound was the way to go. When (or if) we were attacked, everyone could run outside, jump down into the trenches (a la World War I) and be protected. Great idea – except for one thing. No one in America had any understanding of the fauna that lives in Vietnam. We dug the trenches; the snakes, including cobras, immediately took up residence. They loved it down there in the dark, wet, dirt. When a GI would jump in on top of them (and quickly jump out) they would become very excited! Well, we weren't rocket scientists, as the saying goes, but it didn't take us long to learn that trenches may have worked in France in 1917, but not in Vietnam at any time. – *Alton P. Gorbett.*

Guillermo H. Tovar

Age 15 – United States Marine Corps

I was once asked if my first name was Italian and my last name was Russian. Actually, both of my names are Mexican, although I have joked over the years that if we lost the Cold War, I might change

> We all agreed that we would walk in like Marines, with our heads held high.

my name to Tovarish. I was born in Los Angeles, California, on 10 May 1928, and raised in Jackson, California, where my father was a gold miner.

I joined the Marines at age 15 on 28 September 1943. After boot camp in San Diego, I was stationed at Attu, in the Aleutian Islands, and stayed there until the end of November 1944. After a 30-day furlough, I was assigned to the Marine Barracks, Bremerton, Washington, where it was discovered that I was only 16 years old. I was almost 17, so the commanding officer recommended retention for me. I was then sent to Mare Island, California, for sea duty aboard the USS *Haan*, an APA.

The bomb had been dropped on Hiroshima and Nagasaki and the war was coming to a close. While aboard the USS *Haan*, I went to the Marshall Islands, the Marianas, and the Philippines. We transported one of the first groups of Philippine Scouts from Manila to Cebu and Tacloban for mopping-up operations. We also transported Army troops to Nagasaki and Nagoya, Japan.

I was discharged the first time on 30 April 1946 with 33 months' service, ten days before my 18th birthday. I re-enlisted on 6 November 1946 and was assigned to the Marine Barracks, Moffett Field, California. I was again assigned sea duty, this time aboard the USS *Mann* (APA-112). My next assignment was to the Marine Barracks, Pearl Harbor,

Hawaii. While I was there, Colonel Chesty Puller promoted me to sergeant. It was one of the proudest moments of my life.

Soon after being promoted, I was assigned to a Military Police Company, 1st Marine Division, and it wasn't long before the Korean War started. I spent the first two days after the Inchon landing on Wolmi-do Island at a traffic-control point, bringing in the 11th Marines (artillery). We also guarded the bridges between Inchon and Seoul, guarded prisoners of war on the Han River, and patrolled in jeeps in and around liberated towns and villages.

By the later part of November 1950, we were on our way to the Chosin Reservoir, fighting our way through many Chinese divisions. I was part of Task Force Drysdale that was given the task of moving the 11 miles from Koto-ri to reinforce the troops at Hagaru. We were in firefights all the way. This area would later be known as Hell Fire Valley.

Late in the afternoon of 29 November we came under fire. I jumped off a truck and made it to a ditch by the side of the road. I pulled the pin of a grenade and started to throw it just as I was hit by a .45-caliber slug. It went through my left earlobe and into my head just behind my left ear and came to rest at the base of my skull just above my neck. I carried the slug for a week and a half until it was removed at the U. S. Naval Hospital at Yokuska, Japan. I never found the grenade. Apparently the lever was frozen and did not allow the striker to hit the primer.

A corpsman gave me a shot of morphine and he and several others put me under a truck. For the next few hours some of the fiercest fighting that took place in Hell Fire Valley was occurring, and I was under this stupid truck feeling no pain. I thought that I was in Heaven – or going there.

At about 0100 the morphine had worn off and I managed to get back on the line. Later, at about 0430, four men tried to make it back to Koto-ri for help. The Chinese stopped their jeep about 300 yards down the road. They sent one of the four back to our lines to advise the senior officer to surrender his troops. Major McLaughlin kept asking for a volunteer who spoke Chinese to go meet with them. I finally volunteered, although I didn't speak Chinese. I thought that they might have an interpreter.

Major McLaughlin told me to tell the Chinese to surrender to him
and that they would be well taken care of. He said, "I know they are
going to laugh at you, but try to sell them the goods. Tell them we will
feed them well and we will treat them good."

I took my interpreter with me and walked down the road toward
Koto-ri. After walking about 100 to 150 yards, a group of Chinese
officers met us. They had a Korean-Chinese interpreter, and I had a
Korean-English interpreter. When I told the Chinese what Major
McLaughlin had asked me to tell them, their reply was for me to go
back and advise the major that they would give him 10 minutes to
surrender. I went back and told the major this. He told me to go back
and tell the Chinese that he would surrender at 0630 in the morning.
He said to tell them that he needed that time to take care of his
wounded. Actually, the major wanted to stall until morning in hopes
of getting air support. I relayed the message that the major would
surrender at 0630 to the Chinese. Their response was that we had five
minutes to surrender. The major came to talk with the Chinese, and
after a few minutes, he handed over his pistol. We had no choice; we
were surrounded by more than three regiments of Chinese.

The Chinese took a group of us to a farmhouse where we were kept
under guard. On the second day we were told that all the men who
were able to walk would be leaving for Manchuria. Since I had a head
wound and could walk, I got in ranks with the others. My interpreter,
who had been with me since Inchon, came to me and said, "Sgt. Tovar,
if you go with them you'll never come back." He advised me to pretend
that I was sick from my wound. I suddenly appeared very sick and
staggered back to the farmhouse and fell to the floor until well after
the Chinese had taken away our troops and my interpreter. I would
never see him again.

On the fifth day, with only the severely wounded remaining, we
found that the Chinese had left. Three of us, Chief Warrant Officer
Meek, Pfc. O'Brien, and I, decided to try to reach Koto-ri. On the way
I learned what hell really was.

As we approached the road, we stopped to decide which way we
should go. While we were trying to decide, we looked behind us and
discovered that we were over a foxhole in which two Chinese soldiers
were sleeping. We moved away and headed down the left side of the
road toward Koto-ri. All of a sudden we saw a Chinese soldier coming

out of a small hut. I think he had come outside to urinate. He looked at us and we looked at him, but none of us had weapons. While we were deciding what to do, a flight of four Marine Corsairs made the decision for us. They thought we were Chinese and started to strike us. The first plane shot a rocket that didn't explode, but subsequent rockets did. I caught some shrapnel in my back, but it didn't penetrate very deep.

We took off our parkas and waved them at the planes, hoping that they would realize that we were not the enemy. It didn't do any good. The second plane dropped napalm on us. I looked up and saw what appeared to be a large football coming down end-over-end. I just knew that this was going to be *it* for us. How ironic, I thought, to have come this far and to be killed by mistake by your own planes – and Marine planes at that! We all jumped into the same hole, the napalm exploded, we felt the heat, but the flames didn't reach us. The flight made five or six passes at us.

The Chinese in the area now knew where we were because of the attention the aircraft had given us. A Chinese patrol started yelling and firing at us, but they were distracted by another patrol that was heading north. We made it back to Koto-ri just before dark. We all agreed that we would walk in like Marines, with our heads held high. It had taken us seven hours to travel six miles.

Before leaving Koto-ri, Meek, O'Brien, and I made sure the regimental intelligence unit knew that there were more American troops in the farmhouse where we had been held captive. We wanted to get the word to Colonel Puller so that he could notify the Air Wing, because they were shooting rockets and strafing our men in the farmhouse. We all volunteered to take a rescue mission back to the farmhouse, but we were informed that the 5th or the 7th Marines would pick them up on their way back from Hagaru-ri.

We were flown out of Koto-ri and hospitalized near Hungnam. Later we were transferred to the Yokuska Naval Hospital, Japan, where the bullet was removed from my skull.

I returned from Korea in January 1951 and was assigned escort duty, escorting Korean War dead to their final resting place. Three years later, I did a tour of duty with the 3rd Marine Division in Japan. My last 11½ years in the Corps was with the Criminal Investigations

Division at Camp Pendleton and El Toro, both in California. I retired from the Marine Corps as a gunnery sergeant on 31October 1963.

Gil Tovar was awarded the Purple Heart, two Presidential Unit Citations, and a number of other service medals. After his retirement from the Corps, Gil worked for the San Mateo County District Attorney's office and retired as a senior investigator, after 24½ years of service. He has been employed as a deputy U. S. Marshal serving as a court security officer in San Francisco for the past six years. Gil and his wife Nancy have a son and a daughter. Gil has two sons, a daughter, and three grandchildren from a previous marriage. Gil and Nancy reside in San Carlos, California.

✓ INCIDENTally — Roll your own! – When it rained on Guadalcanal, it was so heavy that you could take a shower in it. Many of us would strip down and do just that.

The island's natives loved American cigarettes and were willing to work to get them. They would bring the troops fresh bananas and build covers from the rain for them. I asked a native to build me one, but I didn't have any ready-made cigarettes. When he finished I gave him a bag of Bull Durham and some cigarette papers and began to explain how to do it. He grabbed the bag from my hand, threw it to the ground, stomped on it, and walked off steaming. I really can't blame him, but it was still good for a laugh. – *Jack T. Venables.*

Donald C. Peltz
Age 16 – United States Navy

My family moved from Edholm, Nebraska, where I was born on 28 June 1927, to Woodburn, Oregon, when I was about 8 years old. I have always considered Oregon as my home state.

> The messages were coming in at 30 words per minute, but I could only copy 20.

In July 1943, a friend of mine and I went to the Navy recruiting office in Salem, Oregon. I had turned 16 just a few days before, my birth date being 28 June 1927. The recruiter informed us that we had to have the enlistment papers signed by our parents and returned to them along with our birth certificates. I put my birth year as 1926 on the papers and talked to my parents about enlisting. I don't think they really understood that I had to be 17 to enlist. My older brother was already in the Navy, and they just glanced at the papers and asked me, "Do you really want to go?" I said, "Yes," and they signed. But I still didn't know how to get around the age problem because my birth certificate indicated that I was born in 1927. I decided to wait and see what developed.

I called the recruiting office and told them that I had the papers signed and I was ready to go. I was told that they would be in touch with me. High school started on the first of September, so I enrolled for my senior year. Within a week or so, I received a letter from the Navy stating that a bus would be in Woodburn to pick me up on 20 September 1943, and I would stay overnight in Portland, Oregon. The bus picked me up, we went to Portland, and no one asked for my birth certificate. The next morning we boarded a train for Spokane, Washington. From there we went by military bus to Farragut, Idaho. I was sworn into the Navy on 29 September 1943.

After eight weeks of boot camp at Camp Benton, one of eight training camps at the Farragut Naval Training Center, I was given the choice of attending electrician's school or radio school. I chose radio school, hoping to be sent to Madison, Wisconsin, or San Diego, California, but when they called my name, I was told to prepare for a 15-minute ride – I would be attending radio school at Farragut.

The radio-school course was mainly to learn Morse code. I could copy about 12 words a minute, but seemed to be stuck at that speed. I worked on it day and night and finally brought my speed up to 16 words per minute and graduated from the school as a radioman third class.

I was assigned to a new escort aircraft carrier that was at Bremerton, Washington. I went from Farragut to Seattle by train and went aboard the USS *Attu* (CVE-102). The *Attu* was a brand new ship. We put her into commission and took her on a shakedown cruise in the Straits of Juan de Fuca. After 10 days of training, we went to the Alameda Naval Air Station near San Francisco, then on to North Island, San Diego, California, where we loaded the flight deck with wrecked airplanes. While people were saving aluminum at home for the war effort, we took those wrecked planes and dumped them into the ocean when we were two days out from San Diego.

We did not have a full radio crew, so we worked four hours on, then four hours off. The messages were coming in at 30 words per minute, but I could only copy 20. I told the chief radioman that I couldn't copy that fast. He said, "You are on duty, so do the best you can." I would sit there and get maybe one letter out of five. I would sit there for four hours, then go to bed for four hours. I would copy more code in my sleep than I would on duty. After about three days, I finally got it and was able to copy over 30 words per minute.

We approached Pearl Harbor in late July 1944. Our flight squadron flew out to meet us and made several practice landings and takeoffs. For several days we held gunnery practice, firing at targets towed behind aircraft. While in San Diego, we had picked up a cat as a mascot. The first time the antiaircraft guns were fired, the cat ran down the flight deck and jumped off the end, and was never seen again.

We docked at Pearl Harbor and picked up the rest of the crew, supplies, and ammunition. We went to Guadalcanal where our pilots and planes were transferred to Henderson Field. We went to New Guinea and anchored offshore for a couple of days. Many natives rowed out in their small outriggers to trade seashells for American money. They wanted paper money, and no matter if you gave them a $1 bill or a $10 bill, they would never give you change.

We went to Espiritu Santo in the New Hebrides and picked up elements of the 4th Marine Division to take them back to the States. We were at sea for a couple of days when we ran into a terrific typhoon. The swells must have been 20 to 30 feet high, and the winds over 100 miles per hour. The bow of the ship would go up, and then it would shake and shudder all the way down. During the first night of the typhoon, the bow of the ship went head-on into one of the swells, and the flight deck was folded back like a sardine can.

Since we were in a war zone, we had to maintain radio silence and sail in a zigzag pattern to help avoid Japanese submarines. We were on submarine alert for a few hours, but finally shook him off. We always monitored Tokyo Rose to see what kind of propaganda the Japanese were broadcasting. That night, to our surprise, she announced that one of the Japanese submarines had sunk the USS *Attu* (CVE-102) off the Marshall Islands. This report was picked up at Pearl Harbor and also in the States. When we approached Pearl Harbor and radioed in for docking instructions, they were really surprised to hear from us because they assumed that we had been sunk.

We arrived in San Diego on 6 January 1945. I was transferred to Camp Pendleton for reassignment, but was given a 30-day leave first. My folks knew that I was O.K. but many friends still thought we were all lost at sea. After my leave, I reported to Camp Pendleton and was immediately transferred to San Francisco where I boarded the USS *Benson* (AP-120) in March 1945, and headed for the Philippines. While on our way, it was announced that President Roosevelt had died on 12 April 1945, and Harry Truman was now president. A very sober calm came over the entire ship. Everyone really felt a great loss.

We landed at Guiuan, Samar, in the Philippines. We handled the radio communications for most of the southern part of the Philippines. I made a good friend by radio with an operator in Tacloban. Eventually, we both ended up on the USS *Cocopa*. I was on radio watch on 26 July 1945 when the heavy cruiser, USS *Indianapolis*, sailing unescorted toward Leyte, was sunk by a lone Japanese submarine. No one knew that she was sunk until a patrol plane spotted survivors in the water 84 hours later. Of her crew of 1,200 men, only 316 were rescued. There was an intensive investigation about why no distress signal was heard. I was questioned along with other radio operators about whether we had heard anything on the distress channel.

On Monday, 6 August 1945, the B-29 "Enola Gay" dropped the first atomic bomb on Hiroshima, Japan. We heard about the mass destruction it created, but we had no idea what it really meant. Two days later another bomb was dropped, this time on Nagasaki, Japan. We still couldn't comprehend the magnitude of these bombs. Shortly after the bombs were dropped, Japan surrendered. We had expected to be among the forces to invade Japan if the war had continued.

Although the war was over, I still had almost two years to go on my enlistment. I enjoyed being at sea, so I put in for a transfer. I called my friend that I had made by radio and told him that I was being transferred to the USS *Cocopa* (ATF-101). He called back and said he, too, was being transferred to the *Cocopa*. When we boarded the ship, it was the first time we had met in person.

We had a crew of about 21 aboard, and the skipper was really great. We were headed for Finschhafen, New Guinea. The sea was calm and the skipper said that he thought he had seen sharks in the area and wanted to see if he could catch one. He had us get a 4" x 10" x 8' plank to use as a float. We used a 2-foot hook tied to a ¾-inch rope, with about a 30-pound piece of beef as bait. We put this overboard and let out from 600 to 800 feet of rope. Sometime during the night a shark took the bait and was hooked. That morning we were entering the harbor at Finschhafen, so about five of us tried to pull the shark out of the water but had no success.

The skipper docked the ship and borrowed an Army jeep. We rigged up pulleys and tied the rope to the jeep on the dock. After much pulling, we got the shark alongside the ship. We had to use our .45s and carbines to kill it. We rigged up a hoist and pulled the shark up in the air so the skipper could take a picture of it. It was close to noon and many of the Army personnel were out in the bay swimming and relaxing. When they saw us raise that shark in the air, they scattered like flies to the beach. The shark was 18 feet long and was estimated to weigh over 500 pounds.

Later, we went to Eniwetok to tow a ship that had been in the atomic-bomb tests back to Pearl Harbor for further tests. We needed to replenish our water supply, but because of the radiation, Eniwetok did not have any water to spare. Our skipper then asked how their beer supply was. He was told that they had plenty, so we loaded the ship up with beer. We were rationed on water for our trip, but we had no problem getting beer when we were thirsty!

I really liked the Navy and being at sea, but I decided to further my education on the GI Bill. I was discharged from the Navy on 14 June 1947.

Don Peltz attended several technical schools to further his education in electronics. He worked as a radio engineer at radio stations in Frankfort, Kentucky; Yuma, Arizona; and Corvallis, Oregon. He moved to Wenatchee, Washington, and started a company called Central Communications. He retired from the company in 1990. Don and Jessie, his wife of 49 years, have three children, five grandchildren, and three great-grandchildren. They live in Wenatchee, Washington.

Patrick H. Taylor

Age 13 – Missouri State Guard
Age 15 – United States Merchant Marine

My mother died giving birth when I was born. This occurred in Concordia, Kansas, on 26 April 1928. I was taken to St. Joseph, Missouri, four days later and lived there until I joined the Merchant Marine.

> *I was often stopped on the street and asked why I was not in the service.*

At the time of the attack on Pearl Harbor, I was 13 years old and 6-feet tall. My uncle, who was the postmaster of St. Joseph, called me on 10 December and asked me to come and help out at the post office during the Christmas rush. He told me not to mention my age. I worked there during Christmas of 1942 also. This was my first underage government service.

When I enrolled in the Missouri State Guard, I told them I was 18, although I was only 13. I also took ROTC in high school during the 1942-43 school year. Because of my height, I was often stopped on the street and asked why I was not in the service. One guy said to me, "My son is only 5-feet tall and *he* is in the Army!"

I wanted to join the Army and tried and tried to get my maternal grandparents to sign that I was 17, but they said, "No, it's too dangerous." But, in the summer of 1943, when the story came out that men of 16 were need for the Merchant Marine, I asked my grandparents to sign because I had only seven months to go to be 16. They agreed, and a priest at our parish gave me a baptismal certificate with the year left blank, probably to ease his conscience. I filled in the year as 1927.

On 1 October 1943, I was put on a troop train in Kansas City, Missouri, and we headed for Catalina Island, off the Pacific coast near Los Angeles. We picked up more kids and cars along the way. One morning we arrived on the pier at San Pedro, California. We went by boat to Catalina. It was the first time that I was on an ocean. We were all waiting to see who got seasick first!

There wasn't a better place than Catalina Island to take basic training. Because of my vast military experience, I was made a section leader. This meant that I never pulled KP and was always the coxswain in our lifeboat class. I went on to advanced training in the engine room and earned papers as a wiper, fireman, water-tender, and oiler, and I also earned a Coast Guard lifeboat certificate.

I caught my first ship in May 1944 after turning 16 on 26 April. The ship was the SS *Netherlands Victory*. We carried a cargo for an airfield – bombs, machine-gun ammunition, tents, rations, trucks, and pierced-steel planking. After many stops at islands across the Pacific, each time to form new convoys, we were in the invasion of Lingayen Gulf, on the northwest corner of the Philippine Islands, and unloaded there.

On the way back to San Francisco, the port-side hull developed a crack, so every day we checked to see how much the crack had widened. However, we made it back in one piece.

I took a 30-day leave and went to New York to avoid a return to the Pacific. I went aboard a T-2 tanker, the SS *Esso Annapolis*. We went to Port Arthur, Texas, to load aviation gas, then went through the Panama Canal and on to the Pacific where we refueled aircraft carriers at Iwo Jima and later at Okinawa. After the war, we came back to the States through the Panama Canal and docked at New York. I went back to St. Joseph, Missouri, but I got there after all the parades had been held and all the girls kissed.

After being in a world war, St. Joseph was the pits. I was told that if I enlisted in the Army before 31 December 1946, I would qualify for the World War II GI Bill. So I signed up in the Army on 4 October 1946, figuring that if I didn't like it, I could at least go to college.

I went to Fort Knox, Kentucky, for basic training which was supposed to last for 13 weeks. In the middle of the fourth week, four other prior-service trainees and I were interviewed by our company commander. I asked the first sergeant, "What's up?" He said, "You are going to Japan." I asked, "At the end of basic?" He replied, "At the end of the week!"

In Japan, I was assigned to Headquarters Troop, 7th Cavalry Regiment, 1st Cavalry Division, as a truck driver. We carried Japanese munitions to Yokohama for dumping at sea. One day we carried gold bars from a canal to the Bank of Japan.

In the summer of 1948, I applied for OCS (officer candidate school). I was interviewed by a board of seven officers and a chaplain. All except the chaplain wore the Sam Brown belts, boots, and spurs of cavalry officers. When I was asked which branch I wanted, of course I said, "Cavalry, sir!"

At Fort Riley, Kansas, our OCS class started with 250 candidates and graduated 93. I was commissioned a second lieutenant in the field artillery on 27 May 1949. After completing the basic officers course at Fort Sill, Oklahoma, I joined the U. S. Constabulary at Wetzlar, Germany, where I was assigned to the 517th Field Artillery Battalion. From there I went to Munich, Germany, and served as an instructor in tactics at the 7th Army NCO Academy. I returned to the States and was stationed at Fort Carson, Colorado, with the 45th Field Artillery Battalion.

From Colorado, I went to Korea where I commanded Headquarters and Headquarters Battery, I Corps Artillery. When I returned to the States, I served with the 1st Infantry Division Artillery at Fort Riley, Kansas, and then attended the advanced course at Fort Sill, Oklahoma. My next stop was in Germany with the 3rd Infantry Division, where I served as S1 in the 2nd Brigade, and later as the public-affairs officer for the 3rd Division.

Upon returning to the States, I served as S1 at the Army Training Center at Fort Bliss, Texas. Then it was off to Vietnam. I was assigned as assistant G1 of the Americal Division. I extended my tour and was assigned as an escort officer for MACV (Military Assistance Command, Vietnam) protocol.

I retired from the Army at Fort Bliss, Texas, at the rank of major on 30 October 1968, after serving for 22 years. There were a lot of funny stories along the way, and I loved it all. Would I do it all over again? In a minute!

Pat Taylor was awarded the Bronze Star (administrative) and three Army Commendation Medals. After retiring from the Army, he worked for the Bureau of Labor Statistics, Department of Labor, collecting data for the Consumer Price Index. His main avocation is acting. He received a B.A. in theater from the University of Texas, El Paso, in 1976. His first performance was in Tokyo, Japan, in 1947. Since then he has performed in 155 plays and musicals, usually as a comic character. Pat has seven children and seven grandchildren. He lives in Arlington, Texas.

✓ *INCIDENTally* — *Not a good day!* —

It was mid-1944 in Florida, and I was scheduled for a pre-dawn anti-submarine patrol over the Atlantic. I was awakened about 3:00 a.m., wolfed down my breakfast, arrived at the two-seat dive bomber an hour early, did the pre-flight check of the aircraft, put on my seat-pack parachute, climbed in, buckled my seat belt, and promptly went to sleep. Unbeknown to me, the pilot arrived, decided to let me sleep a little longer, and promptly took off. Suddenly, I was rudely awakened by the engine exploding, bursting the oil and fuel lines, and thus catching the plane on fire. Now wide awake, completely disoriented (and frightened), I instinctively tried to bail out. I had stuck my head out into the slip stream, blinding myself with oil on my goggles so I couldn't see. I disconnected the seat belt, partially slid over the side, then remembered that my phone cord was still connected to my cloth helmet that had a chin strap. Knowing that this would break my neck, I struck a couple of slicing blows with my left arm, but it did not disconnect. About that time, I heard a calm, female voice say, "Queen Seven, Queen Seven, what is your aircrewman doing?" I then tore the goggles off, and though I still could not see well, I could see the runway only a few feet away. Panic stricken, I slid back into the plane, and about that time we came to a stop in a bunch of trees on the edge of the Everglades. The engine was on fire, so we both got out and ran away. Out of breath, the pilot asked, "Just what were you doing?" Also out of breath, I answered truthfully, "I was trying to bail out!" He screamed, "Three feet off the deck going a hundred miles an hour?" It was not one of my better days. A month later, I turned 16. – *Frank Durbin III.*

Roland R. Petty

Age 16 – United States Navy

I was born in Belton, Texas, on 30 December 1926. By 1943, there was a lot of pulling and picking going on in Belton, as the weeds and grass grew, the corn turned brown, and the cotton turned white.

> *I soon became of age by signing my mother's name as good as she could, ...*

My brother William, who was a year and a half older than I, got his draft notice. William and I were very close and I couldn't see him going any place without me. So after giving some thought about how I could go with him, I unhitched the team from the wagon and headed for Temple, Texas, to enlist in the Navy, because that's what my brother was drafted into. The recruiter found out that I was too young, but he told me what I had to do in order to enlist.

I soon became of age by signing my mother's name as good as she could, if you know what I mean. So, I was sworn into the Navy on 2 November 1943 and was off to San Antonio, Texas, and then put on a troop train to San Diego, California. I believe we were assigned to Company 511, but I'm not sure. I am sure that the date was 22 November 1943. I had beans for my first meal at 0530 in the morning – and we thought we had had it rough on the farm!

After boot camp, I was sent to the University of Illinois for training at the signal school and brother William drew amphibious training off the California coast. From Illinois, I was sent to Maryland for amphibious training, then to Portland, Oregon, to pick up a new ship. I was assigned to the *LCS(L)-31*. The letters LCS(L) stand for Landing Craft Support (Large). Actually, our ship was a 158-foot gunboat whose purpose was to move in close to shore and lay down a barrage of rockets and gunfire in support of ground troops.

We sailed down the California coast for more training, off to Hawaii for more training, and then to the hot spots which included the Marshall Islands, Saipan, Tinian, then Iwo Jima and Okinawa. I saw the flag go up on Suribachi.

At Okinawa, my ship was assigned to Radar Picket Station #1. We were to take on the Japanese aircraft before they reached Okinawa, and boy, did we ever take them on! We shot down eight aircraft, but three hit us mid-ship. I was on a 50-caliber machine gun at first, then moved to a 20mm antiaircraft gun. Of the twelve men manning guns in that area, eleven were killed in action. I was the only one to survive from that group.

The attack lasted about two hours, but the major portion of the action took place within 18 minutes. Within that short period of time, we were hit by three kamikazes and we shot down six enemy aircraft. Those 18 minutes earned the *LCS(L)-31* a Presidential Unit Citation. When the attack was over, our ship was dead in the water. We were towed to Okinawa by another ship, after transferring our dead and wounded. My brother William was also at Okinawa, aboard the USS *Bell Grove*. He came aboard my ship to see me and to look over the damage.

From Okinawa we went to the Philippines to get ready for the big one – the invasion of Japan. One night all hell broke loose and we found out that the war was over. We went to Japan to clear mines from Wakayama Harbor, then on to Korea to collect all the Japanese small arms and take them out to sea and dump them overboard. We left Korea at Christmas time in 1945 and went to Tsingtao, China. We headed home after a stop there. We had to stop in Hawaii to replace our worn-out engines, then went on to California. I was discharged on 25 February 1946 at Houston, Texas.

I stayed out of the service for three months and 20 days, then enlisted in the U. S. Army and stayed in until 1971. During this time I served five years in Japan, six years in Germany, three years in Hawaii, two years in Vietnam, and at a number of bases in the States. I served with the engineers in Korea, switched to aviation in 1952, and played the helicopter game in Vietnam. I retired as a command sergeant major.

All of my eight brothers served in the military. Three of us served over 20 years and retired. We were represented in the Army, Navy,

Marines, and Air Force. My only sister married her high school sweetheart, and he spent 22 years in the Air Force.

Roland Petty was awarded two Air Medals and earned Master Crewmember Wings in addition to the Presidential Unit Citation he received while he was in the Navy. After he retired from the Army, he went to work as a painting contractor, then into the civil service, and then back to farming. He and his wife Betty have two sons, two daughters, and eleven grandchildren. They live in Fort Worth, Texas.

✓ INCIDENTally — *Mother's Day greetings!* –

I was stationed on the USS *Shangri La* (CV-38) in 1947. During an overhaul, radioteletype equipment had been installed. This was when ships-to-shore radioteletype communications was in its infancy. We tried it while off the coast of California, and it worked quite well. On a goodwill cruise to the Pacific, we stopped at Sydney, Australia. While in Sydney, we decided to test it to see if we could reach the communications station in Hawaii. It worked! This was the first time any ship had ever communicated that far using radioteletype. It worked so well that the admiral gave permission for members of the crew to send Mother's Day greetings while we were tied up in Sydney. This was really a morale builder. This was the first time that a Class E telegram was sent directly from a Navy ship by radioteletype to Western Union in the U. S. and to its final destination. – *Richard L. Bowlby.*

Harley E. Landrum
Age 16 – United States Marine Corps

In 1943, Raymond Weaver, a friend of mine who was 17 years of age, and I caught a train from Chillicothe to Cincinnati, Ohio, where we enlisted in the Marine Corps. We went to the

> My mother had written to President Roosevelt and told him that her son was only 16.

recruiting station where we filled out our applications and were given physicals. I put that I was born in 1926 on my application, although my true birth date was 12 July 1927. We were given papers to take home to have our parents sign, and we were told to send them back to Cincinnati, along with our birth certificates.

We then went to Columbus, Ohio, to pick up our birth certificates. I actually picked up three or four copies. We tried to change the date on mine, but to no avail. I ended up sending in just one copy, along with the papers my mother had signed. In about two weeks, we received orders to report to Cincinnati.

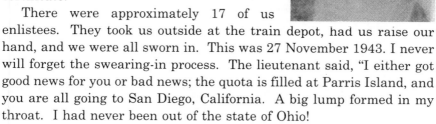

When we arrived at the recruiting station, they went through my papers again with me. I had a folder with all my paperwork in it. I went from desk to desk with my folder. When they came to my birth certificate, they just glanced at it and went on. There must have been five or six people who went through the folder. Apparently, no one had noticed the year on the birth certificate.

There were approximately 17 of us enlistees. They took us outside at the train depot, had us raise our hand, and we were all sworn in. This was 27 November 1943. I never will forget the swearing-in process. The lieutenant said, "I either got good news for you or bad news; the quota is filled at Parris Island, and you are all going to San Diego, California. A big lump formed in my throat. I had never been out of the state of Ohio!

During the last two weeks of boot camp we were at the rifle range at Camp Mathews. It was a Sunday morning and we were cleaning our rifles. Corporal Pratt yelled, "Private Landrum, report to my office!" This was at the front of the barracks. I knocked three raps on the door and he said, "Come in." Of course, I stood at attention until he gave me the order, "At ease." He told me that I was to report to the Marine Corps Base at 0800 Monday morning, and he asked if I knew what this was all about. I said, "Sir, I am only 16 years old." We figured that was what it was all about, and they wanted to question me on how I enlisted. He then told me that I could catch the bus to the base (we called it a cattle car).

I reported where I was supposed to. It was an office in a Quonset hut. There were seven or eight of us there. You could hear the lieutenant talking to each one as they were called in. I could hear him say, "Yellow bellies, you have a yellow streak up your back!" Then he would ask, "Do you want out of the Marines?" When they replied, "Yes," that's when he really tore them up. I didn't know that they were conscientious objectors. I was the only one underage. When my name was called, I walked in and stood at attention. He told me, "At ease," and I sat down. I saw a letter from my mother on his desk.

My mother had written to President Roosevelt and told him that her son was only 16. I had to explain to the lieutenant how I got in. Then he asked if I wanted out of the Marines. I said, "No, sir!" He said that I would have to take a complete physical, and if they found one little thing wrong with me, they would kick me out.

I took the exam and passed. The last thing I had to do was have my DI sign the papers. Corporal Pratt asked me if I wanted out. I said, "No, sir!" I had been through most of boot camp by that time. He informed me that they would probably send me to radio school. I had passed with fairly high grades on the test they gave me. I then took a test from the Marine Corps Institute to qualify for my high school diploma, which I passed. I graduated from boot camp with platoon 1178.

I was given a 10-day leave and I went home, then reported back to California. I then took two-weeks' infantry training and went aboard a ship for the South Pacific. I didn't hear any more about my age until July 1944. We hit the beach at Guam on 21 July 1944. I had turned

17 on 12 July 1944, just a few days earlier, while aboard ship on the way to Guam.

I was in a foxhole with my buddy when a runner came yelling my name. I said, "Here I am!" He stood in front of me with a piece of paper in his hand and said, "You are only 16." I said, "The hell I am – I am 17!" He left, and that is the last I heard about my age. When I was being discharged in 1946, the sergeant said, "I see you have a fraudulent enlistment." So I told him all about the procedures I had gone through.

I joined the Marine Reserves in 1948 in Columbus, Ohio, and was recalled to active duty in 1950 after the Korean War started. I went to Korea with the 1st Replacement Draft and assigned to the 1st Service Battalion, 1st Marine Division. We landed at Wonsan in November 1950 and made our way north. I got as far as Koto-ri before the Chinese intervened. We made it back to Hungnam where we boarded ships and went back to South Korea.

Early in 1951 we were near Pohang looking for guerillas. I was in a foxhole when a guy came running up to me with a telegram. I thought that someone at home was sick or had died. He said, "Your wife and son are doing fine!" I was very surprised because she wasn't due for two more months. My son was premature.

We kept pushing north, and after I had been in Korea for about 10 months, I was notified that I was relieved of duty and would be going home. Shortly after I received that word, a lieutenant came to me and said, "Sergeant, take this convoy of ammunition up to the line." I told him that I had been relieved of duty, but he ordered me to take the three-truck convoy to the front lines. We were greeted by a hellacious mortar barrage about the time we arrived at the front. The next thing I knew, I was on a stretcher and being taken to an aid station. When I woke again, I was strapped in a bed on the hospital ship, USS *Haven*. During the day, they kept bringing in wounded men. I watched as the doctors removed shrapnel from the backside of one of the wounded. When I woke the next morning, I was strapped in my bunk. I looked around and didn't recognize anybody. I asked the corpsman what was going on. He said that I was in the psycho ward. He told me that the night before, the guard at the bottom of the gangplank had caught me walking down the gangplank. He had asked me where I was going, and I am told that I said, "Home."

I finally got off the hospital ship and was put with a group of men who were being sent back to the lines. I told the person in charge that I had been relieved of duty and was to be sent home. He ordered me to get on the weapons carrier that was to take us back to the division. I sat in the very back of the vehicle. As we passed a Marine guard, I rolled out of the truck and hit the road. The guard came toward me with his rifle pointed at me. I told him to call the officer of the day. He did, and I explained my situation to the officer. He called division headquarters and confirmed that I was indeed relieved of duty and was to be sent home.

I thought the ship would dock in California, but we went to Seattle, Washington, and we were sent to a nearby naval base. I thought I would be released there, but I was ordered to take a group of 23 Marines to San Diego. I did and was finally released from active duty.

In spite of everything, I have never been sorry that I joined the Marine Corps.

Harley Landrum is the chairman of the board of the Landrum News Agency, a wholesale distributor of magazines and out-of-town newspapers, an enterprise that he has been involved with for 30 years. Harley and Lorraine, his wife of 55 years, have three children and three grandchildren. One grandson is currently serving in the Marine Corps. Harley and Lorraine live in West Jefferson, Ohio.

C. E. "Ace" Burdett
Age 16 – United States Navy

As a youngster, I ran with a group of boys who were a couple of years older than I was. They started enlisting in the service during 1943. I was only 16, having been born on 19 July 1927, but I was determined to follow them. I

> So I went to the school office, took the transcript from the files, modified my date of birth, and replaced it.

talked to the Navy recruiter in Columbus, Georgia, and was told that I would have to have a birth certificate. I told him that I didn't have one, and I asked if my school transcript would be good enough. He replied in the affirmative. So I went to the school office, took the transcript from the files, modified my date of birth, and replaced it. This was rather easy to do because it was a country school and the secretary was also a teacher. When she was in class, the office was empty, but not locked. The next day, I asked the school secretary for a copy of my transcript because I wanted to enlist in the Navy. She copied directly from the changed copy, so my date of birth was in her handwriting, not mine. I enlisted in the Navy on the second anniversary of Pearl Harbor, 7 December 1943.

After graduating from boot camp at Jacksonville, Florida, I was sent to the Naval Air Training Command, Norman, Oklahoma, for aviation-mechanic training. I didn't like blind riveting, so I failed that course in short order. I was transferred to an LCT (landing craft tank) which was being transported on an LST (landing ship tank). We headed for the South Pacific via the Panama Canal.

I wasn't ready to go to sea on an LCT, so en route to the Canal Zone, I developed a case of appendicitis and was removed to the wardroom of the LST. The doctor gave me a spinal, so I remained awake during the operation. There was a battle lamp mounted on the ceiling so I could watch the cut. I looked over my shoulder and saw two officers standing in the wardroom door planning to watch the surgery. When the first cut was made, they vanished!

I was transferred to the naval hospital in the Canal Zone where I was a mess cook for a couple of months before being assigned to the USS *YMS-366*, a yard minesweeper. I spent the remainder of the war sweeping mines all around the Southwest Pacific.

I was discharged after the war and was a civilian for about three months. I re-enlisted and retained my rating of YN2 (2nd class yeoman). I served on a couple of ships until I made YN1. I was then transferred to Washington, D.C., where I was the first Navy enlisted man ever assigned to permanent duty in the Pentagon in the Office of the Secretary of Defense.

After my tour in the Pentagon, I was assigned to AFSOUTH (American Forces, South) Headquarters in Naples, Italy. My next station was back in the Pentagon, this time with the ONI (Office of Naval Intelligence). While with the ONI, I was commissioned an ensign under the LDO (Limited Duty Officer) program and sent to OCS (Officer Candidate School) in Newport, Rhode Island.

Following graduation from OCS, I was assigned to the USS *Saint Paul* (CA-73). Shortly after my arrival, we were assigned as the flagship of the Seventh Fleet, with Yokosuka, Japan, as our home port. I was promoted to lieutenant junior grade, and on completion of my sea duty, I was transferred to EPDOPAC (Enlisted Distribution Office, Pacific) in San Diego, California. From there, I was assigned as security officer at the Naval Ordnance Plant, Forest Lake, Illinois. My final duty station was at the Naval Administrative Command, Great Lakes, Illinois, where I was director of the security division until my retirement from the Navy on 1 October 1967 with the rank of lieutenant.

One of the most valuable lesson that I learned in my life was when I was personnel officer of the USS *Saint Paul*. Shortly after I went aboard, it was time to do the annual check of the personnel records. That task has to be completed pronto, so we were at it full-time, day and night. Having done that check many times when I was in the enlisted ranks, I jumped in and was assisting the staff in getting the job done. After a couple of hours, the two senior enlisted men in department came over and gave me a lesson which I never forgot for the remainder of my Navy career. In effect, they suggested that I go up to the wardroom, get a cup of java, and let the staff do the work. I immediately recognized my mistake and took off. I will never forget the most important lesson I have ever learned, nor the people who taught it to me. Since that time I have lived by the philosophy, "Surround yourself with competent people and leave them alone to get the job done."

Ace Burdett earned four battle stars on his Asiatic-Pacific ribbon and recently received the Combat Action Ribbon. He went to work for the DuPage County, Illinois, Sheriff's Department after his retirement from the Navy. He rose through the ranks from patrolman to detective sergeant, to captain, and to the commander of the Patrol Division. He retired from the department as deputy chief and commander of the Corrections Bureau. Ace and his late wife Lila had one daughter who has favored him with two grandchildren and a great-granddaughter. Ace lives in Lillian, Alabama.

Lyle H. Warren

Age 16 – United States Navy

The small town of Marvel, Colorado, located about 25 miles southwest of Durango, is where I was born on 29 July 1927, the youngest of four siblings, one girl and three boys. During my childhood, the Depression was adversely affecting almost everyone, and my family was no exception. My father could not find work, and there were times when we were out of food. Trying to help, my next-older brother Herb and I hunted (poached) game in the surrounding hills. We harvested very little, but we learned to shoot quite well. We managed to stay together as a family until the death of my father, who at age 48, contracted pneumonia and was gone within a week. There was no doctor available to treat him because we were very isolated where we lived.

> Now I tell my wife that was the only lie I ever told!

Soon after my father's death, when I was about 8 years old, we went to stay with my grandmother in Marvel. She lived on an old-age pension, was nearly blind, and was crippled from a childhood accident. Nevertheless, she was always pleasant and helpful. She stands out as a very important person in my life. Almost a year after my father's death, my oldest brother was killed in an automobile accident. Needless to say, my mother didn't deal with this too well and went into a depression from which she didn't recover until well after World War II.

On a battery-powered Ward's Airline radio, we listened to President Roosevelt give his famous "Day of Infamy" address after the attack on Pearl Harbor. On 8 December 1941, reflecting the great patriotic wave that was to sweep America, several of the young men around Marvel traveled to Durango in order to visit the local recruiting offices. I considered going too, but was told that at age 14 they would probably throw me out. At least that is what I was lead to believe by some of the elders in town.

My brother Herb and I attended the small high school in Marvel. However, because of a teacher shortage and other shortages due to the war, the 12-student school was closed. This left some of the older boys with the choice of finding work or joining the service. As soon as he turned 17, Herb joined the Navy. He paved the way for me by telling the recruiter that I would be along sooner or later. I first approached the old chief in charge of the recruiting office late in 1942, but he gave me no encouragement at first. However, in early 1943, after I had pestered him enough, he decided to send me to Denver for the physical and, I hoped, for induction. I still think he just wanted to get me off his back. I managed the age question by stating that I was born two years earlier than I actually was. Now I tell my wife that was the only lie that I ever told! Of course, I had to present a letter from my mother granting me permission. She definitely was not happy about doing this, but I had become very efficient at pestering by practicing on the old chief recruiter.

Disaster struck during the physical because, certainly due to excitement and anticipation, my pulse would not go below 130. I can still see the yeoman stamping my papers, "REJECTED." They gave me a bus ticket back to Durango, and I dejectedly returned to my grandmother's house in Marvel. With no available school to attend and no work to be found for a 15-year-old, I definitely felt left out of the mainstream.

At that time my sister was living in Bakersfield, California, where her husband worked. I accepted with appreciation her suggestion that I come there and find a job in one of the smaller war plants. Once there, I found that hard-working women and older men filled all of the choice jobs in aircraft plants, but I did manage to go to work in a foundry helping to make engine parts for Sherman tanks. I worked the graveyard shift doing hot, dusty, sand-tamping into molds for engine parts. The pay was excellent, and I did send money to my mother and grandmother.

I managed to stay with that job for a few months, but I was not happy. I wanted to be in uniform. Consequently, if they would pay any attention, I became acquainted with most of the recruiters in town. The Marine recruiter showed some interest, but wouldn't act unless I could produce a birth certificate or some other positive proof of age. He did make the comment that I was "pretty scrawny to be a Marine." Finally, the Navy decided to give me a break. Again, I had to provide a letter of consent from my mother, but I was 16 years old at that time, and she agreed to sign. At 0600 hours on 22 December 1943, I was aboard a bus en route to Los Angeles, and after the physical and swearing-in ceremony, by 2200 hours that day we had arrived at the Naval Training Center in San Diego. Even now I can hear the "old salts" shouting, "You'll be sorry!" as we green recruits left the bus. That teasing didn't bother me at all because I was finally in the Navy!

All my training, boot camp, torpedo school, and submarine school, was completed in or off San Diego. I had no particular difficulties, except that I couldn't march in step very well at first. Our recruit CPO soon gave me some "remedial exercises," and I learned how to keep in step. Only once was there anything said to us about being underage. An officer addressed us while we were in formation and threatened that the Navy would discover those under the age of 17 and deal with them appropriately. I felt that he was looking directly at me during his entire lecture; however, nothing ever came of it. Anyway, I had very little time to worry about it.

We were allowed to volunteer for submarine school during our trade (rating) schoolwork. It seemed almost everyone wanted to be in the "silent service." Fortunately, I was one of the few who were accepted. I attribute this in part to the fact that I had done quite well while on the firing range. I particularly liked the 20mm gun and made a good score while shooting at a target towed behind an aircraft. At least I never hit the towing plane, as was rumored had happened.

About the middle of 1944, with never any chance to go home to show off my new uniform, I was shipped to Majuro in the Marshall Islands, along with 10 or 12 other submariners. For over a week we traveled that big Pacific Ocean on a hot, crowded, stinky, Army transport ship. We found that it was easier to stay alive by remaining topside as much as possible, and I learned to play poker quite well on that trip.

At Majuro, we were assigned to the submarine relief crew attached to the USS *Howard Gilmore*, the submarine tender anchored there. I was eventually assigned to the USS *Steelhead* and later to the USS *Apogon* as a torpedoman third class. During the later part of the war, big enemy ships were not easily found, and we had to work hard for what was available. My stations of duty on the boat usually consisted of manning the bow or stern planes while submerged, and as a lookout while on the surface. I had excellent vision, and because of previous experience as a hunter and shooter, I did well as a lookout, particularly at spotting aircraft.

I can't make the claim that I single-handedly won the war or even saved the boat. I am, however, proud of the fact that I always did my jobs well. There were only two times during the war when I thought for certain that I would die. Most of the time, like many young men, I felt immortal. Nevertheless, as submariners, we knew that we had very little room for error, and therefore we always cooperated and endeavored to put forth our very best efforts. For the most part, we had a lot of respect for and faith in our officers, especially the captain, and in the senior enlisted personnel, many of whom had survived previous harrowing patrols. It is true that we were not always required to observe the "spit and polish" that was prevalent elsewhere in the Navy. And no doubt we did enjoy the best food the Navy could provide.

We were at Midway Island when we were informed of the big bomb and, we hoped, the imminent surrender of Japan. The scuttlebutt was that all submarine sailors were to receive ground combat training and would be involved in the invasion force against Japan. We didn't look forward to that possibility, but we would have given it our best had it come to pass. After the surrender of Japan, many of my shipmates had accrued sufficient points to be sent back to the States for discharge. Because I was younger and had no dependents, I was not eligible until approximately eight months after VJ Day.

In the interim, I remained aboard the *Apogon*, which was used for training and eventually was scheduled for the Bikini atomic bomb tests. During one training voyage in the deep waters off Hawaii, we almost lost the boat because of too much down-angle while submerging. We were saved by the skipper who took control and managed to level the boat. Needless to say, we had gone much deeper than the maximum recommended depth. Another narrow escape occurred when a tidal wave devastated the waterfront area of Hilo, where we had visited the day before. Had we not gone back to Pearl Harbor when we did, our submarine would have become a landlocked vessel. These incidents demonstrate that not all the dangers in submarining occur in wartime. However, I still get a very solemn feeling when I remember that one out of four World War II submariners are on eternal patrol.

Like most of my shipmates aboard the *Apogon*, I was encouraged to ship over and help to build the postwar Navy. They offered me a significant boost in rating and a 30-day leave. However, during my tour of duty, I could see what a few years of college had done for some of the officers, and I decided that I wanted to continue my education. Therefore, I left the Navy as soon as I had sufficient points, and was discharged from Camp Shoemaker, California, on 16 April 1946.

Would I serve again? Absolutely! Serving my time in the Navy was one of the highlights of my life. Hanging on the wall, alongside my college and medical school diplomas, I have my framed discharge certificate and a letter of appreciation from President Harry Truman. I am proud of them.

Lyle Warren obtained a diploma from Durango High School in Colorado on the basis of his military service. He enrolled in Bakersfield College where he met his future wife, and they both graduated from there. He went on to the University of California at Berkeley and majored in zoology. He worked as a forensic investigator for the state of Nevada, and while in that job, earned an M.S. in biology from the University of Nevada. He decided he wanted to be a doctor, and he was accepted by the University of Colorado School of Medicine. After earning his M.D., and after three years of post-medical training, he opened a practice in what was then the small town of Atascadero, California, where he has practiced family medicine in the same office for over 40 years. His daughter Linda has worked alongside him for the past 20 years. He states that he has never desired to be anything but an old country doctor. Lyle and Bette, his wife of 54 years, have three sons and a daughter who have favored them with six grandchildren. Their two oldest sons served in the military, one in the Army and one in the Air Force. Lyle, Bette, and their three sons are all pilots. On a number of occasions they have flown to Sonora, Mexico, to provide medical help to some of the isolated villages that frequently do not have a physician. Lyle and Bette live in Atascadero, California.

Orrin D. Smith

Age 15 – United States Navy

After running away from home one time and getting in all kinds of trouble, my folks agreed that the service was the best place for me. They said that if I could get into the Navy on my own, they would not protest. At

> ..., my folks agreed that the service was the best place for me.

that time, the draft was taking men as young as 18.

Shortly after my 15th birthday, I went to the local draft board office. I waited until lunch time to go in so there would be only one clerk on duty. I went to the clerk and she asked me what I was there for. I told her that today was my 18th birthday and that I was ready to sign up for the draft. She was a little reluctant to do it, so she questioned me. I finally convinced her that I was 18, so she signed me up. Actually, I was born on 25 July 1928, in Brooklyn, New York.

Within four weeks I was called to have a physical. Four weeks later, on New Year's Eve, 31 December 1943, I was sworn into the Navy and was on my way to the Naval Training Station, Sampson, New York. After boot camp I was sent to an Armed Guard Gunnery School at Camp Shelton, Virginia. The Armed Guard consisted of gunners, signalmen, and radiomen who were assigned to help protect merchant ships. For the most part, the merchant ships were armed with old World War I weapons.

I served aboard three merchant ships and sailed to places such as Cuba, Panama, Ecuador, Peru, Chile, Scotland, Wales, England, and France. On VJ Day, I was on a tanker pulling into Mobile, Alabama.

With the war over, the Armed Guard was quickly disbanded. I was sent to Treasure Island, California, for a shore job. While there, I re-upped for two more years and was assigned to my first fleet ship, the USS Shangri-La (CV-38), an Essex-class aircraft carrier. We were qualifying young pilots for aircraft carrier duty. We operated out of San Diego, with a trip to Pearl Harbor.

We were assigned to make a good-will trip to ports in Guam, Philippines, Australia, and Japan. However, after ten days of great liberty in Australia, we were ordered back to a San Francisco shipyard where the ship was to be decommissioned. I stayed aboard until my hitch was up. I was discharged in October 1947.

Orrin Smith returned to his home in Brooklyn, New York, after his discharge. He was employed by the marine department of the Erie Railroad and worked on tugboats in New York Harbor. He retired after 42½ years with the railroad. On 18 December 1948, he married Lucille, his childhood sweetheart. They raised four children and now have nine grandchildren and three great-grandchildren. Orrin and Lucille live in North Bellmore, New York.

✓ *INCIDENTally* — **Mind the teacher!** – In 1945, I was assigned to the *LST-464.* After the war, we took the ship to Beaumont, Texas, for decommissioning. While berthed at Beaumont, I was working as a deck hand. One day we had a large number of school children visit the ship. At the conclusion of the visit, the school teacher, thinking that I was part of her group, started giving me hell because I wasn't leaving the ship with the rest of the students. I was 16 at the time and no doubt looked younger in her eyes. It took a lot of talking on my part to convince her that I was in the Navy and assigned to the ship. We all got a big kick out of the situation later that day. – *Harry R. Wallace.*

Rudolph J. Millen
Age 16 – United States Navy

I enlisted in the Navy while I was in the 11th grade. I was born in Highland Park, Michigan, a city within the city of Detroit, on 15 May 1927. I was one of ten children, six boys and four girls. By the time I was 16, I was not getting along well at home because

> ... I saw him drop the torpedo that sent the Pennsy *into the mud in Bruckner Bay.*

my father was very strict. My brother was in the Army, and I felt as though I just had to do something for my country, so I decided to join the Navy. I went to the city clerk's office and told them that I was working on a project in school and I needed a couple of blank birth certificates. I filled in all the spaces and signed the city clerk's name. The clerk happened to be our neighbor. It worked, and I enlisted. When I asked my mother to sign the papers so I could go into the Navy, she said, "Go, if that is what you want," and signed. I was sworn into the Navy on 2 January 1944.

Having never been out of Michigan, I asked the recruiter to send me as far from Detroit as possible, so they sent me to Camp Farragut, Idaho. I swear it took us over three days to get there. After six weeks of boot training and a short leave, I wound up in Camp Shoemaker, California. There I boarded a troopship called the *General Scott*, which took me to Pearl Harbor where I was assigned to a battleship, the USS *Pennsylvania* (BB-38). I was a gunner on a 20mm cannon at first, then on a 40mm cannon later.

We participated in the landings at Parry Island, Eniwetok, Japtan, and Engebi islands. From there we went to Australia, then to the Solomon Islands. We took part in the landings on Guam, Saipan, and Tinian. It was at Guam that I turned 17. We took part in the operations on Peleliu and Angaur, and was the first ship into Leyte

Gulf. We took part in the Battle of Surigao Strait and assisted the landing of troops in Luzon.

The USS *Pennsylvania* was the only battleship to take part in every combat amphibious operation in the Pacific from May 1943 until February 1945. The Japanese reported us sunk three times. Ensign Johnny Carson, later to become a famous TV talk-show host, was a member of the crew.

We were in Bruckner Bay, Okinawa, when we were hit by an aerial torpedo. This event occurred 36 hours before the war was over. Aircraft based on the airstrips that we controlled on Okinawa would have to circle over Bruckner Bay before landing. It was just starting to get dark, and a number of our aircraft were in the landing pattern with their landing lights on. A Japanese plane with its lights on got into the landing pattern. When it got over the ships in the harbor, it turned and headed for us. I was on watch, and my buddy Elmer Bodnar and I saw him drop the torpedo that sent the *Pennsy* into the mud in Bruckner Bay.

At the time, the *Pennsy* was flagship of the Seventh Fleet. We were told that the peace treaty with Japan would be signed aboard our ship, but after we were hit, they transferred the flag to the USS *Missouri*, the second choice. I also think that President Truman had something to do with it, since he was from Missouri. I stayed aboard the *Pennsy* until after the war, then served aboard the USS *Essex*.

I was discharged from the Navy in May 1946. I really liked the Navy and was proud to have served. To this day, I don't know why I didn't stay in. I go to two *Pennsy* reunions each year. My five brothers also served in the military, and one of my sisters served in the Navy. Three sisters had husbands in the service during World War II.

Rudy Millen participated in nine naval battles in the Pacific, earning several commendations. After his discharge from the Navy, he worked at several jobs, then went into the bar business. He owned several bars, the last one a night club called the Copa Lounge, located on the west side of Detroit. He completed high school in 1974. He married in 1949, and he and his wife Anita (who died in 1992) had three sons and a daughter. Two sons were career military, one retired from the Navy and one from the Coast Guard. In 1994, he remarried. Rudy and Belle live in North Port, Florida.

Betty J. Adams

Age 14 – United States Army (WAC)

I was born on 2 October 1929 in Manchester, Tennessee, which is seventy miles from Chattanooga. I also lived in Chattanooga and went to school there. For generations, the Adamses have lived .in

> There I was promoted to sergeant – a hard-stripe sergeant at age 15!

those areas. After my mother died in 1942, I went to live with an older sister. Three months after my 14th birthday, I decided to join the Army. My sister helped me obtain the necessary documents.

I went to Charlotte, North Carolina, and was sworn into the WAC on 25 January 1944. From there, I was sent to Fort Oglethorpe, Georgia, for basic training and was subsequently stationed there for over a year. It was like returning home, as it is only seven miles from Chattanooga. As a child, I had four uncles, an older brother, and a brother-in-law stationed there. We have a long family history with the 6th Cavalry and Fort Oglethorpe, going back as far as World War I. When the Army decided they no longer needed horses, they converted the fort into the 3rd WAC Training Center.

My family was still involved with the fort. One uncle, who was retired from the Army, worked in the finance office, and another, also retired from the Army, worked in the fire department on post. An aunt had gone to work there as a seamstress, unbeknown to me. None of them knew that I had joined the Army. My age was my secret. One day I needed to have my uniform altered, and the seamstress turned out to be my aunt! Not a word was said, but we were both stunned. She never told on me.

After basic training, despite the fact that I could not type, I was given the MOS of clerk-typist and assigned to the personnel office. I learned how to type. My first job was typing information on dog tags for new recruits, using an addressograph.

No one ever said anything about my age, although I am sure my CO at least suspected that I was underage. One day she said, "We're all over 21 here, or at least most of us are." I saw her again later when I was boarding a ship bound for Germany. She grabbed me, turned me around to inspect my rank of sergeant, grinned at me, and left. I felt that she had known all along.

After a year at Fort Oglethorpe, I was sent to the ORD (Overseas Replacement Depot) at Ft. Des Moines, Iowa. There I was promoted to sergeant — a hard-stripe sergeant at age 15! I was a platoon sergeant in charge of a two-story barracks. I had my own room. For the most part, I had no discipline problems, although once a trooper under me remarked, "I'd like to shut that little pipsqueak up!"

When the war ended in Europe, the ORD was no longer needed. I was transferred to Camp Blanding, Florida. We lived in an old barracks with only a pot-bellied stove for heat. I worked in the orderly room. It was there that I met my future husband.

We were married while we were at Camp Blanding. I was only 16. I got out of the service for about six months, but since my husband was sent overseas, I went back in the WAC when they offered re-enlistments at the same rank if you would go overseas. My husband was first stationed at Nurenburg for the war-crimes trials, but had been sent to Augsburg, Germany, about the time that I re-enlisted. They promised I'd go where he was, but instead I was sent to Oberstdorf, Germany.

My re-enlistment and leaving the States was so quick that I decided to surprise my husband. We were taken off the train in Augsburg to spend the night in a hotel. We were to go on to Oberstdorf by military bus the next day. Our CO was waiting for us there. A male captain came from the camp to tell us that we were restricted to the hotel for the night — all but me! I could go anywhere I wanted. The captain sent a jeep to get my husband. Boy, was he surprised to see me walking down the street, back in uniform and in Germany. He rode with me to Oberstdorf the next day. Our CO was surprised, but she had gotten a husband, too.

There were fifty Wacs and three officers at Oberstdorf. We were the only Wacs there. We lived in two side-by-side hotels and traveled to and from work in Sonthofen in a military bus. We were assigned to the Constabulary School in Sonthofen, which had been a Hitler-youth camp. I worked in the payroll department in the personnel office.

My husband was eventually transferred to Sonthofen, where he became the NCO in charge of the MP detachment that was assigned to Oberstdorf. We lived there for several years. Oberstdorf is a beautiful little ski-resort village completely surrounded by the Bavarian Alps. It hadn't been touched by the war, but the large cities were left with shells of large buildings. A shock to see!

The stores weren't open because they had nothing to sell. The only place we could buy anything was the PX. We had to send home for many items. We had a lot of electrical problems and no refrigerator in which to keep things. My husband designed an old-fashioned ice box which opened chest-style and put it on our balcony. I don't know where he got the ice, but he did. We gave it to another family when we came home. I hope the man who made it for us got the idea and made more of them. Most people just had a cupboard in the kitchen which had a opening to the outside, and that was their cooler. I guess it worked well in the winter time, but not in the summer.

Our first son was born in Munich. In order to get a discharge in a foreign country, I had to show them a birth certificate and proof of housing. It took five months for the consulate to do the paperwork. That is when they found out that I was underage, but they didn't say anything. In fact, my honorable discharge has "recommended for further duty" on it.

I first heard about the Veterans of Underage Military Service when my cousin sent me a newspaper from Chattanooga, Tennessee. The newspaper had an article about underage veterans with a picture of Penny Lawson who had joined the WAC at age 15. Penny's picture looked so much like me at that age that I thought maybe she was a relative. My children thought it was me. My daughter asked me how they had gotten my picture. After talking with Penny, I became a member of the VUMS.

Betty Adams attended Phoenix City College for two years on the GI Bill while living in Phoenix, Arizona. She moved to California in 1953 where she held a variety of jobs over the years. The work she enjoyed most was when she owned and operated a neighborhood plant shop, which was essentially a mini-nursery. She raised a family of four children, with two of her sons and a daughter serving in the military. The oldest son, a Marine, was awarded the Silver Star for his actions in Vietnam. The second son was a gunner on a helicopter in Vietnam. Her daughter, now a registered nurse, was a linguist with the Army Security Agency in Germany. Betty lives in Temecula, California.

✓ *INCIDENTally* — ***Fruit of our labor.*** – Prior to the of invasion of Guam in 1944, we knew our amphibious unit was to be assigned to a boat pool on the island after it was secured . Knowing this, my bowhook, L.V. Jones, and I secreted all the necessary ingredients to brew "raisin jack," including eight wooden, 8-gallon water breakers, or kegs.

About ten days after the invasion we had a rare opportunity to relax, so Jones doled out the proper amount of raisins, sugar, and dried yeast to each keg. He completed the task by screwing their brass caps tight. I told him that the kegs would explode if he left the caps in. He was adamant and refused to loosen them even though I told him they could not stay in my LCVP's bilges. In a huff he took his share of the concoction to a shipmate's boat.

Three days later, an explosion was heard in Guam's Apra Harbor. Jones's fermenting brew blew the bilge boards out of his host's boat, leaving raisins scattered from ramp to stern. Two weeks later, six of us, including a repentant L. V. Jones, gathered in my boat and enjoyed the results of the "fruit of our labor." – *Robert N. Quinn.*

James M. Jackson

Age 16 – United States Navy

I was born on a 29-acre strawberry farm two miles north of Warrens, Wisconsin, on 23 October 1927. While I was growing up, World War I seemed as far back in history as the Battle at

> My face was covered with blood and I thought the enemy had finally got me.

Gettysburg. We watched war movies such as "All Quiet on the Western Front," "The Dawn Patrol," "Sergeant York," and "The Fighting 69th." But it was clear to me that the war was over and that there would never be another chance for me to serve our country.

And then came Pearl Harbor! How could it be that there was another war upon us and I was still too young to go? My hurt was as deep as any I have ever known as we marched down to the depot with the guys who were old enough to go. At age 15, I decided that I wanted to be a Marine. The Marine recruiting officer in La Crosse, Wisconsin, told me to go home and come back when I grew up. I was devastated!

I took what money I had and bought a ticket on the next train going whichever way it would take me, for as far as it would take me. That was Winona, Minnesota. From there I walked, rode freight trains, and hitchhiked. While hitchhiking, I was picked up by what turned out to be a Navy recruiting officer from Jamestown, North Dakota. I told him I wanted to join the Navy, and he gave me all the papers I needed for my parents to sign. I hopped another train and came back to Milwaukee, Wisconsin, where my father was a patient in the VA hospital. I talked him into signing the papers indicating that I was 17. Elated, I rode another train back to La Cross to join the Navy. There I was told that my father had called and told them that I was not 17.

I was devastated, but remorse soon turned to anger. I decided to try another way to get into this war or die trying. With a whole new set of enlistment papers, ink eradicator, forged signatures, and a notary who needed a buck or two, I reported to the same Navy recruiting officer in La Crosse on 15 December 1943. He didn't remember me. I was two months past my 16th birthday and I was in the Navy! The next step was passing the physical in Milwaukee. I was worried about my flat feet, but I passed the physical. I entered active duty in the Navy on 25 January 1944.

After boot camp, I was assigned to the USS *LST-667* at the Ambridge Shipyard, Pittsburgh, Pennsylvania, in May 1944. We brought her down the Ohio River to the Mississippi. At Baton Rouge, Louisiana, the ship lost her steering and we rammed our first beach, missing a tied up river-boat barge by inches. We went on to New Orleans, then through the Panama Canal. Somewhere along the way I became known as the right man to have on the helm during tight situations. I was assigned to the helm to take the ship through the Canal, not too shabby for a 16-year-old kid who had never driven an automobile.

Our destination was Hollandia, New Guinea. We left Hollandia on 16 October 1944 to rendezvous with other ships in preparation for the landing on Leyte in the Philippine Islands. I was given the helm. As the orders came from above to add ten – or minus five – or put the helm this way – or that way – I became confused. I was asked if I was bringing the ship around as I was told to do. I said that I was. I was told to bring her around a little more, so I gave the wheel a little extra nudge, and I did bring that ship around nearly all the way and into the path of oncoming ships! I was quickly pulled from the wheel and spent the next 90 days washing pots and pans in the galley. I didn't man the helm again for a year.

Our ship, the *LST-667*, made nine landings during 1944 and 1945. They were: Sansapor, New Guinea; Morotai Island; Leyte, Philippine Islands; Lingayen Gulf, Luzon, Philippine Islands; Corregidor, Marivales Bay on Bataan, and Manila Bay; Panay Island; Negros Island; Tarakan, on the east coast of Borneo; and Brunei, on the island of Borneo. The *LST-667* was designated as a D-Day hospital ship. We would off-load tanks, trucks, bulldozers, etc., on D-Day, then hose down the tank deck and prepare to board the wounded.

We were laying down smoke while coming out of Leyte Gulf on 25 October 1944 when two or three Japanese planes attacked us. I was a pointer on a 20mm gun, and I missed all of them! The 40mm-gun tub just below me was hit. There was smoke all around, so I started to climb down to the boat deck. Either I fell, or was overcome by smoke. In any case, I landed on my head. The next thing I knew, I was lying on a mess table. I heard someone say, "This guy is O.K." I said, "Are you talking about me?" He said."Yes," so I thought I had better get back to my gun. The ship was rolling, and as I climbed back to the boat deck, I got hit in the face with a turnbuckle that was on a swinging chain. My face was covered with blood and I thought the enemy had finally got me. It was back to the mess table again.

At Lingayen Gulf, I watched as a transport ship right next to us was hit by a Japanese kamikaze. The plane crashed and exploded just forward of the superstructure. I did not know at the time that the ship was the USS *DuPage* and that I would see her again.

After the Japanese surrender, we loaded troops at Batangas, Luzon, bound for occupation duty in Japan. About three days out, we came into a heavy storm in the South China Sea. I was ordered to the helm! I guess the skipper thought it safe for me to be back on the helm because the war was over and there were no ships around to slam into.

We learned later that we just thought that this South China Sea storm was a big one. Between the 9th and the 15th of October, we were sailing from Okinawa to Tokyo bay, again with occupation troops, when we came into a typhoon that made all other storms we had been in pale. I was ordered to the helm again. We put our stern to the heavy sea, or it blew us that way. Some of our small boats (LCVPs) came loose. The galley was closed. The troops were seasick. If they had been given the choice of riding that death-driven roller coaster or landing on another beachhead, they would have chosen the beachhead! The seas were like moving mountains of water, coming from astern and moving faster than we were. You could look up and see them coming, then look down as the trough went by. The stern would lift completely out of the water and the screws would be churning in the air. When looking forward along the tank deck, you could see the ship bend. We spent three days and three nights in this storm!

At Guam in early December 1945, I left the *LST-667* to go home for discharge. As I went aboard a troopship in the harbor I realized that this was the USS *DuPage*, the same ship that I had seen hit at Lingayen Gulf in January 1945! The ship had been repaired and a new crew was aboard. The *DuPage* brought us to Portland, Oregon, and tied up at Swan Island Naval Base.

I was sent to a barracks at Swan Island and assigned to a bunk that was at the far end of the barracks near a big round stove. For some reason, I did not throw my seabag on my bunk, I just tossed it into a corner and lay down to get some rest. In the evening I went to town with some of the guys and had quite a few drinks. With a little help, I returned to the barracks sometime after midnight, just in time to see that firemen were just leaving. The stove had exploded, and had I been in that bunk, I would have been burned to a crisp!

The next morning I was on a train going east. I was discharged at the Great Lakes Naval Training Center on 12 January 1946. When I returned home, my mother handed me two letters from the draft board that were postmarked October or November 1945. I just tossed them aside. Mother then told me that a man from the draft board was by a week before looking for me. She told him that I was in the Navy, but he inferred that I had run off and he would find me. I became very angry and caught a bus to go to Sparta, Wisconsin, 18 miles away, to confront the draft board. I did, and it was not very pleasant. As I said, I was angry. The sheriff took me to his jail to talk to me. He told me to go home and get whatever papers I had and bring them to the draft board. I did, and the draft board left me alone after that. I admit that I spoke a few choice words to the clerk.

Jimmy Jackson had problems settling down after the war. He went back to high school under the GI Bill, then moved around, ending up in Dallas, Texas, in 1957. There he met a girl named Shirley who changed his life. They were married in 1958. He sold Cadillacs for 23 years in Dallas. Jimmy and Shirley have two sons, one daughter, and four grandchildren. They live in Grand Prairie, Texas.

John E. Collins

Age 16 – United States Marine Corps

"Who is Collins?" came a roar as only an Old Breed sergeant can roar.

"Here, sir!" came a high-pitched reply from a frightened 16-year-old kid.

> ..., we spotted the American flag on the top of Mt. Suribachi.

"Who changed this birth certificate?" the sergeant demanded.

"No one, sir!" I replied.

"The name on this certificate has been changed, and hell, the date has also been changed!" he roared.

"Oh, no, sir, that is the way it has always been!" I stammered.

I still remember that deep, rumbling "Aughhh...", as the sergeant, shaking his head, turned and left the room filled with young kids at the Milwaukee Marine Recruit Processing Center. It turned out to be one of the least stressful moments of my short life in the Marine Corps. While my efforts with chlorine bleach, an old pen, and coffee stains did not go unnoticed, I did get sworn into the Marine Corps that day, 27 January 1944. I had altered my older brother's post-card type birth certificate to indicate that I was 17 years old.

I was born in Onalaska, Wisconsin (population 1,240), one of four boys. Hard Depression times, loss of our mother, getting a good stepmother and stepbrother, and the onset of World War II, made for an interesting childhood. I vividly remember where and how I learned of Germany's invasion of Poland and of the Japanese attack on Pearl Harbor. I saw all the movies, papers, and *Life* magazines. Like so many young boys, I dreamed of becoming a fighter pilot.

After my older brother Ted enlisted in the Marines in April 1943, I became obsessed with doing the same. I just had to give up the impossible dream of getting two years of college, joining the Air Corps, and becoming a fighter pilot. I was afraid that the war would be over before I could finish all the schooling required. No doubt, I was responding to the Hollywood-type call for patriotism. It took several more years for that sense of patriotism to mature and for it to develop into something deep and meaningful.

When my parents initially refused to approve of my enlisting, I simply quit high school during my junior year and worked full-time at a local grocery store. My parents said that if I wouldn't go to school, I would have to pay room and board in order to continue to live at home. Ultimately, my frustrated father signed the approval forms for me to enlist in the Marines. Two months later, my parents took me to the train to go to Milwaukee where I had encountered the nice old sergeant. As I boarded the train, my stepmother gave me back all of the room-and-board money that I had paid.

Boot camp at San Diego was fun and games to a 16-year-old kid. I was soon dubbed, "the feather merchant" because I was the shortest "boot" in the platoon. I weighed 123 pounds. The only disappointing thing I recall about boot camp came after I had fired the highest expert-rifle score of all in our 60-man platoon, thus winning the betting pool. About a fourth of the guys wouldn't pay up their money. Apparently, being bested by the little kid touched their ego. I used most of the winnings to go back home on leave. It was about a 3-day train ride, standing up each way, with three days at home. It really felt good to walk around in my sharp, green uniform and talk tough in front of old friends.

Boot camp was followed by combat training in that luxury resort in the hills called Camp Pendleton, California. A memorable 3-day liberty in Los Angeles was pretty hot stuff for a 16-year-old who had never before been more than 30 miles from his birthplace.

In early August 1944, I sailed from San Diego to Pearl Harbor, Hawaii, on the old aircraft carrier, USS *Ranger*, which was being used to haul new planes to the Pacific. Some of us were sent to the island of Maui to join E Company, 2nd Battalion, 23rd Regiment, 4th Marine Division. We helped ready the base camp for the return of the division from their battles for Saipan and Tinian. The sight of those beat-up grunts and listening to the description of their combat experiences raised some doubts in my mind as to the wisdom of my decision to join the Marines.

We combat-loaded onto the *LST-761* in January 1945 and formed up with a convoy of ships at Pearl Harbor. It was a 6-week trip to Iwo Jima.

My introduction to combat, on 19 February 1945, was to land in the first wave of troops on Iwo Jima's Yellow Beach 2. Our amphibious tractor was crowded by other landing crafts, so when we hit the beach we bumped the stern of a shot-up and beached Japanese freighter. On the third attempt, our driver pulled up about eight feet onto the steep beach. Our big platoon sergeant fell back on me, and I fell on the guy behind me, and so on, like dominoes. After I managed to slither out, I was the first to drop over the right side. A wave was just going out, and I dropped onto the coarse black sand and struggled up the loose sand to the first terrace with dry feet and a very dry mouth. While dropping off the tractor, I saw a bullet strike the wet sand under me. That was the first of several such visuals I have retained. It was fairly quiet for about 20 minutes while the platoon gathered on the flat area between the first and second terraces. It was then that the Japs started to come out of their daze from the pre-landing shelling and bombing. They fired everything they had at us. Thereafter, for 17 days, it was pretty constant hell, broken up by a few memorable moments.

Four or five days after landing, we spotted the American flag on the top of Mt. Suribachi from our location near the first airfield. Contrary to recent books and accounts, I don't recall hearing any shouting or yelling, only comments of relief that the Japs would no longer be shooting down at us from the volcano.

The longest day I had on Iwo Jima was 28 February 1945, when I was on a patrol of 13 men led by Lieutenant Herman "Chuck" Drizin. We left our lines and crossed the second airfield into enemy-held territory to scout out their location and strength. We were out front (some said lost) from before daylight until well after dark. While the "old hands" were destroying three dug-in Japanese tanks, a couple of us were sent to guard the right flank. While we missed the tank action, the two of us were fired on by fellow Marines from across the airfield. They missed! Later, the Japs also missed several shots at us as we were trying to circle back toward our lines. We dug in along a taxiway as it grew dark. We could hear the sound of a moving tank in front of us. Later, we shot a few Japs coming over the skyline. Our patrol finally got back to our lines safely. About the time we got back, the Japs started their frequent nighttime 9-inch-rocket mortar firings. They sounded like a freight train going over. Ultimately, our bazooka man, Pfc. Eugene Frederick, was awarded the Navy Cross for destroying the three enemy tanks.

On 6 March, we made the long march in the dark from the first airfield up to the lines northwest of Tachiiwa Point. By then we were pushing the Japs toward the northeast coast of the island. When placed in the lines after a heavy artillery barrage, we made only minimum progress in the hilly, broken terrain. Enemy mortars caused very high casualties. At dark, while trying to dig in for the night, I got hit by shrapnel from a mortar round and was evacuated to the hospital back on the landing beaches. After treatment, I was assigned to a cot in a tent, but I did not sleep much until morning since the island and the fleet were under a Japanese air attack. I was more afraid of being hit by the falling shell fragments from our antiaircraft barrage than I was about an enemy bomb.

On 7 March 1945, I was flown up through dark clouds into the bright sunshine and south to Guam. Later, I was flown to Hawaii, then went by ship to San Francisco, and by train to the Great Lakes Naval Hospital. After surgery and therapy, I received a medical discharge on 20 September 1945, six months after leaving Iwo.

When I got back to Wisconsin, I was told that it was necessary to register for the draft. When I did, it created quite a stir. It seems that they had been looking for me since my actual 18th birthday, about three months earlier.

Fifty years later, I joined a military tour and returned to that small volcanic island, Iwo Jima, on 14 March 1995, to observe the 50th anniversary of the battle. We flew in from Saipan and were greeted by active-duty Marines who looked after us old-timers all day. I cut short my attendance at a Japanese and American memorial service to head down to Yellow Beach 2. I was still unhappy that the island had been turned back to the Japanese in 1965, and I didn't need to hear any more speeches.

In the 50 years and 23 days since I was last there, the beach had been cleared of the major debris of war by man and wave action. Even the old Japanese freighter, which we had encountered on D-Day, was gone. There were only a few remains of pill boxes, guns, and shell fragments. During this, my second visit to that beach, I planted two U. S. flags, buried some Texas soil, gathered black-beach sand, and buried a crystal-glass plaque inscribed "In memory of our departed comrades, from the survivors of E-2-23, 4th Marine Division." I then caught a Marine truck ride to the top of Mt. Suribachi, unfurled some U. S. flags, took pictures and gathered some volcanic rock and shell fragments. As the volcano top got crowded and there were more "dignitary ceremonies," I got out of there and circled the island by shuttle trucks and saw much more of the island in a few hours than I ever håd in 17 days from foxholes.

We visited the hot, cramped, cave complex that was said to be the cave where the Jap commander, General Kuribayahi, committed suicide. As the road rounded the northeast end of today's jet runway, I passed by the rock-jumbled area where I was wounded on 6 March 1945.

After a hangar reception, our pilots said, "Saddle up," and we took off from Iwo Jima for the return flight to Saipan. It was my second plane ride off from that dark island, and it closed the book an a kid's story, which I wouldn't believe if I hadn't lived it.

If there is a conclusion to be drawn from this tale, I hope it is that my fellow Marines who did not survive Iwo Jima would approve of how "the feather merchant" utilized the years he was given by being lucky enough to survive 17 days and get off that island alive.

Like many other veterans of underage service, my experience shows you can make questionable decisions when very young and sometimes come out of it O.K.

John Collins was awarded the Purple Heart for wounds received on Iwo Jima. After his discharge he worked at various jobs in Wisconsin and Texas, then at the insistence of his wife, he enrolled in the University of Texas and graduated with a degree in petroleum engineering. He worked for a large oil company in field operations for 15 years, then was a manager for natural-gas sales and utilization for 15 years. His wife of 37 years died in 1989 and he remarried in 1993. John and Bonnie have a combined family of four children and two grandchildren. They live in Denver, Colorado.

282

Robert E. Allen

Age 15 – United States Navy

I was born in Hartford, Connecticut on 26 July 1928. When I was 12 years old, my family relocated to San Diego, California, where I attended junior high and high school. My father was an

> What an eerie feeling it was, watching the torpedo come right towards me!

alcoholic, and I received many beatings. I left an unhappy home at age 15 and worked at various jobs. I wanted to join the Navy but didn't know how to, with no one to sign for me.

On 30 January 1944, I went to the draft board in Fort Smith, Arkansas, to register. I told them that I was 18 years old on that day. They did not ask for any proof of age and registered me. I passed the physical examination and declined the two weeks that I could have taken to put my affairs in order. I was sworn into the Navy on 16 February 1944 at the age of 15½.

After boot camp, I was selected for gunnery school at the San Diego Repair Base, California. Following graduation, I was assigned to the Armed Guards, naval personnel who were the gun crews on merchant ships. We went to San Pedro, California to be assigned to a Liberty ship. According to the book, the *Fighting Liberty Ships*, by A. A. Hoekling (published in 1990 by the Kent State University Press), some 2,700 Liberty ships were built during World War II. They carried supplies to American forces in every theater of war.

I was assigned as a gunner on the SS *Selma*. We sailed to Finschhafen, New Guinea, with supplies for the Army base there. We survived two torpedoes from a Japanese submarine. The first one just missed us, crossing within a few feet of the bow of the ship. I was on the bow watch and sounded the general quarters alert. The second torpedo was heading straight for midship. It looked like it would be a direct hit. What an eerie feeling it was, watching the torpedo come right towards me! The helmsman, with the grace of God, maneuvered the ship in such a way that the torpedo passed harmlessly alongside the stern of the ship. We thanked God that the Japanese submarine did not have any more torpedoes.

I was discharged from the Navy on 1 January 1946. At that time, I was only 17 years, 5 months, and 4 days old.

My brother, who was two years older than me, became 18 years old on 31 August 1944. He was drafted into the U. S. Navy in September 1944. Six months later, on 19 March 1945, he was killed in action aboard the aircraft carrier USS *Franklin*, which was hit and severely damaged by Japanese bombs while conducting a raid 25 miles off the coast of Japan. When the Korean War started, I was listed by my draft board as a sole-surviving son, and thus was exempt from being drafted during that war.

Robert Allen earned a GED and enrolled at Hillyer College, Hartford, Connecticut. He received a certificate of completion for a three-year course in architectural drafting and design. At that time he was employed by the building department of the Travelers Insurance Company, Hartford, Connecticut. In 1960 he relocated to St. Louis, Missouri, and worked for Sverdrup and Parcel as an architectural draftsman and specification writer. By 1970, his rental property investments became his full-time occupation. He now has a furniture-repair and refinishing business, and he restores antiques. Robert lives in St. James, Missouri.

284

G. Stephen Muethe

Age 15 – United States Navy

I was born in New York City on
25 November 1928. After my father
died in 1938, my mother and I moved to
Schwabmuenchen, Germany, where we
had family. I was sent to school (sixth

> ..., I was allowed to dive in an
> old hard-hat type of diving suit
> in Sasebo harbor, ...

grade) and after less than an hour, the teacher realized that I did not
read or write in the German language. I was promptly sent to the first
grade to learn to read and write. No 10-year-old kid wants to be in the
first grade any longer than necessary, so I learned to read and write
pretty quickly. In 1939, we saw the war coming in Europe, so we
returned to the United States and settled in Wilkes Barre,
Pennsylvania. In 1943 we moved to Bala Cynwyd, Pennsylvania, and
I attended Lower Merion High School, in Ardmore, Pennsylvania.

The war with Germany and Japan had
been going on for two years and I wanted to
do something to help. In 1943, I went to
Groton, Connecticut, as a welder trainee at
the Electric Boatbuilding Corporation,
helping to build submarines for the U. S.
Navy. This was not enough for me, so with
the aid of an altered birth certificate, I
joined the U. S. Navy in Chicago, Illinois, on
16 February 1944. I was sent to the Naval
Training Center at Great Lakes, Illinois.

On 20 April 1944, I was transferred to
the Naval Training Facility at Purdue
University, West Lafayette, Indiana. On 21 August 1944, I was sent
to the amphibious training base at Solomons, Maryland. On 27
November 1944, I was received aboard the USS *LST727* (LCT)(6)
Group 104, for transportation from New Orleans, Louisiana, to West
Lock in Hawaii. In Hawaii, we assembled our *LCT1283* and awaited
further orders. On 18 May 1945, our 250-ton LCT was hoisted aboard
the *LST229* for transit to Okinawa where we assisted in the invasion.

One of the clearest memories of this period of my life was the announcement of the dropping of the first atomic bomb. The announcer declared that this bomb was the equivalent of 500 boxcars of TNT. I could relate to this as being a very large number because I had counted the number of railway cars loaded with coal leaving Wilkes Barre, Pennsylvania, in the evenings. Five hundred cars was the equivalent of about five trains.

In August 1945, the war with Japan ended and we were sent to Sasebo, Japan, a Japanese naval base. On 13 October 1945, I was transferred to the USS *Yosemite* (AD19), because my LCT skipper, Ensign Armada, thought that I was a diver. I had no formal training, but I did save his neck during our training at Solomons Amphibious Training Base in Maryland. I used a gas mask and an air hose to breathe (primitive, but it worked) while I removed a fishing net that was wrapped around one of our propellers.

After some training from a regular Navy chief, I was allowed to dive in an old hard-hat type of diving suit in Sasebo harbor, where it was rumored that the Japanese had dumped some gold. This good duty lasted about a month, then certified Navy divers were assigned to the USS *Yosemite*. I was given the opportunity to join them, but I failed the eyesight test. Instead, I was assigned to the electrical repair shop.

On 18 January 1946, I was issued an honorable discharge from the USS *Yosemite* and the U. S. Naval Reserve as a fireman first class (EM). On 19 January 1946, I enlisted in the regular U. S. Navy, aboard the USS *Yosemite*. On 14 July 1946, I was transferred to the aircraft carrier, USS *Saipan* (CVL48). We were sent to Pensacola, Florida, to be the training carrier for new U. S. Navy pilots. Due to an accident aboard ship, I was transferred to the U. S. Navy Hospital in Pensacola, Florida. On 2 November 1946, I was issued an honorable discharge from the Navy.

As many returning veterans did, I went back to high school, finished, and even tried several colleges, but never received a degree. I did return to sea by obtaining my papers from the Coast Guard, and I started sailing on Merchant Marine ships. I sailed in the engine room as a wiper, fireman, oiler, and electrician, then took the tests for engineer. I spent about five years working for the United Fruit Company (The Great White Fleet) bringing bananas from Central

America to the United States. I also spent about five years sailing to Africa and Europe with the American Export Lines.

Steve Muethe looked for a shore-based job after marrying a girl from Brooklyn, New York. He started working in the sales department of Southco Inc., a small specialty-fastener manufacturer. He advanced in the company and became sales manager for a five-state region. Southco purchased a small company in Konstanz, Germany, and Steve was given the opportunity to open the European market. After six years in Germany, he returned to the corporate office in Pennsylvania. He retired in 1992 after 33 years with the company, and returned to Texas. Steve and Liz, his wife of 43 years, have two children and two grandchildren. They live in Dallas, Texas.

✓ *INCIDENTally* — ***A draw!*** – While aboard the USS *LST-20*, a 22-year-old lieutenant junior grade put me on report. We had disagreed about how I was handling an LCVP landing craft. At a captain's mast, the charges were dismissed. The captain ruled that, as coxswain of the boat, it was my responsibility and my discretion as to how the boat was handled. The officer and I agreed to disagree, man-to-man, behind closed doors. We fought to a draw. You can imagine his embarrassment when he subsequently found out that I was only 15 years old at the time! – *Philip P. Schneiderman.*

James C. McCarthy
Age 16 – United States Navy

I was born in Yonkers, New York, on 25 January 1928, the oldest of four children. When I was a freshman in high school, my father left my mother and us kids for another woman. Mom had to work in a defense plant to

After almost having a heart attack, I was finally a sailor.

support the family. The war had started and I watched as older friends left school and joined the service. I told Mom that when I reached my 16th birthday, I was going to quit school and go to work to help support the family.

I got a job in a carpet factory and lasted two weeks. That type of work was not for me. I changed the date on my birth certificate from 1928 to 1926 and went to New York City to join the Navy. I was in good health and breezed through the physical until the very last station. There sat a guy with a couple of books with colored circles in

them and numbers in the center. I rattled off the numbers until the last page. I told the guy that there were no numbers in the red and green circles. He told me that I was rejected because I was color-blind. I almost fainted. I had never heard of such a thing! He also told me that I could join the Army. I was devastated and went home.

On 9 February 1944, I told the draft board that it was my 18th birthday and I wanted to register for the draft. They did not ask me for proof of age. I then went back and took the physical again, but this time when I got to the color-blind test, I memorized the numbers in the red and green circles by listening to the guys ahead of me. I passed and was told that if I asked for immediate induction, I could choose the Navy or Marines. I chose the Navy and was sworn in on 23 February 1944.

I left for boot camp at Sampson Naval Training Base in upstate New York. Well, the first thing you do when you arrive at Sampson is to get a physical. Again, I breezed through, but the last thing was a color-blind test. This time there was no one in front of me. I rattled off the numbers and recited the same red and green numbers that I had memorized. After almost having a heart attack, I was finally a sailor.

After six weeks of boot training, I went home on leave for a week, then reported back to Sampson for further assignment. A troop train took us to the Boston Navy Yard where there were three light cruisers tied up: the USS *Vincennes*, the USS *Miami*, and the USS *Houston*. I was assigned to the *Vincennes* as a fireman second class.

The three ships left Boston, met up with the cruiser, USS *Indianapolis*, and sailed through the Panama Canal to Pearl Harbor. We got liberty in Honolulu, and a group of us decided to get tattooed. I was reluctant, but I had to be cool and go along with the group. There was a bit of a line and we had time to look at the wall and choose the one we wanted. Guys were saying, "I want the big eagle on my chest," or, "I want the dragon on my arm." When the guy in front of me got his, he was wracked with pain. I chose the smallest one there was, an anchor that said USS *Vincennes*. It cost $3. When I look at it now, I can hardly make it out.

After liberty, our ships joined Task Force 58 and headed for the Marshall Islands. We anchored off Eniwetok. They made me a whaleboat engineer and my job was to take the guard-mail petty officer to the island to pick up the mail. I had to get directions from the coxswain who was on the tiller. He told me that one bell meant stop, two bells meant to go, and three meant to reverse. I became someone important then! We were the only ones from the ship to set foot on Eniwetok.

We were told of the invasion of Saipan and notified that our mission was to escort the carriers *Essex*, *Calpence*, and *Langley* to Tinian to knock out the airfields there and to prevent them from interfering with operations on Saipan. After that, we sailed back to Saipan to participate in the bombardment of the shoreline to help the Marines and Army troops get ashore.

A couple of days later, I was summoned by the executive officer. He had a letter from my father saying that I was 16 years old. I had to admit it, and he gave me the option of staying aboard or going home. My answer was, "Please let me stay!" For some reason or other, the next day I was ordered to pack up and report aboard the USS *Maryland*. The *Maryland* had taken a torpedo across her bow from a Japanese aircraft and had to go back to Pearl Harbor for repairs. At Pearl, I went aboard a troop transport and went to San Diego where I received an honorable discharge on 29 September 1944. I took a troop train back to New York.

On 25 January 1945, I turned 17 and joined the U. S. Merchant Marine. Because of my Navy experience, I did not have to take any training. I joined the National Maritime Union and got my first ship, a T2 tanker carrying high-octane fuel. I wondered why a rookie got the job over an older seaman, but I understood when I was told that if a torpedo from a German submarine hit the ship, there would be no survivors.

We joined a convoy of many ships which were protected by a number of Navy fighting ships. We arrived safely in Liverpool, discharged our cargo, and returned to Galveston, Texas. By this time the war in Europe had ended. I boarded a Liberty ship as an ordinary seaman, and headed for England again. This time it was London. When we tied up to the Royal Albert Docks, people were dancing in the streets and partying. I thought, "These Englishmen really know how to have fun." Later I learned that Japan had surrendered. We had one great week in London.

We sailed back to New York, and after that I made a couple of uneventful trips, then decided to stay home for a while. I went to work for the Maritime Commission as a deck hand on a tugboat on the Hudson River where a mothball fleet was being established.

Jim McCarthy left sailing and joined the County of Nassau, New York, police department. After nine years as a police officer, he decided to change his lifestyle. He and his wife Ann moved to Kingman, Arizona, where Ann worked as a registered nurse and Jim went to work as a test driver for the Ford Motor Company at their Arizona proving grounds. He progressed from driver to supervisor of safety and security with Ford. He retired in 1991. Jim and Ann have four children and six grandchildren. They live in Kingman, Arizona.

Doris J. (Lyles) Slatten Gilbert
Age 13 – United States Army (WAC)

I was born in Houston, Texas, on 8 March 1930. I was the only child born into a dysfunctional family. I spent my formative years in the world of books. My favorites were *The*

> ..., *"Go home, little girl, and come back when you grow up; we need soldiers like you."*

Swiss Family Robinson and *Tarzan of the Jungle*. I spent a great deal of time with adults, so I never really did "childish" things.

My parents divorced when I was 10 years old and I went to live with an aunt. The following year, my aunt left to join her soldier boyfriend in Washington State. I moved in with a Chinese couple who ran a restaurant. They allowed me to help in the restaurant for my room and board while I attended school.

In February 1944, I saw a poster of Uncle Sam saying, "I want you." This spoke directly to me – somebody wanted me!

I went to a recruiting office and tried to enlist, but was told that I was too young. I found another recruiting office and told them that I was of age, but didn't have a birth certificate. I was given a form to fill out to obtain a delayed birth certificate. I forged the necessary information with the help of a friend's mother. The certificate was accepted at the recruiting office, I passed the physical and mental tests, and was sworn into the Women's Army Corps on 5 March 1944, just before my 14th birthday.

I was sent to Fort Des Moines, Iowa, for basic training. The training was tough, and many times I wondered what I had gotten myself into! However, after a while, as I adjusted to the routines and made friends in my barracks, I began to feel I had found my place in the world.

After completing basic training, I was sent to Fort Myer, Virginia, just across the Potomac River from Washington, D. C. While at Fort

Myer, I was trained and served as a medical corpsman, and later as a dental technician.

When we received passes, my friends and I would go to D. C. I remember we walked the five miles around the newly completed Pentagon, and walked the 669 steps to the top of the Washington Monument.

In November 1945, I was called into my commander's office. He showed me a letter from my mother that stated my real age. I flatly denied that I was that person. However, the fingerprints taken at school at the beginning of the year were was my undoing. No matter how I begged, I was told I must be discharged.

I was shipped to Fort Sam Houston, San Antonio, Texas, for discharge in February 1946. I received an honorable discharge by reason of minority about a month before my 16th birthday, after serving nearly two years. General Eisenhower was visiting Fort Sam at that time and was presenting discharge papers to about twenty soldiers. I was among the twenty. The general shook my hand, grinned at me and said, "Go home, little girl, and come back when you grow up; we need soldiers like you." With many tears, I boarded a train for Houston, leaving friends and memories that are with me to this day.

During the next year, I obtained my GED and enrolled in the University of Houston on the GI Bill. I met my future husband at the university. He was studying to enter law school. We were soon married, and after completing our educations, we became parents of seven sons and one daughter.

While my husband, Donald Slatten, pursued his law career, I worked as a juvenile-probation officer in Harris County, Texas. I soon saw the need for a facility for pre-delinquent girls whose only crime was a dysfunctional family life that they had run away from. I enlisted the help of influential people in the court system and the field of child-abuse prevention. Together we established Meadowbrier Home for Girls, where I served as executive director for eight years.

After my husband suffered a series of major heart attacks, we were forced to change our lifestyle, so we moved to a small ranch in northeastern New Mexico. I completed training as an obstetrical technician and worked in the delivery room of a local hospital. I worked my way up and became the assistant CEO of the hospital.

Later, I was appointed a deputy medical investigator for Mora and San Miguel Counties in northern New Mexico.

My husband died of cancer and heart disease in 1990. I moved to Amarillo, Texas, to be near my children. I was unhappy with doing nothing, but unwilling to work full-time, so I volunteered at the Amarillo Police Department where I became the volunteer coordinator. I was assigned to work with a handsome lieutenant by the name of Merrell Gilbert. We worked together for a year and were married on 13 March 1993.

Merrell retired after 25 years and we became volunteer chaplains for the police department and the local sheriff's department. We soon established our chaplaincy and called it the Cross and Badge Ministry. We travel a five-state area to assist law-enforcement agencies in establishing chaplaincy and volunteer programs. We also serve as law-enforcement consultants for the Baptist General Convention of Texas.

Doris Gilbert and her husband Merrell continue to serve as chaplains and coordinators of volunteer programs for the Amarillo Police Department and the Randall County Sheriff's Department. They have a blended family of nine sons, one daughter, twenty-five grandchildren and eight great-grandchildren. Six of her sons served in the military, two in the Army and four in the Marines. Doris and Merrell live in Amarillo, Texas.

Alexis Sandra Leigh
Age 14 – United States Army (WAC)

When Pearl Harbor was attacked on 7 December 1941, my uncle, John Duff, Jr. (my mother's youngest brother), was stationed at Hickam Field. Johnny was my senior by eight years, but he was my favorite uncle and my best friend. He was a rugged and tough

> ..., I had to change my identity and add eight years to my 14-year-old age.

Irish-Catholic kid who took me to school and to church, taught me my daily prayers, and explained how a lady was always to conduct herself. Johnny was always ready to play a joke, have a fight, teach me to ride my bike, shoot a BB gun, or recite naughty poems in German to my teachers, the Sisters of Saint Joseph. Johnny enlisted in the Army in 1939 when he was 17. When he was sent overseas, I watched his transport ship sail out of New York harbor.

As I watched Johnny's ship leave, I had the nagging, unwanted memory of 26 March 1934 – five years earlier – when my brother, Carmen Richard Seigh, and I left our home hand-in-hand to go to the corner store. We were not allowed to cross streets, but the grocer didn't have what we needed and he said to us, "Go ahead, the store across the street has it. I'll watch you cross." For only a second I dropped my brother's hand to say, "We're not allowed to cross!" But when I turned to my brother, he had stepped off the curb just as the wheels of a truck moved. Except for images of my mother's crying and my father's grief-stricken face, during the next two years I became invisible, never speaking or hearing, but always sensing Johnny's closeness, until at age 7, I returned to those who cared about me.

From 7 December 1941 to 20 January 1944, the day I left my family and my home in Philadelphia, I spent my nights and days on a plan to search for Johnny. Since he had been in the Army, I was certain I could find out what had happened to him after Pearl harbor – if I could manage to enlist in the Army, too – and I did.

When I did enlist, I had to change my identity and add eight years to my 14-year-old age. I was born Gertrude Tina Seigh on 21 March 1929, but I told the WAAC recruiting officer interviewing me that I was Alexis Sandra Leigh, born on 21 March 1921, and she never doubted it. I was sworn into the WAAC in Richmond, Virginia, on 6 March 1944, two weeks before my 15th birthday. Actually, I was sworn into the WAC. Officially, the WAAC became the WAC in July 1943, but my paperwork still said that I was in the WAAC, and for all I knew, I was.

My family and those who knew me as a Catholic school girl called me by my first name, Gertrude, or Trudy. My friends in the military and my WAC comrades of days gone by call me either by my then last name, "Leigh" (pronounced Lay), or Alexis. To this day I respond first of all to the name Alexis, rather than Gertrude or Trudy, or even my middle name Tina, which my law associates, peers, and friends in the judiciary call me. I have no difficulty with these identities, or personalities, since they were each a phase of my life – Gertrude until age 14, Alexis from 14 to 21, and Trudy or Tina since then. In fact, when I was assigned to the Tokyo/23rd CID (Criminal Investigation Division) in Japan, my ability to never display the slightest facial or physical emotion with regard to my then identity was my most valued asset.

During the first week of May 1944, I received orders to report to Fort Oglethorpe, Georgia, for basic training. While in basic, we formally went from the WAAC to the WAC. After basic training, I received orders to report to Aberdeen Proving Grounds, Maryland. I was appointed group leader of a squad of Wacs ordered to Aberdeen. Talk about the helpless leading the blind – I was just 15 years old! We arrived there on 15 June 1944.

My first job was inspecting 37mm antitank guns, 90mm antiaircraft guns, and 105mm howitzers. I decided to teach myself to drive during my spare time. I would get in jeeps, pickups, 1½- and 2½-ton trucks, and anything else with wheels and a motor, and risk life and limb, mine and everyone else's, in my attempt to drive. Finally, with a hard-earned (by cheating) GI driver's license, I was assigned to the motor pool at Aberdeen Proving Grounds. I recall one specific occasion. I was told to take a staff car and drive several civilian VIPs to the Pentagon. I not only did not stop for a concrete stop sign, but I hit it and knocked it over! After wrecking and demolishing about 18 staff cars, trucks, carry-alls, etc., the United States Army finally decided that I needed to go to motor transport school.

After motor-transport school, my interest and desire to drive were forgotten, and since I already knew how to type and take dictation at 200/250 words per minute, I asked to be reassigned from the motor pool. I was assigned to the Office of the Commanding General at Aberdeen Proving Grounds and worked as his aide-de-camp.

In October of 1945, when the WAC detachment was being deactivated at Aberdeen Proving Grounds, I was reassigned to the Indiantown Gap Military Reservation in Lebanon, Pennsylvania. What a muddy hell-hole that was! I stayed there until March 1946 and was then assigned to the 2nd Army Headquarters at Ft. Meade, Maryland, with the rank of 1st sergeant. I enjoyed Ft. Meade, but I still decided to take my discharge at Ft. Dix, New Jersey, on 5 July 1946. I felt it was time for me to continue my schooling and return to what some thought was a "normal" postwar civilian life.

Life as a civilian lasted only one month, since I found myself out of place and I missed my sister Wacs. I easily obtained great employment, and under the GI Bill of Rights, was accepted at New York University. However, I was not able to adjust to civilian dress and lifestyle, so I re-enlisted on 4 August 1946. I chose my assignment to General MacArthur's staff at 8th Army Headquarters in Tokyo, Japan. I was sent to Camp Stoneman, California, for additional overseas training, and then to Tokyo where I was assigned to the Tokyo/23rd CID for intelligence training by what was then the CIC (Counter Intelligence Corps).

I cannot begin to count the number of unauthorized trips that I made to the Pentagon in search of information about my uncle, Johnny Duff, while I was stationed at Aberdeen Proving Grounds. I was in Tokyo during the Japanese war-crimes trials and made a good number of trips to the Japanese Ministry of War Records in search of information about Johnny. All that I learned was that he was a prisoner of war in the Philippines and that he died in a prison camp. To this day, I search for anyone who knew him.

I remained in the Women's Army Corps until July 1947. I was honorably discharged at age 18. This time I was successful in adjusting to civilian life, but I remained close to the military. I worked for the Veterans Administration in Detroit for a short time, then the 2nd Army Headquarters at Ft. Meade, Maryland until 1950. From 1950 to 1955, I worked as a conference reporter and shipbuilding statistician in the Bureau of Ships (BUSHIPS) in Washington, D.C., and the Naval Shipbuilding Scheduling Activity (NAVSHIPSA), in Philadelphia, Pennsylvania, under then Captain Hyman Rickover, the granddaddy of the nuclear submarine *Nautilus*. Although these were civilian jobs, I remained connected to my military roots and, at long last, made the adjustment to civilian dress and life.

Today, I continue to love small arms and especially the old Army .45, and my children are amazed and shudder at my driving skills – similar to a good many of my WAC friends at Aberdeen Proving Grounds years ago!

Alexis Leigh became interested in the law and the judiciary after working for the Navy. She has worked as a court reporter, as a free-lance conference and court reporter, and as a legal assistant to the Honorable Judge Millard L. Midonick, a past Surrogate of New York County Court in New York City, and a former Presiding Judge of both the Criminal and Family Courts of New York City. In June of 1997 she moved to the Pocono Mountains of Pennsylvania. She still takes classes at the local university and continues her education in law and computer science. An avid animal lover, she has three dogs. She goes kayaking and belongs to several gun clubs – she can't give up the old Army toys. She has a son and a daughter. Alexis lives in Tobyhanna, Pennsylvania.

Frances L. (Cochran) Brown
Age 18 – United States Army (WAC)

I was born on a farm in Paulding County, Georgia, on 4 April 1925, the fifth of seven children. During the Depression years times were hard, but we raised plenty of food.

> Being far from home, I became homesick and confided in someone that I was underage...

World War II started during my senior year of high school. After graduation at 17 years of age, I worked for the Goodyear Rubber Company in Rockmart, Georgia, making fabric for tires. Circumstances at home were changing and I wanted to "join the war." I first tried the WAVES, but was not accepted because I was color-blind. Then I signed up with the Women's Army Corps. Being young and healthy – and a high school graduate – I was accepted. I obtained a falsified birth certificate by having a doctor sign an affidavit which I used to get a new one.

I was sworn in on 15 March 1944 and reported to Fort Oglethorpe, Georgia, for basic training. From there I went to Fort Benning, Georgia, to attend parachute-rigger and repairman school. I was in the only class of women ever trained there as riggers. We received paratrooper wings with an "R" on the parachute and were proud to wear our Riggers Wings. We were a part of the Parachute School Airborne Command.

I was transferred to Postal Battalion in New York City to work locator files on mail returning from the European theater of operations. Being far from home, I became homesick and confided in someone that I was underage and wanted to go home. A few days later, I was called before the company commander and was soon on my way to Fort McPherson in Atlanta, Georgia. I was given an honorable discharge on 4 December 1944.

I worked in civil service at Opa Locka Naval Air Station, Miami, Florida, as a sheet-metal mechanic, then went back to Fort Benning to work in the post office again on locator files. After I became 21 years old, on 14 May 1946, I went to Columbus, Georgia, and re-enlisted. I was sent to Orlando Air Base, Florida, and then to Elgin Field, Florida, where I worked as a parachute rigger.

I received an honorable discharge in April 1947. I married William H. Blankenship, a career Air Force sergeant, in 1947, the day after I was discharged. The marriage ended in divorce in 1976. I raised two sons. My second husband, Walter E. Patterson, a World War II disabled veteran, died 1½ years after we were married. My third husband, D. C. Brown, also a World War II veteran, suffered a stroke in 1985 and died in 1992, after eleven years of marriage.

Frances Brown is now a 76-year-old widow on 30 percent disability. Her hobbies are making jewelry and collecting dolls and angels. She lives in Fort Walton Beach, Florida.

Edgar E. DeLong

Age 15 – United States Navy

I was born in New Orleans, Louisiana, on 15 August 1928. My mother died four years later. My father remarried, but things were not the same. I ran away from home to join the circus when I was 13 years old. My

> All anyone talked about was, "What is an atomic bomb?"

stepmother had sent me to buy some butter one day, and I just kept going. I hitchhiked from Louisiana to California, slept in police stations at night, and ended up with the Russell Brothers Circus, training horses and riding a camel.

After a year on the circus circuit, roaming throughout the Southwest, I broke my foot and had to return home. It was then that I decided to join the Navy. I was 15 years old. I had to eat a lot of bananas and drink a lot of milk to get my weight up to the required 112-pound minimum. I had a fake birth certificate, but no one at the recruiting office asked to see it. In 1944, they only wanted bodies for the war. I was sworn in on 12 April 1944.

After boot camp and radio school I was assigned to the USS *Eldorado* (AGC-11), an amphibious command ship, as a radioman. Our ship was involved with the landings on Iwo Jima, Okinawa, and the Philippines. One day I was assigned to a unit that was to go ashore. I happened to be far back of a motor launch when a mortar round landed right in the middle of the men as they waded ashore. I was the only one left alive.

On 15 August 1945 – the day Japan surrendered – I celebrated my 17th birthday. We were in Manila harbor. The word came over the ship's loudspeaker that an atomic bomb had been dropped on Japan, and the war was over. Every ship in Manila Bay started shooting off guns and flares. We were all ecstatic and sleep was far from anyone's mind that night. All anyone talked about was, "What is an atomic bomb?" and "How soon can I go home?"

One day an AlNav (all Navy) message announced that there would be a test of an atomic bomb in Bikini Atoll, wherever that was. Those interested in participating could extend their enlistments and do so. I quickly decided that I wanted to see this new weapon, so I volunteered. After the *Eldorado* returned to Pearl Harbor I was assigned to the USS *Sylvania* (AKA-44). I was a radioman 2nd class at the time.

On the day of the test, we were 18 miles from ground zero. A few of the officers had dark glasses, but the crew had none. We were told not to face the blast until notified. We all waited expectantly. There was no boom, but rather a hiss of sorts and a very bright light, even with your back turned. A few moments later a heat wave, similar to what you feel when an oven is opened, hit us. Finally, we were told we could turn and look. The cloud was immense. In it you could see colorful explosions (or what looked like explosions). As the mushroom grew, we were frightened that it would cover us as well. It didn't.

A few weeks later, the underwater blast known as "Baker" was detonated. We were somewhere between 12 and 18 miles from the center of the target area. Since there would be no flash from the underwater test, we were allowed to watch without goggles. When the bomb detonated, there was a stream of water which erupted into the air, and steam started spreading from it in all directions. We were all concerned that if the radioactive steam covered the ship, there might be a problem. Fortunately, it didn't happen. Later, I volunteered to be a radio operator in a party that went to the Japanese battleship *Nagato*. The destruction was terrible. Little did I know that I would encounter atomic bombs many times during my career.

After the bomb tests, we returned to San Francisco, then went on to Bremerton, Washington. Shortly after we arrived, I was transferred to Pensacola, Florida, for discharge. A year later, after sailing with the Merchant Marine as a radio officer, I re-enlisted in the Navy.

My career progressed and I was promoted to warrant officer. I was assigned to the Electronic Officers School in Great Lakes, Illinois, a school for officers who had many years of electronic experience, but not much formal education in the subject. We were taught by Massachusetts Institute of Technology instructors. We studied math, physics, and other subjects, in order to make us understand why we were doing what we were doing. It was the most gruelling period of my Navy career.

Two days before graduation, I was informed that I would not be graduating with the class. I was given my graduation certificate and orders to report to the Nuclear Weapons course in Albuquerque. The course started in five days!

The classes in nuclear weapons were intense. After completion of the course, I was sent to the Special Weapons Units, Atlantic, in Norfolk, Virginia. I was assigned to an aircraft carrier, the USS *Intrepid*, which had just been overhauled and would be loading weapons while at anchorage in Hampton Roads.

Later, I was accepted for officer candidate school. I graduated as an ensign and assigned to the USS *Galveston* where I was a fire-control officer for the Talos-weapons system. The Talos system also had nuclear capability, but I never let on that I knew anything about nuclear warheads, so I finally got out of the nuclear program.

At age 32, when I was sure that the statute of limitations had run out, I wrote to the Bureau of Naval Personnel and reported that my birth date was wrong. They replied that I should tell the truth and say why I lied, so I did. I told them that I lied about my age to participate in World War II because it was the patriotic thing to do. Not only did the Navy accept my confession, but the Veterans Administration sent me a check for $600 to cover the extra insurance premiums I had been paying for the previous 17 years.

In November 1969, after 26 years of service, I retired from the Navy as a lieutenant commander. I was director of Surface Missile Systems Training at the U. S. Navy Guided Missiles School, Dam Neck, Virginia, at the time.

Ed DeLong earned the Navy Commendation Medal and a number of campaign medals during his years of service. After retirement, he worked for several computer hardware and software companies, and later as an automation consultant for Aetna Life and Casualty Company. He has published in Military Living *and has won numerous writing awards. He has written a book titled* Navy Mustang, *which is awaiting publication. He is currently writing a biography of James Bland, composer of the former Virginia state song, "Carry Me Back to Old Virginny." Ed and Ruth DeLong reside in Virginia Beach, Virginia.*

James R. Yocom

Age 15 – United States Navy

During the winter of 1943, when I was 15 years old, I was caught up in the hype about the world war in progress in Europe and the Pacific theaters. In my hometown

> We did not think we were going to survive the storm.

of Louisville, Kentucky, where I was born on 16 March 1928, the war was about the only thing that anyone talked about. Every serviceman was looked upon as a hero, and I was eager to do my part to serve my country. My two older brothers were in the Army. I had tried to enlist in the Navy with a forged birth certificate, but was denied because my age was easily detected.

Shortly after I was turned away from the Navy, I met a 15-year-old classmate who told me he was leaving for the Marines the following

week. I asked him how he got in the service. He said that he went to the draft board and an 80-year-old man was in charge that day. He told the man it was his 18th birthday, and he was drafted two weeks later. I was eager to give it a try, so I went to the draft board the next day, which was 29 February 1944. Since 1944 was a leap year, I could not be 18 and be born on 29 February; I had to be either 16 or 20. However, the gods were smiling on me, and I got my draft notice in about two weeks. I passed the physical, was accepted by the Navy, sworn in on 12 April 1944, and started boot camp. My discharge still has my birthday as 29 February 1926.

After boot camp at the Great Lakes Naval Base, I was sent to Camp Bradford, Virginia, for amphibious training. We trained on a concrete slab made to the dimensions of an LST (landing ship, tank). After completing the training, we went aboard the USS *LST 1023* for a two-week training cruise and gunnery school. My general quarters station was as a pointer on a 20mm gun. A pointer is the person who sites and fires the gun.

From Camp Bradford, we went to Chicago where we awaited assignment to a ship. We picked up our ship, the USS *LST584*, at Evansville, Indiana. We arrived at Evansville at 4:00 a.m. and began preparing the ship for the week-long trip to New Orleans. The ship's mast was lying on the main deck so we could go under the bridges that spanned the Ohio and Mississippi rivers.

At New Orleans, we completed work on the ship and went on a shakedown cruise. We practiced tying up to docks, landing on beaches, unloading tanks, and firing our antiaircraft weapons. After the shakedown, we went to Gulfport, Mississippi, where an LCT (landing craft, tanks) was mounted on our main deck for transportation overseas. We were finally going to war!

We went through the Panama Canal and ended our 33-day trip in the New Hebrides Islands. This was the longest trip I had ever made in my life. We arrived in Espiritu Santo, unloaded our Stateside cargo and loaded a new cargo for Manus Island. At Manus, we waited about 50 days for orders to beach and unload the cargo. On 16 January 1945, we proceeded to Humboldt Bay, Hollandia, New Guinea, and joined up with a convoy of LSTs and proceeded to Biak Island where we loaded army personnel and cargo which we transported to Leyte, and then to Mindoro, in the Philippine Islands, where personnel and cargo were discharged. On 20 February 1945, we left Mindoro, joined a convoy, and proceeded to Leyte where we again loaded army personnel and cargo, then took them to Mindoro.

On 8 March, after loading troops and equipment, we shoved off for our first combat operation, destination Zamboanga on the Island of Mindanao in the Philippines. On 10 March we successfully landed our troops and equipment on the beach without suffering damage, although enemy mortar fire came uncomfortably close. While going in towards the beach, we could not keep the troops away from the lifelines. Everyone wanted to see what was going on. As soon as the first shell exploded near the ship, they all ran for cover. After we hit the beach and unloaded both troops and cargo, we brought the soldiers who were wounded during the invasion on board for treatment and removal to a hospital ship. When we tried to retract, we could not free our ship from the shore. We had to remove the wounded by carrying them on stretchers to the LST beached next to us. We continued to try to retract and finally succeeded. We returned to Mindoro and again loaded troops and equipment and returned to Zamboanga. After fulfilling our mission, we returned to Leyte and underwent repairs.

Right after the invasion of Mindanao, the ship's captain called me to his cabin. He was furious! He said that he had been notified that I was underage and he was going to have to send me home. He was mad because replacements were hard to come by and underage kids were creating hardships for keeping a full crew. The next day, I was taken ashore by Lieutenant Bradley to see a Navy captain and the Red Cross. They said that I would be home in two weeks. I told Lieutenant Bradley that I did not want to go home, that I wanted to stay and finish what I had started. It was during this time that I received a letter from home telling me that my brother, Private Dewey Yocom, had been killed in Germany on 12 January 1945. Dewey was 24 years old. Suddenly the war felt very real. I learned recently that someone on my ship had written to my mother and told her he suspected that I was underage and she should try to get me out of the Navy. She was in a state of shock and worried, so she went to the Red Cross. However, I was discharged under the point system 14 months later.

On 2 April 1945, we proceeded in convoy to Manus Island in the Admiralties where we were outfitted with pontoon causeways. From there we went to Morotai Island in the Netherlands East Indies and loaded Australian troops and equipment in preparation for the invasion of Tarakan Island, Borneo. During this trip we made many friends with the Australians on board. Some were killed in action on the first day of the invasion.

On 1 May 1945, after having a Japanese submarine fire a torpedo at us that missed us by only inches, we successfully landed our troops and equipment on the beach at Tarakan. We were at high tide. At midnight we went to general quarters because we were under heavy shellfire from enemy shore artillery. Several shells landed 10 or 20 yards on either side of us. No damage was sustained by the ship, but another sailor and I received shrapnel wounds. I was treated by a pharmacist's mate and stayed at my duty station all night. It was the longest night of my life.

At low tide the ship was high and dry, the sea being 300 or 400 yards astern. We were stranded, and the tide would not be as high as on the day that we beached for some time. After 12 days, with the help of tugs, we retracted and proceeded to Morotai. After repairs, we loaded Australian troops and their equipment for our third and final operation. On 10 June 1945, we invaded Mwara Island, Brunei Bay, Borneo. We discharged our cargo with little difficulty. We shuttled another load of troops and cargo from Morotai to Brunei Bay and returned to Morotai. On 15 July we loaded army cargo in Hollandia and proceeded to Manila in the Philippines. From there we took army personnel to Panay and Cebu Islands, then continued on to Leyte.

On 10 September 1945, we proceeded to Manila where we loaded army troops and equipment for transportation to Yokohama, Japan. We beached in Tokyo Bay, unloaded our troops, and proceeded back to Manila. Three days after leaving Japan, we were hit by the worst typhoon ever recorded in the South Pacific. We did not think we were going to survive the storm. We did, and picked up troops at Batangas in the Philippine Islands, and took them to Japan.

In November we went to Saipan. On 7 December 1945, we got underway for Sasebo, Kyushu, Japan, which is 30 miles from Nagasaki where the second atomic bomb was dropped. Upon reaching Sasebo, elements of the 5th Marine Division were loaded aboard for transportation back to the United States. It took 28 days to reach San Diego where we off-loaded the troops. We then went to Galveston, Texas, where the ship was decommissioned. I was sent to Great Lakes, Illinois, where I was discharged on 20 May 1946 as a seaman first class.

I returned to Louisville, Kentucky, and joined the Air Force Reserve unit at Godman Field, Fort Knox, Kentucky. I was called to active duty for 15 months during the Korean War. I was a staff sergeant at the time I was released from active duty.

James Yocom took a GED test, enrolled at the Neon Electrical Engineering School, and later attended the University of Louisville, the University of Kentucky, and the University of Nevada at Reno. He worked for, and retired from, the American Synthetic Rubber Company, now owned by the Michelin Tire Company. He spent 27 years in public service. He was elected to two terms in the Kentucky House of Representatives, was appointed Kentucky State Secretary of

Labor by two governors, was appointed Director of the Federal Black-Lung Program by the U. S. Secretary of Labor, and was appointed Deputy Superintendent for Education, Commonwealth of Kentucky. James and his wife Lynda have three children and eight grandchildren. They live in Naples, Florida.

✓ *INCIDENTally* — **Arrested!** – While the 386th Bomb Group was at Selfridge Field, Michigan, in 1943, the Mt. Clemens River overflowed. We had to move our 54 aircraft onto higher ground. We worked like beavers. Around 1 p.m., my crew and another crew were told by our squadron commander that we were free to go eat. The 12 of us went to the flight-line grill. Afer we entered, the grill door was closed and locked. Our ground crew chief, T/Sgt Bill Griffith, and I were first in line. We each had blueberry pie and ice cream. As soon as we were seated, there was a thunderous rap on the locked door. The manager hurriedly opened the door. It was our group commander, Colonel Lester J. Maitland. He charged over to our table. We stood at rapt attention. He bellowed, "What's your organization?" Bill spoke for us, "386th Bomb Group, sir." "Oh Lord," the colonel screeched, "Here I am out here, working my balls off and you're in here sitting on your asses eating blueberry pie and ice cream! You are under arrest! Both of you! Don't you move!" He then charged over to the other 10 officers and airmen: "Fall outside, all of you!" He ordered a second lieutenant to double-time us to the hanger where, he said, "You will work for your money today!" There was no need to explain to the colonel that we had been told to go eat, no way! Bill Griffith and I retired from the Air Force in later years and are probably the only ones in Air Force history to retire honorably while still under arrest. – *Billie B. Boyd*

James H. Simon

Age 16 – United States Navy

I was born in Long Beach, California, on 9 April 1928. I contracted polio on 29 June 1940 and spent some time in the Los Angeles County Hospital. With the advent of World War II, my mother went

> *Being over 6-feet tall at the time, I had no problem convincing them that I was old enough.*

to work in the Long Beach Naval Shipyard. I joined the California State Militia in 1942 at the age of 14. Being over 6-feet tall at the time, I had no problem convincing them that I was old enough. In 1943, we became B Company, 39th Infantry, California State Guard. In order to attend NCO school, I had to have a draft card, so I registered for the draft.

I volunteered to be drafted and took my physical on 1 April 1944. My mother thought that I would fail the physical because of having had polio, but I passed. I was sworn into the Navy on 13 April 1944, and went through boot camp in San Diego with Company 44-227.

After boot camp, I was supposed to go to electrician's school in San Diego. While waiting for the class to form, I found out that the physical training at the school was more extensive than we had at boot camp. I have not been able to run long distances since my bout with polio in 1940.

To avoid the physical activity at the electrician's school, I volunteered for general detail and was sent to the Pearl Harbor Receiving Station as a replacement. I was assigned to the Naval Civilian Affairs Group, Army Garrison Force 248 at Fort Kamahaina, Hickam Field. We had 47 men and 11 officers who boarded the troopship *Young America* and ended up in the Philippines. In January 1945 we joined Headquarters, 77th Infantry Division. Our new name was Naval Military Government Detachment C-13. Our unit, composed of 26 men and nine officers, was attached to the 305th Infantry.

We were aboard the USS *Stokes* off Okinawa in March 1945. One battalion went ashore on Kerama Rhetto on 26 March 1945. We sailed in circles until 1 April 1945 when we landed at Ie Shima. In early May we were sent to the northern part of Okinawa to a town named Kushi and later Orowan Bay, where we stayed until the war was over.

I went home on leave on Christmas Day 1945, then boarded the USS *Stokes* (AKA-68) and went to Samar, Philippine Islands. I was discharged in June 1946. In February 1947 I joined the Army. They were so messed up that I made it through basic training at Fort Lewis, Washington, in spite of having had polio. There were seven ex-Navy men in our company.

I was sent to Japan where I joined the 1st Cavalry Division. I didn't like it, so I ended up in the Signal Corps and assigned to B Company, 72nd Signal Battalion. I was at the old base transmitter at Yamata, Japan, where Tokyo Rose broadcast during the war.

After I left the Army, I joined the Naval Air Reserve at Los Alamitos and was on flight status. I was taking electronics courses at Long Beach City College at the time. After a year in school without a break, the Korean War came along. I volunteered. I was with VF-781 as a master-at-arms until January 1951. We spent two weeks at the Naval Air Station, El Centro, California, where I worked as an aviation ordnance man.

I was subsequently transferred to Commander, Carrier Division Three, as a coxswain on the admiral's barge. We were aboard the USS *Boxer* (CV-21). We arrived in Korean waters, then went to Japan. That's how I did the Korean War.

I was discharged from the Navy in 1951, and in 1964, I enlisted in the Naval Reserve. They brought me back as a chief electronics technician under the Special Rating Program. Later, due to where we were living, I transferred to the California National Guard, from which I retired. I have post-polio problems with my left leg and use a walker.

Jim Simon had completed this story before he died on 10 November 2001. While in the military, he earned the Combat Action Ribbon, the Navy Unit Commendation, and other service ribbons. He worked for the Flight Test Division of the Douglas Aircraft Company, for eighteen years. Jim and Gayle, his wife of more than 50 years, had five children, nineteen grandchildren, and two great-grandchildren. They lived in Barstow, California, at the time of his death.

Melville J. Aston

Age 12 – United States Army
Age 13 – United States Army
Age 15 – United States Air Force

At the age of 12, I was living with my mother and grandmother in Philadelphia, Pennsylvania, where I was born on 6 January 1932. My father, a career Navy medical officer, was aboard the USS *Solace*

> The fact that by age 12 I was already shaving every day helped.

in the Pacific. My Uncle Bill was on Tulagi, and my brother was going into the Naval Academy. I hated being at home with my mother and grandmother.

Because my father was a career officer, we moved a lot. We lived in Boston, Norfolk, and Portsmouth, in addition to Philadelphia. I was raised on Navy and Marine lore. Dad had served with the Fleet Marine Force, Medal of Honor Marines ate dinner with us, and my surrogate "uncles" were petty officers and Marine Pfcs. I was proud that I could keep "my" '03 rifle shinier and the leather sling polished better than anyone else. My dad never knew that I practically slept in the Marine Guard company barracks.

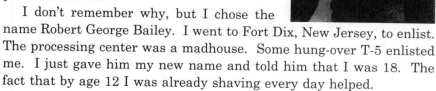

Anyway, in April 1944, I was ready to go! The question was how to do it. Obviously, I needed an alias. I knew that my family's influence extended throughout the Navy and the Marine Corps, as well as the police networks. My grandfather and other relatives were, or had been, Philadelphia police detectives.

I don't remember why, but I chose the name Robert George Bailey. I went to Fort Dix, New Jersey, to enlist. The processing center was a madhouse. Some hung-over T-5 enlisted me. I just gave him my new name and told him that I was 18. The fact that by age 12 I was already shaving every day helped.

I lasted about three weeks, then I said something or did something that tripped me up. My enlistment was voided and I was sent back to Philadelphia — to the same conditions that had caused me to leave before.

In the spring of 1945, my South Philly neighborhood pal, Arthur Henry Hood, and I were fed up with all the old women in our lives. His dad had died, and mine was overseas. We hitchhiked from Philadelphia to Cheraw, South Carolina, en route to Florida where we would become millionaires picking oranges — so Henry said. We ran out of money and rides in Cheraw, and worst of all, Henry became homesick. I wasn't homesick! Henry told me that he was headed home, but he promised not to squeal on me. We were staying in a cheap, dollar-a-night, cabin.

I walked down a fork of the road and asked a tenant farmer and his wife for food and work. They had little food, and no work, but they were very empathetic when I gave them a cock-and-bull story. I concocted the scheme of having them adopt me as 17-year-old Robert Bailey for the sole purpose of signing me over to a recruiting sergeant. We went to the nearby courthouse, met a skeptical legal official who trusted them, and secured the deal, all in one day. I thanked my new "parents" and walked down the street to the Army recruiting office. After filling out the usual papers which my new "father" signed, I was driven that night to Columbia, South Carolina. A bored corporal enlisted me, gave me tickets for food, and bussed me to Fort Jackson, South Carolina, where Private Robert G. Bailey began basic training and eventual (as I dreamed) assignment to Patton's Third Army!

All was fine for ten weeks or so. Then a Philadelphia, Pennsylvania, police lieutenant (a distant relative) showed up in the orderly room to claim me. All hell broke loose when the extent of my scam was realized, especially since I was only 13! The upshot was that the Army voided my enlistment and I was taken in manacles on a train back to Philadelphia, where I stayed with my family until 1947. I was singularly unsuccessful at school and desperately wanted the camaraderie of the barracks.

My third underage escapade began when we were living at the Navy shipyard in Portsmouth, Virginia. My travels had so discombobulated any educational learning program opportunities that I didn't understand "shit from Shinola" in my junior year of high school. But I did make the football team! I was in a family. Unfortunately, I screwed up again. I was driving a jeep that my buddy and I had "misappropriated" and had an accident on High Street in Portsmouth. We smashed through the front door of a pool room. After making the proper phone calls and providing names to the authorities, we both heard the message, "Your Country Needs You!" I worked the second shift in a cork factory in Norfolk for a couple of weeks, then again using the name Robert G. Bailey, I enlisted in the Air Force at Langley, Air Force Base, Virginia, in October 1947.

All was fine until I graduated from the 32-week radio-operator course at Scott AFB, and was assigned to a flying job in Alaska. We were told to correct our military records for insurance purposes, so I told the CO (Capt. Jack Frost) my story. He asked if I wanted to stay in and I hollered, "Yes, sir!" All was back on track until the Air Training Command said, "No!" because I was still under 17. So, I was given an honorable discharge with 1 year, 1 month, and 28 days of active duty. My discharge "special orders" were a classic – in addition to myself, there were 17 other underage chaps listed, headed by a sergeant, a corporal, and us Pfcs.

I was sent back to my parents' home again and hung around until February 1949 when they reluctantly signed the papers allowing me to re-enlist.

I served for 22 years, 7 as a radio operator and 15 as an air-traffic controller. I had some terrific assignments. I was the radio operator on the aircraft of Lieutenant General Paul W. Kendall, Commander Allied Forces Southeastern Europe, from 1954 to 1955. We were stationed in Izmir, Turkey. One time we had the general and 14 other NATO generals aboard and tried (mistakenly) to land at Leninakan Airdrome, a Russian fighter base. I served with the Royal Canadian Air Force in the Northwest Territory for five months, resupplying our listening posts with a ski-equipped C-47. I retired from the Air Force as a chief master sergeant at the age of 38. In the meantime I married a lovely lady who turned my life around.

Mel Aston was awarded three Air Force Commendation Medals for various actions and a Meritorious Service Medal. During the Korean War, his unit, the 3rd Air Rescue Squadron, was the first outfit awarded the Presidential Unit Citation during that conflict. After retiring from the Air Force, he completed his undergraduate studies and earned a master's degree at night while working for the U. S. Department of Agriculture. He retired from the USDA when he reached 55 in 1987. Mel and his wife Mary Claire have three daughters and a son. The daughters all have advanced degrees and the son travels the world for the International Finance Corporation. Mel and Mary Claire live in Williamsburg, Virginia.

✓ *INCIDENTally* — **Keep-em flying!** – In June 1947, as a 15-year-old Coast Guardsman, I was sent to the air detachment in Argentia, Newfoundland, as the only storekeeper. I had a pickup truck that I couldn't drive (but soon learned) and a storeroom full of flight gear and aircraft parts for two PBY and two PB1G (B-17) aircraft. We were flying international ice-patrol daily to plot icebergs that could possibly enter the shipping lanes, or that were already in the shipping lanes. Messages were sent out as "notice to mariners." We were burning loads of aviation fuel, and we ran out of money to pay the Navy for it. One day, Murphy, a Navy civilian employee at the fuel farm, told me we had to pay the Navy $1,700 for aviation fuel. We didn't have even $1.00 in our fuel account. It was then I noticed Murphy eying up the flight gear. I told him I would make a deal with him. I would give him a new goatskin flight jacket for the $1,700 and have his name sewn on it by the parachute rigger. Deal! From then on it was a navigational watch, a shortwave radio, a leather down-to-the-ankles transport coat, and you name it. We made it through 1947 and into 1948 with plenty of aviation gas. I was transferred to Cleveland in the summer of 1948 and have no idea what happened after that. – *Baker W. Herbert.*

Paul W. Shockley

Age 15 – United States Merchant Marine
Age 15 – United States Coast Guard

I was taking care of my grandfather on a farm near Oleander, Alabama, when I decided to join the service. I was born in Albertville, Alabama, on 14 December 1928, and I

> I can honestly say that I was in the movies!

changed the date on my birth certificate so it would appear that I was 17 years old. The Merchant Marine was my first choice. I left Birmingham, Alabama, and went to New York where I was sworn into the Merchant Marine on 19 May 1944. In August 1944, my mother went to the Red Cross, who notified authorities, and I was discharged. About three weeks later, I joined the U. S. Coast Guard in Birmingham, and was again on my way to New York.

After training, I was assigned to a new ship, the *Army FS-282*. We sailed through the Panama Canal to the South Pacific, where I stayed until 1946. We stopped at Pearl Harbor, Australia, the Philippines, and many of the islands in the South Pacific.

On 3 January 1947, I joined the Army Air Forces. I was 18 years old by this time. In April 1948, I transferred to the Army Airborne, and later became a master parachutist. While I was in jump school at Fort Benning, Georgia, the movie "Jumping Jacks" with Dean Martin and Jerry Lewis was filmed there. We made all the jumps for the movie. I can honestly say that I was in the movies! I met my future bride in 1949 while stationed at Fort Benning. She was an Army private and I was a sergeant. We were married in the main chapel at Fort Benning.

During my time in the Army I attended cook and baker school, mess management school, food-service technician's school, and meat and dairy inspector's school. At one time I was a food advisor with the Military Assistance Advisory Group in Saudi Arabia. Later, I served as food-services manager of the cadet mess at the United States Military Academy at West Point.

In 1953, while serving as a sergeant first class in an airborne battalion at Fort Benning, Georgia, I was given a direct commission as a second lieutenant. I was discharged as a first lieutenant in April 1958.

Paul Shockley earned a Master Parachutist Badge, a Glider Badge, two certificates of achievement, and nine letters of commendation. After his discharge, he attended the Marshall County High School Veterans Class and completed the requirements for a high school diploma. Utilizing his Army experience in food handling, he entered the restaurant business. He owned and operated a Holiday Inn restaurant in Florence, Alabama, for several years before selling it. He then founded a chain of Shockley Pancake Houses throughout the South. In 1968, he sold his interest in the chain and took part in founding the Little Jimmy Dickens Fast Foods Corporation. Forty years after he first entered the service, he joined the Merchant Marine and became a boat captain. He has been a Mason for 51 years. Paul and Wynelle, his wife of 52 years, have four children, seven grandchildren, and three great grandchildren. They live in Florence, Alabama.

Walter R. "Bus" Lunt

Age 16 – United States Navy

I was born 26 June 1927 in Morenci, Arizona, and grew up within a 40-mile radius of Clifton, Arizona. I had to lie about my age to get in because I was only 16. I was sworn into the Navy on 6 June 1944, the day of the Normandy

> ..., some residents of North Platte turned out and treated us to the best cup of coffee I had ever had in my life.

invasion, and I was feeling very patriotic that day. From then on everything seemed like it was written somewhere and we were just following a script.

After boot camp in San Diego, California, I asked to be assigned to the submarine service, but I was sent to sonar school at Point Loma, California. After about three months in sonar school, five of us were transferred to Fort Lauderdale, Florida, where we were assigned to the USS *Sylph*, a converted yacht. Even with the two diesel engines that the Navy installed, the top speed was eight knots.

We were on Atlantic sub-patrol duty for a few months, then the five of us were transferred to Norfolk, Virginia, to await further transfer. At Norfolk, we joined about 500 other sonar operators who had been there for up to six months awaiting further transfer. We were told to be patient and we might be out of there within six months.

The very next morning, my name was called, right out of the middle of the list. We were transferred to Shoemaker, California, for further transfer. On the way to California on a troop train, we stopped at North Platte, Nebraska. It was about 2:00 a.m., the temperature was 20° below zero, and a north wind was blowing at about 40 miles per hour. In spite of the time and the weather, some residents of North Platte turned out and treated us to the best cup of coffee I had ever had in my life. To this day I remember and appreciate the good will that the North Platte residents showed to everyone who was on the troop train.

We arrived in California to find 500 or 600 people there, mostly sonar operators, waiting further transfer. As in Norfolk, we were told that we would be out of there within six months. The next morning, again right out of the middle, the names Likens, Love, and Lunt, were called. We were assigned to the USS *Oakland*.

We were aboard the *Oakland* by 10 o'clock that morning and by 2 o'clock that afternoon we were on our way to the Hawaiian Islands. We had been underway about 45 minutes when I was handed a telegram. My grandfather had died and my folks wanted me home for the funeral. After taking on ammunition and provisions in Hawaii, and shooting at one of the islands for target practice, we sailed for the Philippines. After a little R&R at Tacloban, we headed for Okinawa.

We joined Bull Halsey's operation off the coast of Okinawa and soon were involved with bunches of kamikazes. My general quarters station was in the lower sonar compartment, way down in the ship. Each time I went down the many ladders to reach the compartment I would have to dog the hatches behind me. The hull of the ship in the lower sonar room was only about three feet wide. When the guys topside would report, "We have three bogeys (unidentified aircraft) on our starboard beam at five miles and closing," the pause from that to the next statement seemed like five minutes. Then I would hear, "Two of them still on their way in." Then, "We got one!" I would hear nothing more for what seemed like an eternity. When the phones were clear I would ask, "Where is it now?" The reply would come, "Oh, we splashed it."

Most of the time the *Oakland* was stationed dead center in the task force, possibly because we had so much antiaircraft fire. When we were up to standard cruising speed, we only heard the noise of the ships around us on the sound gear. After a few days, we were told to retract the sound gear, but to stay on watch in the upper sonar room. The ship's navigator asked us to keep the coffee fresh so that he could have a fresh cup from time to time. This was great duty! Some of the radar operators, radiomen, and quartermasters, started to grumble about us not doing our share of the work, so we were given jobs to help them out. Mine was on the sky-search radar.

One time I was given a set of phones and stationed outside on the deck above the second combat-information center, which was right by the second stack of the ship. There were enemy planes coming in, and I gave reports on where they were and where they were going. This information was given every few minutes to the guy below in the lower sonar room, just to let him know he was down there. It does make you feel alone when you dog that bottom hatch.

One afternoon, a kamikaze came in so low that its prop was kicking up froth from the sea. I could see the pilot's goggles and the white silk scarf around his neck. He looked at me and I looked at him. I thought that he was aiming right for me. I just stood still and looked eyeball-to-eyeball with the pilot. He came within 40 or 50 feet of me, not yards – feet! He pulled up and turned the plane on its side so his wings would not hit the two smoke stacks as he went through. When he did that, a 20mm gunner clobbered him, and the kamikaze hit the water about 50 yards away.

Just a few days later, the USS *Bunker Hill* was hit. I was standing air-search radar watch. About forty minutes before the *Bunker Hill* was hit, I picked up two planes on the radar. I put the IFF (Identification - Friend or Foe) on and reported two bogeys due north at 180 miles. The officer in charge, a lieutenant junior grade, asked, "Where are they?" I said, "I had them just a couple of sweeps back, due north of us about 180 miles." He replied, "Let me see them." I said, "Well, we can't pick them up now, but they are out there. I put the IFF on and there are bogeys coming in from due north at 180 miles." He said, "Well, let me know when you get them again."

A few minutes later they again appeared on the screen. I reported two bogeys at 160 miles due north, closing. The lieutenant said, "Let me see them." I said, "They are out there." He asked, "Where are they?" I said, "They were there just a few minutes ago." He said, "I can't see them; there aren't any bogeys out there." I said, "Yes, there are. Can't you call someone and verify it?" He said, "Ya, O.K., I'll call the USS *Washington*." So he called the USS *Washington* on the TBS (Talk Between Ships). They said, "No, we have no contacts anywhere, north, south, east, or west. Everything is clear." Instead of saying, "Well, we have a sighting of two bogeys on our radar due north at 160 miles." He said, "Thank you." He came over to me and said, "They don't have any bogeys, so you can't see any bogeys." I said, "There are two bogeys coming in. It's about time for me to get off watch, so I'm going to go down on the fantail and watch the excitement."

At that time we were heading due south. The planes were coming in from due north, and the *Bunker Hill* was directly behind us. When I was relieved from watch, I went by the lieutenant and said, "I'm going down on the fantail. You want to go with me and watch it?" He said, "No, there are no bogeys out there." On the way aft, one of my buddies met me. He wanted to see what was going to happen also.

It was just a matter of minutes after we reached the fantail that two planes each dropped a bomb on the island of the USS *Bunker Hill*. When they started to pull out, both of them were hit by antiaircraft fire. They dived right back on the island. For days afterward, electronics people would discuss "fade charts" on the TBS and wonder how those planes got through undetected by the radar units.

The memory of that incident has haunted me for more than 50 years. I feel so sorry for the people on the *Bunker Hill* who were wounded or killed, and for their families. I feel that somebody ought to know that this episode took place.

We had a small ship's band, with only seven or eight of us, but we played all the popular music of the day. After the war, we returned to the States with other ships, including the *Washington* and the *Missouri*, which had relatively large bands. As a ship would pass under the Golden Gate Bridge, its band would be on the fantail in dress whites playing various songs. When the *Oakland* passed under the bridge, our little band was playing just as loud as any of the others!

We went into dry dock at Bremerton, Washington, in late 1945 or early 1946. On a shakedown cruise about four months later, we were pulling into Astoria, Oregon, in a storm and damaged a screw shaft. We had to return to the dry dock. While the screw shaft was being repaired, six or seven of us were sent to San Francisco to learn how to mothball a ship, but I was discharged before that happened. I was discharged on 10 June 1946 and returned to Arizona.

Walter Lunt worked in the copper mines for about three years after leaving the Navy. He then spent a year at Arizona State University on the GI Bill. Later, he completed a sheet-metal apprenticeship and worked at that trade in Phoenix, Arizona. During the last 36 years, he was involved with design-engineering of grain installations and cattle-feeding operations in the southwestern United States, Mexico, Florida, and North Carolina. Walter lives in Phoenix, Arizona.

Dorothy M. (Craven) Hall
Age 17 – United States Army (WAC)

I grew up in Georgia, and times were hard in the rural South during the Depression. My dad had a real hard time supporting us. I was born on 28 December 1926 in Collinsville, Georgia.

"Mrs. Craven, how old is Dorothy?" She replied, "Well, she says she is 21."

During the Depression years we got very little, maybe a bit of candy and fruit for Christmas. Since my birthday was three days after Christmas, I *never* got anything for my birthday.

When I was in the fourth grade, I was kept back a year because I had been sickly. When I went back to school, I was older and bigger than other kids in my class. When I was in the sixth grade in 1940, my sister asked me to go stay with her and keep her three kids while she and her husband worked in a textile mill. I was 13 at the time. I have often questioned why my parents let me quit school at that age, but it was very hard to send anyone to school in those days.

I was 14 when I added a few years to my age and went to work at a textile mill in my hometown, Thomaston, Georgia. I told them I was 18! I guess they wanted to believe me because there was a shortage of men to work in the mills.

I went to Atlanta, Georgia, to work in a restaurant when I was 15. I worked in several restaurants, then I would go back home and work in the textile mill for a while, then back to Atlanta to work in the restaurants again. My niece was living in Atlanta and we would go to the movies. Before or after the feature, there would be advertisements about joining the service. I would see women marching and I thought they were glamorous. Here I was, a poor country girl who didn't have anything, and those women looked glamorous. I don't know if that was the reason I decided to join the service or not.

The wife of my brother who was in the Army and I went to the Federal Building in Atlanta to join the Women's Army Corps. We had to take a test. As I was trying to take my test, my sister-in-law kept asking, "What's the answer to this one?" and "What's the answer to that one." I said, "Be quiet so I can answer mine." Having very little education, I was surprised to learn that I passed the exam, but my sister-in-law didn't.

At that time, the age requirement was 21 and I was only 17. Being born in rural Georgia, there was no record of my birth, so they gave me some papers to take home and have my mother sign, attesting that I was 21 years old. I must have driven my mother crazy. The recruiter sent a letter telling me when to report back. In fact, I got several letters. Finally, I got my mother to sign. She didn't want to, but I kept begging her until I finally wore her down.

We went to the county seat, Thomaston, Georgia, to sign the papers. Mother was asked, "Mrs. Craven, how old is Dorothy?" She replied, "Well, she *says* she is 21." So they accepted that. I also had to have three letters of recommendation. I didn't have any money, so the recruiters sent me a ticket to go to Atlanta. I went back to the Federal Building and on 11 July 1944, I was sworn in, along with some other girls. During all the time I was in the Army I was never questioned about my age.

We were sent to Fort Oglethorpe, Georgia, for training. When we were walking towards the reception center, Wacs were hollering at us, "You'll be sorry!" They probably had been there only a day or so and were about as green as we were. We were in basic training for six weeks. While there, a lot of girls got discharged because they were underage. I lived in fear that they would send me home. Every time they called, "Dorothy Craven, come to the orderly room," I thought for sure that they had found out about my age.

I don't believe I ever was homesick. I can't remember saying, "I want to go home." At home, we had an outhouse, no running water, no electricity. The only time we ever had electricity was when my papa would go out to the fuse box and put a penny behind the fuse. It was hard times back in those days!

I was very happy in the WAC. We had three meals a day; we had a place to sleep; we had clothing; we had running water and indoor facilities.

After six weeks of basic, I went to motor-transport school for eight weeks. I already knew how to drive, but we learned to drive jeeps, staff cars, and trucks. While I was in school, they made part of a movie, "Keep Your Powder Dry," there. They made all of us who weren't in the movie stay inside.

I was sent to Camp Shelby, Mississippi, after motor-transport school, and was assigned to the motor pool. We would drive people around the base and sometimes take an officer into town for a meeting.

Everyone was happy when the war ended in Europe. I was in the hospital in Camp Shelby when the Japanese surrendered. I had to have my tonsils removed. That was the only time I had any real health problems.

Captain Tucker was in charge of the motor pool. There was another male in the pool, Master Sergeant Reed. I was a buck sergeant. Sergeant Reed was the reason I got out of the WAC in 1946. One time I had to go home on emergency leave. I had my bus spic-and-span clean when I left. When I got back, someone had used my bus and it was dirty. I was mad and I let Sergeant Reed know that I was mad! He just chewed me out. I had planned to re-enlist, but he made me so mad that I got out of the Army. Now that is what is known as cutting off your nose to spite your face, because I wasn't hurting him, I only hurt myself. I was sent to Fort Bragg, North Carolina for discharge.

I stayed out for 15 months. I went back to work in the cotton mill and clerked at a grocery store. I didn't like that, but I did it and drew some of my "52-20," the $20 a week for 52 weeks that they gave to veterans. I didn't like it at home and I didn't like working in the mill, so I re-enlisted.

I was sent to Fort Benning, Georgia. They didn't need women truck drivers, so they sent me to typing and administration school. After training, I went to work in the personnel office. When a request came in for a Wac to go to Germany, I jumped at the chance. In the fall of 1949, I was off to Heidelberg, Germany. I was assigned to the 7774th Signal Battalion. I was to train as a cryptograph operator and work in the code room. I had to sign an oath that I'd never reveal anything that I knew about the code room or anything I had ever done to code or decipher messages. Don't let anyone fool you, being a code clerk back then was *not* exciting. I couldn't remember any messages coming in or going out except for one, and that was the day that North Korea invaded South Korea.

In December 1950, several of us received orders to go to Paris with a group of women from another company to work in General Eisenhower's headquarters. He had been president of Columbia University and was called out of retirement to open the office in Paris. When we got to Paris, they put us in a hotel a few blocks from headquarters. While another Wac and I were registering at the hotel, our picture was taken. Our picture was on the front page of a Paris newspaper, in the *Stars and Stripes*, and in the *Atlanta Journal*. That was my 15 minutes of fame.

When NATO headquarters was set up, the Americans took over the entire hotel. We had to show our passes to get into the building, to get on an elevator, to enter the code room, and another pass was required to go up to General Eisenhower's office. The guards were military police. I was on the elevator one time going up to the code room with one of the MPs. I thought, "Boy, that's a cute looking little MP." He was my future husband. He had been a prisoner of war during World War II and had a lot of health problems.

We were married on 17 July 1951. I didn't like being four years older than my husband, so I asked my mother to get me a delayed certificate of birth and had my age corrected. I even got a small amount of money back from my GI insurance. I was discharged on 3 December 1951.

Dorothy Hall raised two children, a boy and a girl. She and her husband Layton now have six grandchildren and four great-grandchildren. On her 70th birthday her daughter arranged for a surprise birthday party for her. It was the first birthday party she had ever had. Dorothy and Layton live in Jacksonville, Alabama.

Leonard E. Anderson

Age 15 – United States Navy

It was June 1944; I was 15 years old. My two buddies, Richard Peffley and Joe Manley, and I were afraid the war and all the adventure it would provide was going to pass us by. I had just completed my sophomore year in high school and had

> The savage fighting and destruction for the capture of this island was almost beyond description.

traveled around the country with my parents since my birth on 18 August 1928. My father worked in construction and we followed the various construction jobs. Until I was in the eighth grade, I never spent a year in any one school. There were serious gaps in my education, and academic matters were not at the top of my priority list.

Without our parents' prior consent, we went to the Navy recruiting office in Phoenix, Arizona, where I was living at the time, and enlisted. We each told the Navy recruiter that we were 17 years old. He

advised us to return home and get our parents' signatures, and that we would be leaving the next day for boot camp. There was no discussion by the recruiter as to how young we looked, or that we could not possibly be 17.

At first my parents told me, "Absolutely no!" My mother said she would never sign or give her consent. However, after many threats to run away and never finish school, my dad relented and signed the enlistment papers. Perhaps my dad understood my desire for adventure because he had left his home in Finland at a very early age to come to the United States. He had served in World War I, wanting to help protect his new country.

At the time, my father was working on remodeling the Adams Hotel in downtown Phoenix, just across the street from the recruiting office. When we left for boot camp on 26 July 1944, he walked over to the recruiting office as we were getting on the bus. I don't remember exactly what he said, but it was something to the effect "to be careful." He was not a demonstrative man, but I could tell he clearly wished that I had not made this decision.

Boot camp at that point in the war was very short – four to six weeks at most. On about the second day, while our company was lined up on the "grinder" (marching field), we were informed that one out of every five or us would not come back from the war. I remember looking around at the guys on either side and wondering which one would not return. With the optimism of youth, I never once thought that the one person might be me.

Because my test scores showed an aptitude for engineering, I was informed that I would be spending the next sixteen weeks at a basic engineering school somewhere in the South. Fifteen-year-olds are not known for their logical thinking, and I turned down this school. I wanted to go into combat. I volunteered for the amphibious forces and was sent for amphibious training at Coronado Island, California. I was also sent to gunnery school and learned to operate a 20mm antiaircraft gun, which became my battle station aboard ship, except when launching our landing craft.

In addition to operating an LCVP landing craft, I became coxswain of the captain's gig. My many experiences in this role included getting the captain and our boat lost during a storm because I had neglected to activate the electric compass on our return trip to the ship. I finally discovered my error, but not before a considerable amount of time had elapsed. I have been forever grateful that the captain took it good-naturedly. Perhaps he excused this infraction because he could see how young I was.

We completed amphibious training on 1 December 1944 and went to San Pedro, California, by train at night. We boarded a newly commissioned ship, the USS *Attala* (APA-130). By a remarkable coincidence, Joe and Richard, my two buddies with whom I had enlisted, had been assigned to the same ship. Arriving at night, midst all the security and secrecy that war demands, was an eerie and unsettling experience. It brought home the realization that we were not playing war games and that we would soon be headed for the Pacific, and war. After a shakedown cruise, we loaded artillery and infantry, and sailed for Pearl Harbor.

At Pearl, we loaded combat troops and sailed for Eniwetok in the Marshall Islands, where we joined a convoy and sailed for Iwo Jima where we landed our combat troops. The savage fighting and destruction for the capture of this island was almost beyond description. It took approximately 45 days to secure the island, at the cost of approximately 7,000 Marines, sailors, seabees, and UDTs (Underwater Demolition Teams - now called Navy Seals).

The beaches at Iwo were clogged with brave men who had been severely injured or killed almost immediately upon landing. Damaged boats and equipment made it additionally difficult to land more troops and supplies. Marines already ashore were having difficulty getting off the beach because of the intense fire from Japanese forces on Mt. Suribachi. Several days later, I watched our Marines block cave entrances with a tank, fire the flame thrower into the cave, then back away and wait for the surviving Japanese to emerge. When they did, they were shot by the Marines. These images remain with me to this day.

Before leaving Iwo Jima, we evacuated several hundred wounded men for transportation back to the naval hospital in San Francisco. I volunteered to help care for the wounded, giving shots, changing dressings, and feeding those who could not feed themselves. Many men died and were buried at sea. To this day, I think of them and the other courageous men who went ashore on that island to face the terrible enemy fire.

After debarking in San Francisco and placing our wounded in the naval hospital, we sailed to Everett, Washington, and went into dry dock for repairs to the damage done to our ship during the battle for Iwo Jima. On 15 April 1945, we loaded replacement personnel and were underway for Pearl Harbor again. We performed amphibious exercises at Maui in anticipation of the invasion of Japan. On 11 May 1945, we embarked replacement personnel and sailed for Eniwetok, Saipan, and Ulithi Atoll. At Ulithi, we loaded Navy replacement personnel and sailed for Leyte – Samar in the Philippine Islands. In July 1945, we sailed back to Pearl Harbor, picked up combat units and UDTs, and left for Eniwetok, Ulithi, and Okinawa, in preparation for the invasion of Japan.

The Japanese surrendered on 15 August 1945, after President Harry Truman authorized the dropping of atomic bombs on Hiroshima and Nagasaki. Of course, we knew nothing of the destructive nature of an atomic bomb. All we knew was that the war in the Pacific would soon be over and we were grateful. Over the years, I have said many times that President Truman probably saved my life and the lives of countless others. Dropping the atom bomb on Japan was a monumental decision for any man to make, but I think it was the right one. Mainland Japan would have been our next island to invade, at the cost of hundreds of thousands of lives.

After the surrender, we landed the 2nd Battalion, 17th Regimental Combat Team, at Jinsen, Korea, to disarm the Japanese troops in Korea. We then took the 1st Marine Division to Taku, China, to disarm the Japanese troops that were occupying China. Landing the occupation troops in China and Korea was frightening as we came face-to-face with the enemy who was still armed. We hoped that some diehard would not decide to kill one more American. Fortunately, there were no incidents. I think they were also glad it was over.

A severe typhoon hit Okinawa from 16 through 18 September 1945. The typhoon destroyed all Army and Navy installations on the southern end of the island and destroyed all but two planes. Six ships were sunk and many bodies were washed ashore. Our ship came close to capsizing several times. She was damaged, and we lost most of our landing craft. There were quite a few injuries to our crew and to the 1st Marine Division troops on board. Being aboard ship in a typhoon of this magnitude is an experience that will live forever in my memory. We were at the mercy of the sea, an experience none of us would ever want to repeat.

After the occupation troops had been landed in Korea and China, we took some Nationalist Chinese troops from Hong Kong and landed them near the Chinese Communists who were coming down from Manchuria.

After transporting the Chinese, we returned to the States and decommissioned our ship. When my 30-day rehabilitation leave was up, I returned to San Diego and was discharged at San Pedro, California, on 10 June 1946. I was 17 years old, still too young to register for the draft.

Some 25 years later, I returned to Pearl Harbor with my wife. We visited the Arizona Memorial. Tears filled our eyes as we stood there, realizing that 1,100 men are entombed in this now famous battleship and memorial.

Leonard Anderson, fulfilling a promise to his father, returned to high school after his discharge. He completed his junior year, then received a GED. He enrolled in the College of Engineering at the University of Arizona in 1950, receiving a B.S. in engineering in 1955. After graduation he went to work as a structural engineer at the firm of Johannessen and Girand. He later became a partner in the firm of Hamlyn, Mann, and Anderson. He is one of Arizona's most highly respected structural engineers. He designed many of the buildings on the Arizona State University and University of Arizona campuses, and a number of the high-rise buildings that now grace the skyline of Phoenix. He designed the Van De Graf Accelerator Building for the University of Arizona, and won a national award for the structural design of the Tempe City Hall, a building that received national attention because of its unusual upside-down pyramid shape. Leonard and June, his wife of 53 years, have four children, eight grandchildren, and three great-grandchildren. They make their home in Paradise Valley, Arizona.

Richard B. Shivley

Age 14 – United States Navy

I was born on a cold winter day in Chicago, Illinois, 3 February 1930. I had a tough childhood because my parents divorced when I was three. I

> The fires were very intense and were burning everywhere.

spent most of my childhood living in orphanages or with my grandparents. I did what most Depression kids of our time did – I delivered newspapers and groceries for pocket money. As I reached my teens, I began to realize that the war was all around us, in the paper, on the radio, and it was only a matter of time before I would participate.

On 29 July 1944, some older friends and I decided it was time to enlist. Although I was only 14 years old, I thought this was the time to serve my country as well as see the world with my friends. I forged my parent's signature on the enlistment papers, was sworn in, and was on my way to Great Lakes for boot camp.

After boot camp, I went to Madison, Wisconsin, for radio school, then to San Antonio, Texas, for gunnery school. On 2 February 1945, the day before my 15th birthday, I was assigned to the aircraft carrier, USS *Franklin* (CV-13), which was part of Task Force 58.2 under Admiral Davidson. I was a radioman-gunner on a TBF torpedo bomber.

We were at general quarters on Monday, 19 March 1944 and were preparing for a strike on the island of Honshu. At that time, we were the closest to Japan of any American aircraft carrier, approximately 60 miles from their shore. I was in my bunk catching some shut-eye and the rest of my shipmates were up in the hangar deck in the chow line. I was not aware that we were under attack by Japanese aircraft until two bombs hit, one forward and one aft. The fire and smoke became very intense. The only possible escape route was through the escape hatch on the 40mm-gun mounts.

Once I made it up to the deck, I saw bodies literally strewn everywhere. Some were seriously injured, and several shipmates were dead. The fires were very intense and were burning everywhere. We had to fight the fires and the Japanese at the same time. It didn't look like the ship could be saved. Trying to contain fires and trying to fight the enemy at the same time was at best a battle within a battle, and no one was certain at the moment who would win. We had lost over 700 men. The ship was dead in the water and had a 13° starboard list.

Finally, after we began to contain some of the fires, a line was attached from the deck of the burning *Franklin* to the cruiser *Pittsburgh*, which towed us to the island of Ulithi. Soon after, we were able to get some of the boilers going in the engine department and were able to begin the slow trek (6-8 knots) back to Pearl Harbor for repairs.

When we arrived at Pearl, I was reassigned to the destroyer *O'Bannon* where I served out the war. We operated in the Philippines and provided fire support at Tarakan, Borneo, in April and early May of 1945. We then rendezvoused with a group of small carriers (CVEs) off of Okinawa. We escorted them while they struck Akashimi Gunto. At the close of the war we patrolled the coast of Honshu, Japan, until 1 September 1945, then we headed for San Francisco and home. I was discharged from the Navy in June 1946, at the age of 16.

Richard Shivley was awarded a Presidential Unit Citation as a member of the crew of the USS Franklin, *and earned several other service ribbons. After his discharge from the Navy he became an ornamental ironworker and worked at that profession for 45 years. Jane, his wife of 40 years, passed away in 1994. They had seven children. Richard lives in Northlake, Illinois.*

Philip R. Schneiderman

Age 13 – Massachusetts State Guard
Age 15 – United States Coast Guard

I served in Company E, 126th Infantry, Massachusetts State Guard, at the age of 13 and began making plans for enlisting in the regular military early in 1944 while I was still 14. In Boston, where I was born on 19 March

> *I dreamed of sallying forth to destroy Nazi submarines, ...*

1929, it was possible to obtain birth certificates from a number of sources. Over several months, with the help of friends, I was able to obtain a total of 26 birth certificates. My friends at the local furriers were able to alter one certificate so that the correction was undetectable.

The U. S. Coast Guard was an obvious choice for a Bostonian because of their major presence in the area. I dreamed of sallying forth to destroy Nazi submarines, returning with medals that I could exhibit in my former school yard and the local soda shop.

My mother left for the Army the day before I was to be sworn into the Coast Guard. My father had recently been discharged from the Army and was serving in the State Guard with me. On the day of my enlistment, I failed my physical because of low blood pressure. I urged the doctor to relent. He noted that I was employed at the General Tire Company and commented that he had been unable to find the tires he needed for his large Buick Roadmaster. With a phone call, I was able to arrange for five tires to be installed that afternoon. My medical examination was then stamped "waived" and I became the newest member of the United States Coast Guard on 16 August 1944.

After five weeks of boot camp at Manhattan Beach, Brooklyn, New York, we boarded a troop train for Treasure Island, San Francisco, California. At seven weeks to the day from my enlistment, our contingent boarded the Dutch steamer DMS *Brastagi* and headed for New Guinea.

The *Brastagi* was a rusty tramp-steamer that had been hastily converted to a troop carrier. It was built in Bremerhaven in 1926 and was commanded by Dutch officers with a turbaned and loin-clothed Javanese crew. Raw wood bunks had been constructed in the holds of the ship in tiers of five. There was no means of circulating the stale air, and no below-deck toilets. Toilets consisted of wooden shacks built to extend over the sides of the ship, with open holes positioned over the ocean. No showers were available for the over 500 Army, Navy, and Coast Guard troops aboard. Food service was rather unique. One stood in line for breakfast, was served, and then went to the end of the line to consume the meal. With 500 troops aboard, the line moved slowly and you arrived at the serving position in time for lunch. The same procedure was followed for the evening meal. The voyage took 30 days!

Shortly after arriving at Finschhafen, New Guinea, I joined the crew of the USS *LST-20*, which was manned by the Coast Guard. I was assigned as a radar striker (apprentice) and found myself in combat in the Dutch East Indies within weeks. Our ship saw action in New Guinea, the Dutch East Indies, the Philippines, and Okinawa.

I was found to be underage shortly after my 16th birthday. At this point the story becomes interesting. At that time, the Coast Guard did not "knowingly" enlist persons under the age of 17. However, the legal enlistment age, dating back to the founding of the service in the late 18th century, had not been changed from age 14. As an underage enlistee, I was given the option of remaining in the service, if my commanding officer would so recommend and attest that I was performing a necessary service to the war effort.

My records were changed to reflect my true age. I received a letter from the commandant of Coast Guard forces in the South Pacific commenting that I was the youngest serviceman "of record" in his command.

Some months later, having returned with the ship to the States, I overstayed my liberty by 22 hours to attend a family wedding. Our ship's captain had been transferred and we were awaiting a new captain at the time, so the Navy, not the Coast Guard, convened a deck court-martial. I was pressured by the Navy officers to accept an underage discharge. The Navy apparently had little tolerance for underage personnel or for the Coast Guard practice which permitted it. I refused to accept the minority discharge and was awarded three days on bread and water and 12 days at hard labor in a Navy brig located on Pelican Island in Galveston Harbor. In those 12 days, I learned to castrate pigs and to build a corduroy road across a swamp, both rather unusual activities for a native of Boston!

I received an honorable discharge from the Coast Guard in May 1946, shortly after my 17th birthday.

Philip Schneiderman attended college and graduate school and became the executive director of a United Cerebral Palsy association. He then became executive director of United Way organizations in several cities: Pasadena, California; Omaha, Nebraska; Indianapolis, Indiana; and Baltimore, Maryland, where he was located when he retired. During the Vietnam War, while he was at Pasadena and at Wilmington, Delaware, he served on the local draft board. He had little tolerance for those who sought to avoid military service without a valid reason. Fifty-five years after leaving the 10th grade for wartime service, the City of Boston awarded him a high school diploma in 1999. Phil and his wife Elaine have two sons, two daughters, and seven grandchildren. They live in Lords Valley, Pennsylvania.

Jack L. Lutz

Age 16 – United States Navy

I was born in Salem, Oregon, on 6 July 1928. During the summer vacation after my sophomore year in high school, I learned that a few of my older school buddies had decided to join the Navy. That sounded like a great idea to me, and since I had recently had a

> My most harrowing experience ... was when we ... rode out a ferocious typhoon.

couple of brushes with the law for partying too hard, I convinced my dad that it was a good idea, too. With my documents "in order," and my dad by my side, I was enlisted into the Navy on 23 August 1944. I began my naval service in Company 870-44, Regiment 4, Battalion 15, U. S. Naval Training Center, Farragut, Idaho, graduating on 7 November 1944.

After boot camp, I was assigned to the Small Craft Training Center, Terminal Island, California, and then to the newly commissioned attack troop transport USS *Gasconade* (APA-85). The *Gasconade* joined the fleet too late to participate in any of the invasions for which she was built. Okinawa's beaches, the last for which Americans were to fight, had already been successfully secured when the ship left the States with personnel and cargo for the Philippines in May 1945.

The biggest operation of all – the invasion of Japan – was already planned, and I'm sure the *Gasconade* was to participate. We lay at anchor in Leyte Gulf just prior to our departure for a training exercise when we received news of the Japanese surrender, which was brought about by the dropping of the atomic bombs.

Had that turning point in the war not occurred, I probably would not be writing this history, because my assigned station during landings was as forward hook man and machine gunner on an LCVP. I was real cannon fodder. As it worked out, the *Gasconade*'s entrance into Tokyo Bay was made somewhat more peacefully than planned, though it was hardly less dramatic, for the date was 2 September 1945, and the occasion was the signing of the surrender documents aboard the USS *Missouri*. The ceremonies were in progress on the *Missouri*, which was 8,000 yards to the starboard, as the *Gasconade*, in company with a huge transport task force, steamed in from Manila to land the first seaborne Army forces on the shores of Japan. Overhead, swarms of American planes signified the finality of the victory. Not a single maneuverable enemy combat ship was in sight.

Later, the *Gasconade*, again in company with other transport and cargo ships, landed occupation troops at Kure and Nagoya, on the island of Honshu, Japan. After that, it was "magic-carpet duty," that is, returning veteran personnel from forward areas and replacing them, where needed, with fresh personnel.

My most harrowing experience aboard the *Gasconade* was when we were at sea off the island of Okinawa and rode out a ferocious typhoon. History has recorded that this was the worst storm to ever hit Okinawa. Most of the military facilities on the island were destroyed and many naval vessels were lost. We had a very rough ride during those four or five days.

I was transferred off the *Gasconade* at Pearl Harbor in April 1946, where she had been taken for refitting for testing of the atomic bomb at Bikini Atoll. To this day, I do not know of her final fate, but she served me very well.

My last couple of months in the Navy were spent on the *LST-990*, and the *LSM-371*, which transported me from Pearl Harbor, through the Panama Canal, to the Chesapeake Bay, where I was discharged at the U. S. Naval Personnel Separation Center, Shelton, Virginia, on 20 June 1946, 16 days before my 18th birthday.

Jack Lutz returned to high school after his discharge from the Navy and graduated with the class of 1947. He had a very successful tenure with the Oregon State Department of Agriculture and with the U. S. Department of Agriculture, retiring after 43 years of combined service. Jack and Mary, his wife of 49½ years, raised four children who blessed them with six grandchildren. Mary died in 1998. They lived in Salem, Oregon, in the summer and in Surprise, Arizona, during the winter. Jack has remarried. He and his new wife Carol spend most of their time playing golf in either Oregon or Arizona, depending on the season.

L. "Sonny" Salkind

Age 14 – United States Navy

I was born in Chicago, Illinois, on 26 January 1930. This was during the Great Depression and the struggles of that time made a lasting impression on me. I wanted to leave home and I didn't like school, so I left the eighth grade in 1944 to

> *I knew that when I went to the recruiting office, the officer would call home to confirm my age, ...*

join the Navy at age 14. I knew that when I went to the recruiting office, the officer would call home to confirm my age, so I conned my 17-year-old sister Sylvia into being home to answer the phone. I told her that when the recruiting officer called, to say that she was my mother, and that I had her permission to enlist in the Navy.

It worked, and I was sworn into the Navy on 6 October 1944. After boot camp at the Great Lakes Naval Training Station, which was an experience that you can only appreciate by being there, I was assigned to the repair ship, USS *Xanthus* (AR-19). Going to sea was an exciting event in my life, but after a few days, the routine started to creep in.

We went to the Canal Zone, Pearl Harbor, Alaska, and Okinawa. We were assigned to the Third Fleet. We arrived at Okinawa just as the war was over. We were one of the first to be in Japan after the peace treaty was signed.

When the war was over, I went to my skipper and told him that I had lied about my age. He told me to go see the chaplain. It took a lot to convince the chaplain that I was underage, but he finally believed me. I was honorably discharged on 12 April 1946 after 17 months of service. I was 16 years old.

I returned to Chicago but decided that I still wanted to travel, so I hitchhiked all around the country in my uniform. I returned to Chicago again and decided to marry and settle down. I have three children from that marriage. We were later divorced.

After several years, my mother died and my father remarried, but he had a problem. His wife-to-be was much younger than he was, so he fibbed about his age, trying to make himself younger, while I had fibbed to make myself older.

Sonny Salkind has been involved in the real-estate business for the past 30 years. From the time he was young, he had the desire to buy land and build on it. He accomplished his goal by developing a shopping center in Temecula, California, and later sold it for 2.3 million dollars. He owned and developed a 50-acre site for manufacturing homes in Temecula. He also sold recreational properties and was recognized by Dart Resorts as a top sales producer and awarded an honor ring for his achievements. Currently, he is sales manager for Triangle Reality in Desert Hot Springs, California. Sonny and Annie have a combined family of four children and five grandchildren. They live in Temecula, California.

✓ *INCIDENTally* — *You'd better not!* – It was 1948, I was 16 years old and had been with the Army in Japan for about a month or two, when I got a letter from my school principal. He said he was going to get me sent home. I wrote to him and told him if he did, I would burn the school down. I never heard from him again. – *William Ignatz.*

Roland D. Mower

Age 15 – Utah State Guard
Age 16 – United States Navy

World War II was a challenging time for most American young men, particularly for those in the armed forces who were called upon to make the greatest sacrifices.

> You should be in the Boy Scouts, not the Marines!

Very often, their younger siblings shared the burning desire to serve their county. They were still too young to contribute to the war effort by working in essential war industries. However, strange as it sounds, some were able to convince military officials that they were old enough to enlist or to be drafted into the military.

Like so many of my peers, I was determined to enlist. In 1944, at age 15, a few of my friends and I managed to join the Utah State Guard. We received limited military training that was intended to qualify us for service on the home front should an emergency occur. This was a good start, but I really wanted to be overseas where the real action was. That same year, at age 15, I attempted to join the United States Coast Guard. I obtained some altered documents, convinced an old street derelict to sign as my father, passed the physical exam, and was sent home to await active-duty orders. When the orders arrived about ten days later, I packed a few things and departed for Salt Lake City, where I was to pick up my train tickets, meal tickets, and orders. I was to go to Alameda, California, for boot training. When I arrived at the recruiting office, I was greeted by some extremely irate comments by USCG

NCOs. such as, "Get out of here, kid! Don't come back until you are old enough!" I was devastated – someone had discovered that I was underage.

I fell back, regrouped, and decided on another option. I would join the U. S. Marines. I immediately walked to the Marine Corps recruiting office. When I entered their front door, I was greeted by a rather large-bodied woman Marine who looked at me and said, "What do you want here?" I replied in my deepest voice, "I want to be a Marine." She quickly responded in a very loud voice, "You look just like my little baby brother – get out of this office. You should be in the Boy Scouts, not the Marines!" I departed forthwith and went home to mother. I didn't tell her what had happened, but I later presented her with my next plan, which was for enlisting in the Navy. She agreed, but things were on hold until I turned 16.

The documents that I presented to the U. S. Navy recruiters were carefully scrutinized and determined to be authentic. My parents had decided to sign my enlistment application if I would agree to and abide by some rather strict constraints – to which I agreed. On 2 April 1945, I departed my home in Fairview, Utah, where I was born on 25 December 1928, for the U. S. Naval Training Station, San Diego, California.

I was finally in the service, and I was really excited. Boot camp, on the other hand, was quite difficult; I had to work extremely hard just to keep up with my peers. But this was what I had dreamed about since the war started, and I was not about to fail. After graduation, I was assigned to the USS *Pensacola* (CA-24). Within 20 minutes after boarding, the ship was underway. Shortly thereafter, we passed the Point Loma light as we departed the North Island Channel. As the sun slowly slipped into the sea, I looked around. All I could see was water – the Pacific Ocean. I slowly came to realize that I was a crew member on the Navy's famous "Grey Ghost," or "Pukey P" as she was affectionately known by her ship's company. It was a dream come true for the dumb farm kid from rural Utah.

Shortly thereafter, the *Pensacola* sailed to the North Pacific where she operated out of the Aleutian Islands. We were at Adak when the two atomic bombs were dropped on Japan. We departed Attu, and on 9 September 1945 anchored in Japan's Ominato Bay as part of a large fleet of American warships. It was there that Japanese officials boarded the USS *Panimint* (AGC-13) and surrendered all Japanese forces in northern Japan to Vice Admiral Jack Fletcher, USN.

The *Pensacola*'s crew remained as part of the occupation forces in the northern Honshu and Hokkaido regions until early November 1945. At that time, the ship was reassigned to "magic-carpet duty," which involved returning U. S. servicemen who were no longer needed overseas to the United States for separation from the military. After two cruises, one to Iwo Jima and another to Guam, the *Pensacola* was back in the States. However, I had enjoyed Christmas Day 1945, my 17th birthday, in Apra Harbor, Guam.

In April 1946, the USS *Pensacola* sailed to Bikini Atoll for "Operation Crossroads." The atomic bomb tests, "Able" and "Baker", were conducted in July 1946. They involved some 200 ships, 42,000 men, and 150 aircraft. The *Pensacola* was part of the target fleet. It received considerable damage during the second (underwater) test. The *Pensacola's* crew returned to Terminal Island, California, on 3 September 1946, where most were assigned to other ships. My next assignment was to the USS *Columbus* (CA-74). My 18th birthday was celebrated in Long Beach Harbor, California, where the *Columbus* was anchored.

On 17 January 1947, the USS *Columbus* departed for an East Asian tour of duty. In Hawaii, our skipper, "Mad Dog" Moore, was replaced by Captain Milton E. Miles. The latter was one of the finest officers in the U. S. Navy. During the next five months, we were stationed in Shanghai and Tsingtao, China, and in Tokyo Bay, Japan. We returned to our home port of Long Beach long enough to witness Howard Hughes flying his huge seaplane, the "Spruce Goose," on 2 November 1947. Our next port of call was Bremerton Navy Shipyard, Washington, where our ship underwent several months of needed overhaul and repair.

In April 1948, the *Columbus* went to Norfolk, Virginia, in preparation for a European cruise. Crew members who were slated for discharge within a year were assigned to other ships. I reported for duty aboard the USS *Missouri* (BB-63). One week later, we picked up a horde of midshipmen from the Naval Academy at Annapolis, Maryland, and departed for Lisbon, Portugal, with further stops in Nice, France, and Algiers, Algeria. The highlight of the return trip occurred about mid-Atlantic. The sea was extremely calm. It looked like a pane of glass. The skipper stopped the battleship and sounded swimming call. Probably 500 sailors leaped from the ship into the inviting sea. Our next stop was in Cuba for some rum and coke. Then we took our pampered cargo of future naval officers back to their swank country club at Annapolis.

About ten days before Christmas 1948, I was transferred from the *Missouri* to the Norfolk Naval Base for discharge. I became a civilian on 17 December 1948, eight days before my 20th birthday. I spent Christmas and New Year's Day with my new wife, then we sat down to inventory our assets. She was a high school graduate and employed; I was an unemployed high school dropout who had barely completed the ninth grade. Most people who attempted to counsel us about our future were kind, but they usually smiled and wished us well as they walked away shaking their heads. It was obvious that I needed to return to school if I ever expected to support my family.

I attended a technical school in Chicago for a year, then found work as a technician at Eitel McCullough Inc. in Salt Lake City, Utah. They arranged my work schedule so I could attend the University of Utah. Upon graduating in 1955 with a degree in geography, I was commissioned as a second lieutenant in the U. S. Air Force and selected for pilot training.

After primary pilot training at Spence Air Force Base, Georgia, and basic pilot training at Vance AFB, Enid, Oklahoma, I was selected to remain at Vance as a B-25 instructor for two years. During this period I completed an M.S. at Oklahoma State University. In January 1960, I was transferred to James Connally AFB, Waco, Texas where I completed an advanced flying course offered by the USAF IPIS (Instrument Pilot Instructor School). Again, I was chosen to remain as an instructor with IPIS. In 1961, the entire squadron relocated to Randolph AFB, Texas, where we were assigned new, supersonic aircraft which were exciting to fly.

I applied to become an academic instructor in the Department of Geography at the U. S. Air Force Academy in 1963. To my surprise, I was selected. It was a dream tour for my entire family. The dream ended when I volunteered for duty in Vietnam. I arrived in Saigon in December 1967.

My first six months in Vietnam were spent flying from Tan Son Nhut Air Base in Saigon to military installations and activities throughout South Vietnam and Thailand. Occasionally, we went to Australia, Malaysia, Okinawa, Japan, the Philippines, and Hong Kong. I had the pleasure of flying with the 7th Air Force's "Scatback" Squadron, and the U. S. Army's Razor Backs, Decca, and Red Baron units. For a thrill, I flew missions with the Vietnamese Air Force, and Air America.

During my second six months "in country," I was a faculty advisor at the Vietnamese National Defense College. I departed Vietnam in December 1968. After spending Christmas holidays with my family in Utah, I reported to the University of Kansas where I enrolled in a new Ph.D. program specializing in remote sensing. I received a Ph.D. in 1971, complements of the U. S. Air Force.

Following graduation, I reported to Wright-Patterson AFB, Ohio, where I joined the Reconnaissance Branch, Aeronautical Systems Division. Somewhat more than a year later, I was transferred to the Reconnaissance and Surveillance Division, Air Force Avionics Laboratory, at Wright-Patterson. This was my last tour of duty with the Air Force. I retired on 31 August 1974 as a lieutenant colonel.

Roland Mower was awarded the Bronze Star with an oak leaf cluster, the Air Medal with four oak leaf clusters, the Meritorious Service Medal, the Air Force Commendation Medal, and a number of other service medals. During his Vietnam tour, Roland flew nearly 400 sorties, logging 275 hours of combat and 350 hours of combat-support flight time. After retiring from the Air Force, he became a professor at the University of North Dakota where he taught and conducted research in remote sensing for 14 years. He retired from the University in 1988 and accepted the position of Head, Aviation Division, Embry-Riddle Aeronautical University, Prescott, Arizona, and retired from that position in 1993. Roland and Nona, his wife of 52 years, have five children, sixteen grandchildren, and eight great-grandchildren. They live in Mt. Pleasant, Utah.

Donald R. Osborne

Age 16 – United States Army

When I was 16 and my sister was 18, our family separated and I went to live with distant relatives. I quickly became unhappy with my situation and decided to make one last heroic effort to

> *I had become known as "the kid" in every recruiting office within a 25-mile radius.*

get into the U. S. Army. I had tried many times before, but could never produce a reasonably believable, altered birth certificate. I was born on 19 June 1928 and needed to change that year to 1926 in order to fool the recruiters. They had been too sharp for me in the past, and I had become known as "the kid" in every recruiting office within a 25-mile radius.

Finally, in desperation, I took a train from Sunnyvale, California, to San Francisco, where my sister was staying and looked up the draft board in the neighborhood where she lived. It was at 34th and Taravale Avenues, so I took a trolley there. I passed in front of that august place to steel myself for what I was about to do, which, if unsuccessful, could land me in jail. I summoned up my courage, boldly marched into the office, and approached the lady behind the desk. Trying to appear nonchalant, and hoping I didn't faint from nervousness, I said, "Ma'am, tomorrow, March 15, is my 18th birthday. Is this where I sign up?"

They were so happy to get an applicant that they didn't require any proof of my age, and they allowed me to volunteer for immediate induction. Over the next two weeks, I was given a physical, formally notified of my classification as 1A, and inducted into the Army of the United States. I was sent to Camp Beale, California, where I was sworn in on 7 April 1945. I was given a thousand shots, issued a set of uniforms, and put on a troop train with a couple of hundred other recruits bound for Camp Hood, Texas, and infantry basic training. While on that train we learned that President Roosevelt had died.

We were in advanced combat training 17 weeks later when the war ended in August. We were being trained to invade the Japanese home islands and had been told that we were prepared to lose a million men in that operation. The Army may have been prepared to lose a million men in that invasion, but I was determined not to be one of them. I volunteered for the paratroops so that I could avoid landing on Japan in an LCI (Landing Craft, Infantry). Somehow, the idea of jumping out of an airplane didn't bother me as much as a daylight invasion from the sea.

With the war over, we were destined for occupation duty. I was sent from Camp Hood to Fort Ord, California, to Vancouver Barracks, Washington, where we were given the choice of going to Japan to occupy it, or to re-enlist in the regular Army and go wherever we chose. I re-enlisted, was promoted to private first class, given $350 as a re-enlistment bonus, and sent to Fort Benning, Georgia, to jump school. From Fort Benning, I was sent to Fort Bragg, North Carolina, and joined the 504th Parachute Infantry Regiment of the 82nd Airborne Division.

I still carried my California driver's license, and that got me into the motor pool as a truck driver. From there, I became a jeep driver, then I was sent to mechanics school at the Aberdeen Proving Grounds. Thereafter, I became a shop foreman and was promoted to motor sergeant. My enlistment was up in October, 1948. I was discharged as a staff sergeant at age 20, having served almost four years, and after making 21 parachute jumps.

While still in the Army, I finished the requirements for a GED and got my high school diploma. Soon after my Army discharge, I enlisted in the newly formed U. S. Air Force as an aviation cadet and went to flight training at Randolph Field, Texas. I took and passed a two-year, college-level equivalency exam in order to get into flight training. After 13 months, I graduated as a second lieutenant pilot, fifth in my class of 55. This was on 15 September 1950.

The Korean War had just begun, and although I volunteered for combat duty, I was assigned to the Training Command as a flight instructor. They made up for their oversight 17 years later when they sent me to Vietnam where I served two tours and flew 243 combat missions. The first tour was at Tan Son Nhut Air Force Base in Saigon, South Vietnam, where I flew the RF-4C. The second tour was at Takhli Royal Thai Air Force Base, Thailand, where I flew the EB-66 "spy plane."

I attained the rank of major before being forcibly retired in 1970. I had flown almost every fighter in the Air Force inventory, and also a few bombers. At one time, I was a test pilot and current in seven different airplanes, including four first-line fighters. Over the years, I flew the F-51, F-80, F-84, F-86, F-89, F-94, F-102, T-33, T-6, T-28, B-25, C-47, C-45, RB-66, and RF-4.

Don Osborne was awarded the Distinguished Flying Cross, 14 Air Medals, and a number of other decorations. While in the Air Force, he earned a degree in civil engineering. After retiring from the Air Force, he earned a master's degree in education and was a math instructor at a technical college. During the subsequent 20 years, he was an instructor, department head, division chairman, and dean before he retired again in 1990. Currently, he is a part-time math instructor at Central Carolina Technical College, in Sumter, South Carolina. Don and Mabel, his wife of 53 years, have two sons and three grandchildren. In 1999, he had the honor of swearing in his granddaughter as an Army second lieutenant as she entered medical school on an ROTC scholarship. Don and Mabel live in Sumter, South Carolina.

William F. Thames
Age 15 – United States Army

I was born in Vernon, Florida, on 21 February 1930, the oldest of six children, all boys. This was in the midst of the Great Depression. There was no money, not much food, and no work. We were considered dirt

> ... I had to find a way to get into the military so I could do my part.

poor, as were most other people during that time. To this day I can vividly remember the cold winters and attending school without a good coat to keep warm. Shoes were not available for us poor folks, and I will never forget how my feet would crack due to the cold and no shoes.

When I was 11, in 1941, I heard the radio broadcast of the Japanese bombing of Pearl Harbor. I had to continue in school while most of my older friends were being drafted into the Army or the Navy. I felt that I had to do something to help our men in service. It was late 1943 when I first falsified my age, at age 13, to obtain work in the new shipyard in Panama City, Florida. I was able to get into a school to learn welding and burning. After completing school I worked as a welder until early 1945. I got tired of going home with burned eyes. I would spend almost all night treating them so that I could work the next day.

I had kept in contact with my friends who were serving in the military. One was in the Army and had been seriously wounded in Europe. The other was in the Navy and had been on two ships that were torpedoed and sunk. At that time I had to find a way to get into the military so I could do my part.

On 14 May 1945, at the age of 15, I proceeded to the Washington County, Florida, Selective Service office and registered for the draft, stating my birth date as 14 May 1927. I was not asked for proof of age. One month later I was ordered to report for a physical exam. I was put on a Greyhound bus with others and sent to Camp Blanding,

Florida, for a physical. About one week later, on 30 June 1945, we were sent to Montgomery, Alabama, and sworn into the Army. We were promptly put on a bus and sent to Sheppard Field, Texas, for basic training. Following that, I was sent to Fort McPherson, Georgia, for field artillery training. Shortly after arriving at Fort McPherson, I received orders to attend camouflage school at Geiger Air Force Base, Spokane, Washington, and from there to Brooks Field, Texas, for a short stay. From Brooks Field I was sent to Tyndall Field, located in Panama City, Florida, where I was to train as a cook, but cooking was not my game.

I had always made it a point to keep a close check of the bulletin board where they would post notices for volunteers. One of the first things you learn in military service is not to volunteer for anything because you would most likely get the opposite of what you asked for. However, when a notice was posted for volunteers for duty in the Panama Canal Zone, I promptly placed my name on the list. I was selected for this duty and was immediately sent to New Orleans, Louisiana, where we were placed on a troopship and sent to Panama. After arriving in Panama, I was assigned to the 628th/629th Aircraft Control and Warning Group under the 6th Fighter Wing at Albrook Air Force Base. I worked for a wise, old, first sergeant. To this day, I believe that he knew that I was underage, just a kid, but he never said anything to me about it. He took me under his wing and made me attend every school he could put me in, two of those being teletype and radio school. This was my first real job in the Army Air Forces.

We had a large number of outposts located throughout the countries of Panama and Columbia. These outposts consisted of a crew of about 10 to 12 men, a sergeant-in-charge, a cook, a medic, two radio operators, a diesel mechanic, a supply clerk, a clerk, a truck driver and mechanic, and two to four men for as-needed duty. I was assigned to outpost station #6, located on top of a mountain. The only way to the outpost was by riding in a truck or walking. They had made a small road with just enough room to drive a 3/4-ton truck up to the station. Our supplies were delivered by boat and had to be trucked up the mountain. Mail was dropped by plane. Our job was to report to headquarters all aircraft and ships that came near our station. This was for the protection of the Panama Canal. I enjoyed my 16th birthday there.

After my tour of duty was up, I was sent back to Howard Air Force Base for a short stay. Our units were sent back to the States by air transport and assigned to an underground station at Rosyln, Long Island, New York, where I worked as a teletype operator until I was discharged in November, 1948.

At the start of the Korean War in 1950, I was recalled to active duty in the Air Force. I decided to go down to the local Navy recruiter and join the Navy. I was immediately sent to Montgomery, Alabama, where I took the oath. From there I was sent to Great Lakes Naval Training Center for two weeks of refresher training, after which I was stationed aboard the heavy cruiser, USS *Albany* (CA-123). This was followed by a tour of duty at the Naval Air Station, Jacksonville, Florida, then to the Naval Air Station, Guantanamo Bay, Cuba. From there we were stationed at the U.S. Naval Submarine Base, New London, Connecticut. Sea duty followed. I served a tour of duty on the following ships: the aircraft carrier, USS *Essex* (CVS-9); the fleet oiler, USS *Canisteo* (AO-99); the aircraft carrier, USS *Antietam* (CVS-36); and the fleet supply ship, USS *Alstede* (AF-48). My last tour of duty before retirement was on the staff of Commander, Service Force, U.S. Atlanta Fleet. I retired in 1967 at the rank of radioman first class with 22 years of service.

While in the Navy, I fulfilled a promise I had made to my parents: I would get my high school diploma if they would let me remain in military service. I obtained my GED in 1959. I received my authentic high school diploma from the State of Florida in October 2000.

Bill Thames returned to Pensacola after his discharge from the Air Force in 1948 and enrolled in Pensacola Junior College. He was living with his uncle and aunt, and had to catch a bus to school. A gorgeous 15-year-old girl who lived two houses away caught the same bus. She had long, dark, flowing hair. Bill made it a point to walk close behind her to the bus stop. After about three days of this, she stopped one morning and said to him, "You might as well walk with me." They were married on February 24, 1950, just before his naval career began. Now, 51 years later, Barbara and Bill have six children (five daughters and one son), nine grandchildren, and eight great-grandchildren. After he retired from the Navy, Bill went to work for Sacred Heart Hospital and retired as Director of Physical Plant and Engineering after 28 years. Bill and Barbara live in Milton, Florida.

Robert Davidson

Age 16 – United States Army

I joined a para-military group called Future Marines at age 14 in 1943. This was a group of youngsters ranging in age from 14 to 17 who wanted to be Marines when they turned 17. This group was based in

> *Whenever my name was called I thought, "This is it!"*

Milwaukee, Wisconsin, where I was born on 3 February 1929.

I stayed with the Future Marines until 1945 when I tried to join the Marine Corps. I didn't pass the physical. I then talked my mother into signing papers for me to join the U. S. Army, stating that I was 18. I passed the physical and was inducted into the Army at Fort Sheridan, Illinois, on 15 August 1945. I enjoyed being in the Army and didn't have any problems except that I was fearful that someone would find out that I was underage. Whenever my name was called I thought, "This is it!"

My father had been away in the service when I joined the Army. When he returned home and discovered what my mother and I had done, he was extremely upset and demanded to know where I was. He then notified the military authorities and I was returned to the separation center at Fort Sheridan where I was processed, given the ruptured duck, and discharged in December 1945 because of a fraudulent enlistment.

My father died soon after I was discharged, so I legally enlisted in the Army when I turned 17. I was sent to Fort Knox, Kentucky, for basic training for the second time. I did not have the same drill sergeant, but I was in a training company near the one I was in the first time. I did see my old drill sergeant, but he did not remember me all that well.

I served in several foreign countries and with a number of units while with the regular Army and with the Army Reserves. I spent quite a bit of time in Korea and in Germany, in addition to being stationed at a number of posts in the United States. Some of the units I served with include: the 7th Infantry Division Military Police, the 17th Infantry Regiment, the 62nd MP Highway Patrol, 7751st MP Customs, 540th MP Railway Guard Battalion.

I was involved in a riot in Munich, Germany, in 1954. We were trying to break up a fight in a bar when a hand grenade was thrown through the bar window. I don't remember much more. I woke up in a military hospital in Heidelberg, Germany, to find that a portion of my nose had been blown away. But unbeknownst to me, the portion that had been blown off had been found, and the doctors reattached it. I underwent many weeks of treatment and surgery. Today, I have only a small scar to remind me of that incident.

After I was released from the hospital in Germany, I returned Stateside and underwent more treatment at Walter Reed General Hospital. I was discharged from the Army after being released from the hospital. I stayed in the reserves and was recalled to active duty in Korea. I was later released to inactive duty but served several more tours of active duty. While on active duty, I did a second tour in Korea during 1957-58, and while there, I married a Korean girl who has been with me since then.

I retired as a master sergeant in 1989 after 35 years of service. I will never forget my service and have never regretted the time I served. I would gladly do it again!

Bob Davidson, when not on active duty with the Army, worked for the Springfield, Missouri, police department as a motorcycle patrolman and as a supervisor in the traffic division. He retired from that job in 1980. Bob and Chin, his wife of 44 years, have a daughter. They live in Nixa, Missouri.

Joseph J. Jenkins

Age 16 – United States Army

I thought I was born on 22 August 1929. At least that's what Mom had always maintained. I could say something about being raised during the great Depression, but for those who lived it, no explanation is necessary. For those who didn't, no explanation would suffice.

> I was only 15, but what the hell, I could try.

During the Second World War, my hometown was host to the Deshon Army Hospital. I often met some of the soldiers who were patients there in the Butler, Pennsylvania, facility. They were from all over the country – mostly young fellows not much older than myself. I listened to their stories over a cup of coffee or a soft drink in the local restaurants, and wanted to be one of them. There was no way I was going to get into the service legitimately, I reasoned.

The war was going hot and heavy in the Pacific on that afternoon in 1945 when I felt I had to do something, anything, to get involved. I was only 15, but what the hell, I could try.

I went to the local courthouse where young men of 18 had to register for the draft. It was 15 June 1945. I hesitated a bit before going into the room where one lady sat at a lonely desk, seemingly uninterested in her surroundings. I went in and said that I wanted to register for the draft, fully expecting her to tell me to, "Get the hell out of here, kid!" She looked at me and asked, "When did you turn eighteen?" I said, "Two days ago," not even knowing what day that would turn out to be. O.K. No problem. I signed up, checked the calendar to see that "two days ago" was the 13th of June, and that was it.

At that time they apparently really didn't give a damn about my real age. They needed soldiers (the term "cannon fodder" now comes to mind), and they wouldn't look a gift horse in the mouth. I was never asked for a birth certificate or other proof of birth. Hell, I was there, so I must have been born!

Three weeks later I was ordered to Pittsburgh for a physical. Again, no problem. On 5 September 1945, just two weeks after turning 16, I was to report for active duty, less than three months after registering for the draft.

Basic training was at Fort McClellan, Alabama. As soon as basic was over, I took a short discharge to re-enlist in the regular Army, for with the enlistment went a choice of overseas assignments. I was a bit disappointed that the shooting war had ended before I got overseas; nevertheless, overseas is where I wanted to go. There were four of us in a little "group," and two locations for assignment were open: Alaska and the Panama Canal Zone. We flipped a coin, two of us going south and two going north. I went south, to serve with the Army Air Forces. I enjoyed Panama for over two years, mostly at Albrook Field, then served a while in the Galapagos Islands. I got out of the Army in 1948.

I was still interested in the military, so I joined the local National Guard, mostly to play softball with them. I thought I could be a good second baseman. Before I even got to see the field, the Korean War came along and we were activated. I went in early to help process the others, since my military specialty was in the field of administration at the time. My younger brother gave the supreme sacrifice in the Korean War, an act which only gave me more incentive to stay with the military.

Even though I had been in and out of the service without any problem with my fake birth date, I kept my old records for purposes of longevity, or continuity, or whatever. It always bothered me that my birth date was wrong, and I agonized over how to go about correcting it. There were stories about those who, having enlisted too young, were given less than honorable discharges, and that sort of bothered me. I finally decided to take the bull by the horns and look the situation right between the eyes. So, later, while serving in Germany, and now a master sergeant, I went to the personnel department to have my records corrected. I told them that they had the wrong birth date and that it was not in June, but in August. I was asked to produce a birth certificate, and I had to write to Harrisburg, Pennsylvania, to get one from the official state-records branch. My mother was off by one day, according to the official records. I was born on 23 August 1929, not on 22 August, as I had been led to believe. To her dying day, Mom insisted that the doctor was wrong and she was right, for, after all, as she would say, "I was there!"

I attended officers candidate school in Fort Sill, Oklahoma, and was commissioned a 2nd lieutenant. Commissioning was followed by assignments in the artillery. While in Alaska, commanding a Nike-Hercules battery, I couldn't help notice that the war in Vietnam wasn't going too well. My old outfit, the 101st Airborne Division, was taking some serious hits. I called the Pentagon, where I had a friend, and asked about the possibility of going to Vietnam to help out. He first asked me in what capacity I would go, and when I told him as a field artillery officer, he asked me how fast I could pack my bag!

I went home that day and asked my wife which one of these United States she would like to live in. I explained that I would be going to Vietnam, and that she and the family would be settled in whatever state she desired while I was there; she just about fainted. It didn't take her long, however, to decide on El Paso, Texas, where I had gone to school at the Antiaircraft Artillery Training Center at Fort Bliss.

In Vietnam I was assigned as a battery commander. I commanded Battery A, 2nd Battalion (Airborne), 320th Artillery Regiment, 101st Airborne Division, a 105mm outfit. My tour was from 1966 to early 1967. I spent the entire tour as a commander, as opposed to the standard practice at the time of rotating commanders after six months to allow more officers to have combat command time. I reasoned with my commander that this was not a training exercise, and he agreed.

One of the memorable accomplishments of the tour was the time we fired the "fleschette" round for the first time in active combat against a charging enemy. This was the beehive round, loaded with small darts that would cover an area the size of a football field if set to detonate at a certain height. We fired the round point-blank at the enemy, which stopped them cold.

I returned to the States and spent the last part of the year (1967) in the Air Defense Command at Pittsburgh, Pennsylvania, during which time I was promoted to major. I retired on the last day of 1967, and it was one helluva New Year's Eve party we had!

Joe Jenkins was awarded the Purple Heart and the Bronze Star with combat "V" and an oak leaf cluster for his actions in Vietnam. After retiring, he went to work as a special agent with the FAA

(Federal Aviation Administration) in 1972 at the time that airport security was something new. His role as special agent was coupled with the role of a federal air marshal, which required him to be ready to go on a mission to any part of the world at a moment's notice. After 21 years with the federal government, he retired and returned to Pennsylvania. Joe and his wife Joann have a combined family of nine children and sixteen grandchildren. They live in Butler, Pennsylvania.

✓ *INCIDENTally — Wheels down?* – In 1944, our squadron's final training before combat included a stay on Maui in the Hawaiian Islands. Towards the end of that training, they would wake us up about 3:00 a.m., and we would fly practice radar-runs up and down the coast until dawn. After three tedious hours, I would be half asleep on the flight back to our base. Needless to say, the pilot was equally drowsy. Anyway, one morning as we arrived back to the base, I was jolted awake by an urgent shout from the tower, "TBM in final, take a wave off, your wheels are up!" The tower had spotted us about to touch down on the runway with no wheels.

Following that near miss, the pilot and I agreed that before all future landings, I would read him the following check list, "Wheels down? Flaps down? Mixture rich? Prop in low pitch?" We never had that problem again. – *Thomas J. Craig.*

Gerald Mooneyham
Age 15 – United States Army

I was born in Chanute, Kansas, on 5 November 1930, the youngest of twelve (six boys and six girls). Our family moved to California in 1935 or '36 in an old Whippet automobile. My brother Jim and I were the

I must have washed every pot and pan that Fort Lewis had, ...

only kids still at home. My mother died in 1938, and Jim and I were left to fend for ourselves. After spending time in several homes, we eventually wound up working on adjoining farms in Laton, California. When I was 13, my oldest brother Vernon found me and took me to his home in Lewiston, Idaho.

In October 1944, Vernon and Jim encouraged me to go with them to enlist in the Army. The recruiter asked me about my age. I told him that I was 16, but would be 17 the following month. In the meantime, my brothers chickened out, but both served later on. On 5

November 1945, I went back to the same recruiting office to enlist. I asked the sergeant if he remembered me. He said, "Yes, sign here." I was sworn into the Army on 6 November 1945 at Fort Lewis, Washington, at age 15.

I learned very quickly what a life I had to look forward to when I was horsing around and failed to answer to roll call. I was still in civilian clothes, but I wound up on KP. I must have washed every pot and pan that Fort Lewis had, and I peeled enough spuds for the entire U. S. Army.

I had signed up for the military police, so I was shipped to Camp Robinson, Arkansas, for basic training. After basic, I took MP training at Camp Robinson.

In February 1946, I was sent to Le Havre, France, and wound up in the newly formed 73rd MP Company in Marseille, France. A short time later, that company was broken up and our unit was shipped to

Nuremberg, Germany, where we were assigned to the 793rd MP Battalion. I went to the trials at the Palace of Justice a couple of times, but I wasn't impressed, so I missed out on a lot of history.

My enlistment ended in 1948. I re-enlisted in 1949 and was shipped to Tokyo, Japan, where I was assigned to the 720 MP Battalion. In June 1950, we were advised that North Korea was attacking South Korea and that a few American troops were there. Hell, I had never heard of Korea! I immediately volunteered for duty in Korea, but I didn't get there until September 1950 when we made the invasion at Inchon. I was a member of the newly formed 10th Corps MP Company. We had brought thirteen motorcycles from Japan to Korea. It was rather eerie coming off the landing craft at midnight with artillery and small-arms fire lighting up the beach. We all landed safely without mishap.

While working on my motorcycle near Seoul, someone kicked me from behind and I came up ready to fight. Lo and behold, it was my twin brothers, Bob and Bill, who had somehow found out that I was in Korea. The three of us were all quite tall; Bob was 6-feet-4 inches, Bill was 6-feet 5-inches, and I was 6-feet 5-inches.

My brothers talked me into requesting a transfer to the 6th Medium Tank Battalion, 24th Infantry Division. I objected because I knew nothing about a tank. They convinced me that they would teach me everything I needed to know in less time than it would take to find their outfit, if and when my transfer was approved. They were both master sergeants at the time and had influence with someone, because my transfer was approved. My first sergeant advised me that the 24th Division was near the Yalu River. I hopped a flight at Kimpo Air Base to Pyongyang where I caught a ride on a 2½-ton truck heading toward the Yalu River. I located my brothers' outfit which was seven miles from the Yalu River. We celebrated that night.

The next night the Chinese crossed the Yalu and all hell broke loose! I hopped into a supply truck and we started back toward Seoul. We didn't lose anybody or any tanks in our march to the rear. I quickly learned about the M46 tank and was promoted to master sergeant shortly after my 21st birthday. Bob was wounded and returned Stateside. Bill was given a battlefield commission as a second lieutenant and went home shortly thereafter. Bob was given a commission to second lieutenant shortly after he returned to duty.

Both Bob and Bill retired after 20 years of service. I have talked only about brothers Bob and Bill, but all five of my brothers served in the military. Combined, the six of us have over 70 years of service.

I retired on 1 January 1966 as a first sergeant after 20 years of service.

Jerry Mooneyham was hired as a deputy sheriff in Santa Cruz, California, immediately after he retired from the Army. After 7 years, he moved to Oregon where he retired from the Phoenix, Oregon, Police Department after serving 14 years as a patrolman, sergeant, lieutenant, and captain. Jerry has nine children, eighteen grandchildren, and five great-grandchildren. He lives in Lewiston, Idaho.

✓ *INCIDENTally* — **Drink – or else!** – While on board ship in San Francisco harbor in 1946, I went to the head about midnight to relieve myself. A member of the crew came up to me, handed me a bottle of "rotgut," pointed a .45 pistol at my head, and demanded that I drink it. I did, and he left. Evidently, he did the same thing to other crew members, including the captain, until he was captured and taken off the ship in a straightjacket. I never saw him again after that weird event. – *Harry R. Wallace.*

Donald L. Streeter

Age 13 – Texas State Guard
Age 14 – United States Army Air Forces

Although I was an "A" student, I quit school while in the eighth grade at the age of 12. Things were a bit tough for my family, and we got a little hungry. I went to work making ice cream for a

> The recruiter saw my sloppy work and sent me home with a pat on the head.

small family-owned operation. This was in Dallas, Texas, where I was born on 3 January 1931.

I joined the Texas State Guard when I was 13. I told them that I was 16, which was the age requirement. In six months I was a corporal and a light machine gunner. I loved the military regimen and the discipline from the start. I had a burning desire to get into the war.

At age 13, I would occasionally go on day trips with a friend who drove an 18-wheel tractor-trailer. I learned to drive an 18-wheeler by watching him closely. He let me drive twice. Later, another friend told me about a company in Irving, Texas, that needed drivers. I

walked in the company office, the owner handed me some keys, pointed to a tractor-trailer, and told me to take it to Ballinger, Texas, with a load of 20-inch diameter pipe, 49 feet long. I drove off, scared to death. I was a few months shy of 14.

My driving career went very well. I drove for the Curtis Candy Company out of Dallas, and drove throughout Texas, Arkansas, and Mississippi for another company whose name I can't remember. But above all, I wanted to get into the war.

I doctored up my birth certificate and went to the Navy recruiting office in Dallas. The recruiter saw my sloppy work and sent me home with a pat on the head. I found out afterwards that all I needed to do was to get my parents to sign that I was 17 and I would be accepted.

I obtained a consent form for enlistment in the Army Air Forces. I approached my mom with the form, and both she and dad signed it. She told me later she had two choices: to say no, and I would continue driving tractor-trailer rigs, which she considered too dangerous, or to sign.

I was sworn into the U. S. Army Air Forces in Dallas, Texas, on 12 November 1945. I was 14 years old, 5-feet 10½-inches tall, and weighed 133 pounds.

On the day of my enlistment I was sent to Fort Sam Houston, Texas. After three weeks there in "tent city," I was sent to Sheppard Field, Texas, for basic training. Since I had served more than a year in the Texas State Guard and had infantry training at Camp Wolters in Mineral Wells, Texas, they cut my basic short by three weeks and made me part of the permanent party at Sheppard. They made me a cook!

There was an epidemic of bacterial spinal meningitis at Sheppard in March 1946. I caught it and almost died. After I recovered, I couldn't lift any significant weight, so they sent me to Boca Raton, Florida, as a military policeman. I spent seven years in law enforcement and loved it. When I attained the grade of technical sergeant, they changed my career field, promoted me to first sergeant, and assigned me to Pittsburgh, Pennsylvania, where I met the love of my life, my future wife.

I spent the next 13 years in the Strategic Air Command. In 1965, I was the wing sergeant major of a B-52 Wing at Homestead Air Force Base, Florida, and was selected for assignment to the Strategic Air Command headquarters. I was to be the top-secret control officer in the Inspector General's office at SAC. I had to have a top-secret clearance, which required a background check. Naturally, I entered my correct date of birth on the background information request. That produced a "blip" on the record of investigation when it came back. My boss, Brigadier General Nichols, called me into his office and told me there was a little discrepancy on the background investigation results. After saying that, he stood up, extended his hand, and said two of the most beautiful words in the English language, "Welcome aboard!" He signed off on the investigation results, and that was it.

I retired on 1 July 1967 as a senior master sergeant after nearly 22 years of service. I was 36 years old. After I retired, an Air Force accounting office sent me a form letter which stated that there was a discrepancy in my birth date and asked me for a copy of my birth certificate. I sent it to them, and that's the end of the story.

Don Streeter was awarded the Air Force Commendation Medal with three oak leaf clusters. He never attended high school, but he earned a GED in 1951 and an A.A. in liberal arts in 1981. Twelve days after his retirement from the Air Force, he was hired by the Army and Air Force Exchange Service, and retired after 24 years as chief of their Labor-Management Relations Division. He now owns and operates a successful consulting business in federal labor-management relations. Don and Jeanne, his wife of 49 years, have two children and four grandchildren. Sadly, their only granddaughter, 14-year-old Natalie Prince, was killed in a sight-seeing helicopter accident in Maui, Hawaii, on 21 July 2000. Don and Jeanne live in Grand Prairie, Texas.

✔ *INCIDENTally — The Rose Bowl.* – In 1944 while my ship was in the States for repairs, the Salvation Army gave my friends and me six tickets to the Rose Bowl game. I wasn't a drinker, and on New Year's Day I found myself with five guys who had passed out from partying the night before. I went to the game by myself and gave away the other five tickets. – *William P. Mazzoni.*

Cres C. Baca

Age 15 – United States Army Air Forces

I was born on a dirt-poor ranch near Santa Rosa, New Mexico, on 18 October 1930. Our home was approximately two miles (if you were a crow) from the school I attended as a child. It was close to 3½ miles

> In 1945, barely 15 years old, I began looking for ways to enlist.

when we walked following the road and using the bridge to cross the Pecos river. On 8 December 1941, I was on my way to school, and as I passed the local drug store, I spied the *Albuquerque Journal* with headlines reading "Japs Attack Pearl Harbor, War Declared." I recall running all the way back home to inform my parents that we were at war. I don't know what I thought I would accomplish by doing so, but I did manage to skip school that day.

From that day forward, I can remember that patriotism in America was feverish. My mother moved to Albuquerque as a result of divorce in 1942, and for the following three years, my only ambition was to enlist in a uniformed service. All my friends felt the same way. It was all we could talk about. However, most of my friends were about two years older than I, and their day to enlist came sooner than mine.

In 1945, barely 15 years old, I began looking for ways to enlist. My motivation at this point was that my best friend, now 17 years old, was enlisting with parental consent. At the Navy recruiting station, I was not accorded a very warm welcome. But at the Army station, I was told that if I was 17, I only needed a notarized statement to that effect from my parent, and I would be able to enlist. On 18 October 1945, my 15th birthday, I began pestering my mother to sign such a statement. She fought a great battle, but I finally wore her down and she agreed to sign if I would wait until after Christmas to depart. I agreed. The next hurdle was to get the statement notarized. The problem was solved when my mother admitted that the owner of a real-estate company who knew the family was also a notary public. He was well known in the city because of his huge height; everyone referred to him as "Seven-Foot Pickett." When I took that statement to the recruiter, it passed muster without question. On 26 December 1945, I was on a Greyhound bus to Fort Bliss, Texas, a proud soldier in the United States Army Air Forces.

I was processed in at Fort Bliss, issued uniforms, and then sent to Wichita Falls, Texas, for basic training. After basic, it was to military-police school, then directly to Germany. I was part of the replacement forces relieving the World War II combat troops that were being sent home. My MP unit moved several times while in Europe. I saw service at Erlangan, Erding, and Landsberg, Germany.

While at Landsberg, my patrol partner and I were in pursuit of black-market operatives that were operating out of a displaced-persons camp. We drew small-arms fire and my partner was shot once in the head. Because we were crawling toward the camp in about four inches of snow, I did not realize immediately that he had been hit. However, when he failed to move up with me, I turned and saw the unmistakable color of blood in the snow. I returned to our jeep and radioed for help. My partner was dead. I was 16 years old, and visibly shaken. I asked to see a Catholic chaplain. I recall he was a tall, rugged-looking man. I told him that I was only 16 years old and wanted to go home immediately. He talked to me for about three hours, calmed me down, and sent me back to my quarters. I never saw him again, never heard any more about it, and didn't get to go home. Perhaps he didn't believe me, perhaps he did not care, but I finished my tour.

I returned home in July 1948 with instructions to immediately register with my local draft board. When I went to register, I took my birth certificate. I was told that I could not register because I was not yet 18 years old. So there I was, a full-fledged veteran of World War II, unqualified to register with the draft board!

If I learned one thing during that first tour of duty, it was that I was sorely in need of a decent education. I was determined that one day, I too, would be a college "ring knocker." I finished high school, re-enlisted in the Air Force in late 1949, and started taking college courses in the evening. By 1957, when I was a Korean police-action veteran, and a staff sergeant with almost three years of college, I was asked to take the examination for officers candidate school (OCS). I did, and in September of that year, I was enrolled in OCS Class 58-A, at San Antonio, Texas. On 21 March 1958, I was commissioned a second lieutenant.

My first assignment as an officer was back to Germany as an air-police officer, followed by a tour at Colorado Springs, Colorado, as a security inspector, then to Thule, Greenland, as a squadron commander, then to Fort Leavenworth, Kansas, as an exchange officer to the Army. Next, I went to Panama for a time, then to Kirtland Air Force Base, New Mexico. I then went to Thailand where we secured a large air base, the home of the B-52s used in the Vietnam War. There were two more tours at Stateside bases and an assignment with the Department of Defense as a nuclear surety-inspection team chief.

When I was a second lieutenant, General Curtis LeMay was the Air Force Chief of Staff. In a speech outlining his vision for America's Air Force, he detailed what the successful Air Force officer would need to advance through the ranks. I took him at his word, attended all of the military schools required, and earned a master's degree from an accredited university. I went where I was told, stayed as long as they wanted me to, worked hard, and complained little. The result was on-time promotions and retirement as a colonel on 30 June 1986. I served more than 39 years.

I have been asked numerous times, if I had it to do over again, what would I change, or do differently. My answer has always been the same: I would change nothing! My life has been full and exciting. I have been very scared several times, but I survived. I married a great lady and supportive friend, and together we raised a fine family. I loved military life and will die a happy man.

Cres Baca was awarded the Department of Defense Superior Service Medal, the Legion of Merit, the Air Force Meritorious Service Medal with oak leaf cluster, the Air Force Commendation Medal with oak leaf cluster, the Army Commendation Medal, the Royal Thai Supreme Command Forward Badge (Thailand), and a number of other medals. After his retirement he was asked by Governor Garrey Curruthers to chair the New Mexico Adult Parole Board, which he did for 3½ years. In 1991 and 1992 he was the New Mexico State Director of H. Ross Perot's "United we Stand America" presidential campaign.

Since 1993, he has been involved in volunteer work, primarily with the Benevolent and Protective Order of Elks, which he served as New Mexico state president in 1999-2000. Cres and Betty, his wife of 49 years, have five children and eight grandchildren. They live in Los Lunas, New Mexico.

✔ *INCIDENTally* — **Dismissed!** – I was a 16-year-old recruit at the Marine boot camp at San Diego in the fall of 1950. I lived in fear that my age would be discovered, so I tried my best to be the best and follow all the rules. Whatever was said, I was there to do all that was called for. One day when we were marching to chow, another platoon was coming around the corner and right toward us. Someone had to move. Our squad leaders started getting out of the way of the other platoon without waiting for a command from the drill instructor. Our DI, Sergeant Annese, was a muscular man who looked like a human bulldog and barked like one. He was very upset about this, and when we marched back to our tents to close the day, he said, "RIGHT FACE, listen up. FROM NOW ON, anytime anyone gets in your road, knock them down and run over them!" He repeated that order loud and clear, followed by, "IS THAT CLEAR?" We all responded, "YES, SIR!"

Unfortunately, he was standing right in front of me with his arms folded. He was right in my way when he yelled, "DISMISSED!" Without hesitation, I knocked him down and was on top of him so quickly that we were nearly trampled by the others running from the formation. I will never forget the look in his eyes as we were eyeball-to-eyeball. He grabbed me by the lapels and growled, "Get out of here!" Nothing further was ever said.

Years went by. I was married and my wife was opening mail at Christmas time. She said to me, "Who is Joseph A. Annese?" I smiled and said that he was my DI in boot camp. She said, "Of all the people he put through boot camp, how would he remember your name, or anything about you, and send you a Christmas card?" I laughed and said, "No, Ann, the proper question would be: 'How could he ever forget me?'" – *William C. Morgan.*

Bruce L. Salisbury

Age 15 – United States Army

In the middle 1940s, I was a teenage boy living in the small and boring town of Farmington, New Mexico. World War II was just ending, and I felt as though I had been cheated out of the

..., I drifted off to sleep that night owning the proud title of regular Army soldier.

opportunity to show them what kind of warrior I could be. I was born several years too late to be a part of the "war that saved the world."

In the fall of 1945, I decided that I could not stay in this town of 3,300 souls with its dirt streets and sidewalks that were rolled up promptly at dark. A dysfunctional family caused me to make the decision to find another life. I had already quit school after a dispute with my mother over playing football. For some reason, she didn't want me to go out there and bang heads with the big boys. So at age 15, I climbed on a bus and rode to Durango, Colorado, where I was determined to join the Army and find some excitement.

I walked into the Durango post office and entered a room with a big sign above the door that read "Draft Board." I told them that I had come to sign up for the draft. A rather bossy woman told me to go home and come back after the end of the year and after the holidays. I told her that she could go to hell and that I was not coming back. This caused some commotion. She jumped up and demanded that I tell her when I would turn 18. I was pretty good at math and quickly invented the date of 30

December 1927 instead of the more familiar, correct date of 13 May 1930. The lady demanded that I get myself back in there, and the fingers flew on those old typewriters as I gave them my information.

I had been staying in Durango, and when it was time for me to go for a physical in Denver, Colorado, an old soldier who knew my plan suggested that I not go in when requested, but let the police come and get me. As a result, two other guys and myself were loaded onto the little narrow-gage train in Durango with some military guy who was assigned the job of guarding the three of us until we got to Fort Logan, near Denver. The rest of the draftees glared at us, but we managed the slow and scenic trip without event. Shortly I had been examined, questioned, prodded, and poked, and was declared fit for service in the U. S. Army. They gave us draftee serial numbers and sent us off on another train bound for Fort Leavenworth, Kansas. I was sworn into the Army on 16 January 1946.

After arriving in Fort Leavenworth, we milled around, learning the ropes. One morning a big, burly, sergeant came and ordered us to fall in on the street for a little lecture. Part of what he told us was, that if we wanted to really get ahead in the military, we should transfer to the regular Army. This seemed like a good plan, as I intended to stay awhile. I also thought that it might be less likely for a regular to be asked for a birth certificate. When the request was made to step forward, I was among the first to do so. By nightfall, my serial number that had served me as a draftee now had the letters RA in front of it. With only a few days' experience, I drifted off to sleep that night owning the proud title of regular Army soldier.

On a number of occasions I was asked for a birth certificate, and my answer was always the same, "Don't have one. Never had one." Soon enough, the question was not asked again. I got into military life and managed to make the deception work, even though my military age made it look like I had been born a few months after my eldest brother and ten months before another older brother, who was also serving in the Army Air Forces.

I was assigned to the Army Air Forces and trained in aircraft maintenance. I went through the basic aviation school in Biloxi, Mississippi, then went on assignments with reconnaissance squadrons at several locations: Guam, Hawaii, Fairfield Suisun Air Force Base in California, Shemya Island in the Aleutians, and then to Japan where I was in the 512 Reconnaissance Squadron during the Korean War. Our unit flew out of Yokota and Misawa Air Force Bases. I rotated home in late 1951.

When I returned to the States, I was assigned to the Strategic Air Command at Biggs AFB, Texas. I worked on, and flew with, KB-29 refueling tanker aircraft and with B-50 bombers. I was sent to Walker

AFB, New Mexico, and was trained in the giant B-36 bombers. During this time we were constantly under deployment. One memorable flight home brought us non-stop from Guam to Roswell, New Mexico.

On 1 November 1952, I married Airman Third Class Dorothy Barter in the chapel at Carswell AFB, Texas. In 1956, I left the Air Force, but soon returned. I re-enlisted in Denver, Colorado, and was assigned to the Air Defense Command at Peterson Field and Ent AFB, Colorado. From there, my career took me to Alaska, once more in reconnaissance squadrons. Four years in Fairbanks taught me to love inland Alaska, but by then I was married and we had three little kids. Because of the long, hard, winters, my wife was not happy in Alaska. We came back to the States and were assigned to Minot, North Dakota. I had to learn all about the F-106 Delta Dart on this tour with the Air Defense Command.

After completing my tour at Minot, I returned to Alaska, and to Shemya Island. Not too many men are lucky enough to pull two tours on that remote island. I was there in 1964 when the earthquake hit Alaska, but we hardly felt it. I returned to Fairchild AFB, Washington, where I retired on 1 March 1966. I was one of the youngest American servicemen to retire with 20 years of service at the age of 35. I still loved the Air Force, but our children wanted to attend the same high school and play football and run track.

Bruce Salisbury had not finished his first semester of high school before entering the Army. In 1979, he graduated from New Mexico State University with honors. Actually, his college years were a family affair. His wife and youngest son were enrolled at the same time, lived in a small family-housing unit, had a great time, and graduated together. His oldest son served 20 years in the Air Force, and his daughter served in the Air Force for eight years. Bruce and Dottie, his wife of 49 years, live in Aztec, New Mexico.

Robert F. Feikema
Age 16 – United States Navy

I was born in Grand Rapids, Michigan, on 7 August 1929, but soon moved to Holland, Michigan, to be near family. I quit school at age 15 in the summer of 1945 and tried to join the

> *I badly wanted to get off that rock, so I thought it was time to use my ace-in-the-hole.*

Navy. I didn't know that I needed proof that I was 17, and that even at 17, I would need someone to sign for me. To this day, I don't know why I didn't say that I was 18.

After my first attempt to join at age 15, I had two copies made of my birth certificate. I altered my birth date and had a photo copy made to cover up any defects. I showed it to my dad. The answer was the same, *"No!"* He took the birth certificate to the kitchen sink, lit a match, and burned it. That was that for now, but I didn't give up.

Two months later, the day after the first atomic bomb was dropped on Japan, I turned 16. I altered the other copy of my birth certificate like I had done the first one, but this time I went to a different photo shop in fear that they might remember me and report me to the Navy. I nagged Dad until he finally signed. I enlisted in the Navy on 7 December 1945, but I was not sworn in until 22 January 1946.

I went to the Great Lakes Naval Training Center for boot camp. We had some free time one night, so I was playing basketball with the guys. I got a bad pain in my side and fell to the deck. I woke up in the base hospital. I opened my eyes and a doctor was looking down at me. I thought that I was home because the doctor was our family doctor. I didn't know that he was in the Navy.

I was put into a scarlet-fever ward for 21 days, but I didn't have scarlet fever! I had had scarlet fever when I was 12 years old. It's a good thing that I had a GI haircut or I might have pulled all my hair out. It was like 21 days in jail!

After boot camp, I was sent to Treasure Island, California, for reassignment. From there, I went to Guam aboard the USS *Oneida* (APA-221). I worked on aircraft and trucks at the Naval Air Station, Guam. I didn't like Guam very well. I wanted to be on a ship, but my name just didn't get on the out-going unit list.

I badly wanted to get off that rock, so I thought it was time to use my ace-in-the-hole. I went to headquarters, where a lieutenant commander asked me what I needed. I told him I was 16 and wanted to get out of the Navy. He asked, "Who signed for you?" I told him, "My dad." He said, "Do you want your dad to go to jail?" Boy, the answer to that was a big *no*! He told me to get back to work ASAP. That was the end of my ace-in-the-hole.

Shortly after that incident, I was assigned to the USS *Antietam* (CV-36). We were part of Task Force 77 with the USS *Boxer* (CV-21). The task force conducted extensive fleet maneuvers en route to Manila, Philippine Islands, for the celebration of their independence on 4 July 1946.

We were out in the Pacific most of the time, with stops at Pearl Harbor, Guam, Saipan, Truk, China, Japan, etc. We came back to San Francisco, then to San Diego, to pick up new pilots. On 18 November 1946 we pulled in to Hunters Point, California, and put in dry dock for overhaul.

Later, there was a gas explosion on board. I had gone down to the ship's store to get soap and toothpaste, and on the way back I stopped in the mess compartment to visit with a buddy who was reading there. I had just left the compartment when the explosion occurred and I was blown into some tables and lockers. I lay on the deck for I don't know how long. The smoke was so thick the overhead lights looked like matches. There was dead silence. It seemed like an eternity while I was trying to understand what happened. I got on all fours, trying to stay close to the deck for better air, and groped around until I finally found a ladder to the next deck. I could see better there, but there was still a lot of smoke. Someone bumped into me. I could see well enough to tell he was burned quite badly. He was yelling, "Where is the sick bay?" He turned away from me and ran down a passageway into more smoke. I tried to help him, but lost him in the smoke. Other men were running in the other direction, trying to get out.

I found out later that the burned man was my buddy. Some of the fire and blast came out of a bomb elevator near where he had been sitting. He died later from his injuries. I was very lucky to come out with only a sore body. It was a very sad day for me.

We went to Pearl Harbor during April 1947. On 1 May 1947, we left Pearl as part of Task Force 38 with the USS *Shangri La* (CV-38) as flagship, on a 10-day good-will trip to Australia.

We returned to the Mariana Islands and remained there until October 1947, then returned to the States. I left the ship on 19 November 1947 and was discharged at Treasure Island, California, on 28 November 1947.

Bob Feikema did auto-body repair work until he retired in 1991. He had a reputation for doing very good work. Bob and Sue, his wife of 52 years, have three children, but no grandchildren. They have lived in Holland, Michigan, (Tulip City, USA) all their lives.

Charles E. Trite

Age 15 – United States Navy

I was born in Waynesboro, Pennsylvania, on 14 March 1930, the youngest of six children. My father died when I was 4 months old. When I was 4 years old, four of my sisters and I were placed in an orphans' home in Loysville,

> His reply to me was, "Sailor, you asked for it!" I was stuck.

Pennsylvania. I stayed in the home for 12 years, then went to live with my mother, stepfather, and two half-brothers. I spent a lot of time with my sister and brother-in-law.

My brother-in-law was drafted and chose to go into the Marines. He lost his life on Iwo Jima in February 1945. My brother Marshall was drafted into the Army in 1942. In 1944 he was in Europe with the 551st Engineer Battalion, U. S. Third Army, under General Patton.

I was almost 15 years old when we learned of my brother-in-law's death. That is when I decided that I wanted to join the Navy. One of my school buddies who had enlisted at age 16 told me what to do. I obtained a letter from a doctor stating that I was 17 years old. The letter was accepted at the recruiting office, but the recruiter said that I would have to have proof of my birth date when I got to boot camp.

I was sworn into the Navy on 22 January 1946 and was off to boot camp. The issue of my birth date was not pursued. After boot camp, I went to Providence, Rhode Island, where I was assigned to the USS *Massey* (DD-778), and went to sea for three weeks. After returning to Providence, we went to a Leonardo, New Jersey, pier to unload ammunition. While getting ready to dock aft of the USS *Solar*, a destroyer-escort, there were several explosions on the *Solar* that blew the bow off the ship. There were five killed and 130 wounded.

We went to another dock, unloaded our ammunition, then went to a dry dock at the Brooklyn Naval Yard. This was quite an experience for me. I helped to sandblast the ship while it was in dry dock. One day, I was on gangway watch when the OD (Officer of the Deck) told me that I was being transferred to the Armed Guard Center in New York City the next day. At this time I told the OD that I was only 16 years old. His reply to me was, "Sailor, you asked for it!" I was stuck.

My next assignment was aboard the *Zebulon B. Vance*, a naval transport. We sailed to Southampton, England. While there, I was assigned to the USS *Houston* (CL-81), the flagship of the Sixth Fleet, which was under the command of Admiral Hewitt. My duty was to keep the admiral's passageway clean at all times. My general quarters station was as a fuse-setter on a 5-inch gun mount. We went on a good-will tour, visiting nine different countries.

In October 1946, I left the *Houston* in Southampton and went to London, England, then flew to Bremen, Germany. This is where I saw the results of war. Bremen had been completely wiped out. From Bremen, five of us were driven to Bremerhaven Naval Base. At Bremerhaven, I boarded the M.I.T. Victory ship to return to the States. There were about 5,000 Army troops on the ship. I volunteered for mess duty so that I could have fresh-water showers.

When I arrived in the States, I was sent to the Long Island Naval Hospital with a kidney problem. I was discharged from the Navy at the hospital on 11 November 1946.

Years later, when I applied for a security clearance to work for my company at Camp David, Maryland, they discovered my true age. I was asked why I had never told them. I replied, "Nobody asked me." I was able to keep my clearance.

Charles Trite worked for a painting contractor for a number of years. In 1953, he began working for an electrical contractor and decided to take some courses in the electrical trade. He completed his courses and received his diploma from Hagerstown Junior College. He then worked for Local Union 307, International Brotherhood of Electrical Workers, for 38 years. Charles and Betty, his wife of 50 years, have two sons, a daughter, and seven grandchildren. They live in Cascade, Maryland.

Francis C. Sealy

Age 15 – United States Marine Corps

I was born in Uniontown, Alabama, on 8 January 1931. These were hard times. My daddy was working six days a week for $7 a week. World War II started, and all the young

> *He made me proud to be underage.*

men were volunteering for the service. I was 10 years old and wanted to go. I was told that I was just a kid and I would have to wait. I did.

The war brought us south to Mobile, Alabama. I was in school, and upon reaching the age of 13, I tried to enlist in the Marines. My brother had already enlisted. I was told to come back when I grew up. The next year at age 14, I tried again and was accepted, with the help of a friend's birth certificate. All the paperwork was completed and I was sworn in on 30 January 1946, three weeks after my 15th birthday. The fighting was over, but I still wanted to go so I could relieve those who had been fighting.

I received my boot training at a beautiful resort in South Carolina called Parris Island. It has the most gorgeous setting of swamps I have ever seen outside of Louisiana. The wildlife is abundant, lots of cottonmouth snakes and alligators. Our camp guides (drill instructors) for Platoon 32 (1946) attended to our every need. This was a real experience for a 15-year-old. Being from a poor family, we only had an outhouse for a toilet. At Parris Island, we lived in a wooden barracks, but it had indoor plumbing. We were assigned different clean-up jobs. Luckily, the job I received was cleaning the commodes, 12 in all. My

DI said, "These commodes are yours to clean and they better be kept clean. The magic word was "yours." Imagine! When I left home in Alabama, I had no indoor commodes, now I had 12, and they were all mine. I felt rich!

After eight weeks, we headed to the rifle range, which was on a different side of the base. It was a bit less restricted and we felt a little freer. During boot training, you were allowed to go to the PX only twice. Our platoon was an exception. One time we were allowed a third trip. This is how we earned this privilege:

One member of our platoon slipped off during a break one Sunday afternoon, went to the PX, and later was caught eating a half-gallon of ice cream in the last place he thought he would be caught, the latrine.

We were ordered to fall in and were standing at attention. Our DI – I'll call him Corporal Pleasant to preserve his identity – had a gleam in his eye and a smile on his face. We smelled death! He had obtained from our personal belongings 25¢ for every man. He asked if we liked ice cream. No one uttered a word. He shouted, "Do you like ice cream!" We shouted back, "Yes, sir!" Our corporal gently said, "One of your buddies has already had ice cream. I believe all of you deserve ice cream." That came to be known as the coolest, sweetest, march that we would ever experience.

First we were marched to the PX and back to the barracks for a total of 10 times. When we were finally brought to a halt, we were hot, sweaty, and tired. Thoughts were going through my head, "Do I really need this ice cream?" By this time, I was sure all of my buddies, except one, were feeling the same.

After lining up to buy ice cream, I got chocolate, my favorite kind. When we were reassembled in formation, Corporal Ples (what we called him behind his back) ordered us to disassemble the top lid of our newly bought containers. Being smartly trained Marines, we held the containers in our right hands and opened the lids with our left hands – in unison. By this time, under the hot sun, the ice cream was beginning to drip. Corporal Ples explained that upon his next command, we were to remove our caps with our left hands, and with our right hands, we were to place the ice cream upon our shaven heads. Then came the command we were all anticipating, one very loud, "Hooo!"

A cool feeling caressed my shaven head, even down to my inner being. This was the best ice cream that I never tasted. There we were, 30 recruits, complete with ice-cream helmets, 29 with vanilla and one with chocolate. I learned the lesson to always do the same as the others, to never be different, and you won't be remembered.

Streaks of goodness were flowing down both cheeks. Then suddenly, without warning, came the sand fleas. Do they bite? Yes, they bite! Corporal Ples kept shouting, "Don't you dare kill a sand flea! They are government property!" Relief was in sight in the form of a lieutenant colonel. This officer walked up to Corporal Ples, received his salute, and saluted the corporal in return. The colonel asked, "What in the 'heck' is going on?" The corporal explained that it was a matter of discipline. The colonel told the corporal that if he was finished with his cold manner of discipline, to get us cleaned up. From that moment on I always liked lieutenant colonels.

We were marched back to our huts with the now soggy ice-cream containers smartly tucked into our left sides and with our right arms swinging as we marched. Aye, we looked as proud as any British marching team!

After boot camp at Parris Island, I received demolition training at Camp Lejeune, North Carolina. I had always liked to blow things up, but that's a different story.

In October 1946, I was sent to Guam, where I stayed for two years. Shortly after I got there, I experienced one moment in my life that I will always remember. The Communists were taking over China at that time, and the Marines were being pulled out. MATS (Military Air Transport Service) aircraft were bringing men from China to the States via Guam.

Many of us volunteered (with the help of our sergeant) to serve a hot meal to those men on their short layover for refueling. I was dishing out chow to them when I spotted a very young looking guy. I asked him his age. He replied, "Sixteen!" I proudly responded, "I'm only fifteen!" He looked at me and said, "Yeah, but I've been in four years." I crawled back into my shell and continued serving chow. I couldn't resist one last look at this "man." At the same time he looked back at me, smiled, and gave me a thumbs-up. He made me proud to be underage.

I returned to the States in 1948 and spent 27 months at the Naval Operating Base Annex, Norfolk, Virginia. I was discharged in March 1951 and returned to southern Alabama. I had spent five years in the Marines and still was not legally old enough to buy a beer!

Francis Sealy was a police officer for ten years following his discharge from the Marines. He worked for a chemical company for 24 years, and retired in 1992. Francis and Dorothy, his wife of 50 years, have two children, six grandchildren, and one great- grandson. They live in Daphne, Alabama.

✓ *INCIDENTally* — **Let there be light!** – On 22 March 1945 (D+31 on Iwo Jima) our battalion occupied the extreme left flank of the entire 5th Amphibious Corps line attacking toward the north end of the island. My command post (CP) was situated on somewhat of a plateau with a number of small fissures leading into the position. At night, we would circle the plateau with trip flares. Should a Japanese soldier attempt to crawl up one of the small ravines, his presence would be announced by the light of a flare he had set off. However, once the flare ignited, that area would be dark for the remainder of the night. During the day of 22 March, I decided to have three concentric circles of flares installed to preclude the gaps that had existed with only one line of flares. About midnight, all was quiet when suddenly all the flares ignited at one time, and no enemy soldiers were in sight. All remained quiet until about 2:00 a.m. when all hell broke loose about 100 yards to our right. About 60 Japanese attacked Company D's command post and pushed the Marines from their position. In time, they fought their way back into the CP, killing about 50 Japanese. At first light, we discovered the answer to the mystery of the flares. Japanese soldiers equipped with ropes with a rock tied to one end had surrounded my position. At a signal, they all threw their rocks toward the interior of my position and drew the lines in, catching all the trip flare wires, and giving us an early Fourth of July. To this day, I have no idea why the Japanese did not attack Company E's CP. – *Dave E. Severance.*

John P. Hollern

Age 15 – United States Army Air Forces
Age 16 – United States Army

I was about 5 years old when my father's friend, Joe Grant, who was in the Coast Guard, visited our family. Since that time, I wanted to be in the Coast Guard. Throughout my elementary school years, my friends wanted to be garbagemen, policemen, or

> *I passed all the tests for the Navy, but one chief thought that I looked too young.*

firemen, but I wanted to be a Coast Guard sailor. Even though my uncle Johnnie was a fireman and my paternal grandfather retired as a captain of the fire department, I wanted to be a Coast Guard sailor.

I was born in Covington, Kentucky, on 29 July 1930. In 1943, at age 13, I heard that the Merchant Marine would enlist 13-year-olds as cabin boys. I attempted to enlist, but the cabin boy story was not true. When World War II came to an end, there was a big need for

replacements in the services. In February 1946, I changed my birth certificate so I would be old enough, and went to enlist in the Coast Guard. No Coast Guard recruiter was available, so I went to the Navy recruiting office. I passed all the tests for the Navy, but one chief thought that I looked too young. He had called the county record office to check my date of birth, but each time the telephone was busy, or wasn't answered. He then told the other chief that he would try once more, and if there was no answer, I was in. I'll never forget that call because just as he was about to hang up, some one answered and verified that I was only 15. The chief then told me to come back when I was old enough, and they would be glad to enlist me.

I was now fired up with patriotism, so I headed to the Army recruiter and was successful in enlisting. I was sworn into the Army on 12 February 1946. I was processed at Camp Atterbury, Indiana, shipped to Sheppard Field, Texas, then to San Antonio for basic training.

One night, ambulances took several soldiers to the hospital with what was thought to be meningitis. A friend with whom I had gone to school was one of them. When I told my mom on the telephone what had happened to my friend, she decided to get me out of the service for being underage. So my short career as a 15-year-old soldier came to an end. I was shipped back to Camp Atterbury for discharge. During the discharge briefing for about 50 men, mostly veterans of the war in Europe, we were told to check in with the draft board so we would not be drafted. I did check in with my draft board, and it paid off later.

Several months after being discharged, after turning 16, I went to the draft board to register so I could use my draft card to prove that I was 18. The comment was made in the draft-board office to the effect that now that I was old enough to be drafted, I probably would not want to be in the service.

In December 1946, I decided to use my draft card as proof of age and join the Coast Guard. I tried to enlist in the Coast Guard, the Navy, and the Marines. Not one would take a draft card as proof of age. I then went to the Army recruiter, and on 11 December 1946, I was successful in enlisting at age 16. My plan was to finish my hitch in the Army, and then I would be old enough to join the Coast Guard.

After basic training, I was shipped to Germany and joined the United States Constabulary there. At the end of my tour, I realized the work I was doing was vital towards keeping the peace, plus I was in the top-notch unit in Germany, so I stayed and made a career of the Army. I retired from the Army in 1968, but went back in on voluntary recall in 1970. I went to Vietnam in time to make the Cambodia incursion.

I retired again in 1972 as a sergeant major. I had a very satisfying Army career, but I am sure that it would have also been satisfying had it been spent in the Coast Guard.

John Hollern was awarded the Bronze Star with two oak leaf clusters, the Army Meritorious Service Medal, the Army Commendation Medal with two oak leaf clusters, and a number of other service medals. After retiring from the Army in 1968, he worked as a warehouse foreman for the Kroger Company in Cincinnati, Ohio. After his second Army retirement, he enrolled in a new college program in real estate and received the first degree in that field in the state of Kentucky. He worked as a real-estate broker until he retired in 1996 because of his wife's illness. His wife Trudy died in 1996. They had four sons and three grandchildren. He remarried in 1999. John and Brenda live in Vine Grove, Kentucky.

✓ *INCIDENTally* — **Sailor's lament.** — The phrase "the Navy gets the gravy and the Army gets the beans," was probably invented by a hungry GI gnawing on a spoiled K-ration in a beleaguered foxhole. The chow line on my ship, the USS *Badoeng Strait*, formed on the hanger deck, wound down a starboard ladder, descending into the mess hall below. While our mess fare was not exactly "gravy," the ship's crew always lined up in the chow line before the best "pickins" were depleted. On 13 January 1952, we lined up to eat dinner as usual. I had worked my way down the ladder, advancing short of getting my chow tray. Looking back, I noticed my shipmates were no longer coming down the ladder, creating a large gap in the queue. The chief cook, anxious to finish the dinner and start the clean-up, popped out of the galley and hollered, "What's holding up the chow line?" No one could explain. With growing impatience, he stepped out on the mess deck, shouting another bellicose demand for an explanation. All chatter stopped. Only the heavy breathing of the cook could be heard. Finally, a footstep fell on the ladder. One of the ship's rescue crew slowly emerged from above, carrying a stretcher, followed by another of the rescue crew. They carried our comrade, a Marine fighter pilot killed in action earlier that day, down to sickbay. We all finished our dinner in thoughtful silence. — *Douglas L. Miller.*

Gordon L. Saint

Age 15 – United States Army

During my school years, we said the morning prayer and the Pledge of Allegiance every day. I was taught to love and respect my fellow man and to love my country and what it stood for. I sold newspapers at Fort

> *We were one of the last units to depart Hungnam on 24 December 1950.*

Benning, Georgia, during much of World War II. I learned from the soldiers about love of country, what freedom was all about, and the cost of having the right to call America home. With all of this behind me, I just couldn't wait to enlist in the U. S. Army. I was born in Taylor County, Georgia, on 17 March 1930, and enlisted in the Army on 13 February 1946. I changed my birth certificate to read "1928" and my father signed for me.

Due to my small size (118 pounds), I was shipped to Keesler Field, Mississippi, for basic training with the U. S. Army Air Forces. This was in February 1946. After basic, I went to Lowery Field, Colorado,

to attend ordnance supply school, and from there I went to the 4th Air Force at Hamilton Field, California. My mother wanted me home for the Christmas holidays, so she told the Army that I was only 16. After serving only 11½ months, I was given an honorable discharge and a train ticket home. This was in January 1947.

After being out for two months, I re-enlisted for three years. This meant that I had a choice, and I wanted to stay out of the Air Force, so I selected the airborne infantry. After jump school at Fort Benning, I was shipped to Japan to join the 11th Airborne Division. Shortly after joining the 11th, I was transferred to the 1st Cavalry Division in Tokyo because the 11th was returning to the States. After 30 months in Japan, I returned to the States.

When our ship was two days out from Washington, the North Koreans crossed the 38th Parallel, invaded South Korea, and the war was on. As I was crossing the United States on my way home, U. S. forces were sent into Korea. My orders were changed and I joined the 3rd Infantry Division and went to Korea with them in November 1950. My unit, the 3rd Battalion, 7th Infantry Regiment, was formed into a task force (Task Force Dog) and ordered into the Chosin Reservoir, where about 12,000 men were surrounded by 120,000 Chinese. After fighting our way there, we served as the rear guard as the forces fought their way out to Hungnam. As the troops were shipped out to South Korea, my unit remained behind. We were one of the last units to depart Hungnam on 24 December 1950.

By February 1951, we were advancing back north and had gotten as far as the Han River when I was wounded. I spent the next three months in a hospital in Japan. I was released from the hospital and returned to my unit about the time that the Chinese had started a counterattack. By August 1951, we were at the Iron Triangle. At that time I was rotated home.

I was a drill sergeant for the next two years, then was assigned to the 82nd Airborne Division. I re-enlisted in 1953 and requested to be assigned to my old outfit, the 3rd Infantry Division in Korea. However, the Army in all its wisdom, sent me to Germany where I spent the next four years. All was not bad, as I returned home with a new wife, whom I married in October 1955.

I was stationed at Fort Benning with the Honor Guard on the Main Post. This was mostly parades, and I wanted to serve with a field unit, so I transferred to the 3rd Infantry Division as a scout section-leader with the Recon Platoon of the 4th Infantry Regiment. In May 1958 we were shipped to Germany where I spent the next five years. During this time, the Recon Platoon was rated the best in the division. I transferred to a line company where I won the Expert Infantry Badge. My rifle squad won the Battle Group test. In 1960, I was then sent on TDY to V Corps Long Range Reconnaissance Patrol (Provisional). We were the first LRRP deployed and tested the concept for the Department of the Army. The Army later assigned an LRRP Company to all divisions.

I returned to the States in March 1963 for duty as an advisor to an infantry battalion in Texas. I stayed there for three years. When I received orders transferring me to Korea, I called Washington, D.C., and asked that my orders be changed to the 1st Infantry Division in Vietnam. They changed my orders and I served seven months as a rifle-platoon sergeant with the 1st Division.

After being medically evacuated Stateside, I re-enlisted and was ordered to the Signal School at Fort Gordon, Georgia. My duties there were taking care of the troops, marching them to and from class, keeping up the barracks and the outside area, and insuring that all student records were kept up to date. After several phone calls to Washington asking to return to Vietnam were refused, I put in for retirement. I retired on 30 October 1967 after more than 21½ years of service, of which more than 13 years were overseas.

Gordon Saint was awarded the Purple Heart, the Combat Infantryman's Badge for Korea and a second one for Vietnam. He was also awarded the Vietnam Cross of Gallantry with palm, and a number of other service medals. After his retirement from the Army, he worked for Beal's Lighting and Decorating Gallery in Columbus, Georgia, for more than 20 years and was their warehouse manager when he retired. Erna, his wife of 45 years, is also retired. They have one child. Gordon and Erna live in Phenix City, Alabama.

382

Sidney Jones, Jr.
Age 15 – United States Army

I was born in Beaumont, Texas, on 9 November 1930, the second of nine children. We were a very poor but happy family. Being raised during the Great Depression taught us to rely

> ... I can truthfully say that I had a real adventurous, happy, rewarding, military career.

on each other and our Christian upbringing during those times.

When World War II began, I was 11 years old and an avid reader of world events. Although my parents couldn't read, I was always intrigued by books and would try to read anything – newspapers, funny books, the Bible, etc. By the fourth grade I was a very good reader and I was able to follow the movements of the armed forces, both in Europe and the Pacific.

During the week of my 15th birthday, 9 November 1945, my school's football team was to travel to New Orleans to play a game against a prep or junior-college team. I had played football as long as I could remember, and in the 11th grade at 15 years old, I was nearly 6-feet tall and weighed 150 pounds. During practice I skinned and bruised my knee when the knee pad moved during a tackle. When my father saw that, he told me, "No more football!" Needless to say, I was broken-hearted. Neither the coach or relatives could get him to change his orders. No trip to New Orleans for me! That is when I began planning to run away.

The big bomb had been dropped on Japan in August, and the war was over. The military needed men badly to replace the returning warriors. I ran away from home on 5 March 1946. A cousin who had just returned from the war helped me enlist in the Army. On the enlistment forms we wrote that I was 17 and he signed as my parent.

I went to Houston for a physical, was sworn in, and put on a train for Fort Sam Houston, all in the same day. After receiving uniforms, orientation, etc., I was put on a troop train for Fort Eustis, Virginia, for basic training. I met some Texas farm boys in my company who couldn't read or write. Soon I had a little business going. For 50¢ I would help them compose and write a letter home to family and girlfriends.

After basic, many men in my company were chosen for technical training as DUKW drivers. A DUKW is a truck-boat with a propeller and is operated on both land and water. We were sent to Fort Story, Virginia, for eight weeks to learn to operate this vehicle. During this period we spent a week at Little Creek Naval Base learning to unload LSTs a mile from shore. It was my first time to see so much water, and it was my first experience with seasickness.

After completing technical training, I was shipped to Camp Stoneman, California, for assignment to the Pacific theater of operations, with a 30-day leave in route. From California, I went by troopship to Inchon, Korea. I was assigned to a trucking battalion near Inchon with the 8th Army's 24th Corps, Korea Base Command. That was my home for two years, from about August 1946 until September 1948.

On my 17th birthday, 9 November 1947, I was promoted to T/5 and was promoted to sergeant before my 18th birthday. Upon my return to the States in September 1948, I was sent to Fort Belvoir, Virginia. I was discharged in February 1949 and returned to Beaumont, Texas. I had completed my high school education at the U. S. Army High School, Seoul, Korea, at night. The Beaumont School District accepted my certificate as credits, and I graduated in absentia with my class of '47.

By June 1949, I had had my fill of job hunting and was trying to decide whether to leave home for college or return to the military. I enlisted in the U. S. Air Force on 10 June 1949 and reported to Lackland Air Force Base, San Antonio, Texas. During the next few years I served at a number of bases, including a couple of six-month TDYs (temporary duty) to Okinawa and Guam in '51 and '52. I was part of an armament crew. We loaded bombs on B29s headed for North Korea.

I volunteered for duty in Korea and was sent there in May 1953. I was at Taegu from June '53 until June '54. The war had ended and this tour of duty was a vacation compared to the occupation duty in Korea during 1946-48. On my return to the States, I attended a number of schools, including the A & E Mechanics School. I was a crew chief on a KC-97 tanker until that aircraft was phased out at March AFB, California. Later, I was trained and certified as a flight engineer on C-47s, C-54s, C-123s, C-131s, and T-29s, all propeller-driven aircraft.

During my career, I went overseas to places like England, Tripoli, Australia, New Zealand, Guam, Okinawa, Japan, and Hawaii. I was in Vietnam for one year, 1963-64. I retired on 31 July 1966 as a technical sergeant at Los Angeles Air Force Station, California, which was the best duty station of my military career.

As I look back over my life, back to 5 March 1946, I can truthfully say that I had a real adventurous, happy, rewarding, military career. Not bad for a 15-year-old runaway whose only reasons for running away were freedom, adventure, and patriotism.

Sidney Jones worked for the U. S. Postal Service for three years after retiring from the Air Force. He found his second career in trucking. He owned and operated a tractor-trailer rig and carried freight all over the United States and Canada until retiring in 1990. Sidney and his wife Dee have a combined family of four children, twelve grandchildren, thirty-eight great-grandchildren, and one great-great-grandchild. They live in Apple Valley, California.

John N. "Buz" Broussard

Age 15 – United States Navy

I was born in Port Néches, Jefferson County, Texas, on 4 August 1930. Soon after my birth, my family moved back to Scott, Louisiana, where my parents, two brothers, two sisters, and I lived and subsisted on a 50-acre cotton farm. I attended the local public schools and did well, but I was bored by the teachers who did not challenge me.

> At boot camp, I marveled at the amount of food I could scarf up!

I quit school in 1945 to work as a short-order cook in the daytime and to pack sweet potatoes in the evening. Not only was it the patriotic thing to do, but I was making $1.50 a day, which was a terrific wage then! In December 1945, I got restless and doctored my certificate of baptism, which had been handwritten by a priest in Port Néches. I wet the "30" in 1930, dried the runny ink, then wrote "28" in place of "30" so that my date of birth became 4 August 1928. I was now 17! I wanted to join the Navy to emulate my brothers who both were sailors, and for adventure.

My dad finally agreed to sign, putting his "X" on the papers, since he was illiterate. I was sworn into the Navy on 17 March 1946 in New Orleans, Louisiana, and sent to the Naval Training Center, San Diego, California, for boot training.

At boot camp, I marveled at the amount of food I could scarf up! I had a great time for about three weeks, then I got terribly homesick. I went to see our chief petty officer, Chief Gunner's Mate Toma, and told him I was only 15. The grizzled old chief jumped up, drew his sword, brandished it at me, let out a string of curses, and said, "If you ever mention *that* to anyone again, I'll cut you in two!" I got over my homesickness then and there! The chief was like a god to us, so I assumed that he *could* decapitate me at will.

From San Diego, I traveled by a slow-moving, military-chartered train to Bainbridge, Maryland, where I attended cook and baker school. It took seven days (with no baths) to get to Bainbridge. I graduated from the school near the bottom of my class. I was transferred to the Naval Operating Base, Norfolk, Virginia, where I was promptly detailed to help a skeleton crew decommission the battleship, USS *Mississippi*. From Norfolk, I was sent to the Naval Air Test Center in Patuxent River, Maryland, and assigned to Squadron VR-7. From there I went to VR-6 at the Naval Air Station, Agana, Guam. I enjoyed the duty at Guam, except for getting shot at by a Japanese holdout near the Barrigada Tank Farm.

I returned to the United States in early 1948 and was honorably discharged as a seaman second class. After a few weeks on the 52-20 club (a government program that paid ex-GIs $20 a week for 52 weeks, or until they could find a job), I got my GED, then attended the Nashville Technical College, Nashville, Tennessee, under the GI Bill for nine months' training as a mechanic. I worked for the Southern Pacific railroad until my first wife and I broke up in 1951, whereupon I joined the U. S. Marine Corps.

I enlisted in the Marines on 9 June 1951. Boot camp at the Marine Corps Recruit Depot in San Diego took my mind off my marital discord. I went to Korea aboard the troopship, USNS *William V. Weigle*, landing at Sokcho-ri in January 1952. I was a naval-gunfire spotter with the First Marine Division. I served with the 7th Marine Regiment for a while, then with the Republic of Korea I-Corps. I was a spotter for the 16-inch guns of the USS *Wisconsin* and the USS *New Jersey*. What an experience it was to see and hear the 2,000-pound bullets rumble overhead toward the enemy positions and to see the enemy ripped apart! There were only two Americans at the ROK I-Corps, so we lived like royalty and dined with the top officers, occasionally including the I-Corps commander, Lieutenant General Lee.

I returned to the States in January 1953 and was assigned to "Exercise Desert Rock V," in the Nevada desert, under the command of Brigadier General Wilbert "Bigfoot" Brown. It was awesome witnessing the power of a 20-kiloton bomb (the shot named "Badger") detonated atop a 300-foot tower less than two miles from our trenches. A few minutes after the blast, we boarded helicopters and were dropped off near ground zero. We walked through the devastated bunkers, warehouses, jeeps, and dead and dying goats, sheep, and chickens. I remember in particular a white goat that was still alive, whereas all the dark animals were toasted dead.

I was discharged as a sergeant in June 1954, but re-enlisted shortly thereafter. From 1959 until 1962, I was radio chief of the 3rd Marine Air Wing at El Toro Marine Air Base, California. During this time I kept busy by taking extension courses. I completed the Quantico Basic Officers Course and the Communications Officers Course. At the end of my tour at El Toro, I was selected to attend the Defense Language Institute (DLI) in Monterey, California.

At the end of my studies at DLI, I aced my finals, both oral and written, in cryptic French military jargon, economic and banking parlance, and civilian French. I had the highest average of all students in the 18 different language schools. For this accomplishment, I received the Maxwell D. Taylor Award. I also received a handwritten letter of congratulations from General David Shoup, then Commandant of the Marine Corps. I credit this accomplishment to my mother, who taught me Cajun French as a boy.

After completing the DLI course, I asked for a transfer to the 2nd Radio Company at Camp Lejeune, North Carolina. Shortly after reporting to Lejeune, I received orders to report to Company F, Marine Support Battalion, Washington, D.C. Although this was our "home" base, I was actually at Karamursel, Turkey. This was at the height of the Cold War. It was nothing for me to attend a midnight briefing on the USS *Forrestal*, have breakfast six hours later in Naples, Italy, fly around the Black Sea and the Dardanelles all day, then sleep over in Rota, Spain, that night.

I was transferred from Karamursel to a Navy security group in Bremerhaven, Germany, in 1966. This was dull duty after the heady tour in Turkey. In 1966, I was promoted to master sergeant with the MOS (Military Occupational Speciality) of electronic-warfare chief. While there, I studied German at the University of Bremen.

On 6 May 1966, I received a warrant for immediate promotion to second lieutenant, which I tried to refuse. The answer from the Commandant of the Marine Corps was travel orders to the Philadelphia Navy Yard to pick up a tailored USMC officer's uniform. I went.

I returned to Bremerhaven, but was bored with the duty there. I kept applying for a transfer to Vietnam, and finally, in early 1967, my request was granted. I completed combat training at Camp Pendleton, California, then reported to the 3rd Marine Division near the DMZ (Demilitarized Zone) in Vietnam. I served as the officer in charge of the 1st Special Security Communications Team at Dong Ha and points west. On one sad day, I lost both my commanding general, Major General Bruno Hochmuth, USMC, and my immediate boss, Colonel Spark. Both were killed in action near the DMZ in a chopper crash.

I returned to the United States in September 1968. In 1969, I transferred to the Fleet Marine Corps Reserve and reverted to master sergeant. In 1976, after completing 30 years of service, I retired from the Marine Corps as a captain.

Buz Broussard returned to Louisiana, taught school for several years, entered Louisiana State University Law School, but didn't graduate because of family problems. He then worked for the Shell Oil Company at the Geismar Louisiana Refinery until he retired as a supervisor in 1990. Now he edits Scuttlebutt, *a newsletter of the Acadiana Detachment of the Marine Corps League. Buz and his wife Verna have a combined family of three children and three grandchildren. They live in Lafayette, Louisiana.*

Robert J. Andrews
Age 16 – United States Navy

I was born in Bellview, Illinois, on the morning of 9 July 1929 at the home of my favorite aunt. My family had bounced from one home to another all over Chicago's South Side and the suburbs. I quit school at the age of 14

> The Navy and I hit it off right from the very beginning.

and went to work on a dairy farm owned by a relative in Wauconda, Illinois. In February 1946, my mother and stepfather went to Florida to check out a new business. I called Mom and begged to come down for a couple of weeks. She agreed and I hopped a Greyhound bus in Chicago and arrived in Hollywood, Florida, one afternoon just as the rain had stopped. As I stepped off that bus, I could smell orange blossoms in the air, and I immediately became a Floridian for life.

While sipping a soda in the local drug store one afternoon, I struck up a conversation with two sailors stationed at the nearby Opalaca Naval Air Station. They took me on a tour of the air station. That evening when Mom and Dad came back to the motel we were staying in, I told them I was going down to the naval recruiting station first thing in the morning to enlist. Mom was all for it and helped by using some ink eradicator on the year of birth on my birth certificate. A 16-year-old became 17 instantly!

I went to the recruiting office where the chief recruiter gave me a simple test, looked at the birth certificate, winked, and said, "Welcome aboard, sailor!" I left by train the very next morning for Jacksonville, Florida, where I took the physical and was sworn into the U. S. Navy on 19 March 1946.

After a couple of days in Jacksonville, 15 or 20 other young guys and I were shipped by train to the Recruit Training Depot in Norfolk, Virginia. We were assigned to Company 95. Ours was the last boot company to graduate from the Norfolk facility. Boot training was moved to Bainbridge, Maryland.

I seemed to have found my niche in life. The Navy and I hit it off right from the very beginning. Apparently, my company commander saw a certain leadership quality in me because I was made platoon leader of Company 95.

After returning from two weeks of boot leave, I received my first set of orders. I was to report to the USS *Washington* (BB-56), a first-line battleship. She was tied up at the Norfolk Naval Station and was preparing to depart on a midshipman cruise to the South Atlantic. I was assigned to the gunnery department's small-arms armory. My primary duty was to inspect the gunpowder magazines daily and record the temperature of each magazine.

Like all new recruits, I had to take my turn at mess cooking. I worked in the scullery for about two weeks before being relieved by one of the 1,000 Middies (Naval Academy Midshipmen) we had aboard for their annual cruise. Who knows, the Middie that relieved me might one day be my commanding officer.

After about eight weeks of cruising, we disembarked the Middies at Annapolis and sailed to Bayonne, New Jersey, where the *Washington* was scheduled for decommissioning. I was transferred to the Brooklyn receiving station to await further orders. On the second day there, at morning muster, a first class petty officer asked who in the group had a driver's license. This sounded like just what I needed. I could get out and see the sights around New York. Three of us were picked and ordered to report to the back of the building. Our vehicles were waiting – three shiny wheelbarrows and a large pile of sand that needed moving. For this we needed a driver's license?

I was assigned to the USS *Purdy* (DD-734), at anchor in Newport Harbor, Newport, Rhode Island. The *Purdy* was a World War II destroyer built for a one-way trip to the Pacific. But here she was, still steaming. I was assigned to a five-inch gun mount where I spent many hours chipping paint. I came close to losing my life in that gun mount. I was using a heavy-duty (240 volt) electric wire brush to sand off the rust. Apparently, there was a short in the wiring because suddenly I was being electrocuted and could not let go of the wire brush. Fortunately for me, the first class gunner's mate, a big Swede named Anderson, stepped in the gun mount and gave me a hard kick against the bulkhead with his big foot, causing the wire brush to fall from my shaking hands. My body shook for several hours after that close call.

While I was aboard the *Purdy*, we made a six-month cruise to the Mediterranean Sea. When we returned to Newport, I was sent to Radar School, Boston, Massachusetts. While there, I met and married a beautiful, loving, French Canadian girl who would be the mother of our four wonderful sons and the best Navy wife any sailor could ask for. Terry Therese Vachon Andrews died on 6 March 1971.

After radar school, I again reported to the USS *Purdy*, and in September 1948 we departed for an extended cruise. I received orders to report to the USS *Sarsfield* (DDE-837), in May 1949. The *Sarsfield* was an experimental destroyer whose duties were to test and evaluate new sonar equipment and antisubmarine weapons. Duty on the *Sarsfield* was a brown-bagger's paradise. We were underway each morning at about 0800 and returned to our permanent berth at Key West at 1600. While cruising off the coast of Florida at Cape Canaveral, we had cameras rigged to photograph the first launching of the WAC Corporal missile. This was the beginning of today's space program.

President Harry S. Truman made the Key West Naval Station his "Little White House." He spent a lot of time in the area, and when he was there, he chose the *Sarsfield* for deep-sea fishing and relaxation cruises. I had the opportunity to meet and talk with the President and his guest, General Omar Bradley.

In September 1951, I received orders to attend Class C Instructor's School at Norfolk, Virginia, then to report for duty at the Fleet Sonar School at Key West. I was the only radarman at the school, and the only enlisted man assigned to teach in the prospective commanding and executive officers antisubmarine warfare classes. While at the sonar school, I received my GED high school diploma and also took several college-level courses. In the 1950s, living and working in Key West, Florida, was like living on an island paradise.

I reported for duty on the USS *Pritchett* (DD-561) in August 1954. Our ship was soon assigned to home port at Long Beach, California. The *Pritchett* spent more time in the Far East than it did in Long Beach. I was away from my family for many long periods of time.

I was promoted to chief radarman in November 1956 and taught radar at the radar school at Norfolk, Virginia, for nearly three years. After attending electronics school at Treasure Island, California, I was assigned to the USS *Waller* (DD-466).

In the fall of 1962, I was assigned to the USS *Harry E. Yarnell* (DLG-17), which was under construction at the Bath Iron Works. Shortly after the *Yarnell* was commissioned in Norfolk, I found myself in the Portsmouth Naval Hospital. In June 1963, I was assigned to the U. S. Army Air defense Station at Norfolk, Virginia. I vividly recall the afternoon at Norfolk when we heard the radio broadcast announcing the assassination of President Kennedy.

After serving about 18 months aboard the USS *Franklin D. Roosevelt* (CVA-42), I found myself back in the hospital at Jacksonville Naval Air Station. After a brief tour at the U. S. Naval Ordnance Test Center at Cape Kennedy, Florida, I was back in the hospital. I spent the next five years under temporary orders at home in Melbourne, Florida. Once or twice a year I would receive orders to report for a physical at Jacksonville, and then on 31 May 1971, after 25 years of service, the Navy placed me on permanent retirement as senior chief radarman with a 50 percent disability.

During my Navy career, I served on seven ships and two shore stations. I made eight trips to Guantanamo Bay, Cuba, two Mediterranean cruises, one northern Europe cruise, and three Far East cruises.

Bob Andrews, after retiring from the Navy, went to work for a company that manufactured electronic-communications equipment for NASA. He moved to El Paso, Texas, in 1973 and became an independent contractor, representing a company out of Watertown, Wisconsin, that manufactures money-processing equipment for banks and major retail stores. After the death of his first wife, he married Cleatis Marie Strauss. They have a combined family of six sons, eleven grandchildren, and two great-grandchildren. He is now living his dream – skipper of his own boat. Bob and Cleatis Marie live in Astor, Florida.

James E. Carpenter
Age 16 – United States Army Air Forces

In December 1945, my brother Bill was 17 years old and wanted to join the Army. I went with him to the recruiting center in Kalamazoo, Michigan. While I was waiting for Bill, a recruiter asked if

> My dad did not know where I was until he received the chaplain's call.

I wanted to join the Army also. I said no, I wanted to be in the Army Air Corps. He said okay and sent me to a soldier at another desk, and I signed up.

The recruiter said that he would send a telegram the first part of January 1946 to let us know when to report. He told us to bring a birth certificate and written permission from our parents.

We received a telegram that told us to report to the train station in Kalamazoo on 19 March 1946. We reported! I didn't have a birth certificate or a note from my parents, but they didn't ask for either.

We were told to go down the tracks until we saw a car with a big "6" on it. We were going to Fort Sheridan, Illinois, for an induction physical and to be issued uniforms and equipment.

According to the papers we had with us, my brother Bill was born on 3 July 1927 and I was born three months and nine days later, on 12 October 1927. Actually, I was born on 12 October 1929. Bill went to Fort McClellan. He was killed in action in Korea on 2 November 1950.

I went to the Air Cadet Center in San Antonio, Texas, for basic training, then to a school at Camp Bullis, Texas, to become a 786 toxic-gas handler. After school, I was sent to Fort Bragg, North Carolina, to work in aircraft ordnance. One day while I was delivering some ordnance to an aircraft, a piece exploded. The explosion ruined a good jeep and trailer, broke my right shoulder, compressed three vertebrae in my lower back, and dislocated my right hip.

I was flown to a hospital in Hot Springs, Arkansas, for repair and recuperation. The chaplain at the hospital called my dad and he told the chaplain that I was only 16. My dad did not know where I was until he received the chaplain's call. After I had healed, they sent me home with a ruptured-duck pin and a 3-6-11 minority discharge.

Forty-two days later, on 12 October 1946, I was 17. With a birth certificate and a letter of permission from my dad, I re-enlisted. I was sent to March Field, California, and assigned to the 1st Pursuit Group, the first unit to get the P-80 Shooting Star jet aircraft. My unit was to take Shooting Stars to Ladd Field, Fairbanks, Alaska, for cold-weather tests. We started with seven aircraft. Four crashed before it was learned that kerosene gels at low temperatures. The solution was to mix gasoline and alcohol, and JP-2 jet fuel was born.

While I was in Alaska, my dad was killed in a storm. After an emergency leave, I was sent to Selfridge Field, Michigan, to await assignment. I was put to work in a bakery and later sent to Oscoda Air Force Base, Michigan, as a baker. When I arrived at Oscoda, Hollywood was making a movie there called "Fighter Squadron," with Robert Stack, Edmond O'Brien, and Rock Hudson. About two dozen other airmen and I were dressed in German uniforms. They had us run through some trees. We got that right the first time, but when we were strafed, we had to do four shoots before we got "killed" the right way.

Some days later, I met John Tosh, who had also been in the movie. John was either 15 or 16 at the time. We both married local girls and have been friends for over 50 years. John is also a member of the Veterans of Underage Military Service. (His story appears on page 481 of the first volume of *America's Youngest Warriors*.)

While at Oscoda, I soon learned that baking wasn't for me, so after a tour in air technical intelligence at Wright-Patterson Air Force Base, I retrained as an equipment-cooling technician, and worked in cooling of electronic and computer equipment. Nine of the last eleven years of my Air Force time were spent underground, from Kinsbach Cave in Germany to my last duty station at the NORAD facility at Cheyenne Mountain, Colorado Springs, Colorado.

In 1957, three other airmen and I took an R&R flight to Edinburgh, Scotland. While at Edinburgh Castle, Red Skelton came up to us. He was with his son who had cancer. Red was taking him on an around-the-world trip. While visiting with him, he asked us where we were staying. We were at the same hotel as he was. People kept asking him for his autograph. I asked if he ever got tired of being pestered. He said that when people asked him, "Who are you? I've seen you before." He would respond with, "I don't know. Have you ever been in prison?" When we checked out of the hotel we learned that Red Skelton had paid all of our hotel bills!

I retired from the Air Force in Colorado Springs on 1 August 1966, after 20 years of service. I was 36 years old.

Military service was good to me. I was the seventh of twelve children. Six brothers and one sister served in uniform. One grandson served in Desert Storm as an Army engineer. He was injured and received a medical discharge.

I entered the service with an eighth-grade education. While in the service I took advantage of correspondence courses from the University of Maryland and the General Motors Institute. I completed high school, received a four-year degree as a design-test engineer, studied for two years in industrial maintenance, two years in industrial air-conditioning, two years of moral and ideology courses, and two years in hand, shoulder, and base defense weapons.

Jim Carpenter was awarded two Air Force Commendation Medals, eleven letters of appreciation from the Air Force, and a number of service medals. After retiring from the Air force, he worked as a union pipe fitter in heavy construction which included five years at the Cook Nuclear Power House in Michigan. He spent seven years as a superintendent with Allied Boiler, installing industrial boilers, six years in construction of two cold-roll steel mills, and five years doing industrial maintenance at Bendix Aircraft Wheel and Brake plant at South Bend, Indiana. During that time he farmed 200 acres of corn and soybeans and owned and operated a 58,000-bird, egg-laying house that produced 48,000 to 52,000 eggs a day. At age 62, he retired to Florida to fish, travel, and enjoy the good life. Gloria, his wife of 48 years, died in April 1997. He has five daughters and nine grandchildren. Jim lives in Palm Coast, Florida.

396

Volley H. Cole

Age 14 – United States Army Air Forces

I was born in the farming community of Richland, Arkansas, on 3 September 1931. My parents raised cotton on the farm that my forefathers had homesteaded. In 1933 or 1934, our home burned while my folks, my

> *My commanding officer told me that I was the youngest master sergeant in the Army. I was 20 years old at the time.*

two older brothers, and I were in the fields working and gathering wood. This was during the Depression and my father had no monetary assets, so he turned the land over to a brother and moved us to Harrison, Arkansas, where he worked for a railroad.

During those years, I had a difficult time with my father. I was rebellious and wanted something more exciting than attending school. I always looked older for my age, and I hung around with a cousin who was 18. In early March 1946, my cousin received his notice from the draft board. He suggested that I go to the draft board and tell them that I was 18, register for the draft, and ask for an immediate call-up. I was 14 at the time, but I went to the draft board and told them that my birth date was 10 March 1928, which made me 18. There was never a question raised about my age.

My cousin and I were sent to Camp Robinson at Little Rock, Arkansas, for our physicals. We both passed with flying colors. The only comment from the doctor at the examining facility was, "You are a little skinny son, but we will fatten you up." When I returned home, the Army recruiter contacted me and said, "You don't want to let them draft you and wind up in the infantry." So he signed me up for the U. S. Army Air Forces, using the documents from my draft board.

I was sworn in on 19 March 1946 at Camp Chaffee, Arkansas, where I saw my first German prisoners of war. After a few days during which some items of clothing were issued, we were on our way to Sheppard Field, Texas, for basic training. After basic, we went by troop train to Geiger Field, Washington, where I attended heavy-equipment operators school. From there, I was off to McDill field, Tampa, Florida, where I was assigned to the 621st Aviation Engineer Equipment Maintenance Company. In 1947, I drew my first overseas assignment. It was to Greenland, Labrador, and Newfoundland, where we repaired emergency landing strips for the Air Forces planes being shuttled to Europe.

I was transferred to Rhein Main Air Force Base, Frankfurt, Germany, in 1948, where I was assigned to the 862nd Engineer Aviation Battalion. The 862nd was part of SCARWAF (Special Category Army Regular With Air Force). My battalion worked at both Rhein Main and Templehof Air base in Berlin during the Berlin Air Lift.

My company was transferred to Bitburg Air Base, near Bitburg, Germany, in 1950. We participated in the construction of this base as well as the airbases at Hahn and Spangdalin. The first winter there we lived in tents. Our first enlisted-men's club was a large tent that had been shipped to us from Furstinfeldbruck Air Base. I recall that a lot of beer was consumed in that tent.

In 1952, I was promoted to master sergeant (E-7), which at that time was the highest enlisted grade in the Army. My commanding officer told me that I was the youngest master sergeant in the Army. I was 20 years old at the time.

On weekends, one of my men who spoke French and I would pull patrol with the French authorities in Trier, Germany, to help keep the American soldiers under control. Trier, as was Bitburg, was in the French occupation zone. Bitburg was an excellent assignment because it was a fun town and was close to Luxemburg. We could wear civilian clothes there. Also, George Patton is buried there.

During my assignment at Bitburg, I was given a choice to go with the U. S. Air Force or remain with the Army. I elected to stay with the Army because of my limited education.

I returned to the States in early 1953 and was assigned to the Transportation Division at Camp Kilmer, New Jersey. We were responsible for shuttling troops to and from New York for further transport to and from Europe and Korea. I hated this assignment and looked for a way to get back overseas. My boss, who also was a master sergeant, received orders for Europe, but he didn't want to go. I asked for, and was granted, permission to do so.

Back in Germany, I was assigned to the U. S. Armed Forces Recreation Center at Garmisch. When I arrived, my commander told me that I had to do something about my education, which I did. I enrolled in the U. S. Armed Forces Institute and earned my eighth-grade diploma, and later my high school diploma. Later in my career I obtained a bachelor's degree in business management.

My assignment at Garmisch was as the operations NCO for the post engineers, overseeing all maintenance and repairs for 17 hotels, ski resorts, and a variety of other facilities in Garmisch, Berchtesgaden, Fussen, Murnau, and Obberammergau.

During the latter part of 1953, the vice president of the International Bobsled Federation paid a visit to our commander. He asked him to provide some members of the Army to participate in a new winter-sledding sport called "luge sledding." Three other NCOs and I volunteered. We were placed on TDY (temporary duty) in Switzerland to learn what "luge sledding" was all about. Switzerland was not only a good place to learn about sledding, but for extracurricular activities as well.

For the next four years, as time and TDY assignments would permit, I continued my sledding career. I was transferred to the U. S. Army Aviation Center at Fort Rucker, Alabama, in 1957. I was soon sent to Korea where I remained until the later part of 1960. After Korea, I was assigned as maintenance supervisor for an Engineer Construction Battalion at Fort Bliss, Texas.

For all of these years, I had never corrected my records to reflect my true age. My commander ordered me to apply for a warrant officer position, which required a birth certificate. I told the battalion personnel NCO that I had a problem. After explaining my dilemma, he told me that the law had been changed, and that as long as I had honorable service, I didn't have a problem. I contacted my mother in Arkansas. She sent me a copy of my birth certificate and my records were corrected. I did not become a warrant officer, but at least I could breath easier from then on.

In the early 1960s, I was assigned to the U. S. Army Recruiting Command and sent to Minden, Louisiana. Shortly after I arrived, I was contacted by the United States Olympic Committee (USOC) and asked if I was interested in forming a luge team to represent the United States at the Winter Olympics in Innsbruck, Austria. I jumped at the chance. The Army transferred me back to Garmisch, Germany, where bobsled and luge runs were available. I selected some military personnel, and we started to train in earnest. We trained in Germany, Austria, Poland, and Switzerland.

Neither the Army or the USOC had funds to support the training, so we had to hit the black market to raise funds to keep us going until the games in 1964. In February 1964, I took the first United States luge team to the Winter Games in Innsbruck, Austria. I was selected to head up a six-man contingent to carry the Olympic flag into the stadium for the opening ceremonies. In 1968, the USOC asked me to act as team advisor for the Winter Olympics in Grenoble, France.

I was promoted to senior master sergeant and transferred to Sacramento, California, to take charge of Army recruiting in northern California and western Nevada. In 1969, I left for Vietnam where I was assigned to the 16th Combat Aviation Group. The 16th CAG was part of the 23rd "American" Infantry Division.

I was injured in my right eye and was medically evacuated to Japan in 1970. After I recovered, I was transferred to Sacramento, California, again with the Recruiting Command. In 1972, the International Luge Federation, which I helped form and of which I was a vice president for eight years, asked me to serve as an official at the Winter Olympics in Sapporo, Japan. I did, and was associated with the Winter Olympic Games in one capacity or another until 1994.

I was promoted to sergeant major in 1973. In mid 1974, I started making plans to retire. I was transferred to Fort Carson, Colorado, and retired at that location on 1 October 1974, after 29 years, 6 months and 13 days of service. What would I do differently if I had it to do over? In a word, nothing.

Volley Cole was awarded the Bronze Star, the Air Medal, and a number of campaign medals during his 29+ years of service. He also received a number of awards from the United States Olympic Committee, the Olympic Organizing Committees, the Olympic Alumni Association, the International Luge Federation, and many others. After his retirement from the Army, he was the superintendent of the transportation division of the public transit system in Colorado

Springs, Colorado, until 1978. He then worked for Morrison-Knudsen on a construction project in Saudi Arabia, and later went with McDonnell Douglas Aircraft Company where he worked with the F-15 fighter program. His military career made it difficult to maintain a normal family life and two marriages failed. In 1974, he married Mary Dawson at the Air Force Academy Community Chapel in Colorado Springs, Colorado. Between the two of them, they have nine children and ten grandchildren. Volley and Mary live in Sun Lakes, Arizona.

✓ *INCIDENTally* – **Rainbow liberty!** – We were at anchor at Manila Bay, Philippine Islands, in 1946. We had gone ashore by LCVP, and later in the day we were going back to our ship, the USS *Antietam*. The bay was a bit choppy and we took on a little water. Two sailors who had been partying too much got sick and upchucked, then lay down on the bottom of the LCVP. They had leis around their necks. The leis got wet and the dye bled out on their white uniforms. We had to drop a cargo net and roll them into it to get them aboard the ship. They looked like two rainbows as they were lifted aboard. The four of us who put them in the net looked a bit like rainbows also. The officer of the deck was not a happy camper. He gave us a bad time about our stained uniforms. One of the guys said as he walked away, "Just like an officer, no thanks for helping our shipmates." Oh well – just one of those days.
– *Robert F. Feikema, Jr.*

Robert W. Fry

Age 16 – United States Army

I was born in Memphis, Tennessee, on 6 August 1929. My mother and father were not happy together, so they divorced in 1940. My mother said that my father was ordered to pay alimony and child

> During my Army career, I achieved 14 enlisted and commissioned ranks.

support to her, but he stated that he would go to jail before he would give her a penny. To the best of my knowledge, he never paid her anything, nor did he go to jail.

I was 10 years old and the child-labor laws had not been established, so I worked at a bakery next door to our home, washing pots, pans, and dishes. My mother started to move around and took me to live with different relatives in several locations: Memphis and Martin, Tennessee; Fulton, Kentucky; Springfield, Illinois; Richmond, California; and St. Louis, Missouri. I attended schools in Memphis, Springfield, Richmond, and St. Louis.

Wherever I was living, I worked at many different jobs such as cutting grass, delivering groceries, cleaning stores, and delivering newspapers. I worked in a cabinet shop and at the Union Ice Company in Richmond, California, and the Coca Cola Company in St. Louis, Missouri.

My mother felt that my brother, sister, and I were old enough to leave home at age 16. My sister married when she was 16, my brother enlisted in the Navy at age 16, and I enlisted in the Army when I was 16.

I was sworn into the regular Army on 28 March 1946. After six weeks of basic training at Camp Lee, Virginia, I was shipped to the Philippine Islands and was assigned to the 618th Ordnance Base Armament Maintenance Battalion on Luzon Island.

I returned to the United States in 1947, was discharged at Camp Stoneman, California, and returned to St. Louis. After one visit to the local unemployment office to sign up for the 52/20 club, as I had been advised to do, I decided that I was better off as a buck sergeant in the Army, so I re-enlisted. I was assigned as NCOIC (non-commissioned officer in charge) of a troop train from St. Louis to Keesler Field, Mississippi. From there, I went to Fort Jackson, South Carolina. After attending the Signal Corps Photographic Center, Long Island, New York, I went to Fort Dix, New Jersey, for shipment to Germany.

In February 1948, I was assigned to the 6th Constabulary Regiment in Schweinfurt, with temporary duty to the 53rd Constabulary Squadron in Schwabach and Weiden. The 53rd was reorganized as the 15th Constabulary Squadron with the mission of keepers of law and order in Germany along the borders of the U. S. Zone, the Soviet Zone, and Czechoslovakia.

My duties were: official U. S. Army photographer, Special Investigations Section investigator, provost sergeant, NCOIC of the Special Police Platoon, commander of the honor guard, and first sergeant of Headquarters Troop.

I was commissioned a 2nd lieutenant in January 1952 and assigned as a reconnaissance platoon leader. I served as trial counsel on several special court-martials. I remained with the 15th Constabulary Squadron until 11 July 1952 when I returned to the States.

I held several command and staff assignments at Fort Leavenworth, Kansas, until January 1956 when I was transferred to Keflavic, Iceland, for duty with the 2nd Battalion Combat Team. In December 1956, I went to Fort Benning, Georgia, until May 1957, then to Fort Lawton, Washington, until September 1960. I went back to Germany and served with the 21st Infantry Regiment of the 24th Infantry Division. I was captain of the 1st Battalion marksmanship team and we took second place in the NATO shooting matches.

I returned to the United States in May 1963 and was assigned as the senior officer advisor in the VI U. S. Army Corps General Officer Command in Pontiac and Flint, Michigan.

During my Army career, I achieved 14 enlisted and commissioned ranks. The *Stars and Stripes* newspaper thought this worthy of an article in their May 1966 issue shortly after I was promoted to major. I was selected for promotion to lieutenant colonel, but I chose to retire on 30 April 1966.

My best memories of more than 20 years in the U. S. Army are, without a doubt, during the time I spent with the United States Constabulary.

Bob Fry was awarded the Army Commendation Medal and received a number of other awards and service medals. After his retirement from the Army, he held progressively more responsible staff, management and consulting positions as an employee and owner of several national and international companies located in the Pacific Northwest. He met his future wife in Schwabach, Germany in 1948, and they were married in 1952. Bob and Irma have a daughter and triplet grandchildren. They live in Federal Way, Washington.

✓ *INCIDENTally* — *Navy chow.* – It was my first morning at boot camp at the Naval Training Center, San Diego, California, in 1942. The bugler sounded mess call and we fell in and marched to the mess hall. I picked up a mess tray and proceeded down the counter. The fare was Boston baked beans. I had never tasted Boston baked beans in my life and was not able to eat them. What was worse, it being Friday, fish was served at noon. I couldn't eat the fish either! However, at the evening meal, I ate everything. Later, while talking with the other guys, we agreed that the Navy needed to be coached on what Southern folks ate. In the course of these events I learned lesson number one – keep your mouth shut. – *Herman I. "Ike" Hargraves.*

404

Edward W. Peifer
Age 15 – United States Army

I was born in Palisades Park, New Jersey, on 26 February 1931. My mother moved to the Bronx, New York, with my 3-year-old sister and me after my father was killed in an accident. When I was 5 years old, my mother remarried. The person she married was a

> *I found that it was a tough transition from being a kid to becoming a man.*

gambling, drunken, wife- and child-beater. My mother had a makeup kit that she used to cover her bruises and black eyes.

We moved to Washington, D.C., when I was 11 years old. When I was 14, I came home and found that beast beating my mother. He was a big man, 6-feet 2-inches tall, and weighed 220 pounds. I was about 5-feet 9-inches tall, and weighed 150 pounds. I tried to stop the beating. He turned on me, swinging his belt. I ducked, and the belt wrapped around my head, tearing an ear. I shouted at him, "You are

a dead man!" He asked what I meant. I told him, "When you go to sleep, or pass out, I'll kill you!" He must have believed me because he left the house and was never heard from again.

I was always in trouble. I used to steal, mostly food and other necessities that my mother needed. I was caught more than once and finally wound up in the National Training School for Boys, a reform school, where I spent three months. After I was released, I was caught breaking into a store

and had to appear before a very familiar judge. He told me that he could give me big time in jail, but he thought that maybe there was some hope for me, and he would drop the charges if I went into the Army. I told him that I was only 15 years old. He told me to register for the draft and then use the draft card as proof of age at the recruiting office. He said if that wasn't enough, he would sign for me.

It was enough, and on 28 March 1946, I was in the Army. I had field-artillery basic training at Fort Belvoir, Virginia. I received a summary court-martial there for a traffic violation. I was sent overseas right after basic and was assigned to the 1st Infantry Division in Bad Tolz, Germany. It was not long after I arrived that I received my second court-martial for hitting a lieutenant. It was self defense and everyone knew that, but I got a six-month sentence and served four months. The first year in the Army was difficult for me. I found that it was a tough transition from being a kid to becoming a man. I always tried to act like a big shot and had many fights trying to prove myself.

One escapade I will never forget. It was New Year's Eve, 1946, a very cold and blustery evening. I was full of beer. My girlfriend had left the club before me and was waiting for me in her room in a small house on top of a hill. The road to the house was cobblestone, coated with ice, and very slick. Being slightly drunk, I kept slipping. As I slipped and stumbled my way up the hill, a new problem emerged – I was attacked by a large goose which had been trained to guard the road at night. The goose, furiously flapping its wings, pecked at me with its very hard beak. I was determined to rendezvous with my girlfriend, so I tried to punch the goose out of my path. But with each ill-aimed, beer-guided blow missing the mark, I found myself sliding backward on the icy cobblestones. The goose was winning the battle.

Finally, I landed a haymaker on its hard head, and the stunned goose staggered away. A bit worse for this encounter, I wobbled up the hill and sneaked into the house. The elderly couple my girlfriend lived with would not allow male visitors, so I very quietly snuck into her room.

The room was tiny, containing just a small dresser with a water pitcher and basin, and a bed with a large, inviting, feather quilt. By now, the large quantity of beer that I had consumed was demanding its toll. I had to pee – and pee fast. I could not use the downstairs bathroom, as I would awaken the elderly couple, so I did the next best thing. I opened the window and peed. As I urinated, I suddenly heard sounds like machine-gun fire. Glancing out the window, I noticed a wood shed with a metal roof about 10 feet directly below. My own need to answer the call of nature had created this terrible racket! My girlfriend tried to get me to stop, but the beer wouldn't allow it.

Naturally, the racket woke the elderly couple and I was promptly thrown out.

By now, I was in a bad frame of mind. Here I was, shivering miserably in the cold night, denied the bed with the large feather quilt and my girlfriend's hugs. To make matters worse, I knew that the goose awaited me.

Luckily, the goose was still somewhat stunned, and I managed to get past it without any trouble. Thinking my woes were finally over, I quietly staggered my way down the slick cobblestones. That's when I found myself caught in the glare of a jeep's headlights. Inside the jeep were two stern-looking MPs. It didn't take long for me to see myself through their eyes – out late at night on New Year's Eve, uniform in disarray, hair disheveled, hat missing (I suddenly realized that I lost it during the earlier goose encounter), and an unsteady gait. I could see that, to them, I was just another drunk to deal with, and that I was going to get a citation. Resignedly, I answered their questions, but as the goose story unfolded, the unexpected happened. They laughed! Instead of a well-deserved citation, I got a ride back to camp!

I was 17 when I received court-martial number three. This one was for stealing a truck, which I did. I was a division middle-weight boxer and was well-known, so the court-martial drew a crowd. I pleaded not guilty, and thanks to Lieutenant Evans who defended me, I was found not guilty. Although Lieutenant Evans gave me a good dressing down, he thought I needed a break in life and that there was hope for me. He talked his good buddy, Lieutenant Kostis, who was the commander of the 1st Infantry Division Honor Guard, into taking me into the Honor Guard. Kostis didn't want to do it, but he did. He told me that I would not make the grade. I fooled him, and made the Honor-Guard first team. For the first time in my life, I had pride in myself. I wore a pressed uniform second to none. When the guard was disbanded because we were going on four months of maneuvers, I was assigned to the 1st Quartermaster Company. I went from private to buck sergeant in a matter of months.

I was discharged on 13 January 1949, just before my 18th birthday. I worked as a baker's helper for a year and a half. I was in the inactive reserves and was called back to active duty in September 1950. I served in Korea with the 1343rd Combat Engineer Battalion from January 1951 until February 1952. I returned to the States as a sergeant first class. I re-enlisted and was assigned to Fort Belvoir, Virginia, where I was promoted to master sergeant at the age of 21. After eight months at Fort Belvoir, I was shipped back to Germany where I had served as a 15-year-old. I was assigned to the 91st Antiaircraft Battery as a first sergeant.

When my hitch was up in 1954, I returned to the States. I called on the judge who had strongly suggested that I join the Army. I was wearing my uniform with 1st sergeant's stripes. He took one look at me and said, "My God, you stole a uniform!" We both had a long laugh.

I was discharged at the age of 23. I had earned a GED while in the Army, with only a sixth-grade education. The Army was a good place for me. It turned a kid who was always in trouble into a man.

Ed Peifer enrolled in the American University in Washington, D.C., on the basis of his GED. He was awarded a full-tuition scholarship and earned a B.A. in economics. He entered the business world and became general manager and vice president of a business for six years. He changed jobs and was the president of another business for 20 years. He retired in 1988 at the age of 57. He has three children and four step-children. Ed and Judy, his wife of 24 years, live in Hartfield, Virginia.

Charles C. Deits

Age 15 – United States Army Air Forces

I was sworn into the U. S. Army on 29 March 1946, six days after my 15th birthday, which legally is 23 March 1931. Of course, I didn't tell the recruiter that I was 15. To him, I was 17. With the help of a forged birth

> As near as I can figure out, it was just for the adventure.

certificate and a parental-consent form signed by my girlfriend and her brother, plus being warm-bodied and still breathing, I was in like a tall burglar.

Why did I join? I still don't know why! One day, two friends (also underage) and I skipped school and hitchhiked to the big city of Petoskey, Michigan, about 15 miles away. For the lack of something better to do, we ended up at a recruiting office. Was it patriotism? I doubt it! Was it because we were in trouble at school or with the law? No way! Was it because of an undesirable home-life? Not at all! As near as I can figure out, it was just for the adventure.

Our first stop was Fort Sheridan, Illinois, for processing. That is where some guardian angel started looking over me. All three of us were parted right away. Somebody decided that I should be in the U. S. Army Air Forces, so I was shipped to Buckley Field, Colorado, for basic training, all 128 pounds of me (dripping wet, with my pockets filled with fish sinkers). After making it through basic, they asked me what school I wanted to go to. For the lack of something better, I chose cook and baker

school. Again, somebody was looking out for me; they sent me to clerk-typists school at Lowery Field, Colorado, a career field that stood me in good stead for the rest of my career.

I was sent to Eglin Field, Florida, and assigned to the 857th Chemical Company as a company clerk. I spent the remainder of my 18-month enlistment there and was discharged as a T/5. While at

Eglin, I passed the GED test and received a diploma from the Florida State Board of Education, two years earlier than I would have by staying in school. Despite passing the GED, I went back to high school under the GI Bill, and also took flying lessons under the GI Bill.

After finishing the football season in 1948, I decided that civilian life was a bit dull and re-enlisted on 13 December 1948. I was still too young to enlist without my parents' consent. I spent the bulk of this hitch at various bases doing personnel work, eventually ending up in Korea at K-2 Airbase.

Upon returning Stateside in August 1952, after a two-week troopship cruise, I was discharged as a staff sergeant. This time I planned to stay out of the military for good. After a couple of years in a series of nondescript jobs, a brief stint in the Michigan National Guard, and having met my future wife, I decided I'd better try the military again.

After two years of civilian life, I enlisted in the Aviation Cadet program in 1954, but soon washed out because of poor eyesight. I went ahead and re-enlisted, but after a two-year break in service, I lost all of my rank and had to go through refresher basic training and through personnel school again. This was not a very smart career move on my part, but I decided that I had better stay in or stay out. I stayed in until June 1970, when I retired as a chief master sergeant.

During my Air Force career, I worked in personnel, ground radar, airborne-radar operations, and as a first sergeant for the last five years. My overseas assignments included Canada, Alaska, Japan, and Korea, with plenty of TDYs (temporary duty) around the world when on aircrew status.

In retrospect, I think that I can safely say that enlisting the first time at age 15 was probably one of the *dumbest* things I have ever done, but finally serving in the Air Force for over 22 years and retiring was one of the *smartest* things that I have ever done.

Charles Deits returned to northern Michigan where he worked in a number of different jobs. He was a sales manager for a farm-implement company, then a real-estate broker. He moved to Alabama to avoid the long, cold, snow-filled Michigan winters, where he worked in a variety of jobs in the mobile-home business. Charlie and Joie, his wife of 47 years, have three children and two grandchildren. They live in Foley, Alabama.

Robert L. Koble, Jr.

Age 15 – United States Navy

At age 15, I moved to Phoenix, Arizona, along with my mother, father, sister, and brother, from Cleveland, Ohio. I was born in

> ..., it was very obvious that the certificate had been altered.

Roseville, Ohio, on 12 June 1930. In a short time, my uncle, aunt, and their two children followed and moved into our one-room cabin that measured about 20 feet by 20 feet. It was not a good situation. I slept in the car, an old Hudson Terraplane. The year was 1945.

Each night I would pretend that I could start the engine and drive off to places unknown. For a while, it was an exciting adventure knowing I could (in my mind) just take off. I would look forward to the nights.

One day I heard of a guy who had forged another person's birth certificate and was able to join the Army. I met the forger and asked if he would forge my birth certificate so I could join the Navy. He said, "Sure!" I told my mother that I needed a copy of my birth certificate for some reason other than my true intentions. After the forger looked at my birth certificate, he confessed he could not alter it because it was typed rather than handwritten, as many certificates were at that time.

My heart sank! Again, in my mind, I was already in the Navy. I confided in one person what I was trying to do, and how the forger was unable to alter my birth certificate. My new confidant was an 18-year-old girl who lived across the street from me. She had just graduated from high school and obtained her first job as a clerk at the Valley National Bank. She looked at the certificate and said that she could remove the "30" from the year 1930 and replace it with "28," thereby instantly making me 17 rather than 15. After work the next day, she handed me the document. Again my heart sank, for lo and behold, while the document now read "1928" rather than "1930," it was very obvious that the certificate had been altered. There were heavy eraser marks along with roughed-up paper where the number "28" had been placed. I was devastated. I not only had an obviously altered document, but I no longer had a clean birth certificate to work with.

Several days later, I was walking past the Union Title Company in downtown Phoenix. On the sidewalk, next to the curb, was a sandwich-board type of advertisement stating: SPECIAL, TODAY ONLY! PHOTOSTATIC COPIES 50 CENTS EACH. Photostats were the precursor of Xerox copies. However, they were positives, that is, all black print was white and the white background was black.

I wasn't about to waste too much good money on this new experiment, so I ordered only one copy to be made of my terribly forged certificate. When I returned in four hours to pick up the copy, I could hardly believe my eyes. It was truly beautiful, sharp, clear, and no sign of erasures – a masterpiece! For the next two weeks I carried the folded photostat copy in my rear pocket in an effort to give it age and make it look as if it had been in the family for a while.

Now, being fully prepared, I went to enlist. My plan was to write to my mother after I was in and tell her what I had done. Instead, they never asked to see my birth certificate at the recruiting office! They just asked how old I was, I took some tests, filled out a lot of forms, and signed a lot of papers. About four hours later, I was told that I would be sworn-in in two days, and I was to bring in proof of my age and a parent to sign a consent for me to go in at age 17.

I asked myself, "Why didn't someone tell me that at age 17, one was required to have parental consent?" I could have made myself 18 as easily as 17. I concluded that I now had to confess to my parents what I had done, and what I wanted to do, and ask them to please sign the papers for me. My mother said, "Absolutely not!" I discovered then, and also in later years, that some of my best thoughts occur to me when I am under extreme pressure. I stepped back, and with a calm and clear voice, told my mother, "Mother, if you do not have Dad sign the papers, you will wake up tomorrow and not know where I am, or you can get him to sign, and you will wake up tomorrow and know I am in the Navy. What'a ya want to do?"

As my father drove me to the recruiter's office to sign the papers, not one word was spoken between us. The recruiter looked at the superb forgery and said, "Well, you can't forge a photostat, can you?" I meekly said no. But, as I look back in my older years, I think he knew it was a fake. I was sworn into the Navy on 8 April 1946.

I was sent to the Naval Training Center at San Diego for boot camp. When we graduated, our commander gave us a pep talk and commented that we were now men. He went on to say that in the past there were cases of young kids getting into the service underage. Most could not take the rigors of boot camp and called for their mommies to get them out. Yet, there were others that proved themselves as men and were never discovered. I swear to this day that the commander was staring at me, and that he knew I was underage. On the other hand, it could have been my pride that made me think that.

After boot camp, I was sent to Pearl Harbor where I was in vehicle maintenance at the Aiea Naval Hospital. Later, I was transferred to the submarine base for training as a submarine crewman.

During my entire enlistment I told no one my true age, with the exception of a Navy family by the name of Lee who lived near the submarine base at Pearl Harbor. The father was a Navy lieutenant junior grade. At 17, I would be too old to hang out with his daughter Barbara and son Woody, who were 15-year-old twins, so I told them my true age. This family adopted me, and for the first time, I really enjoyed family life. I went to all the high school functions, football, track, and dances. It was just a wholesome family atmosphere. Unfortunately, I have lost contact with them.

I was discharged from the Navy on 21 January 1948 at the real age of 17. Soon after my 18th birthday, I received a notice to report to the draft board. I told the elderly lady (she may have been 30) that I had already been in the service. I explained to her that I had lied about my age and showed her my discharge papers. She said, "You lied to the government?" She went on to yank my chain, telling me that I would have to go back in because it doesn't count if I lied. For several years after that, I never told anybody but close family what I had done. I was afraid that I would lose my GI Bill of Rights benefits.

Robert Koble studied at Phoenix College under the GI Bill, then went to work as a lab technician for the International Metal Products Company in Phoenix, Arizona, ending up as their chief engineer for research and development. He left that company to start his own business, manufacturing fluorescent-lighting fixtures. During his career, several patents were issued to him. Currently, he consults and markets his inventions. Bob and Dixie, his wife of 52 years, have three children, six grandchildren, and one great-grandchild. One of his sons is currently a senior master chief in the Navy. Bob and Dixie live in Camp Verde, Arizona.

Clifford Boyd

Age 15 – United States Army

I was born in The Hollow, Virginia, on 26 July 1930. Our nearest neighbor was my Uncle Snuffy Smith. The nearest town was Mt. Airy, North Carolina, located about six miles from

> This 15-year-old moonshiner from Virginia became 18 years old on 9 March 1946.

my home. Some people call it Mayberry because it is the birthplace of Andy Griffith. During the 1930s, everyone in The Hollow fell upon hard times. We referred to this period as the "Hoover Times." One couldn't find a ground hog, possum, squirrel, or any kind of wild game to put in the pot. My dad worked for the coal mines in Coalwood, West Virginia. Later he came home and worked for the WPA (Works Progress Administration).

In 1941, I told my first lie about my age. I had to be 12 years old or older to get a job picking apples. So, I told the foreman that I was 12, but I was only 11. I was hired at the enormous wage of 5¢ an

hour. I thought I was rich! I picked apples again during the fall of 1942 and was paid 8¢ an hour this time. Things were looking up due to the war. My dad had gone to work for the Shipbuilding and Dry Dock Company at Newport News, Virginia.

During the spring of 1943, my older brother and I decided that picking apples was not bringing in enough cash. We had found our dad's 50-gallon copper still and we started making whiskey. Sugar was rationed, but since there were 11 kids in the family, we had enough sugar to make whiskey and brandy. The military men on furlough were always looking for some good "likker" and we were happy to supply it. There were other factors in our favor relating to sales. One was that my county (Patrick) and other neighboring counties were dry (no legal sales of whiskey). Another factor was that most "revenoors" had been drafted, so there was little danger of being caught. We made whiskey until the war ended, then we put Dad's still back where we had found it. When the shipbuilding industry was about to close down, Dad came home. I don't believe he ever suspected what my brother and I had done while he was away.

By 1946, I was looking for something exciting to do. I figured out a plan to get drafted. I lived 30 miles from the county seat, Stuart, Virginia, but I lived only six miles from Mt. Airy, North Carolina, so I decided to go there to register. This 15-year-old moonshiner from Virginia became 18 years old on 9 March 1946. At the draft board in Mt. Airy, they could only register me and forward the paperwork to my county seat, which they did. It worked like a charm, and shortly thereafter, I received my greetings from the President. I went to Roanoke, Virginia, to be examined. I had already signed papers stating that if I passed the exam, I would go directly into the armed forces. So on 19 April 1946, I was sworn into the United States Army.

I was sent to Fort Meade, Maryland, where everyone referred to me as "Peach Fuzz." After a week, I was then sent to Fort McClellan, Alabama, for infantry basic training. Basic was a little rough for most city guys, but for this 15-year-old ridge-runner, it was no problem. In fact, it was a lot of fun – except for the time my commander kicked my ass for not being in step. When I settled back down to the ground, I was in step, and I stayed in step for the rest of my 24 years in the military.

After basic training, I was sent to Camp Kilmer, New Jersey, and from there it was on to Hawaii through the Panama Canal. We arrived in Manila in the Philippine Islands about 1 September 1946, and I was assigned to the 50th Military Police Battalion at Quezon City. I learned how to drive a jeep as a patrolman. They didn't ask me if I could drive, and I didn't tell them that I couldn't. My partner was an ex-moonshiner from Henry County, Virginia, who had made much liquor prior to entering the Army. Needless to say, he was a good teacher. He showed me how to slide a jeep around in the middle of the road and all the other tricks he had learned from being chased by the law. However, I didn't like being an MP, so I asked for a reassignment.

My transfer came through and I ended up with the 3008th Graves Registration Company at Palo, Leyte, in December 1946. There were 35 military troops assigned there and about 1,000 Filipino workers.

They mostly painted and replaced the wooden markers located at each grave. With 14,000 graves, this was quite a chore.

I was assigned as a clerk, which at first seemed great. However, I was soon to learn that my job involved going throughout the southern Philippine Islands looking for deceased American military. My job took me to all provinces on Mindanao, Cebu, Negros, Panay, and elswhere. We recovered hundreds of American bodies during these operations, including bodies at aircraft crash sites.

A trip to one crash site was memorable. Four Filipinos and I went to get the remains of a pilot who went down in his L-5 aircraft on top of the highest mountain in Leyte. We were driven to Ormock, Leyte, and from there we commenced walking east toward the mountain. We spent the first night halfway up the mountain. I spread my poncho and blanket on the ground, hoping to get some sleep. However, this wasn't to be, for there were bugs and other creepy things I'd never seen before. When I pulled off my boots, they were full of my blood. I could wring blood from my socks. This was my first encounter with dry-land leeches. When they were full from sucking blood, the blood kept flowing due to their anticoagulant secretions. My ankles were totally black with leeches and blood. The only way I could get the leeches off was by using my trusty Zippo lighter.

The next morning we commenced the second leg of our trip. At about noon, we arrived near the top of the mountain. I was dying of thirst, as my canteen was empty. I saw a beautiful, bubbly stream with a pool of water suitable for drinking. I lowered myself push-up style and started drinking the cool mountain water. When I raised myself up to breathe, I saw what was making the pool. There were at least 50 Japanese skeletons lodged together forming the dam. I was no longer thirsty.

There were several acres of level ground on top of the mountain, and the sight there was something I will never forget. The ground was covered with what seemed to be thousands of Japanese bodies, and tons of their army gear. I also saw much American stuff, including bombs and unexploded artillery shells. A few feet off the trail, I saw two skeletal remains of what appeared to be Americans. There was paratrooper gear around them, they were at least six-feet tall and they had no gold teeth. At this point, having seen many thousands of

Japanese skulls, I was convinced that they were American soldiers. I marked the place and we continued on our journey.

We went down the other side of the mountain and spent the night at a fast-flowing river. The next morning we located the L-5 aircraft and the pilot's remains. He was still in the cockpit of his plane and his wedding band was still on his fleshless finger. I put his remains in a rubberized laundry bag for return to Palo.

We stopped and picked up the two bodies I had found the day before. After arriving back at Palo, I gave them to our bone technician, a civilian, and he started laughing. It seems as though the remains I had brought back were Mongolians who had been conscripted by the Japanese. I was furious.

We went to the Devao Penal Colony, near Devao City. The Japanese had converted a civilian prison to a POW camp. They had starved at least a dozen POWs to death. I helped disinter remains of bodies at this place of horror. I interviewed local Filipinos about what had happened to the American POWs and was told some horrible stories. They told me that the POWs would sing American songs in which they would ask for food. For example, the Americans would sing, "You are my sunshine, please give me some eggs." The nearby Filipinos would sneak bananas, eggs, and what food they could to the POWs. However, at some point, the Japanese found out what was going on, so they lined up over 50 people from the nearby barrio and shot them.

I ran into many American escapees from the Philippine Death March. They fought guerrilla warfare during World War II, mostly in the southern islands. Many married local women and had children. Some came back on active duty, some didn't. Some became very prosperous. I met several Death March veterans who were POWs until the end of the war. I will never forget those courageous men who gave so much for their country.

I was discharged at Fairfield Army Air Base, in California, on 7 October 1947 and returned to my home in Virginia. I had just turned 17 and everything looked rosy. I tried my previous civilian occupation, but this time the competition was much greater, and also there were more lawmen. A lot of discharged veterans tried making moonshine for a living because jobs were very scarce. Many of them were caught and served time in prison.

While I was going to school on the GI Bill, the Korean War started. I quit school and went to the same post office where I had registered for the draft in 1946 and enlisted in the U. S. Air Force. I was sent to Lackland AFB, Texas, then to Carswell AFB, Fort Worth, Texas. After three years at Carswell, I served a tour in French Morocco. From there I went to Lake Charles AFB, Louisiana, then to Ernest Harmon AB, Newfoundland. After three years, I was assigned to Robins AFB, Georgia, then to Westover AFB, Massachusetts, where I worked as a management analyses superintendent. After six years, I was sent to Anderson AFB, Guam.

By then I was a senior master sergeant and became the non-commissioned officer in charge of management analysis in 8th Air Force Headquarters. My main responsibility was being in charge of all combat statistics for the Strategic Air Command (SAC) in Southeast Asia. I kept a tally of all sorties and flying hours by crew members, the total JP-4 (fuel) used, and a running total of all bombs dropped by type and tonnage. I also did many analyses of war damage by B-52 aircraft in Southeast Asia. I briefed the 8th Air Force commander and staff on all SAC activity in southeast Asia on a weekly basis.

My last Air Force assignment was at SAC Headquarters, Offutt AFB, Nebraska. After two years there, I retired on 1 August 1972, and moved back to Virginia. I now live about five miles from my birthplace. I have only one regret – I never made it to Vietnam. I was on the volunteer list for 12 years, but they didn't have an opening for an E-8 in management analysis at that time.

Clifford Boyd was awarded two Meritorious Service Medals, two Air Force Commendation Medals, three Outstanding Unit Awards, and a number of other service medals. After he retired from the Air Force, he was a deputy sheriff in Patrick County, Virginia, for more than two years and a supervisor for four years. Prior to accepting the job, he told the sheriff that he would not have anything to do with people who made or drank moonshine whiskey because they would be either relatives or friends. Clifford and Jewell, his wife of 53 years, have three children and three grandchildren. They live in Ararat, Virginia.

Melvin Rudolph

Age 13 – United States Army
Age 15 – Illinois National Guard

It was a beautiful night on 29 April 1946 in Chicago, Illinois. I was hanging out with my buddies, George Ferber and Jerry Harris. During the course of the

> *So I filled out the papers with my brother's name.*

evening, George announced that he was going to enlist in the military the next day. George asked Jerry if he wanted to tag along. I volunteered to ditch school the next day and ride with George to the recruiting office, even though I was supposed to be in school. We made arrangements to meet the following morning at the El (train).

When we arrived at the recruiting station, we were told to sit on benches in a big room. After a few minutes, an Army sergeant came up to George and me and asked George if he wanted to enlist. George said yes, and added that he was 17 and had all his papers signed. When the sergeant asked me if I was enlisting, too, I was so shocked I just blurted out, "Yes!" The sergeant asked me if I had my papers

and if they were signed by my parents. I said, "No." He said, "Let's do the physicals first for both of you, and then you can go home and get your papers signed by your parents and be back before 5 p.m. today."

After the physical, the sergeant told me I was fit to join the Army. He gave me a few papers to fill out. As I started to fill them out I realized my birth certificate would show my real age as 13, that I was born on 15 August 1932. Thinking hard and fast, I remembered that my brother Herbert had just turned 17. So I filled out the papers with my brother's name. Then I was told by the sergeant to go home and get the papers signed and notarized.

By this time it was 1 p.m. and I had no idea how I was going to get my mother or father to sign for me. I went home, and knowing where the family papers were kept, I went straight to my mother and father's room and took my brother's birth certificate. The only one home at the time was my sister Helen, 18 months younger than I. She didn't know where my father was, but she told me my mother was shopping. I told my sister what I was doing and she said, "I'll sign for Mom." Which she did. Now I needed to get the papers notarized. I knew a man who owned a bicycle shop down the street. I went to his store and asked him to notarize the papers for me. I told him my mother was sick and couldn't come in. He said okay and notarized the papers.

I had second thoughts about joining the Army because of my age, but I was caught up in the moment and went back to the recruiting office, arriving about 4 p.m. All of us "men" went into a big room and were told to stand at attention. An officer came in and told us all to raise our right hands, repeat the oath after him, and take one step forward. Then he said, "You're all in the Army now." This was 30 April 1946.

I was still with my buddy George as we marched out of the building to a train station across the street. We were informed that we would be going to Fort Sheridan in Illinois for induction and assignment. Boy, I thought, this is all so exciting, and at my age, it was. We got into Fort Sheridan about 6 p.m., went to a barracks, were told to pick out a bunk and to leave our luggage or whatever we had on our bunk. We went outside and they marched us over to a large mess hall.

After dinner, I quickly found a phone and called my mother and father. My father answered the phone and asked me why I wasn't home for dinner. I said, "Dad, I'm in the Army and at Fort Sheridan." There were a few moments of silence. Then in his very strong, deep, voice he said to me, "That's the best place for you!" Dad was a World War I veteran and knew all about the Army. He turned the phone over to Mom, who started to cry and begged me to come home. I told her I couldn't, that I was a soldier now, and I told her how I joined. After a lot of tears, I told Mom I would be at Fort Sheridan for a week or so and that she could probably come and see me. That weekend, a car pulled up in front of my barracks and my mother, father, and two sisters got out. We all went to the PX and had some ice cream and talked. My mother was still very upset about the whole thing and again asked me to come home.

When they left, it began to dawn on me just how serious the whole thing was, and I began to get scared. I found my buddy George and stayed pretty close to him. Since he knew the truth, he offered me encouragement.

After four or five days, we were told we would be shipping out to Texas. I remember the troop train as being all green inside. It was not a pleasant trip to Texas. When we arrived in the middle of the night, we were right in the heart of the camp then known as San Antonio Army Air Field, now known as Lackland Air Force Base. We were assigned to a barracks and told to pick out a bunk. George and I got a lower and upper bunk. The sergeant said, "See you at 5 a.m.," and he did!

My first experience of being Herbert Rudolph came the next morning when the sergeant out in the street was yelling for Herbert. I had forgotten it was me. George said, "They are calling you," and I got out of the barracks as fast as I could. It happened a few times after that, but I soon learned to answer to the name of Herbert. Everything was going good for me. My father was still saying it was the best place for me, my mother was still crying, and I was getting used to my new name.

Basic training was difficult for me because I was not as strong as the other men. My buddy George helped me get through a lot of tough times. During the second month of training I was ordered to report to the commanding officer. I was scared to death when he said to me, "You are not Herbert Rudolph, are you? You are Melvin Rudolph and we know you are 13 years old." I was so tired of lying that I just said, "Yes, sir." He said, "Your mother wants you home as soon as possible, so after they submit all the paper work and your records have been changed, you will be sent back to Fort Sheridan for discharge." I knew then that any hope of my remaining in the Army was over.

I was assigned to a barracks while my paperwork was being processed, which took about a month. I was sorry to have to go and wished my mother would have left things alone. But she said I belonged at home, in school, and there was nothing I could do about it. I took another train ride back to Fort Sheridan where I was processed out of the Army along with thousands of GIs. I remember being so awed to be in their presence because they were real heroes with a lot of medals.

I was issued an honorable discharge under Article 615, minority. I also received $300 mustering-out pay, a ruptured-duck pin, and the World War II Victory Medal. It was a thrill for me to be a "veteran" at age 14 and to graduate from the eighth grade and go on to high school. All my friends had a million questions for me. I was the only student able to wear a World War II Victory Medal and a ruptured duck.

I joined the Illinois National Guard at age 15 and was on their rolls until I joined the Army at age 18. I volunteered for the draft and entered the Army on 23 September 1952. I was assigned to the 101st Airborne Division Infantry Division at Camp Breckenridge, Kentucky, and then to the Japanese Logistics Command as a photographer, and served in both Korea and Japan. I was finally able to accomplish what I tried to do at the age of 13 – to serve my country.

Mel Rudolph worked as a police officer in the Chicago area after his discharge from the Army in 1954. He became chief of security for the Del E. Webb Corporation when they started building Sun City, Las Vegas, and served in that position for 12 years. Mel and Rose, his wife of 51 years, have four children and three grandchildren. They live in Las Vegas, Nevada.

Clayton D. Hibbard

Age 16 – United States Army

I was born in Lewiston, Idaho, on 31 July 1929. My parents divorced when I was 7-years old. From that time on, I spent the school months with my grandmother, and the rest of the year I stayed with aunts and uncles on their cattle ranches.

> ..., I asked myself why I was always volunteering for everything.

From the time that World War II started, I had a desire to join the Army. When I reached the age of 16, I talked my grandmother into helping me lie about my age. After enlisting, five of us young men from Lewiston, Idaho, boarded a train for Seattle, Washington. On 2 May 1946, we were sworn into the United States Army.

The five of us were given a choice of the branch of the Army in which we wanted to serve. I asked for the infantry paratroopers. To this day, I do not know where the other four from Lewiston went. I was sent to Fort McClellan, Alabama, for eight weeks of infantry training. At the close of training, they asked if anyone wanted to volunteer for the paratroopers. There were about 200 men in the company. I was the only one that volunteered. I was sent to Fort Benning, Georgia, for six weeks of parachute and glider training. From there, I went to Camp Stoneman, California, where I boarded a ship for Japan. I was assigned to  the K Company, 3rd Battalion, 187th Regimental Combat Team, 11th Airborne Division, stationed on Hokkaido, Japan's northernmost island.

Soon after I joined the 11th Airborne, they put out a call for boxers. I always liked to fight, so I decided to try it. After a couple of fights per month for a year, they held a division tournament. I won the lightweight championship. I held that title until I was discharged on 1 May 1950, after completing my 4-year hitch.

After my discharge, I went home to Lewiston, Idaho, and married my hometown sweetheart. I re-enlisted in the Army on 23 June 1950, two days before the North Korean army invaded South Korea. I was stationed at Fort Lawton, Seattle, Washington, for about six months, then was sent to Fort Warden, Port Townsend, Washington. At that time they were closing down Fort Warden and were sending all the men to the Nevada Atomic Bomb Test Site. Not knowing a thing about atomic bombs, I asked for, and received, a transfer to Korea where I was assigned to the 9th Infantry Regiment of the 2nd Infantry Division. After arriving in Korea, I asked myself why I was always volunteering for everything. After 1 year, 1 month, and 15 days, I was sent Stateside to Fort Lewis, Washington, where I was discharged on 22 June 1953 with the rank of sergeant first class.

Clay Hibbard earned the Combat Infantryman's Badge during his service in Korea. After his discharge, he attended several schools, received a GED, and accumulated a couple of years of community college credits. He joined the Plumbers and Pipefitters Union, served a 5-year apprenticeship, then worked at the trade for 40 years. He is still married to his hometown sweetheart. They have two daughters, one son, and five grandchildren. Clay and Luella live in Seattle, Washington.

Bernard J. Doyle

Age 16 – United States Navy

When I was 4 years old, my father took me aboard the USS *Colorado* (BB-45) to visit my uncle who was an electrician's mate aboard the ship. We had traveled from Laramie, Wyoming, and arrived at Long Beach, California, in time to see the fleet come into

> The day that we visited the Colorado was the day my blood turned Navy blue.

port. Although I was very young, I still remember the flags and pennants flying, the Navy band playing, and the sailors coming ashore in the liberty launches. The day that we visited the *Colorado* was the day my blood turned Navy blue. All I ever wanted to be was a sailor.

I was born in Laramie, Wyoming, on 20 May 1930. At about the time I started school, we moved to North Platte, Nebraska. When I was 14, I decided to try a bit of military life, so I joined the Nebraska State Guard. We drilled in the local armory and I went to summer training twice at Camp Ashland, Nebraska. The second year, they made me corporal of the guard and handed me keys to a jeep so I could

check the posts on the perimeter. I had to be very careful where and how I parked because I didn't know how to get the jeep in reverse, and I didn't know how to drive while backing up.

In May 1946, at the age of 15, I had a chance to construct a new birth certificate for myself. One of my classmates came to school with a pad of forms. His dad was a physician, and he had picked up a pad of blank birth certificates from his dad's office. The next day, while the nuns were in the convent praying and having lunch, I recruited two girls to type the information from my original certificate, change the date, and add two signatures. I then used a silver dollar to emboss two raised seals, one heads, the other tails. Nine days after I turned 16, on 29 May 1946, I was in the Navy.

While in boot camp, I volunteered for immediate sea duty. The aptitude-test people told me I should be an aviation radioman. They scheduled a Morse-code test. I knew the dots and dashes from my Boy Scout days. At first, I tried my best, then realized that if I did well, I would be flying around in an airplane and not going to sea right away. I purposely missed everything from then on.

My first cruise was to Tsingtao, China. As I stood on the deck of the ship passing under the Golden Gate Bridge, I was 16 years old, weighed 129 pounds, and felt 10-feet tall! My dream had come true. To paraphrase a line by Ishmael in *Moby Dick*, I had my Yale College and my Harvard in a Navy ship on the high seas. Later, I went to finishing school at the University of Nebraska, the School of Aerospace Medicine, and Marquette University.

In 1947, Mao's army was skirmishing with government troops and coming down into north China. One day the word was passed for all hands not on watch to report to the main deck, on the double, to repel boarders. We were at low tide and the main deck was nearly at the level of the pier. About 100 Chinese men and boys were throwing rocks and metal objects and trying to use large bamboo poles against us. We manned the fire hoses and rolled their butts around the dock until they decided they had had enough.

After several months in China, I returned to the States for a 10-week service school in San Diego. We stopped in Japan on the way back, and I got to see General MacArthur leaving his Tokyo headquarters in all his glory. What a sight!

I was transferred to the 19th Fleet in San Diego. I had completed high school correspondence courses while in China and now had an opportunity to take night courses at the local school. By transferring credits and completing the GED tests, I graduated from St. Patrick High School, North Platte, Nebraska, with the classmates I had left behind.

I loved the Navy then, and still love it now. I didn't even mind my five days with the Marine Corps on a diet of bread and water, otherwise known as cake and wine, or was it piss and punk? After a captain's mast, they assigned my best friend Smitty as an armed guard to take me off the ship and deliver me to the brig. In those days, if the prisoner escaped, the guard had to do the time. Smitty told me at least four times that if I tried to escape, he would have to shoot me.

I told him I had to do only five days and that I would be glad to get inside where the Marines could protect me from him.

Inside the brig, I was processed, issued a set of whites with a great big "P" on the front and back, and assigned to a cell. I asked my cell mate what he was in for. He said that he was a pay clerk and was accused of stealing $70,000 (a lot of money back then). Across the passageway there was a guy in a cell by himself. He constantly walked in a circle ten times clockwise, then ten times counterclockwise. When I asked what he was in for, my cell mate said, "Murder." He then asked what I was in for. When I told him I was in for not saluting an officer properly, he gave me an incredulous look and said, "You gotta be shittin' me!" But there I was, doing my time with thieves and murderers. No wonder we grew up fast!

After my 3-year enlistment was up, I took my discharge and enrolled at the University of Nebraska, since I had the GI Bill. I took an aptitude test administered by the Veterans Administration. After a week or so, they called me in and told me that I should be a mortician, a musician, or a real-estate salesman. I told the counselor that I was registered in the pre-dental program and that I wanted to go to dental school. He gravely reviewed my tests and announced that I would never be admitted to dental school. He then added that even if I got in by some fluke, I would never graduate. For some fortunate reason, I disregarded his advice. I was not only admitted to dental school, but I graduated sixth in my class. Furthermore, I completed two specialty programs, one at the School of Aerospace Medicine, and one at Marquette University. I am a board-certified periodontist. Not bad for someone who was supposed to play the organ at funerals and sell grave plots!

After graduating from dental school, I was on the other side of the bars. I was with the U. S. Public Health Service, assigned to the Federal Reformatory for Women at Alderson, West Virginia. I had a number of notorious patients, including Machine Gun Kelly's wife Katherine, his mother-in-law Ora Shannon, Axis Sally (Mildred Sisk) and the Communist spy, Myra Soble. After nearly a year, I decided that this duty was not for me, so I resigned.

Later, I was commissioned as a dental officer in the U. S. Air Force and served in Vietnam during the first Tet Offensive in 1968. I retired from the Air Force as a colonel in 1976.

Bernie Doyle was awarded the Bronze Star and the Vietnamese Honor Medal for his service in Vietnam. After his retirement, he taught at the University of Texas, then spent several years in Saudi Arabia with the Arabian-American Oil Company, followed by private practice in Dubai, United Arab Emirates. He ended his dental career as a contract periodontist at the Naval Hospital in Corpus Christi, Texas. He volunteered for Doctors Without Borders but was told that they wanted medical doctors, not dentists. So he entered medical school and became one of the oldest medical school graduates in history. He received an M.D. in June 2001 at the age of 71, and then did postgraduate studies in tropical medicine at the Royal College of Surgeons in Dublin, Ireland. He plans to spend his time working for humanitarian medical groups around the world. Bernie has a son and a daughter. His home is in San Antonio, Texas.

✔ *INCIDENTally* — **Grenade!** – While the 101st Airborne was in a rest area in France in March 1945, one fellow was doing his duty in a five-holer when he heard a distinct click and recognized what he believed to be the click of a grenade primer. He leaped off the hole, and at that moment a white phosphorous grenade went off in the mire below, scattering white phosphorous and foul-smelling excretion in all directions. Only his pride was injured. – *Walter Holy.*

Charles A. Hoyt, Sr.

Age 15 – United States Army

I was born in Winfield, Kansas, a small town 35 miles southeast of Wichita, on 7 April 1931. I was 10 years old when the Japanese bombed Pearl Harbor. Growing up during the Depression and

> *I was questioned many times about my age, but I always stuck to my story ...*

World War II was quite an experience. I worked at many different jobs, one of which was at Strother Field, an airfield outside of town. That was my first contact with the military.

In 1944, I went to work at the local fairgrounds for a guy who broke and trained horses. In the fall of 1945, he moved his stable to Hollywood Park, and later to Santa Anita racetrack, both in California. I really didn't like school, so I talked my dad into letting me go with him. I guess my dad figured that if he couldn't keep me in school, he might as well let me go. At least he would know where I was.

We loaded our horses on the streamliner, *Kansas Citizen*, and headed for California. I saw one of the greatest sights I think I have ever seen when we went through Kingman, Arizona. After the war had ended in 1945, the military stored aircraft in the desert outside of Kingman. There were thousands of World War II aircraft, stretching as far as the eye could see. I remember it as if it was yesterday.

My oldest brother was in the Navy and my other brother was in the 82nd Airborne Division. So, I started getting the bug to go into the service. I had a chance to go home to Kansas in April 1946. After I had been home a short time, I decided to enlist in the Army.

I talked to a recruiting officer and he told me that if my dad would get a notarized affidavit that I was 17 years old, he would take me. I talked to Dad, but I didn't tell him that I had already talked to the recruiter. After a lot of begging, he agreed to sign for me, provided that the Army recruiter knew that I was just 15, even though he would say I was 17. So, the recruiting officer came to the house and talked to Dad. On 27 June 1946, at the age of 15, I was sworn into the United States Army.

I was inducted at Smoky Hill Air Base in Salina, Kansas, went to Fort Leavenworth, Kansas, to receive my uniforms, then was put on a troop train to Fort Knox, Kentucky.

Basic training was an eye-opener for me. I don't know what I expected, but I got used to it. I was questioned many times about my age, but I always stuck to my story that I was 17. They would just say, "Oh, sure, you are 17," and let it go. I guess as long as I was doing my job, nobody would say anything.

Following basic training and a 7-day leave, I was ordered to Camp Kilmer, New Jersey, for shipment to Germany. While I was waiting for orders, the corporal who was in charge of the barracks told me to report to him that evening. He said, "Hoyt, I am going to make you my assistant and put you in charge of getting the guards out for guard-mount and for getting the KP detail to the mess hall. Think you can handle that?" I assured him that I could. For the next several days, I would see that the KP detail was up and reported to the mess hall on time. Then I would see that the guard-duty detail was ready for guard-mount. I didn't think anything about it at the time, but everybody was leaving but me.

Well, I had a good job, eating good and getting plenty of rest, so I didn't worry about it. I figured that they would send me overseas when they were ready. What I didn't know then was that I was doing the work of the barracks corporal and he had not submitted my name for overseas shipment.

This went on for a couple of weeks. One day, a captain came in the barracks when I was there. He said, "What are you doing here?" I replied, "Sir, I am the assistant to the barracks corporal and he put me in charge of the KPs and the guards." He said, "Who in the hell told you that?" I replied, "The barracks corporal made me his assistant." The captain then asked, "How long have you been here?" I told him, "About two weeks." That ended my first job in the Army. Needless to say, about three days later, I was on a boat to Germany. I don't know what happened to the corporal because I never saw him again.

This was to be the first of seven ocean crossings I would make over the next 23 years. It was, without a doubt, the roughest crossing I would ever make. We hit an Atlantic storm that was really something. We were aboard the *Marine Angel*, a WWII Liberty ship. These ships were like the proverbial cork in a washing machine. We were kept locked in our compartments during the roughest part of the storm, which lasted for two to three days. I would sometimes wonder if the ship would right itself after some of the rolls. Needless to say, I was very scared during the storm.

During one of the breaks in the storm, they asked for volunteers to box. I stuck up my hand, which I determined later was a mistake. I weighed about 125 pounds, but said I weighed 145. My second mistake! As my opponent, I drew a merchant seaman who easily weighed 150 pounds. I did O.K. for a couple of rounds. I stung him a few times, but I think I just made him mad because he really hammered me in the third round. We were using a hatch cover as a boxing ring. During one of the rolls of the ship, I lost my balance and fell off the hatch and sprained my ankle. That ended my boxing career. If I had stayed in the ring much longer, I would have gotten killed. I learned a lesson: quit volunteering!

Upon arriving in Germany, I was assigned to the 17th Cavalry Squadron in Heidleberg. Later, I was assigned to the 2nd Cavalry Regiment in Friesing, Germany. When the United States Constabulary was formed, I was transferred to the 11th Constabulary Regiment in Straubing, Germany. We were sort of a super police force in the U. S. Zone of Germany with the responsibility of border patrol and interzonal patrols. We operated much like a state highway patrol in our country.

During my first year or so in the Army, I wasn't doing all that great. I couldn't seem to stay out of trouble. Finally, I had the good fortune to be assigned to a platoon sergeant by the name of Tom Estridge, who made me his special project. He shaped me up and I began to be promoted. I made buck sergeant when I was 16 and staff sergeant when I was 17. Tom was my best man when I got married, and we are friends to this day.

One other thing happened during that period of my life that helped shape my future. I was lying on my bunk one day when the Information and Education NCO came into my room and asked what

I was doing. I replied, "Nothing." He said, "Come with me." The end result was that he gave me a series of tests: the GED, an IQ test, and an officer candidate test. These would play an important role later in my getting a direct commission to second lieutenant.

When I returned to the States, I was assigned to the 3rd Cavalry Regiment at Fort Meade, Maryland. I was promoted to sergeant first class and was made a platoon sergeant in 1949 at age 18. We were training recruits at this time.

When the Korean War broke out in June 1950, I wanted to go to Korea. I talked to my friend, who at the time was the sergeant major of the battalion, into volunteering to go with me. He had been in World War II, but agreed to go with me. We volunteered, then waited quite a while for orders, but they never came. In the meantime, there was an Army circular offering direct commissions to the top three enlisted grades. We both applied for a direct commission. I made a high enough score on the tests that I had taken in Germany to qualify. On 26 February 1951, I received a direct commission to second lieutenant with a concurrent call to active duty on the next day, 27 February 1951. We both stayed in the 3rd Cavalry Regiment, but changed battalions. I was later sent to the basic officers course at Fort Knox, Kentucky, and in 1951, I was assigned to the 14th Cavalry Regiment in Bad Hersfeld, Germany.

It was during this period that the Army required all officers to obtain a secret clearance. Knowing that my minority age would be exposed, I wrote a letter to the Adjutant General of the Army and explained the circumstances of my enlistment. They simply wrote a letter to the battalion personnel officer, instructing him to correct all erroneous entries on my service record. I then reverted to my correct age. In 1962, Congress passed a law that allowed minority service to count for retirement. Up until that time it would only count towards longevity.

After my second tour in Germany, I decided that I had had enough of the Army and let my commission revert to inactive status. This didn't last long. After a couple of months, I re-enlisted at my permanent grade of sergeant first class and was assigned to the U. S. Army Reserve Advisory Group in Wichita, Kansas.

After a couple of years, a circular came across my desk requesting qualified Army Reserve Armor first lieutenants and majors to apply for active duty. I applied and reported for active duty in 1955 as a first lieutenant. I was assigned to the 1st Armored Division at Fort Polk, Louisiana. Next, I served a tour in Korea, returned to Fort Knox, Kentucky, attended the advanced class for Armor officers at Fort Knox, and then began a third tour in Germany with the 4th Armored Division.

On returning to the States in 1964, I was assigned as the Armor advisor to the Oregon National Guard. In 1967, I was assigned to the advisory team in Turkey as the Armor advisor to the Turkish 3rd Army. My final assignment was at Fort Knox, Kentucky, back where I started. I retired as a lieutenant colonel in November 1969 after 23½ years of service. I was 38 years old.

Charlie Hoyt was awarded the Legion of Merit, two Army Commendation Medals, and a number of other service medals. After his retirement he sold real estate for a time, then went into the golf industry. He worked in the pro shop at the Phoenix Country Club, Phoenix, Arizona, and managed a golf course in Flagstaff, Arizona, for a time. Charlie and Joyce, his wife of 52 years, have five children, seventeen grandchildren and five great-grandchildren. They live in Mesa, Arizona.

Melvin E. Hobert
Age 16 – United States Army

When I was 8 years old, my parents were divorced. My father disappeared, leaving me, my mother, and two younger brothers alone. It wasn't easy to survive in those Depression years. We were living in

> *It was obvious to me that this was the answer to all my problems.*

Bedford, Indiana, where I grew up. I was born in Monroe County, Indiana, on 15 June 1930.

By the time I was 11 years old, I was working after school and during the summers washing dishes in restaurants. At age 14, I was a meat cutter in a supermarket. I learned a lot working with adults during the years 1941 to 1944. There was no time for youth activities, nor for after-school functions.

I could accompany my boss into any bar in town and order a beer without being questioned. I could drive his car, and I was dating girls older than me. When one of my older friends was home on furlough, I borrowed one of his uniforms and we went on double dates as soldiers. I was not a delinquent, but I was growing up faster than a child should. The movies during the war years were a great influence on my life. I was thrilled and inspired by the Army, Navy, and Marine hymns, and desperately wanted to be part of it all.

The most important thing that ever happened to me in my life occurred on 1 July 1944: I met the most beautiful girl in the world.

In June 1946, I finished my second year of high school. Our local newspaper printed a full-page ad soliciting volunteers for an 18-month enlistment in the military services. It was obvious to me that this was the answer to all my problems. I could get a high school GED instead of attending high school for two more years, which was unlikely because of the way I was working to help support my mother and brothers. If I was in the service, I could get a dependents' allotment sent home to them. The girl I was in love with was going to graduate in one more year. It would be better for her if she were to marry a veteran than a high school dropout. To top it all off, the ad promised the GI Bill for veterans.

I approached my mother about signing for me, but she said no. I got my birth certificate, altered it, and finally convinced her that my decision to go in the service was best. She signed a notarized statement that I was 17 years old.

I went to the Navy recruiter and was rejected because I was wearing glasses. I hitchhiked to Louisville, Kentucky, went to the Army recruiting office, and enlisted without any problems. I was sent to Fort Knox, Kentucky, for my physical, which I was worried about passing. I was second in a long line of guys all stripped down to their shorts. When the guy in front of me stepped up to the eye examiner, I heard the doctor tell him to take off his glasses and read the lowest line possible. He said to the doctor, "I can't see the big letter without my glasses." The doctor told him to get dressed, the Army couldn't use him. I stepped up to the doctor and took a quick peek down the hallway at the eye chart. I took off my glasses and could not see the big letter either, but I remembered what it was. I said, "I see the big 'A' very well." Another lie to get into the Army. I could see 20-20 with my glasses.

I was sworn into the Army on 10 July 1946. After basic training at Fort Dix, New Jersey, I went home on leave for two weeks, then reported to Camp Stoneman, California. I was soon on a troop train to Fort Lawton, Washington, to await shipment overseas. I was sent to Japan as a member of the occupation forces and served as a cook in the 58th Signal Battalion. After about a year in Japan, I returned to the States and was honorably discharged on 12 November 1947.

Mel Hobert married the beautiful girl he met in 1944 and went to work for the Milwaukee Railroad shortly after his discharge. He spent 41 years doing about everything there was to do in railroading: steam-locomotive mechanic, Morse-code telegrapher, train dispatcher, and terminal supervisor. He started his railroad career in Chicago, Illinois, but transferred to Terre Haute, Indiana, where he worked until he retired in 1988. At the age of 36, while working nights on his railroad job, he started taking day courses at Indiana State University and received a B.A. in 1971 and an M.S. in 1973. Mel and Rose Ann, his wife of 54 years, have two sons, five grandchildren, and two great-grandchildren. They live in Port Charlotte, Florida.

✓ *INCIDENTally* — **Conned!** – After our swearing-in ceremonies at Drew Field, Florida, on 10 June 1947 we boarded a train for (what is now) Lackland AFB, Texas, to begin basic training. I was put in charge of a group of seven other enlistees. I had all the records, travel orders, meal tickets, and most importantly, the train tickets, including the Pullman berth reservations. We departed Tampa, Florida, and had to change trains in Jacksonville, Florida.

All went well until late that afternoon. I was standing in the aisle of our car talking with a couple of other trainees when we were approached by a very friendly man in a coat and tie, looking quite distinguished and important, who inquired as to our status. Being quite anxious to impress all and sundry that we were brand-new soldiers, we began to converse with him.

At one point while he was talking, I heard a voice over my shoulder saying "Tickets, please." Glancing around and seeing a man wearing what I took to be a conductor's cap, I handed over the envelope containing our tickets without hesitation. All the while, the first stranger continued to talk and occupy our attention. After a few seconds, the person behind me returned the envelope and I stuffed it into my pocket. Soon thereafter, the stranger departed, wishing us well.

We had to change trains again in New Orleans for the trip to San Antonio. When I presented the ticket envelope to the agent, I discovered to my horror that the Pullman reservations had been removed. I HAD BEEN CONNED! Fortunately, the coach tickets were still there. I explained what had happened, but the agent was less than sympathetic. There was no military-assistance desk in the terminal, and even had there been one, I would doubtless have had to sign a statement of charges for additional Pullman reservations.

We had to sit up all night and well into the next day in coach, and I'm sure my companions never forgave me for my carelessness. – *William Brown.*

Lee R. Bishop

Age 15 – United States Army Air Forces

I was born in Des Moines, Iowa, on 14 October 1930. Although the country was in a depression, we lived well, for my father was a very successful bootlegger. The latest cars and Oriental carpets were the order of the day. In 1934, the good life came to an

> ..., my immature appearance caused a doctor to remark, "Are you sure you are 17?"

end with the death of my father from pneumonia. There was no penicillin in those days.

My mother was unable to work and take care of me, so I wound up in the Des Moines Children's Home and a series of foster homes after that. I finally wound up at Father Flanagan's Boys Town in early 1942. It was at Boys Town that I began to develop an interest in the military, partly as a result of being caught up in the patriotic fervor of World War II. Bugle calls for reveille, mess call, and taps, governed our lives at Boys Town. Hospital corners on our beds were the order of the day, and the military routine became second nature. Our high

school graduates began to populate the Navy's V-12 Officer Training Programs. Pete Bucher, future commander of the USS *Pueblo*, which was captured by the North Koreans, was my classmate.

In 1944, my mother married a returning Army veteran who was being medically retired, and I was taken out of Boys Town. No one in our family had ever graduated from high school, and Mother's idea for me to escape poverty was to join the Navy and "learn a trade." There was no thought of

college. My stepfather was an old Army man who had served under General Patton during World War II, and it was he who piqued my interest in the Army.

How taken I was with military life really came to me during an exciting air show at San Bernardino Army Air Field in August 1946.

I suddenly felt that life in the U. S. Army Air Forces would be much more satisfying than two more boring years of high school. There was a recruiting booth at the air show, and on impulse, I got into the enlistment line with all the others, even though I was only 15. I signed up as being 17 and was told I must have a permission form signed by my parents to enlist. Home I went, promising to deliver the form the next day. I was able to persuade Mother to sign the papers, under the condition that I finish high school. I was no doubt aided by the fact that one less mouth to feed on a small military pension would remove the strain from the family budget.

The next day, 6 August 1946, I returned with the permission, was sworn in and given a jeep ride home. The jeep ride was probably to verify if Mom had actually been the one to sign the permission paper. During my recruit physical exam, my immature appearance caused a doctor to remark, "Are you sure you are 17?"

I was sent to San Antonio by way of Camp Beale, California, for basic training. At Camp Beale, we were issued used uniforms that had been turned in by soldiers returning from overseas, and we received our first inoculations. I learned in the shot line that size and bravery do not correlate. The biggest fellow in the line, who was making fun of all the puny guys like me, fainted and had to take his shots while unconscious. I took my aptitude tests in basic training and was offered the option of being either a B-29 turret-system technician or a radar repairman. Having seen a radar scope in a recent newsreel, I opted for radar and was soon on a troop train headed for nine months of radar school at Boca Raton Army Air Field in Florida. I was so frail upon graduation from basic training that our flight instructor had to carry my duffel bag to the troop train for me.

In September 1947, I was in the last class to graduate from Boca Raton. A hurricane had completely destroyed the base and I got to skip my last week of school. My first assignment was as a radar repairman with the 635th Aircraft Control and Warning Squadron at McChord Field, Washington. McChord was interesting, but I wanted to see the world, so I volunteered for overseas duty. Six months later, I was on a troopship headed for Japan. I had the good fortune to be assigned to the 7th Signal Radio Maintenance Team, Far Eastern Air Force, at Showamae, Japan. The 7th was the only unit allowed to maintain the electronics on General MacArthur's aircraft, which was based at Haneda Air Base, Tokyo. Haneda used to send vehicles to transport our technicians back to their base to work on their equipment.

The 7th Signal also had the task of installing all the radars in the Far East. When we were not installing, we were rebuilding radars from battle-damaged and discarded systems that we had salvaged throughout the Far East. No new systems were available because the Cold War had just started. I had the chance to work on the old radar systems that helped win our World War II victory in the Pacific. I worked on systems such as TPS-1B, SCR-717, SCR-720, MPS-5, and the APQ-7 that made possible precision bombing through overcast. I got to see all the islands of Japan while installing the Japanese Air Defense Network radars. When the Korean air war first started as a "commuter" war, those radar systems we had installed guided our planes to and from Korea.

In May of 1949, at the ripe old age of 18, I left Japan on a troopship for the States. I was discharged at Camp Stoneman, California, sewed on my ruptured duck, and went to Los Angeles to visit my family and scope out my future. After looking at some unexciting civilian options, I went to the main Los Angeles recruiting office to begin in earnest a military career that lasted 26½ years and took me from the U. S. Embassy in Rome to Vietnam in such diverse assignments as a B-36 radar tail-gunner, interpreter, editor, instructor, and military advisor. I met my future wife Chao-Ying (Mary Jo) in 1956 while serving as military advisor to the Chinese Nationalist Air Force in Taiwan.

I retired from the Air Force as a chief master sergeant in 1973. I had earned a high school diploma, a bachelor's degree, and started on a master's degree. Mother was proud!

Lee Bishop is one of a very few enlisted men who have been awarded the Legion of Merit. He also earned the Army Commendation Medal and the Air Force Commendation Medal. After his retirement from the Air Force, he worked for Electronic Data Systems (EDS) in San Francisco, California, and Dallas, Texas. He then worked for the federal government as a scientific analyst, and after completing a master's degree, he was reassigned as an engineer. He retired from federal service as a GS-15 in 1992 and was technical director of the U. S. Air Force Radar Target Scatter Division (Stealth Testing) at Hollomon Air Force Base, New Mexico at the time of his retirement.

He has worked part-time as a senior radar and senior consulting engineer for Dimensions International of Alexandria, Virginia, since 1992 and occasionally teaches classes in mathematics and radar at a local college. Lee and Mary Jo, his wife of 46 years have two daughters, a son, and four grandsons. Both daughters served in the military. One retired as an Army major. Lee and Mary Jo live in Las Vegas, Nevada.

✓ *INCIDENTally* — *Down to the beautiful sea!* –

Someone paraphrased John Masefield this way: "I must go down to the beautiful sea, where the wind blows strong and the waves run free. I must go down to the beautiful sea – damned right I must, they're sending me!" And so upon leaving boot camp in early March 1947 at the age of 15, I was assigned to the Coast Guard Cutter *Bibb*. The ship was en route to a North Atlantic Ocean station with a stop at Argentia, Newfoundland, for refueling. It was vernal-equinox weather, so we new guys were sick, and I hated it. When we were out to sea a few days, someone asked if anyone of the seamen could type. I asked why, and was told that the commodore in Argentia needed a storekeeper striker. I said I could type and was assigned to Commander, North Atlantic Ocean Patrol in Argentia. I couldn't type a word, but I met two really understanding yeomen who gave me a typing book and a typewriter that Friday evening. I typed all day Saturday, went to church Sunday morning, and returned to my typing. On Monday morning, I reported to the finance officer, typed nine words a minute without looking – and I was hired! – *Baker W. Herbert.*

Bob Robinson

Age 15 – United States Marine Corps

Trying to recall one's early years can be a challenge. I was born in Spokane, Washington, on 16 November 1930, during the Great Depression. But from what I can remember, the struggles of that time gave me a greater respect for the

> *"Wow! I didn't know mines were that big."*

struggles in my later life. The cliche that "I had to walk five miles to school, and in a snowstorm, too," was true for me. It was five miles to school, and it wasn't flat most of the way. During my sixth year I had a serious mastoid operation, and at the same time, suffered from a broken collar bone. In those days, mastoid operations were often fatal.

My journey into adolescence was not unusual, unless you think catching a 20-inch rainbow trout (at age 7) with a string and a willow pole in a local Pierce, Idaho, creek is a daily occurrence. I still

remember with joy the amazed look on my mother's face as I slowly displayed my prize that I had hidden behind my back.

When I reached the age of 15, restlessness overcame me. I used my brother's birth certificate and joined the U. S. Marine Corps on 12 August 1946. Since I was becoming a burden to my mother, she signed for me.

Going into the Marine Corps at age 15 was an enlightening experience, and then some. I have never really regretted it. Going through boot camp is something you can only appreciate in person. After boot camp and after some additional training, we were scheduled to ship out to China. Going to sea was an exciting event in my life, but after a few days, the routine started to creep in. We stopped briefly in Hawaii, then went on to Guam.

I was standing by the ship's rail, daydreaming, when I noticed a huge mine floating by. I remember thinking, "Wow! I didn't know mines were that big." Suddenly, the battle-stations alarm sounded and the ship made a turn back towards the mine. The 20- and 40-mm guns missed their target, but the rear 3-inch gun destroyed the mine.

Several days went by and I was sitting on the aft hatch reading a magazine. I noticed a picture of President Truman placing the Congressional Medal of Honor on a Marine. Somehow, the picture struck me as familiar, but I couldn't understand why. As I pondered the dilemma, I heard a low chuckle from the Marine sitting next to me. I must have had a puzzled look on my face. I glanced at him and back at the photo. I still didn't understand why I was so puzzled. Eventually, as I turned back and forth from the photo to the Marine beside me, I said to him, "Is this you in the picture?" Laughing, he said, "Yes." His name was Corporal Doug Jacobson. I was a little flustered, to say the least. To shake the hand of such a brave warrior was one of my most memorable experiences. Later, I read the citation for the Medal of Honor that he received for the remarkable feats of bravery he performed on Iwo Jima.

From Guam, we went to the Philippines. Entering Subic Bay was quite a shock. As we approached Manila, our ship had to zigzag through the dozens of sunken Japanese ships still there in the harbor. As we left Manila headed for China, we passed by Corregidor. We all silently paid our respects to the brave men and women who died there during World War II.

We arrived in China in November 1946, in the dead of winter, 40° below zero. I was a 15-year-old Marine, freezing to death, waiting to be loaded into a cattle car. I thought, "I must be nuts!" The days and months that followed were filled with danger, laughter, and learning experiences too numerous to mention. As time passed, we adjusted to the oriental ways and enjoyed the cultural changes and differences in lifestyles. What I didn't realize at the time was that the many Marines who were killed in action or wounded in China were never mentioned in the press back in the United States.

As the Communists gained more ground in the civil war, American bureaucrats decided to pull us out of China. We packed up, put on full battle gear, and marched to the train station. As we marched, the roads were lined with thousands of Chinese of all ages. It was an incredible sight: men, women, and children weeping as we passed by them. It was if they were seeing their last hope of freedom slowly marching down the street. I will never forget it. One Christmas I received a card from Chaing Kai-shek and his wife. Regretfully, it was later lost in a fire.

Leaving China, we headed for Guam for the second time. I was a 16-year-old veteran Marine, anxious to succeed. We were surprised and disappointed when we arrived. There was nothing there! No barracks, nothing! We set about and within a few short weeks we had a reasonable camp set up. I soon wished we were back in China. It was work, work, work, train, train, train, out in the jungle, 35-mile hikes, battle conditions, mosquitos, mud – you name it. What I didn't know at first was that we were sent there to establish the new First Provisional Marine Brigade.

One Saturday morning our commander, Brigadier General Edward A. Craig, pulled a snap inspection. Our squad leader, a real Marine's Marine, stood six-foot-two and was built like a tank. He was not around at the time, and our squad had to have a leader for the inspection. The guys picked me. Not thinking, I picked up the squad leader's carbine rifle, but failed to adjust the sling to my much smaller bulk. As General Craig came by to inspect our squad, I brought the rifle from my shoulder. Because of the loose sling, the rifle swung out much farther than I expected and just missed the bridge of the general's nose. I swear you couldn't put a sheet of newspaper between the rifle and his nose. Stopping abruptly, the general glared at me with steel-riveted eyes. What to do? As he stood there, I thought that he might thrash me for trying to rearrange his nose. A few seconds later he moved down the line, but glanced back at me with a stare that I remember to this day.

After completing my tour on Guam, I was sent back to San Francisco for discharge. For three days during April 1948 we were wined, dined, and given the blue-ribbon treatment. Fresh steaks! Fresh milk! Fresh eggs! I hadn't had those in two years. Then they gave us a lecture on Marine history and urged us to sign up for the Marine Reserves. For some reason I did not join the reserves. Some 1,500 Marines were discharged during three days, and only six did not join the reserves. What I didn't know on that fateful day, and neither did the others, was that these same Marines would find themselves on battlefields in Korea: at Pusan, on the beaches at Inchon, and fighting the Chinese at the Chosin Reservoir. Many would never return.

I had served in Fox Company, 2nd Battalion, 5th Marines, 1st Marine Division. The same Marines that I ate and drank with in San Francisco would see heavy action in Korea. But I hadn't joined the reserves.

Bob Robinson took college courses in automotive mechanics and photography after his discharge. He worked as a driver and salesman for Consolidated Freightways and Oregon-Washington Transport. He has seven children and five grandchildren. Bob lives in Portland, Oregon.

✔ *INCIDENTally — **Mine hunting.** –* I was a radar operator aboard the USS *LST-20*. In 1944, while in mid-ocean, I detected a floating mine on the radar. The captain, who was a native of France and spoke poor English, ordered us to destroy it with gunfire from the old 3"-50 guns. When this failed, he ordered the 40mm guns to fire at the mine. Two birds that had been perched on the mine flew into the air, but returned to their perch when we failed to hit the mine. The captain had a fit and ordered us to move into close range and use the 20mm cannon to fire at the mine. At this point, the gunners made little effort to hit the mine, which further disturbed our frustrated commanding officer. He then ordered us to move in even closer and had the boatswains fire at the mine with model 1903 rifles. If we had hit the mine with the rifle fire, the ship would have gone up in the explosion! – *Philip P. Schneiderman.*

John E. Terry

Age 16 – United States Army

I was born in St. Johns, New Brunswick, Canada, on 15 May 1930. My family moved to Napanee, Ontario, when I was 4. My mother had grown up there and had studied nursing in nearby Kingston. During her nursing training, she met and married my father, who was being treated for injuries sustained during World War I. I was the youngest of three children.

> I was determined to enlist immediately to avenge my brother's death.

By the time I was a 8 years old, the clouds of war were forming over Europe. Throughout the British Empire, men were being called to duty, as England's very existence was in peril. My dad and my 15-year-old brother David enlisted in 1939.

My mother, sister, and I moved to the United States where nursing jobs were more plentiful and the wages better. We settled in Detroit, Michigan. In late 1943, my mother received notice from the Canadian government that David had been killed during the invasion of Sicily.

I was determined to enlist immediately to avenge my brother's death. I crossed the border and boarded a train for Ottawa without a ticket. With conductors bearing down on me, I jumped off the moving train and hitchhiked to my old hometown.

I met a soldier on the street and asked, "How can I become a soldier?" Seeing my pink cheeks and sparse facial hair, he laughed, then he suggested that I might be able to join the Home Front Defense; then, when older, I could join the army. I played soldier with the Home Guard until my mother found out where I was. She insisted that my uncle get me a ticket to Detroit and put me on a train home. Mom understood my anguish at losing my brother, but she didn't want to risk losing me, too.

Without her knowledge, I continued to visit recruiting stations in and around Detroit. I needed a birth certificate so that I could change my birth date to make me 18. Finally, in 1946, I sent a letter to the New Brunswick Department of Health asking for a birth certificate, and they sent me one.

One of my friends, Joe Stack, had agreed to enlist with me. I went to his house to tell him that I now had a birth certificate and had changed it so I would be 18. Joe had gone to visit relatives for the summer. His younger brother Frank answered the door. At age 13, Frank was 5-feet 11-inches tall and well-developed. As a joke, I asked him about enlisting with me and if he had access to his birth certificate. He said yes to both questions.

I had visited the Navy and Marines recruiters so often that I was sure they would catch me with an altered birth certificate, so I met Frank after school and we stopped by the Army recruiting office. We showed our birth certificates, took the physicals, and were told to meet at the train station at 7 a.m. the next day. We would be sworn in at Fort Sheldon, Illinois. I was so happy and excited that I didn't even know that we had joined the Army Air Forces, and not the Army! As far as I was concerned, that was just a technicality. The uniform was the same, just a different patch on my shoulder. We took the oath on 23 August 1946.

We were issued clothing, given shots, and were on a train to Randolph Field in San Antonio, Texas, in three days. The four days on the troop train took its toll. The cattle cars they called coach accommodations were drafty and didn't have heat or bathroom facilities. Twice a day they stopped the train in the countryside so we could relieve ourselves. Frank got sick and was sent to the hospital as soon as we got to Randolph Field (now Lackland Air Force Base). Because of his illness, he started basic training a week after I did. This one week of hospitalization resulted in our being separated for the duration of our enlistments.

Following basic, I was assigned to Keesler Field, Biloxi, Mississippi, to train as an aircraft mechanic. Frank was sent to Japan. I had routine Stateside assignments until June 1948 when a call came for aircrews to participate in the Berlin Airlift after the Russians had cut surface transportation into and out of Berlin. The threat of World

War III hinged on the outcome of "Operation Vittles," which would soon be known as the Berlin Air Lift.

I was sent to Frankfurt, Germany, and assigned to a squadron of C-54 Skymasters. We moved to a former German fighter base at Fausburg in the British Zone of Germany. When we flew over the area for the first time, it was so well-camouflaged that we missed it. It was in a dense forest, and the single landing strip was painted to match a meadow. The small hangar doors were painted like the edge of the tree line that circled the strip. All buildings and roads were concealed in the dense forest. There were no signs that it had ever been attacked during the war.

The British had a small garrison there, but no aircraft. Air Force personnel flooded the base in short order. We hired German mechanics, cooks, maids, and office workers. Perimeter security was assigned to the free Polish Army soldiers who wore British uniforms that had been dyed black. The Poles would shoot first, then ask, "Who goes there?"

Aircraft began arriving from all over the world. We had C-47s and C-54s, and the Navy had two R5D (C-54) squadrons. The British Royal Air Force brought in an air supply operation. We worked 12-hour days, seven days a week.

Promotions were slowed because many veterans who were officers during World War II were re-enlisting as technical and master sergeants. Five months before I was to be rotated back to the States, I made acting sergeant and started making flights into Berlin and to Brentwood, England. I was asked by the first sergeant if I wanted to re-enlist and stay with the squadron. I declined the offer and was sent back to the States in August 1949 at my permanent rank of corporal. I shipped out of Bremerhaven for New York City in the first week of August. We docked at Pier 8, Brooklyn, New York.

I was honorably discharged at Camp Kilmer, New Jersey on 23 August 1949. I enlisted in the Air Force Reserve for a 4-year hitch at the time I was discharged. I toured New York City and bought a 1940 Ford coupe that a buddy and I drove home to Detroit, Michigan.

John Terry used the GI Bill to obtain a GED while working for the Chrysler Corporation, and again with the GI Bill, to attend a radio-television school while working for the WWJ-TV Studio in Detroit. In 1960, he moved to Las Vegas and was employed by the Aerojet General

Corporation. He was assigned as an electronics technician to a research and development project that was testing drone aircraft at a remote desert site north of Yuma, Arizona. When he returned to the Las Vegas area, he worked in a number of casinos, then started a construction company that built and repaired residential and commercial properties. He retired in 1996. John has two sons and two granddaughters. He lives in Las Vegas, Nevada.

✓ *INCIDENTally* — **Pluto and the mail bag.** – While serving on the USS *Dortch* during World War II, we joined Task Group 38.3 and were assigned as the mail ship for the group. This meant picking up mail from the tankers and distributing it to all ships in the task group. We were assigned this duty because our CO was junior to the other ships' commanders in the group.

A few months later, a new CO came aboard who was senior to the squadron commander. The new skipper resented the mail-ship assignment immensely. He called in one of the crew members who was noted for being a cartoonist and asked him if he could paint a cartoon depicting "dog psychology" on each side of the bridge. When asked what he meant, he replied, "If you can't eat or drink it, urinate on it." We ended up with a picture of Pluto urinating on a mail bag on both sides of the bridge. Thereafter, the entire task group recognized us immediately. When we arrived in San Francisco, the first thing we had to do was to paint out Pluto. – *Charles R. Johnson.*

Frank J. Stack

Age 13 – United States Army

When I was 13 years old I went with a bunch of my friends to a canal off the Detroit River that was the property of a brick factory. We were swimming and diving off a ferry boat when the police came and arrested us for trespassing. I was

> *My mother chased me to the recruiting office and tried to take me home, but I wouldn't go.*

mortified. I didn't want to face my mother, a single parent. We were living in Detroit, Michigan, where I was born on 22 December 1932.

My friend, John Terry, who was 16, was looking for my brother Joe. He wanted Joe to join the Army with him. Joe was out of town, so John asked me to join with him. I didn't want to go to court, so I decided to go along with John and give the Army a try. We went to the Army recruiting office, and the first thing the sergeant asked us was whether we had a draft card. We told him no, so he sent us to the draft board. I thought I was all done, but the lady did not ask for a birth certificate. She gave me a draft card right then and there. To

make sure, I went to a friend and she changed the birth year on my birth certificate so I would be 18. One thing in my favor was that I was a big guy. I was almost 6-feet tall and weighed a solid 160 pounds.

John Terry and I were sworn into the Army on 23 August 1946 and were assigned to the Army Air Forces. At no time did I back out, or even want to back out. My mother chased me to the recruiting office and tried to take me home, but I wouldn't go. On the way to basic training in Texas, I contracted pneumonia and was separated from Terry, but I went on and finished the training.

My mother tried to get me out of the military once again. She wrote to the base chaplain, told him I was underage, and asked that I be sent home. I was called into the base commander's office. The master sergeant at the desk asked, "All right, Stack, what do you want to do about this? Do you know, if you stay in the service, you can retire when you're 33 years old?" I told him that I didn't want to go home. The sergeant threw the letter in the trash.

I received orders to go to Japan and got off the ship there on my 14th birthday. I was an aircraft and engine mechanic, military occupational specialty (MOS) 747B, and worked on P-51 fighter aircraft. During my 30 months in the Pacific, I witnessed the aftermath of World War II. I flew over Manila and saw all the damage and the sunken ships in the harbor. The wreckage on Okinawa was shocking.

Although I worked on aircraft, I wanted to be a pilot, but I didn't have the education. I had only finished the eighth grade when I enlisted. I completed a GED and even passed a 1-year college equivalency test, but I still was not accepted for flight school. I was very upset about this and decided to end my military career after completing my 3-year enlistment. I was discharged from the Air Force on 10 August 1949 at the age of 16. I had served three years and was still not old enough to legally enlist!

Frank Stack worked at a number of jobs in auto plants while attending radio-electronics school. After graduating from radio school in 1953, he went to work for the Michigan Bell Telephone Company. He retired from the company in 1989 as an equipment engineer. He never lost the urge to become a pilot, so in 1982 he achieved his goal by obtaining his pilot's license. He also obtained a building-contractor's license and built the home they now live in. Frank and Dee, his wife of 48 years, have three children, three grandchildren, and one great-grandchild. They live in Attica, Michigan.

450

Noble J. Craft, Jr.

Age 16 – United States Army

I was born at home in Freedom, New Hampshire, on 9 January 1930. My father was in the trucking business and the family moved a lot. By the time I was 6 my parents divorced and I moved from one grandparent to another until I was put in

> ..., I was a member of a team that monitored the first free election for Korea's first president.

an orphanage for three years. In 1943, my mother got a job in a shipyard in Boston, Massachusetts, as a welder, and could then afford to get me out of the orphanage.

I was very much caught up with patriotism while living in Boston during World War II. It was a feeling shared throughout the nation. Enlisting in the military seemed the only patriotic thing for me to do. Naturally, my mother objected, but I altered my birth certificate and went to enlist. I tried the Marine Corps first. They took one look at me and my crudely altered birth certificate and told me to go home. So I got another birth certificate, over my mother's objections, and

tried the Navy. Again I was sent home, to my mother's delight. Finally, I got another birth certificate and told my mother I was going to join the Army. She didn't think I would make it, but she told me that if I did, she would sign the papers.

When I went to the Army recruiting station, they gave me some papers, told me to get my parents to sign them, and come back the next day. It took me all night to get my mother to sign them, but she did. The next day, 3 September 1946, I was sent to Fort Banks, Massachusetts, given a physical and all kinds of tests, and sworn into the Army.

The following day I was on a train on my way to Fort Dix, New Jersey, where I was issued uniforms and awaited assignment. Then I was off to Fort Eustis, Virginia, for basic training in the Army

Transportation Corps. After basic, I was off to Fort Warren, Wyoming, by troop train for further schooling as a railroad-signal repairman. Upon completion of the school, and after a leave, I reported to Camp Stoneman, California, for shipment to Korea. I spent two years on occupation duty in Korea where I was assigned to the 500th Railway Grand Division, 790th Railway Battalion. I was a brakeman in Seoul for a short time, then I became a baggage man on the Seoul-to-Pusan run, then a conductor on the Seoul-to-Taejon run and return. I worked a short time as assistant yardmaster in Taejon.

In 1948, I was a member of a team that monitored the first free election for Korea's first president. A short time later, I returned to the States and got an early discharge so I could return to school. I had taken the GED test and received my high school diploma. I enrolled in Embry Riddle School of Aviation at Opa Locka, Florida. While there, I enlisted in the Navy Reserve at Masters Field.

When the Korean War came along, I enlisted in the Marine Corps and was sent to Parris Island for boot training. Thanks to the schooling at Embry Riddle, I was able to go into Marine aviation and receive further aviation training. I became a helicopter mechanic and served a year with VMO-6 (Marine Observation Squadron 6) in Korea.

After returning from Korea, I served a 3-year tour at the Naval Air Station, Squantum, Massachusetts, and the Naval Air Station, South Weymouth, Massachusetts, as an aviation mechanic, as a recruiter, and as a drill instructor for a 30-day Marine Reserve boot camp. After another overseas assignment with Marine Aircraft Group 12, Iwakuni, Japan, I served three years at the Naval Air Station, Millington, Tennessee. This was followed by another overseas assignment in Iwakuni, Japan with VMGR-152.

Upon returning to the States, I completed schooling to become a flight engineer on the GV-130 aircraft. This was followed by a tour at Futema, Okinawa, and Danang, Vietnam with VMGR-152, and temporary additional duty tours out of El Toro, California. The main purpose of these flights was in-flight refueling and resupply of troops. From June 1964 until July 1967, I accumulated 2,572 flight hours.

I retired from the Marine Corps in 1968 after 22 years of service. I have but one regret, and it is that I did not stay in the service for 30 years.

Noble Craft started his own trucking company after retiring from the Marine Corps. After 25 years in the trucking business, he retired again. In 2000, he toured the United States and Canada on a motorcycle and had a ball. Noble has five children, eleven grandchildren, and seven great-grandchildren. He lives in Fountain Valley, California.

✔ *INCIDENTally — **Manhunt in a tank!** – During the 1950 Christmas season, our division was at Camp Cooke (now Vandenberg AFB), California. We were expecting the word to ship out for Korea, so the entire division was confined to the post. Our tank company had been training all over the wilderness area of the post and we knew our way around. Our company commander said that if we had a full 5-man crew, we could sign out a tank and do some individual maneuvering. Well, we did just that, and while out in the boondocks, a man in a truck waved us down. He was a guard from the federal prison at Lompoc (which was at the southern end of the base), and was looking for a prisoner who had escaped just a few hours before. He couldn't go anywhere in his truck because there were no roads, so he asked if we could help him look for the missing guy. We spent the next five hours whipping through the brush in our tank, but we never saw hide nor hair of the escapee. The guard got a radio call to the effect that the guy had just been picked up in Ventura, almost 100 miles away. I don't think it was discovered just how this escapee managed to travel 100 miles in less than eight hours, while still in a uniform clearly marked "PRISONER." – Murray L. La Hue.*

Harold D. Pershall
Age 16 – United States Army Air Forces

I was born in Wakefield, Kansas, on 19 March 1930. My two older brothers, Wayne and Bob, served in the Navy and the Marines during World War II, but I was just too young – the war had passed me by. By 1946, I had

> I finally found a home among veterans just like me.

turned 16 and couldn't wait any longer to enlist. On 3 September 1946, I caught a ride to Fort Riley, Kansas, where I met a recruiting officer, a Captain Jordan. The captain gave me a choice: I could go in the Army for eighteen months, or in the Army Air Forces for three years. I chose the Air Forces.

Captain Jordan told me that I needed a birth certificate and that I was to go home to Clay Center, Kansas, to get one. He informed me that the train was leaving at 0800 the next morning, and I was scheduled to be on it. They had issued me my GI clothes, so I did not go home, but stayed on the base. The next day I was on the train for San Antonio, Texas. I was never again asked for my birth certificate during my 3-year tour. In San Antonio, I was assigned to Flight 1157 for basic training.

After graduating from basic training, I was assigned to the officers candidate school physical-training program. In March 1947, I joined the paratroopers and was sent to Fort Benning, Georgia.

Meanwhile, my younger brother Gene, age 15, saw that I had made it in the Air Forces, so he joined. After basic training, he was transferred to Ladd Field, Fairbanks, Alaska. At Fort Benning, I could not make my first jump, so I put in for a transfer back to the Air Forces and asked to be stationed in Alaska. I was sent to Hamilton Field, California, the replacement depot for the Air Forces, and from there I went to Whittier, Alaska, aboard the troopship, *General*

Eltinge. From Whittier, I was assigned to Marks Field, Nome, Alaska, some distance from my brother. Gene and I did visit when we could catch a weekend hop.

In late 1948, my father passed away and I was reassigned to Walker Field, New Mexico. I was discharged from the U. S. Air Force at Roswell, New Mexico, on 2 September 1949.

I am proud to have served my country, but I was afraid to let anyone know that I was an underage veteran. On Veterans Day in 2000, I attended a meeting of underage veterans at the Ramada Express Hotel in Laughlin, Nevada, and immediately joined the Veterans of Underage Military Service (VUMS). I finally found a home among veterans just like me. I told my brother Gene about the VUMS and he has joined also.

Harold Pershall obtained a GED after his discharge from the Air Force. He worked eight hours a day and went to college six hours a day for three years. He moved to Arizona and became a deputy sheriff. He attained the rank of chief deputy and later was selected to become a judge, serving 10 years on the bench. He was appointed to several state boards by the governor. After retiring from the bench, he was appointed as deputy director of the Arizona State Liquor Control Commission and served in that position for several years before retiring again. He still sits as Judge Pro-Tempore when called upon. Harold and Janelle, his wife of 52 years, raised a family of four girls and a boy. They live in Kingman, Arizona.

Robert W. Gares

Age 16 – United States Army Air Forces

I was born in Newport News, Virginia, on 24 December 1929. Although I had a rotten life as a child, I finished high school early, graduating in 1946. I signed up for a post-graduate course at Newport News High School.

> *... as time went on, I began to really enjoy the military.*

I felt that 16 sounded too young to be taking a postgraduate course, so I told them that I was 17 and listed my birth date as 24 December 1928.

Later, I decided to go into the military, primarily to get the benefits of the GI Bill of Rights. I talked with an Army Air Forces recruiter, and he asked me to get my parents' permission. I asked my mother to sign the paper, which she did. The recruiter then asked for a birth certificate. I told him that he could call the school to check on my birth date, and he did.

So, on 26 September 1946, I was on a train to Richmond, Virginia, where I was sworn into the Army Air Forces. From there, I was sent to Fort Meade Maryland. The next day I was issued uniforms and given a bag to send my civilian clothes home. We were put on a troop train destined for San Antonio, Texas, for basic training. At St. Louis, Missouri, our train stayed on a siding for 24 hours. We didn't have any food during this time. Finally, they took us into town and fed us.

After basic training, I was sent to Spokane, Washington, by troop train. It was so crowded that we had to share bunks. I was in a bunk with a Mexican-American. One night he woke me up. He was yelling, "Look at the snow!" He had never seen snow before.

When we arrived at the base in Spokane we were sent to a barracks where we made our bunks, then went to eat. At 3:00 a.m. the next morning, we were awakened and told that we were in the wrong barracks. We moved to another barracks, and after we had made our bunks, we were told we were at the wrong base.

We were taken to Fort George Wright, Spokane, Washington, where I was assigned to the medics. This was in December 1946. At this point I didn't like the military and didn't like the medics, so in January 1947, I put in for a minority discharge. I didn't hear any more about it, and as time went on, I began to really enjoy the military.

I put in for, and was granted, a 30-day leave in September 1947. I was on a train to Virginia when two military policemen got on the train, found me, and said, "Let's go – your discharge came through." They made me go back to Fort Wright. I reported to Master Sergeant Cherko and told him that I didn't want out. He said that I had no choice, that I must go.

I enlisted in the Air Force on 12 February 1952 and served until 28 February 1956. I had a bad drinking problem at the time. However, I haven't had a drink since 10 May 1965 at 4:15 p.m., and I'm very proud of that.

Robert Gares worked in a Newport News, Virginia, shipyard and for Bowditch Ford and other shops. He has six children, six grandchildren, and one great-grandchild. Robert lives in Versailles, Missouri.

Joseph D. Buffington
Age 16 – United States Army

I was born in Reinerton, Schuylkill County, Pennsylvania, on Christmas Day, 25 December 1929, the fourth of six children. My mother died 25 days before my 5th birthday. My father kept the

> He also promised the three of us that we would stay together if we joined.

family together until 1944. My two older sisters were married by then, my older brother was in the Navy, and my two younger sisters were placed with family members. I was placed on a chicken farm and worked for $28 per month, plus room and board, while attending high school.

On 30 September 1946, two friends (one was 16 and the other 17) and I attended the Gratz Fair in Gratz, Pennsylvania. While there we talked with an Army recruiter about joining the Army. He said that we would be paid $50 per month, plus medical care and room and board. He also promised the three of us that we would stay together if we joined. We all wanted to go into the AAA (Antiaircraft Artillery).

The recruiter met us in Gratz on Monday, 2 October 1946 and took us to the recruiting station in Harrisburg, Pennslyvania.

The woman who was processing my paper work asked my age and I said that I was 18. She asked for my draft card (they were still drafting men in 1946). I told her that I was 18 on Saturday, 30 September, and I did not have time to register. She accepted that and completed my enlistment papers. I was sworn into the Army that day and was sent to Fort Meade, Maryland, for processing.

Later, I found out that my 16-year-old friend enlisted in the Army Air Forces and was sent to Langley Air Force Base, Virginia, after basic training, and the 17-year-old went to Fort Lewis, Washington, for his basic training. The three of us never met again while in the military.

About 10 days after arriving at Fort Meade, I was on a train to Fort Bliss, Texas, where I was assigned to the 58th AAA Training Battalion. After four weeks of basic, everyone received orders to go overseas. I was selected to stay at Fort Bliss as cadre to train others. However, for reasons unknown to me, two weeks later I left for Japan. I was given a 30-day leave en route to Camp Stoneman, California, where I reported in on 24 December 1946. I left by ship on 1 January 1947 and arrived in Japan on 15 January.

I remained in Japan until November 1951. While there, I met and married a lady from Hawaii. She was working in Japan as a civil-service employee at the headquarters of my unit, the 40th AAA Brigade.

When I was assigned to the S-2 (intelligence) section in 1948, I was required to have a security clearance. At that time I told them that my true birth date was 25 December 1929, not 30 September 1928. My clearance application was sent to GHQ in Tokyo, Japan. General MacArthur's headquarters processed the clearance and directed that my records be changed to reflect my true birth date.

I stayed in the Army for 27 years. I was assigned to various places, including Fort Knox, Kentucky, where I attended OCS (Officer Candidate School). I graduated from OCS in February 1953 and was assigned to the 11th Armored Cavalry Regiment, Fort Carson, Colorado. I served in Germany with the 2nd Cavalry Regiment from 1954 to 1995.

In 1960, I attended a television equipment repair course at Fort Monmouth, New Jersey. I graduated from the course on 28 February 1961 and was assigned to the Cable TV Section, Fort Huachuca, Arizona. From Arizona, I moved to Alaska where I was chief engineer for Channel 8, AFRTS (Armed Forces Radio & TV Service), Wildwood Station, Kenai, Alaska, for two years. I remember well the great earthquake of 29 March 1964. Over 120 people died in the quake.

I returned to Fort Huachuca, Arizona, in 1964 and spent four years in the Service Test Division of the U. S. Army Electronic Proving Grounds (USAEPG). We tested items of communication from radios to field wire. I served in Vietnam from September 1968 until September 1969.

After returning from Vietnam, I was assigned to the U. S. Army Advisory Group, Phoenix, Arizona. I served as a unit advisor to the 6224th U. S. Army Reserve School (C&GS). I retired from the Army on 30 April 1973 in Phoenix, Arizona.

Joe Buffington was awarded the Bronze Star for his service in Vietnam and two Army Commendation Medals, along with a number of service medals. After his retirement from the Army, he completed an A. A. in banking and finance, and another in middle management. He also attended Arizona State University (ASU). He went to work for the Valley National Bank of Arizona, (later, Bank One of Arizona), in the real-estate department. He retired from the bank as an assistant vice president after 17 years. His son and daughter graduated from ASU. Joe was divorced in 1979. He married Lorraine R. Goughnour in January 1998. Joe and Lorraine live in Phoenix, Arizona.

✔ *INCIDENTally – Welcome to Japan!* – In 1947, I was shipped to Japan aboard the *Admiral Mayo*, a big ship, as I recall. There were about 2,800 soldiers aboard, and about 300 wives and children of officers who were stationed in Japan. We arrived in Yokohama Bay on a beautiful, sunny morning. I was standing by the rail, feeling tremendous pride as the tugs slowly pushed us toward the dock. I could hear an Army band playing and saw a large sign that said "Welcome to Japan." I was a proud 16-year-old soldier. When we got closer to the dock, the second line of the sign became clear. It said "wives and children." The gangplank went down and the civilians immediately departed. A few hours later, trucks arrived to take the 2,800 soldiers to a tent city. I still have a good laugh when I think about it. – *Melvin E. Hobert.*

John L. Shaughnessy

Age 16 – United States Army

I was born in Baltimore, Maryland, on 18 July 1930. Baltimore was a port city with many blue-collar plants and factories. In the 1930s, many were closing because of the Depression. Baltimore's approximately 750,000 residents were made up of various ethnic groups. My

> *I look back fondly and with great pride at this period in my life.*

parents lived in an Irish enclave. The homes were two-story, brick row-houses. The neighborhood had many churches, predominately Catholic. Our home had formerly belonged to my grandmother who died one year before I was born. I was an only child.

When I was 5 years old, my parents separated and I was placed in a hospital orphanage because I was underweight and possibly had rickets. I stayed there for a year or so. My mother moved to a smaller home and worked cleaning neighborhood taverns. My education began at age 7 in a Catholic school. I was a discipline problem and received

the typical punishment from the sisters, rulers across the knuckles and a yardstick or a pointer across the back.

At age 9, I began selling newspapers on streetcars. The conductors would let us kids jump on the car, sell the papers for three or four blocks, then make us jump off.

At this time I had been placed in a foster home because my mother was unable to earn enough money to support us. The Catholic Church had placed me in a home with a family who had two daughters. I stayed with this family for six years. The home was near my mother, but I didn't see her very often. It was not a warm or comfortable place to raise a foster child.

During that time, Pearl Harbor was bombed and World War II was declared. I was too young to enlist, but I read every newspaper and listened to radio broadcasts about all the strange countries where our troops were fighting. I became a messenger for the Civil Defense Agency, collected scrap metal, and got a job as a helper on a milk truck.

When I was 14 years old in 1944, I left school and moved back with my mother. Since I was not in school and earning my own salary, I stayed on the streets until 2 a.m. I always made it home before my mother, who came home from work at 2:30 a.m. I started to think about going into the Merchant Marine or the Marines, but I could not figure how to do this at my age.

In July 1946, I was 16 years old and I knew my self-training was going to take another turn, one that changed my life forever. I went to the Catholic church and got my baptismal certificate. I then got a bottle of ink eradicator, and my master plan began. I had to change "1930" to "1929," so I had two numbers to alter. It was the world's worse job of altering, but I now had a document that would take me to a new life.

I entered the U. S. Army on 30 September 1946, after getting my mother to sign the documentation stating that I was 17 years old. I received my medical exam and shots and was issued clothing at Fort George C. Meade, which was just outside of Baltimore. The sergeant in charge of new recruits assigned several of us to stencil the last four digits of each recruit's serial number on his newly issued clothes. After we were finished, the sergeant collected $2 from each recruit. Since there were several hundred recruits that passed through there each week, I figured this sergeant was doing very well financially.

The next day, we were on a train bound for Camp Polk, Louisiana. The next two months my brain and body were given over to a 5-foot 5-inch, tough-as-nails, three-striper (sergeant) from Waco, Texas, whose job was to make us into soldiers. One thing I had a tough time learning was how to do an "about-face" while marching. After three nights on the parade field under lights, constantly marching and doing "about-face" about 1,000 times, I became the best in the company.

I received a 30-day leave after basic, then reported to Camp Kilmer, New Jersey, to await a ship for Italy. Twelve days after boarding the ship at Staten Island, New York, we arrived in Livorno (Leghorn), Italy. Upon debarking, some men left the ship with much more money than they came on with. Every day of those 12 days, there was every type of gambling going on. It was a floating casino!

I was assigned to Company C, 350th Infantry Regiment, 88th Infantry Division, as a radio operator, at Plava, Italy. This area, part of the Julian Alps, was near the border of Italy and Yugoslavia, just north of Trieste, Italy. There was a dispute over which country should control it. Our job was to protect a power-generating plant that served much of the surrounding area. There were many small roads in the mountains that were used mainly by farmers. We had checkpoints set up to check IDs of those crossing the border. Yugoslavian troops were stationed just past our outposts. The area was always tense, and small skirmishes occurred from time to time. This was the beginning of the Cold War.

Our living quarters consisted of about 50 units of two-story apartments, and one three-story unit. These units were originally built for the workers at the generating plants. There were three men to a room. The units were without bathing facilities. During the summer we bathed in the Izonzo River. In the winter, we would fill our helmets with hot water in the mess hall and carry them back to our rooms and bathe. A Quonset hut had been added for a mess hall and recreation room. The area was fenced with a guard post at the entrance and 24-hour roving patrols.

At meal time, we usually let three to five kids into the camp, but they were not allowed into the mess hall. As the troops left the rear door of the mess hall, the kids would be standing outside with one-gallon cans with a wire handle. We would scrape the remains of our meal into their cans. Sometimes the scraps of our meals went into the wrong cans they were holding, such as jello into the potatoes. All of us saw to it that the kids left with full cans. Many large families were fed by their 7- and 8-year-old kids who stood in the freezing cold to collect what we did not eat. I thought to myself that I was only eight years older than they were, but I didn't have to walk for miles in freezing weather with only a thin coat for warmth to get a meal.

As a radio operator, I was on call 24 hours a day, 7 days a week. I spent time as a lineman repairing phone lines, and I also manned the radio and switchboard. The radio room was in the three-story building which also served as the officers' quarters. It was directly over the captain's bedroom. Everyone on the night shift took his boots off while on duty.

I took advantage of the courses offered by the USAFI (United States Armed Forces Institute) in Madison, Wisconsin. I completed the necessary courses and received a high school equivalency diploma.

While I was at Plava, there were many parades for visiting dignitaries and generals at battalion headquarters, including General Bradley and General Eisenhower.

We stood our last review as the 88th Division on 2 October 1947. The division commander, Major General Bryant E. Moore, and his assistant, Brigadier General Ridgley Gaither, told us about the fine job the men of the 88th Division had done facing the Yugoslavians. Troops in the Trieste area were now called "Trust Troops," and the work of our division was done.

The 88th Division had received high honors during the war. It was rated among the top ten of American, British, German, and Italian Divisions. The 88th left Italy on 11 October 1947 and the men were reassigned to bases throughout the United States. I was assigned to a battalion which trained troops going to the officers candidate school at Fort Benning, Georgia.

I was discharged on 18 March 1948. I have always felt that military service was the pinnacle of my growing-up. I look back fondly and with great pride at this period in my life.

John Shaughnessy became a Baltimore City police officer at the age of 21 and was assigned to a high-crime area. He worked as a patrolman and later as a detective, investigating all types or crimes. He left law enforcement after 14 years, and with his wife, bought a small moving company. They built the company as a family enterprise and in 1988, after 24 years, they sold it to a California firm. Four of their sons are still employed by that company. He moved to Florida and worked as a real-estate agent for a short time. He was a legislative assistant to a Florida state legislator for 2½ years. John and his wife Mary have a combined family of eight sons and two daughters, twenty-two grandchildren, and sixteen great-grandchildren. They spend winters in Florida and summers at their home in Newcomb, Maryland.

Michael K. Mitchell
Age 14 – United States Army

My story is not one of great heroism or valor, but one of cunning. I was born in Philadelphia, Pennsylvania, on 27 October 1932. I was not a very compliant youth, and I was in trouble in school most

I actually loved basic training!

of the time. This resulted in a deep and abiding dislike of school.

I ran away from my home in Philadelphia in September 1946 at the age of 13. I traveled to Dallas, Texas, where I landed a job on a soda fountain in a drug store. Although this job provided enough for me to eat, it was not a well-paying position, so I decided to join the military. I first went to the Army Air Forces recruiter. I was told that I was color-blind and not eligible to join. I had the same experience when I tried to join the Navy and the Marines.

Finally, I went to the Army recruiter. He said that I would need the signature of my mother, father, or a legal guardian in order to enlist. Obviously, I couldn't get my mother's signature because she had died when I was 12. My father had no idea where I was. Since I couldn't get anyone to forge the signature of my mother or father, I went to a lawyer's office and told him that I was an orphan and wanted to enlist in the Army. He said that he could take out a legal guardianship and then could legally sign the enlistment papers, which he did.

I took the properly signed paper to the recruiting office and was sworn into the Army on 8 November 1946. I was sent to Fort Lewis, Washington, as a member of the 1st Cavalry Division, and received basic training there. I actually loved basic training! I was learning things that I believed were important, and I was firing the M1 rifle. The main reason I loved my Army experience was that I was treated like an adult. As long as I did what I was asked to do, and I did, I was treated like everyone else. I learned to drive a 2½-ton, 6x6 truck at age 14!

I finished basic training and was preparing to go to Japan. I was eagerly looking forward to going to Japan. I wanted to find out if it was true that the Japanese women would show an American soldier great personal gratitude in exchange for chocolate, silk stockings, or cigarettes. I was told that all these "gifts" were available in the post exchange at a very low cost.

Unfortunately, it was discovered that I was only 14 years old, and I was asked by a chaplain to call my father. I was not given a choice, and call I did. My dad said that he would be in touch. I was afraid that I would be in *big* trouble, but I waited.

My dad worked for Senator Joseph Grundy, the most powerful politician in Pennsylvania at that time. Senator Grundy called the Pentagon and demanded that I be flown home at once. He was told that an airplane was not available, but I would be given an honorable discharge, travel orders from Fort Lewis to Philadelphia, $300 mustering-out pay, and VIP treatment. I was made eligible for the GI Bill and all the rewards that came with it.

I never really knew why I got such preferential treatment. However, on 13 February 1947, my discharge was final. I was 55 years old when my dad revealed to me the role that Senator Grundy played in my discharge.

Many times I have regretted that I did not go to Japan, but then I remember that the soldiers of the 1st Cavalry were among the first to go to Korea, and many of them were killed. I honor and respect all members of the Veterans of Underage Military Service who joined, fought with valor, stayed in, and retired after a long military career.

Michael Mitchell made his peace with schooling and finished high school at the Valley Forge Military Academy, Valley Forge, Pennsylvania. He attended the University of Miami and graduated with, of all things, a bachelor's degree in education. After teaching for 20 years, he went back to school and earned a master's degree and a Ph.D. from Texas A&M University. He continued to teach until 2001, the last 13 years at the state reform school in Anchorage, Alaska. His experiences as a youth prepared him well for this challenging teaching opportunity. Michael and Nell, his wife of 42 years, have two children and two grandchildren. They live in Anchorage, Alaska.

Pasquale "Pat" Varallo
Age 16 – United States Army

I was born in the front bedroom of a small house in North Philadelphia, Pennsylvania, on 15 November 1930. My father abandoned my mother when I was about 9 years old, leaving her with six children to raise. Most of the time

> ..., "Peewee, go back to the barracks and shave."

I was under no supervision and was pretty much a juvenile delinquent. I quit school and went to work when I was 15 years old.

In 1945, a friend, "Rabbit" Flynn, and I went downtown to the U. S. Army recruiting office to sign up. I was 14 and Rab was 15. "Airborne!" we told the recruiter. "Airborne!" he said, "You'll be airborne when I put a foot up your ass. Go home and grow up first." We left with his laughter ringing in our ears.

In 1946, we went to the recruiting office again to enlist. By this time the war had been over for several months and they needed new men so that they could rotate all those vets back home. There was no

derision from the recruiter this time. He told us that we needed proof of age and at least one parent's consent. I didn't think I could get my mother's consent.

In November 1946, I turned 16. By this time I was getting into trouble. So when I asked – really – pestered my mother to let me sign up, she figured I would be better off under a tough Army sergeant than running the streets. My mother and I obtained a copy of my baptismal certificate from our parish church. A little ink remover and "1930" became "1929," and I was no longer 16 but 17.

Armed with "proof" I went to the recruiter and was welcomed with open arms. I was sworn into the Army on 7 February 1947 and sent to Fort Dix, New Jersey. I had enlisted for 18 months. After about a week in basic, we were marched into an orientation hall. Our platoon leader stood on a platform and started speaking to us. He cut right to the point, no build up. It was a bombshell. "We know that some of you men are underage," he stated. "What we want you to do is go back to your barracks, get your gear, and report to building such and such. You're going home." The jig is up I thought, and then he continued, "No questions, no punishment, no nothing. We'll put you on a bus and send you home. You were never in the Army."

While I was sitting there, thinking about what my mother had said – you pestered me to join, now don't come home till you've done your time and with an honorable discharge – the lieutenant let the other shoe drop. "If you don't report to building such and such by xx hours, you are in the Army and any attempt to get out by claiming that you are underage will result in a court-martial and a dishonorable discharge." I kept quiet and was relieved. I have no idea how many in that company were underage. As far as I know, only one opted out. So there were at least two, and it was clear that the Army was giving us a choice.

I finished basic in April and was given orders to report to Ft. Myer, Virginia. The company was out on details and I was alone except for the barracks orderly. I was putting my things away when the orderly came up to me and introduced himself. I can't recall his name. He was surprised to find out that I didn't understand what kind of outfit I was in. He told me that I was in the Ceremonial Detachment, a spit-and-polish outfit. The detachment furnished a White House detail, did military funerals at Arlington National Cemetery, guarded the Tomb of the Unknown Soldier, and much more. And all this was done by this one company of 100 men.

One day we had fallen in for inspection prior to an officer's funeral at the cemetery. Officers' caskets are borne to the grave site on the famous caisson, followed by a platoon-size escort of riflemen. Staff Sergeant Pickerel was in charge of the escort and was inspecting us. When he came to me, he peered into my face and said, "Peewee, go back to the barracks and shave." While standing before the mirror in the latrine, I thought, "Pick's nuts." I couldn't see a whisker anywhere on my face. But, orders are orders, and I lathered up and had my first shave.

On Army Day, 6 April 1948, we reactivated the 3rd Infantry Regiment, the oldest regiment in the Army, aptly called the Old Guard. After receiving the regimental colors, we kicked off the Army

Day parade. We were the first unit behind the Army band. On Pennsylvania Avenue, at the White House, we were given the command, "Eyes right!" and there, about 20 feet away in the reviewing stand, was the President of the United States, Harry S. Truman. He had a large grin on his face. That moment is fixed in my memory like a photograph.

Near the end of the 1947-48 winter, I was given the very distinct honor of being chosen as a guard at the Tomb of the Unknown Soldier.

One of the biggest events to occur while I was at Fort Myer was when General of the Armies John J. Pershing died. He had been retired and living at Walter Reed Hospital. I was detailed as honor guard to Walter Reed Hospital. A guard was posted at the foot and head of the open casket. On the day before the burial at Arlington National Cemetery, I was chosen for the great honor of being in the firing party for the salute at the graveside services.

On July 29, 1948, I left Ft. Myer and went home. I handed my mother my honorable discharge. My Army records show at that time I was 5-feet 6-inches tall, and weighed 120 pounds. I was still growing. There were no jobs at that time for a high school dropout. I decided to re-enlist. I had always wanted to go to sea, so I went to the U. S. Navy recruiting office. I was told that their quota was filled and that there was a waiting list. I enlisted in the Coast Guard on 20 January 1950.

After boot camp, I was assigned to the Cross Rip Lightship in Nantucket Sound, Massachusetts. I wrote a story about my experience aboard Cross Rip for the U. S. Lighthouse Society's magazine, *The Keeper's Log.* For those who might ask, a lightship is the same as a lighthouse, except it is placed where it isn't feasible to build a lighthouse. After six months aboard Cross Rip, I applied for and was accepted at the U. S. Navy Sonar School, Key West, Florida. I was there from November 1950 until May 1951.

After sound school, I reported aboard the USCGC *Duane* (W-33) at Constitution Wharf, Boston. I made four patrols in *Duane.* In July 1952, orders came through transferring me to the CGC *Ramsden* at the Philadelphia Navy Yard. I made one patrol on the *Ramsden.* We left Philadelphia, with stops at Curtis Bay in Baltimore, Maryland; Miami, Florida; both sides of the Panama Canal; Acapulco, Mexico; San Diego, California, and on to Honolulu. From there I was sent back to the

States for separation. Because of the Korean War, it was rumored that we might be extended. It never happened. I was discharged at Alameda, California, in January 1953.

Pat Varallo signed on aboard a tanker that carried crude oil from Texas to Philadelphia for the Atlantic Refining Company. After completing a trip on another oil tanker, he was fired for union-organizing activity. He spent the rest of his post-service life driving busses, trucks, and big rigs for a living. He obtained his GED at age 55. His wife Eileen died on 4 June 2001 after a long illness. He has four children and three grandchildren. Pat lives in Philadelphia, Pennsylvania.

✔ *INCIDENTally* — **Yeast brews trouble!** – During the initial assault on Saipan in 1944, the galley oven on our landing craft *LCT962* was broken. Later, we had to dispose of many full cartons of dehydrated yeast. Applying our Yankee, and Rebel, ingenuity, we sold the yeast to the native men who were working on the docks for Uncle Sam. The natives used the yeast to make home brew, and we used the money to buy Stateside rye whiskey from merchant seamen. When the yeast ran out, we substituted powdered milk, which doesn't make a potent brew. We were lucky that our skipper was able to get us, boat and all, reassigned to Guam just in time to avoid an attack by outraged Saipanese. – *Cornelius F. Murray.*

Jess D. Todd

Age 16 – United States Army

Both sides of my family came from about 15 miles east of Parkersburg, West Virginia. I had an older brother who was born on 24 August 1929, and I was born on 3 October 1930, more than a year later. My mother

..., so I decided to come clean and disclose my true birth date.

died when I was about 18-months old, leaving my 22-year-old uneducated father with three small children. My younger sister died a short time later. As a result, my brother and I were raised by my maternal grandparents for about ten years.

My grandparents operated a country store and the only beer hall in a very large area. This was the gathering place for the drinkers in the area. There was a considerable number of World War I vets residing in the area, and they fought the war many times over, especially when they had a few drinks in them. We were exposed to many war stories at an early age. At the time, it sounded exciting to us. I actually

learned to count money and make change when I was 6 or 7 years old by selling beer at 10¢ a bottle, three for 25¢.

My brother and I started school at the same time, but because I was more studious, I skipped the third grade. I was a year ahead of him in school and many people thought I was the oldest, but he was more than a year older than me. I attended two years of high school, but I skipped many days. I failed to start my junior year, even though I was only 15.

On 14 January 1947, shortly after turning 16, I went to the local draft board and registered for the draft. The person with whom I talked asked me my birth date. I told him, "Today." He asked me who my relatives were, then said, "Are you the oldest?" I replied, "Yes." He registered me without asking for any proof of birth. I learned later that he knew my entire family.

With my new birth date, I became seven months older than my brother. About this time, my brother went to the recruiting office in Parkersburg and enlisted in the Army. His serial number was RA15250661. Shortly after my brother left for the Army, I went to the recruiting office and enlisted in the Army for three years, using my registration card showing my birth date to be 14 January 1929. I was sworn into the Army on 12 February 1947, six days after my brother. I was issued serial number RA15250790. It was only 129 numbers higher than the one issued to my brother.

I went to Fort Bragg, North Carolina, for basic training. In June 1947, I arrived at Camp Zama, Japan, for further assignment. A large number of names were called and the men assigned to General Headquarters (GHQ) in Tokyo. After that, my name alone was called. I was told that I was going to the 441st Counterintelligence Corps (CIC) in Tokyo, and would go there with the large contingent going to GHQ. This really concerned me because I thought that my fraudulent enlistment had been discovered and I was in a lot of trouble. I believed that I was the only one of the contingent in this position. I had no idea what CIC was.

A few days later we arrived in a transient area in Tokyo. Shortly after arrival, I was summoned over the PA system to report to the orderly room with all my gear. When I arrived at the orderly room, I was met by a Japanese driver who addressed me as Mister Todd and wouldn't even allow me to carry my own gear to the nearby jeep. Now, for a 16-year-old private with about five months in the Army and whose enlistment was fraudulent, I didn't know what was going on. I was either very lucky, or in a lot of trouble! My only choice was to go along and see what happened.

We drove for several miles through bombed-out Tokyo and arrived at a building called Norton Hall, which was across the moat from the Emperor's Palace. The driver parked the jeep and a corporal came out to help unload my gear. He, too, addressed me as Mister Todd. This was shortly after basic training and I still believed corporals were the nearest thing to God! I believed that I was going to like the Army even though I didn't know what was going on or what the future would hold, but it was sure great at this point. That night I experienced my first earthquake, and it scared the hell out of me.

A few days later we were taken to an office building in downtown Tokyo and processed into the 441st CIC. At that time we learned that a complete background check would be made for a required security clearance. We had to fill out a four-page pink form that listed our entire life history. At this point, it became very clear to me that I had to do something because the background check would certainly disclose my correct age. I knew that if anyone was going to do any singing, that I might as well lead the choir, so I decided to come clean and disclose my true birth date. I talked with the personnel officer in charge. He didn't seem surprised or concerned. He flipped the form over to the back, referenced the date of birth entry, and noted the correct birth date.

Later, I was placed in charge of the parts room at the motor pool. I soon started getting promotions and was a sergeant shortly after I had really turned 17. The men I worked with were a great group of individuals. There was not much military activity required, and the benefits were outstanding. At our mess hall, we sat four to a cloth-covered table. We could order from menus and choose what we wanted to eat and how we wanted it prepared. We had our own club where we could buy inexpensive drinks. We were allowed the use the jeeps for recreational purposes. This was the best assignment that I had in more than 20 years. I spent the next 17 years trying to duplicate it, but with little success. My only regret for this period was that I was not old enough or experienced enough to avail myself of the many opportunities that were presented to me.

When the background check was complete, I was sent to the colonel's office. He explained that the background investigation was satisfactorily completed and they learned that I had been truthful earlier when I reported my correct birth date. The colonel said that if I wanted, I would be sent home and given a minority discharge. I replied that if it was up to me, that I wanted to stay in the Army. He said that he wanted me to stay, signed the papers, and I returned to my assignment. During this enlistment no effort was ever made to change the birth date on my records. The subject never came up again, although practically everyone in the unit knew that I had enlisted underage.

I was discharged from the Army at Fort Lawton, Washington. I went back to West Virginia and found that things there had not changed much, but that there had been a big change in me. On 28 April 1950, I was sworn into the Army for a 6-year enlistment. I was required to use my original DD-214 form which had my fictitious birth date, so now I had enlisted fraudulently twice. I ended up with a military police unit at Fort Holabird, Maryland. I talked with a friend who worked in personnel and had him correct my birth date in the records.

I arrived in Korea in February 1952 and was assigned to the 7th Infantry Division. I thought I would be in the infantry, but instead I was sent to the 13th Combat Engineer Battalion. Later, I transferred to the 7th M.P. company and completed my Korean tour.

After returning to the States, I was offered an opportunity to join the investigations section. Later, I attended the CID school at Fort Gordon, Georgia. I served three tours of duty with the 62nd CID detachment at Fort Ord, California, the first from 1954 to 1957, then from 1959 to 1963, and again from 1966 to 1967. When not at Fort Ord, I was with a CID detachment in Germany. I was promoted to warrant officer while in Germany. On 1 June 1967, I retired from the Army as a CWO-2 after more than 20 years of service. I was 36 years old.

Jess Todd earned an Army Commendation Medal while in Korea. After his retirement from the Army he worked for the Department of Corrections at Soledad prison in California. During this time he completed several classes at Hartnell College in Salinas, California, and at San Jose State University, and in 1971 received a B.S. in law enforcement and corrections from the University of Nebraska at Omaha. Later he became a special agent with what became the Bureau of Alcohol, Tobacco, and Firearms of the U. S. Treasury Department. Jess and Bertie, his wife of 48 years, have two children and nine grandchildren. They live in Federal Way, Washington.

Clifford H. Whalen

Age 15 – United States Army Air Forces

I was born in Wiergate, Texas, a small sawmill town in southeast Texas near the Louisiana border, on 16 September 1931. My mother was divorced and she, my older brother, and I, lived with her mother, as many families did in those days.

> I boarded the bus with a bag of bananas and a jug of milk.

As a child, I can remember the talk among the adults about the war in Europe. With a childlike mind, I often thought that one day I would be grown up and I would go help fight that war. I was 10 years old in December 1941 when the Japanese attacked Pearl Harbor. I thought I should be doing something to support my country.

I was 15 years old in 1947, and on 26 May 1947, I enlisted in the Army Air Forces. I gave the recruiting officer 20 April 1929 as my birth date. This was actually my brother's birth date. It was not changed on my military records until 1962.

I still had to have permission of a parent to enlist. An uncle signed for me. Mother was very unhappy, but she decided to let me stay through boot camp. She thought it might make me change my mind. When she realized that I was serious about a military career, she decided to say nothing about my age but made me promise to get my high school education, which I did some years later.

Before leaving for Lackland Air Force Base, San Antonio, Texas, I was told to eat all the bananas and drink all the milk I could because I was underweight. I boarded the bus with a bag of bananas and a jug of milk. Every stop we made, I bought more. It worked! I weighed in at the right weight. I did 13 weeks of training at Lackland during the hottest time of the year.

In early September 1947, a few weeks before my 16th birthday, I was sent to Scott Field, Illinois, to attend control-tower school.

In December 1947, hundreds of others and I were headed for occupied Japan aboard the USS *Miggs*. We were packed in like sardines in a can. I was proud of myself on this voyage because I never got seasick. Standing up to eat didn't bother me. There were so many aboard this ship that we were issued different colored meal cards so that we had to rotate to eat our meals. We also "island hopped," stopping at Pearl Harbor first, on to Guam, then to Yokohama, Japan. In Yokohama, we were billeted in what once had been a stable.

Three days after arriving in Japan, I was assigned to another school, this time radio-operators school. It was close to Mount Fuji. My next stop was Itami Air Force Base near Osaka. I was there for the next 30 months. There was much poverty in Japan at this time. Hardly any buildings were still standing, and there were a lot of homeless people. The atomic bombs had been dropped in 1945.

Although the Army Air Forces had become the U. S. Air Force, I was still wearing Army olive-drab with Air Force stripes. By the time I was 17, I had three stripes. It was in late 1950, when I was back in the United States, before I got my first Air Force blues.

In June 1950, I was aboard a ship heading for the States when we got word that war had broken out in Korea. We were to turn around and go back to Japan, but we kept on going to the States, arriving in San Francisco in mid-July. For the next year I was in El Paso, Texas, and then I attended ground-control approach (GCA) school at Keesler Air Force Base, Biloxi, Mississippi.

In November 1951, I was in Korea. We flew into Seoul in "Old Shakey," a C-124. We spent the night in an old church, sleeping on church benches. The next day we left for Kimpo AFB by truck. At Kimpo, a tent shared with seven other men became my home. One of the men was "Ajax," Albert J. Baulmer, an ex-Flying Tiger. He fought for the Chinese before America entered the war. When America entered the war, he fought in the Army Air Forces under General Chennault. When Ajax and I shared a tent, he was just a two-striper. He had been an officer with General Chennault.

How well I remember the cold and "Bed Check Charlie," who tried so many times to bomb us but was never successful. One incident that sticks in my mind was a day when we had an aircraft coming in to land with an injured pilot. To keep him from passing out, those of us operating the GCA equipment kept talking to him. Then we learned that he had a 500-pound bomb hung on his wing. Our GCA unit was 250 feet from the runway and was surrounded by sandbags. We were given an order to evacuate, but none of us did. When we got the pilot on final approach, we were again instructed to leave. On landing, the bomb came loose from the wing and tumbled all the way down the runway, but it never did explode. We were told later that if it had rolled, it would have exploded. The pilot was rescued and all ended well.

On my return to the States in December 1952, I was once again stationed at Keesler AFB, this time as an instructor. In 1954, I served a tour at Yokota AFB, Japan. In 1960, I found myself in England at the Brizenorton AFB in the Cotswold countryside. It was here that I met the girl who became my wife in 1961.

When we left England, I was stationed at Tinker AFB, Oklahoma, and was assigned to the 3rd Mobile Squadron. We were mobile all right! I spent time at Ben Hua in Vietnam, the Dominican Republic, Panama, Brazil, and remote Alaska. These are just a few of the places we went to. Whenever a runway or GCA unit was needed, the 3rd MOB was there.

I retired from the Air Force on 1 April 1969. I have never regretted my military career. There were good times, bad times, happy times, and sad times. Some of the horrors of war will forever be buried in my memory. I am proud to be an American, and I am proud of having had the privilege of serving my country.

Clifford Whalen went to work for the FAA as an air-traffic controller after he retired from the Air Force. He left the FAA for health reasons and became a sales manager for Auto Zone Auto Parts from which he retired in 1993, again for health reasons. Clifford and Elizabeth, his wife of 41 years, have a daughter and three grandchildren. They live in Vivian, Louisiana.

Richard E. "Gene" Pershall

Age 15 – United States Army Air Forces

I was born in Clay County, near Clay Center, Kansas, on 1 March 1932. My father was a farmer and my mother a seamstress. They were parents of 13 children, nine boys and four girls. I was the seventh to be born and came along at the height of the Depression.

> Harold and I wanted to go whip the enemy, but we were too young.

When I was very young, my father could no longer cope with the wheat dust at our farm, so he moved our family into the small town of Clay Center with a team and a wagon.

As a child, I grew up thinking that I wasn't wanted. My brother just younger than I died in infancy, and my folks had another, and another, and another child. I was just there – one of many with an open mouth. There really seemed to be three families in one: the older ones, the younger ones, and my brother Harold and I who were in the

middle. We felt like the black sheep of the family. My school days were happy ones even though there was never enough of anything to go around.

I remember very well the Pearl Harbor tragedy and the ensuing war. My older brother Wayne served in the Navy and Bob served in the Marines. Harold and I wanted to go whip the enemy, but we were too young. I well remember the war years; the attitudes of the people in our town were of patriotism and pride in all our service people. My oldest sister was the clerk of the draft board in our town. I really wanted to go fight somebody, sometimes anybody.

I was really excited when the Army guys came from Fort Riley, Kansas, to do maneuvers in our town. A group of us would go and talk with them and dream of being soldiers. It was an interesting time at the end of the conflict when my older brothers came home. Brother Wayne had married and moved away. Brother Bob didn't find work and also moved away, but he left his Marine clothes behind. Well, guess what? They fit me – well, almost – and I became a soldier after all.

I tended to grow up a little too early and wanted to be older than I was. I dated older girls and ran around with Harold's group because they were older and my group was so *immature*! Well, when Harold went off to the service, it was hard for me to deal with being the only one left. I thought that I ought to be doing my part, too.

I remember very well my ninth grade in school. School was never hard for me, but there were too many things on my young mind, so after the football and basketball seasons were over, I quit school and went to the next big town to get a job and be a *man*. I came in contact with a group of soldiers from Fort Riley. They showed me the barracks and the chow hall. Wow – they had three big meals a day, every day! I was more impressed than ever. They encouraged me to join. They said, "It's no big deal, just tell the recruiter that you are 17 and he will sign you up." Uh-huh, well, there was one small detail – a birth certificate. They said, "No big deal. Just get your parents to sign the permission form." A big problem arose. My mom and dad said, "No way!" But after a week of my behaving as a "teenager" (I could have used a more descriptive word), my dad was ready to sign anything.

On 27 May 1947, at the age of 15, I found myself in the Army Air Forces. They quickly showed me what it was like to be a soldier and sent me to San Antonio, Texas, to do basic training. Actually, I enjoyed everything but the heat. Boy, it was hot the summer of 1947! But I made it – I graduated – so what to do with me after that? All the schools that I wanted were full. Finally, they shipped me to the Radio Fundamentals Branch at Scott Field, Illinois. I thought that was the dirtiest place I had ever been in, and I didn't care one bit about radios or how they functioned. That was a disaster.

They asked me what I wanted to do. I told them that I wanted to be an airplane mechanic. They granted my wish and I was off to New Mexico to work on P-51s. I was happy, especially since my folks had moved to Clovis, New Mexico, for my dad's health. I was transferred to Alaska and assigned to the 10th Air Rescue Squadron at Fairbanks. I spent 18 months there.

I acquired my GED at age 16. I was honorably discharged at Lubbock, Texas, in May 1950. No one had discovered my age. I had really grown up. I grew two inches and gained 40 pounds.

All of my family grew up to be honorable citizens. As I matured, I realized that this was due in large part to our parents. Now I understand that what I had felt as a child was because we were such a large family, and love was spread throughout the family.

Gene Pershall worked for the Santa Fe Railroad, married, then went to college. Thanks in part to the GI Bill, a working wife, and a good job, he graduated from college with a B.S. in elementary education in 1955 and earned an M.S. in 1965. He spent his career in teaching and loved it. He taught elementary school, junior high, high school, and college. He was an elementary school principal for seven years and then was a school superintendent for 10 years. He has been very active in Kiwanis Clubs. Gene and Margaret, his wife of more than 50 years, have two children. They live in Clovis, New Mexico.

Donald P. Appelbaum
Age 16 – United States Army

I was born in St. Louis, Missouri, on 16 April 1931, the second oldest of seven children. Like so many others, our large family was suffering from the effects of the Depression. I was 10 years old when World

> I had a baby face and hid my nervous fears behind a smile.

War II started, and I was immediately affected by the waves of patriotic feeling that swept the country. As a boy, I was determined to fight for my country as soon as possible. I hero-worshiped Audie Murphy and other popular military figures of the early days of the war. As a kid, I was adventuresome, a risk-taker, undisciplined, and a showoff.

In 1945, when I was 14, the war was in its final months. I had heard through the teenage grapevine that in San Pedro, California, they were so desperate for seamen in the Merchant Marines that kids as young as I could go to sea. I immediately began planning.

In the fall of 1945, I ran away from home and began hitchhiking west. I had $20 and a lot of nerve. I bummed rides along the old Route 66, and accepted any charity I could find. I finally came to Deming, New Mexico. I was broke, hungry, and gratefully took an offer of a job on a ranch. I never made it to San Pedro, but I learned a lot about life. I returned to St. Louis in 1946, still determined to serve in the military.

I hatched another plan in the spring of 1946. I took my older brother's draft card (he was in the Army of Occupation in Japan), and went to the recruiting station and used it to enlist. They accepted it and I was sent to Ft. Riley, Kansas, to be processed and sworn in. Everything went well until we were to be sworn in, then my trickery was discovered and I was sent home.

Finally, in 1947, at the age of 16, I changed my birth certificate with ink eradicator, had a photostat made of it, and was accepted for enlistment. I was sworn in on 5 June 1947.

I was sent to Fort Knox, Kentucky, for infantry basic training. I was 5-feet 6-inches tall and weighed about 135 pounds. I had a baby face and hid my nervous fears behind a smile. I was determined to handle anything to be a good soldier.

I went through the 13 weeks of training with no problems. I was full of enthusiasm and volunteered for the paratroopers. The cadre looked at my physical size and baby face and told me I would never make it. I was sent to Fort Benning, Georgia, and graduated from the infantry school as a paratrooper and gliderman on 15 November 1947. I was sent to Fort Bragg, North Carolina, and assigned to the 504th Parachute Infantry Regiment.

Everything went smoothly until my mother contacted the Red Cross and reported my deception. I hadn't written to her for a long time, and she got worried and turned me in. I was given an honorable minority discharge and sent home. I was sorely disappointed.

In early 1948, as soon as I became 17, I re-enlisted in the Army, this time with parental consent. I asked to go back to the 82nd Airborne Division, but the recruiting officer offered me an opportunity to be trained in military intelligence because of my high aptitude scores, and I accepted. I was sent to Fort Knox for a 3-week orientation, then transferred to the Army Security Agency headquarters in Arlington, Virginia. After two months of training, I was sent to Fort Monmouth, New Jersey, and trained for six months as a high-speed, radio-intercept operator. After graduation, I was immediately shipped overseas, arriving in Bremerhaven, Germany, at the end of 1948.

I served at several locations in Germany and Austria for over three years. My duties were interesting and exciting. I worked on top-secret intelligence. When the Korean War started in 1950, the intensity of our mission was doubled. I am very proud of the contribution we made to our country during the period of the Cold War.

I returned to the United States and was discharged on 24 May 1952. Later I joined the Missouri National Guard and had the thrill of shaking hands with then retired President Harry Truman in Casper,

Wyoming, when he reviewed the troops at a Missouri National Guard summer camp.

I look back on my service as a teenage soldier with pride, and I would do it again if given a chance. I celebrated my 70th birthday with a parachute jump!

Don Appelbaum completed a GED while in the Army and enrolled at St. Louis University on the GI bill after his discharge. He worked as a journeyman electrician in commercial and industrial electrical construction for 45 years. Don and Patricia, his wife of 50 years, have five children, ten grandchildren, and two great-grandchildren. They live in O'Fallon, Missouri.

✓ *INCIDENTally — I don't want to jump!* – It was my sixth jump during parachute training at Fort Benning. There were 1,250 of us waiting for an aircraft. During our wait, one aircraft had run off the runway and the 24 men aboard were marched back to board the next available aircraft. I didn't like the looks of this, so I told the officer in charge, "I quit!" knowing full well that this would get me guardhouse time. The officer said, "Go up and you'll be O.K." I asked, "You will kick me out?" He asked, "What will your girlfriend think if you quit?" I said, "I have no girlfriend." He asked, "What would your mother think?" I said, "She would be damn glad that I did." In the end, I did go up, made the jump, and stayed with the paratroopers for two years. – *Walter Holy.*

William Brown

Age 15 – United States Army Air Forces

I was born in Frostproof, Florida, on 16 March 1932, in the middle of the Great Depression. I suppose that I couldn't have come at a more inopportune time. Both of my parents had been people of the soil in

> So I'd probably leave home just as I did in 1947 and never look back.

Georgia, dirt farmers in the eyes of some, as their parents had been before them and their parents' parents. As the Great Depression grew worse and my daddy could no longer find farm land to work, he did what many others in his position did – he moved his family to Florida and looked for work of any kind.

Shortly after my birth, my dad moved us to Haines City, Florida, in the northern part of Polk County. I grew up there and attended school some of the time. For the most part, I had an unremarkable childhood; no worse than most, better than some. I had my share of

scrapes with the law and caused my parents more tears than they deserved. It took a run-in with a juvenile court judge to get my attention and make me realize that I had to get away from life in Haines City.

On the day school let out for the summer in 1947, I hitchhiked over to Lakeland, where the nearest Army recruiting office was, and enlisted in the Army Air Forces. Bear in mind that I had just passed my 15th birthday on 16 March. The recruiting sergeant eyed me very closely, and I don't think he really believed me when I told him that I had turned 17 in March. He gave me some papers and told me to take them home and have my parents sign them and come back with my birth certificate.

I knew my dad was not about to sign the papers for me to go in the service, so I approached my mother first and begged her to intercede for me. She argued at great length with him and he finally signed. My brother Wallace, who was home on furlough from the Navy, altered my birth certificate to make my birth year 1930 instead of 1932. I should point out that in those days we didn't have photostats of birth certificates; we had the actual card-stock form. Wallace very carefully picked out the "2" in 1932 with a needle, took the form to a druggist friend who had a typewriter, and typed a "0" where the "2" had been. I became two years older instantly. To this day, I don't feel the recruiting sergeant believed that I was 17, but he enlisted me anyway, and the rest, as they say, "is history." I was sworn in on 10 June 1947.

Some events in my military career warrant special mention solely for their nostalgic value. I tasted my first beer at a place called the Riverside Café on the San Antonio, Texas, River Walk in August 1947; I was 15½ years old. At that time, I was stationed at what is now Lackland AFB, undergoing basic training. I had my first Mexican food in Denver, Colorado, in the fall of 1947, and also saw my first snow at Lowery AFB.' I saw the Pacific Ocean for the first time when I sailed with a group of GIs from San Francisco to Seattle en route to Fairchild AFB in Spokane, Washington, in early 1948. I took my first airplane ride from McChord AFB, Washington, to Elmendorf AFB, Alaska, in March 1948. I saw downtown Anchorage when only the main street was paved, and a hamburger-steak dinner with mashed potatoes and a roll was 75¢. A glass of iced tea was 10¢ more.

In the summer of 1948, after the Air Force separated from the Army, a group of parachutists from the Airborne School at Fort Benning, Georgia, came to Elmendorf AFB making a pitch to get people to join the Army Airborne. We were sitting in the theater one morning when the troopers came onto the stage. They were wearing heavily starched khaki uniforms with creases so sharp it looked like you could cut a finger on them. And the boots! The boots were polished so shiny you could see your face in them. The troopers all had lots of ribbons on, plus the Combat Infantryman's Badge and, of course, jump wings. A lieutenant was in charge and as soon as he started speaking, I knew in my heart what my next move would be. I took a "short" discharge from the Air Force in September 1948 and re-enlisted in the U. S. Army Airborne. I took parachute and glider training at Fort Benning, Georgia, and made my first jump in January 1949. I was not yet 17 years old; wouldn't be for another two months.

I served 3½ years with the 82nd Airborne Division and two years with the 11th Airborne Division before I was transferred to Germany in April 1954. I was serving in a non-jumping artillery battalion in

Darmstadt, Germany, when I made what would be one of the few defining decisions of my life. I applied for Special Forces duty in the summer of 1954, was accepted, and transferred to Bad Tolz, Germany. While there, I applied for and was accepted for officer candidate school at Fort Benning, Georgia.

Another defining moment came when I "volunteered" for service in Vietnam three times during that ill-fated war. You see, early on I had realized that I was not made from the same mold as Patton, MacArthur, Eisenhower, or any of the great combat leaders in our history. And, if I was to have any semblance of a respectable career, it would take hard work and daring. I am satisfied with the level I reached, even though the price was high in terms of things I had to forego, like watching my children grow up and being separated from them and my wife. But when one is not born with a silver spoon in one's mouth, there are certain trade-offs in life.

My military career lasted 24 years, 7 months, and a few days, during which time I rose from a "slick-sleeve" private to a lieutenant colonel. I retired from the Army on 28 February 1971. Incidentally, I corrected my official records in 1953 to reflect my actual birth year.

Knowing what I know now, would I do anything differently? Probably not. I've always been sort of unconventional in my approach to life, even to the point of almost becoming a rebel. So I'd probably leave home just as I did in 1947 and never look back. But this time around, I would get everything in writing. When I signed up in the Air Forces, I told the recruiter I wanted to be a tail gunner on a B-29 and he told me in so many words, "No sweat, son. There are plenty of openings." The closest I ever got to a B-29 was watching one on the screen in a theater.

Bill Brown was awarded the Bronze Star with oak leaf cluster, the Army Commendation Medal, the Combat Infantryman's Badge, a Master Parachutist Badge, and a number of other service medals. Along the way he continued his education and earned a master's degree. After his retirement from the Army, he worked as a public accountant and taught business subjects in the Orange County, Florida, public school system. He is also active in several veterans organizations. He married Margaret Earlene "Peggy" Williams in December 1950. They have six children and nine grandchildren. Bill and Peggy live in Orlando, Florida.

William J. Burns

Age 14 – United States Army Air Forces

In 1940, my family moved to Snohomish, Washington, from Mitchell, South Dakota. I was born in Rapid City, South Dakota, on 23 August 1932. One Sunday afternoon after my freshman year in high school, I was

> ..., then he looked over at me and asked, "You want to join, too?"

walking down 1st Street in Snohomish when I ran into a friend from school. I asked him, "Where are you going?" He replied, "I'm going to join the Army. I'm meeting the recruiting officer at his home on Beard Street. Walk down there with me." I said O.K., and twenty minutes later we were sitting in the front room of the recruiter's home, with the curtains partly drawn to keep out the hot July sun.

I listened as the officer talked to my friend for a while, then he looked over at me and asked, "You want to join, too?" I didn't think they would take me. I was 5-feet 9-inches tall, weighed 130 pounds, and didn't look older than my 14 years. But out of my mouth came the

words, "Might as well." The recruiter gave us some papers to fill out and have our parents sign for proof of age. My mother didn't want to sign, so I promised to get a GED in the service, and I did. My mother signed, and one week later I was at McChord Field, Washington. An officer told us we would be waiting for two weeks to be sworn in. They were getting a lot of recruits together to make the largest group to enlist at McChord. The event took place on 1 August 1947.

We were put on a train to Lackland Field, San Antonio, Texas, for basic training. They didn't have any khaki uniforms at McChord, so they had issued us winter olive-drab uniforms. The ribbing that we took at Lackland in August because of our uniforms was not funny. Besides, it was very hot!

After 13 weeks of basic training, most of our squadron went to Langley Field, Virginia. We bunked in a barracks and every morning we would fall out so we could volunteer for job openings on the base. I was hoping for a mechanic's job, but there were no openings in that field. I ended up being a firefighter. Since I wanted to see some of the world, the next May I signed up for overseas duty, and I was assigned to Guam, in the Pacific. I went home to Washington on a 30-day leave, then on to San Francisco to catch a ship.

As we went under the Golden Gate Bridge, all the servicemen were on deck watching as the mainland was getting smaller. I started getting the feeling that I might be the first man on the ship to upchuck. We stopped at Hawaii and got off the ship for about six hours. I would not have minded staying there.

When we left Hawaii, I had trouble with my sleeping accommodations. The hole we bunked in on the troopship, USS *Hasse*, was really starting to stink of vomit. I knew that if I kept sleeping there, I would soon contribute to it. When it became dark, I took my blanket, went up to the deck, found a cozy spot on the steel deck, looked at the stars, smelled the fresh air, and slept like a baby. This was against the rules, but by the time we arrived in the Philippines, four of us were sleeping on the steel deck.

The next stop was Guam. I got off the ship with my duffel bag and got in a 6x6 GI truck. About 300 of us were headed for the military base. When we arrived, we got out of the trucks, fell into ranks with our bags, and waited for someone to show us our next home. About an hour later, an officer came over and told us some of us had a change of orders. He said, "When I call your name, grab your bag and get back on the trucks. You will be going to the Philippines."

My prayers came true – they called my name. In two seconds I was on a truck and soon was back on the ship. We arrived in Manila Bay on 23 August 1948, my 16th birthday. While standing on the ship's deck before getting off, I looked down into the water and it was just full of sharks swimming around. Then I looked out across the bay and saw masts and bows of ships that were sunk during World War II sticking out of the water. I thought that the men on those ships had no chance – if the explosion didn't get them, the sharks would.

Our next mode of transportation was a narrow-gauge railroad train that took us to Clark Field. On part of the way to Clark we traveled along a small river. I saw Filipino women and children on the bank of the river pounding clothes with rocks to get them clean. It struck me that it was quite different than at home.

Clark Field was our new home for a couple of years. One of my jobs as a fireman was to check and recharge fire extinguishers around the base. One stop was at the water-purifier station that supplied the base with water. The water came from a small river that came out of the jungle, and it really looked enticing in the hot weather. One day my partner and I left our vehicle at the station and walked up a trail along the river for about a half a mile and found a nice spot and went swimming.

On a couple of different occasions when we went swimming at that spot, a tribe of Negritos would come walking along the train heading to their jungle homes. The men were all five feet or less in height and carried rifles that were bigger than they were. The women carried all the supplies on the top of their heads. They smiled as they passed, and to our amusement, their teeth were all filed to a point, even the kids' teeth.

One time when we were there swimming, I got out of the water and got a cigarette our of my shirt pocket, but I couldn't find a match. The other guy didn't have a light either, so I put the cigarette back into my shirt and went back in the water. About 10 minutes later, a little boy ran out of the jungle with a smoldering stick, put it on a rock, then ran back into the jungle. I went over and got the stick and lit my cigarette. I hollered, "Thank you!" and waved toward the jungle. Those little kids had probably been watching us every time we went swimming.

In early 1950, a buddy and I were heading to the mess hall and noticed a new announcement on a bulletin board. It said:

> Anyone wanting to go TDY with the Navy to Hong
> Kong, sign up below. Only 10 men from the base, one
> from each squadron, will be allowed to go.

The sign-up sheet was already full of names, so we decided that we didn't have a chance and didn't sign. Two days later, the first sergeant called me into his office. He said, "Burns, I think you need to get away for a little while. Do you want to go to Hong Kong?" I replied, "Yes, sir!"

The next day I went to Subic Bay and boarded a Navy ship and headed out to sea. The sleeping accommodations were much better than on the troopship that brought me to the Philippines. We anchored in Hong Kong harbor. The harbor was full of Chinese junks and other types of boats, many of them people lived on. It was just like a city on the water. Needless to say, I had a great time in Hong Kong!

In June 1950, they posted shipping orders on the bulletin board for us to catch the next ship home. This made a lot of guys happy. About a week later, the shipping order to the States came down and was replaced with orders for Korea. A few days later, the first sergeant called me into his office and said, "Clear the barracks today. Tomorrow you will get on a plane to go back to the States. Your 3-year enlistment is up."

Back in the United States, I had another good break when they offered to send me anywhere I wanted to go. The sergeant said that McChord AFB was the closest to home and he supposed that I would like to go there. I told him no, I would like to go to Westover AFB in Springfield, Massachusetts; so that is where my orders were made out for. I had a friend at Clark AFB who was stationed at Westover and liked it there, and I had never been to New England. I thought this might be my only chance to see that part of the country.

I caught a bus in California for Boston, Massachusetts, then on to Springfield. They had allowed me five days, but it took six days of travel time. What I thought would be a short stay at Westover AFB lasted a little longer than I had figured. President Truman gave me a 1-year extension to enjoy the East Coast a little more, so I did. I was discharged in September 1951.

I really enjoyed being in the service. Everywhere I went – Texas, Virginia, Philippine Islands, and Massachusetts – the men I worked and played with were all young like myself. We had fun and just enjoyed life, like being with our families.

Bill Burns worked at a paper mill in Everett, Washington, for 14 years. During that time he and his wife Margaret purchased a café in Snohomish. After leaving the paper mill, he began selling recreational vehicles as well as operating the café. He retired in 1994. Bill has two daughters, a son, twelve grandchildren, and three great-grandchildren. He lives in Snohomish, Washington.

Olen Allison

Age 14 – United States Army

This is my story of underage military service. It's not very exciting compared to some others, but I'll just write it as it happened.

> *...the idea of going into the Army came to mind, so I did just that.*

I was born in Wichita Falls, Texas, on 9 May 1933. I got out of the seventh grade at Avondale, Arizona, in May 1947. That summer I worked as a farm laborer in the area west of Phoenix, Goodyear, Litchfield Park, etc. I got tired of that kind of work fast, and the idea of going into the Army came to mind, so I did just that.

I told the recruiter that I was 17 and got my mother to sign for me. I used my correct name, and no proof of age was required other than my mother's signature. I was sworn into the Army on 4 August 1947 and left immediately for Fort Ord, California, and basic training.

I believe basic training was for 17 weeks. I was in excellent physical condition because of the work I had been doing. A lot of guys thought basic was hard and very demanding, but for me, it seemed easy. In December 1947, I reported to Camp Stoneman, at Pittsburg, California, where I boarded the USS *John Pope* for a trip to Japan.

After arriving in Japan, I was assigned to B Company 19th Infantry Regiment, 24th Infantry Division. I found out that B Company was in Kokora at the division headquarters doing honor-guard duty. Thus began my rifleman duties. I was on guard duty for 24 hours, two hours on post, and four hours off for rest. The days we weren't on guard duty, we trained. I did that for a few months until the company went back to the regiment at Beppu, Japan.

The rest of my tour was spent doing infantry training. At that time, an overseas tour was two years, so in December 1949, I came back to the States and was assigned to the 15th Regiment of the 3rd Infantry Division at Fort Benning, Georgia. I was due for discharge on 4 August 1950, but the Korean War started in June 1950, so my enlistment was extended for one year. By this time, my 3-year enlistment was almost over and I had not been discovered to be underage.

The 3rd Division was sent to Korea via Japan. When we went into Korea, I did what infantry folks do during wartime. I was a corporal at the time. On a very cold day, the lieutenant came up to where I was and said, "Allison, get your gear, you're going home." What I didn't know at the time was that my mother had gone to the Red Cross and to a congressman to get me out of the Army.

I received an honorable discharge from the Army on 6 April 1951, eight months past my original 3-year enlistment. I was 17 years old. On 4 March 1952, I enlisted in the Air Force and served until I retired on 1 July 1970.

Olen Allison earned the Combat Infantryman's Badge while serving in Korea. After retiring from the Air Force, he went to work at McConnell Air Force Base, Wichita, Kansas, as a plumber foreman. After 19 years in that job, he retired on 1 July 1989. Olen and Thelma, his wife of 43 years, have two children and eight grandchildren. They live in Derby, Kansas.

James M. Andre

Age 15 – United States Army

I was born in New Orleans, Louisiana, on 22 May 1932, and grew up in rural communities surrounding the oil refineries of southern Louisiana. As kids during World War II, we boys would play war. We would

> I made the mistake of telling some friends that I was only 16.

dig trenches, carve weapons out of soft pine, and look at the German POWs through the fences of the nearby POW camps outside of our towns. We were all anxious and willing to join the Army, and when the war ended in 1945, we were disappointed that we missed it. We all wore the soldier and sailor suits that our parents bought for us at Sears and Roebuck.

In early spring of 1947, five of us went to a recruiting station in New Orleans to join up. We were all underage. I was 14 and the smallest of the five. I told the sergeant that I was 17, but I'm sure he didn't believe me. I was told to return home and get my parents' permission in writing.

I tried to join again just before my 15th birthday, but I was too light and was told to go home and eat bananas and drink milk shakes until I weighed 105 pounds. It was two and a half months later, on 4 August 1947, that I was sworn in. I was sent by truck to Camp Shelby, outside of Hattisburg, Mississippi, for processing, then on to Fort Benning, Georgia. I was told that I was to be a paratrooper. I was delighted until I heard the stories about what happened to paratroopers during the Normandy landings, then I was scared.

I had just started paratrooper training when, during barracks inspection, a sergeant flipped a coin on my bed and told me to strip it and make it over. I made the mistake of asking what was wrong with the way I made it. I think he screamed at me for an hour or so. I've never sassed anyone since then!

A short time later, a lieutenant came through looking for volunteers to transfer to the Army Air Forces, since it soon was to be made into a separate service. I jumped at that opportunity, and within days I was sent to Keesler Field, Mississippi, and then to Lackland Field in San Antonio, Texas, for basic training. While in basic training the Army Air Forces became the U. S. Air Force and the prefix of my serial number was changed from "RA" to "AF."

I was looking forward to being a pilot like everyone else going into the new Air Force, but it was out of the question for me because I had only completed the eighth grade. A chaplain told me to take a test called the GED, which I did in late 1947 and promptly forgot about. However, it was to be the turning point of my life.

After completing basic training in San Antonio in December 1947, I was sent by troop train to Chanute Field, Illinois. That was the first time I had ever seen snow. After two months at Chanute Field awaiting assignment, I was again sent by troop train to Selfridge Field, Michigan. This was near the last of the troop trains to be used, but I remember it well because the MPs would not let us get off at stops or even leave the car to which we were assigned.

I really loved the service and progressed through the ranks. I made buck sergeant while I was only 16, but I made the mistake of telling some friends that I was only 16. That's how the Air Force found out that I was underage. The base commander called me into his office and said that if I wanted to get out I could go home that night, but if I wanted to stay in, I could, and the matter would be dropped. Needless to say, I jumped at the chance to stay, and vowed to keep my mouth shut about my age. I stayed in the Air Force for 12 years, the last seven in the active reserves. I left the Air Force as a master sergeant in 1959.

In 1950, at the age of 17, I met and married a 17-year-old girl named Doris. We have been married for 51 years now. That year I tried civilian life for a few months, only to be recalled to active duty for the Korean conflict, as it was called, on April Fools' Day, 1951.

In 1954, while in the active reserves, I tried to get into college with my GED. I fully intended to return to active duty after graduating. Because I had not attended high school, I was allowed in as a non-matriculated trial student on the basis of my GED. After completing college and medical school, I rejoined the service, but this time with three college degrees, thanks to that GED, the GI Bill, a very supportive wife, and three children. Since public health was my interest, I chose the U. S. Public Health Service (USPHS), a uniformed service. I was commissioned a lieutenant in 1964.

While on active duty as a USPHS physician, I was first assigned to the USPHS Hospital in Norfolk, Virginia, for my internship. I was selected by the National Institute of Mental health as one of ten special fellows from across the nation for residency training in psychiatry and neurology. I was the only one selected from the uniformed services that year.

After training for three years, I ask for and was assigned to the Indian Health Service (IHS). I was fortunate to receive accelerated meritorious promotions from lieutenant to lieutenant commander in 1969 and lastly to captain in 1973 (equivalent to an Air Force colonel).

In 1974, I was honored to be made the first senior clinician for alcoholism and substance abuse of the Indian Health Service. I provided training, education, and consultation to all Native-American tribes and to physicians, nurses, and other health personnel who were serving the nation's American-Indian clinics and communities. While in this position, I authored about 40 medical papers and a training manual for physicians for the IHS and the National Institutes of Health.

After retiring from the Public Health Service in 1980, I served as an evaluator and consultant for the Joint Commission on Accreditation of Health Care Organizations for 12 years, evaluating some 500 hospitals in the 50 states.

Although my parents were very reluctant to sign a paper falsifying my age to allow me to enlist in the Army in 1947, they later came to be pleased that they did. For me, going into the service as a kid was the best move I ever made. It helped me to grow up and focus on some real goals. I will be forever grateful to the service and all those who helped guide me in those early years, including that paratrooper sergeant who screamed at me. I cherish his memory as one of the best teachers I ever had.

Jim Andre is somewhat modest about his educational achievements. His wife Doris provided a bit more information. The admissions counselor at the university laughed when Jim wanted to take pre-med courses when he didn't know that H_2O was the symbol for water.

However, he let Jim enroll as a trial student, figuring that would be the end of it. Some 15 credits later, Jim was allowed to matriculate and went on to major in chemistry and English. He graduated from Wayne State University, Detroit, Michigan, with a bachelor's degree, and four years later graduated from Wayne State College of Medicine, third in a class of 125 students. He won eight scholarships for scholastic excellence as a medical student. He was one of five students who received a Doctor of Medicine with Distinction. Jim also received his specialty training and a Master of Public Health degree from the University of Michigan at Ann Arbor. Jim and Doris Andre live in Albuquerque, New Mexico.

✔ *INCIDENTally* — *A set-up!* – After arriving in Korea in August 1951, I was assigned to the 1st Battalion, 38th Infantry Regiment, 2nd Infantry Division. While waiting for assignment to a company, I overheard a couple of old-timers in the chow line say that Company C did a lot of fighting but had few casualties. That appealed to me, so the next morning when we were all asked if we had a preference for a company to be assigned to, I asked for Company C. When I reported to Company C, I found out that they were in bad need of replacements because they had suffered serious casualties. It then dawned on me – the chow-line conversation had been a set-up to get volunteers for the company! – *Wilbur G. Corbitt.*

496

James T. "Tom" Flannery
Age 15 – United States Army

I was born in Tulare, California, on 18 July 1932, during the Great Depression. We moved around a lot in those days. I remember when I was about 5 years old, we were living near the Sacramento River. I left

> ... and my mother said, "So, that's where you have been. Surprise!"

and went to the movies one day without telling anyone where I was going. It was a triple feature about seven Texas Rangers who were ambushed. An Indian named Tonto showed up and found one of the Rangers still alive. This was the beginning of the Lone Ranger series. When I returned home from the movie, I found the authorities dragging the river for me. They thought that I had drowned. Needless to say, I was in deep trouble.

We also lived on Sugar Loaf Mountain in Poteau, Oklahoma, for a time. I started school there and had to ride a mule down the mountain, put it in a pasture, and catch a school bus. I remember being scared because my brother kept telling me to watch out for bears.

We moved back to Lindsay, California, in about 1938. I continued school in Lindsay, but soon lost interest. I became bored and just wanted to get out of there. Just what I was going to do wasn't clear until one day in June 1947. My cousin and I were in Tulare, California, and we noticed a U. S. Army recruiting office. We decided to go in and talk with the recruiter.

One of the first things he asked us was how old we were. I told him I would be 17 on 18 July. My cousin told him that he was already 17. The recruiter then gave us a short aptitude test. He handed us forms to be filled out by our parents, confirming our age. My cousin signed mine and I signed his.

However, we soon had second thoughts about the whole idea, thinking that we might get into trouble. By August, we decided to go ahead and join up. We went back to the recruiter's office and he sent us to Fresno, California, by bus for physicals and to be sworn in, if accepted. At some time during that process, I was told I needed to gain a few pounds because I weighed only 116 pounds. Someone suggested that I should eat as many bananas as I possibly could, which I did, and consequently reached the desired weight of 118 pounds.

During the physical, as we were lined up to go from one room to the next, with my cousin in front of me, some officer looked at my cousin very sternly and said, "You are not 17, are you?" My cousin replied, "No, sir." The officer took him aside and I finished my physical and was sworn in with 15 other men. This was 19 August 1947. We were then sent to Fort Ord, California, for basic training.

I was assigned to the 3rd Squad, 3rd Platoon, F Company, 4th Infantry, Division for basic. On the first day that we were in formation, the unit commander made an announcement. He said, "I know that a number of you are underage. Fall out now, line up in front of the orderly room, and you will be processed out today. No charges will be brought against you." I was too scared to fall out! We had started with 240 men. After the announcement, we wound up with 180. The training lasted for 13 weeks.

Early in the training there was another announcement. There was going to be a GI party! I was really excited and was looking forward to the food and drinks. You can imagine my surprise when all that was there was scrub brushes, buckets, and mops. The sergeant announced, "Welcome to the Army!"

After basic training, I went home on leave, now weighing 168 pounds. I walked into the house wearing my uniform and my mother said, "So, that's where you have been. Surprise!"

I reported to Camp Stoneman, California, after my leave. I was put on orders to the Far East. Meanwhile, someone in the barracks came down with the mumps, so we were quarantined for 21 days. My orders were changed and I was sent to the Pine Bluff Arsenal, Arkansas, and assigned to the 12th Chemical Maintenance Company. From there I went to Germany.

I spent 14 years in Germany, with intermittent Stateside duty. I was stationed in Augsburg, Mainz, Nuernberg, Marnheim, Baumholder, Wiesbaden, Mannheim, Fuerth, Grafenwoehr, Wuerzburg, and as an instructor at the chemical section of the Combined Arms School at Vilseck.

My Stateside assignments included Fort Ord, California, with the 50th Chemical Service Platoon. We participated in Operation Teapot, nuclear tests at Camp Desert Rock, Nevada (also called Camp Mercury). We were the first units into the areas after the blast. We measured and marked radiation contamination levels. I was over-exposed to gamma radiation while there.

Another Stateside assignment was Fort Dix, New Jersey. From there I was sent to Fort Drum, New York, to train National Guard and Reserve units. I was also stationed at the Chemical School at Fort McClellan, Alabama.

Other overseas duties were tours in Korea and Vietnam. I retired from the Army in December 1971 after 24 years of service. I loved the Army, and if they would let me, I would enlist again in a heartbeat!

Tom Flannery earned two Army Commendation medals, a number of service medals, and several Certificates of Achievement during his 24 years of service. After his retirement from the Army, he went to work for the American Building Maintenance Company. He began as a foreman, then became a supervisor, and finally, sales manager. He had never tried selling anything before, but after the second year, he was recognized as the company's top salesman in the United States and Canada. Tom met his wife Margarete in Nuernberg, Germany. They have two daughters, a son, four grandchildren, and three great-grandchildren. Tom and Margarete live in Des Moines, Washington.

Henry Martinez

Age 16 – United States Army

I was born in La Coste, Texas, on 19 May 1931, the baby of a family of eight. My family moved to Houston, Texas, when I was 1 year old. While I was growing up I wanted to do everything my brothers did,

> *I learned so much, and I had such unbelievable experiences.*

but they always told me I was too young. My world changed on 7 December 1941, when Pearl Harbor was bombed and we were at war. I was only 10 years old, but I began to notice that our neighborhood was changing. My oldest brother, some cousins, my brother-in-law, and their friends were going off to war. Eventually, all three brothers served in the Army.

My brothers returned after the war, but I had made up my mind to enlist. I went to the Army recruiting office before my 16th birthday and was told to come back in two years. In September 1947, I decided to try again. I was 16 and a friend was 15. We wanted to enlist in the

Army Air Forces, but the recruiting sergeant told us the Air Force had split from the Army. He looked at us rather strangely, but told us to go ahead and take the written test. We passed the test and he gave us some forms for our parents to sign. We were never asked for our birth certificates.

My mother refused to sign the papers. I did some tall talking and finally my father agreed to sign. After about two hours of discussion, my mother finally agreed to sign. My friend's parents also wouldn't sign at first, but finally did. That afternoon, 9 September 1947, we went back to the recruiting office with the signed forms. We were sworn in and the sergeant exclaimed, "You are now in the Army!"

I had never been out of Texas and had only left Houston to go to San Antonio to visit relatives, but now I was going to California! We arrived at Fort Ord, California, in the early morning. During basic training the drill sergeant was very hard on me, but I didn't know why until much later.

We shipped out from San Francisco and arrived at Inchon, Korea, in February 1948. The weather was cold and miserable. We worked at the Inchon docks, loading supply ships. When I pulled guard duty there, I would watch the tide come in and go out. For miles, all you could see was mud, mud, and more mud. Then the tide would come back.

By April, I had had enough of that miserable country. I was still 16, so I decided to write my mother and see if somehow she could get me out of that miserable place. I had never been so cold, and we really didn't have proper clothes. While I was sitting there thinking and writing my letter, my sergeant came in and said that they were forming baseball teams and I was going to be a pitcher. I looked down at my letter and decided to tear it up. I thought to myself, "You got yourself into this; don't ask your mother to get you out." That was the last time I thought about trying to get out.

We stayed in Korea until January 1949 when we received orders to Japan, where I was assigned to the 8th Army. What a beautiful country! It was heaven to us. We formed baseball teams and competed with the 24th and 25th Infantry Divisions, and others. We had a great time while it lasted. We just didn't know what the future held.

I was 19 in May 1950 and my sergeant told me that I had orders to go home, although I wouldn't be discharged until September. On 25 June 1950, everything changed. A bunch of us GIs were on pass, sitting around on a Sunday morning, when we heard on the radio that North Korea had attacked South Korea, and that all GIs should report back to their company. My sergeant did not know what to do with me. I was still scheduled to go home. I decided to go with my buddies, although they told me I was crazy and didn't know what I was doing. We were in Korea on 29 June 1950, four days after the war started.

After a month and a half, I had seen more than enough combat. I was scared, really scared. I saw the miseries of war that summer, plus the weather was 105 to 115 degrees in the shade. It was very hot and very wet.

In August 1950, my company commander told me I was going home and would be discharged within a month. When the time came, I reported to the port at Pusan where hundreds of GIs were lining up to go back to the States. Soon a whistle sounded and the captain of the ship announced, "Now hear this, now hear this: Mr. Harry Truman, the President of the United States, has just given you one more year, a 1-year extension. Please report to your units." When I reported back to my company commander, he said, "I just can't seem to get rid of you!"

After the Marines landed at Inchon in September, we moved north rapidly. One late afternoon in mid-October, we arrived at Kimpo Airport in a convoy of trucks. Our sergeant told us we would be getting a hot meal at the Kimpo mess hall. When we entered the mess hall, the sergeant and two officers came to me and asked if I spoke Spanish. I said I did, and they described a Korean serving at the chow line. They said that if he spoke Spanish to me, to give him false information. When I came face-to-face with the Korean, he asked me in Spanish if I spoke Spanish, and I said that I did. He then proceeded to ask in Spanish where we were going. I knew the area quite well because I had been stationed at Inchon in 1948, so I told him that our convoy was going south (instead of north) to the Port of Inchon with supplies. He asked why we were not going north, and I told him that we were just following orders.

As I walked away and was ready to sit down to eat, the officers looked at me and I nodded my head in a "yes" motion. Before I had even set my tray down, the sergeant told me to step outside. I went outside to where our officers, the ROK (Republic of Korea) MPs and some ROK officers were huddled. They wanted me to identify the Korean to make sure that he was the one who asked me where we were going. He was the same guy, but the ROK MPs had beaten him to a pulp. The Korean officer told me that he was a very dangerous spy.

The next day we continued north. The rumors were that we were not to cross the 38th Parallel. Since I knew the area quite well, I asked my sergeant why we were crossing the 38th Parallel. He responded, "Orders are orders!"

We were soon in Pyongyang, the capital of North Korea. General McArthur said that we would be going home by Christmas, but the day after Thanksgiving, the Chinese intervened. By now, the weather was miserably cold, 20 to 40 degrees below zero. The weather killed many of our men as well as Chinese. You could see frozen men everywhere. We withdrew to the port at Chinnamp, southwest of Pyongyang, and boarded a Navy ship. Ships were bombarding the port and aircraft were bombing the area. Everything was blown up. We later returned to Pusan where our headquarters were.

One night in Pusan I went to a club. I heard a sergeant say, "Martinez, don't you remember who I am?" I looked at the sergeant and said, "No, I have seen so many sergeants in the last few months I don't know who is who."

He then said, "I'll give you one guess. How about 1947 in Fort Ord, California?"

I replied, "You are the one who gave me basic training. Why did you pick on me so much?"

"First," he asked, "were you too young to be in the service in 1947?" I told him that I was 16.

"Well," he said, "that's the reason you got the extra detail, the extra march and everything, but it paid off didn't it?" I asked him what he meant.

"You're still alive." he said.

"Well, sarge," I said, "you trained me very well and maybe that's why I'm still alive. But the real reason I'm still alive is that God didn't want me yet, but thank you, sarge, for training me, thank you very much."

That sergeant had been a Ranger during World War II. He really put me through hell in basic training.

I was sent home in June 1951 and was discharged at Fort Bliss, Texas, on 1 August 1951 at the age of 20. I don't regret going into the Army so young. I learned so much, and I had such unbelievable experiences.

Henry Martinez earned a number of service medals including two Presidential Unit Citations during his service in Korea. When he returned to Texas he worked in the glass industry. He has been very active with veterans' organizations and is past commander of the American Legion Post 416 in Houston, Texas. He is presently Color Guard Commander of the Texas Lone Star Chapter of the Korean War Veterans Association in Houston. Henry and Eva, his wife of 48 years, have two daughters, one son, and eight grandchildren. They live in Houston, Texas.

Franklin P. Tilghman

Age 16 – United States Army

I was born on a farm near Hughes, Arkansas, on 26 January 1931. Dad was always looking for a better job, so our family would frequently move from one farm to another.

> ..., a Chinese mortar shell seriously wounded me, resulting in the loss of both legs above the knee.

I failed several grades in school by 1947, due to the fact that I had to stay home and work on the farm much of the time. When I was 16, I decided to join the Army. Although I was legally underage, my mother, at my insistence, signed a paper given me by an Army recruiter which stated that I was 17 years old and had her consent to join the Army.

I left home with $1.65 in my pocket, dressed in a suit of clothes one size too large. I looked like a "sad sack." When I arrived in Little Rock, Arkansas, the MPs had no difficulty in recognizing me as a new recruit. They drove me to the YMCA where I spent the night. The next day, 17 September 1947, I was sworn into the Army. At 4 p.m., I was on a train bound for basic training at Ft. Jackson, South Carolina.

When it came time for the evening meal, the porter announced that dinner was being served in the dining car. I was really hungry from all the day's excitement, but when I looked at the menu, the prices were very high. My Army meal ticket had the words, "VALID FOR $1.00 ONLY," but I still had the $1.65 that I had left home with.

I was worried. If I took the minimum order, it would still cost over $1. Then I overheard some of the recruits at another table give their order. I heard one say, "I'll take the steak, ah...ah the baked potato, tossed salad, apple pie, and...ah...ah... and ice cream." As the waiter picked up his menu and started to walk away, the recruit yelled, "And add a good cigar to that order, please!" When the waiter came to my table I'm sure he could detect my concern over the prices. He said, "Don't worry, your meal ticket will cover anything on the menu." With a sigh of relief, I replied, "I'll have the same thing that the other person ordered, but add two Baby Ruth candy bars and a pack of Camel cigarettes." Next came Fort Jackson, and basic training.

In early 1948, I was sent to Korea where I was assigned to Company F, 31st Infantry Regiment, 7th Infantry Division. Our company was located on the east coast of Korea in an isolated area near the town of Kangnung. About once a week, a C-3 cargo plane would land on a nearby dirt landing field and bring mail. About once a month, a doctor would be on board. Our unit guarded the 38th Parallel (the line between the Russians and us). In October, the CO made me the company carpenter. With a Korean assistant, we constructed packing crates for all of our equipment and weapons.

In November 1948, the 7th Division moved to the island of Hokkaido, Japan. Our company replaced a unit of the 11th Airborne at Camp Haugen, near the city of Sapporo. Within a few days of our arrival, the CO appointed me the company arms artificer and supply clerk.

I was sent back to the States in 1950 after two years and two days of overseas duty. My new assignment was Company C, 12th Armored Infantry Battalion, 2nd Armored Division, Fort Hood, Texas. When the Korean War started in June, our unit began training recruits and reservists. In August, I was promoted to sergeant. My enlistment was up in September, but a presidential decree added a year to all enlistments. To insure that I would remain a true volunteer, I re-enlisted for four years.

In January 1951, I was transferred to Camp Chaffee, Arkansas. My duties were as a platoon sergeant, training new recruits. About two months later, I was transferred to Combat Command Headquarters as a first-aid instructor, although I taught and assisted in other subjects. In early 1952, I was ordered to combat duty in Korea.

I was assigned as platoon sergeant of the 3rd Platoon, Company G, 32nd Infantry Regiment, 7th Infantry Division. In October 1952, my platoon was in position opposite Hill 598 (Triangle Hill). On 9 October I was slightly wounded during a night attack on Hill 404, a part of the Triangle Complex. In mid-October, elements of the 31st Regiment attacked Triangle Hill. On 22 October, our unit replaced the battle-weary soldiers on that hill. On that day and night, my platoon had about seven casualties from Chinese artillery and mortar fire.

On the afternoon of 23 October 1952, while preparing for an attack on a nearby hill, a Chinese mortar shell seriously wounded me, resulting in the loss of both legs above the knee. After over eight months of hospitalization, I was retired from the Army as a sergeant first class (E6), after 5 years, 8 months, and 14 days of military service. I was 4 months and 5 days past my 22nd birthday.

Frank Tilghman was awarded the Bronze Star for his actions on Hill 598, although the award wasn't presented to him until 14 December 1999, 47 years later. He also earned the Combat Infantryman's Badge and received two Purple Hearts for wounds received in action. In 1951, he took the GED test and obtained a high school diploma. In 1954, he enrolled at Austin College, in Sherman, Texas, where he received a B.S. in 1958. In 1971, he received an M.S. in rehabilitation counseling from Arkansas State University. Subsequently, he worked in community services as a counselor and job developer. Frank and his wife Edna have two daughters, four grandsons and one great-granddaughter. They live in West Helena, Arkansas.

Milton D. Grismore

Age 15 – Colorado National Guard
Age 15 – United States Army

According to family records, I was born on
5 February 1932, during a ground blizzard on
an eastern Colorado hardscrabble farm. It
was during the Depression, and like everyone
else, my family lived as we could and where

> We came face-to-face
> with a tiger and stood
> stunned until it left.

we could. In 1936 we moved to Denver and things improved for us.
I never knew that we were poor. We had more than most of our
neighbors. We had plenty to eat, a big house, and I had a bike.

In 1942 we moved to the inner city so my dad could walk to work.
We lived in a multi-ethnic neighborhood where a kid had to be tough
to survive. I survived! I quit school and ran away from home, going
from job to job when my true age was discovered. I joined the National
Guard, then transferred to the regular Army on 13 October 1947. I
was 15 years old, but my age was never questioned. There were at
least six underage boys in my basic training company at Fort Ord,
California. Five of the six took minority discharges. I graduated from
basic as a private first class. After a leave, I shipped out to Asia. My
first port of call was Shanghai, China, then Inchon, Korea, where I was
assigned to the 6th Infantry Division.

The year 1948 was a wake-up year for me. I was given an Article
104 for an offense which I was not guilty of. I was transferred from
Pusan to Kwangju where I got into real trouble and spent 56 days in
the stockade. I was sent to Taegu where, in November, we were
attacked by Korean Army insurgents whom we captured and turned
over to loyal Korean troops. We listened as the bad guys were
machine-gunned. My first taste of live, incoming rounds was when the
bad guys sprayed our compound with .50-caliber machine-gun fire.

We moved to Pusan and ran into more trouble. The Korean
Nationalist hot-heads were beating and stripping our troops while they
were on pass. Another kid and I went into Pusan where we were
accosted by a gang of the young insurgents. My buddy was clobbered
in the head with a club and went down. I was attacked by a youth

with a sickle who swung at my neck. I had a knife which I drew, crouched, and planted into his belly. This dispersed our antagonists. I took my companion to the Railway Transportation Office from where he was taken to an emergency room. The MPs brought the Korean to the emergency room and I was tagged. The next morning my CO gave me an Article 104, restricting me to the post. We shipped out for Japan two days later.

We arrived in Fukuoka, Japan, on 28 December 1948 and were transported to Camp Hakata for reassignment. I requested and was granted assignment to the 52nd Field Artillery Battalion. Occupation duty in Japan was a dream world for a 16-year-old kid.

I returned to the States in March 1950 and was assigned to the 15th Field Artillery Battalion, 2nd Infantry Division at Fort Lewis, Washington. Life was good until the North Koreans invaded South Korea. By presidential order, my enlistment was extended for a year and I shipped back to Korea. We landed at Pusan near the last of July and moved right up on the line on the Naktong River. I boasted to the section troops that I knew this country and the people. I shouldn't have done that, because within 24 hours, I was assigned to a reconnaissance party and was up on the line the next morning. One time while I was driving a jeep, I was chased by a T-34 tank.

After the Inchon landing, the North Koreans bugged out into the mountains and to the north. We crossed the Naktong River, went into firing position, and immediately came under incoming enemy artillery fire. I was in one of two parties that were sent up on nearby peaks to triangulate the enemy fire. We were successful and the enemy artillery was destroyed.

The only enemy we saw on those peaks were dead, smelly, well-chewed-up North Korean kids. Tigers were living off the remains. We came face-to-face with a tiger and stood stunned until it left. What a night we spent on that mountain!

We convoyed to Seoul, thence to P'yongyang where we bivouacked for a few days. My sidekick and I liberated a Korean bullock from the owner, but we never did get a bite of it. My recon party moved to Kunu-ri at 0300 the next morning.

The day after Thanksgiving, we brought in infantry stragglers dressed only in their underwear. They told of Chinese infiltrating their unit and bayoneting the troops as they slept. I was assigned to a battery of the 503rd Field Artillery to work as a fire-direction controller. I remember fire missions, noise, and action, but all else is blacked out of my memory. I remember rejoining my battery five days later. We, along with the 23rd Infantry Regiment, rather than go through Kunu-ri Pass, boarded our vehicles and went north, then east, then south towards P'yongyang. We stopped for a rest in the early morning and were harassed by a Chinese recon plane that dropped grenades on us but caused no damage. We went through P'yongyang and Seoul, crossed the Han River, and went into bivouac. While there, I met a cousin who was passing through the town with his company.

In January, we moved into Wonju. It was cold! In February, we moved into Heonsong, in support of the South Koreans. Several Chinese field armies opposed us. At about 0200 on 12 February 1951, the Chinese infiltrated all artillery units. They entered our tents in silence, and using bayonets, quietly wreaked havoc. My tent mate and I escaped to a ditch where we sniped at the Chinese until mortar rounds chased us out. We were almost out of the area when we found some howitzers set up, but all personnel were wounded. We fired those guns, line of sight, until dark. Some of us were sent to get help. Under fire all the way, we made it to the river. While crossing, still under fire, I slipped on the icy rocks and went down. I got up and ran, finally reaching the main supply route where I intercepted a convoy and was taken to a town. I was treated at the aid station and later evacuated to Japan. Out of my battalion, there were twelve enlisted men, one officer, and six howitzers present for duty.

I returned to duty in Korea in April 1951. I was in the Chorwon Valley, the Iron Triangle, and hills later known as Heartbreak and Porkchop. I spent my last six weeks in Korea as a staff sergeant, assigned to teach combat artillery fire to new second lieutenants. Believe me, no other duty was as tough or more rewarding. I rotated home in September of 1951 and assigned to Fort Lewis for discharge. I re-enlisted and served tours in Korea, Japan, Germany, and, of course, Vietnam, for a total of about 10 years overseas. I retired after more than 21 years in the Army.

Milton Grismore was awarded the Bronze Star with "V" for valor for his service in Korea. He also received a number of other medals for service in Vietnam. After retiring from the Army, he earned an LPN license and worked in physical-rehabilitation nursing for a time. He earned a B.A. in anthropology and later worked for the U. S. Postal Service, earning a number of awards for his work. Milt and his wife Janean have six children, fourteen grandchildren, and one great-grandchild. They live in Shoreline, Washington.

✔ *INCIDENTally* — **The regulations say...!** – Late in the afternoon of 21 February 1945, the 28th Marines penetrated the Japanese defenses at the base of Mount Suribachi, Iwo Jima. As it was turning dark, I moved my company around to the east side of the volcano, taking up a defensive position in the rocks near the shoreline. In our haste and in the darkness, we had by-passed some enemy positions, and in the morning found ourselves cut off from our battalion. I was unable to reach the battalion by radio. This did not present a problem until some Navy F6F fighters, armed with 100-pound bombs, mistook us for Japanese and started making bombing runs on our position. We had red flares to be shot from rifle grenade-launchers for just such an emergency. Unfortunately, we had suffered 30% casualties, and though we had the flares and the launchers, no one had bothered to obtain the necessary cartridges from the casualties who were first carrying the launchers. Taking the only course of action left open, I switched to the regimental commander's frequency on my radio and the conversation went something like this:

"Red Wing Six, this is Bayonet Easy Six, over.

Bayonet Easy Six, this is Red Wing Six, over.

Red Wing Six, friendly planes are bombing our position, over.

Bayonet Easy Six, say again your message, over.

Red Wing Six, friendly planes are bombing the hell out of us, over."

At this time there was silence, and I visualized the radioman running to someone on the staff with my message. Shortly, the regimental radioman came back on the air with: "Bayonet Easy Six, you are not authorized to come up on this frequency, out!"

Fortunately, my battalion commander was nearby and asked the radioman about the call and then saw to it that the Navy planes changed their target. – *Dave E. Severance.*

William G. Ignatz
Age 15 – United States Army

I was born in West Homestead, Pennsylvania, on 26 December 1931. I tried to join the Army at age 13, and again at age 14, but was not successful either time. At age 15, I altered my baptismal papers to become the right age and went to Pittsburgh, Pennsylvania,

> I soon learned that a Partisan is one who is inserted behind enemy lines.

to join the Army. This time I was successful and was sworn in on 6 November 1947.

I took basic training at Fort Ord, California. In February or March 1948, I was sent to Japan and assigned to the 11th Airborne Division's 187th Glider Infantry, which, after several name changes, became the 187th Airborne Regimental Combat Team (ARCT). We were stationed at Camp Crawford in Northern Japan, near the city of Sapporo.

I graduated from glider and parachute school in Yamoto, Japan. I parachuted into North Korea in October 1950 as a pathfinder with the 187th ARCT. I was wounded at Wonju on 14 February 1951 while

serving as a rifleman and radio operator with K Company. I returned to the States, and in 1952 I was assigned to 511 Parachute Infantry at Ft. Campbell, Kentucky.

In 1953, along with 99 other paratroopers, I volunteered to go back to Korea to rejoin the 187th ARCT. When we got to Japan, the other 99 were sent on to Korea, and I was left behind. In a few days, I was asked if I would like to be a Partisan. I wasn't sure what the word meant, so I volunteered. A few days later, I was taken into a black room with "secret" marked on the walls. I soon learned that a Partisan is one who is inserted behind enemy lines.

I was questioned about what I knew about the Partisan Forces in North Korea. Of course, I knew nothing. I was told that my skills and knowledge made me eligible to become one. I agreed. The Partisan

Forces were the forerunners of today's Special Forces and were kept secret until declassified in 1995.

After a couple of plane rides, a two-day briefing, and a boat trip, I was on the North Korean island of Suwi-do, where I became an operational Partisan. My code name was "Donkey 13." My position was overrun on 21 July 1953, six days before the war ended on 27 July 1953. My team leader, an American officer, was killed in action. Two North Korean Partisans and I retrieved his body. I placed it on a English frigate that had supported us with naval gunfire.

Shortly after the war was over, I was on my way back to the 187th ARCT. We rotated back to Ft. Campbell, Kentucky, where we changed designations again and became the 327th Regiment of the 101st Airborne Division. I became an instructor in the jumpmaster school at Ft. Campbell. At the time, I was a sergeant first class.

When Vietnam came along, I volunteered and was sent to the 1st Special Forces. I was an operations sergeant. My tour of duty was from 1963 to 1965.

I retired from the Army as a master sergeant in 1968 after 20 years of service.

On 27 July 2001, the 48th anniversary of the ending of the Korean War, I received the Honor Medal from the Korean War Commemorative Community, Federation of War Veterans, 8240th Army Units, Partisan Forces, Korea. This came as a total surprise to me.

Bill Ignatz was awarded the Purple Heart for his wounds received in Korea and the Cross of Gallantry for his service in Vietnam. He earned two Combat Infantryman's Badges, one for Korea and one for Vietnam, and received the Army Commendation Medal for valor. He earned a Master Parachutist Badge, the Pathfinder Torch, and a number of other service medals. He was an instructor pilot at Fort Rucker, Alabama, in 1969-71, and flew the U. S. mail in 1972-73. He was the first full-time district pilot hired by the Alabama State Forestry Commission with the primary mission of fire detection, locating southern-pine beetle infestations, and marijuana detection and eradication. Currently, he owns and operates the Northport Detective Agency in Northport, Alabama, and is the commander of the Military Order of the Purple Heart, Chapter 22-11. Bill and his wife Jean have five children and two granddaughters and one grandson. They live in Northport, Alabama.

Robert D. Burgess

Age 15 – Illinois National Guard

The year was 1946, I was 14 years old, and I had just completed my sophomore year in high school. I could hardly wait for my 15th birthday. This was the time when many soldiers and sailors were getting their

> I am very proud of all my family who served in the military.

discharges after serving in World War II. My family was very much involved in that war. My father and several uncles served in the Army, Navy, and Seabees. My two grandfathers served in the military, one in World War I and the other in the Spanish-American War. My great-grandfather was a Civil War veteran and is buried in the Soldiers Cemetery at Fort Leavenworth, Kansas. I am very proud of all my family who served in the military.

The big day arrived. I was 15 years old. I was torn between wanting to stay home and make some money and wanting to be a soldier. That summer, I watched my older brother Bill join the Illinois

National Guard. He came home with a new uniform, new high-top boots, hat, shiny belt buckle, and brass buttons on his uniform. That was what I wanted.

I thought it over, and without telling my parents, the next day I went to the National Guard Armory in Urbana, Illinois. I told them I was 17 and wanted to join the Guard. Much to my surprise, I was accepted. They told me I had to sign up for three years, and that was all right with me. I was enrolled in Company B, 106th

Mechanized Cavalry, Illinois National Guard, on 13 November 1947. I was just 15, having been born on 24 July 1932 at Champaign, Illinois.

That summer, our unit was sent to Camp Ellis, Illinois, for two weeks' training. It was there that I learned how to shoot guns and drive tanks and jeeps.

I was 16 the next summer. In full army dress, we loaded up in trucks and jeeps for a caravan trip to Camp McCoy, Wisconsin. I was so proud of this special time. On 10 February 1949, our unit was redesignated Company B, 106th Heavy Tank Battalion.

In June 1950, the Korean War started. I was planning to get married on my 18th birthday, 24 July 1950, and I knew that I would need to go to summer camp at Camp McCoy shortly after the wedding. During the last days at camp, I was in a tank accident and ended up in the base hospital. When I was released from the hospital and returned home, our unit had been mobilized and was going to Korea. Because of the injury to my back, I was discharged on 12 November 1950 and did not go to Korea with my buddies.

I am proud that I served in the military and I'm proud to be an American.

Robert Burgess worked for the Kroger Food Company for 12 years, then became the national sales manager for the HRI (hotel, restaurant, institution) Division of Cudahy Foods. His last position prior to retirement was as a meat-product manager for Lady Baltimore Foods. Robert and Beverly, his wife of 52 years, have two daughters, seven grandchildren, and two great-grandchildren. They live in Bradenton, Florida.

Angelo Stamelos, Jr.

Age 13 – Missouri National Guard
Age 15 – United States Army

I was born in Saint Louis, Missouri, on 20 August 1933. In 1939, when my mom and dad divorced, I, along with my brother and sister, lived with my dad, with side trips to stay with my grandmother.

So today, according to the record, I was baptized three years before I was born!

I graduated from grade school, but I quit school after one year of high school and went to work.

While attending high school, I joined the 138th Infantry of the Missouri National Guard, enlisting on 12 December 1947. I was 13 at the time, but had no trouble enlisting as they did not require proof of birth. I served for one year and eight months before asking for a transfer to the regular Army.

To transfer to the Army, I had to have some proof of my age. I went to the church where I was baptized and convinced the priest that a mistake had been made and the record should read "1930" instead of "1933." He said, "No problem," and changed the date. Years later, when I tried to get the date changed back, I was told that it couldn't be done. So today, according to the record, I was baptized three years before I was born!

I entered the regular Army on 20 July 1949 at the age of 15. I was sent to Fort Chaffee, Arkansas, for three months of basic training. I was then sent to Battery B of the 67th Antiaircraft Gun Battalion at Fort Bliss, Texas. I had only enlisted for a year so, I was due for discharge in July 1950. When the Korean War broke out, I re-enlisted for three years.

When they took personnel for service in Korea, I was put on the cadre list. I stayed at Fort Bliss until 1951 when I was sent to Worms, Germany. I was promoted to sergeant during my one year and 10 months there. In 1953, I returned to the States and was sent to Camp Breckenridge, Kentucky, where I was discharged on 21 July 1953.

Angelo Stamelos returned to St. Louis where he worked at several different jobs, retiring from the Sysco Food Company in 1997. He married, but later divorced. He has five children. Angelo lives in Elsberry, Missouri.

✓ *INCIDENTally* — **Learning to drive.** – I was a teen-age sailor in Guam in 1947 and had just been issued a well-used 2½ ton Ford truck with six forward gears and four reverse gears. The problem was, I didn't know how to drive! A chief assigned a petty officer to teach me how. He detested the task and told me how he hated dumb Cajuns.

We drove out to an isolated refrigeration-storage area and the petty officer went through a short drill explaining how to shift gears. Then he got out to check a noise coming from a refrigeration unit, and I moved into the driver's seat.

Suddenly, the loud crack of a bullet split the air and the petty officer jumped behind a revetment. I jammed down the clutch and threw the truck into gear – any gear. I barreled out of there like a bat out of hell, grinding the gears and double-clutching all the way. This dumb Cajun wasn't staying there.

Both the petty officer and I made it back safely, but no one would believe our story. I forgot about the incident until I read about the death of a Japanese soldier who hid out on Guam for years after World War II. I sometimes wonder if he wasn't my motivation to learn to drive in less than five minutes! – *John "Buz" Broussard.*

Robert F. Coucoules

Age 16 – United States Army

I was born in Savannah, Georgia, on 1 January 1932. At that time families were still feeling the effects of the Depression. Since my divorced mother was unable to take care of me, she agreed to have me sent to a Catholic orphanage located in

Because of my persistent efforts to join the service, my stepfather, ..., offered to help me.

Washington, Georgia, where my two older brothers had been previously sent. I went to the orphanage in the mid or late 1930s, and I remained there until 1947, so I was there during the entire World War II period. I ran away from the orphanage three times and had completed only the seventh grade by the time I left. This could probably be attributed to emotional problems caused by the departure of my older brothers who left the orphanage when they reached the maximum age.

In 1947, when it came my turn to leave the orphanage, I was placed in a boys' boarding school in Savannah. Again, I became a disciplinary problem, since I ran away from that institution also. Another problem was that the school had so few boys that I was the only one eligible to enter the eighth grade. Therefore, they decided to pass me on to the ninth grade, a situation I could not handle.

I was sent home to live with my mother and stepfather, but it was another situation that I had a problem handling. In those days, many of the kids were anxious to join the military. In a way, we were somewhat disappointed that the war was over. While still 15 years old, on my own and without my parents' knowledge, I attempted to join the Navy and then the Marines. They turned me down because I was unable to prove my age. I also tried to join the Army, but mistakenly told them that I had had asthma.

Because of my persistent efforts to join the service, my stepfather, an old Army friend of the recruiting sergeant, offered to help me. In early January 1948, he and my mother signed the enlistment papers indicating that I was 17, even though I had only turned 16 on 1 January. A birth certificate was not required at that time.

I traveled by train to Fort Benning, Georgia, where on 9 January 1948, I was processed and sworn into the Army. It was nine days after I had turned 16. The Army was looking for enlistees to join the Army Security Agency, so I decided to look into it. However, when I was given forms to complete, I decided that it was not very wise of me to lie about my age, since they were going to do background checks.

I took basic training with the 5th Infantry Division at Fort Jackson, South Carolina. After basic, I was assigned to the division band-training unit and taught to play the saxophone. I made that decision because my older brother had played that instrument in his high school band. After about three months I decided that the band was no place for me, and I requested a transfer.

I received orders to report to Fort Lawton, in Seattle, Washington, where I was assigned the duties of the unit mail clerk in an Alaska Replacement Company. While there, I began to realize that without a high school education, I would not go very far in the Army. So I visited the post-education center. I received help in devising a course of study to meet high school requirements. I subsequently passed a test and was awarded a high school certificate from the state of Georgia. As far as the Army was concerned, I was now a high school graduate. While at Fort Lawton I met my future wife. She was 16 years old and attending high school. I was only 17 at the time. In 1950, I was transferred to the 9th Army Postal Unit on Okinawa. After a 2-year tour, I returned to Seattle and we were married.

My subsequent assignments included: two tours in Korea, the first from 1955 to 1956, and the second 20 years later, 1970-72; Whittier, Alaska, 1956-60; Augsburg, Germany, 1962-65; Ingrandes, France and Worms, Germany, 1966-68; Vietnam, 1968-69; and several assignments in the continental United States.

While stationed with the Army Command and Communications Agency at Fort Myer, Virginia, I informed my commanding officer about my real age. Since I was required to obtain a secret clearance, I though it best that I do so. He escorted me to the Pentagon personnel section and had my records changed to reflect my true birth date. There was no action taken. Later, I read that Congress had passed a bill pardoning those who entered the services underage and awarded us retirement credit for the time served underage.

While assigned to the 24th Division Army Post Office in Augsburg, Germany, I visited my older brother in Munich where he was assigned as a criminal investigations agent in the Munich Provost Marshal's Office. Upon being introduced, the provost marshal encouraged me to apply for assignment to the Criminal Investigations Division (CID). He explained that the CID had recently created an apprentice program and provided me with the regulations.

Shortly thereafter I applied for the CID, but I still had a couple of years left on my overseas tour. By agreement between my commanding officer and the division provost marshal, I was attached to the provost marshal's office as an investigator. I was to obtain on-the-job experience that would prepare me for attendance at the CID school at the end of my tour. The presumption was that my CID application would be approved. I could see no problems with my career change. My grandfather, father, and uncle had been police officers, and my brother was already a CID agent.

The application was approved, and when my tour was over, I was assigned to the Military Police School, Criminal Investigations Course, Fort Gordon, Georgia. As required by regulations, I was then assigned the new rank of specialist 6. I completed the CID school at Fort Gordon and was assigned to the CID unit at the Presidio of San Francisco, California, as an apprentice agent. Within a year, I received my accreditation, and shortly thereafter, I was discharged as an enlisted man and sworn in as a warrant officer.

I retired from the U. S. Army as a warrant officer-3 on 31 July 1975, after serving 27 years, 6 months, and 22 days.

Bob Coucoules continued his education after retiring from the Army. He earned an A.A. in law enforcement, a B.A. in criminal justice, and graduated from Pacific Lutheran University with a master's degree in human relations. He then went to work for the State of Washington's Attorney General's Office as a fraud investigator. He retired from state service in August 1996. Bob and Claudine, his wife of 49 years, have four children, six grandchildren, and one great-grandchild. They live in Auburn, Washington.

Joseph D. Passalaqua
Age 15 – United States Army

I was born in Chicago, Illinois, on 11 May 1932. The Depression was on and times were hard. I had three older brothers and two older sisters.

> *I wanted security, education, and a chance to see the world.*

My father was a good Catholic and a hard-working man. He and Mom came from Sicily, Italy. They met and married in the United States.

Dad, who worked as an upholsterer, was the sole support of the family. To make ends meet, he and my oldest brother played guitar and sang old Italian songs in the evenings at the local speakeasies. The Chicago winters were brutal, and by the time I reached the age of 10, Dad became seriously ill. On doctor's orders, we moved to Arkansas, seeking a better climate.

The Second World War had started and my two older brothers went into the Army, fought in Europe, and returned safely. While they were gone, my one older brother and I were left to support the family. I was taken out of school in the seventh grade to work on the farm. We sold hay, cotton, and corn, and even had an ice-delivery route.

After the war ended, my third oldest brother joined what at that time was the Army Air Forces. Meanwhile, my dear mother had three more children, all boys. Now we had nine in the family. By this time my older brothers and sisters had gone their own separate ways. The burden of supporting the family fell on me, and I was not a happy camper, to say the least. I was devastated by my father's decision to remove me from school. We argued and fought constantly.

Being a fairly smart kid, I just knew that I would probably never amount to anything in those Arkansas hills without at least a high school education. A dirt farmer I did not want to be! I wanted security, education, and a chance to see the world. With this in mind, looking at my three older brothers and their service time, and three younger brothers coming up behind me, the service seemed to be my ticket to success and a chance to show my patriotism.

On 1 March 1948, two months before my 16th birthday, I talked two of my best friends into joining the Army with me. We had sworn each other to secrecy. Both were older than I was by a few months, but they were turned down. One was color-blind, and the other was accused of being too young. We used no documents regarding age. My story was that I was born on 11 May 1930 and was going to be 18. I told them that my family had lost my birth certificate during the move to Arkansas. They believed me, and on 13 March 1948, two months before my 16th birthday, I was inducted into the United States Army as a private.

When I broke the news to my family, my father was not at all pleased, but he was proud that I had taken the same road as my older brothers. On the other hand, my mother was a totally different story. She felt that eventually she would lose a son, if they all kept going into the service. Needless to say, it was very hard for her to let me go.

I took my basic training at Fort Knox, Kentucky, and from there I went to Fort George G. Meade, Maryland, where I began my military police training. In 1949, I went to Japan and served there with an MP company during the occupation. I was stationed at Kōbe and also served in Kyōto, Japan.

The Korean War broke out on 25 June 1950. My MP company was divided into two parts. I was attached to the 19th Regiment of the 24th Infantry Division. My company landed in Korea on 5 July 1950. Most of my friends went to the 27th Regiment of the 25th Infantry Division. They were all killed in the first three days of fighting.

I was assigned to do reconnaissance work with the 19th Regiment. This consisted of knowing where the front line was, which roads, bridges, tunnels, and railways were open and not occupied by the enemy. Another duty consisted of escorting stragglers back to their front-line duties. The hardest thing for me to do was to escort the wounded and the dead back to the rear lines for aid, hospitalization, and disposition. There were many with missing limbs, half of their faces missing, etc. There were so many to be sent to the rear that they were loaded on flatbed railcars. This was, and is today, the most traumatic thing I have ever had to endure. But we did what had to be done.

When we retreated to Pusan, Korea, we aided in establishing a police presence and started an R&R center for all troops within that theater. I returned to the States in January 1952. When I arrived home, my mother told me that my dad had gotten into a barroom brawl defending my honor as a soldier fighting for our country in Korea.

I stayed in the military, married, and earned some college credits. College credits did not come easy for me. There was a lot of burning the midnight oil. In my early years in the Army, they offered what they called the end-of-course test, at the local Army education center. Three months of study and successfully passing the test would earn you three college credits. While at Fort Polk, Louisiana, I earned a number of credits through Louisiana's McNiece State College, and through San Antonia Community College.

I was thinking of retiring in 1969, since after a presidential proclamation by President Kennedy, my fraudulent service would count towards retirement. However, I was encouraged by my commanding officer to apply for a warrant officer's appointment. I did so, and was appointed a warrant officer on 29 December 1969. My college studies continued while I was serving as a warrant officer. In all, it took me more than five years of day and/or night classes to earn the equivalent of two years of college credits.

I was assigned to the United States Army Criminal Investigations Division Command in Washington, D.C. I made short trips to Vietnam and many other countries, assisting in investigating cases. The Mi Lai Massacre and the Jeffrey McDonald – Green Beret cases were among them. I was reassigned to the personal security division and served on the staff of the Secretary of Defense, who at that time was Melvin Laird. This was during President Nixon's administration.

I retired on 30 September 1973 as a chief warrant officer-2, after serving a total of 25 years, 6 months, and 18 days. I was 41 years old. All circumstances being the same, I would do exactly what I did. The military was good to me; after all, I grew up there.

Joseph Passalaqua was awarded the Army Commendation Medal, the Meritorious Service Medal, and a number of other awards and medals. His military police background was advantageous when he applied for a job with the Jefferson Parish Sheriff's Office, Metairie, Louisiana. He was hired as a deputy and served for 24 years, retiring as a full colonel on 31 December 1999. His wife passed away after 34 years of marriage and his three children were grown. Joe remarried and his wife Kim has presented him with two children, a girl and a boy. They live in River Ridge, Louisiana.

✓ *INCIDENTally* — **Halt! Who goes there?** – Going from boot camp at Parris Island, South Carolina, to guard duty in Taku, China in early 1946 was quite an experience. I was assigned a post on the road going to the dock area. Due to the raids being made on supplies, I was told to allow no one to pass without a trip ticket. When I saw a car approaching, I stepped out with my carbine leveled at it and brought it to a stop. I could see a man and a woman in the front seat. As I approached, the driver's side, I got a real shock when I saw the driver had eagles on his collar. Having never been in contact with anyone of higher rank than a lieutenant, I thought, "Oh hell, I've done it now!" But as any good Marine would do, I shouldered my weapon, gave a snappy salute, and asked where he was going. He said, "To the dock area." When I asked him for a trip ticket, he looked at me and said, "Son, colonels don't have trip tickets." I said, "I'm sorry sir, but nobody goes down that road without one." He pulled his wallet out and started showing me several IDs, all the time mumbling to himself. That's when, as a smart Marine, I figured I'd better get him on his way.

A month later, our regiment had a change of command. As our company lined up for inspection, the same colonel came marching down the ranks. He stopped right in front of me and asked. "Don't I know you, son?" Being at attention, I managed to blurt out, "I don't think so, sir." With a smile, he continued on his way. – *John Stamelos.*

Edward C. Andrix, Jr.

Age 16 – United States Marine Corps Reserve

I grew up in the same neighborhood where I was born in Columbus, Ohio, on 24 April 1932. With my parents' consent, I enlisted in C Company, 7th Infantry Battalion, U. S. Marine Corps

> *My squad leader guessed that I was underage ..., but he told me he would keep my secret.*

Reserve, on 27 April 1948. The unit was located at Fort Hays, in Columbus. I was 16 years old. I joined the Marine Reserve for several reasons: I had always had the desire to be a Marine, and I wanted the adventure, the discipline, the training, and the experiences of summer camp. I attended the weekly training sessions at Fort Hayes, and went to the 2-week summer training at Camp Lejeune, North Carolina, in 1948 and 1949. My squad leader guessed that I was underage while we were at summer camp in 1948, but he told me he would keep my secret. He also became a good friend and mentor, which helped me get through the rigid training at summer camp.

I completed my 2-year enlistment on 27 April 1950 and had attained the rank of corporal. I re-enlisted for another two years. On 25 June 1950, the North Koreans attacked South Korea and the Korean War began. My unit was ordered to stand by for further orders. We were told that our summer-camp training was cancelled.

On 4 September 1950, my reserve unit boarded a troop train at Fort Hayes and joined other reserve units from the East Coast that were also on their way to Camp Pendleton, California. I was sent to Tent Camp 2 at Camp Pendleton where I received advanced infantry training. Other reservists from my unit and from many units from all over the country received their training there. Some reservists who had never been through boot camp were sent to the Marine Corps Base in San Diego, while others were not. I am one of a very few Marines who served in combat without first experiencing the rigors of boot camp.

We were shipped to Korea in February 1951. I was assigned to D Company, 2nd Battalion, 1st Marine Regiment, 1st Marine Division. I spent the next seven months with this unit and traveled up and down the Korean Peninsula as the front lines kept moving back and forth. When the 1st Marine Division was sent into reserve status in September 1951, I was transferred to the Headquarters Battalion and became a cook with the 2nd Battalion. I remained with that battalion until I returned to the States in March 1952.

I was released from active duty, transferred to reserve status, and returned to Columbus, Ohio. I remained in the Marine Reserves until 1956, then I requested to be discharged. I had completed eight years of service.

Edward Andrix earned the Combat Action Ribbon and a number of other service medals. His unit was awarded the Navy Presidential Unit Citation. He spent 36 years in the printing trade as a linotype operator and typographer, and worked four years in the sign-manufacturing business. He learned the upholstery trade and worked four years at that trade before retiring in 1993. He has been active in the Veterans of Foreign Wars, the American Legion, Marine Corps League, the 1st Marine Division Association, and the National Association of Boxcar Hobos, a clown organization that is affiliated with the Forty and Eight, the American Legion honor society. Ed and Saundra, his wife of 49 years, have six children, sixteen grandchildren, and six great-grandchildren. They live in Westerville, Ohio.

Salvador Cantu
Age 16 – United States Army

I was born in Mercedes, a small town in the lower Rio Grande Valley of Texas, on 22 July 1931. I am the fourth of nine children born to Rafael and Gregoria Cantu. My family moved to Weslaco, where I went to school. I had to quit school in the third grade and go to work. In the south part of Texas, the only work available was picking cotton or doing seasonal field work.

> *It was July 1999 before I was able to fulfill the promise made to my buddy Virgil.*

When I was 14 years old, I became interested in joining the military. My oldest brother Rafael enlisted in the Army Air Forces and made it seem easy for anyone to join. One day I went to the recruiting office and tried to join, but I was turned down because I was too young.

I worked for the next two years and waited anxiously to turn 16. Eighteen buddies and I went to the recruiting office to enlist in 1948.

After completing the paperwork and taking the test, only two of us were accepted, my 18-year-old cousin, and I, at age 16.

Both of my parents forbade me from joining at this time. My oldest brother had just returned home from the Philippines and was honorably discharged after serving for four years. My second-oldest brother, Jerry, had just enlisted in the Air Force and was on his way to Germany. This did not make it any easier for me. My oldest brother convinced me to go ahead and join. He forged my father's name and told me that under no conditions could I return home if I could not fulfill this responsibility. My parents were very upset with both of us, but after I left, they accepted the fact.

On 12 May 1948, when I was just 16 years old, I was sent to Fort Ord, California, for basic training. On my 17th birthday, I was sent to Okinawa where I spent 14 months. I returned to the States in 1950.

By this time the war had started in Korea, so I volunteered to go. I was assigned to C Company, 9th Regiment, 2nd Infantry Division.

I was promoted to staff sergeant and assigned a platoon. We fought at the Pusan Perimeter, Wonju-Sowon, and the Naktong River. About this time, I received word that my third oldest brother, Susano, had enlisted in the Army and was sent to Germany.

We moved into North Korea and engaged in a number of battles. My platoon suffered many casualties. My best buddy, Virgil Volk, was killed in action. I will never forget the moment when Virgil and I were sharing a foxhole during a specially ferocious battle. We made a promise to each other that if one of us survived the battle and the other didn't, the survivor would visit the other's family, pay his respects, and tell them of their last words.

During this time, my family was notified that I was missing in action in North Korea. While my parents were dealing with this devastating news, my 14-man platoon and I were fighting our way back to South Korea. We were found a month later, and after being examined by medics, I was shipped to Japan for medical treatment. My family then received telegrams telling them of my recovery.

I was sent back to my unit in Korea, and since my enlistment was nearly up, I was looking forward to being discharged. However, President Truman signed me up for another year.

In 1951, I was sent to Camp Roberts, California, where I was promoted to sergeant first class. I was 20 years old, three months short of my 21st birthday. I was honorably discharged on 1 April 1952. About this time, my youngest brother, Emilio, enlisted in the Marines. I am proud to say that all five of my brothers served honorably in our military services: Air Force, Air Force, Army, Army, and Marines.

It was July 1999 before I was able to fulfill the promise made to my buddy Virgil. I visited his family and visited him at his grave site. Since this visit, my family and I have become good friends with the Volk family, and we share our stories of Virgil.

Sal Cantu earned the Combat Infantryman's Badge and was awarded a number of service medals for his service in Korea. He worked in construction and is now semi-retired from Laborers Union Local 89. He and Virginia, his wife of 48 years, raised five children and have six grandchildren. Sal and Virginia have lived in Carlsbad, California for the past 48 Years.

George R. Fredin
Age 16 – United States Army

I was born on 24 February 1932 at the Swedish American Hospital, Rockford, Illinois. My Swedish immigrant parents, Thor and Elsa Fredin, were divorced when I was three. I lived with my mother in a predominately Swedish neighborhood, attended local schools, and worked at odd jobs whenever I could.

> *At the age of 16, here I was, a military policeman, and loving every minute of it!*

I had two mentors who influenced my life. Lee Winquist, a local pharmacist, advised and counseled me and my friends. We hung out at his store, and I frequently did my homework there. Don Chesak taught us about living outdoors, camping, fishing, and hunting.

At age 16, while at the local bowling alley where I was a pinsetter, an Air Force recruiter approached me. He asked me two questions: what grade was I in school, and how old I was. I replied that I was a senior and that I was 18 years old. The conversation continued and I got interested in the Army. All I had to do was to get my mother to sign for me. This was in April 1948.

My mother consented to sign for me. I talked to my school counselor, who advised me to take the GED tests during basic training and wished me well. With a little ink eradicator on my birth certificate and my mother's signature, I was inducted into the U. S. Army on 18 May 1948. Looking back, I don't think the recruiter believed that I was 18, but figured that I would be better off in the Army than being where I was.

I was sent to Fort Knox, Kentucky, for eight weeks of basic training with the 32nd Tank Battalion, 3rd Armored Division. During the second week of basic I was promoted to acting sergeant and was a squad leader, then a platoon sergeant. I did very well on the rifle range, firing expert. I took to land navigation and enjoyed being in the field. I climbed Agony and Misery Hills a couple of times.

I was promoted to private first class after basic training and sent to Fort Monmouth, New Jersey, to attend a signal maintenance school. While there, I took the GED. The results were sent to my old high school, and I received a regular graduation certificate.

Upon completion of the signal school, I received orders shipping me to Okinawa. I rode a train to Camp Stoneman, California, with a short delay in Rockford, Illinois. While in Rockford, I wore civilian clothes and kept a low profile. At Camp Stoneman, we were issued field gear and took a 12-day cruise to Okinawa. At the replacement company, 20 of us were selected to be military policemen and were assigned to the 524th Military Police Company. We spent the next five weeks at MP school. At the age of 16, here I was, a military policeman, and loving every minute of it!

Okinawa is an island of roughly 454 square miles. Only the central half was on-limits for us. Our company was in one of the new typhoon-proof barracks at Sukiran. I was TDY to the detachment in the south half. It was good duty, mainly patrolling the roads and trying to keep both civilian and military personnel out of the area.

Typhoon Gloria hit the island with winds up to 140 miles per hour in March or April 1949. The local villages did O.K., but the rest of us sustained a lot of damage. Cables over Quonset huts were pulled up, and sheets of wood and tin were flying through the air. The open-air theater at Easley Bowl was destroyed. The next day, a four-by-eight sheet of plywood had the following message painted on it: "Now playing – Gone with the Wind."

I had a good friend while on Okinawa, Louie Paoletti from Miami, Florida. Louie and I always carried a bag full of candy while on patrol in the village. Small children would stand by the road waving and saying, "Otto," instead of, "Hello." We would stop and Louie would tell them his name was "Louie," not "Otto," as he was passing out candy.

The tour of duty on Okinawa was 12 months. I was rotated back to the States in November 1949 and was assigned to the 10th Military Police Company, 10th Infantry Division, Ft. Riley, Kansas. My duty assignments were mostly post patrol and town patrol in Junction City, Kansas.

About the time the Korean War broke out, I was promoted to corporal. They asked for volunteers and I raised my hand. I was soon off to Camp Stoneman and another cruise across the Pacific. At Camp Drake, Yokokama, Japan, I was slotted for the X Corps, but ended up in the 2nd Battalion, 32nd Regimental Combat Team, 7th Infantry Division. I did my job like everybody else, and the rest is history.

I came home with another stripe in December 1951. At Fort Sheridan, the assignment officer was my old executive officer on Okinawa. He offered me an assignment with the MPs at Fort Custer, Michigan. I accepted and was assigned to the 116th Military Police Battalion. My duty was night town-patrol in Battle Creek, Michigan.

One day the supply sergeant issued me full field gear. I asked, "What is this for?" He replied, "In three weeks we are going to Texas for a training exercise." Three weeks later, a second lieutenant and I were the advance party and I drove a ¼-ton truck to Fort Hood, Texas. I was discharged in April 1952 and returned to Rockford, Illinois.

I went to work at a local industry and joined the Air Force Reserves. I left the Air Force Reserves to join the Army Reserves, 337th Infantry Regiment, 85th Infantry Division in December 1953. I attained the rank of master sergeant while with the 337th. During this time I met my wife Mary Ann, who was the loving mother of our three daughters.

My civilian job was as a tile and marble setter, but I answered an ad in the paper and became a member of the Illinois State Police. After graduating from recruit school at Springfield, Illinois, I was assigned to my home county, which allowed me to continue in the Army Reserves. I stayed with the Illinois State Police for 28 years.

In the Army Reserves, I became first sergeant of the 388th Smoke Generator Company. In December 1962, I accepted the assignment as first sergeant of Company C, 863rd Engineers. I held this position until 1978, when I was asked to be the battalion command sergeant major. I could write for hours about Company C, but we will leave it to history. The names Pawlus, Herbig, Sandona, Zanin, Leslie, Wendell, Hallin, LeCausi, CW-4 Myers, CPT Bucalo, are all part of the history. All have retired now, and we get together periodically. I served as command sergeant major for two years, then was transferred to Headquarters, 416th Engineer Command, Chicago, Illinois.

In 1979, my wife passed away. My three daughters and I carried on. I remarried in July 1982 and gained two more daughters.

During my tour at the 416th Engineer Command Headquarters, I served as a construction-operations sergeant and command re-enlistment NCO under Colonel Bordenaro, a former Marine. While with the 416th, I watched a career officer whom I first knew as a second lieutenant, Max Baratz, attain two-star rank and become both chief of the Army Reserve and commanding general of the United States Army Reserve Command.

Tenure caught up with me in 1983. After 35 years of service I was transferred to the Individual Ready Reserve, with a mobilization designee assignment at the Signal Center, Fort Gordon, Georgia, as a command sergeant major. I did several short 15- to 30-day tours there.

In 1985, I retired from the Illinois State Police and accepted a long active-duty tour out of the Army Personnel Center, St. Louis, Missouri. My assignments were: operations NCO, Fort McCoy, Wisconsin; command sergeant major at the U. S. Army Signal Center, Fort Gordon, Georgia (three tours); sergeant major at the U. S. Army Engineer School, Fort Belvoir, Virginia; and sergeant major for the 100th Infantry Division, Fort Knox, Kentucky.

The finale for my Army career was in January 1991. I was ordered to active duty for one year in support of Operation Desert Storm. I reported to Fort Leonard Wood, Missouri, and after two weeks' processing, I was transferred to Fort Benjamin Harrison, Indiana. I completed advanced training and was waiting for orders to ship out. While I was waiting, the war was over and we were demobilized.

On 24 February 1992, I became 60 years old and was placed on the retired list with 43 years, 10 months and 23 days of active duty and active reserve credit.

George Fredin earned a Combat Infantryman's Badge and a Bronze Star while in Korea. Later he was awarded the Army Meritorious Service Medal, the Army Commendation Medal with oak leaf cluster, and the Army Achievement Medal with three oak leaf clusters. George and his wife Shirley have five daughters and twelve grandchildren. They live in Roscoe, Illinois, in the summer and in Naples, Florida, in the winter.

George V. Cobb

Age 15 – United States Navy

I experienced a very unhappy teenage home life primarily because of my father's illness. I was born near Waco, Texas, on 9 August 1932, but was raised in Houston, Texas. During World War II, my mother, brother, and I stayed in

> ... "as long as you keep up with the older guys, I will not say anything, but one mistake and you are out!"

Houston while my father went to work at Oak Ridge, Tennessee, at the plant where the atomic bomb was developed.

Because of his work, my father was a stranger in our home during the war. After the bomb was dropped on Hiroshima, he came home and started implementing rules that were terribly difficult to follow. My brother and I found it impossible to keep him off our backs. Late in 1945, at age 15, my brother left our home in Houston, got a job in Waco, Texas, and enrolled in a technical school.

My brother and I thought that our father was very mean. Later in life we came to realize that he was not mean, but that he was sick from all the radiation he was exposed to during the construction of the bomb. He experienced a heart attack almost every year until his death from leukemia at age 60.

After my sophomore year in high school, I had had enough. With the help of friends, I started planning an early enlistment in the military. My father discovered what I was trying to accomplish and a confrontation followed. He gave in finally and decided to support my effort. He went to the recruiting office with me and signed paperwork that supported my age as 17. He also signed the parental-consent form that was needed for enlistment at age 17. I was sworn into the Navy on 1 June 1948, and was sent to the Naval Training Center, San Diego, California. I was extremely happy to be in the United States Navy. It had been my dream during and after World War II.

While I was in boot camp, my company commander called me into his office and told me that he had learned I was underage, which I denied. I felt intimidated and afraid. He continued to try to get a confession from me, but I never conceded. He concluded the confrontation with a statement implying that "as long as you keep up with the older guys, I will not say anything, but one mistake and you are out!" That worked – I got the message.

After boot camp, I was assigned to the USS *Mississippi* (AG-128) for a short time, then to the USS *Newport News* (CA-148), and finally to the USS *Des Moines* (CA-134). During my tour of duty I enjoyed four 4-month cruises to the Mediterranean, three to the Caribbean, and a cruise inside the Arctic Circle.

One day while I was aboard the *Newport News*, I was approached by the ship's educational officer. He introduced himself, then stated that he had noted I had not graduated from high school. He didn't mention my age. I admitted that I was a dropout. He asked if I might want to do something about my lack of a high school diploma. I replied, "What are you talking about?" He explained the extension program and added that if I was interested, he would assist me. I was more than happy to take part in this program. He talked to my division officer, who supported the plan. I was permitted to go to the ship's library after noon chow on most days to work on my GED.

In a little over 18 months, I had earned my GED and had finished a few hours of college work. Not many of those hours were accepted as transferable, but I did learn a little about college work.

During my 3-year enlistment, the Korean War started and all enlistments were extended a year by order of President Truman. I was discharged on 25 March 1952.

George Cobb enrolled at the University of Texas under the GI Bill, earned a B.S. in mechanical engineering, married his college girlfriend, and went to work for North American Aviation in Los Angeles, California. He worked in the Liquid Rocket Division at Canoga Park, California, and was transferred later to their Solid Rocket Division in McGregor, Texas. That division was purchased by Hercules Inc. in 1978. After working at a number of different levels of engineering and management over a 38-year period, he retired from Hercules Inc. in 1994. George and Jeanine, his wife of 45 years, have three daughters and six grandchildren. They live in Waco, Texas.

Robert D. Caulkins

Age 15 – Massachusetts National Guard
Age 16 – United States Marine Corps

I was born in the kitchen at home in Pawtucket, Rhode Island, on 30 June 1933. My father was at work at the time. He was a deliveryman for the Downy Flake Donut Company and was fired that day for giving

> But I was prepared to fight to get into my Marine Corps.

away much of his inventory to people who, because of the economic depression, could not afford a box of donuts.

I remember during World War II of being electrified by the reports of the gallant Marines fighting on Wake Island, Guadalcanal, Tarawa, and Iwo Jima. It was during those war years that I made up my mind that I would, one day, wear the uniform of a United States Marine.

On a chilly day in April 1950, I went to the Marine Corps Recruiting Station in the Federal Building in downtown Boston. I was not yet 17, but I had convinced my parents to let me attempt to join the Marine Corps Reserve. My mother had been adamant that she would not sign the papers for me to ship out in the regulars, but the meeting-a-week reserves were okay with her. My father was all for my joining up, reserve or regular. He had joined the Navy at age 15 and had gotten as far as the USS *Arkansas* before his parents, whose permission he did not have, asked the Navy to send him home. Actually, neither of my parents believed I would even pass the physical. So I guess

they felt on firm ground when they said that they would sign me into the Corps if I passed all the tests required to join.

The reason my parents had doubts about my being accepted into the service was that I had undergone a serious kidney operation at the age of 12. It had left me with a 14-inch horizontal scar on my left waistline. As a matter of fact, I had been discharged from the

National Guard because of the scar. I had joined the Guard on 15 November 1948 and served for five months before being discharged. The Guard unit used a contract doctor who gave physical examinations to those who had joined the Guard during the previous 6-month period.

On the night I was to have my physical, the doctor came from a party and was "three sheets to the wind." He took one look at the angry-looking scar on my side and screamed, "What the hell is that?" As I attempted to tell him about the operation and that I was now healthy and feeling fine, he interrupted me and said, "You're physically unfit, boy. Get the hell out of here."

So ended my career as a private, serial number 21264875, with the Ammunition and Pioneer Platoon, Headquarters Company, Headquarters Battalion, 101st Infantry, 26th (Yankee) Division, Massachusetts National Guard. I was discharged at the age of 15. My brother Don who had joined with me as my bogus 17-year-old twin, left the Guard shortly thereafter. He had no big, scary scar; he just decided to resign. He was 14 years old.

As I rode the bus and then the subway to the Marine recruiting station on that brisk April day, I had serious thoughts about what might take place. My first worry was that I might run into one of the recruiters, Sergeant Wolf, who had grown weary of my repeated visits asking for recruiting material. But, I had not been there for about a year, and I hoped he might have been transferred or that he would not remember me.

The second worry, and the biggest, was the long, ugly scar on my left side. If the National Guard had kicked me out, the Marine Corps and Sergeant Wolf would certainly do the same, after beating me to a pulp for messing up his quota.

But I was prepared to fight to get into my Marine Corps. I would not easily accept defeat. Before I left home that morning, I took a 20-foot length of quarter-inch clothesline cord and wrapped it snugly around my waist, under my clothes. Looking in the mirror, I was careful to make sure that the cord covered the scar. I had tried it out before, and looking at my reflection in the mirror, it appeared as though I had worn a belt very tightly and had a humdinger of a belt mark all the way around my waist. I hoped that it would also look that way to the Navy doctor.

I got to the recruiting station, and my nemesis, Sergeant Wolf, was nowhere to be seen. I asked a Marine corporal if Sergeant Wolf would be coming in later, and I was informed that he was on leave. Whew! One critical worry out of the way. I sat down and filled out the enlistment papers and was then told to take my physical examination forms upstairs to the medical department. I asked if I could use the bathroom before I went up and was told to go ahead, but not to lollygag. I didn't know what lollygag was, but I certainly didn't intend to do anything but uncoil the rope from around my waist and get up to the medical department. In the men's room, I entered a stall, dropped my trousers and my underpants, and uncoiled the rope. I dropped it into the used paper-towel container, straightened out my clothing, and went upstairs to the physical exam room.

There were several other guys there who were applying for the Navy. At least, I would not be the sole object of the examiner. At one point in the exam, a corpsman checked me over for the "marks and scars" section of the exam report. My heart was in my mouth as he tapped my side with his pen and asked, "What's that?" But, as soon as he asked the question, he answered it himself by saying, "Oh, a belt mark." He then wrote "none" under "marks and scars." My hearing was tested by the doctor who clicked two coins together and asked me how many times I heard the click.

A short time later, I was bounding down the street, a mile-wide smile on my face, whistling the Marines Hymn. In my hand I had a large, brown, manila envelope containing enlistment papers. I had been ordered to report to the Second Infantry Battalion, United States Marine Corps Reserve. I had made it — I was going to be a Marine!

My mother and father, true to their word, but with a bit of apprehension on my mother's part, signed the parental-consent forms. On 12 April 1950, I was sworn into what was known then as the Organized Marine Corps Reserve. Two months later, the United States went to war. So did the Marine Corps, and so did I, at age 16.

Bob Caulkins served in Korea and later in Vietnam. His personal decorations include the Purple Heart and the Combat Action Ribbon. He retired from the Marine Corps as a master sergeant after 22 years of service. He was hired by the CIA in 1976 and served with that agency for 17 years, mostly in Europe as a case officer. Bob and Ursula Caulkins live in Brunswick, Georgia.

Darryll D. Wolfe

Age 16 – Washington National Guard

I was born in Seattle, Washington, on 28 March 1933, during the Great Depression. My father was an immigrant from Sweden and my mother was from Iowa. When I was about 1½ years old, my parents separated and

> I have worked very hard to close the door to those memories.

I was sent to live with my maternal grandmother and an uncle whom I thought of as an older brother. My uncle was killed on Iwo Jima on 20 February 1945.

Between the ages of 6 and 12, I lived with aunts and uncles, and occasionally with my mother and stepfather. During the summers, I worked on nearby vegetable, poultry, and pig farms, and for my uncle in his taxi and trucking business.

My father gained legal custody of me when I was 10, and the sixth grade was the first time that I spent a full year at the same school. I lived with him until I was 14, when I was sent to Sweden to live with

my grandmother and to start vocational training.

My father's illness required me to return to the United States. I lived independently in a small room that I shared with a fellow worker. I worked for a cafeteria company as a busboy six days a week for $32 before taxes. I attended vocational school in the afternoons and worked part-time with a baking company. I also worked in service stations, for the Northern Pacific Railroad, and as a Swedish-language interpreter.

At age 15, I started attending weekly meetings at the National Guard armory without officially being enrolled. I spent two weeks one summer with the Guard at the Yakima firing range. Some of these meetings consisted of going on field trips such as ski trips to Snoqualmie Pass using military vehicles. I now realize that these adventures are one of the reasons some Guard units earned a bad reputation.

I was sworn into the Washington National Guard on 1 January 1949 at age 16. I had obtained a Washington State driver's license at age 14, giving my age as 16. I used that document as proof of age. Many of my fellow guardsmen were underage.

In July 1950, I was granted a leave of absence from the National Guard to leave the United States and become a civilian employee of the Military Sea Transportation Service, North Pacific Marine Service. During the next 20 months, I served aboard the USNS *General M. C. Meigs*, the USNS *General Hugh J. Gaffey*, the USNS *Marine Adder*, and the USNS *James O'Hara*.

While I was in Japan in November 1950, my seaman's documents were confiscated by the United States Coast Guard and I was issued a conscript's certificate for emergency service with Coast Guard. I never learned the reason for this action.

Our vessels shuttled between various Japanese ports such as Kōbe, Yakuska, and Yokohama, and the Korean ports of Inchon and Pusan, with shore landings at other locations. During these shuttle trips, many of the soldiers we transported and cared for, some still in their teenage years, were physically wounded and/or mentally fatigued. Some of the individuals we transported were prisoners of war, and the treatment they received from the Marine guards was less than desirable.

I was a storekeeper aboard ship, so during many of the shore trips in Korean ports I would be sent to deliver supplies to special units or to "procure" supplies and parts for the ship. I still have memories of the destruction I saw during these trips ashore. On several occasions I delivered supplies to orphanages where many of the children were severely wounded. I have worked very hard to close the door to those memories.

While I was in Korea in 1952, I was informed by the Washington State Selective Service Board that they would not renew the certificate (form 300) which permitted me to be outside of the United States. I was ordered to return to the United States. At first, my ship's captain refused to release me, but he soon discovered that the Selective Service Board had more authority.

I was classified 1-A. No military service would allow me to join without a release from the draft board, and no employer would hire me because of my draft status. I finally found a job as a night cashier in a combination service station and parking lot.

I was drafted into the U. S. Army infantry in February 1953 and served as a cadre in basic-training units at Fort Lewis, Washington. I held the rank of sergeant (E-5) at the time I was released in February 1955. I served in the Army Infantry Reserve until 1959.

Darryl Wolfe went to work for the Pacific Telephone and Telegraph Company as an installer and repairman in 1955. Later he became a supervisor and a plant engineer. He and Elaine, his wife of 49 years, have a son, a daughter, and six grandchildren. They live in Camano Island, Washington.

✔ *INCIDENTally* — **Fire in the water!** – I was a 16-year-old Marine aboard a troopship going to China in 1946. The head (toilet) on the ship was an open trough with running water flowing down to carry away the waste. When guys were sitting down doing their thing, we would ball up some toilet paper, set it on fire, and let it float down the trough. Needless to say, when the burning paper passed under the guys sitting there relieving themselves, they would jump! – *William G. Hood.*

Charles L. Simmons

Age 16 – United States Army

I was born in Winchester, Virginia, on 5 November 1932. My mother and father were separated and we lived with a man and his brother who hired my mother to care for their invalid mother. Both men were physically abusive, and the abuse

> I attribute my achievements to the training and discipline I learned in the military ...

continued until I was big enough to fight back. At age 15, I quit school to work in the apple orchards picking apples for 10¢ a bushel. Later in the fall, I worked in the apple-packing shed for 35¢ an hour. The workday was 10 to 13 hours, six days a week.

I turned 16 in November 1948, and after a very violent fight with the man who raised me, we decided that I should leave home. On 3 January 1949, with him verifying to the Army recruiter that I had turned 18 on 1 January, I was sworn into the United States Army.

I went through basic training at Camp Pickett, Virginia, with the 17th Airborne Division. After basic training and a short leave, I was shipped to Camp McGill in Japan where I was assigned to the 507th AAA AW Battalion, a coastal artillery outfit. I was a secondary gunner on a quad 50-caliber machine gun in a squad of 13 men.

We had an outstanding commander and first sergeant, but I was your typical 16-year-old screw-up. I cleaned the guns by day and slipped through the fence on many nights to drink and generally raise hell. The military police caught me and returned me to my first sergeant. I learned several new skills because the first sergeant was very innovative in thinking up things I could do for extra duty to keep me busy in the evenings and on weekends.

After I had been in Japan for a few months, I wrote and told my mother that I wanted out of the Army. She was in favor of that since she didn't want me to enlist in the first place. She sent a copy of my birth certificate to my commander in November 1949 and I was sent back to the States. I was honorably discharged from the Army on 23 January 1950 at Fort Lawton, in Seattle, Washington.

I rode a Greyhound bus from Seattle to Winchester, Virginia, a 3-day and 3-night trip. I married a childhood playmate in March 1953 when she was 16 and I was 20. During the winter of 1953-54, I couldn't find any kind of work, so in May 1954, I went to see the Army recruiter. Since I had a dependent, the Army wouldn't take me, but the Air Force would. I was sworn into the Air Force on 19 May 1954. After a 15-day refresher course at Sampson Air Force Base, New York, I was sent to Cheyenne, Wyoming, to attend a supply technical school.

During my Air Force career, I was stationed at several Stateside and overseas installations including Morocco, Guam, Shemya, and Vietnam. While in Vietnam, I was the non-commissioned officer in charge of the Maintenance Supply Liaison Section of the 35th Tactical Fighter Wing at Phan Rang AFB, from January 1969 until January 1970. I supervised 23 airmen and non-commissioned officers. Our job was to support the wing in carrying out its bombing missions and other classified missions involving over 100 combat aircraft.

I retired from the Air Force in 1975 as a master sergeant (E-7) with more than 22 years of service. I entered the Air Force as a seventh-grade dropout and retired with an associate's degree, needing only one year to complete a bachelor's degree. I attribute my achievements to the training and discipline I learned in the military and to the love and support of my girl-bride who saw something in a trouble-making teenager that other people didn't see.

Charles Simmons was awarded the Bronze Star for meritorious service, two Air Force Commendation Medals, an Air Force Outstanding Unit Award with "V" for valor, the Vietnamese Cross of Gallantry with palm, and a number of other service medals. After his retirement from the Air Force, he completed his bachelor's degree, earned a master's degree, and has finished all but his dissertation for a doctor of philosophy degree. He is an ordained Southern Baptist minister and is retired from the business world. He lost his wife Janet to cancer in November 2000 after 48 years of marriage. Charles lives in Anchorage, Alaska.

Floyd L. Herring

Age 16 – United States Army

I was born in Colorado Springs, Colorado, on 11 July 1932, the sixth of eight children. For most people living in that area, times were very hard because of the Depression. I believe one of the problems was that there were so many

> Some of the guys were whispering about what would happen to me if I was caught underage.

people who were uneducated. I had no knowledge of what the world was about. All I knew was that we were very poor, but everyone else was too, so we accepted it. My first encounter with the military was in 1944. Some other young people and I got jobs selling newspapers to servicemen at Camp Carson, just outside of Colorado Springs.

In 1945, we moved to Salem, Oregon, so all of the family could pick

fruits and vegetables. My father decided to leave us and moved to California by himself. We never saw him again. The war was over, so with all the servicemen and women coming home, there were few jobs to be had except field work. One of my brothers, who was two years older than me, was always in trouble. I was afraid that I would get into trouble, too, if I didn't do something, so I went to a lady who ran the truant office. She gave me the money to get some ink remover and then she changed "1932" to "1931" on my birth certificate. My mother signed for me, so on 14 January 1949, I was sworn into the Army.

I was sent to Fort Ord, California, for eight weeks of basic training, then I was given a 1-week leave to go home. Upon returning to Fort Ord, we were sent to Camp Kilmer, New Jersey, and a few days later, we boarded a troopship, the *General Haun*, and headed for Germany. That is when I got to wondering if I had gotten on the wrong ship. Some of the guys were whispering about what would happen to me if I was caught underage. They said that I would have to pay back all the money for food, lodging, and training, and they would kick me out. Then I really got scared!

We landed at Bremerhaven, and from there we took a troop train to Hanau, Germany. Upon arriving at our post in Hanau, I was asked what I wanted to do. I started working on trucks, jeeps, graders, cranes, and all sorts of equipment. We repaired all the government equipment that was sent to us, then painted it olive-green. I worked at the Hanau Engineering Depot for three years, eight months and three days. I returned to the States and was discharged on 16 September 1952.

I returned to my home in Oregon and went back to school. Two years after I was discharged, the older brother who I was afraid I might follow, was killed in a holdup in California. I think that the military saved my life. I am very proud to have been part of the armed forces, and if I had it to do over again, I would do the same thing. I have had a successful civilian career and I attribute all that I have today to my Army service in Germany and to all of the older men who looked out for me.

Floyd Herring went back to school and operated heavy equipment for a time. He became a stock broker in 1962 and has been involved in all phases of financial planning. He has been involved in insurance sales, real-estate sales, general contracting, and property development. Floyd and his wife Janice have a combined family of four children and five grandchildren. They live in Bend, Oregon, during the summer and in Arizona during the winter.

Frank C. Calandriello, Jr.
Age 15 – New Jersey National Guard

I was born on 8 July 1933 in Red Bank, New Jersey, the middle child of three, to Frank and Rose Calandriello. To make things easier, the name was shortened to Callo.

Much to our surprise, they never asked for proof of age.

When I was 15, my friend Bill Heyers and I had been out to see a movie. On the way home we passed the National Guard Armory. A sergeant was standing in the doorway smoking a big, black cigar. He said to us, "Hey, you two, would you like to join the National Guard?" We both said, "Hell, yes!"

We went in, filled out the necessary paperwork, and were sworn into Company B, 644th Tank Battalion, New Jersey National Guard. Much to our surprise, they never asked for proof of age. Naturally, we made ourselves two years older. We spent the rest of the night in the S-4 supply room being issued all our uniforms and equipment. That was 2 March 1949. I was still in the ninth grade.

We had drill and classroom instruction every Wednesday night. Since I had always liked to fool around with guns, they gave me technical manuals and training on the .30-caliber M1 carbine, 1911A1 Colt .45-caliber pistol, the 1911 Browning .30-caliber light machine gun, and the Browning M2 .50-caliber machine gun. So here I was, a 15-year-old kid in Company B with a light armor MOS (military occupational specialty).

My mother and father knew nothing of this until I had to go to basic training at Fort Dix, New Jersey. At first they were against it, but with a lot of persuasion on my part, they reluctantly signed the necessary papers. I spent my school vacation, from June to August, assigned to Company E, 2nd Battalion, 47th Infantry Regiment, 9th Infantry Division.

I was with the New Jersey National Guard for one year, four months, and seven days when the Korean War started. At that time, I was in the 10th grade. I quit school to go on active duty, and eventually got my high school diploma while I was in the Army.

I was on active duty from 28 July 1950 until 27 July 1953. I started out in Fort Bliss, Texas, with my original unit and we were soon shipped to Korea. I was there for eight days when somehow, somebody realized that I was only 17 and in a combat zone. The rule was that one had to be 18 in a combat zone. I was given an Article 15 court-martial for lying about my age and sent posthaste to Germany.

I have always suspected that my father had something to do with my age being discovered. He managed the New Jersey estate of the U. S. Ambassador to Denmark and knew a number of politicians. I surmise that he managed to get word to the Army through his political connections. I accused him of this, but he wouldn't even respond.

In Germany, I was assigned to Headquarters Battery, 63rd Antiaircraft Artillery Gun Battalion, and later to Headquarters S-2 Section of the 27th Anitaircraft Artillery Automatic Weapons Battalion in Mittenwald, Germany. Our unit was on detached duty from the Army to the Air Force to guard the air bases.

After I was discharged in 1953, I stayed out of the service until 1957. I missed service life so much that I went to McGuire Air Force Base, New Jersey, and joined the USAF Reserves. Because I was a policeman in Red Bank, New Jersey, they assigned me to the 1611th Air Police Squadron. But my real desire was to fly, so after a year with the air police, I transferred to the New Jersey Air National Guard, then to the 514th Military Airlift Wing as a flight-crew member. I made a total of 11 combat cargo missions to Vietnam with that unit.

I served a total of 29 years in the military. I loved the military and serving my country. Imagine, they used to pay me to fly all around the world on cargo missions that I thoroughly enjoyed! Given the opportunity, I'd do it all over again – no question.

Frank Callo received 18 awards and decorations during his 29 years of military service. As an Air Force Reserve air-crewman, he accumu-lated 4,893 flight hours, 14 of which were combat hours. His civilian job was in law enforcement, in which he worked for 35 years. Frank and Robyn, his wife of 32 years, live on a ranch near Deming, New Mexico.

Clyde C. Stewart

Age 15 – Tennessee Air National Guard
Age 16 – United States Army

I was born on 7 December 1933, eight years to the day before Pearl Harbor. This event occurred while my parents were visiting my grandmother in Isola,

> My size was just right for those small plane doors!

Mississippi. I decided to come early. I guess that is the reason I'm always early for everything, even enlisting in the military at the early age of 15 years.

We were living in Memphis, Tennessee, and I wanted to join the Tennessee Air National Guard. I begged my mother to sign the papers and she finally did. She thought that since I was so small for my age, I wouldn't pass, but I did! I enlisted on 18 August 1949 and served in the Guard until March 1950.

One Saturday night I lost the boxing match for the North Memphis Lightweight Golden Gloves Championship. The following Monday, 15 March 1950, four buddies and I joined the U. S. Army. The next day we left by train for Fort Knox, Kentucky, for basic training. One of my friends had a big brother who was in the paratroopers, and that is what I wanted to be.

After finishing basic training, I went to jump school. My size was just right for those small plane doors! I graduated on 23 June 1950 and was sent to Fort Campbell, Kentucky, where I was assigned to the 187th Airborne Regimental Combat Team. About a year later, I was transferred to the 408th Airborne Battalion Quartermaster. Both the 187th and the 408th were part of the 11th Airborne Division.

In early 1952, I was stationed in Times Square in New York City as a recruiter for the airborne. On weekends, we demonstrated parachuting to the guys we recruited. After four months of good times,

I was sent to Germany. We jumped supplies and equipment all over Europe. I made my 36th and last jump over Holland, landing in the water. This earned me my senior parachutist wings. I returned to the United States and was discharged in July 1953.

I visited Memphis where I was raised and looked for work, but I was unable to find anything. I decided to go back into the airborne, but the quota was filled for the month. When I walked out of the recruiting office, a Marine recruiter was standing on the sidewalk. After talking with him, I was on my way to Parris Island, South Carolina, and another boot camp.

The Marines gave me something I'll never forget. As we crossed the equator, they put us first-time guys through a memorable initiation that transformed us from "polliwogs" to "shellbacks." After almost two years in the tough Marines, I was offered an "early out" and took it. I stored my belongings in a rooming house in Florida and never went back to get them.

I went to Memphis, bought an old car, and headed for California. I thought I would play a while, then join the Navy and serve in a third branch of the military. My car broke down in Houston, I met a girl whom I married, and it was 1999 before I ever got to California.

Clyde Stewart sold heavy-duty trucks for Peterbilt for many years, then for Kenworth and later Mack. In 1988, he opened his own used-truck dealership. He retired in 1998. Clyde and Janiece, his wife of 46 years, have two children and eight grandchildren. One grandchild is serving in the Air Force in Operation Enduring Freedom. They live in Manvel, Texas.

Murray L. La Hue

Age 15 – California National Guard
Age 16 – United States Army

I was born in St. Louis, Missouri, on 24 May 1934. We moved to California when I was 3 years old. At age 15, I felt the need to do something more than goof off or go to school, so I decided to join the

> *I have a sneaky suspicion that he already had some idea of my age, ...*

California Army National Guard. At that time, in order to enlist, one merely had to fill out an application and have it signed by a parent, as long as you were 17.

I obtained an application for the Guard, took it home, and filled it out. Actually, my mother thought this was a pretty good idea, so she signed it. I became a member of the 223rd Heavy Tank Company, 223rd Infantry Regiment, 40th Infantry Division, on 11 October 1949, at age 15.

It became a real thrill for me to put on my uniform, including a helmet liner, and go to the unit meetings. I lived in Baldwin Park, California, and the unit was in El Monte, California, about seven miles away. I was too young to drive, so one of my parents drove me to the meetings and picked me up, or I scrounged a ride to and from the meetings, or I walked – which I did on numerous occasions. I was assigned as a loader on an M4A3-E8 Patton tank. This weapons system was equipped with a 76mm cannon whose shells were almost as big as I was.

In June 1950, we were advised that the 40th Division would probably be activated because of the Korean conflict. I argued long and hard with my parents, who now planned to send a letter to the company commander advising him of my correct age.

At that time, I had gotten in with a rather bad crowd which was involved in a number of things that were not really acceptable in polite society. I had completed my sophomore year of high school and had already decided that, unless I was forced, I would not go back to school. After all, I told my parents, I already knew all that I needed to know and probably knew more than the teachers. The news of the pending activation came at a rather opportune time. I was smart enough to realize that the activities I was involved with were going to lead to my downfall, and I felt that going into the Army would be an advantage. My parents reluctantly agreed and did not send any notice to the unit about my age.

In July 1950 the rumor was confirmed, and on 1 September 1950, the 40th Infantry Division was activated and became a part of the U. S. Sixth Army. Very early on 1 September, we congregated at the company facility, loaded on buses, and went to Santa Maria, California. We were taken to Camp Cooke, an old base which had housed German POWs during World War II. It had been abandoned in 1945, and the buildings boarded up. The entire base, which is now Vandenberg Air Force Base, was in a terrible state of disrepair.

We arrived very late at night and were herded into the dilapidated barracks. Metal bunks and mattresses were piled in a corner. We each grabbed a mattress and crashed on the floor. In the morning, we started on a project of rehabilitating these buildings. It was felt by our leaders that since we were already soldiers, we didn't need to jump right into a training program, but we would spend the first portion of our stay in getting the facility into a livable condition. This took longer than they had anticipated. The cracks in the walls were so large that sunlight, and the fierce winds that blew in off the Pacific Ocean, came through almost unaltered.

During Christmas of 1950 we were confined to the base, so my parents drove up from Southern California. All of the visiting families joined the troops in the company mess hall for Christmas dinner. When we had finished dinner, the company commander (Captain Thomas T. Tomkinson, who had served as a tank commander under General Patton) called for everyone's attention. He announced that we had been working hard to fill up the division to proper strength, and we were now at that point. We would soon depart for Japan for a short training period, then go on to Korea.

At this time my parents became a bit excited, and after a conversation from which I was excluded, advised me that they were going to tell Captain Tomkinson of my age. They did!

I have a sneaky suspicion that he already had some idea of my age, primarily because of my diminutive size. He was upset because he had been asking everybody if they were "legal" ever since we had been advised of our activation. I had always assured him that I was old enough. He had no choice but to start the paperwork for my honorable discharge, which took place on 12 January 1951. I was told that if I re-entered the service at a later date, my time would count.

I stayed out of the service, but I wasn't really happy. I did not want to return to school, so I found work as a flunky in a plastics manufacturing shop. I thought long and hard about my time in the military and recalled that I had actually liked the regimentation and the controlled atmosphere. In January 1952, one year and two days after being separated from the Army, I joined the Air Force. This time I was 17 and had my parents' permission.

Because of my prior service, I re-enlisted as a private first class, and I was assigned to March Air Force Base, Riverside, California, a 45-minute drive from my home. Since there wasn't much call for tank crewmen in the Air Force, and since I had taken a typing class in high school, I became a clerk-typist.

During the next four years we converted to the blue Air Force uniform. I cross-trained into the transportation career area, and was promoted to airman second class, then to airman first class, and finally to staff sergeant. I stayed at March AFB for my entire 4-year enlistment. After I was discharged, I worked in a lumber yard and went to college. But after nearly six months of civilian life, I re-enlisted in the Air Force. I retained my E-5 (staff sergeant) rating, and asked for an assignment to Europe.

I reported in to the Manhattan Beach Air Force Station in July 1956. After a few days, my European assignment arrived from the personnel office. I was going to APO 231 (Armed Forces Post Office), which I thought was either in Germany or in England. It turned out that it was at Wheelus Air Base, in Tripoli, Libya. Of course, I had no choice but to board a plane for Libya.

When my 18-month tour was about half over, I met a lovely Italian girl who worked in the American Express Bank on the base. After a totally old-world-style courtship, we were married.

When we returned to the States, I was fortunate enough to be reassigned back to March Air Force Base. There I applied for and was accepted into the Air Force officer candidate school program. I was commissioned a second lieutenant on 22 September 1961.

My first assignment as an officer was to Westover AFB, Massachusetts. After a year there, I joined the second group of Air Force personnel to go to Vietnam on a permanent rather than a temporary assignment. I went to Pleiku Airfield, Republic of Vietnam, where I commanded Detachment 3, 8th Aerial Port Squadron.

I spent the next 10 years at various locations in the United States and overseas, ending up at Sheppard AFB, Wichita Falls, Texas, where I was in charge of a transportation training organization. This assignment was probably the most enjoyable of any during my 22+ years of service. It was extremely rewarding to see kids come from basic and leave trained to a degree that I would like to have them work for me as a base transportation officer.

I received an advisory that I was being considered for another overseas assignment. I was told it would be a great "career-broadening" assignment. It was to be the chief of transportation for the 814th Air Division at Osan, Korea. It was a colonel's position and I was a fairly junior major. I told personnel that I did not really want my career broadened, and I applied for voluntary retirement. I retired from the Air Force on 1 July 1973.

Murray La Hue was awarded the Bronze Star with oak leaf cluster and the Air Force Commendation Medal with oak leaf cluster. On two occasions he was selected as the Air Force Outstanding Transportation Officer, after his professional performance was compared to all Air Force transportation officers world-wide. He also received the Stanley H. Morgan Award for operating the best traffic-management office in the Strategic Air Command. Several years after his retirement, he was recruited by the Northrop Corporation to go to Saudi Arabia as transportation director for their Peace Hawk program. He stayed with Northrop for 14 years, retiring in July 1990. Murray and his wife Margherita have two daughters and four grandchildren. They live in Phoenix, Oregon.

Robert W. Burlingame
Age 15 – Arizona National Guard

At the time that I was born in East Alton, Illinois, on 21 June 1934, my dad was in the Navy. He spent much of his time in China. Men who served in Chinese

> I am proud of my military service, as I come from a military family.

waters for extended periods were known as "China Sailors." Dad contracted tuberculosis while in China, so the Navy sent him back to the States to die. He was given the choice of living in Phoenix, Arizona, or Denver, Colorado. He chose Phoenix.

He moved the family to Phoenix in 1939, but he didn't die. After the attack on Pearl Harbor, he started pestering the Navy to take him back, but they refused on the basis that he had TB. He pestered them so much that in the spring of 1942 he was told to go to a hospital in Tempe, Arizona, and be tested for TB. He did and was found to be free of the disease. He reported for active duty in June 1942 and

immediately joined the crew of the USS Wasp (CV-7), which soon set sail to the South Pacific. On 15 September 1942, while escorting a transport convoy to Guadalcanal, the *Wasp* was torpedoed and sunk by a Japanese submarine. The torpedo struck the ship near the gasoline-storage area where my dad was working.

I was only 8 years old when my dad was killed in action, but I knew that he had done his part for our country, and I wanted to do mine. By 1949, I was young, patriotic, and impatient. I joined the Arizona National Guard on 24 October 1949 at the age of 15. I wanted to get the training and experience, so when I turned 18 and joined the Army, I wouldn't have a hard time getting accustomed to military service. Back in those days, it was an honor and a duty to put your time in the service and then get out and start your own life.

When the Korean War broke out, it took me from June 1950 until the middle of October 1951 to talk my mom into letting me go on active duty. After getting her permission, I found out that one had to have prior service to ask for active duty, so I joined the Army. I did get to keep my National Guard serial number, but not my private first class rank. I had to go into the Army as a private.

I took basic training at Fort Ord, California, and advanced training in antiaircraft artillery (AAA) at Fort Bliss, Texas. From Fort Bliss, I was sent to Camp (now Fort) McCoy, Wisconsin. I was there two months and received orders to go to Korea. The troopship stopped at Okinawa on the way to Korea. The AAA command on Okinawa was short of trained personnel, so all trained AAA troops were taken off the ship and assigned to the 97th AAA Group.

I served with B Battery, 22nd AAA AW Battalion, 97th AAA Group, from August 1952 until October 1954. I was a section leader on an M55 machine gun. I came back to the States in October 1954, returned to Phoenix, and got married in May 1955.

I went back in the National Guard and then, in June 1957, re-enlisted in the Army. I went to Germany twice in four years and spent some time at Fort Sill, Oklahoma, as an instructor in fire control at the U. S. Army Artillery Training Center, in the 7th Training Battalion. I developed arthritis in my left leg, which resulted in a medical discharge in May 1961.

I am proud of my military service, as I come from a military family. Besides my father, my brother served in Korea, and I have two nephews who served in Desert Storm. I really wish that I could have made the Army a career, but I developed a severe case of arthritis in my legs.

Bob Burlingame was discharged at Fort Sheridan, Illinois, and returned to Phoenix. He worked in land surveying for a few years, then became a letter carrier for the U. S. Postal Service. In 1979, he was forced into early retirement because of his arthritis. He has four children from a previous marriage. Bob and his wife Norma live in Black Canyon City, Arizona.

Walter R. Cassady

Age 16 – Oklahoma National Guard
Age 16 – United States Army

My first recollection of war was when my family gathered around an automobile battery-powered Crosley radio and listened to reports of the Nazi blitzkrieg into Poland and Eastern

> *It was a tough sell, but I was persistent in begging my mother to let me enlist.*

Europe. I was not yet 6 years old, but I understood that war was a bad thing.

I was born in Oklahoma City, Oklahoma, on 5 November 1933. I was the fifth child and was reared with five sisters, four older and one younger. My mother was given a small amount of money by her father, and during the worst part of the Great Depression, she purchased an acreage with an old house and a water well several miles east of Oklahoma City. She believed that children should be raised on a farm. Because my father was a plumber and worked in town, he had to live in Oklahoma City. The cost of gasoline and tires, and the sometimes very muddy roads, made it impossible for him to live in the country with us. Dad would deliver groceries on Saturday evening and

stay until daylight on Monday morning. Mother raised crops, calves, pigs, chickens, and her kids, virtually by herself. Only in later years did I come to appreciate what a feat she had accomplished, all in a leaky wooden house with no plumbing, no washing machine, no telephone, and no gas or electricity.

World War II was the prime factor in my yearning to be in the military. In 1940-41, with the war raging in Europe and China, a group of Oklahoma City businessmen bought several square miles of land one and a half miles south of our place. They donated it to the U. S. Government as the location of the Army Air Corps Midwest Air Depot. Our family and neighbors witnessed the construction of what became Tinker Field, now Tinker Air Force Base, the Douglas Airplane Company's manufacturing plant, and the towns of Midwest City and Del City.

The servicemen from Tinker Field and the numerous other military installations nearby became my heroes. Of course, having dating-age sisters attracted a lot of servicemen to our home. Our family befriended guys from all over the United States. From age 8 to age 13, I had many military buddies, some whom I am sure had to tolerate the inquisitive little brother.

In 1947 at the age of 13, I joined the Civil Air Patrol as a cadet at Tinker Field. During the next two years, I went with other members on orientation flights in C-47s and often flew as an observer and cross-country navigator in a Piper Cub. I wore my uniform with pride and was never late for a squadron meeting, although I had to walk four miles round-trip to attend the evening meetings.

During my junior year in high school, a number of the older guys were joining the Oklahoma National Guard's famed 45th "Thunderbird" Division. They wore their uniforms to school on Thursdays and were picked up by a truck after school and taken to the armory in Oklahoma City for drill. In October 1949, with my mother's permission, I rode to the armory with the older guys and was taken to see the first sergeant, a World War II veteran. He listened to me tell about the Civil Air Patrol and all the military subjects I knew, looked at my slick cheeks, and asked me my age. I lied and boldly told him that I was 17 and that I really wanted to be a soldier. He asked if I could get my parents' consent to enlist, and bluffing, I told him I was sure that I could. He said that I had to get written permission from my parents, but when I told him my birthday was 5 November, he said I could just come in after my birthday if I wanted.

It was a tough sell, but I was persistent in begging my mother to let me enlist. She finally gave in. I enlisted in Headquarters and Headquarters Company, 45th Infantry Division, on 21 November 1949 at the age of 16 years and 16 days. I was not required to produce a birth certificate or have papers signed by my mother.

In May 1950, a customer on my country paper route who was a WWII airborne veteran and a sergeant in the 45th Signal Company, talked me into transferring into the Signal Company so that I could attend an active-duty Signal Corps school in the summer of 1950.

In June 1950, the unit was preparing to convoy to the annual summer camp at Fort Hood, Texas, when the North Koreans invaded South Korea. Our orders were changed, and the Thunderbird Division was notified that it would be federalized on 1 September 1950 and ordered to Camp Polk, Louisiana. The division had been activated ten years earlier, so for many of our older soldiers, it was *déja vù*.

I was on state orders for 30 days in August prior to federal mobilization. I was inducted into the federalized National Guard on 1 September 1950, about two months before my 17th birthday. I had to really talk to keep my mother from telling my commanding officer about my correct age.

In February 1951, the 45th Division was ordered to Japan, then on to Korea. I had been in signal school for three months and had not completed all phases of combat training, so I was reassigned as cadre to a training battalion that was left behind to complete the training of draftees who would rejoin the 45th as replacements. I had the feeling that the Korean War would be over and that I would have spent my tour at Camp Polk and at Camp Gordon, Georgia.

A high school buddy who had joined the Air Force told me that it was easy to get overseas if you were in the Air Force. I had heard about underage soldiers getting minority discharges, so I came up with a plan. I would get a minority discharge, then enlist in the Air Force, giving my correct age. On 22 May 1951, I was discharged from the Army and went back to Oklahoma City. Twenty-eight days later, I enlisted in the Air Force. I lost a stripe, but I didn't have to lie about my birth date anymore.

I spent two months at Vance Air Force Base, Oklahoma, then I was on orders to the Far East. I spent 18 months at a radar site in Niigata, Japan. I returned to the States in March 1953 and was assigned to a radar site on San Clemente Island, off the southern coast of California. This was great duty; we worked 21 days straight, then had a 7-day break on the mainland. This enabled me to hitchhike to Little Rock, Arkansas, to date my future wife. Her husband had been killed in action in Korea when their daughter was 20 days old. She was fearful of losing another husband in the military, so we agreed that I would complete my enlistment, then I would re-enlist as an active reservist.

I completed my 4-year enlistment in the Air Force on 19 June 1955, and was discharged as a staff sergeant. We were married in September. I adopted her daughter and we had a son and another daughter. My wife died of Hodgkin's disease in May 1971.

On 8 September 1955, I re-enlisted in the 45th Infantry Division's 45th Signal Company, the same unit that I was in when I was inducted at age 16. I balanced my civilian working career and my part-time soldiering for more than 38 years without a break in service. I attended officer candidate school as a guardsman in 1957, made a branch transfer to the Army Medical Service Corps in 1968, and volunteered for as many active-duty tours as my civilian occupation would permit. I completed the U. S. Army Command and General Staff College in 1976 and served in numerous medical battalion and command headquarters staff assignments. As the Superintendent of the Oklahoma Military Academy, I was promoted to colonel in May 1984.

I transferred to the Army Reserve on 1 January 1986 and was assigned to the Academy of Health Sciences, U. S. Army Medical Services at Fort Sam Houston, Texas. I enjoyed very rewarding active duty as the medical coordinator at the U. S. Army Garrison, Fort McCoy, Wisconsin, in 1987 and 1988.

In the summer of 1988, I was encouraged to apply for selection as a brigadier general. I was not selected because there were only eight assignments for about 20 highly qualified Medical Service applicants. As a former high school dropout, I was pretty satisfied with the road I had traveled. I was asked to apply for the 1989 selection cycle, but at age 55 with 32 years of commissioned service, my mandatory removal date occurred before the next general officer selection round took place.

But I was not ready to leave the active reserves. Through a chance meeting with a former colleague, I learned that I could vacate my commission and re-enlist as a staff sergeant. At that time, a gray area existed where retirees under the age of 60 received virtually no retiree privileges until they reached the age of 60. Re-enlisting, however, would allow me to continue to soldier and earn additional retirement points. I was offered the assignment at a troop medical clinic at the Oklahoma Army National Guard's training-site detachment at Camp Gruber, Oklahoma. What a choice job!

While attending a business conference in Boston in my civilian occupation with Rockwell International, just after Thanksgiving in 1990, I received a call from the unit administrator. My unit, the 245th Medical Company, had been ordered to active duty on 6 December 1990 in support of Operation Desert Shield. It had been a little more than 40 years since I was first inducted as a slick-faced, 16-year-old, enlisted Thunderbird, and now I was being inducted as a gray-beard, 57-year-old, enlisted Thunderbird. We were deployed to Rhein Main Air Base near Frankfurt, Germany. While in Germany, I ran into a lieutenant colonel friend from our days at Fort Sam Houston. He greeted me with, "Hello, colonel." Then he looked like a deer caught in the headlights when he saw my staff-sergeant insignia. He exclaimed, "How bad did you mess up to get busted from O-6 to E-6?" We had quite a laugh!

Our short stint in Germany was one of long hours, hard work, and the reward of "mission accomplished." I had no complaints about that, but I did wrestle with the experience of living in a barracks with soldiers young enough to be my grandchildren. Their all-hours-of-the-night heavy-metal rock music and my Glenn Miller ear didn't blend well – but I survived!

At the conclusion of Operation Desert Storm we returned from Germany and I resumed my assignment at Camp Gruber. I was the last Thunderbird to actively serve in the Oklahoma National Guard who had been mobilized with the 45th Division in September 1950. On my 60th birthday, 5 November 1993, I retired from the Army of the United States with the rank of colonel, 43 years, 11 months and 14 days after I had first enlisted. What a privilege – what an honor!

Walt Cassady's civilian career included working in electronics and weapons system management at Tinker AFB, Oklahoma, from 1955-65. From 1965-1991, he held various technical and project management positions with the North American Aircraft Operations of Rockwell International Corporation in Tulsa, Oklahoma. He retired from Rockwell a month after returning from Desert Storm. Walt and Starr, his wife of 30 years, have a combined family of three daughters, two sons, and 12 grandchildren. One daughter is an Air Force lieutenant colonel. Walt and Starr live in Tulsa, Oklahoma.

William J. Boggs

Age 15 – West Virginia National Guard

I was born on 8 May 1934 in my parents' bedroom on a farm near Moatsville, Barbour County, West Virginia. I am the oldest of six boys; there were no girls. We moved to Cleveland, West

> Drowning was preferable to remaining at "Fort Lost in the Woods."

Virginia, when I was 6 years old. I attended a one-room school, used a slate board for writing and ciphering, and studied a McGuffey's reader.

I enlisted in Company B, 150th Infantry, West Virginia National Guard on 30 November 1949. I was 15 years and 7 months old at the time. My younger brother John joined about a week later. We have consecutive serial numbers. His is one greater than mine.

I quit school after completing nine years. In May 1951, I left West Virginia and went to work as a psychiatric aid at a psychiatric hospital in Sykesville, Maryland. While working at the hospital, I completed a course in practical nursing. While there, I received a general discharge under honorable conditions from the West Virginia National Guard for being underage.

In July 1952, my mother informed me that the Selective Service Board in Weston, West Virginia, was looking for me because I had failed to register. I resigned my position at the hospital and returned home. I immediately visited the draft board and was informed that I would be called to report for an induction physical no later than the following Monday. I contacted the local Army recruiter, took a battery of tests, and volunteered for airborne training. All of this activity took place at the Armed Forces Entrance and Examination Station (AFEES) in Fairmont, West Virginia. Thirteen years later, after returning from my first tour of duty in Vietnam, I would return to command the station as a captain of infantry.

I entered active duty on 11 August 1952. Basic training consisted of 16 weeks' light-weapons infantry training at Camp Breckenridge, Kentucky, as a member of Company A, 502nd Airborne Infantry Regiment, 101st Airborne Division. Because I was an airborne volunteer, I missed being shipped immediately to Korea, which was the fate of 210 of my 220 classmates. I completed airborne basic at Fort Benning, Georgia, and was assigned to the 508th Airborne Regimental Combat Team at Fort Benning. Because of the practical nursing course I had taken, my light-weapons infantry MOS was ignored and I was assigned to the medical company as a field medical-aid man. This was a blessing in disguise.

I became the day-room orderly and mail clerk and was promoted to private first class. Next was cook and baker school, which I completed as an honor student, and I was then promoted to corporal. I visited my brother John at the Aberdeen Proving Grounds, Maryland. I was a corporal and he was a sergeant. Our paths would cross occasionally throughout our service.

I rose to the rank of sergeant and became the mess steward. The 508th was moved to Fort Campbell, Kentucky, and eventually shipped to Japan. I chose not to accompany the unit and was transferred to the Ambulance Company, 11th Medical Battalion, 11th Airborne Division, also at Fort Campbell, and became the motor sergeant.

This success, which took place prior to my 21st birthday, came to a screeching halt. I allowed demon rum to cloud my judgment and was reduced to corporal, then converted to specialist-3. I was discharged on 10 August 1955.

I returned home and married an old grade-school chum. I re-enlisted in September 1955 and was assigned to Fort Jackson, South Carolina. I was immediately shipped to Korea and assigned to Medical Company, 34th Infantry Regiment, 24th Infantry division. I spent about 16 months on the DMZ. When I returned to the States I was stationed at Upper Marlboro, Maryland, as the senior emergency medical technician on site. This was one sweet tour of duty.

I was transferred to the Medical Platoon, Headquarters and Headquarters Company, 1st Battle Group, 34th Infantry, 24th Infantry Division, Augsburg, Germany. This was the tour that changed my career orientation. I was not able to be promoted because of an overabundance of sergeants first class, so I decided to apply for officers candidate school.

I reported for officer training at the Infantry Officers Candidate School, Fort Benning, Georgia, in March 1961. I fell in love with the infantry. Of the 1,000 candidates that commenced training, 550 fell by the wayside. In the entire U. S. Army, only 450 officers were commissioned through OCS in 1961. I was extremely fortunate to be one of those officers. I could have been commissioned in the medical service, but I chose the infantry.

Fort Leonard Wood, Missouri, was my next home. During the Korean War, Walter Winchell, a news commentator, lost a son during basic training at Fort Leonard Wood. Winchell would close his newscast with this admonition: "Write to the boys in Korea, pray for the boys at Fort Leonard Wood." I understand the reason for this feeling on Winchell's part. The weather was a killer: boiling heat in summer and frigid winters. I spent the better part of two years conducting basic training at Fort Leonard Wood.

I became desperate to escape that torture chamber. A memorandum came across my desk stating that the U. S. Army Special Forces was looking for volunteers. One of the qualifications was that the volunteer must be able to swim. I couldn't swim. All of my brothers learned to swim, but I never did. During my airborne duty, I had to swim a specified distance with a full field-pack and a weapon. However, the rubberized, waterproofed inside of the pack made it into a flotation device. I escaped notice and always qualified. I was desperate, so my application was submitted with a slight administrative oversight – on paper, I swam. Drowning was preferable to remaining at "Fort Lost in the Woods."

Fort Bragg was the home of the Special Warfare Center and Special Forces. I was assigned to the 6th Special Forces Group Airborne, with further assignment to the Special Forces School. I learned to swim and completed the course in March 1964. I deployed to Pakistan for a military training mission in desert survival as an A-Team commander. I also commanded a modified B-Team that trained infantry battalions from Fort Benning, Georgia, in counterinsurgency.

I was transferred to the 5th Special Forces Group to prepare for deployment to Vietnam. I trained an A-Team and left for Vietnam with that team in March 1965. I was promoted to captain, wounded, and med-evacuated to Walter Reed Army Medical Center, Washington, D.C.

After release from the medical center, I was placed on light duty for six months. I was assigned as the commander of the AFEES Station in Fairmont, West Virginia. I had come full-circle. I was home.

I was transferred to the U. S. Army Recruiting Main Station, Beckley, West Virginia, in November 1966. Initially I was the executive officer, then became the commanding officer of the station. This duty was demanding. The Vietnam War made it quite difficult to meet all assigned objectives. It was difficult to sell death. I was responsible for 22 counties in Eastern Kentucky, 49 counties in West Virginia, 5 counties in Southern Ohio, and 5 counties in Western Maryland. We never missed a quota. I had a group of recruiters that was second to none.

My next assignment was to the Infantry Officers Advanced Course, Fort Benning. Prior to completing the course, I volunteered to return to Vietnam and the 5th Special Forces Group Airborne. I was promoted to major in August 1968.

Upon completion of the course, I traveled to Egland Air Force Base, Florida, and to Fort Clayton in the Panama Canal Zone to receive training in personnel infiltration interdiction that I would be utilizing in Vietnam. I reached the 5th Special Forces Group in early November 1968. I was further assigned to MACV-SOG-CCN (Military Assistance Command, Vietnam, – Studies and Observations Group – Command and Control, North). Here I was involved in the infiltration and extraction of reconnaissance teams into Laos, Cambodia, and the DMZ.

In January 1969, I was assigned to the 4th Corps Mobile Strike Force, where I spent the remainder of my tour, alternating between the positions of executive officer and commanding officer. I applied for and received an inter-theater transfer to Europe upon completion of my tour. I was assigned to the 1st Battalion, 51st Infantry Mechanized, 1st Armored Division, at McKee Barracks, Crailsheim, Germany, in January 1970.

I retired from the Army on 30 September 1972 at the rank of major with more than 21 years of service.

Bill Boggs was awarded the Purple Heart, the Bronze Star Medal, the Air Medal, the Army Commendation Medal, the Meritorious Service Medal, a Presidential Unit Citation, the Combat Infantryman's

Badge, the Expert Infantryman's Badge, a number of parachute badges, and other service medals. After his retirement, he spent 12 years as an office manager and as a maintenance and construction supervisor for a Kentucky Fried Chicken franchisee. He was self-employed for three years, and the assistant chief of Central Service of the Veterans Administration Medical Center in Clarksburg, West Virginia, for eight years, retiring from that position in December 1996. He completed a four-year B.A. in accounting and is preparing for the CPA examination to be held in November 2002. He is active in veterans affairs and maintains membership in a number of veterans organizations. Currently, he is chief of staff of the Department of West Virginia, Military Order of the Purple Heart, and commander of the 3rd District of the American Legion, Department of West Virginia. Bill and Barbara , his wife of 47 years, had four sons (two deceased), and one grandchild. They live in Salem, West Virginia.

✓ *INCIDENTally* — **The enemy knew first!** – When the 508th Parachute Infantry Regiment received orders to return to the States in June 1946, many of us wanted to transfer out of the 508th and remain in Germany. Our officers told us that we could not transfer out because the unit was to remain intact in the U. S. Our German contacts told us the unit would be deactivated upon reaching the U. S. We did indeed deactivate; so much for truth from our superiors. – *Walter Holy.*

Lloyd W. Pate

Age 15 – United States Army

I was born on 11 January 1934 on the Olympia Mill Hill in Columbia, South Carolina. Most of my people worked in a cotton mill. My formative years were during World War II. I would recite the Pledge of

> All that stuff about American prisoners of war giving up is a crock.

Allegiance at school every morning and say a prayer for victory and the safe return of our fighting men. In the evening, I would listen to the radio or read the newspaper about our victories and our losses in Europe and the Pacific. I made up my mind then that I wanted to be a soldier.

I enlisted in the Army on 6 December 1949 at the age of 15. I had started to shave when I was 14, and by this time I had a pretty good face of hair. I was just shy of 6-feet and weighed a solid 165 pounds.

I told the recruiter that I was 17, upping my age by two years. He didn't bat an eye, but told me I would still have to have my parents' signature. I could have told him that I was older than that and proved

it by my Social Security card, as I had gotten it when I was 12. I told them I was 16, because you had to be 16 to get a card back then. You could not work without a card, and I needed to work. I took the enlistment papers home and told my mother I needed her permission to get a job. She signed, and the next day I was sworn into the United States Army. Of course, my mother was mad and threatened to turn me in, but I talked her out of it.

I took basic training at Fort Jackson, South Carolina, and after basic, I was assigned to the Far East Command. I was stationed in Yokohama, Japan, when the war broke out in Korea.

I volunteered for duty in Korea on 27 August 1950, and was assigned to Company K, 3rd Battalion, 19th Regiment, 24th Infantry

Division as an ammo bearer for a 57mm recoilless rifle. Less that two months later I was a corporal and a squad leader. It didn't take long for your turn in the barrel to come around. On 17 September 1950, we started our push north, and by the end of October we were sitting a few miles south of the Yalu River. Then the Chinese came into the war.

The Eighth Army and the Tenth Corps made a hasty strategic withdrawal to the rear. When the Chinese made their big push across the 38th parallel on 31 December 1950, my hours of freedom were numbered. About 0300 on 1 January 1951, our company was ordered to withdraw to other positions. My squad, occupying the right flank of the company's perimeter, never got the word. We were the only ones holding the hill. We held it.

At about 0500, we heard a voice to our rear. It was my section sergeant, Graham Cockfield, who had found that we were missing and came back for us. Shortly after we rejoined the company, we were told to make our way to our lines as best we could. Sergeant Cockfield went with my squad. Shortly thereafter, we were hit with mortar fire and Cockfield was hit in the legs and side. I was hit in both legs and one of my men, Cletys "Bill" Nordin, was hit. We sent the squad on their way, and Bill and I started to carry Sergeant Cockfield. After several miles we came upon a makeshift aid-station where we left him. He lost both legs and is now deceased.

We soon joined another group of 14 men, led by a lieutenant. We were moving up a gully when all of a sudden it seemed as though the snow had risen up several feet all around us. It was the Chinese. We were now guests of the Chinese People's Volunteers. To the best of my knowledge, Bill and I were the only ones who made it back.

I was in several Chinese prison camps during my 31 months and 19 days in captivity. We were continually bombarded with communist propaganda. All that stuff about American prisoners of war giving up is a crock. Generally, the POWs did themselves proud. I remember being thrown into solitary confinement with my arms shackled tightly behind my back. The guards threw food on the floor, and I had to eat it like a dog.

I refused to sign a confession, so they tied a rope under my armpits and hung me from a ceiling beam with my toes inches from the floor. When the rope stretched enough for my toes to touch the floor, the guards would come into the room and yank me up a few inches. After three days of this, the guards finally gave up. It was so painful that I was passed out much of the time. However, I wasn't about to succumb to "give-up-itis." I was determined to fight until the end. If I was to die, it would be by a Chinese bullet.

I learned that as a prisoner, you have no defense. You realize very quickly that your captors can kill you at any time. At least on the front line you have a weapon and can go down fighting. I've been both places, and I tell you, I'd much rather be on the front line with a fighting unit than in a prisoner-of-war camp. My experiences as a POW left me with two enduring passions: a love of freedom and a hatred of oppression.

After we were released I returned to the States determined to stay in the Army. I served for another two decades, which included two tours as an infantryman in Vietnam. I retired from the Army as a first sergeant, very proud that I was able to serve my country.

Lloyd Pate earned the Combat Infantryman's Badge, three Bronze Stars, the Purple Heart, three Army Commendation Medals, the Air Medal, the POW Medal, and more than 20 other awards, including foreign medals. He wrote Reactionary, *a book about his experiences as a prisoner of war, the title coming from the name that the Chinese called those who resisted their attempts at communist indoctrination. The book was first published by Harper Brothers in 1955 and reprinted with revisions in 2000 by Vantage Press. In the revision titled* Reactionary - Revised 2000, *he put back a lot of material that the Army censored out of the first edition. After he retired, Lloyd went into the major-appliance sales and repair business. Lloyd and Juanita, his wife of 48 years, have four children, four grandchildren, and two great-grandchildren. They live in Grovetown, Georgia.*

John A. Boggs

Age 14 – West Virginia National Guard

I was born at home on a farm near Moatsville, Barbour County, West Virginia, on 2 July 1935.

My service began on 7 December 1949 (Pearl Harbor Day) as an underage

> *... he suspected a number of us were not the age that our records indicated.*

enlistee in Company B, 150th Infantry, West Virginia National Guard. The date was by chance and not by design. After a review of past events and consultation with my older brother, the documents used as proof of age and who signed what, is somewhat unclear to both of us. I have always been under the impression that I had used the services of a local female bootlegger by the name of "Ma Bragg." A local doctor by the name of Chapman gave me my induction physical. I do remember that his reputation for physical exams was said to consist of only "looking up your ass to see if your hat was on straight." If you wanted to join the military, Doc Chapman was noted for finding you 1-A.

Company B was at Fort Knox, Kentucky, in July 1950 at the beginning of the Korean conflict. I remember that our 1st Sergeant White called a company formation and announced the news. At that time he also noted that he suspected a number of us were not the age that our records indicated. He then asked all who fit this category to step forward. I told my section leader that I needed to talk to my brother Bill who was in a different platoon. I then went to see what he was going to do. We were both underage and I was going to be affected by his decision. He said, "Let's stay put. We have a good deal going for us. They provide

clothes, good food (I became addicted to 'shit on a shingle' forever), and money." He added, "We get to shoot guns and run around in the woods as well." Then he said, "There will be a problem if we go on extended active duty. Mother will be mad as hell if we don't get back and put the hay up." We decided that we could just send a few bucks back to a neighbor and get him to do the haying for us. I don't remember anyone stepping forward to declare he was underage. I know that there were at least two or three others who were underage. However, we were not activated, and Bill and I returned home on schedule.

I attended drills, participated in summer camp at Fort Knox, Kentucky, in 1950, 1951, and 1952. My assignment was in the weapons platoon.

From 1 October 1952 through 14 January 1953, I was on active duty, attending an 18-week combined light/heavy weapons and leadership course at the Infantry School, Fort Benning, Georgia. I went on extended active duty from 3 November 1953 until 22 November 1954. During this period, I was stationed at Fort Meade in Maryland, Aberdeen Proving Grounds, Maryland, and I did an overseas tour with the 5th Regimental Combat Team in Korea, and with the 7th Infantry Division in Korea.

On 23 November 1954, I was discharged from the West Virginia National Guard and enlisted for a 3-year term in the regular Army. My duty station at that time was with the 48th Field Artillery Battalion, 7th Infantry Division, in Korea.

I returned to the States in 1955 and was assigned to the XVIII Airborne Corps Artillery at Fort Bragg, North Carolina. In 1956, I was stationed at Fort Benning, Georgia. It was there that I met a member of the Women's Army Corps who would become my future wife. In November 1957, I elected to enter civilian life.

My civilian career lasted until early April 1958. My next duty station was Fort Carson, Colorado, then I returned to Fort Benning, Georgia. In early 1959, I was ordered to Germany, and the following year I was assigned to a 7th Army unit at Seckenheim, Germany.

I returned to the States in 1962 and went to Walter Reed Army Medical Center. In early 1963, I was transferred to Fort Belvoir, Virginia, for a time, and then I went to France. In late 1964, I returned to Fort Benning and attended "Benning's School for Boys," which terminated in a commission as a second lieutenant of infantry.

I was assigned to the 1st Cavalry Division's airborne brigade as a platoon leader in July 1965. Our unit deployed to the Republic of South Vietnam (RSVN) in late July 1965.

I went back to Fort Benning in August 1966 and was assigned to the Infantry School. Our mission was to train personnel to become second lieutenants of infantry. My next assignment was as company commander of the 44th Company (Airborne), 2nd Student Battalion (Airborne).

I returned to RSVN in 1968 with intermediate stops at the John F. Kennedy Special Warfare Center, Fort Bragg, North Carolina, and the Defense Language Institute, Fort Bliss, Texas. My assignment was with the Military Assistance Command, Vietnam (MACV). My directions, orders, and guidance came from a mixed bag of organizations and commands. My second tour ended in April 1969 via the medical evacuation route, about one month earlier than scheduled. After a brief stop in Japan, it was on to the Eisenhower Memorial Medical Center, Fort Gordon, Georgia. After a short period, I headed for the University of Nebraska Omaha, where I obtained a B.G.S., a bachelor of general studies degree.

I then returned to Fort Benning to attend the Infantry Officer Advanced Course (IOAC) and the Instructor Training Course (ITC). I became an instructor in the Brigade and Battalion Operations Department at the Infantry School.

By 1972, my term as an active-duty reserve commissioned officer was about to close because of a law that limits reserve officers to 20 years of active duty. I found a regulation that allowed a commissioning in the medical service under a different law. I was accepted by the Medical Service Corps in 1972 as a regular Army officer. By this time I had graduated from Georgia State University with a master's degree in education (M.Ed.) and was an instructor in the Office of the Staff Surgeon, the Infantry School.

I attended the Medical Service Corps Advanced Course at Fort Sam Houston, Texas, then returned to Fort Benning as commanding officer of the 546th Medical Company (Clearing), 34th Medical Battalion. During the year 1974, I graduated from Georgia State University with an education specialist degree in psychological services and counseling (Ed.S.).

In early 1975, I became the executive officer of the 34th Medical Battalion. In May 1975, the battalion was directed to prepare for the arrival of some 170 Vietnamese orphans. I was the officer in charge of "Operation Benning Babies." My responsibility was to meet and welcome them at Lawson Army Air Field, transport them to a pre-arranged facility, which was to be their home/hotel until their placement with adopted families had been completed.

Upon the successful closure of "Operation Benning Babies" in June 1975, I departed for Letterman Army Medical Center at the Presidio, San Francisco, California. My assignment was as chief of the Operations and Training Division and Medical Library. In July 1975, I applied for retirement. As a regular Army officer, I had at least another seven years of tenure, but my 26-year love affair with the Army had ended and it was time to go. I retired at Fort Benning, Georgia, on 1 January 1976. I have never given my underage service much thought and certainly never considered it as other than ordinary. For that matter, I still don't.

John Boggs earned the Purple Heart with one oak leaf cluster, the Bronze Star Medal with one oak leaf cluster, the Air Medal, the Army Commendation Medal with two oak leaf clusters, the Combat Infantryman's Badge, the Expert Field Medical Badge, both the U. S. Army and Vietnamese Parachutist Badges, and a number of other service medals. He moved to Minnesota in 1977 and briefly taught in the public schools. He worked for 15 years as a program director of services for mentally ill, retarded, and physically handicapped persons. He retired in 1992 and now travels, performs unpaid community service, and is immersed in family genealogy. John and Ruth, his wife of 46 years, have three sons, a daughter, and eight grandchildren. All three of his sons have served in the military. His second son recently joined a Minnesota National Guard medical unit, and his youngest son is an Army major. John and Ruth live in Milaca, Minnesota.

Wilbur G. Corbitt

Age 15 – Florida National Guard
Age 16 – United States Army

I was born in the small city of Pearson in Atkinson County, Georgia, on 19 May 1934. I attended grade school in Pearson, Waycross, and Argyle, Georgia, and high school in Homerville, Georgia, and in Lake

> The weapon and the ammo belt seemed to weigh as much as I did.

City, Florida. While in the 10th grade, I enlisted in the Tank Company (Medium), 124th Infantry Regiment, Florida National Guard, on 27 April 1950. I used ink eradicator on my birth certificate, which had been handwritten, and changed only the year from "1934" to "1932." It seemed like most of the boys in my 10th-grade class enlisted. The National Guard recruiter knew what we had done, but decided to overlook it. I was running around with a pretty rough crowd, so my parents had no problem with me enlisting.

I was in the 11th grade when, on 19 January 1951, some friends and I went to Jacksonville and enlisted in the regular Army. I must admit that I first tried to enlist in the Marine Corps, but failed the color-

blind test. So I went to the Navy, and then to the Air Force, but they both had waiting lists. The Army recruiter was glad to see me. I used the same birth certificate that I had used to join the National Guard. Once again, my parents had no problem with my enlisting because I was still running around with the wrong crowd.

We were sent for basic training to Fort Jackson, South Carolina, where I trained with the 28th Field Artillery Battalion, 8th "Golden Arrow" Division, located on Tank

Hill. I was assigned as acting platoon sergeant because of my National Guard experience, but I lost that when I was hospitalized for two weeks with pneumonia.

When we finished basic, I was given a 2-week leave and ordered to report to Fort Lawton, Seattle, Washington, for transport to Japan. When I arrived home from basic training, I visited my old crowd. They were easy to find as most of them were in the Columbia County Sheriff's jail. They had stolen something and were destined for some time in prison. I'm sure that my entry into the Army saved me from the same fate.

I reported in to Fort Lawton, and within a few days I was on a troopship to Japan, arriving there in July 1951. I was sent to Eta Jima, Japan, to take a 4-week pole-line construction course. Why I was sent there, I have no idea, because after completing the training I never climbed another pole or worked with telephone or power lines. From Eta Jima, we went to Sasebo, Japan, and from there to Pusan, Korea, via a Japanese fishing trawler. It was early August 1951.

After a few days, several hundred of us were loaded on a train and moved up to the 2nd "Indianhead" Division. Here we were divided into three equal groups, one for each infantry regiment. That is how I was assigned to the 1st Battalion, 38th Infantry Regiment. I was assigned not by name, but by where I was standing. Regardless of the training we had received or our MOS, we were all assigned to the infantry. We were loaded in trucks and taken to the battalions, where we were given a hot meal.

I was assigned to C Company and given a Browning Automatic Rifle (BAR). The weapon and the ammo belt seemed to weigh as much as I did. During my first night on the line while on watch, I thought I kept seeing movement and a tank to our front. I guess it was a combination of nerves and being scared, because the next morning I saw that it was only terrain features, bushes, and trees. I'm glad I did not panic and wake everyone up that night.

On 29 August we were ordered into an assault position. Early in the morning of the 30th, we moved up to attack a Chinese-occupied ridge line and found that the Chinese were moving to attack us. We met in a draw and slugged it out. At the end of the day, both sides withdrew. Company C could only muster 19 men and one automatic weapon, the BAR that I had. We were ordered to resume the attack the next day. The remnants of our company were formed into a platoon and we were part of the first assault line. Our attack succeeded, and I had gotten almost to the top of the hill when I got hit in the side of my chest. The bullet knocked me down and drained me of all my energy. My right lung was punctured and air bubbles were coming out when I breathed. It was raining and dark by the time we reached the aid station. There were wounded lying all around.

The next morning I was given a shot of morphine and sent to a med-evac hospital. I was operated on and held there for a few days. I remember waking up and seeing that I had been cut open, and that there was something like a small, silver, jack stuck between the ribs that held the cut open. I could see my guts, and it scared the hell out of me! I was told that they had removed part of my lung. I was in a haze during my entire stay there because of the morphine. I was flown to the Tokyo Army General Hospital where they did the final sewing up. Until then, I was wide open from underneath my right shoulder blade to the middle of my stomach. They were trying to make sure that my wound did not become infected.

I returned to the States and was given a leave. I then reported to the 47th "Viking" Division at Fort Rucker, but soon was reassigned to Fort Benning, Georgia, where I became friends with a personnel clerk who was able to get me orders to go back to Japan. Initially, I was assigned to the mail room at the Tokyo Army General Hospital. I kept trying to go back to Korea and finally did in July 1952. I was still designated light duty, so I served as a mail-handler in the postal unit of the 179th Infantry Regiment, 45th "Thunderbird" Division.

I returned to the States in October 1953 and was assigned to the G-3 training section, U. S. Army Infantry Center, Fort Benning, Georgia. I had to apply for a security clearance. One day a CID agent came to my desk and asked, "Exactly how old are you, Sergeant Corbitt?" I was caught, and I told him the truth. He told me to get my personnel records corrected immediately, and I did. I also got my security clearance.

I was an advisor to the U. S. Army Reserve in Gainesville, Florida, for two years. where I met my future wife. I then returned to Fort Benning and joined Company D, 2nd Battle Group, 38th Infantry, 3rd Infantry Division. The entire Division was sent to Germany to replace the 10th Mountain Division in early 1958. I returned to Fort Benning in 1961 where I was designated as a principal instructor in the Ranger Department of the Infantry Training Center. A few months later, I asked the director of the Ranger Department, Colonel Robert B. Nett (a Medal of Honor recipient), if he would recommend me for officer candidate school. He said no, but if I would put in for a direct commission, he would recommend me for that. I put in the paperwork.

Some months later I was called into Colonel Nett's office. He told me that I had screwed up, and he removed my stripes. Then he had my wife come out of hiding and pin a 2nd lieutenant's bar on my collar. I then attended the infantry officers basic course, then the Ranger course, and earned my Ranger tab. I was promoted to captain in January1966 and remained with the Rangers until April 1966.

After some special training, I was assigned to the Military Assistance Command Vietnam (MACV) as an advisor to the Vietnamese Army Basic Training Center in the Mekong Delta. We had a small airstrip there, and I flew as an artillery spotter many times. One day we were very surprised when a helicopter landed and the actor John Wayne got off and stayed with us for a couple of hours. Another surprise arrival was Chubby Checkers and a group of female dancers.

In December 1966, I was transferred to the Vietnamese Infantry Training Center outside of Nha Trang, where another officer and I were given the mission of establishing a Long Range Reconnaissance Patrol School (LRRP). The school was unique in many ways, but one of them was that the training patrols were actual combat patrols.

I returned to the States and attended the advanced infantry officer course in Fort Benning for nine months, then returned to Vietnam in June 1968. I served as company commander of Company D, 2nd Battalion, 14th Infantry Regiment, 25th Infantry Division. The unit was a light-infantry airmobile rifle company. We conducted a lot of search-and-destroy missions. It seemed like we were in a firefight almost every day. For me, this war was different from the Korean War.

I led one of the few night assaults against an enemy position during this tour. We had landed in a hot landing-zone where another company was in trouble. We had a lot of wounded, and we had to do something so we could get them evacuated. The only thing to do was a night attack. We were successful, and the enemy withdrew. While on a company-size patrol in August 1968, we set up the company perimeter in darkness, not knowing we were over some tunnels. Early the next morning, two enemy soldiers who were not more than two or three feet away shot off my left thumb at the knuckle. My weapon deflected the bullet and prevented more serious injury. Although my wound was not that serious, the doctors decided to send me back to the States.

After a brief stay in a hospital and a 2-month tour as an Army Reserve advisor, I was called by the Pentagon and asked if I was ready to return to Vietnam. I agreed and returned to the same regiment of the 25th Division that I was in before, and I was assigned as the commander of B Company. This was in November 1968, and the company was operating from a fire-support base outside of Cu Chi base camp. I was wounded by shrapnel twice during this tour, once in the left hand, and later in both knees, and my leg was broken. A cast was put on my left leg from my ankle to my hip, and I had a cast midway on my right leg. While I was lying totally incapacitated on a cot, the enemy penetrated the base-camp perimeter and blew up several aircraft. A couple of bullet holes appeared in the top of my tent, and I expected the Vietcong to enter my tent at any time and put me to sleep, but they didn't.

When I was able, I became the only S-3 air operations officer flying around the battle area with casts on both legs. My tour ended in November 1969 and I returned home. I retired from the Army as a major on 31 July 1972 at the age of 38, with 22 years, 3 months and 5 days service.

Wilbur Corbitt was awarded two Silver Stars, the Bronze Star with "V" device and three oak leaf clusters, four Purple Hearts, the Air Medal with "V" device and seven oak leaf clusters, the Combat Infantryman's Badge with star (one for Korea and one for Vietnam), two Army Commendation Medals, and a number of other service medals. During his last tour of duty as Army Reserve advisor to the Florida National Guard, he received a B.S. in business administration from the University of Tampa. Later, he earned an M.S. in public administration from Florida International University. He has been employed as an investigator with the U. S. Department of Justice, Drug Enforcement Administration since June 1975. Will and Doris, his wife of 46 years, have five children and seven grandchildren. They live in Davie, Florida.

Titus O. Lee

Age 16 – United States Army

Some time during World War II, as a preteen, I decided that I wanted to be a soldier. Of course, I was much too young, and I put the thought out of my mind. The year that I was in the ninth grade was not a good one for me, and the thought of joining the Air Force kept creeping into my mind.

> *I told him my true age. The two officers looked at each other, looked back at me, and ended the interview.*

I was born in Cullman County, Alabama, on 2 April 1934. Shortly after my 16th birthday, I stopped by a recruiting office in Cullman, my hometown. I told the sergeant that I was interested in entering the Air Force. I had seen the movies and had learned that the Air Force personnel slept in tents, while the Army lived in a hole in the ground. He gave me a quick look and said that I would need a birth certificate for the Air Force, but he could enlist me in the Army without one. The sergeant was looking at a 16-year-old who, at age 25, was carded in a bar before being served a beer, and as a 30-year-old master sergeant, was called "The Boy Master," behind my back, of course. But, he added, your parents must give their written permission.

Okay, so the Army spent time in foxholes. I thought that a foxhole would be better than going to school. My grades were passing, not good, just O.K., but as I said, it was not a good year. I spoke to the principal and he agreed to allow me to skip the last couple of weeks and receive a passing grade for the ninth grade. It apparently had not been a good year for the principal either.

Then I was properly armed to approach my parents for their approval. My father was first with his, "O.K., if your mother will." I went to Mom and got her approval with less effort than I had thought it would take. I went back to the recruiter, looked him in the eye, and *lied* about my age. The papers were processed and I entered the United States Army on 10 May 1950.

I was sent to Fort Knox, Kentucky, for basic training. On the second or third day of being processed in, we were given a lecture on fraud. We were told, "All fraudulent enlistees would be found out, and would be sent to jail! But, if those who have lied will come forward and confess, you will be sent home with no punishment." I did not sleep that night. The next day, a Saturday, I went to the orderly room to make my confession. The CQ (charge of quarters) on duty was a corporal and to me, the ruler of the universe. I confessed to him that I was only 16 years old. He told me to return to my barracks and he would handle the matter. I was happy that I had confessed and was free of the lie that I had told. After that day, if anyone asked my age, I did not lie, but told my true age.

Toward the end of basic, I applied for leadership training and was interviewed for the school by two officers. The Korean War had started by then. I remember one of the officers saying to me that soon draftees would be inducted into the Army and would be coming to Fort Knox for training. They would be much older and would be reluctant to take instructions from someone so young. Then he asked me my age. I told him my true age. The two officers looked at each other, looked back at me, and ended the interview.

Basic training was completed in August 1950, and I was sent to Korea, arriving in early September 1950. I was assigned to E Company, 7th Regiment, 1st Cavalry Division, and joined my unit near Taegu, Korea. My first night in a foxhole was uneventful, but I was too tired to care.

The platoon leader, Lieutenant John Fatum, now a retired colonel living in Columbus, Georgia, made me the platoon runner. It seems as though my youthful appearance led to my adoption by most, if not all, of the men of the 2nd platoon. I remember one night after we had been ambushed, we were told to dig in and expect an attack on our position. I was doing my best to dig a foxhole, but not making much progress because the ground was so hard. Another soldier told me to move and he finished digging for me. By the way, the attack never came and we continued our march north the next day, meeting no resistance.

Later, while on an extended march, one of the men got several blisters on his feet. When it was suggested to him that he should fall out and wait for a jeep to pick him up, he refused and said, "As long as that kid is walking behind the lieutenant, I'll keep walking." His blisters were so bad that he had to spend a few days at an aid station.

Often, if I were sent on an errand to deliver a message or obtain some information, the lieutenant or the sergeant would send someone with me, but not often enough, if my memory serves me. One night as we were preparing to move out, the lieutenant sent me to ask or tell someone something. I returned and gave my report. He said, "Thanks," then added that he appreciated the way I repeated messages verbatim. He said that maybe I could do that because I was so young. Then Lieutenant Fatum asked me my age. I told him that I was 16 years old. He dropped his bedroll!

It was early December 1950 and the Chinese army had entered the war. I was sent to the division rear and waited for the order to send "The Kid" back to the United States. I was honorably discharged on 30 December 1950.

I got a job flipping hamburgers and was happy and content until my mom began to talk about my returning to school. To avoid going back to school a year behind my peers, I enlisted in the U. S. Air Force in July 1951. I was assigned to Maxwell Air Force Base, Montgomery, Alabama, but that choice assignment lasted less than a year. I was sent to Johnson AFB, Japan, where I was assigned to the 38th Fighter Wing Headquarters Air Operations. I found that my job required more than my ninth-grade education could handle, even though I had already taken and passed the high school GED. I started to attend night school and took high school English.

Night school became habit forming. When I returned Stateside and was assigned to Craig AFB in Alabama, I enrolled in the University of Alabama's night-school program. My education was interrupted by a tour in Vietnam from May 1963 until May 1964. I was assigned to Nha Trang, a seaside resort town south of Da Nang, where I spent the longest year of my life, being separated from my wife and two children.

Upon returning from Vietnam, I was again assigned to Maxwell AFB, Alabama. I continued my education and received a B.S. from the University of Alabama. Again, my assignment to Maxwell was much too short, even though it was three years. In the summer of 1967, my family and I went to Clark Air Force Base in the Philippines. Again I enrolled in night school. This time I entered the University of the Philippines and earned an M.A. in political science. Not too bad for a kid that joined the Army and the Air Force to avoid going to school!

After two years at Clark, the family and I returned to K. I. Sawyer AFB, Michigan. One year later, my goal of 20 years was met, and I retired as a master sergeant on 1 December 1970.

Titus Lee earned the Combat Infantryman's Badge, the Air Force Commendation Medal with one oak leaf cluster, and a number of other service medals. After his retirement he was employed in the insurance industry, mostly in administrative and management positions. He was designated a Chartered Property Casualty Underwriter (CPCU) by the American Institute for Chartered Property Casualty Underwriters. He entered night school again and obtained an M.B.A. from Campbell University's night school program at Fort Bragg, and later became a part-time economics instructor in the night school program. He was transferred by his company to Atlanta, Georgia in 1985, and taught political science in Reinhart College's night school program. In 1995, he retired from his insurance company and from night school. However, he joined a senior citizen group to study Spanish. Titus and his wife Sharon have a son and a daughter. Their son received a commission in the U. S. Air Force and served for five years. Titus and Sharon live in Marietta, Georgia.

Vincent P. Gambino

Age 14 – New York National Guard
Age 15 – United States Army

I was born in Brooklyn, New York, on 16 September 1935. My parents were Italian immigrants with nine children. Things were a bit crowded around the house at times. I participated in some

> *Just after my 15th birthday in September 1950, my mother turned me in, ...*

youth-gang activities and was "detained" by the police several times before I was 14. I was sent to a school for truants at age 13 after getting in a fight with an instructor.

My older brother, whom we all looked up to, joined the Army at age 17 and I also wanted to join. I changed my birth date on my birth certificate, "borrowed" a notary seal to authenticate my parents' signatures, and enlisted in the 245th Antiaircraft Artillery Gun Battalion, New York National Guard, on 12 June 1950. We trained at Fort Devens, Massachusetts, that summer. The Korean War broke out in late June, and we were federalized in August 1950 and sent to Fort Bliss, Texas.

Just after my 15th birthday in September 1950, my mother turned me in, and I was given a minority discharge on 9 October 1950. In May 1951, I enlisted in the regular Army under my next-older brother's name. I obtained a copy of his birth certificate and forged my parents' consent and the notary's signature. Again, I "borrowed" a notary seal to authenticate the signatures on the enlistment form.

I was sent to Fort Dix, New Jersey, for my second go at basic training. From there I went to Orleans, France, as a military policeman – yes, me a policeman! I volunteered to join my older brother in Korea, but never made it. I ended up with the 22nd Infantry Regiment, 4th Infantry Division, in Germany. I was promoted to sergeant and was a squad leader before my 18th birthday. We served on the tactical ready positions in Germany, waiting for the Russians to come over the line. When I turned 18, I "fessed up" and I was able to use my own name again. No disciplinary action was taken. I finished my enlistment and was honorably discharged in April 1954.

Six months later, I re-enlisted and was assigned to the Military Police Unit, First Army Headquarters, Governor's Island, New York. While at Governor's Island, I received my GED without even attending one hour in high school in my life. After serving a little more than six years, I was honorably discharged on 16 December 1957.

Vince Gambino enrolled at New York University and graduated four years later. After several accounting jobs, he joined the Intelligence Division (now the Criminal Investigations Division) of the Internal Revenue Service as a special agent. He served in New York City, Washington, D.C., Rome, Italy, and Sao Paolo, Brazil. He retired in 1991 after 28 years of government service. During his IRS career, he received several high-level awards for his work on organized crime investigations and undercover activities. He has two daughters and four grandchildren. Vince lives in Rome, Italy.

Douglas L. Miller
Age 15 – United States Navy

In the very early hours of a Sunday morning in November 1950, I left home on an incredible adventure. As far as my father and stepmother knew, I was setting out for a local distribution branch of *The*

..., and decided that I would become a completely new person, ...

Portland Journal, Portland, Oregon, to deliver the Sunday morning paper. Instead, I took my savings, abandoned my bike, my paper route, my French horn, and my family, to seek adventure. I took a bus to the train depot and asked for a one-way ticket to the most distant city in the country I could think of, Miami, Florida. I was born in Gothenburg, Nebraska, on 21 April 1935, and going from one coast to the other was truly an adventure.

The trip took several days. I began to realize that when I arrived in Miami, I would be out of money and have to face the reality of the need for food and shelter. I planned to seek out the local military recruiting stations to see if I could enlist and ride the wave of patriotism which was embracing the country as American boys were fighting tenaciously to keep Communism from swallowing South Korea. I foresaw a problem in attempting to enlist under my true name, so I considered the names of movie stars, high school friends and acquaintances, and decided that I would become a completely new person, Robert Allen Gardner.

After arriving in Miami, I registered at the "Y" and began searching for the recruiting stations. My first choice was the U. S. Navy. When I was 14, a Navy destroyer had docked on the Columbia River in Portland, and I toured the ship with the public. My impression of shipboard life was vividly exciting. I climbed steps to the Navy recruiting office wondering how quickly I would be thrown out, or even worse, be carried away in a patrol car after being reported by the Navy officers as a delinquent. Instead, a secretary gave me a brief form to fill out. I completed the form, using some creative fiction as to my education and employment history. I was approached by a recruiter and asked for my draft card. I confessed that I did not have one. The recruiter sent me to the local draft board, where I registered under my new name, then returned to the recruiting office. During a dental exam, the dental officer exclaimed, "When did you guys start recruiting 15-year-olds?"

Later, the recruiter asked me to place a call to my high school to verify my date of graduation. I called a small town in Nebraska where I had attended kindergarten under another name. The school secretary searched diligently for a graduate named Robert Gardner, to no avail. She apologized, and I felt certain that I would be out in the street the next day. The recruiter told me to come back the next day. I returned early the next day, anxious to learn my fate. The recruiter announced that he was going to certify that he had seen a baptismal certificate brought in the office by "Bob" to verify that he was of legal age to enlist without parental permission. The document did not exist. I was sworn into the Navy on 10 November 1950.

Arriving at the Great Lakes Naval Training Center in mid-November from Miami was a shock. There was deep snow. We were issued uniforms and handed a large box in which to pack our civilian clothes. We were told to complete an address label for the box and the Navy would mail the box home to moms, dads, or wives. Panic struck me. I could not send my things home; my father would come and get me. I could not use a false address because the box would be returned, and the Navy would want to know why. Desperate, I asked the kid next to me if I could send the box to his home. Although the reason I gave was suspicious, the kid agreed, and I placed the strange address on the box. I never saw my civilian clothes again.

After boot camp I was assigned to electrician's mate school, still at Great Lakes. Three months later I was given orders to report to the USS *Badoeng Strait*, an escort carrier at the Bremerton Naval Shipyard, near Seattle, Washington. In about six weeks we were underway, bound for San Diego on a post-shipyard shakedown cruise. From there it was to Pearl Harbor and on to Japan.

The *Badoeng Strait* served six months in Asia, three of which were in Korean waters, before returning to the States for routine maintenance. She then returned to Yokosuka and Sasebo for renewed antisubmarine warfare and close air-support missions in Korea. Later, we went to Okinawa and anchored offshore at a place called "White Beach" as there were no docking facilities available. We went ashore in a liberty boat and sailed through broken hulks of landing craft which had been sunk during the assault on the beaches during World War II. From Okinawa, we sailed to Formosa and got caught in a typhoon that was broiling the East China Sea.

We returned to San Diego and I was transferred to the USS *Valley Forge*. I was hoping that the ship would eventually go to Europe, but we went to Guantanamo Bay in Cuba, Nova Scotia, and ports on the East Coast of the United States. Near the end of my 4-year enlistment, I reported to the mustering-out station in Norfolk and was assigned to shore patrol duty. I found myself patrolling the night spots of Norfolk, inspecting bars frequented by noisy seamen who occasionally became unruly. Ironically, I was 19 years old and technically violating the law by frequenting places which served alcoholic beverages while I was obliged to enforce the laws of the land.

I began to think about what I should do to rectify my false name and age. I approached the chaplain and told him my strange tale. He told me I had two choices: I could remain in the unit for several months and have the Navy officials make the necessary changes, or I could go home and ask the help of a veterans' organization to get things changed. He assured me that no ill would befall me either way I wished to pursue the corrections. I opted to go home.

Doug Miller was successful in getting his records corrected to his true name and age. He had taken the GED while in the Navy, so the state college at Kearney, Nebraska, accepted him as a freshman. He graduated in 1959 and taught school until he entered the federal service in 1962. He was an investigator with the Civil Service Commission, a special agent with the U. S. Information Agency, and was in charge of the personnel security program of the Federal Energy Administration, which later became part of the new Department of Energy (DOE). Doug's assignments with DOE included inspection and oversight of the Pantex weapons assembly at nuclear weapons facilities. In 1981, he was detailed to the White House Security Office to evaluate difficulties they were having in processing clearances for officials who needed access to the President. He was also commander of the security program for the Forrestal Building in Washington, D.C. He retired from government service in 1995. Doug lives in San Antonio, Texas.

✔ *INCIDENTally* — **Missiles from Russia!** – During the period 1 January 1960 to September 1962, I was assigned to the staff of the Naval Forces, Continental Air Defense Command (CONAD), Ent Air Force Base, Colorado Springs. The large tunnel in Cheyenne Mountain had not been constructed. Ent AFB units occupied old WWII temporary wooden buildings near the center of town. All were above ground and there were no bomb shelters. A local insurance salesman, a friend of my Navy captain boss, used to frequent our offices. If my boss was elsewhere, the insurance man made himself at home in our large five-desk office. He would find an unoccupied desk and sit with his feet on it and sometimes use our phones. Needless to say, he was a thorn in our side, but we were not at liberty to complain because our boss knew what was going on and did nothing. One day a siren sounded on the base which only meant one thing – "Condition Red!" Sure enough, when our admiral called the operations office, they reported that the new, large radar in Alaska, the Ballistic Missile Early Warning System (BEMEWS) had picked up an object coming out of Russia. Mr. Insurance became panicky and wanted to run home. We advised him he was stuck because the main gate was closed. As time went by, he became pale and began to sweat. The admiral made another call – and "an object coming out of Russia," was the report. But the BEMEWS had been unable to detect the speed of the object in order to estimate its target. For about a half hour we sat under "Condition Red." Finally the siren sounded an end to the emergency and the gate opened. Mr. Insurance made a beeline for the gate, and we never had to entertain him in our offices again. Several months later, our boss retired, and when he went to work for Mr. Insurance, we understood his tolerance. Oh yes, the missile! The command ultimately discovered the target was the moon! – *Dave E. Severance.*

Ronald D. McKinney

Age 16 – United States Marine Corps

To begin with, I am an Okie. That is, my mother, father, sister, and I left Marlow, Oklahoma, in October of 1934, bound for California. I remember nothing of the trip, as I was born on 18 September 1934, and was less than a month old. I

> The ... gunnery sergeant said to me, "Hey kid, where'd you find the water to shave in out there?"

was told by reliable sources that had I not been nursing, there was a fair chance I might have starved to death.

When we arrived in California, along with thousands of others, the opportunities which my mother's older sisters and brothers had found when they arrived in the 1920s were no longer available. My father became discouraged before the year ended and departed. Fifteen years would pass before we discovered that he was alive and well, living in Tennessee.

Meanwhile, my sister and I lived with a series of families in what were then called "boarding homes," while our mother worked to pay for our keep.

Having an older sister was a boon to me, as I was taught to read and write by her before ever going to public schools. Since most of the schools that I attended were of the one-room variety, I had an advantage over the other students. This proved to be a mixed blessing. On the one hand, I was placed in classes based on my level of competence, without regard for my age. On the other hand, this resulted in my being a 14-year-old junior in high school.

Not being large enough to participate in normal athletic activities such as football or basketball, I turned to the ROTC for extracurricular activities. I did not enjoy wearing the World War 1 uniforms, but I did enjoy participating on the drill team and the rifle team. These experiences possibly planted the notion that my future lay in military service.

Following a summer of independent camping and surviving in the Sierra Nevada mountains, I felt competent to quit school, leave home, and set out to see these United States. I made it as far as Michigan before the winter set in. I decided that my clothing would be more suited to Florida and set off in that direction.

My journey took me through Tennessee, where by sheer chance, I met my father. Since he had completed only three years of schooling, my father did his best to encourage me to resume my education. To please him, I enrolled in White County High School.

The principal of the school judged that I would fit well in their senior class, but it was more difficult for me than he imagined. Having come from California, my accent set me apart. Therefore, when the school closed for a week during the county fair, I continued my journey to Florida.

In the winter of 1950, I was working in a dime store in Winterhaven, Florida. The newspaper headlines were then covering the defeat of the U.N. forces in Korea by the Chinese "Volunteer" Army. It seemed to me that all of the dire predictions made by my ROTC instructor a year earlier had begun to come true.

One day, while having lunch at the dime store lunch counter, an old, salty, Marine master sergeant sat on the adjacent stool. After finishing his soup and sandwich, he turned to me and said, "Boy, we could sure use you."

I was 16, and his assumption that I was older seemed a compliment. I followed him back to his office in the post office and obtained the parental-consent form. I was afraid that telling him I was 18 would be stretching my luck, so I said that I was 17.

He told me to get my parents to sign the consent forms. I told him that my parents were divorced. He wanted to know who my legal guardian was. I told him that my mother was, but that she lived in San Francisco, California. The recruiter told me she would have to sign.

I phoned my mother collect and told her of my plan to enlist in the Marines. She said, "It is your life. I'll be glad to sign the papers, just as soon as you return to San Francisco."

I hitchhiked back to the city, and she signed an affidavit that I was born in 1933 and filled out the consent form. With the documents in hand, I went to 100 Harrison Street and was sworn in by the CO of the Marine Detachment on 4 June 1951. I was given a travel voucher and went by train with several other recruits to San Diego, California.

At the Marine Corps Recruit Depot, my ability to march was recognized, and I was made a squad leader. Immediately after firing for qualification at Camp Matthews, I volunteered to go to Korea. I was assigned to the Advanced Infantry Training Regiment at Camp Pendleton, where I trained for combat and waited for my birthday to roll around. On 18 September 1951 I was assigned to the staging regiment and was sent to our new Cold Weather Training Center in the Sierra Nevada mountains, not far from where I had spent my 14th summer. After two weeks in the mountains, I boarded ship with the 15th Replacement Draft.

As the MSTS troopship *General Pope* pulled away from the Navy pier in San Diego, a Navy band on the pier played "So Long, It's Been Good to Know You."

I looked at the pier and recalled that on the 7 December 1941, I had been standing on that spot awaiting the liberty boats to bring sailors ashore from the ships at anchor in the bay. I had a shoeshine kit in hand when a cop approached and told me I had to get off the pier. The Japanese had just bombed our fleet in Pearl Harbor, and an attack on San Diego was expected at any moment.

Although the expected attack never materialized, my mother, who worked at North Island for the Navy, felt we kids were in danger. So she sent us to live with the wife of a Navy chief petty officer who had property in the Mojave Desert. The chief was listed as missing in action at that time. Shortly after we had mucked sand out of the old ranch house and made it livable, the chief was located and returned Stateside. His family naturally followed him to his new shore-duty station in Norfolk, Virginia. My sister and I were pawned off on a boarding ranch near Apple Valley.

Life on an irrigated alfalfa ranch was exciting. There were 14 kids ranging in age from 6 to 16, and we were the labor force which mowed and baled the hay, fed the hogs, cattle, horses, and chickens. My specific chore was to supply the household with fresh cottontail rabbits. I was given a single-shot Stevens .22 rifle and a box of ammo. In short order, I became a marksman; fried, roasted, or stewed rabbit became a staple in our diet.

All of my experiences prior to enlistment in the Marine Corps seemed to prepare me for my part in the Korean War. I served with Item Company, 3rd Battalion, 1st Marines, 1st Marine Division, and with the Reconnaissance Platoon, H&S Company, 3rd Battalion, 1st Marines. My initial assignment was as a BAR man, but my marksmanship skill was discovered and I served as a scout-sniper with my good friend, Robert Lee Fowler.

It was rather obvious to everyone in our company that I was underage. We came off an outpost after 67 days and everyone had grown beards. The company gunnery sergeant said to me, "Hey kid, where'd you find the water to shave in out there?"

I was wounded on Bunker Hill on 13 August 1952, just as our outfit was being relieved. I was surrounded by body parts from two other men, and thought that my arm was hanging by a thread. The shrapnel wounds were treated by our corpsman, who merely plucked out the slivers with his hemostat and covered the holes with merthiolate and Band-Aids. I felt like an ass for having worried so much about it. Being afraid that my fraudulent enlistment would be discovered, I failed to press the issue about not receiving my Purple Heart at the time.

I returned to the States on 21 December 1952 and immediately applied for any overseas-duty station, including Korea. I was sent to Adak, in the Aleutian Islands. While there I completed the course for a high school equivalency diploma, then was tested and found qualified for the Naval Aviation Cadet Program. As the Korean War had ended, the demand for pilots diminished, and only college graduates were being accepted in the flight-training program.

I served for two years, 1954 to 1956, in the 1st Provisional Amphibious Reconnaissance Company, FMFPac. In November 1955, we were trying to make a rubber-boat landing in heavy seas and the boat capsized. Half of the boat team drowned, including my swimming partner, Donald McCreery. He had celebrated his 17th birthday just a week before. I escorted his remains to Mitchell, South Dakota, then reported to the State Department Security School.

I served at the American Embassy in Bern, Switzerland for 18 months and at our Consulate General's office in Geneva for six months.

I was on the dignitary protection detail. When I returned to the States in March 1958, I was sent to Quantico, Virginia, to compete for a commission. I graduated second in a class of 325, won a regular, unrestricted commission as a second lieutenant, then reported to Pensacola, Florida, for flight training.

During the final week of advanced flight training, my wife departed. Her motivation was the fiery crash of my squadron commander only 50 yards from our house. It was not the first crash she had seen. She issued an ultimatum to me: either quit flying or she would file for divorce. I quit flying and requested an infantry officer billet. I then reported to Lima Company, 3rd Battalion, 6th Marines, at Camp Lejeune, North Carolina.

In 1962, while in Cuba, I resigned my commission, took a reserve commission, and was reunited with my family, although the marriage didn't last. I resigned from the Corps in 1969. My age on the official records was not corrected until 1997. At that time I went to the Florida Department of Motor Vehicles to obtain a new license with my correct birth date. The clerk asked, "Why spend ten bucks? This license is valid until 2000." I said, "I just want to get a year younger," and gladly paid the $10.

Ron McKinney did not receive his Purple Heart until 1998. It was presented to him by the Marine Corps in a formal ceremony in Orlando, Florida. His commanding officer while he was in Korea was present. After he left active duty, Ron flew demonstration hops for Beechcraft and sold real estate, securities, and insurance. He also worked as a high-scaler/driller/blaster, and as a carpenter. He has three children from his first marriage. He and Christine, his wife of 30 years, have a daughter, Allison. They live in Seminole, Florida.

Donald R. Wilkinson

Age 16 – United States Army

I was born in Pittsburgh, Pennsylvania, on 25 December 1934. I was raised in a single-parent family consisting of my mother, an older brother, and two older sisters. Although I was too young to remember much about it, until the start of

> *..., and the most vivid and lasting memories are the odors and the bone-chilling cold.*

World War II, our main source of income was welfare.

Soon after the attack on Pearl harbor, my brother enlisted in the Navy. He served on the USS *North Carolina* during the war years. I think that growing up during those times, hearing the stories told by my brother and other veterans, had a marked influence on my decision to enlist in the Army.

My attitude towards school was one of forced tolerance. I knew from the time that I was 12 years old that I would quit when I was 16 years old. I did just enough to be promoted, but I had no interest in what I did, or in school itself.

I left school for Christmas vacation in December 1950 and never went back. After a few short-lived and disappointing jobs, I decided to alter my birth certificate and enlist in the Army. I found this task much more difficult than I had first thought. I ruined my original and had to get a copy. I put the copy in a mixture of warm water and ink eradicator and the ink lifted off clean. I then placed the blank birth certificate on a mirror to dry. After it dried, I filled it out.

I enlisted in the Army on 9 July 1951 and was sent to the induction center at Fort George G. Meade, Maryland. From there, I went by troop train to Fort Knox, Kentucky, for eight weeks of basic training followed by eight weeks of truck-driving school. After finishing driving school, I went to Camp Stoneman, California, and embarked for Korea.

After two miserable weeks aboard the USS *Meigs*, we disembarked in Yokohama, Japan. From there we took a train to Iwakuni, Japan, where we received our issue of cold-weather gear. Then it was on to Korea.

I was assigned to Charlie Company, 811th Engineering Aviation Battalion, located at K-16, Korea. The 811th was tasked with building, rebuilding, and maintaining landing strips in Korea. In retrospect, my year in Korea seems like a month. The days run together, and the most vivid and lasting memories are the odors and the bone-chilling cold. I did not believe I would ever be warm again.

After returning from Korea, I was assigned to Logan Heights, at Fort Bliss, Texas, as a jeep driver. On the surface, this sounds like good duty, but I found it boring and mundane. I guess the bars in El Paso and the close proximity of Juarez were too much for me to cope with. I was put on morning report four times for being late for work call. I had a long talk with my company commander and found myself on another ship, this one headed for Okinawa.

In Okinawa, I was assigned to the 50th Truck Company, driving a semi tractor-trailer. I was kept busy all day, and stayed out of trouble for the year that I was there. I liked Okinawa; it was good duty.

I was discharged from the Army at Fort Meade, Maryland, in 1954. I had thought about re-enlisting, but I realized that I was not cut out to be a professional soldier. I think that I made a sound decision both for the Army and myself. I have no more illusions about war. I realize how fortunate I was to come home unscathed, and I shed a tear for those who were less fortunate. God bless them, and all warriors.

Don Wilkinson worked at different jobs for a few years, then began a career in engineering design. He and his wife also owned a sub-shop franchise for 8½ years. He and Patricia, his wife of 38 years, have three daughters and ten grandchildren. They live in Starke, Florida.

Samuel T. Hambrick

Age 16 – United States Marine Corps

I was born in Dallas, Texas, on 9 December 1934. By the time I was 16, I was bored with school and had no plans for the future. I took the family Bible and put a new family register inside of it. I used water and ink to put the

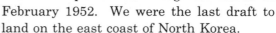

I took the family Bible and put a new family register inside of it.

names in it, and in the process, added two years to my age. I then ironed the pages to make them look old. I took one of my older sisters to the recruiting office to vouch for the Bible, and the recruiter accepted it. It was 14 August 1951, and I headed for San Diego with my 15-year-old buddy, Jackie D. Elliff.

I endured boot camp at San Diego until graduation in October 1951. I was sent to Camp Pendleton and assigned to the 2nd Infantry Training Regiment at San Onofere. Upon graduation and completion of cold-weather training at Bridgeport, California, I was assigned to the 18th Replacement Draft and departed San Diego for Korea in

February 1952. We were the last draft to land on the east coast of North Korea.

After my tour of duty with Headquarters Battery, 2nd Battalion, 11th Marine Regiment, 1st Marine Division in Korea, I returned to the States in April 1953 and joined Chesty Puller's 3rd Brigade at Camp Pendleton's Tent Camp Three. I volunteered to go back to Korea, but the truce was signed and I was transferred to the 1st 155mm Gun Battalion at Twentynine Palms, California.

I was assigned to embassy duty and served in Bonn, Germany, in 1954 and in Belgrade, Yugoslavia, in 1955. In 1956, I joined the 3rd Marines at North Camp Fuji, Japan, and later that year went to Okinawa with the 12th Marines. I returned to the States and was discharged from the Marines in August 1959.

I enlisted in the Army in August 1959 and was assigned to the artillery school at Fort Sill, Oklahoma, then it was back to Okinawa where I served in a Nike-Hercules missile battery. I served with missile units in Kansas, Greenland, and Rhode Island. I went to Kissingen, Germany, in 1966 and served with a 155mm gun battery. Vietnam beckoned in 1967, and I was assigned to a Hawk missile battery and a civic-action platoon in the Mekong Delta. I returned from Vietnam in 1968, was stationed at Fort Bliss, Texas, for about a year, then it was back to Okinawa. My final Army assignment was as assistant NCOIC (non-commissioned officer in charge) of the Topper Club, Sukinsan, Okinawa. I returned to the States and retired from the Army on 1 September 1971.

Upon my arrival in the States, I found that all my household goods, hold baggage, and automobile had been lost. After contacting my congressman, my missing items were finally located in October 1971.

Sam Hambrick was awarded the Combat Action Ribbon for his Korean service and the Vietnam Cross of Gallantry with palm for his Vietnam service. After his retirement from the Army, he joined "Mensa," the high-I.Q. society. He graduated from the University of Houston, Clear Lake, with three degrees in four years and received a master's degree in public administration. He was a security officer at the Port of Houston, then joined the Houston airport police as a patrolman. In 1978 he was promoted to aviation management at Hobby Airport, Houston, and retired as airport superintendent in April 1994. He married Sayoko Toguchi of Osaka, Japan, in 1960. They have three sons, one daughter, and five grandchildren. Sam and Sayoko live in Alvin, Texas.

594

Jackie D. Elliff
Age 15 – United States Marine Corps

I was born in Brownsville, Texas, on 17 November 1935. When I was 15 years old, I was hanging around with several 16-year-old friends. They were always saying how they were going to join the Marines and fight in Korea. Several of

I was lucky that I didn't end up in Denmark ...

us were to go, but everyone backed out except for Sam Hambrick and me. (See his story on pages 592-593.) When Sam made the new family register to put in his family Bible, he added my name, listing me as his cousin. Of course, we made sure that my birth date was such that enlisting was no problem. Sam and I were sworn in on 14 August 1951. The two of us went to San Diego, California, and graduated from boot camp with Honor Platoon 239 in October 1951.

Sam and I were split up after boot camp. We both went to Camp Pendleton where I was assigned to G Company, 2nd Battalion, 1st Infantry Training Regiment at Camp Pulgas. Sam went with the 2nd Regiment at Camp Onofere. After three tough months of training, I

was shipped to Bridgeport, California, for cold-weather training. We had the good luck of being the only training unit to be snowed in for 17 days. The Air Force had to fly in supplies to us – how degrading!

I was with the 17th Replacement Draft to Korea in January 1952. Upon arrival in Korea, I was assigned to the Fuel Platoon, 1st Service Battalion, 1st Marine Division. The Division moved from the east coast of Korea on 19 March 1952 and took up positions in the west-central section.

On 20 March 1952, I stepped on a land mine. After being patched up by a corpsman, I was flown south to an Army medical station. Within a day or two, they placed me on a railroad car to Pusan where I was put aboard the hospital ship, USS *Constitution*. After about two weeks, they started transferring patients from the *Constitution* to a

Danish hospital ship. During the transfer, the corpsmen carrying my stretcher made a wrong turn and placed me in a hold with the Danish wounded and their nurses. No one spoke English. I had no hospital records. The only food offered me for the 4-day trip to Japan was something between cream of wheat and grits.

When we arrived in Japan, all the wounded who were on stretchers were placed on the deck. As an American corpsman walked by, I grabbed his leg and asked him to move me over to where the other Americans were. When I finally got to the Yokosuka Naval Hospital, the staff told me they had been looking for me for a week. I was lucky that I didn't end up in Denmark because all the Danish wounded were flown there the day they arrived in Japan.

After 19 months in the hospital and 14 operations, I was medically retired from the Marine Corps in 1954.

Jack Elliff was awarded the Purple Heart by a Navy captain while he was in the Yokosuka Naval Hospital. After being medically retired from the Marines, he returned to school for three years. He worked for a dairy in San Antonio for 17 years, then worked as an outside sales representative for a paper company for 20 years. Jack and his wife Chris have three sons. They live in Boerne, Texas, during the winter months and in Colorado from May until October.

John R. Vigil

Age 16 – United States Navy

I was born in Brighton, Colorado, on 24 June 1935, the oldest of four children. Our family moved to California in 1942 after the war broke out in the Pacific.

> ... we got caught in the middle of Hurricane Hazel. We really rocked and rolled!

My dad was too old to serve in the military, but he worked for Lockheed Aircraft for 36 years. During World War II, he helped build the P-38 fighter planes.

When high school got boring, I told my mother that if I could not go into the service, I would run away from home. She agreed to fibbing about my age and signing for me.

I joined the Navy on 16 January 1952 and went to boot camp in San Diego, California. From there I went to submarine school at Mare Island, California. After completion of the school and more training,

we were shipped to Japan aboard the USS *Telfair* (APA-210). At Yokosuka, Japan, I was assigned to the submarine SS *Bass*, a K-2 type boat.

We did a tour through Korean waters between Inchon and Pusan and also dropped underwater demolition teams (UDT) – forerunners of the Navy Seals – behind enemy lines. Later we would go back and pick them up. It was interesting at times!

After that I was assigned to shore duty in Yokosuka and Kuriama, Japan, where I spent nearly three years in the fire department as a tiller-driver and dispatcher.

Later the Navy needed crews for four mine destroyers that were to go back to the States. The personnel needed to have been overseas for more than two and a half years to qualify to sign up. It was a one-way trip; the ships were to be decommissioned and most of the men were to be discharged.

I got lucky and was assigned to the USS *John L. Sullivan* (YAG-37), and we sailed for the States. We went through the Panama Canal and headed for Florida. In the area between Cuba and Florida we got caught in the middle of Hurricane Hazel. We really rocked and rolled! The hull of the ship split, so we took her to Mobile, Alabama, for dry dock.

I was reassigned to the Navy base at Panama City, Florida, where they had minesweepers and trained UDT teams, and completed my enlistment. When my time came for discharge I was sent to Pensacola, Florida, where I was discharged on 26 November 1955.

John Vigil returned to California and worked for a vending company. While in California, he coached baseball and football in a junior-high school and received a Coach of the Year award in 1964. He was also an assistant director for parks and recreation. He moved to Cheyenne, Wyoming, in 1974 and worked for a Coors Beer Distributor. He is a member of the American Legion Honor Guard, serving at military funerals, flag presentations, and other veterans' services. John and Betty, his wife of 46 years, have four children and ten grandchildren. They live in Cheyenne, Wyoming.

598

Robert R. Blackwell
Age 16 – United States Marine Corps

I was born in Saint Louis, Missouri, on 11 August 1935. My parents divorced while I was young, so I spent part of the time with my father and part with my mother. I alternated between Saint Louis and Centerville, Illinois.

> *Needless to say, it really took a long time before I could eat bananas again!*

I wanted to serve my country, so in January 1952 at the age of 16, I tried to join the Navy. Every time I went to the recruiting office, they would tell me that they had a 6-month waiting list. In the same office, there was a U. S. Marine Corps recruiting sergeant. Each time, he would tell me that there was no waiting list for the Marines. I wanted the Navy because my best friend had joined the Navy.

I went back to the recruiting office every month until May 1952. The Marine recruiter kept telling me, "We can get you in now – no waiting." So I finally said, "Give me the papers and I'll have my parents sign them." They wouldn't sign, so I got my brother's birth certificate (who would have been a year older than me, had he not died). I had two of my friends sign my parents' names on the Marine Corps papers. Off to the Marine recruiting office I went, with documents in hand. I was sent to get a physical. I was 5-feet tall and weighed 100 pounds. The sergeant wrote down 105 pounds and told me to eat nothing but bananas all the way to boot camp (which took three days) in order to gain enough  weight. Needless to say, it really took a long time before I could eat bananas again! I was sworn into the Marine Corps on 8 May 1952.

My drill instructor in boot camp, Sergeant Jensen, said to me, "Termite, what are you doing here? I'm going to make you go AWOL." He assigned the biggest man in our platoon to make sure that I shaved every day with a new blade in the razor. At that time, I still had peach fuzz, so I didn't need to shave and especially didn't need a new blade every day. After boot camp, I realized that Sergeant Jensen was testing me to see if I was capable of handling adversity. I would have gone through hell with that man.

I was sent to Jacksonville, Florida, for airman prep school. At that time my father discovered that I had joined the Marines illegally and turned me in. I wrote a letter to the Commandant of the Marine Corps and asked to stay in the service. I was granted that privilege. I changed all my records from my brother's name to mine and continued my stint in the Marines.

I was sent to the Marine Corps Air Station, El Toro, California, where I was assigned to VMO-2, 3rd Marine Air Wing. From there I was sent to Korea and joined VMO-6, 1st Marine Air Wing. After my tour in Korea, I returned to the States and was stationed at Lambert Field, St. Louis, Missouri, training "weekend warriors" (reserves) until my discharge in May 1955.

A month after my discharge, I was watching a news program showing French paratroopers jumping into Dien Bien Phu, French Indochina (now Vietnam). I said to myself – that's for me, and off I went to enlist in the airborne. I spent three years in the 82nd and the 101st Airborne Infantry Divisions. I was discharged in 1958 at the age of 22 with six years of service. I had been more places and done more things than many people have done in their entire lifetime.

Bob Blackwell learned the locksmith trade and worked in that profession for many years. In 1966 he started taking karate and now has a sixth-degree black belt in Shorin-Ryu karate and a first-degree black belt in Budo-Shin jujitsu. His wife died in 1990. He has two sons. Bob lives in Crystal City, Missouri.

George T. Sawyer, Jr.
Age 16 – United States Coast Guard

Having grown up in a naval family, I guess that I was predisposed to follow in my dad's footsteps. He was a retired Navy chief yeoman. I'm sure that the excitement of being on ships and the

> The ship was covered with many tons of ice and was heavy to the starboard.

expectations of visiting ports unknown also played a large part in my wanting to enlist.

As a Navy family, we lived in many places. I was born in Honolulu, Hawaii, on 26 January 1936. We moved back to the States for the second time in late 1941. We lived in various places around the United States until 1947, when we moved to a small farm in Hickory, Virginia. The farm was my home until I enlisted in the Coast Guard.

My first experience with a recruiter was sometime in late 1951. Of course, the recruiter was a Navy chief. During the preliminaries, he looked me square in the eye and repeated the question I'm sure he had asked others, "Son, you aren't really 17 are you?" Of course, my answer was, "No." He looked at me and said, "Why don't you come back when you turn 17?"

By August 1952, I had to try again. Off I went to the federal building in Norfolk, Virginia. I encountered two sailors (whom I thought were Navy) getting on the elevator. One of them asked me if I was joining up. I answered, "Yes, sir, I am!" He said, "Follow us." They promptly led me to the Coast Guard recruiting office.

I had the help of my Aunt Mary in this endeavor. Aunt Mary was every kid's dream of an aunt. She let us do things that Mom and Dad wouldn't, and she made them fun. Having been married seven times, she was good at acting. She helped me alter my birth certificate and presented herself as my mother to the recruiter. With her help and acting ability, I had no problem enlisting. I was sworn in on 18 August 1952.

Before reality had a chance to set in, I found myself in recruit training at Cape May, New Jersey. To say that it was a wake-up call for me would be an understatement. The first time I was allowed to make a telephone call, I called home. The request that I made to my real mother was, "Please get me out of here!" I heard my mom repeat the request to my dad who replied, "Tell him he made his bed, now lay in it!" My dad had also enlisted when he was 16 years old, so I didn't get much sympathy from him. I have always considered that the way my parents handled the situation was the best possible solution to my problem.

The six ships I served on were mostly buoy tenders that also serve as search-and-rescue vessels and fishery patrol. They also had ice-breaking capabilities which proved useful because the first place a rogue fish-processing ship would head to was the ice fields. I have participated in arresting parties on Japanese fishing vessels.

On one patrol, we were heading home through Unimak Pass. The seas were rough and the wind was strong. The temperature was dropping and ice began forming on the ship. We knew that we had a problem that was getting worse by the hour because the ship was taking longer to recover from starboard rolls. We were seeking shelter and found it just in time. The ship was covered with many tons of ice and was heavy to the starboard. It took all hands to chop and beat the ice off. We had gotten most of the ice off when we received a call to return to the Bering Sea on a search-and-rescue mission. So it went!

I served for 20 years and 3 months in the Coast Guard and retired as a senior chief (E-8) in December 1972 at the age of 36. At the time I retired, I was serving on the CGC *Sorrel*, whose home port was Seward, Alaska. I also served on recruiting duty.

The duty that I remember most was in 1959. I served one year with three other men at a completely isolated station at the southern tip of Alaska, called Tree Point. The closest people were 50 miles by water and 100 miles cross-country. The purpose of the station was to transmit a radio signal that aided airplanes and ships to plot their location. There was also a lighthouse. The four of us manned the radios, radio direction-finding equipment, generators, and weather recorders around the clock. There was no TV, no movies, only a pool table and cards for recreation. There were card games (mostly Hearts) with the same three guys every night. The fourth man was on watch.

We took 1-week shifts at cooking the evening meal. It seemed like we tried to outdo each other with our cooking. We produced what I consider outstanding meals. The hunting and fishing was great, but you had to be very alert about your surroundings. You had to be by yourself because the others were sleeping, working, or on watch.

That year taught me that it was indeed possible for people to get along for long periods of time. During that year, there was not a problem that we didn't solve. We learned to accept the imperfections that each of us had.

I consider the training and time spent in the U. S. Coast Guard to be the best experience life could have given me.

George Sawyer worked as an electrical power generation instructor at the Alaska Skill Center in Seward, Alaska, for three years. He was harbor master in Seward for two years, and worked for the Kenai Peninsula Borough for 10 years before retiring again in 1988. George and Kathleen, his wife of 48 years, have four children and seven grandchildren. They live in Tucson, Arizona.

Duane C. "Dewey" Hein
Age 16 – United States Air Force

It was 1952 and my "older" buddies (including my future wife's brother) were talking about "gettin' out of Dodge," Dodge County, Wisconsin, that is, and joining the service. I was only 16, but I was tall for

> ..., I was thinking about all the fun my buddies were having at Minnie's Bar.

my age at 6-feet 3-inches. I decided that they weren't going to leave me behind. I got out my birth certificate and was going to "modify" it, but it was black with white writing and I knew that wouldn't work.

I went to the County Recorder's office and said that I had lost the original and needed a new one. When I got home, I sweet-talked one of the girls in the high school typing class to change my birth year from "1936" to "1935." I was born on 14 May 1936 in Columbus, Wisconsin, but grew up in Hustiford, Wisconsin.

The new birth certificate worked like a charm. I went with all the guys and we signed up in December 1952. However, the quota was filled, so we had to wait until 5 January 1953 before we were inducted. I joined the Air Force and received my basic training at Lackland Air

Force Base, Texas. From there I was transferred to McChord AFB, Washington. While I was stationed there in 1956, a buddy and I drove home to Wisconsin.

I was involved in an automobile accident while on leave and spent a year at the Great Lakes Naval Hospital, Great Lakes, Illinois. The guy that traveled home with me returned to Washington thinking that I had "bit the dust." I didn't find that out until 1999 when a mutual friend from Washington gave him my address and phone number. I still owed him $200 that I had borrowed for my leave, and I finally paid him back.

After I was released from the hospital at Great Lakes, my enlistment was up. I went home and went to work at a canning factory. While I was stocking boxes in a warehouse, I was thinking about all the fun my buddies were having at Minnie's Bar. I took the afternoon off and went down and re-enlisted in the Air Force.

I was stationed at Truax Field, Madison, Wisconsin. My next transfer was to Keflavic, Iceland, for an isolated year-long tour in 1958-59. Russia was still trading with Iceland at that time and all U. S. military forces were restricted to base. The Army and Navy shared the base with the Air Force, which created some interesting brawls at the base clubs.

The Navy had its own hangars, but the Air Force shared a small portion of their hangar with the Army, which delivered food, mail, and supplies to the radar sites. The Navy flew P2V aircraft and patrolled the DEW (Distant Early Warning) line, while the Air Force flew F-89s and the Army had two-seat Cessnas. Above the door of the Army's office hung a large sign, "T. W. A." and under it, in very small print, was "Teenie Weenie Airlines."

When I arrived in Iceland, I had some debts and car payments overdue back home. Gambling was the main pastime on payday, but I was not a gambler. My buddy and I started a small sandwich and drink business and kept the gamblers fed and watered. Not only did I pay off my debts and car, but I had money in my pocket by the time I was transferred back to the States.

When I returned home from Iceland in December 1959, I got married and headed to my next duty station, Dover, Delaware. During the next 13½ years, I was stationed at Kadena AFB, Okinawa; Yokota, Japan; Nellis AFB, Nevada; Osan, Korea; and one year at Udorn AFB, Thailand.

While stationed at Udorn during 1969-70, we were located very close to the Cambodian border. Our duty was to keep the fighter planes maintained for their missions over Vietnam. The base perimeter received occasional sniper fire. There was an elephant that came through the base gates and left any time he felt like it. The monsoon rains made waist-high rivers of the street, in which many dead rats and snakes floated by. If you ventured off the base you had to fight off the monkeys that thought whatever you had belonged to them. They weren't into negotiation. It was an interesting tour, to say the least.

In March 1973, after 20 years of service as an aircraft mechanic, I retired from the Air Force at George AFB, Victorville, California. I was a master sergeant at the time.

I participated in a parade in 1996 in which Arizona Congressman Bob Stump rode in my convertible. Bob is a member of the Veterans of Underage Military Service. He told me about the group and I joined it.

Dewey Hein began a second career as a diesel-truck driver for CONTEL, a local phone company in Victorville, California. He retired from that job after 17 years. Dewey and Rose live in Chino Valley, Arizona.

✓ *INCIDENTally — A black-bread recipe.* – The staple food for prisoners of war in Nazi Germany during World War II was black bread. The recipe for the bread was found in the official record of the Food Providing Ministry in Berlin. It was a top-secret publication with the identifier 24.X1 1941. The recipe was given as:

　　　　50% bruised rye grain
　　　　20% sliced sugar beets
　　　　20% tree flower (sawdust)
　　　　10% minced leaves and straw

Some POWs found bits of glass and sand in the bread. Someone was cheating on the recipe. – *Walter F. Ram.*

Glenn R. F. Logan

Age 16 – United States Army

My father was working on the Los Angeles Aqueduct near Indio, California, where I was born on 23 March 1937. My parents divorced six weeks after I was born. As near as I can recall and figure out from

> *The Army was glad to have me, and never asked about my age, ...*

what I have been told, I was raised by about 24 different families. From age 9 to 13, I worked for room and board on a farm in Canada, then Mom found me and brought me home to Temple City, California.

At school, they put me in the 10th grade for a while, then sent me to Pasadena City College because I'd already passed all the high school courses by examination while in Canada. Meanwhile, I was having friction with my stepfather, who was trying to act like a dad to me, but I was having none of that stuff. I tried to go to the Merchant Marine Academy, but could not for some reason. Finally, I talked Mom into signing an affidavit stating that I was a year older and had been born in a county where we knew the courthouse had burned down.

I joined the Army on 1 September 1953. The Army was glad to have me, and never asked about my age, probably because a college sophomore had to be old enough. I took basic at Fort Ord, California, then went through cook, baker, and meatcutter schools there. Next, I was sent to Fort Lewis, Washington, where I spent three years. During part of this time I was assigned to the general's mess at Camp Desert Rock, Nevada, where, during the atomic tests, I got a radiation overdose.

A tragic romance in Seattle led to a drinking bout, followed by a re-enlistment in which I requested to be sent to Germany. However, I was sent to Fort Carson, Colorado, as a 60mm-mortar squad leader with the infantry. There I met my future wife. Three days after we were married, I was sent to Heilbronn, Germany. My wife finally arrived there 14 months later, but her stay was short. I was transferred back to the States to attend OCS at Fort Benning, Georgia.

I was disillusioned by two years as an infantry lieutenant in Korea, so I tried to resign my commission. My resignation was denied, so I simply took a discharge from the Army after seven years of active duty.

But I wasn't ready for civilian life, so in 1961, I re-enlisted as a corporal in the Army Security Agency and was assigned to study Arabic at the Army Language School in Monterey, California. This led to serving over four years in Ethiopia, a few times to various Middle East destinations, and several tours with the National Security Agency (NSA).

I studied Vietnamese at the Defense Language Institute at Monterey, California, and went to Vietnam in 1969. I served as operations NCO with the 1st Radio Research Company (Aviation) for a year, then I returned to the NSA. I received a letter stating that I'd been nominated as a potential sergeant major of the Army, which triggered headquarters to send me to Korea for a year for "professional development." I applied for retirement as soon as I got back to NSA. I was tired, for somehow or another, I'd seen combat in four wars over the years – not all ours.

I retired from the regular Army as a master sergeant (E-8) and from the Army Reserves as a major and was on the list for promotion to lieutenant colonel.

Glenn Logan earned the Expert Infantry, Paratrooper, and Air Crewman Badges, was awarded 12 Air Medals, two Joint Service Commendation Medals, two Army Commendation medals, and a number of other service medals. After his retirement from the Army, he worked as the CEO of a defense contractor doing translations of technical foreign-language documents. By this time he had used 14 languages professionally. After retiring from that position in 1987, he went to graduate school and received an M. A. in counseling. He was licensed as a senior chemical-addictions counselor and is currently a licensed professional counselor. Glenn and Rosalie, his wife of 45 years, have six children, fourteen grandchildren, and two great-grandchildren. They travel extensively on tours and cruises. They live in Colorado Springs, Colorado.

John C. Franklin, Jr.
Age 16 – United States Army

I did not join the service because we were poor or hungry. Poor we were, but we always had plenty to eat. We always had a garden and got wild game from the swamps of Jay, Florida, where I grew up.

> I turned 16 in the recruiter's office and almost gave myself away ...

I think it was more for adventure and patriotism that I joined.

It all started when I was in the fifth grade. I would read about the knights of old defending the kingdom, etc. Oliver and Charlemagne were my favorites. In the sixth grade, I discovered the novels about Dave Dawson and Freddy Farmer at Dunkirk. They were fighter pilots, and all this just inflamed me with the desire to become a warrior in the service of my country.

I tried unsuccessfully to join the Navy at age 14, but just didn't have the know-how. I was put in a home for truants for a while. There I pretended that I was in the "barracks." I guess I thrived on the strict regime. As the Korean War was going on, I thought of a

plan which might work to get me into the service. I went to the draft registration office and told them that I was 18 years old that day, although I was born on 16 August 1937 in Bluff Springs, Florida.

My given name is John Carlton Franklin, Jr., but I registered for the draft as Johnny Carl Franklin. The clerk asked me for my birth certificate because I did not look like I was 18. My reply to her was, "Man, have you ever heard of the Baby-Faced Bandit?" She said, "Yes, but you are not him." She would not register me without a birth certificate. I had planned long and hard for this, so I had a reply ready. I told her that I had hitchhiked down there, and I was not coming back. There was a war going on, and I didn't want to go anyway. I asked her to please give me a letter saying that I had tried to register, but that she would not accept me. She then made a call to someone, and I guess they told her to go ahead and register me.

Each day I would be the first one to the mailbox, awaiting my draft card. After about six weeks, I finally received my "greatest possession." There was a curfew in our town, 10 p.m. if you were under 18. When I got my draft card, I flaunted it. The cops said that they knew that I wasn't 18, but they couldn't prove it.

I tried to volunteer for the draft, but was unsuccessful, so I devised another plan. The Army recruiter's office was directly across the hall from the draft-registration office. After carefully observing the schedule, I knew that the draft clerks went to lunch at 12 o'clock every day. At 11:59:45, I watched them come out of their office. I also knew that the Army recruiter was looking out of his door. So I said to the clerks, in a voice loud enough for the recruiter to hear, that I wanted to volunteer for the draft. They told me to come back at 1300 hours. I stood outside the office, and as I expected and hoped, the Army recruiter called me in and said that he had a "deal" for me, if I would enlist for three years. I said, "O.K."

I waited for almost a month for my orders. I had to hide this from my parents and friends at school. I turned 16 in the recruiter's office and almost gave myself away by saying, "Today is my birthday." Finally, I went to Jacksonville, Florida, and was sworn into the Army on 10 September 1953. That night, we were put on a troop train to Fort Jackson, South Carolina.

We went through the clothing issue, the shots, etc., and were given a "flying 20," a $20 bill. I was rich! I went to the beer garden and bought a 5¢ beer. Man, was I finally living! About that time, I spotted Corporal Faron Young, a famous country singer. I dared not speak to him though, because a one-striper (private first class) had given me such a hard time that to approach a two-striper (corporal) would be too much.

I was flown to Fort Sill, Oklahoma, for basic training. This was my first plane ride. I was assigned to the 469th Field Artillery Battalion. After basic, I went to the 163rd Transportation Company to become a truck driver. During this time, they asked who wanted to go to Germany, and I said I did. I was assigned to the Service Company, 16th Infantry Regiment, 1st Infantry Division, as a truck driver.

I turned 17 on the top of a mountain named Wildfliken. Shortly after, Mother and Dad got me out of the Army. But 84 days later, they signed for me to go back in, as I didn't go to school or do anything else they wanted me to do. I was at Fort Chaffee, Arkansas, in 1958 when Elvis Presley came in the Army. Although I had the rank to talk to him, I could not, because he was surrounded by the news media. Oh well!

During my Army career, I served at Thule, Greenland, and in Korea. I had four tours of duty in Germany, and two in Vietnam. The units I served with in Vietnam were A Battery, 2nd Battalion, 32nd Artillery Brigade at Xuan Loc, as communications chief, and the 1st Cavalry Division at Bein Hoa.

I would have stayed in the Army a couple of years longer as I had a good job as battalion communications chief of the 2nd Battalion, 18th Field Artillery at Fort Sill, Oklahoma, but I received orders to go to Germany again. I had volunteered for each of my eight tours of overseas duty, but this time I didn't. I told the battalion commander that I wanted to "play Columbus and discover America."

I retired from the Army on 31 January 1975 after serving more than 21 years. During my Army career, I was aboard seven troopships and was seasick every time. I'm glad I didn't make it into the U. S. Navy!

John Franklin went into the trucking business after retiring from the Army. He owns and operates a semi tractor-trailer rig, traveling to all parts of the United States. He and his wife Lu Ann have a daughter, Lisa Marie. They live in Pace, Florida.

George E. Hughes
Age 16 – Texas National Guard

I was born in Houston, Texas, on 21 July 1937. When I decided to join the National Guard and later the Army, I was able to convince my mother to sign the necessary papers. I joined Company G,

> ..., I was able to convince my mother to sign the necessary papers.

143rd Infantry Regiment, 36th Infantry Division, Texas National Guard on 26 March 1954. I served as a heavy-weapons infantryman and was trained on the 60mm mortar and the 57mm recoilless rifle. I was in summer camp at Fort Hood, Texas, on my 17th birthday.

At the time I joined the Guard, I was taking Army ROTC at John H. Reagan Senior High School in Houston, Texas. I was getting poor grades in my other subjects, so in March 1955 I decided to quit school and join the regular Army.

I started my Army career at Fort Riley, Kansas, in the Tank Company of the 85th Infantry Regiment. I took all my training in this unit and was with it during Operation Gyroscope. We went to Germany in November 1955.

I returned to Fort Benning, Georgia, where we retired the colors of the 10th Infantry Division and reactivated the 2nd Infantry Division. From Fort Benning, I was assigned to Fort Eustis, Virginia, where I joined the 557th Heavy Truck Company as a tank driver. I went back to Germany in 1961 and was assigned to the 8th Infantry Division, and stayed there until December 1963. In 1964, I was assigned to the The Armored School at Fort Knox, Kentucky, where I stayed until May 1966.

I went next to the 2nd Infantry Division in Korea for a 4-month tour, then I went to Fort Gordon, Georgia, as an instructor in the Signal Officer Candidate School. I started my third tour in Germany in 1968 and was assigned to the 3rd Armored Division. In November 1970, I finally received orders to Vietnam, where I was assigned to the Military Advisory Command and served as an advisor to the Vietnamese 12th Armored Cavalry from January to December 1971.

I returned to the United States in January 1972 and was assigned to the 1st Cavalry Division where I stayed until I retired in March 1975.

George Hughes was awarded the Army Commendation Medal with oak leaf cluster, the Meritorious Service Medal, the Vietnamese Staff Service Medal, the Vietnamese Armor Badge, and a number of other service medals. After his retirement from the Army, he worked for the General Services Administration as a federal protective officer for 13 months, then transferred to the U. S. Postal Service. He retired from that position in October 1992. George and his wife Bonnie have three children and eight grandchildren. They live in Cleveland, Texas.

✓ *INCIDENTally* — **The wrong way!** – I was a 16-year-old Marine getting ready to go overseas in 1946. Several of us asked our lieutenant if we could put our rifles in our seabags. He said, "I'm not sure, but I don't think it would hurt anything." A couple of other guys and I went ahead and did it. Somebody must have said something to the captain because he got hold of us and really chewed our ass out for that stunt. I don't know what happened to the lieutenant. – *William G. Hood.*

Bobbie Sue (Dunaway) Grape

Age 16 – United States Army (WAC)

As the Korean War was ending in 1953, thousands of men and women were being sent home, many with lost limbs, and many sent to hospitals before they could go home. The news was filled with stories about these great heroes. At age

> ... and there was a full-page picture of Uncle Sam pointing his finger at me and saying, "I want you!"

15, I was engrossed with these stories and I kept newspaper clippings of hundreds of the events that were happening.

Home life was total chaos for me, and I think that somehow, with a lot of imagination, I was with each of these men and women, helping them in some way.

By the time I was 15, I had run away from home six times. My mother and stepfather were very strict with me, and I actually never had what you would call a social life until I entered the service. My mother did her best to control me during an uncontrollable time in my life, but we both knew that I was headed for trouble unless something drastic took place.

I was frequently truant at school, and I had only one special love – music. My music teacher saw talent in me and would often allow me to sing for our spiritual morning prayer. One morning I bellowed out the Andrews Sisters' song, "Company B," for our morning worship. The kids went wild, and I was almost expelled from school. That was the last day that I remember being in school.

My home life was becoming worse. I had total responsibility for two half-sisters, did the cooking and cleaning and chopped wood, among other things. I always related to Cinderella in the fairy tale and wondered when my fairy godmother would come along and rescue me.

I received the newspaper one day, and there was a full-page picture of Uncle Sam pointing his finger at me and saying, "I want you!" It was a cold September day, and I had just turned 16 in July, my birth date being 2 July 1938. I left the house quietly and flagged down a driver to take me into town. I sought out an Army recruiter, filled out some forms, told him I was 18, and he never blinked an eye. He later came by the house to bring me back home and get my mother's approval and proof of my age. My birth certificate was the main component for confirmation of my age.

My heart was in my throat as my mother presented the birth certificate. He looked at it, smiled, and told me to be ready to travel to Knoxville for further testing, a physical examination, etc. I could not believe my ears. He assured me that the USO was a huge part of the Army, and he did not see why I would not fit right in. I sang "Dear John" for him. He shook my mother's hand and left.

I received the usual punishment of my stepfather's leather strap for running away and taking things into my own hands. I think that was the only time I never cried while being punished. After all had settled down, my mother and I scrutinized the birth certificate with eyes of wonderment and awe. It had been folded in half, then half again. The year "1938" was in one of those folds. The "8" appeared as a "6" because of the second fold.

I don't remember sleeping for days! I was finally going to help the servicemen. I knew in my Cinderella heart that I could sing them back to health.

I was sworn in on 12 October 1954 and left for Fort McClellan, Alabama, on a bus. I was in for a rude awakening. What I thought was my fairy tale come true was my worst nightmare. I began to learn a whole new vocabulary: spit-shine, quarter-tight bed-making, ditty bag, attention, at ease, halt, mess hall, and chow. One of my strongest memories is that I would never be able to "shoot" anything again, but I would learn to "fire" the M1 rifle, or I would fail the basic training. I never experienced a bruise at home like the ones I received from the old M1s. To this day, I have a dislike and fear of guns. Fear took on a whole new meaning to me! I feared my staff sergeant, my commanding officer, and black people.

In school, I remember reading Mark Twain's *Huckleberry Finn*. The black man Joe in the story became a reality for me in basic training. We were assigned very small cubicles with two bunk beds in each. My roommate's name was Jeanne, a very beautiful black girl from Chicago. I was so afraid of this girl that I would wait until she was asleep before I went to bed. I don't know what I was afraid of, but never knowing any black people growing up, this was just another new experience for me.

I was continuously being gigged for improper footlocker arrangement, for not being able to spit-shine my shoes, and because my brass emblems were always dull. I received only one weekend pass during my whole eight weeks of basic training. I was called into the sergeant's office daily. Every time this occurred, I could envision my birth certificate lying on her desk with a big "1938" scrawled on it. I had frequent dreams of this and of Jeanne carrying me off somewhere never to be found.

One day, after a grueling morning on the firing range and three miles of practice marching drill, I was exhausted! We were getting ready for one of the generals who was to visit the barracks and see a parade of trainees at the completion of basic. I remember coming into the cubicle and bending down to unlace my boots. My next memory was of waking up in sick bay. I had passed out. The doctor diagnosed me with hypoglycemia and exhaustion. I understood the exhaustion, but he later told me that I was running low on blood sugar. I was kept overnight for observation. I knew my fairy tale had come to an end. I would never be able to sing for my soldiers, and I could not think of ever going back home!

I was released the next morning and returned to my cubicle. I thought that I had walked into the wrong one, but Jeanne and a few others were there. My footlocker was up to military standards, and more. My shoes were shined so that my reflection was beaming in and out of them, my uniform was pressed with creases, and my brass emblems, shining like gold, were pinned on my lapels and lying across my tight bunk. Jeanne bounced a quarter on it, and we all laughed.

Jeanne Taylor was my fairy godmother. She had made it possible for me to see my vision become a reality. She came over and gave me a quick hug and everyone clapped. The next day, the general and other officers did a barracks inspection; no gigs, and I got my first weekend pass. I went with Jeanne and a couple of other girls to, of all things, a USO show. Jeanne had told the director that I sang, and with her assistance (she was a singer, too) we sang, "Sincerely" and received a standing ovation. I will never forget that wonderful evening!

Jeanne taught me everything about keeping all things up to military standards. I learned that she was 23, but she never asked my age, and I never told her.

Our basic training was over in the middle of December 1954. We all had our furloughs and assignments for our next destination. Mine was Fort Riley, Kansas. I didn't get to see Jeanne those last days. Her parents had come early to pick her up for the holidays in Chicago. I missed her, and I did not want to go home! A girl from Florida who had driven her own car to basic training invited me to go to Florida for the holidays, and I accepted. Her family was very kind to me, and that was the first time I had ever seen a beach and sand! I had $200 for my furlough and to get to Kansas.

I arrived in Kansas around midnight on 6 January 1955. My luggage was lost. All I had was the uniform I was wearing. It was the most scary and lonely feeling I had felt in a long time. The train agent called for a military policeman to take me to the WAC Detachment. When I saw three MPs coming toward me, I could see "1938" stamped on each of their foreheads. They had finally found me out! I was shaking so badly that one asked a porter for a blanket to put around me. The other two MPs were there only to make out a report for my lost luggage and promised to get it to me as soon as possible.

I arrived at the WAC Detachment at 2:00 a.m. and was assigned to Unit 1. I was now in the 5th Army, 2nd WAC Detachment, with an MOS of medical technician. Where was my dream of the USO? I was sent for on-the-job training at the hospital for six months. It was not bad. I was fulfilling my dream, taking care of my soldiers – I just wasn't singing to them.

One evening I was working the 11 to 7 o'clock shift on Ward 10 when a soldier came in with a temperature of 104 degrees. He was having delusions about Korea and thought that he was in a prison camp being tortured by North Koreans. I was assigned to him to help bring his temperature down. He was put into restraints, and I continually kept him in cool towels until about 9 o'clock the next morning when his fever came down to 101 degrees. He was in quarantine and suffering from the effects of malaria which he had acquired in a Korean prison camp. He kept looking at me and finally told me that he was the one who had picked me up at the train station. He wanted to know if I ever received my lost luggage. I assured him that I had and told him of my dream of singing for the USO. He was released a week later and gave me credit for nursing him back to health and reality.

One Sunday afternoon, I was contacted by the desk clerk and told that there was an MP in the waiting room who had requested my presence. Again "1938" was all I could see. My lie had now really been found out! But it was my patient. He took me to the USO, introduced me to the director, and asked her to give me a chance. The director, a kind, older woman, told me that there were two USO clubs on the post, and each weekend new basic trainees were allowed to have passes to be entertained. I was again filled with excitement.

I had two tryouts on two occasions for song and dance. I was allowed to do both. With the permission of my commanding officer, I performed at both clubs every weekend. On my second tryout, my greatest thrill and surprise was seeing none other than my Black fairy godmother, Jeanne Taylor. She, too, had been assigned to Fort Riley, but with a MOS of USO assistant. We recaptured our old friendship and caught up on what had been going on since basic training.

The MP's name was Sergeant Richard "Dick" Grape. He tried to never miss one of my shows, and he was there to make sure that I got back to the barracks safely. We were married later. I became pregnant and received an honorable discharge in October 1956. He remained in the Army and retired after serving 23 years. I didn't tell Dick my true age until after our second child was born. He laughed and told me that he had tried on numerous occasions to get into the service at ages 15 and 16, but was caught each time. Until writing this, I have never told any one but Dick about my underage service. I feel such a sense of relief telling about it!

Bobbie Grape received a B.S. in nursing at the University of Seventh Day Adventists Nursing School at Collegedale, Tennessee. She now teaches at the nursing school that she graduated from. Her husband Dick passed away in 1998 of heart complications stemming from diseases he incurred while in prison camp. She is active in the Korean Ex-POW Association and sings at their reunions. Bobbie and Dick had five children and one grandchild. She lives in Cleveland, Tennessee.

Charles W. "Bill" Cutshaw

Age 16 – California National Guard

I enlisted in Company B, 134th Tank Battalion, 40th Armored Division, California Army National Guard, on 8 November 1954 in Brawley, California, at the age of 16. In addition to the friction at home between my stepfather and me, I was manipulated by the NCO cadre in the California Cadet Corps at school. The story was that if we youngsters did well in the Cadet Corps, they would arrange for us to enlist in the local unit of the Army National Guard. The word was that the Guard had great "GI parties!"

> ..., I believe that my duffel bag weighed nearly as much as I did, ...

I busted my hump as the company clerk and was eventually told that I could enlist. I was escorted to the local armory one Monday night and had the parental-consent papers typed up with "1937" as my birth year instead of "1938." My actual birth date was 5 June 1938. I was driven in an open jeep to my residence, where my step-dad and Mom signed the papers. I'm quite sure they were aware of the wrong birth year, but said nothing.

The following summer, our National Guard company was loaded aboard an olive-drab troop train in Brawley, which took us to Camp Roberts, California, for summer camp. Needless to say, I was "ten-feet tall" even though my second-hand fatigues made me look like "sad sack." I was 5-feet 2-inches and weighed 138 pounds. I thoroughly enjoyed the long train trip, even though the mostly underage corporals harassed us all the way. Upon arrival at the industrial area at Camp Roberts, we disembarked and formed up for a good two-mile uphill hike with duffel bags on our shoulders some of the time, to the base of Camp Roberts Hill, where we were billeted for the encampment. Looking back, I believe that my duffel bag weighed nearly as much as I did, but there was no way that I would ever drop it or fall out of formation. I guess that I was just born to be military, and even though the "GI parties" turned out to be scrubbing the World War II barracks from top to bottom, inside and out, I decided that military life was for me.

On 10 November 1955, I enlisted in the United States Marine Corps. Unbeknown to me, it was the Marine Corps' birthday. Twelve weeks later, I graduated from boot camp in San Diego, California. I completed individual combat training at Camp Pendleton, and cold-weather training at "Pickle Meadows," California, near Bridgeport. I spent the next two years as a "grunt" with Marine Corps Test Unit #1 at Camp Horno, at Pendleton. I was transferred back to the same recruit training battalion at the Marine Corps Recruit Depot, San Diego, that I was in during boot camp. I served there as a training NCO for the remainder of my enlistment.

I became bored and decided that if I was going to make the military my career, I wanted a commission. I left the Corps in 1959 as a buck sergeant, enrolled in college, became financially strapped, and started looking for additional income. As it turned out, the local Army National Guard had a civil-service opening in Company D, 224th Tank Battalion, 40th Armored Division. I applied, was accepted in 1961, and by 1963 I was first sergeant of what was now Company B, 2nd Battalion, 160th Infantry, 40th Armored Division. At the time that I was appointed first sergeant, I was a fairly new staff sergeant and had my work cut out for me. Many problems were "worked out" behind the building where I managed to hold my own. As I recall, there were quite a few "tripped over my footlocker" injuries in the company.

During my enlisted time with Company B, I was often encouraged to apply for officers candidate school. For various reasons, I kept postponing applying until I became too old for acceptance. As it turned out, the maximum age for commissioning was raised to 31 during the Vietnam conflict. About this time, someone within my hearing distance said, " 'Top' could never make it even if he was accepted for OCS." That did it! In August 1966, I graduated form OCS at Fort Benning, Georgia, and was commissioned later that year. I was pinned with my gold bar in the same barracks area at Camp Roberts that I had trudged to 12 years earlier.

I was commissioned as an Armor officer, and due to my military background, was initially given command of a detached scout platoon

I was commissioned as an Armor officer, and due to my military background, was initially given command of a detached scout platoon in Placerville, California. I was next transferred back to the 2nd Battalion (Mechanized), 160th Infantry, which had been relocated to Fresno, California, on the same date that I was transferred to a civil-service position there. My branch was changed from Armor to Infantry and the majority of the time I spent as a lieutenant was in a captain's billet as the adjutant.

After I was promoted to captain, I was honored to be given command of the battalion's combat support company. Following that assignment, I served as S2 (intelligence-security officer), and for five years as the battalion S3 (operations officer). While serving as S3, I was informed that my hearing loss would probably prohibit me from commanding a combat arms battalion, and I was transferred to the Transportation Corps where I eventually became battalion commander of the 818th Transportation Battalion, U.S. Army Reserve. I served in this position throughout the Gulf War, and had the war lasted another week, the battalion was scheduled to be mobilized.

I had already attained the age of 53, the maximum age for lieutenant colonels, but since my replacement was on active duty, I had been allowed to stay in the assignment while a request for a special exemption to the age rule was processed. This exemption would have allowed me to go before the full colonel board 19 days after I was to be retired. Because of the end of the Gulf War and the Army's subsequent "build down" posture, my request for extension was denied.

It would have been nice to be promoted to colonel, but I was not too disappointed because the Army had changed just too much from the "ole brown-shoe Army" that I had enlisted in 37 years before. Also, I was missing the job satisfaction that I had back in my enlisted and company grade officer days. I retired form the U. S. Army Reserves on 4 July 1991.

Bill Cutshaw was awarded two Army Meritorious Service Medals and the Army Commendation Medal. He earned a B.A. in business administration and worked in the federal civil-service for 31 years. He has two daughters and five grandchildren from a previous marriage. His wife Cecilia, a registered nurse, also retired from the U. S. Army Reserves as a lieutenant colonel. Bill and Cecilia live in Prescott, Arizona.

Robert E. "Red" Hudson
Age 15 – United States Army

I was born in the little town of Batesville, Mississippi, on 8 March 1939, the middle child of three boys. My father was a sharecropping farmer and money was always short. In 1948, my father got a

> ..., the only thing I could think of was, "What have I got myself into?"

public-works job in town, leaving my oldest brother and me to do a lot of the farm work. It was hard work. I knew then that I wasn't going to be a farmer when I grew up.

In 1952, my mother started working in a hosiery mill. By this time we had moved to town and the farm was history. By mid-1954, my parents were in a very bitter divorce dispute. My father moved out of the house and left it up to us boys to decide where we would live. My older brother and I went with our father, mostly because he had the car. Not having much supervision, I began to hang out late and even tasted a little beer and moonshine. The maverick was beginning to come out in me. I was still attending school most of the time.

In early 1955, I needed some shoes for school. My mother told me to get my "damned ole daddy" to buy me shoes. My daddy told me to get my "damned ole mama" to buy me some shoes. I was already hanging out with some older boys. Some of them had been talking about going in some branch of the service. That sounded good to me, but I was only 15 years old. That Friday night as my father sat reading the paper, I told him I thought I knew where I could get me some shoes. He never looked up, just grunted and said, "All right." I only had two sets of jeans and shirts, a light jacket, and a pair of ragged Keds tennis shoes. I put my extra change of clothes in a paper sack and hid it under the house. I left for school as I always did on Monday morning. I walked to the edge of town and stuck out my thumb.

In Clarksdale, Mississippi, I went to the Army recruiter's office. Two of my older buddies were already there. They told me they were glad that I made it and that they had already told the recruiting sergeant that another one was coming.

The recruiter asked what he could do for me. In my gruffest voice I said, "Today is my birthday. I am 18 and ready to go!" I filled out some papers, signed them, and handed them back to the sergeant. He never asked me for anything to prove my age. That surprised me. By this time two more boys had shown up, all of age but me.

Later that day we were put on a bus to Jackson, Mississippi, where there was a small induction center. The next day , 7 January 1955, we took some written tests and a physical exam, and we were all sworn into the U. S. Army. At 3:30 that afternoon, they put us on a twin-engine propeller plane and took us to Fort Jackson, South Carolina. When that plane lifted off the ground, the only thing I could think of was, "What have I got myself into?"

After a few days at Fort Jackson, I was sent by bus to Camp Gordon, Georgia, for basic training. At my first Saturday morning inspection, I was asked why I had not shaved that morning. All I had was a little peach fuzz, so I answered that I had never shaved in my life. I was informed that I was to shave every day whether I needed to or not. From then on, I shaved every Friday night.

After a shortened period of basic training, we were shipped out to Seattle, Washington, on our way to South Korea. We were told that they had shipped too many troops home after the war. They needed to build the units up to full strength, so they were shipping everybody out that they could.

We boarded the USS *Mann* for the trip to Inchon, Korea. From there we were trucked to Pusan, Korea. My 16th birthday was spent walking guard around an ammunition dump. I was sent to several places in Korea during that year, but I spent most of my time in and around Kimpo Air Base, across the river from Seoul.

I was a good soldier and liked the Army. I had been gone from home about 90 days when I wrote my father a letter. I told him not to worry about me, that I was in good hands, and I had some shoes. I did not tell him where I was, but I did give my correct address. My father had never been off the farm, so my military address meant nothing to him. He wrote me back and wanted to know what in the hell I was doing in San Francisco, my address being APO, San Francisco. I never told him that I was 10,000 miles west of San Francisco. Sometime later he was told that I had a military address, but he never tried to get me out. I was glad of that because I was enjoying the Army.

The tour in Korea at that time was 12 months. I finished my tour and came back to the States on the USS *Mann*, the same ship that I had gone over on. Nothing really exciting happened to me during my time in Korea, except a trip to Japan on R&R for a week. I had been staying at a hotel run by the Army Special Services and hanging out in a nightclub in Tokyo called the Showboat. It had four floors with the center section cut out. It was a real showplace, and I had a lot of fun there. I would return to the hotel by midnight every night, but one night I got too drunk and woke up the next morning lying in an alley like a real bum. All I could think of was, "That ain't the way it is done."

When I returned to the States, I was assigned to Fort Benning, Georgia. I went home on leave and found that Daddy wasn't mad at me. While I was home I met a girl. We got married shortly afterwards and had a daughter, but it didn't last.

I had been back in the States about five months when I got into trouble with a sergeant. I was about to be court-martialed. I talked the CO into sending me back to Korea. I hoped that this would kill my court-martial, and it did. When I got back to Korea, it was for a 16-month tour. I was assigned to the 24th Infantry Division. I was a good soldier and made staff sergeant before I got out. I was discharged in January 1958. I have always regretted that I didn't stay in the Army for 30 years.

Red Hudson returned to Batesville, Mississippi, and the only job he could find was in an upholstery shop. He worked in the shop during the day and took a class in upholstery at night at a nearby junior college on the GI Bill. He retired from the upholstery business 45 years later. Red and Artie, his wife of 44 years, have seven children, and ten grandchildren. They live in Batesville, Mississippi.

Kenneth R. Buster

Age 15 – California National Guard
Age 16 – United States Navy

I was born to a family of construction workers and migrant farm workers on 22 September 1939. My dad was involved with the building of Shasta Dam, and the town in which I was born, La Moine, California, is now under Lake Shasta. As it was the end of the

> *Since he was the first recruiter I could talk to, it was the Navy for me.*

Depression, we didn't have a lot, but we always seemed to get by. My parents divorced when I was 4. My mother later married a much older man who was always more like a father to me than my real father.

At about the age of 10, I began to rebel against everything. I became a real good acquaintance of the juvenile authorities. I was in the juvenile hall several times between the ages of 10 to 15. It was always for petty things, but the pattern was beginning to show, and it was only a matter of time before the petty things became more serious. My mother had instilled a love for reading in me, and I was fortunate that schoolwork was not difficult for me, so my troubles with the law did not affect my progress in school. In fact, I skipped two grades in

elementary school and entered high school much younger than the other kids.

In my junior year, the school began a program called the California Cadet Corps which I thought would be an easy class, so I signed up. That decision became the turning point in my life.

The instructor was a retired Marine major, a veteran of World War II and Korea, who had retired and entered the cadet program as one of its primary instructors. After several months into the school year and after a couple of trips to the juvenile hall, he called me aside and talked to me like nobody ever had before. He told me that I had potential and could become someone that I could be proud of, and other people would be proud of, but I had to change the direction of my life. He asked me if I would be interested in joining the local National Guard unit because he knew the first sergeant and could get me in. He let me know that the discipline and the exposure to the veterans would be good for me. As this was the first time in my life that anyone had really explained to me that he cared about my future, I told him I would. I did not tell my parents because I was afraid they would stop me.

On 27 April 1955, I enlisted in Heavy Mortar Company, 187th Infantry, 49th Infantry Division, California National Guard, in Carmichael, California. The unit sergeant took care of the paperwork, and all of a sudden I was 18 years old. My MOS test was very scientific. The NCO took me to the weapons room and asked me to pick up several different pieces of what looked to me to be junk. He kept this up until I picked up the heaviest piece of this "junk." Then he told me to jog in place while holding it. I did not know the "junk" was parts of a 4.2-inch heavy mortar. On that day I became an 11C mortar man.

On 15 May, we left for training at Camp Roberts, California. It seems so strange now, as I remember us meeting at the armory (really an old store), drawing our equipment and weapons and marching to the train station carrying our duffel bag and rifles. It was late when we boarded the train and we were assigned a sleeping space (a hammock). We placed our duffel bags on the floor under the bottom hammock, and when we asked the squad leader where we would put the rifles, he let us know in very firm tones that we "would sleep with them" and God help us if we let something happen to them.

My one and only train ride was very uncomfortable and memorable. We stopped at Camp Stoneman to pick up more troops, then continued to Camp Roberts. It was a very long night. During that period of training, I began to grow up. Most of the cadre of the unit were veterans of World War II and Korea and the camp-staff members were the men of the 2nd Infantry Division, just back from Korea. I received firm but fair discipline. I was allowed to work hard and was treated like an equal partner in a team, for the first time. However, I was always aware that I was a very junior partner.

The next year when I started school, I had a different attitude and I graduated as the Cadet Commandant. I was a very proud young man! I was going to join the service but I really didn't know, or care, which branch to join. All recruiting offices were in the basement of the courthouse. I arrived about lunchtime on 7 July 1956, with the goal to join the first branch whose recruiter I could talk to. Both the Army and Marine offices were closed for lunch and the Navy recruiter was just about to leave when I walked up. Since he was the first recruiter I could talk to, it was the Navy for me.

I had all of my papers from the National Guard, so there were no problems as far as my age was concerned. Before the lunch period was over, I had joined for four years and was scheduled to report to the Great Lakes Naval Training Station for basic training.

I became a hospital corpsman, and after my schooling was completed, I was sent to Guam. While on Guam I had several experiences that will always remain with me. Volunteers were needed for an Air-Sea Rescue Unit, and I signed up. We took our training right there on Guam, and following the graduation, I was awarded the coveted Gold Navy and Marine Jump wings. When I left Guam I was told I couldn't wear them anymore because all jump training was supposed to be conducted at Fort Benning, Georgia. They did offer me the chance to go through jump school, but I declined.

We had two unique but totally different missions. The first was an airplane crash into the bay off of Agana, Guam. By the time we got to the bodies, they had been in the water for two or three days and had begun to deteriorate. The second was a body-recovery call from the Guam police. A taxi driver had murdered a prostitute and thrown her body off a cliff, hoping it would go into the ocean. Instead it landed on a ledge about halfway down. We rappeled down, recovered the body, and discovered the screened entrance to a cave. We later went back to the cave and discovered quite a cache of Japanese equipment, but it was all rusted and not even suitable for keeping as a wall-hanging.

While in the Navy I served at Guam, Oakland Navy Hospital, and on the USS *Watts*. In the latter part of my tour, I became sick, was diagnosed with multiple allergies, and was discharged. After taking the series of shots to help the allergies, I applied for reinstatement and was accepted but could only go into the reserves.

My first reserve tour was in Oakland. While there, I became acquainted with some Marines and applied for the Fleet Marine Force corpsman's course. I was accepted, and upon finishing the course was assigned as a corpsman to the Marine Reserve unit in Springfield, Missouri. During the next 20 years, I spent several short tours of duty (30 – 60 days) on special assignments, with two of them in Vietnam.

In the mid-60s when the GI bill was reinstated, I started college because I had a wife and three kids and needed the extra money. I wanted to get a commission, but since I was approaching 30, the chances were not looking too good. The Marines were not commissioning anybody from the reserves at that time. I knew some guys from the Army National Guard who told me that if I completed my master's degree, I could apply and would probably be accepted. So in 1967, I enlisted in the Missouri Army National Guard. I completed my master's degree in 1974, applied for and received a direct commission as a captain of engineers, since my degree was in safety engineering.

After retiring from my civilian job in 1988, I went back to active duty with the Kansas Army National Guard as the G-4, 35th Infantry Division, stationed at Fort Leavenworth, Kansas. I was later selected as the commander of the National Guard Marksmanship Training Unit at Camp Robinson, Arkansas, where I retired in 1995 as a full colonel. Upon retirement, I had 19 years of enlisted service and almost 22 years of commissioned service. I had a great career, but I owe it all to a retired Marine major who saw something in a half-wild kid that nobody else could see.

Ken Buster was awarded the Legion of Merit, the Bronze Star with "V" for valor, the Purple Heart, the Meritorious Service Medal with four oak-leaf clusters, the Army Commendation Medal with three oak-leaf clusters, Navy and Marine Gold Jump Wings, Army Air Crewman Wings, Army Distinguished Pistol Shot Badge, Army Distinguished Rifle Shot Badges, and the United States Distinguished International Shooting Badge. He was the first National Guardsman and the 17th person in U. S. history to earn the three shooting badges. While a civilian, he was employed as a correctional officer and later as a safety engineer with the Department of the Army. In 1984, he received a Ph.D. in safety management. He earned all his degrees while working a full-time job. School was a "little bit here and a little bit there" for him. He retired as the senior safety engineer at Fort Leonard Wood, Missouri, in 1988. Ken and Jo, whom he married in 1991, have a combined family of four children, twelve grandchildren, and one great-grandchild. They live in Heber Springs, Arkansas.

George E. Ferguson
Age 16 – United States Air Force

My fascination with the military came at a young age. I was born in Zwolle, Louisiana, on 20 May 1939. Zwolle is located 30 miles north of Fort Polk in northwest Louisiana. Zwolle and the surrounding areas were used for war games in late 1941 and later years. I have a vivid memory of

> He asked me if I could stay out of bars until I was at least 17.

the sights and sounds of tanks, cannon, and antiaircraft guns being all over town. The soldiers would give us kids candy, rations, and even blank bullets.

As kids we spent a lot of time playing soldiers. I found out in later years that General Omar Bradley, General George Patton, and Field Marshall Bernard Montgomery were in the area to observe the maneuvers at one time.

During one of the war games in 1943, our house caught fire from the wood stove my mother was cooking on. My mother got so excited about the fire that she ran outside with the rest of us and forgot about my newborn baby brother. She quickly remembered and ran back

inside to retrieve him. The smoke attracted the firemen brigade that was camped nearby. They quickly extinguished the fire and said that it was good practice for them. There was only moderate damage to the house.

There were three of us underage boys who decided to join the service. The mother of one of the boys was a teacher and had a typewriter. It didn't take much effort to change "1939" to "1938." We had just started the 11th grade when we decided to go

to Shreveport and join the Navy. The other two boys backed out, so I decided to do it by myself. After a lot of talking, my mother agreed to sign for me.

When I got to Shreveport and found the recruiting offices, I walked into the Air Force office by mistake. The recruiter asked me if he could help me, and I said I was looking for the Navy recruiting office. He asked why I wanted to join the Navy, and I said, "To see the world!" He told me that I could do it a lot faster by flying with the Air Force. He signed me up on the spot and had someone take the permission papers to my mother to sign. She told me later that she didn't think they would accept me, and that is why she promised to sign.

I was sworn into the Air Force on 25 October 1955, and the next day I took my first plane ride – to Lackland Air Force Base, Texas. Two or three days after we arrived, the commander came and talked to us. He told us that they were always catching people who enlisted fraudulently. He mentioned people with criminal records or who were underage. He said they would find out. He said if they came forward after he left and told the drill instructor, there wouldn't be any consequences except a discharge. After he left, I went to the drill instructor and confessed to being only 16. He asked me if I wanted to stay and I said, "Yes!" He told me that if I could take all he dished out, that I could stay. The next day, and for the next 11 weeks, I caught pure hell. I was so determined not to give up that I made it through boot camp.

When we filled out papers for ID cards, I put my correct birth date on them. While in basic training, I took the GED test for a high school equivalency diploma. My scores were above average and the high school principal back in Zwolle issued me a regular diploma. I had a high school diploma and was still months away from my 17th birthday.

After basic training, I went to Scott Air Force Base, Illinois, to attend a repairman school for ground communication equipment. One night in a St. Louis bar, the police came in checking IDs. Most of us were under the legal drinking age, but they noticed my ID in particular. I spent the night in jail, and the next morning they let me go back to the base. The commander called me to his office and asked me how I got in the Air Force so young. After telling him my story, he said that I was his first underage case. He asked me if I could stay out of bars until I was at least 17. I made him a promise that I would and kept it.

On my 17th birthday, the guys in the barracks bought a fifth of Old Crow. They told me I would have to chug-a-lug it to celebrate my coming-of-age. I was young and foolish, so I tried to do just that. My memory of the next couple of days is fuzzy. I remember trying to put on a shirt for a pair of pants the next morning. The rascals responsible for this told me that I threw up soon after turning the bottle up and almost emptying it. They made me stay in bed the next day and covered for me by saying I was in sick bay. To this day I can't touch Old Crow, or much of anything else, for that matter.

After tech school, I received orders to go to Japan. One of the guys who was recently married received orders for remote Alaska. He came in crying because he wouldn't be able to take his new bride with him. Since I was an ex-Boy Scout, I offered to trade (one good deed too many). Remote Alaska ended up being Adak in the Aleutian Islands. I was assigned to the 1929th Airways and Air Communications Service Squadron. Adak is known as "The Wind-Swept Pearl of the Bering Sea," and it was said "that there is a girl behind every tree." Only problem is there are no trees.

While I was on this volcanic island, earthquakes were a common occurrence. A day burned into my memory is 9 March 1957. A 7.0 earthquake struck in the early morning hours. I, along with my roommate, was literally shaken out of bed. It was pitch-black except for some transformers exploding and burning. For a few seconds I thought this might be the end of the world. We didn't know whether to jump out the window or go blind. The initial shocks didn't last too long, but there were lots of smaller aftershocks for days. Luckily, the barracks were built on springs to withstand these shocks, but there were several cracks and other damage. Most of the roads had cracks. At least part of one road disappeared. The electricity was out for two weeks and there was no water or heat. The only food the mess hall could fix was roast beef. We had it three times a day for nearly two weeks.

Somehow I lasted my year on Adak without going too crazy. There were several guys not so fortunate. One had to be taken out of the barracks in a straight jacket. A "Dear John" letter didn't help him, I'm sure. Another poor soul walked around with an imaginary dog on a leash and would try to peddle sandwiches to everyone in the barracks.

Needless to say, he didn't have any customers. He finally got to leave early.

I was one of the fortunate ones to be chosen for arctic-survival training while there. They took us to a remote location and dumped us out in the middle of a snowstorm that turned into a blizzard. We did have tents to try and put up during the storm. Most of the guys took off their foul-weather gear and crawled into their sleeping bags inside their tent. I kept everything I had on and crawled inside my sleeping bag. I still shook and shivered all night. The next morning, several of the guys who had removed their fur-lined boots had frostbite. The Air Force decided to call off any more arctic-survival training.

From Adak, I went back to Scott AFB as an instructor. Since I had joined up to see the world, I wanted to go to a new location. I went to see the civilian who was in charge of the instructors. I convinced him that I would not make a good instructor, so they put me in the repair shop. I stayed there for about a year. When they started transferring schools to Keesler AFB, Mississippi, I helped make the move.

I spent my last year in the Air Force at Keesler. My roommate was from Tupelo, Mississippi. He took me home with him one weekend. His wife arranged a date for me with her best friend. This blind date turned out to be my wife of 42 years.

I was discharged from the Air Force at Keesler AFB on 29 September 1959.

George Ferguson worked in New Orleans doing ejection molding with plastic for about a year, then was hired by Western Electric. When AT&T was split into the "Baby Bells," company names changed and he finished his career with Lucent Technologies. He was promoted into management, although he had never completed high school. He retired in 1996 and was hired back as a project manager on a contract basis in 2000. George and Jean have two girls and two boys who have blessed them with nine grandchildren. They live in Brandon, Mississippi.

632

Wallace C. Broadnax
Age 16 – United States Army

I was born on 12 June 1939 in Monroe, Georgia, the third oldest of four children. When I was in the 10th grade, I left school to enlist in the U. S. Army. Three friends and I went

> ... I can truthfully say that I had a real adventurous, happy, rewarding, military career.

to the recruiting office in Monroe. I was told that I needed a birth certificate or a draft card. I went to the draft board and requested a draft card and was told that I needed a birth certificate. I told the clerk that I would be back the following day with my birth certificate, so she gave me a draft card. I went back to the recruiter with the draft card, was sworn into the Army on 21 November 1955, and was soon on my way to Fort Jackson, South Carolina.

I took basic with the 101st Airborne Division. Basic training on Tank Hill was pretty rough, but I suffered it out and graduated in

February 1956. From Fort Jackson, I went to Fort Bragg for jump school with the 82nd Airborne Division. After jump school, I stayed with the 82nd Airborne for about two years. I was assigned to Tank Company 505. I left Fort Bragg in 1958 and went to Fort Stewart, Georgia, and joined the 710th Tank Battalion. I remained at Fort Stewart until May 1960, at which time I re-enlisted for six years. I was sent to Kitzingen, Germany, where I was assigned to the 1st Battalion, 68th Armor. In June 1963, I was

transferred to Fort Carson, Colorado, and was assigned to the 1st Battalion, 77th Armor. In 1965, I went back to Germany and joined the 2nd Battalion, 33rd Armor at Kirch-Goens.

In May 1967, I was transferred to the 2nd Battalion, 34th Armor, in Lai Khe, South Vietnam. In July 1968, I returned to Fort Knox, Kentucky, where I was assigned to the 3rd Battalion, 33rd Armor, and the 194th Armor Brigade. In August 1970, I returned to the Republic of South Vietnam. During this tour, I was assigned to three different units: the 3rd Squadron, 4th Cavalry, 25th Infantry Division in Cu Chi; the 3rd Squadron, 11th Armored Cavalry Regiment at Dian; and the 1st Battalion, 77th Armor at Quang Tri. I was there for about three months and then was transferred to the 2nd Squadron, 11th Armored Cavalry at Camp Fresnell Jones in Long Bien.

After completing my second tour in Vietnam, I was assigned to the 9th Infantry, 1st Battalion, 34th Armor, at Fort Lewis, Washington. I remained there until June 1973 when I was transferred back to Germany and assigned to the 1st Battalion, 81st Armor. In April 1976, I returned to the States and was assigned to the 2nd Battalion, 34th Armor at Fort Carson, Colorado. I retired from the Army on 1 June 1978 as a sergeant first class. As I look back over my life, I can truthfully say that I had a real adventurous, happy, rewarding, military career. I have no regrets.

Wallace Broadnax was awarded the Bronze Star Medal with two oak leaf clusters, the Vietnamese Cross of Gallantry (four awards), and a number of other service medals. In June 1981, he was employed at the Pueblo Chemical Depot and became a supervisor in the Security Division. He retired in November 2001. Along the way he finished high school and earned an A.A. from Pike's Peak Community College in Colorado Springs in 1981. Wallace and Marion, his wife of 32 years, live in Colorado Springs, Colorado. They have two children, a girl and a boy, both college graduates.

634

Alton P. Gorbett
Age 16 – United States Army

I was born in a small town in southern
Indiana on 27 June 1939 and lived there
until I was 15. During my early formative
years my father was in the Navy. He was
discharged in 1946 after serving for eight
years, most of it overseas on a Navy hospital

> I got a copy of my birth
> certificate and used ink
> eradicator to blur the
> date of birth, ...

ship. When he returned home he worked at any available job, and
there weren't many at that time. While we didn't have much money,
I never thought that we were poor – we always had food on the table
and presents at Christmas. The presents were mostly clothing and
other needed things, and the food mostly came out of our garden and
from the chickens and rabbits we raised.

But the town and my school were still in the early part of the
century; at least that's how I felt. I had no problems at school, except
a certain boredom. I had the usual yearning for money. A friend
joined me with a pushcart and we would prowl the alleys collecting
newspapers, glass, and assorted junk which we sold for pocket change.
But I could see that there was little future in my staying in this same
rut, only getting older and not smarter. Having no other direction or
ambition except to get away and see what was out there beyond my
Indiana home, when I was 15 years old, I ran away from home.

Truthfully, I wasn't running *away* from home, I was running
towards a new life. Home hadn't been bad – it just didn't offer me any
opportunity for the future. I hitchhiked my way to Florida, cadging
meals from those kind folks who would pick me up and take me down
the road in their cars. Sometimes I slept in the fields, and sometimes
I was lucky and got a bunk in the local police station. I learned a lot
of American history along the way, something I've loved ever since.
One place I really remember was a small town in Georgia, which I was
told was the first slave market in the state. I was taken there one
evening by the local chief of police. He told me how the market had
begun, about the shiploads of slaves brought in to the ports of Georgia,
and how they were sold at auction. I had no idea that we had such

physical remnants of history left in our country. Today, of course, I know there are many surviving memorials to our past in many areas besides slavery.

These experiences led me to decide that I had to join the military. It was the total answer to what I wanted in life. In the military I would have a good-paying job, a chance to better my education, an opportunity to learn a good trade, and an opportunity to see both the world and my own country. I joined the Army and have never regretted a minute of it.

I got a copy of my birth certificate and used ink eradicator to blur the date of birth, moving the date from 27 June 1939 to 2 January 1938. Eighteen months was all I needed to escape Indiana and join the world of the professionals. On 4 January 1956, I presented myself at the recruitment station in Indianapolis, Indiana, and volunteered for the Army. I quickly passed my physical and was sworn in. I went home that evening (hitchhiking again) to tell my mother what I had done. She said I could not possibly have done such a thing, but of course, I had. At least she understood enough about me to accept the fact, and she never did anything to have me booted out of the service.

Two days later, I was back in Indianapolis, boarding a train which took me and lots of other guys to Fort Leonard Wood, Missouri. Before we boarded the train, the sergeant gave us our military serial numbers and told us we damn well better know them by the time we reached the camp. I spent most of the night repeating that number over and over, never again to be forgotten. We arrived at Fort Leonard Wood at 3:00 a.m. the next morning. I was 16 years old.

Basic training was rough in the winter. We did physical training in the snow, ran for miles, then stood in the freezing rain! We did the rifle range when the ground was frozen. Not only were we frozen to the ground when we tried to get up from the prone firing position, but we had to pick up the fired brass which was also frozen to the ground. An M-1 rifle bolt smacking shut on your thumb hurts like hell — especially when your hands are so cold you can hardly hold the weapon!

During basic, I took all the usual qualification tests, hoping I could make it into the engineers so I could learn to operate earth-moving and construction machinery. I was looking forward to a career after my 3-year enlistment. But the Army had other ideas. Apparently I did very well on the test for Morse code, as I was selected to go to the Army Signal Corps school at Fort Knox after basic training. I became a radio operator, skilled in Morse code, semaphore, and light (those big, blinking lights they use on Navy ships). Then it was off to Germany. We flew from Louisville, Kentucky, to Fort Dix, New Jersey. This was my first time in the air and I kept my face to the window every minute, watching the world pass below. A couple of days after reaching Fort Dix, we were loaded on the troopship USNS *Buckner* en route to Europe.

I spent two and a half years in Germany with the 73rd Antiaircraft Artillery Battalion, providing communications for the organization. Our communications group was small, and the 73rd was a bastard outfit, answering directly to Corps headquarters. The stated purpose of the battalion, should war erupt, was to race to the western side of the Rhine river and stop or slow the approach of the Russian Army. I was in Headquarters Company, and we communicators were rather superfluous to the overall mission. During all the military exercises, we'd pull our communications rigs to the highest hill in the area and provide relay for the units around us. During my tour, I was lucky enough to be selected to attend radio repair school in Ansbach, Germany, and later returned there for a course on radiation-detection devices such as Geiger counters.

In December 1958, I was honorably discharged. In February 1959, I re-enlisted using my correct birth date, but only after confirming that all of my prior service would be credited towards my future service. At this time I think I knew I would make the service a career; I was having a good time, enjoyed my job, and felt that I was providing a service to my country. I went back to school at Fort Devens for more communications training, and then spent three years in Japan. Following Japan, I had a tour in Turkey, then a year and a half in Vietnam. I went to Vietnam as a new E-6 and was assigned as a platoon sergeant in a unit in the northern part of the country. It was an interesting time, to say the least.

Following Vietnam, I served in Japan (again), Burma, Bolivia, Afghanistan, Ecuador, and Turkey (again). I served some short tours in the States attending schools and working for a brief time at Arlington Hall Station in Virginia, making courier trips over to the labyrinth halls of the Pentagon. I also did two tours at the language school at Monterey, California. The first was for six months of Spanish language, then some years later, for nine months of Turkish language.

I retired from the Army in December 1976 at the rank of master sergeant (E-8). I had some really great tours, and I would happily do it all over again.

Al Gorbett joined the Department of State after his retirement from the Army and had a second career in communications. He enjoyed postings to Israel, Chad, Kenya, and Ecuador. After 21 years with the Department of State, he retired for the second time in 1999. Al and his wife, Dale Laura Flashberg, live in Boerne, Texas.

✔ *INCIDENTally — Inspection!* – In 1943, just before we entrained from Lake Charles AFB, Louisiana, to Selfridge Field, Michigan, to receive our new B-26s and head for England, we had a readiness inspection in the barracks. We were lined up in front of our bunks with our clothing displayed on the bunk. Our group commander, Colonel Lester J. Maitland, came through like a dose of ex-lax. He stopped at the bunk adjacent to mine and barked to my buddy, Staff Sergeant Tex Coffman, "Where are your undershirts?" Tex barked back, "I don't wear any, sir." Maitland bellowed, "Goddamnit, I said where are they?" Tex said, "In my barracks bag, sir." Maitland snapped, "Get them out! And get a haircut! Let's see, you are a staff sergeant. Now you are a private! Take his name." He busted about 15 guys in the group that day, but later relented after squadron commanders pleaded mercy. – *Billie B. Boyd.*

George J. Rogers

Age 16 – United States Army

I was born on 22 February 1939 in Rome, Floyd County, Georgia. My father died when I was only 7 years old, and my mother remarried in 1952. My stepfather never mistreated me, but I

> *In retrospect, I think I probably joined for the adventure more than anything.*

guess I had a lot of resentment toward him because I was never really happy after my mother remarried.

My first cousin, with whom I was very close, joined the Navy at age 17 in 1955. I wanted to go with him, but I was only 16. I convinced my mother that I would be better off in the military. She finally agreed to sign the papers, providing that I could convince the recruiter that I was 17. I went immediately to the Navy recruiting office, and told the petty officer in charge that I was 17, but was born at home and did not have a birth certificate, which was not true. Well, it took him about 15 minutes to call my high school and verify that I was only 16.

By this time I was desperate, and I pleaded with him to help me get in. He said that there was no way he could take me because he knew my true age, but that I might get the Army recruiter next door to take me. I went next door and told him my story and asked what I could do to enlist. The recruiter told me to get some official document stating that I was 17 and get my mother's permission, then he would sign me up. I had a birth certificate, written in pen and ink, that had been filled out by the attending physician. It was no problem at all to change "1939" to "1938," and my mother signed the necessary documents.

I quit high school midway through my 11th year and was sworn into the U. S. Army on 9 January 1956 at Atlanta, Georgia, 45 days short of my 17th birthday. But 45 days for a 16-year-old is like a lifetime, and I just didn't feel like I could wait another day. In retrospect, I think I probably joined for the adventure more than anything.

After being sworn in, I was sent to Fort Jackson, South Carolina, for basic training, then to Fort Hood, Texas, for armored artillery training with the 4th Armored Division. After completion of my training I was shipped to Fort Lewis, Washington, by troop train, with a couple of hundred other privates. We were allowed to leave the train in Dallas where we had stopped for 3- to 4-hour layover. At that time, I remember thinking that the Army was making a big mistake, and that we would lose half of the group by the time the train pulled out. But to my knowledge, not a single soldier missed the train.

On the second day out, I got very sick and was taken off the train in Amarillo, Texas, and treated at the Air Force Base Hospital for strep throat. I rejoined my buddies in about a week. A whole bunch of us were assigned to the 40th Antiaircraft Artillery (AAA) in Japan. We shipped out of Seattle on the USNS *Marine Lynx*. We stopped to off-load some troops in Pusan, Korea, and then proceeded to Yokohama, Japan. I have vivid memories of the Korean dock workers coming aboard the ship and eating out of the garbage cans on the fantail.

On arrival in Japan, I was separated from the others who were going to the AAA outfit, and instead was assigned to the 588th Quartermaster Company (petroleum supply) at Sasebo, Japan. There were only about 25 or 30 Army personnel in Sasebo at that time, and we were quartered on the naval base there. I spent two and one-half years at Sasebo working as the company clerk before being sent back to Fort Jackson for separation.

I tried civilian life for a while, but I was bored. In July 1959, I joined the Navy and went to boot camp at San Diego. Subsequently, I was assigned to the USS *Coral Sea* (CVA-43), home-based at Alameda, California. Further assignments were to: the Staff, Commander Fleet Air Southwest Pacific at Cubi Point, Philippine Islands; the Navy Receiving Station, Brooklyn, New York; the Navy Correspondence Course Center, Scotia, New York; the Navy Nuclear Power Training Unit, Schenectady, New York; the USS *Goodrich* (DD-831) at Mayport, Florida; the Enlisted Personnel Distribution Office, Bainbridge, Maryland; and the U. S. Navy Recruiting District, Atlanta, Georgia.

I retired from active duty as a chief personnelman in July 1975.

George Rogers went to work for the Cobb County, Georgia, Police Department, after retiring from the Navy. He had obtained a GED while stationed in Japan, so he enrolled at Kenneasaw State University under the GI Bill and earned a degree in criminal justice. He retired from the police department in January 1997 after 21 years of service. He married Ann Marie Dietz of Albany, New York, in 1965. They have three children and five grandchildren. George and Ann live in Powder Springs, Georgia.

✓ *INCIDENTally* —*I could have danced all night!*

– While our ship was in port in 1944, I was restricted to the ship because I had come back late from liberty. They were having a ship's dance at one of the big hotels. My buddies had really razzed me because they were going to the dance and I was stuck on board ship. The officer of the deck called me and asked if I could drive, and I said yes. I was given keys to a car and told to drive to a hotel and pick up two women and take them to the hotel where the ship's dance was. I was to go to the desk and tell the clerk that I was there. You can imagine my surprise when the women turned out to be actress Una Merkle and singer Martha Tilton, who were very popular at that time. I was to stay with them at the dance and bring them back to their hotel when they wanted to leave. I made sure every sailor that I knew saw me at the dance. – *William P. Mazzoni.*

Tony L. Gallego

Age 16 – United States Army

I was born in Tucson, Arizona, on 10 October 1939. I was raised by an aunt and uncle who provided me with everything a growing boy could want or need. They

> *Joining the service was like a patriotic expectation.*

were my Mom and Dad. My biological mother passed away when I was nine months old. I was about 8 years old when other kids told me that my real mother was dead. I was shattered. It started an unexplainable uneasiness in me that, I believe, I still carry. After that, I started slipping in school and I grew progressively out of control.

I quit high school in the ninth grade and wasn't doing anything productive. My brother, who is a World War II Army Air Forces veteran, convinced my parents and me that the service was the best thing that could happen to me. He said, "They will make a man out of you." Looking back through the years, it seems like someone in my

own family, my extended family, or in the neighborhood, was always in uniform. Joining the service was like a patriotic expectation.

I went to see the Army recruiter and was allowed to take the required entrance exam. I passed, but my parents were reluctant to sign for me. After a while, they were convinced that I really did want to join the Army. We went to see a notary public. I'm not entirely sure if he knew what was going on or not, but we filled out an affidavit stating that I was 17 years of age, and he notarized it.

Bright and early on 13 March 1956, I was off to the induction center for my physical and swearing in. On the way to the induction center from the bus depot, I must have bent over at least five times from stomach pains. I don't know if it was from nervousness or from getting up so early.

I was shipped to Fort Ord, California, for basic training. The first morning at Fort Ord, we were blessed with the presence of a young private first class blowing a loud whistle. It was an awakening that would last a lifetime. Basic training was pretty easy for me. I guess it was because of my age. I could crawl, climb, and run. I welcomed anything physical.

After basic, I was sent to Fort Bliss, Texas, where I was assigned to the motor pool of Headquarters Battery, 2nd Guided Missile Battalion. I was licensed to drive anything from a ¼-ton jeep to a 2½-ton troop carrier. At Fort Bliss, I attended the Nike-Ajax (SAM) radar-operator training school. Upon completion of that training, I was sent to South Dakota where our missiles replaced the antiaircraft artillery. I was privileged to participate in the firing of six Nike-Ajax missiles, three at the MacGregor Range and three at Red Canyon Range Camp, all kills. I remained there for the duration of my enlistment.

I was separated from the Army on 12 March 1959 at Fort Carson, Colorado. I had received my draft notice while I was in the Army. I thought for sure they were going to catch me then. When I was getting my "re-up" talk, the battery commander asked me if I had joined underage. Of course, I said, "No, sir!"

The Army during the Cold War was not a hell, such as serving in combat. But there was always training at all hours, inspections, spit-and-polish, KP, guard duty, CQ, and sometimes boredom. It was not an easy life. While in the Army, I got a lot of advice from the older guys, the 22- to 27-year-old draftees. They saw how young I was and they were always hammering me with the importance of getting an education.

The Army shaped my destiny. It has been the driving force behind anything I have ever accomplished. I believe the eye-opening wisdom one gains in the military cannot be duplicated anywhere else. The service gave me the GI Bill, gave me direction, and showed me how to be a survivor. I didn't think so at the time, but I do now.

Tony Gallego restarted his education after leaving the Army by taking a correspondence course, enrolling in a technical institute, then attending Pima College in Tucson, Arizona. He earned a general electronics-technician diploma from the technical institute, an A.A. in general studies, an A.A.S. in electronic technology (digital), and an A.A.S. in electronic technology (communications), from Pima College.

In 1992 he received the "Best of Pima" alumni-achievement award from Pima College. He obtained an FCC 2ⁿᵈ class radiotelephone operators license, and for a number of years was a lead man of the electronic-service technicians in an electronics-standards laboratory. He was a technical floor support specialist at the time he retired from Hughes Aircraft Company in 1994. Tony credits his biological father for urging him to get into the field of electronics. One of his proudest achievements was getting an elementary school named after his grandfather and a great-uncle for their contributions to the community. Tony and his late wife Christina had four children and eight grandchildren. He lives in St. David, Arizona.

✓ *INCIDENTally* — **The rest area.** – In March 1945, the 101ˢᵗ Airborne Division was in a rest area in France. We lived in tents with a small sheet-metal stove in the center of the living space. Most of us were enjoying the time by writing letters, reading magazines, or just lying on our bunks. All was going well in the serene atmosphere when someone walked into the tent next to mine and very discreetly dumped two handfuls of rifle ammunition into the stove, then quickly exited the tent. Within minutes, the ammunition began to explode and projectiles were flying in the area causing havoc with the tranquility. The stove was blown apart and the tent was riddled with holes, but amazingly, not one injury was sustained. This would not have been the case if that individual had been apprehended! – *Walter Holy.*

644

Larry W. Smith

Age 16 – United States Army

I was born in Campbell County, Virginia, on 15 October 1941, the youngest of ten children. We lived on a tobacco farm with neither electricity nor indoor plumbing. My father was a farmer and a

> When I turned 15, I told my mother that I was going to join the Army.

blacksmith. I worked in the fields at an early age, driving horses pulling a plow. We worked from 6 a.m. until 11 a.m., broke for lunch and a 30-minute rest, then went back to plowing at 12:30, working until dark. I helped my mother gather eggs, feed the chickens, and get the cows in for milking. I had no time to play, or to do things I wanted to do, except on Sundays.

Sometimes I would miss school to help in the fields. My teacher always gave me homework so that I could keep up with my class. We were very poor, but my father and mother made sure that all of us had three meals a day. My mother sewed feed bags together for bed sheets and clothes for my sisters. I would take two or three dozen eggs to the

store and exchange them for salt, pepper, and sugar – things that we needed at home but couldn't raise on the farm. Being on a farm was hard work, but it made me appreciate what I have today.

At the time I was born, my two oldest brothers were in the military. Thank goodness they both came home safely from World War II! Another brother joined the Army in 1950, and one joined the Marines in 1956.

When I turned 15, I told my mother that I was going to join the Army. She said, "No way!" When I was 16, I told my mother she would have to sign papers so I could go into the Army. Again, she said that I was too young, and she would not tell a lie for me to get into the Army.

I dropped out of school at age 16 and went to Lynchburg, Virginia, 32 miles away, and stayed with my older sister. I got a job at Gilliam Esso Station, changing oil and washing cars. I made $1 per hour. After about three months of that, I said, "I am going in the Army!" I hitchhiked to my parents' farm and begged my mother to sign papers saying that I was 17. She said no.

I hitchhiked back to Lynchburg and went to the Army recruiting station to join. When I walked into the office, the following conversation took place:

"Boy, what do you want?" asked a sergeant.

"I want to join the Army," was my reply.

"How old are you?" he asked.

"Seventeen," I said.

"Are you sure?" he asked.

"Yes, sir!" I replied.

"How soon do you want to join?" was the next question.

"Right now!" I said.

So he gave me a test, I passed it, and he took me back to my home, which is a place called Hat Creek, Virginia.

When we drove up the driveway, my mother was sitting on the porch. I got out of the car and told the sergeant to give me a minute. I walked up on the porch and asked my mother to go into the house. She asked me who was in the car. I told her it was an Army recruiter. In the house, she began to cry. I begged her to sign the papers for me to join the Army. I said if she did not sign, I would have my aunt sign them. Finally, she signed them and I waved for the sergeant to come in. When he was inside, he asked my mother how old I was. She said, "Seventeen." I was so happy!

Then the recruiter asked for a record of birth. I picked up the Bible from the coffee table and went to the middle where all births were recorded, and showed it to the recruiter. I kept my finger over the year. The recruiter said O.K. My mother cried for about 30 minutes, and we left. The recruiter took me back to Lynchburg and put me on a bus to Richmond, Virginia, where I took my physical and final test.

I was sworn into the Army on 10 March 1958. The next day I was sent to Fort Knox, Kentucky, for basic and advanced training. From there I went to Fort Bliss, Texas. My first overseas assignment was with the 1st Cavalry Division in Korea. When I returned to the States,

I was stationed at Fort Sill, Oklahoma, then was sent to Turkey. I came back to Fort Bragg, North Carolina, then Fort Lee, Virginia, and back overseas to Germany for three years. I returned to Fort Sill for a time, then it was on to Vietnam where I was assigned to the 23rd Infantry "Americal" Division. I lost some friends there.

After returning from Vietnam, I was assigned as an Army recruiter in Battle Creek, Michigan. From there I went to Norfolk, Virginia, where I retired from the Army. I served for 24½ years and retired on a disability. I was a master sergeant (E-8) at the time. I say thanks to my country for the privilege of serving.

Larry Smith was awarded two Bronze Stars, the Combat Air Medal, the Meritorious Service Medal, the Army Commendation Medal, and earned a number of service medals during his Army career. He has been a car salesman for Perry Buick Company, Norfolk, Virginia, for the past 17 years. Larry and Mary, his wife of 37 years, have three children and three grandchildren. They live in Virginia Beach, Virginia.

Ronald W. Browne

Age 16 – United States Navy

I was born in Baxter Springs, Kansas, on 22 July 1942. One of my two sisters and I were adopted by Clifford C. Browne and Pauline Anderson Browne in 1944. My dad was a Marine during the first

> He said for us to stand shoulders back, eyes forward, and not to speak.

World War, serving in Cuba, and many of my uncles and cousins served during World War II and Korea. I remember them coming home, and I knew then that I wanted to serve, too.

I tried to join the Marines when I was 14, but I was caught by the police in Guymon, Oklahoma, and sent home. I was in the Junior ROTC in high school for a year, but I quit school while in the 10th grade in the spring of 1958. I married Nancy Begnoche in August 1958.

I went with a friend to the Naval Air Base at Hutchinson, Kansas, in May 1958, because he wanted to join the Navy. Chief Petty Officer Bill Terry asked me if I wanted to join the Navy, too. Well, I did. I entered boot camp on 3 December 1958. I was in Company 663 at the Naval Training Center, San Diego.

While in boot camp our company was to be inspected by a captain. Our drill instructor told us how and what to do during inspection. He said for us to stand shoulders back, eyes forward, and not to speak. During the inspection, the captain saw my wedding band and asked me if I was married. Well, the DI had said not to speak. I felt fear for the first and last time. He asked me at least three times, and finally our DI told me to answer. I said, "Yes, sir." The captain was slightly irritated, but I was just following orders. I was told not to speak.

After boot camp I served as the master-at-arms in the main chow hall at the Naval Training Center for a time, then reported aboard the USS *Catamount* (LSD-17). In 1961, our ship was part of a large flotilla that assembled at the north tip of Borneo, preparing to go to Vietnam. We had helicopters aboard that had been fitted with sprayers and tanks filled with yellow-green stuff. They sprayed the top of an island, and three days later, everything that had been green was dead. Agent Orange!

We were on Riverine patrol. In early 1962, we were ordered to bring our weapons to the woodworking shop where wooden plugs were put in them. President Kennedy had ordered this done because, if we were shot at, he didn't want us to shoot back and cause an international incident.

We were commissioned as special forces in April 1962. We were called SEALS-1. We did our jobs and did them well. Vietnam was largely a naval war until 1964 when many of our boats were transferred to the Army.

I was discharged from the Navy in October 1962 and returned to Kansas. I dedicated my life to the service because of Corporal Charles L. Gilliland, my cousin and best friend, who is still missing in action in Korea. His story is on the internet under Korean Medal of Honor recipients. He earned the Medal of Honor in 1951 as a member of the 3rd Infantry Division.

Ronnie Browne worked as a pipe fitter, welder, cowboy, wrangler, and horse trainer. Even while in the Navy, he carried his rodeo saddle. Ronnie was married twice. He has seven sons, two daughters, fourteen grandchildren, and four great-grandchildren. One son is a U. S. Army nurse, another an Army Ranger, and one is in Navy intelligence. Ronnie lives on a farm near Nevada, Missouri.

649

Dale L. Hartman
Age 16 – United States Navy

I was born and raised in the outskirts
of Des Moines, Iowa, the third-oldest of
eight children. Our family of 10 lived in a
three-room house in the community of

> *This was the first birthday
> cake I had ever had!*

Norwoodville. Living with six females in the small house, and because
I was having problems with my father, I decided to enter the service
in the fall of 1962. I obtained two forms of the waver needed to enlist
at age 17 and traced my parents' signatures on one of the forms, then
turned it in to the recruiter. I felt that I should inform my mother
that I was going into the service, so I took the other form to her and
my father and told them that I wanted to join the service. They didn't
know that it was already too late because I had turned in the other

form, but I wanted them to feel that they
still had authority over me. They signed the
waiver.

I informed my best friend, Thomas J.
Williams, who was also 16 years old, that I
was about to leave for the service. He
elected to join also, and obtained his parents'
signatures on the waiver. We were to go on
the buddy plan, but he left about four weeks
before I did. We saw each other three times
while in boot camp. Two years later, Tom
was killed in an accident while he was home
on leave.

All my paperwork and other documents were completed and dated
for my swearing-in and leaving for boot camp on my 17th birthday, 21
March 1963. However, six days before I was to leave, the recruiter
called me and said that because of the large number of recruits, I had
to leave the following day or be delayed for an indefinite period of time.
He said I would be sworn in on my arrival in boot camp.

For over three days and three nights, more than 100 of us who were
on the way to boot camp stayed drunk. When we arrived in San Diego,

California, I was asked when my birthday was so that I could be sworn in. I had totally lost track of time, and I just assumed that because I had arrived at boot camp that day, at midnight I would turn 17. At midnight, I was awakened by an officer and presented with a Hostess cupcake with one candle on it. Everyone sang "Happy Birthday" to me. This was the first birthday cake I had ever had! Upon the conclusion of the song, I was required to repeat the oath for military service.

The following day, in the process of completing military paperwork, I found out that it was only the 20th of March, and that I had given the wrong information on my arrival at boot camp. I didn't say anything for a couple of years, then I began having people change the date of my being sworn into the Navy from the 20th to the 21st.

While I was in boot camp, the person in the bunk next to mine died of spinal meningitis, as did several others in barracks near ours. I came down with it the night of the outbreak, but I survived because I was in better than normal physical fitness and because I sucked on burned stick matches, a home remedy for fever that I had learned as I grew up. I was the first person to survive this illness. I learned that it was because of the sulfur in the matches. The doctors went to a veterinary store and bought and passed out one-inch horse pills of sulfur to everyone in boot camp. I was told that I was in the medical books because of this incident.

After boot camp, I was stationed at the Naval Air Station, North Island, San Diego, California, until June 1965. A high point of my stay there was when eight of us recovered an experimental helicopter that had crashed in the ocean. The recovery process was undertaken during very hazardous weather conditions. We retrieved it from the ocean floor and returned it to the air station on Christmas Eve 1964. For our efforts, we received a Navy Letter of Commendation, and our picture was published in a San Diego newspaper.

From June 1965 until January 1967, I was stationed aboard the aircraft carrier USS *Hancock* (CVA-19). We left for Vietnam in September 1965 and returned in November 1967. Our cruise ended up being longer than the normal six months. I worked the flight deck in the fuels division. During this time I had only seven days of liberty and real dirt under my feet.

I went aboard the *Hancock* weighing 160 pounds and left weighing 119. There were too many times to count that I went two, three, or four days without sleep because aircraft would be landing hourly and require refueling. While we were off the coast of Vietnam, I watched a few aircraft return at night on fire, from which the pilots ejected but were never recovered. One night an A-4 aircraft landed while on fire, and bullets from its magazines were exploding because of the heat. A bullet nicked me near my eye when I ran out to tackle a co-worker who had frozen in place and was in the direct line of fire and was in danger of being hit. I turned down the Purple Heart for the injury.

I watched as aircraft were launched from the bow and ended up in the ocean, from which the pilots were never recovered. I saw a couple of aircraft hanging over the deck, held only by the tail hook. It seemed like hardly a day went by that I didn't have a bomb, a sidewinder missile, or a flare skim along the catwalk towards me. One time I banged my head when I jumped into a refueling station. When I woke up I had a 500-pound bomb essentially sitting in my lap. The bomb was cracked and leaking its black powder that sparkled when it hit the floor. But it did not explode because JP-5 fuel had displaced the oxygen near the deck. I ended up disarming the bomb by myself because of the lack of space for anyone to get in and help me. I watched several people get blown off the flight deck and injured. I was blown off late one night in 1966 during a training exercise. I was in the area when a person was cut in half when he walked into the turning propellor of an aircraft. I heard the cries of a person who had lost an arm, and another who lost a leg by getting caught in one of the aircraft elevators.

Small Vietnamese boats, loaded with explosives, tried to attack our ship. The boats had Vietnamese civilians tied to them as human shields. I listened over the ship's public-address system to the pilots describing having to shoot and sink these boats to protect our ship. I watched the massive bombing of the coastline by B-52s one day. I have just touched on a few events that occurred on our ship. It is too bad that the general public has no concept of what wartime conditions are like on an aircraft carrier.

My biggest regret is that when I returned to America in 1967, I, like other veterans of the Vietnam War, was spit on, pushed in front of oncoming vehicles, and had rocks thrown at me. I was not able to retain employment for several months because I looked military and conducted myself in a military fashion.

I lost several very close childhood friends in Vietnam. I have always thought that if what they and I had done would give more people freedom of choice, then it was worth it. I was discharged after serving 3 years and 10 months. It would be three months before I could legally drink a beer!

Dale Hartman worked as an industrial-machine operator for five years and in the medical field for more than nine years. He entered the civil service and worked in the fuel department at the Naval Air Station, Miramar, California, until taking early retirement at the age of 51 in 1997. Dale has three children from a previous marriage. He and his wife Terri live in San Diego, California.

✓ *INCIDENTally* — *Eat your veggies!* – I was never too fond of vegetables. When I was in Navy boot camp, I had my week of mess duty working on the scullery machine. There was so much water sloshing around that I was constantly wet. On my final day, beets were the veggie of the day. My white leggings ended up beet red. I spent my weekend scrubbing leggings. I used everything I could find, including salt, to get them white again. I couldn't eat beets for over 40 years. I do eat them now, but it took some forgiveness on the part of the beets. – *John Laws*.

Lester S. Delinski

Age 16 – United States Marine Corps

When I was 7 years old in 1960, my oldest brother, who was in the Marines, was ordered overseas for a tour on Okinawa. Up to that point in my life, when my parents mentioned

> *I grew up quickly at Parris Island, ...*

"overseas," they were talking about war. I incorrectly assumed that my brother was going off to some war. My dad explained that there was no war, but my brother and other young men his age still had to serve tours overseas to help insure and keep the peace. After mulling this over, I remarked to Dad that he was unlucky, since World War II occurred while he was in the Army. He laughed and explained that like most everyone else, when the country went to war, he enlisted to do his share. He said that all good men want to serve when their

country is threatened, and every able young man has the duty to serve if called or needed.

My dad died shortly after that and I was raised by my mother. I left high school at age 15 and worked for a year in Washington, D.C. I'd begun a sort of aimless daily existence, working and just hanging around with my friends. The art gallery where I worked was located near Dupont Circle, then one of the centers of the District of Columbia's counterculture. I heard and saw the antiwar side of the Vietnam issue every day. I read the papers and watched the news, so I understood that there was another side.

In early 1969, the war was heating up both in the field and on the home front. I knew that eventually my turn would come. At age 16, I didn't agree with much that people of my parents' age were saying. I felt like going off to serve in a real war, as my father had done, would earn me the right to have a valid opinion. The Marine Corps seemed like the best bet for serving in Vietnam. If I waited almost a year to meet the minimum age requirement, I'd have to join for four years, and I might never make it overseas. If I added a full year to my age, I could join for two years and be almost assured of quick training and a tour in Vietnam.

I changed the date on my birth certificate from 19 May 1952 to the same day and month in 1951, making me one year older. Knowing that I needed both direction and discipline, my mother gave her consent. I had to promise her that I wouldn't tell them my true age just to get sent back home when the training proved difficult or I became homesick. I was sworn into the Marine Corps on 10 March 1969 and was sent to Parris Island, South Carolina, for boot camp.

There were many nights at boot camp when I would lie on my rack at night after a long, grueling day, thinking that maybe I was too young for the situation I was in. I knew that I could leave any time I wanted by just telling them my true age, but if I did, I would have to face my mother. Once during our training, a boy was sent home for medical reasons. He was given a uniform to wear home, but its buttons with the Marine insignia had been replaced with plain black buttons and the insignia on his hat removed. It was the thought of going home to my mother that way that kept me there on Parris Island.

I grew up quickly at Parris Island, and for the first time in my life learned to accept strict discipline. I was taught how to fight with a knife, bayonet, rifle, and bare hands. I was amazed to find that by listening and applying what was taught, I could win even against older, bigger guys. I turned 17 there, and five days later we were sent to Camp Lejeune, North Carolina, for advanced infantry training.

In late October 1969, my name came up for rotation to Vietnam. I received a 20-day leave and was at home until late November. I watched the Vietnam Moratorium and March Against Death on the streets of Washington, D.C. Each person wore a placard with the name of someone killed in Vietnam, and after pausing to call out the name at the White House, marched on and placed the placard into a casket on the Capitol steps. My friends and I watched the march and enjoyed the almost-party atmosphere it had brought to the city.

I reported to Camp Pendleton, California, for a month of hands-on review of infantry skills and staging for overseas. We were to leave in early January 1970. We were taken in trucks to the Los Angeles International Airport to board a civilian plane for the flight to

Okinawa. While we were loading our seabags onto the aircraft, a group of war protesters who had gathered at the airport became agitated and threatened to overwhelm the airport security people who were separating them from us. We were ordered to stop loading and were put back on the trucks, to the cheers of the protesters. They were joyous and amazed that their efforts seemed to have stopped us. There was a good deal of grumbling in the trucks about the "hippies" and how they should have been dealt with. Of course, this is what our officers sought to avoid by reloading us on the trucks.

We were driven to the El Toro Marine Corps Air Station, some distance south of Los Angeles. The civilian airliner had also been rerouted to El Toro. It took hours for things to come together, but we boarded the aircraft late at night and we took off over the Pacific. I remember thinking that the happy protesters from the airport were sleeping soundly down there, after partying half of the night, blissfully unaware that we were still going to war.

Several hours after leaving Hawaii, we approached a speck of an island that looked far too small to hold our airplane even sitting still, let along big enough to land on. As we circled closer, we saw it did have an airstrip, though its runway seemed to have a sharp left-hand turn near the end. Once the pilot turned on his final approach, we could see nothing but water out of the side windows. Guys who had been sleeping were now awakening, and we watched with delight as each one suffered a moment of mounting terror when he looked out the windows to see the swells and whitecaps just below the wings, and no land on either side. When the wheels touched down on tiny Wake Island, we were all tossed forward as the pilot quickly reversed the engine thrust to slow the airplane. We saw that we were headed for an earthen wall at the end of the runway. Just as we realized that the plane couldn't stop before hitting the wall, it suddenly jerked and swung wildly to the left with our right wingtip passing within feet of the earthen wall. I realized then that there was a sharp turn in the island's runway.

Our next stop was Iwakuni Air Base, Japan, and from there we went to Okinawa for final staging, then on to Da Nang, Vietnam. I received orders to report to the 1st Engineer Battalion, 1st Marine Division, at Marble Mountain. There was no transportation available going to Marble Mountain, so I was told to go to the gate and ask each driver if he was going in my direction. I caught a ride going in the general direction, and when we came to a fork in the road, the driver pointed to a distant mountain and said that the 1st Engineers were located over by "that mountain." He was to turn left, so he told me to wait and hitch a ride with someone who was turning right.

It was late in the evening and I was standing beside my seabag, alone and unarmed, on the side of a road, near a village someplace in Vietnam. I watched eagerly as trucks and jeeps approached the fork, and then felt my spirits sink as each one took the road to the left. When the sun was fully down, the village looked much more hostile. I decided to take the next ride that came by, whichever way it was headed. I stopped the next truck that came along, opened the door, and the driver called me by name. I had known him in training back in the States.

At Marble Mountain, I was assigned to taking care of the battalion's 36 mechanical mules. Mechanical mules were about the size of a jeep but were essentially open platforms with wheels and a steering wheel. I had two weeks to learn how to keep the 36 mules running for a year. My mentor, the outgoing mule mechanic, not only taught me how to care for the mules, but how to obtain parts and new ones. One day we drove to the Army's 80th General Services Group, with the objective of obtaining a new mule. We spotted one being driven to the officers' club by a young officer. My mentor told me that he would take the new mule and I was to follow him to the gate, but I was to stop and distract the guard while he left the area. It worked, and we repeated this escapade later.

After my tour, I rotated back to the States and was discharged from the Marine Corps on 13 January 1971.

Les Delinski used his experience with mules by working as a motorcycle mechanic for several years. He then became a general contractor and operated Blue Sky Builders in Washington, D.C., until retiring and moving to Florida in 1997. Les and Denise, his wife of 22 years, have one daughter. They live in Lake Mary, Florida.

✓ *INCIDENTally* — INDEX- continued.

Contibutors to the first volume of America's Youngest Warriors

Adams, Betty Jean	Age 16 · WAVES	Burd, Hershel C.	Age 16 · USA
Adams, Dwight L.	Age 16 · USNG	Burns, Billie R.	Age 16 · USA
Adams, Edgar C.	Age 15 · USN	Burton, Don H.	Age 16 · USMC
Aman, Jacob F.	Age 16 · USN	Butler, Oliver J.	Age 15 · USN(FMF)
Arthur, Edward I.	Age 13 · USNG	Buyanovits, Robert O.	Age 16 · USA
Arthur, Merle M.	Age 16 · USN	Camp, Johnny	Age 14 · USCG
Bartholow, Robert C.	Age 16 · USMC	Cannon, Jack L.	Age 16 · USA
Bates, Warren G.	Age 14 · USN	Champagne, Joseph J.	Age 16 · USA
Belanger, Harry A.	Age 16 · USMC	Chase, Freddie C.	Age 16 · USN
Beno, Gerald J.	Age 16 · USMC	Ciriello, Edmund R.	Age 16 · USA
Boone, James A.	Age 15 · USN	Cline, Robert H.	Age 14 · USN
Boorda, Jeremy M.	Age 16 · USN	Coleman, Tommy J.	Age 16 · USN
Booth, Billie L.	Age 16 · USA	Coronado, Gil	Age 16 · USAF
Bowlby, Richard L.	Age 15 · USN	Cramer, John B.	Age 15 · USNG
Boyd, Billie B.	Age 16 · USAAF	Cranston, William E., Sr.	Age 16 · USMC
Brand, William V.	Age 15 · USNG	Crass, Ray L.	Age 15 · USN
Brandon, Alvie M.	Age 15 · USN	Crass, Roy M.	Age 15 · USN
Brandt, Dorothy H.	Age 16 · WAC	Crepeau, Robert R.	Age 16 · USA
Brinson, Harold M.	Age 14 · USN	Cucka, John M.	Age 16 · USN
Brouse, George R.	Age 15 · USA	Darrow, Harry W.	Age 15 · USN
Brown, Charles E.	Age 14 · USN	Davies, William L.	Age 16 · USN
Brown, Jack H.	Age 15 · USA	DeVos, Darlene E.	Age 19 · WAC
Bruton, Billy E.	Age 15 · USN	DeWitz, George O.	Age 15 · USN
Buckley, Arthur W.	Age 13 · USA	DiNapoli, Frank	Age 15 · USN

Dodson, Robert D.	Age 16 · USA	Jackson, Ray D.	Age 16 · USMC
Dominique, Doughty J.	Age 15 · USAF	Jackson, Spencer B.	Age 15 · USA
Durbin, Frank III	Age 15 USN	Jakaboski, Theodore P.	Age 16 · USNR
Dyer, Delmar J.	Age 16 · USA	Jenke, Clifford R.	Age 15 · USN
Edgington, Richard A.	Age 14 · USAAF	Johnson, Harold B.	Age 16 · USN
Elliott, Lewis E.	Age 15 · USA	Johnson, Richard H.	Age 12 · USNG
English, George W.	Age 14 · USN	Jolly, T. Steve	Age 14 · USMM
Eordekian, George	Age 15 · USCG	Jordan, David M.	Age 14 · USA
Evenson, Ronald E.	Age 15 · USAF	Joseph, Robert E.	Age 15 · USA
Fischer, Wilson R.	Age 14 · USNR	Kibble, Leo E.	Age 16 · USN
Frank, Gordon W.	Age 16 · USN	King, Charles T.	Age 14 · USN
Frasier, Jack L.	Age 15 · USNG	King, Melford A.	Age 16 · USN
Gaddis, Carl O.	Age 15 · USMC	King, Stanley E.	Age 15 · USA
Garcia, Gerald	Age 16 · USNG	Kiser, Buddie C.	Age 16 · USA
Geygan, James W.	Age 15 · USAF	Kloppenburg, Herbert	Age 16 · USMC
Gilley, Edward E.	Age 16 · USAF	Kotan, John A., Jr.	Age 16 · USMCR
Goff, Curtis B.	Age 16 · USA	Kriss, Daniel W.	Age 14 · USN
Goodman, Carl E.	Age 16 · USA	Kulp, Steward H.	Age 16 · USA
Gordon, Eugene A.	Age 15 · USN	Lansinger, J. Ronald	Age 16 · USMC
Gordon, Maxine V.	Age 16 · USMC	Lawson, Wilma P.	Age 15 · WAC
Graham, Calvin L.	Age 12 · USN	Leriche, Robert W.	Age 13 · USAAC
Hamlet, Lawrence E.	Age 15 · USA	Lessin, Roger D.	Age 16 · USA
Hansen, Donald W.	Age 15 · USNG	Long, Otis M.	Age 15 · USN
Hanson, Vilas	Age 14 · USAF	Lowery, Thomas T.	Age 15 · USN
Hanson, William S.	Age 15 · USN	Luster, Herbert R.	Age 16 · USNG
Hartley, Beaufort	Age 16 · USN	Lyke, Thomas A.	Age 16 · USA
Heldman, H. Sherry	Age 16 · USMC	Lyle, Calvin H.	Age 15 · USN
Hennessey, Daniel S.	Age 15 · USN	Mahony, A. W. "Sam"	Age 16 · USN
Herbert, Baker W.	Agé 14 · USN	Malloch, James R.	Age 14 · USMC
Hibbert, Omega Gene	Age 14 · USA	Manson, Willie C.	Age 13 · USN
Hise, Thomas C.	Age 15 · USN	Martinez, Paul Z.	Age 16 · USA
Hoffler, Jackson	Age 14 · USN	Marzolf, Curtis H.	Age 14 · USAAF
Holy, Walter	Age 16 · USA	Mason, Calvin W.	Age 16 · USNG
Hood, William G.	Age 16 · USMC	Mason, Lewis A.	Age 15 · USN
Huddleston, Ben L.	Age 15 · USA	McDannold, Robert H.	Age 16 · USN
Hunt, Donald J.	Age 15 · USN	McGehee, Bill J.	Age 16 · USMC
Huntsberry, Thomas V.	Age 15 · USA	McGinnis, Winston L.	Age 16 · USAAF
Hyatt, Merle E.	Age 15 · USA	Mendoza, Jesus "Dick"	Age 15 · USNG

Michaelson, Jack	Age 15 · USA	Stamelos, John T.	Age 16 · USMC
Miller, Charles L.	Age 16 · USAAF	Stevens, Earl W.	Age 16 · USN
Miller, William S.	Age 16 · USA	Stewart, Archie W.	Age 14 · USNG
Moore, Donald F.	Age 15 USMC	Stewart, Reginald D.	Age 14 · USN
Moore, Jerome A.	Age 14 · USA	Stinnett, Raleigh G.	Age 14 · USA
Morgan, William C.	Age 16 · USMC	Stoupa, Roland J.	Age 15 · USA
Morris, David	Age 16 · USN	Stover, Allan C.	Age 14 · USCG
Mounts, Dennis G.	Age 15 · USA	Stump, Bob	Age 16 · USN
Moynihan, Joseph A.	Age 16 · USN	Sumpter, Orville E.	Age 15 · USMC
Murray, Cornelius F.	Age 16 · USN	Sutor, Chester C.	Age 15 · USCG
Murray, Walter L.	Age 15 · USA	Swanson, Norman J.	Age 16 · USN
Noland, Richard A.	Age 15 · USA	Szczepanski, Stanley B.	Age 16 · USA
O'Sullivan, Jerome R.	Age 16 · USMC	Tabaka, Eugene W.	Age 16 · USN
Ohrn, Lars O.	Age 16 · USMC	Theoldore, Jack A.	Age 12 · USN
Olshefski, Norbert S.	Age 15 · USAAF	Thomas, Harry B.	Age 15 · USMC
Payne, Eddie H.	Age 16 · USN	Thomas, Richard J.	Age 16 · USN
Peck, John E.	Age 16 · USA	Thorpe, Robert G.	Age 16 · USAF
Pelham, Richard L.	Age 16 · USA	Tosh, John D.	Age 14 · USAAF
Peterson, Richard B.	Age 16 · USMC	Trero, William S.	Age 13 · USMC
Pettit, Bobby L.	Age 13 · USN	Underdown, Leon D.	Age 15 · USA
Poma, Nicholas	Age 15 · USN	Wagenbrenner, Blase F.	Age 15 · USN
Popplewell, James A.	Age 14 · USN	Walcott, Gary L.	Age 16 · USA
Potter, James W.	Age 15 · USA	Wallace, Harry R.	Age 16 · USN
Pressley, James A.	Age 16 · USN	Ware, Jack	Age 14 · USN
Price, Donald L.	Age 16 · USA	Weaver, Robert E.	Age 14 · USNG
Puskarcik, Ted R.	Age 15 · USN	Webb, Scott L.	Age 15 · USA
Quinn, Robert N.	Age 16 · USN	Webb, Theodore	Age 13 · USN
Rice, John W.	Age 16 · USN	Webber, Walter F.	Age 15 · USNG
Rockey, Clarence J.	Age 16 · USN	Wedeen, Lennart D.	Age 16 · USAF
Rodriguez, Carl R.	Age 16 · USAF	Wheeler, E. E.	Age 14 · USAAF
Scott, Billy J.	Age 15 · USA	White, Fred L.	Age 15 · USN
Sexton, Elsie	Age 16 · WAAC	White, James R.	Age 16 · USA
Shaw, Norman R.	Age 15 · USN	Wilkins, Verne J.	Age 15 · USNG
Shebley, Howard V.	Age 16 · USMC	Wilson, Jr., Seth T.	Age 16 · USN
Singer, Mike	Age 15 · USMC	Zane, Gordon	Age 16 · USN
Smith, Robert L.	Age 14 · USA	Zdanavage, Tony	Age 15 · USA
Smith, Ronald M.	Age 15 · USMC	Zitzelberger, Donald J.	Age 14 · USA
Snodgrass, Joseph W.	Age 16 · USAAF		